AQA(A)
PSYCHOLOGY
FOR A2

AQA(A)
PSYCHOLOGY
FOR A2

RICHARD GROSS
GEOFF ROLLS

DYNAMIC
LEARNING

Innovate • Motivate • Personalise

HODDER
EDUCATION
AN HACHETTE UK COMPANY

Orders: please contact Bookpoint Ltd, 130 Milton Park, Abingdon, Oxon
OX14 4SB. Telephone: (44) 01235 827720. Fax: (44) 01235 400454. Lines are
open from 9.00 – 5.00, Monday to Saturday, with a 24 hour message
answering service. You can also order through our website
www.hoddereducation.co.uk

If you have any comments to make about this, or any of our other titles,
please send them to educationenquiries@hodder.co.uk

British Library Cataloguing in Publication Data
A catalogue record for this title is available from the British Library

ISBN: 978 0 340 973 530

This Edition Published 2009
Impression number   10 9 8 7 6 5 4 3 2 1
Year   2012 2011 2010 2009

Hachette UK's policy is to use papers that are natural, renewable and
recyclable products and made from wood grown in sustainable forests.
The logging and manufacturing processes are expected to conform to the
environmental regulations of the country of origin.

Cover photo © Clément Contet / iStockphoto.com
Illustrations by Barking Dog
Typeset by Fakenham Photosetting Ltd, Fakenham, Norfolk

Printed in Italy for Hodder Education, An Hachette UK Company, 338
Euston Road, London NW1 3BH

Contents

Acknowledgements

Both authors would like to thank Ruben Hale and Stephanie Matthews who both took over the management of this project mid-voyage, but who have successfully kept us afloat and within sight of dry land! Thanks too to Emma Woolf who helped launch this ship before sailing off in another direction! She was aided for a while by Kate Short. Thanks are also owed to Lynn Brown once again, for her thorough and efficient copy-editing of the text.

RG would also like to thank GR for his continuing support- both pedagogical and moral. This has been a trying and testing journey, which I'm glad I didn't have to make alone!

GR would like to thank RG for being RG. This task would have been impossible without RG. GR would also like to thank Naomi Klepacz for her research, help and guidance with the Eating Behaviour chapter. She tells me this taught her two things: never to even contemplate writing a textbook and to avoid teaching that particular section.

GR would also like to acknowledge the support and expertise of all the other dedicated psychology teachers at Peter Synmonds College, Winchester including Andy Pond, James Larcombe, Michelle Morgan, Kim Palmer, Claire Hindmarsh, Chrissie Rycroft and Julia Adlam.

Dedication

To all those fellow-passengers on the voyage around Psychology: it can be choppy at times but it's always worth a little psi-sickness! (RG)

To Billy, Ella and Eve as always (GR)

Introduction

As the title indicates, *AQA(A)Psychology for A2* is written for that particular Specification, but it could also prove useful for students following other Specifications.

Each of the 11 chapters follows the same basic structure, reflecting the section and subsection headings as they appear in the Specification. However, compared with AS, there's much more scope – on both the authors' and student's part – for interpreting exactly what should be covered within a particular subsection. This sometimes means that chapters are longer than they'd otherwise be, providing readers with additional material; sometimes this additional material will appear in the form of 'Stretch and Challenge' (content that goes beyond what's needed for even a grade A essay but which adds challenging and thought-provoking content for those of you who are happy to be 'stretched and challenged').

Key features in the *AQA(A) Psychology for A2* book include:

- *Practical Learning Activities* (**PLAs**): these occur several times within each chapter and are designed to help you consider methodological aspects of the research studies and theories that make up the content. This can be done either through questions requiring (usually short) written answers or through suggested practical activities / practicals (which can be fairly specific or more open-ended, leaving room for you and/or your fellow-students to design your own). Either way, you're being asked to consider *How Science Works*, a set of concepts which underpin the whole Specification, designed to help students understand how scientists 'do' science in their attempt to explain the world around them. While psychology displays many characteristics of science in general, it's also unique in being about human behaviour and experience (which includes doing science).

- *How Science Works* is assessed in **AO3** (see below). One of the special problems faced by psychologists as scientists relates to the *ethics* of their research; others include the *culture* and *gender-bias* of their theories and conclusions. These are sometimes included within the PLAs and represent a broader view of *How Psychology Works*; they're also dealt with under the heading of 'Synoptic Material', another recurring feature of every chapter.

- *End-of-chapter summaries:* these are detailed summaries, using the same subsection headings as used in the chapter (following the Specification). They're designed to aid revision as well as initial learning.

- **Other features of the text** include *Key Study* boxes. Although you're not required to know about specific studies, these key studies retain a central place within a particular topic. In other words, it's important that you're familiar with them, even though you couldn't be asked in the exam about a specific study. Each study is evaluated in terms of both methodological and theoretical issues. Outside of the Key Study boxes, a theory or research study may be evaluated using a different format, namely, positive criticisms (denoted by a ✔) and negative criticisms (denoted by a ✘). Positive and negative criticisms are of *equal* importance. 'Specification Hints' aim to 'unpack' or 'deconstruct' the Specification content by spelling out what certain terms mean, how different parts of the Specification overlap or are linked, and emphasising the use of terms such as 'including' and 'for example' (what's *required* and what's *permissible/acceptable*).

This text is accompanied by the **Dynamic Learning Student** website, which includes useful further resources and activities such as multiple choice questions, sample essays and visual schema chapter summaries. Details of how to access the Dynamic Learning website can be found on the inside front cover of this book.

Also available is the **Dynamic Learning Network Edition CD-ROM** which follows the new **AQA(A)** specification exactly, and provides teachers with extensive learning and teaching resources, activities and exercises, all in our highly flexible Dynamic Learning framework. The wide range of resources includes lesson starters, revision schemas and interactive activities such as fill-the-gaps exercises. Chapter summaries appear in the form of *schematic summaries* (or *schemas*): these are diagrammatic in nature, combining boxes, links between boxes etc. as well as words. These more visual elements aid memory and reduce a large amount of information to a much smaller, more manageable format. Another way of checking your knowledge and understanding of the topic is to *fill-the-gaps* that appear in written summaries: you'll be presented with a sentence or short paragraph that has one or more words missing. You have to choose from several options the correct word(s) by dragging it into the gap. At the end of the exercise, you'll be told how well you've done.

Other features of the CD-ROM include (a) a multiple-choice test for each chapter, (ii) two Personal Tutor presentations per chapter, which are interactive 'writing frames' for helping you to plan essay writing with which you can compare your own attempt; (iii) and Exam and Study skills section which (a) defines exactly what's meant by AO1, AO2 and AO3, (b) explains mark allocations for AO1 and AO2, (c) provides hints for writing evaluation AO2), (d) provides some examples of how to write your commentaries for AO2, and (e) offers some tips on how to make effective use of your time both before and during the exam.

Just as examiners use 'positive marking', so we are very much on your side. We hope you find this book easy and enjoyable to read, and that it helps you both to learn and to revise what you need to know to achieve a good grade in your A2 exam.

Picture credits

The author and publishers would like to thank the following for permission to reproduce material in this book:

Figure 1.1 BARIL PASCAL/CORBIS SYGMA; Figure 1.2 AP/PA Photos; Figure 1.3 Joe McDonald/CORBIS; Figure 1.4 With kind permission by Martha McClintock; Figure 1.9 CORDELIA MOLLOY/ SCIENCE PHOTO LIBRARY; Figure 1.10 Bettmann/CORBIS; Figure 1.11a Kevin Schafer / Still Pictures; Figure 1.11b Alain Compost / Still Pictures; Figure 1.11c Philippe SURMELY - Fotolia.com; Figure 1.11d Mike Powles / Still Pictures; Figure 1.11e Michel Gunter / Still Pictures; Figure 1.11f PhotoAlto; Figure 1.14 Steve Jacobs/iStockphoto.com; Figure 1.15 Ravi Tahilramani/iStockphoto.com; Figure 1.17 iStockphoto.com; Figure 2.2 Michael Simon / Rex Features; Figure 2.3 The Barnes Foundation, Merion Station, Pennsylvania/CORBIS; Figure 2.4 Sipa Press / Rex Features; Figure 2.7 Roger-Viollet / Rex Features; Figure 2.8 rachel dewis/iStockphoto.com ; Figure 2.9 THIERRY BERROD, MONA LISA PRODUCTION/ SCIENCE PHOTO LIBRARY; Figure 2.10 Reproduced with kind permission by Prof. Judith H. Langlois, Ph.D., The University of Texas at Austin; Figure 2.11 Jim Smeal/BEI / Rex Features; Figure 2.12 Nik Wheeler/CORBIS; Figure 3.2 Arpad Nagy-Bagoly - Fotolia.com; Figure 3.3 Stockbyte/Getty Images; Figure 3.4 Jason Kwan / Alamy; Figure 3.5 Photodisc/Getty Images; Figure 3.8 microimages - Fotolia.com; Figure 3.10 Ljupco Smokovski - Fotolia.com; Figure 3.11 From Crooks. Psychology: Science, Behaviour and Life, 2E. © 1991 Wadsworth, a part of Cengage Learning, Inc. Reproduced by permission. www.cengage.com/ permissions <http://www.cengage.com/permissions>; Figure 3.12 Konstantin Sutyagin - Fotolia.com; Figure 3.13 Vladimir - Fotolia.com; Figure 3.14 .shock - Fotolia.com; Figure 3.16 Frédéric LEVIEZ - Fotolia.com; Figure 3.17 Peter Widmann / Alamy; Figure 3.20 Rex Features; Figure 4.1 David Hartley / Rex Features; Figure 4.2 Jon Brenneis/Life Magazine/Time & Life Pictures/Getty Images; Figure 4.3 Andrew Drysdale / Rex Features; Figure 4.4 Sonny Meddle / Rex Features; Figure 4.5 With kind permission by Prof. Albert Bandura, Stanford University; Figure 4.6 Rex Features; Figure 4.8 Nathan Benn/CORBIS; Figure 4.9 Lawrence Manning/CORBIS; Figure 4.11 With kind permission by Philip G. Zimbardo, Inc; Figure 4.14 jesse Karjalainen/iStockphoto.com; Figure 4.15 Dirk Freder/iStockphoto.com; Figure 4.16 emmanuelle bonzami/iStockphoto.com; Figure 5.1 Sipa Press / Rex Features; Figure 5.4 James McCauley / Rex Features; Figure 5.5 Reuters/CORBIS; Figure 5.6 Olga Solovei/iStockphoto.com; Figure 5.7 NBCUPHOTO-BANK / Rex Features; Figure 5.8 Josef Philipp/iStockphoto.com; Figure 5.9 Norman Pogson/iStockphoto.com; Figure 6.5a Design Pics Inc / Rex Features; Figure 6.5b WILL & DENI MCIN-TYRE/SCIENCE PHOTO LIBRARY; Figure 6.6 Meredith Mullins/iStockphoto.com; Figure 7.4 Allen Ginsberg/CORBIS; Figure 7.8 Mathieu Garçon/ Sygma/Corbis; Figure 7.9 Najlah Feanny/Corbis; Figure 8.3 Charles Sykes / Rex Features; Figure 8.4a Kristin Callahan / Everett / Rex Features; Figure 8.4b Tim Rooke / Rex Features; Figure 8.4c KPA / Zuma / Rex Features; Figure 9.6 Martin Lee / Rex Features; Figure 9.8 Christian J. Stewart/iStockphoto.com; Figure 9.13 Dutch Photo Press / Patrick van Katwijk / Photoshot; Figure 9.16 Everett Collection / Rex Features; Figure 10.1 Bettmann/CORBIS; Figure 10.2a Archives for the History of American Psychology, University of Akron; Figure 10.2b Wellesley College Archives; Figure 10.3 Photoshot; Figure 10.5 JEREMY WALKER/SCIENCE PHOTO LIBRARY; Figure 10.6 Ken McKay / Rex Features; Figure 10.7 2004 Fortean/TopFoto; Figure 10.9 With kind permission by Liz Pyle; Figure 11.3 Milos Stojanovic - Fotolia.com; Figure 11.4 Tony Kyriacou / Rex Features; Figure 11.5 Scott Hortop / Alamy

Every effort has been made to obtain necessary permission with reference to copyright material. The publishers apologise if inadvertently any sources remain unacknowledged and will be glad to make the necessary arrangements at the earliest opportunity.

Biological rhythms and sleep

What's covered in this chapter?

You need to know about:

Biological rhythms
- Research studies into circadian, infradian and ultradian rhythms, including the role of endogenous pacemakers and of exogenous zeitgebers
- The consequences of disrupting biological rhythms (for example, shift work, jet lag)

Sleep states
- The nature of sleep
- Functions of sleep, including evolutionary explanations and restoration theory
- Lifespan changes in sleep

Disorders of sleep
- Explanations of insomnia, including primary and secondary insomnia, and factors influencing insomnia (for example, apnoea, personality)
- Explanations for other sleep disorders, including sleepwalking and narcolepsy

✔ Specification Hint

This is a popular section of the specification and certainly includes some interesting material. However, many of the sub-sections overlap with each other – for example, sleep can be included as both a circadian rhythm (once per day) and the sleep cycle as an ultradian rhythm (less than 24 hours). Rather than repeat material, we've dealt with it in the most appropriate section and referred to this in other sub-sections where it's also relevant. Of course, this means that there may be less material to learn (since the same information can be applied for different questions), but it's more complicated to work out exactly what is relevant for each question. In your exam, you must explicitly state how all material you present is directly relevant to the exam question and then the examiners will have to give you credit.

BIOLOGICAL RHYTHMS

This section deals with biological rhythms, including circadian, infradian and ultradian rhythms, and the role of endogenous pacemakers and exogenous zeitgebers.

Terminology

A *bodily rhythm* is 'a cyclical variation over some period of time in physiological or psychological processes' (Gross *et al.*, 2000). Many human activities take place within a cycle of about 24 hours. These are called *circadian rhythms* ('circa' = about, 'diem' = a day). Rhythms that have a cycle longer than 24 hours are called *infradian rhythms* (e.g. the human menstrual cycle). *Circannual rhythms* are yearly rhythms and are included as a subset of infradian rhythms. Cycles with shorter periods are called *ultradian rhythms* (e.g. the 90–120-minute cycle of sleep stages in humans). Environmental factors such as light–dark cycles, noise, clocks and so on give clues as to external cycles and are called *exogenous zeitgebers* (German for 'time-giver'). In the absence of any zeitgeber, behaviours that show rhythmicity are driven by internal timing devices – internal biological clocks, which are referred to as *endogenous pacemakers*.

Circadian rhythms: research studies

The Underground Cave Studies 1962, 1975

One of the first studies into the effect of the absence of exogenous zeitgebers on human circadian rhythms was conducted by Aschoff and Wever in Munich in 1962. They isolated participants in an underground Second World War bunker in the absence of environmental time cues for three to four weeks at a time. Although the participants could turn lights on and off at will, they had no external cues to provide clues as to the time of day (or night). All the participants followed a circadian rhythm with a sleep–wake cycle of about 25 hours. Experimental changes in room temperature had no effect on their cycle.

Michel Siffre (see Figure 1.1) has conducted a number of similar studies using himself as the sole participant. In 1962 he spent two months in the caves of Scarrasson in the southern Alps. He spent 61 days underground and surfaced on 17 September believing it to be 20 August. In 1972, he spent 205 days in 'Midnight Cave' in Texas, being monitored by NASA, and in November 1999 he spent three months underground, missing the millennium celebrations! Despite being aware of the results of the previous studies, each time he settled into a 24-hour and 30-minute sleep–wake cycle. Siffre reported feeling pessimistic and depressed when his clock was most out of step with the outside world.

Figure 1.1 Michel Siffre is a specialist in chronobiology, the study of man's internal clock

Evaluation of research studies

✔ **Replicated findings:** there have been numerous sleep–wake studies and although some have reported sleep–wake cycles ranging from 13 to 65 hours, there's a fairly consistent finding of about 25 hours. Miles *et al.* (1977) report a 24.9-hour circadian rhythm for a man that was blind from birth. Despite hearing zeitgebers to inform him of the time, he struggled to cope with a 24-hour day–night cycle and had to take stimulants and sedatives at the appropriate times in order to cope.

✗ **Cognitive sense?** It seems unlikely that humans have evolved with a faulty biological clock running every 25 hours. Animal studies show a consistent 24-hour cycle and it would make more sense for humans to follow this pattern (see the reference to the work of Czeisler *et al.* (1999) below).

✗ **Case studies:** many of these studies use very few participants (a single individual in the case of Siffre) and, for this reason, findings may not easily be generalised to a wider population. Indeed, there may be specific factors about these individuals (e.g. age, gender, personality) that also bring into question such results.

✗ **Conflicting research findings:** it's claimed that isolating participants from the environment without *strictly* controlling their behaviour isn't sufficient to reveal the activity of the endogenous circadian pacemaker. Czeisler *et al.* (1999) suggest that participants in earlier sleep–wake cycle studies were inadvertently affected by their exposure to high levels of artificial light, which skewed their results. Czeisler *et al.* claim that allowing participants to switch on bright lights was like giving them the equivalent of a drug that reset their internal clocks. Czeisler *et al.* claim that the cycle is actually 24 hours. In their 1999 study, 24 men and women lived for a month in very low subdued light, with no clues to the passage of time. The participants were placed on an artificial 28-hour sleep–wake cycle by the researchers. During this time, researchers monitored body chemistry and temperature, which mark the action of the body clock. This allowed the researchers to detect when the body clock, or circadian pacemaker, was turned on. Czeisler *et al.* found that the measurements showed that the human sleep clock operates on a schedule of 24 hours, 11 minutes, not the 25 hours widely reported.

Figure 1.2 'All of the textbooks indicate that humans have a 25-hour day instead of a 24-hour day. We now know that is wrong' (Charles Czeisler: one of the world's leading experts on sleep and shift-work patterns)

Infradian rhythms

Infradian rhythms (longer than 24 hours) include bird migrations, hibernation, the human menstrual cycle and many reproductive cycles. Although some reproductive cycles – such as that of the 17-year magicicada genus of North America cicada (see Figure 1.3) – are very long infradian rhythms, we are all familiar with the yearly springtime reproduction cycle of animals. Seasonal rhythms such as this, which last about a year, are called circannual rhythms and are usually associated with long-lived plants and animals.

Menstrual cycle

The best-known infradian rhythm in humans is the human menstrual cycle. Through a series of complex interactions with the brain and reproductive organs, an egg is released approximately every 28 days by the

Although the menstrual cycle was identified many years ago, exactly how it's generated and how it interacts with other factors are not clearly understood. There's no doubt that it is also affected by circadian rhythms since the secretion of luteinising hormone (which starts ovulation) occurs in the early morning hours. In addition, phase shifts that occur due to jet lag have been shown to affect menstrual cycles.

Research studies

Figure 1.3 The magicicada of North America, which reproduces every 17 years – an extremely long infradian rhythm

ovary. During each menstrual cycle, hormones (oestrogen and progesterone) are secreted, and physiological changes occur to the breasts and the reproductive organs, which are prepared for possible fertilisation. Each cycle ends with menstruation unless pregnancy occurs.

Figure 1.4 Martha McClintock was the first researcher to discover menstrual synchronisation among human females while still an undergraduate at Welleseley College; she's now a Professor at the University of Chicago

Key Study 1.1: McClintock's Menstrual Synchrony Studies (1971, 1988)

Aim/hypothesis (A01)

McClintock identified the synchronisation of female menstruation when she observed that the menstrual cycles among her dormitory mates became synchronised. After further research, she concluded that the synchronisation of the menstrual cycles among 135 female friends and dormitory mates (aged 17–22 years) was caused by pheromones transmitted through social interaction. Pheromones are odourless chemical substances that, when secreted by an individual into the environment, cause specific reactions in other individuals, usually of the same species. It was initially suggested that there may be a specific female pheromone that affects the timing of other female menstrual cycles (McClintock, 1971).

Method/design (A01)

In 1988, McClintock and Stern began a follow-up ten-year longitudinal study that involved 29 women between the ages of 20 and 35 with a history of irregular, spontaneous ovulation. The researchers gathered samples of pheromones from nine of the women at certain points in their menstrual cycles by placing pads of cotton under their arms. The women had previously bathed without perfumed products and then wore the cotton pads for at least eight hours. Each cotton pad was then treated with alcohol (to disguise any smell) and frozen. These pads were then wiped under the noses of the 20 other women on a daily basis.

Results (A01)

McClintock and Stern concluded that 68 per cent of the women responded to the pheromones. Menstrual cycles were either shortened from 1 to 14 days or lengthened from 1 to 12 days, dependent on when in the menstrual cycle the pheromones had been collected. The pheromones collected from the women in the early phases of their cycles shortened the cycles of the second group of women (between 1 and 14 days) by speeding up their pre-ovulatory surge of luteinising hormone. Conversely, pheromones collected later, during ovulation, lengthened the menstrual cycles (by 1–12 days) by delaying the luteinising hormone surge.

Conclusions (A01)

It's still unclear how the pheromones trigger menstrual cycle changes. Because the samples were put on the participants' top lips, McClintock admits that 'we know absolutely nothing about where the chemical formula is acting, whether it's through the skin, the mucus membranes in the nose, or a pair of tiny pits in the nose' (McClintock and Stern, 1998).

Evaluation (A02, A03)

✔ **Research support:** Russell et al. (1980), using a similar methodology to McClintock, obtained supporting results. It's unclear why this synchronisation might occur but in evolutionary terms it may have been useful for females in a social group to have their children at similar times in order to be able to share tasks such as breastfeeding or other childcare activities. This certainly appears to be the case with animals such as lionesses in the same pride.

✔ **Animal evidence:** the evidence for pheromonal effects in rats is very strong and in some cases the actual pheromones have been extracted and analysed. However, whether we can generalise from animal findings to humans remains controversial. Animal behaviour, especially when it comes to mating behaviour, is not as straightforward as human behaviour. An ovulating female boar, when exposed to a male boar's saliva, immediately goes into a spread-legged mating posture. Human behaviour is just not that clear-cut!

✗ **Conflicting evidence:** a study that examined a women's basketball team for an extended period of time found no correlation between the women's menstrual patterns. However, it's known that exercise, dieting and stress can each cause changes in women's menstrual patterns as well, and these may have affected any possible synchronisation effect.

✗ **Methodological errors?** It's claimed that apparent clustering of the female menstrual cycle is a myth and is no more likely than would be expected by chance alone. Furthermore, many of these studies use small samples and rely on women recalling the onset date of menstruation, so this method may be inaccurate. One researcher (Wilson, 1992) has claimed that when you correct all the errors, including McClintock's, the evidence for menstrual synchrony evaporates.

Seasonal affective disorder (SAD)

In the dark time of the year the soul's sap quivers – T.S. Eliot

Seasonal affective disorder, or SAD, is a disorder in which sufferers show seasonal changes of mood and/or behaviour. The most common mood change is depression or 'affective disorder'. Symptoms typically include depression, guilt, low self-esteem, lethargy and sleep problems.

In summary, according to Cynthia A. Graham (2002), 'Menstrual synchrony is a difficult phenomenon to demonstrate, its occurrence among women remains uncertain, or at least unpredictable, and if it does exist, its functional significance remains unclear.'

The exact causes of SAD are still unclear. The most common explanation is that lack of light during the night causes the *pineal gland* to secrete a chemical called *melatonin*. The increase of light at dawn tells the gland to switch off this secretion so that we can wake up. Particularly in northern countries in the winter some people do not seem to experience enough light. Put simply, imbalances in melatonin can lead to problems with other chemicals that may lead to depression. When it was found that exposure to bright light suppresses night-time melatonin production, it was suggested that bright artificial light could be used experimentally, and perhaps therapeutically, to manipulate the circadian sleep–wake cycle in humans (Lewy *et al.*, 1980).

✔ Specification Hint

Seasonal affective disorder (SAD) can be included as either an infradian *or* circadian rhythm. Since the disorder occurs mainly during the winter months, it would appear to be a disorder involving circannual rhythms, which are a subset of infradian rhythms (more than 24-hour rhythms). However, it's hypothesised that SAD occurs because of disruption of the body's sleep–wake cycle, which is, of course, a circadian rhythm. Thus, it's possible to include SAD in either an infradian or circadian rhythm essay (or both!). However, you must *explicitly* state *how* SAD fits into the rhythm that you've been asked to write about.

SAD study (Terman *et al.*, 1998)

A total of 124 participants (aged 18 to 65) with SAD took part in this study. Over three weeks, 85 participants received daily 30-minute exposures to bright light from a box mounted above the head. Some had light therapy in the morning, others in the evening. The remaining participants sat for 30 minutes each morning in front of an apparatus called a negative ion generator, which emitted air ions. These treatments were placebos.

Of those who received the morning light therapy, 60 per cent showed marked improvements in SAD symptoms compared to 30 per cent of those in the evening light condition. Winter depression eased in only 5 per cent of participants exposed to air ions.

Evaluation of SAD

✔ **Replicated findings:** other well-controlled studies by Eastman *et al.* (1998) and Winton *et al.* (1989), conducted with adequate sample sizes, suggest morning bright light therapy is effective in treating SAD.

✔ **Practical treatments:** light therapy is easy to administer in outpatient settings, lacks major side effects (although some have questioned long-term effects on the retina of bright lights) and is cost-effective.

✗ **Not just light:** other factors are implicated in SAD. Genetic vulnerability and stress also seem to be major factors in its causation. The exact cause of SAD remains elusive and unconfirmed.

Ultradian rhythms

We've already mentioned how the sleep–wake cycle in humans follows a basic 24-hour cycle, or circadian rhythm. However, within the sleep portion of this cycle, an ultradian rhythm exists. An ultradian rhythm is a biological rhythm that occurs with a frequency of less than 24 hours. Using a number of physiological techniques, we've learnt that sleep is composed of several repetitive cycles, each lasting about 90 minutes. The three standard physiological measures of sleep are as follows.

1. The *electroencephalogram* (EEG) measures brain activity. It records an average of the electrical potentials of the cells and fibres in a particular part of the brain by means of an electrode attached to the scalp. The EEG is an objective measure of brain activity and allows researchers to determine whether people are awake or asleep, and to identify a number of different sleep stages.

2. The *electrooculogram* (EOG) measures eye movements. It's been found that dreaming is usually accompanied by rapid eye movements and is thus called REM sleep. The other stages of sleep are often referred to as non-REM sleep (NREM) or slow-wave sleep (SWS).

3. The *electromyogram* (EMG) measures the muscle activity of the chin, specifically when it is tense or relaxed (see figure 1.5).

Techniques such as these have allowed researchers to discover that infants spend about 50 per cent of their sleep time in REM sleep compared to adults, who spend only about 20 per cent of their sleep time in REM.

There are distinct differences in the EEG, EMG and EOG record at each of the different sleep stages. Figure 1.6 shows the differences in the EEG, EMG and EOG during waking, REM sleep (rapid eye movement sleep) and SWS, or NREM sleep.

In REM sleep the individual undergoes a relatively brief period of vivid, erratic dreams. When the brain is monitored by EEG, the brain activity is similar to the EEG of a person in a state of wakefulness, and

yet it's difficult to wake people from REM sleep; hence it's often called 'paradoxical sleep'. Non-REM sleep is further split into four stages, each of which is identified by different electrical patterns on the EEG. Within the 90-minute sleep cycle the body begins with a cycle of non-REM sleep, followed by a shorter period of REM sleep. These cycles continue throughout the night, with the REM period getting slightly longer as the night progresses (see Figure 1.7). Each stage is associated with different EEG waves. Put simply, they tend to get 'bigger' as the sleep gets 'deeper'.

The characteristics of these different stages of sleep can be summarised as follows.

- *Stage 1:* the period when we 'drift off'. Breathing becomes slower, heartbeat becomes irregular, blood pressure falls and blood flow is reduced. Brain waves become smaller, slower and somewhat irregular, characterised by a low-voltage fast EEG. Initially, these are called alpha waves, but gradually they slow and are called theta waves. It's easy to wake during this stage.

- *Stage 2:* an intermediate stage of sleep that lasts about 20 minutes. The sleeper gradually goes into deeper sleep. Larger brain waves occur and occasional quick bursts of activity (sleep spindles occur and K-complexes are noted on the EEG). Bodily functions slow down, and blood pressure, metabolism, secretions and cardiac activity decrease.

- *Stage 3:* the beginning of deep sleep occurs about 35 minutes after first falling asleep. The brain waves known as delta waves are slow (at the rate of 0.5 to 4 per second) and quite large (five times the size of waves in stage 2).

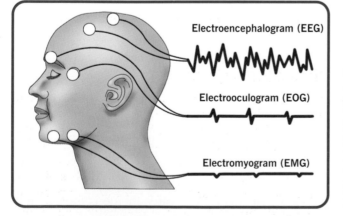

Figure 1.5 Placement of EEG, EOG and EMG electrodes in a sleep experiment

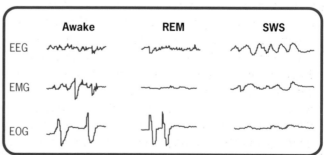

Figure 1.6 EEG, EMG and EOG pattern of different states of consciousness

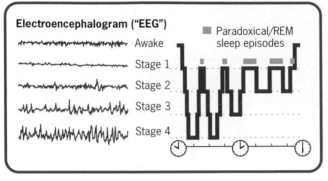

Figure 1.7 The stages of sleep and paradoxical/REM sleep episodes (after Andreasen, 1994)

- *Stage 4:* this is the deepest sleep stage and lasts about 40 minutes. The brain waves (called delta waves) are quite large, making a slow, jagged pattern on the EEG. It's very difficult to wake a sleeper in this stage and bodily functions sink to the deepest possible state of physical rest. The sleeper awakened from deep sleep will probably be groggy, confused or disorientated. He or she may experience 'sleep inertia' or 'sleep drunkenness', seeming unable to function normally for quite some time. In both stages 3 and 4, the EOG shows little movement and the EMG shows the muscles to be relaxed.

- *After stage 4:* we ascend the 'sleep staircase', but instead of entering stage 1 again, we enter REM sleep or paradoxical sleep (see Figure 1.7). During REM sleep, the EMG shows that the muscles are completely inactive, whereas the eyes are extremely active (hence 'rapid eye movement'). Heart rate and blood pressure fluctuate, and the breathing rate is higher. The end of the first REM stage marks the completion of the first ultradian cycle. See the next section for more on REM sleep and dreaming.

The release of hormones also occurs in an ultradian rhythm. Growth hormone (GH) in humans would be a good example of this. Growth hormone has a pulse of hormone every three hours, yet overall its period of highest concentration is found at night.

Ultradian studies

REM and Dreaming Study (Dement and Kleitman, 1957)

By monitoring the EEG record during sleep, Dement and Kleitman (1957) were able to wake participants during each of the different stages of sleep. They asked the participants to report their feelings, experiences and emotions. They found that people awakened during REM sleep reported dreams 80–90 per cent of the time. The dreams were recalled in great detail and included elaborate visual images. Only 7 per cent of the awakenings from NREM sleep led to dream recall. Dement and Kleitman had found the point during the ultradian cycle when people dream. It's perhaps surprising that this discovery had taken so long since it's possible to detect REM simply by looking closely at a sleeping person's eyes.

Characteristics of Dreams Study (Dement and Wolpert, 1958)

Using the same awakening technique during REM sleep, Dement and Wolpert (1958) found out many factors concerned with dreams and REM sleep. These included those listed below.

- All normal humans dream. People who don't report dreams merely forget their dreams. If they are woken during REM sleep and asked immediately if they were dreaming, people report dreams.

- The length of a dream corresponds to the length of the incident that is being dreamed about. Dreams *don't* last only a second or two. However, dreams don't seem to last longer than 15 minutes and it's speculated that, beyond this time, people forget the beginning of the dream.

- Eye movements observed during REM sleep can correspond to a dream's content, but this isn't always the case.

- Dream content can be affected by events experienced during the day. Since it's relatively difficult to wake up during REM sleep, external stimuli can be incorporated into people's dreams. Dement and Wolpert sprayed water on their participants during REM sleep and these dreamers more often reported a dream that involved a water theme compared to a control group. This might be worth trying on a younger brother or sister – purely in the interests of science, of course!

Evaluation

✔/✗ **Other research findings?** Generally, Dement and Kleitman's research findings have stood the test of time and are accepted by the scientific community. However, some studies have reported figures as high as 70 per cent for the percentage of reported dreams during NREM sleep. Foulkes (1967) attributed this difference to confusion as to what constitutes a dream. Vague, dream-like experiences or muddled thoughts have sometimes been incorrectly categorised as dreams.

✗ **Lacks ecological validity?** The artificial and uncomfortable surroundings of the sleep laboratory (given all the electrodes that have to be worn) suggest that such sleep findings may lack ecological validity. Sleep in the comfort of your own bed may be of a qualitatively and/or quantitatively different nature.

The role of endogenous pacemakers

Endogenous rhythms are rhythms that aren't imposed by the environment but generated from within the organism. Since many of our biological cycles follow an approximate 24-hour rhythm, even in the absence of external stimuli (exogenous zeitgebers), it follows that there must be some kind of internal biological clock.

Although studies of one-cell organisms suggest the cellular nature of the system that controls circadian rhythms, the circadian pacemaker in higher organisms, is located in the cells of specific structures of the organism. These include the optic and cerebral lobes of the brain in insects, the eyes in some invertebrates and vertebrates, and the pineal gland, which is located within the brain, in non-mammalian vertebrates. In humans and mammals, the circadian clock is located in two clusters of nerve cells called the suprachiasmatic nuclei (SCN). These are found in an area at the base of the brain called the anterior hypothalamus.

The SCN is located just above the optic chiasm (see Figure 1.8). The optic nerve sends axons directly from the retina of the eye to the SCN. Hence, in humans, the SCN clock keeps to a 24-hour rhythm with inputs from the eye telling it whether it's night or day. If the SCN is damaged or removed, light can no longer reset the clock.

Evidence for the SCN being the site of the clock comes from experiments in which the SCN was removed from rats and this led to the usual rhythmic cycles of activity and sleep being abolished (Stephan and Zucker, 1972).

Further experiments showed that recording electrodes picked up rhythmic bursts of activity from the SCN that varied according to a 24.5-hour cycle. These rhythms persisted even when the hypothalamus was surgically isolated from the rest of the brain – a preparation known as a hypothalamic 'island' (Green and Gillette, 1982).

Even when cells of the SCN were removed and studied in vitro, the 24.5-hour rhythm of neural activity continued. One group of experimenters bred a group of mutant hamsters, which followed a 20-hour cycle. They transplanted SCN cells from these adult mutants into the brains of foetuses with a normal 24-hour rhythm and the recipients produced a 20-hour rhythm. When the experimenters transplanted SCNs from normal, 24-hour cycle hamsters into the mutant breed, the recipients followed a 24-hour cycle within six or seven days. In each case, the recipients' rhythm no longer matched their own genes, but the genes of the SCN donors (Ralph et al., 1990). This provides strong evidence for the importance of the SCN in generating and maintaining the circadian rhythm.

Although similar experimental studies have not been conducted on humans (well, would you volunteer?), it's been shown that circadian rhythms are affected by exposure to light (Czeisler et al., 1989). Anatomical studies show the presence of the SCN in humans, and the presence of a pathway (called the retinohypothalamic tract) from the retina to the SCN, has been proved. There have also been a number of reported studies involving brain tumours, which have damaged the region of the SCN and thus produced disorders in sleep–waking cycles (Fulton and Bailey, 1929). However, such damage is not always restricted solely

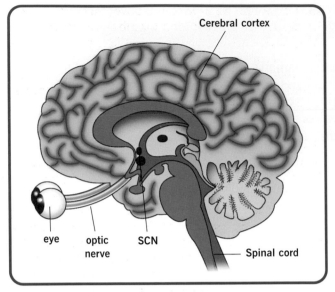

Figure 1.8 Human brain, showing the position of the suprachiasmatic nucleus (SCN)

to the SCN and damages a wider area of the hypothalamus; therefore it's uncertain that it is only the SCN damage that is critical (Carlson, 2001).

Although the SCN has a rhythm of about 24 hours, it also plays a part in longer rhythms. Male hamsters have an annual rhythm of testosterone secretion and this appears to be dependent on the amount of light that occurs daily. Their breeding season begins as day length increases. Lesions (cuts) of the SCN stop these annual breeding cycles and the animals secrete testosterone all year.

Although it appears to be the most important, the SCN is not the only biological clock in mammals. The pineal gland is a pea-like structure found behind the hypothalamus in humans. It receives information indirectly from the SCN. It appears that the SCN takes the information on day length from the retina, interprets it and passes it on to the pineal gland, which secretes the hormone melatonin in response to this message. Night-time causes melatonin secretion to rise, while daylight inhibits it. Even when light cues are absent, melatonin is still released in a cyclic manner; yet if the SCN is destroyed, circadian rhythms disappear entirely.

In animals, melatonin acts on various structures in the brain to control hormones, and physiological processes and behaviours that show seasonal variations. For example, during longer nights, more melatonin is secreted and some animals will go into the winter phase of their circannual (yearly) rhythm. The role of melatonin in humans is not clearly understood and is currently being investigated. The SCN is known to have hormone receptors for melatonin, so there may be a loop from the pineal gland back to the SCN. Researchers now use melatonin levels as an accurate marker of the circadian rhythm in humans.

The locus coeruleus is a group of cells located in the pons. When these cells are removed, REM sleep disappears. Thus, it's concluded that the locus coeruleus must play an important part in activating REM sleep. The locus coeruleus produces noradrenaline and acetylcholine, which are also responsible for the start of REM sleep. The NREM–REM stages of sleep are believed to operate due to an interaction between the raphe nuclei and the locus coeruleus. The raphe nuclei initiate sleep by acting on the reticular activating system (RAS).

Recent research has found that circadian rhythms can persist in isolated lungs, livers and other tissues grown in a culture dish (i.e. in vitro) that were not under the control of the SCN (Yamazaki et al., 2000). These findings suggest that most cells and tissues of the body may be capable of activity on a circadian basis. It's still recognised that the SCN has the key role as the major circadian pacemaker, but also that it may coordinate

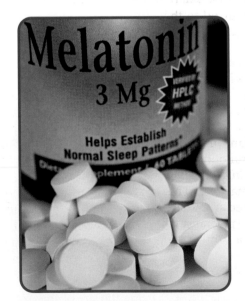

Figure 1.9 Melatonin is a natural hormone that regulates the human biological clock; double-blind research with young adults has shown that melatonin facilitates sleep (Zhdanova et al., 1995)

this in collaboration with the cells, tissues and the whole organism. Although it's known that the SCN sends neural signals as well as neurohormonal signals through the blood to other organs, the specific way in which the SCN 'communicates' to the rest of the body remains unknown (see Stokkan *et al.*, 2001).

The amount of REM sleep people experience as a percentage of total sleep decreases with age (see the section on 'Lifespan changes in sleep', below). Newborns can spend as much as 50 per cent of their total sleep time in REM sleep, whereas this percentage declines to approximately 15 per cent by the age of 50–70 years. Thus age appears to be an endogenous factor that affects the ultradian rhythm of sleep. There are different explanations for why this might be the case (see the section on 'The nature of sleep', below).

✔ Specification Hint

Evaluation that was mentioned in relation to the circadian rhythms section can be used as evaluation of endogenous pacemakers. In addition, you should mention that much of the research on endogenous pacemakers has taken place with either non-human animals or brain-damaged patients. Such evidence is strong, but it might be claimed that it's not so easily generalized to the wider population.

Molecular geneticists have recently found cyclic changes in certain genes that may act as possible mechanisms underlying the internal pacemaker. This hypothesis was supported by the demonstration that a number of species required certain genes for normal circadian function to occur. Researchers produced many random mutations in the DNA of the fruit fly, *Drosophila melanogaster*, until they found rhythm abnormalities. This 'mutant exploration' approach identified circadian clock mutants, which they called period (per) and frequency (frq, pronounced 'freak'). Using a similar process, the first mouse circadian mutation was found and called 'Clock' (see King and Takahashi, 2000).

Exogenous zeitgebers

An important characteristic of circadian rhythms is their ability to be synchronised by exogenous zeitgebers (external time cues) such as the light–dark cycle.

Thus, although we have seen (above) that rhythms can persist in the absence of exogenous zeitgebers, normally such cues are present and the rhythms align to them. Accordingly, if a shift in external cues occurs (e.g. following travel across time zones), the rhythms become aligned to the new cues. This alignment process is called entrainment.

Light

Light is the dominant environmental time cue for circadian clocks. This was not immediately recognised. As seen above, Aschoff *et al.* (1975), in their isolation studies, later reported that the 'light–dark cycle seems to be of little importance for the entrainment of human circadian rhythms' (1975: 64). Again as noted above, Czeisler *et al.* (1999) found out that this was in fact wrong and that the presence of strong artificial light had affected Aschoff's participants' circadian rhythms.

A fascinating study by Campbell and Murphy (1998) is often reported as another study that demonstrates the importance of the light zeitgeber, but this time involved not light that enters through the eyes but through the knees! Campbell and Murphy monitored the body temperatures of 15 volunteers who slept in a lab. The male and female participants were woken at different times and a light pad was shone on the back of their knees. The participants' circadian rhythms fluctuated by as much as three hours away from their normal cycle, depending on the time the light was given. The back of the knee was chosen since light applied here would not reach the participants' eyes and the blood vessels here are very near the surface. The results suggested that humans do not rely solely on the light that enters the eyes, and that blood may be the messenger that carries the light signal from the skin to the brain.

✔ Specification Hint

If you get a question on exogenous zeitgebers you could refer to the effect of light on SAD (see page 5), and the role of pheromones in the synchronisation of the menstrual cycle as reported by McClintock (1971, 1988) (see pages 4–5).

Although the light–dark cycle is clearly the major zeitgeber for almost all organisms, other factors – such as

Evaluation of endogenous pacemakers and exogenous zeitgebers

The persistence of rhythms in the absence of a dark–light cycle or other exogenous time signal (i.e. a zeitgeber) clearly seems to indicate the existence of some kind of internal timekeeping mechanism, or biological clock. However, some investigators have pointed out that the persistence of rhythmicity does not necessarily exclude the possibility that other, uncontrolled cycles generated by the Earth's revolution on its axis might be driving the rhythm (see Aschoff, 1960).

However, these findings should be treated with caution. First, phototransduction via the circulatory system has never been demonstrated in another organism. Researchers have failed to replicate these findings. It was suggested that, despite precautions, participants were exposed to low levels of light reaching their eyes, and even Campbell and Murphy have failed to replicate their study with sleeping participants. Despite such criticisms, there are patents pending for 'knee light pads' to help executives combat the effects of jet lag!

social interactions, activity or exercise, and even temperature – can also modulate a cycle's phase.

Specification Hint

If you get a question on endogenous pacemakers and exogenous zeitgebers, you'll have to refer to the evaluation of the studies associated with SAD and the McClintock Menstrual Synchrony Study (MMSS) (1971).

The consequences of disrupting biological rhythms

As we've seen, the synchrony of an organism with both endogenous pacemakers and exogenous zeitgebers is critical to its well-being and survival; without this, an animal may be led into dangerous situations. For example, if a nocturnal rodent were to venture from its burrow during broad daylight, it would be exceptionally easy prey for other animals. In humans, a lack of synchrony within the environment might lead to health problems in the individual, such as those associated with jet lag, shift work and the accompanying sleep loss (e.g. impaired cognitive function, altered hormonal function and gastrointestinal complaints).

Shift work

Most animals follow the messages from their SCN and let it determine their circadian rhythms. Humans,

however, always like to be different and often try to disobey their 'internal clock' by living a 24-hour lifestyle. The consequences of the increasing trend towards a 24/7 world are still unknown. However, the list of accidents blamed on the effects of incorrect decisions made as a result of a lack of sleep is worrying. These include the Three Mile Island and Chernobyl nuclear accidents, the Challenger space disaster (see Figure 1.10) and the Exxon Valdez oil spill. In addition, workers on night shifts have significantly higher rates of heart disease and diseases of the digestive system. It's estimated that approximately 20 per cent of shift

Specification Hint

The specification mentions 'the consequences of disrupting biological rhythms (e.g. shift work, jet lag)'. Since the words rhythms here is *plural*, you need to know a minimum of two rhythms. Remember, the emphasis here is on rhythms rather than the processes that disrupt these rhythms. Although the spec mentions shift work, we've chosen to look at jet lag as well. We'll deal with jet lag, which mainly disrupts circadian rhythms, and SAD, which disrupts both circadian and infradian rhythms, and sleep deprivation studies (e.g. Jouvet's work and the study of Randy Gardner, see below), which have demonstrated the effects of circadian and ultradian rhythm disruption.

workers report falling asleep during work, which increases the risk of industrial accidents and decreases productivity. Ironically, shift work can diminish the economic gain it is designed to create.

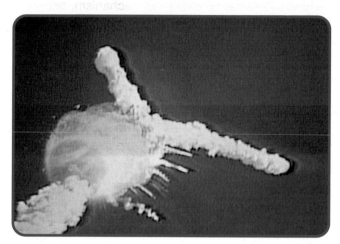

Figure 1.10 The Challenger space disaster: it is claimed that the decision to launch was made in the early hours of the morning when people were at their most tired

Nearly 20 per cent of employees in industrialised countries are employed in shift work, which requires a drastic change to their sleep–wake cycles. Put simply, shift workers don't get enough sleep. Night-time shifts affect the body's natural wake–sleep pattern. This makes it difficult to stay awake during the night and difficult to sleep during the day. Daytime sleep may also be of a different quality to night-time sleep. This chronic lack of sleep harms a person's health, on-the-job safety, task performance, memory and mood, as well as having social costs related to time spent with family and friends who follow more usual sleep–wake cycles.

There are two types of shift work:

1. non-fluctuating, where workers work an unconventional but constant shift, such as 11 pm to 7 am

2. fluctuating, where workers work eight-hour shifts (typically) that change continuously; three different rotating eight-hour shifts enable a 'round-the-clock' operation to occur – the most common ones are 7 am–3 pm, 3 pm–11 pm and 11 pm–7 am.

Both types of shift work produce their own set of effects. In non-fluctuating shift work, the shift in circadian rhythm remains constant once the body adapts to it. Resynchronisation may take a while, but it is possible. However, many shift workers frequently change shifts, thus intensifying the severity of circadian rhythm disturbance.

In shift-work change, exogenous zeitgebers such as daytime and night-time are never permanently synchronised with the start and end of shifts. This means that, for shift workers, the sleep–wake cycle is governed by consistently mistimed circadian rhythms and alternating external cues.

For example, a person may work the night shift for five nights in a row, followed by two days off. During the two days off, the person resumes a normal daytime (diurnal) activity with family or friends. This disrupts the person's previously adjusted circadian rhythm, and he or she must readjust their sleep–wake pattern when they go back to work. Without a constant pattern, biological rhythms remain continually out of synch.

Czeisler *et al.* (1982) studied shift workers and found that the most preferred fluctuating shift pattern is one that rotates every 21 days in a forwards direction. This means that workers move to a schedule that begins later in the day (phase delay) rather than earlier in the day (phase advance). Czeisler *et al.* argued that a phase delay rotation pattern brings increased benefits to workers and employers, such as health improvement, fewer accidents and more production.

Jet lag

Jet lag (or desynchronosis) is a temporary condition that can be experienced as a result of air travel across several time zones in a short period of time. This causes the traveller's internal biological clock to be out of sync with the external environment. People experiencing jet lag have a difficult time maintaining their internal, routine sleep–wake pattern in their new location, because exogenous zeitgebers, like sunshine and local timetables, dictate a different pattern. For instance, if you fly from New York to Paris, you 'lose' hours according to your body's clock. You'll feel tired when you get up because your body clock is telling you that it's still night-time. It might take several days for your body's rhythm to acclimatise to the new time.

The main symptoms of jet lag are fatigue and insomnia, but it can also involve anxiety, constipation or diarrhoea, dehydration, sweating and an increased susceptibility to illness.

Passengers flying north or south in the same time zone usually don't experience jet lag since they remain in the same time zones. Passengers flying east seem to experience the greatest number of problems since they lose time. Passengers flying West still experience jet lag but seem better able to cope with it since they gain time.

Delayed sleep phase syndrome (DSPS)

Delayed sleep phase syndrome (DSPS) also results from a disturbance between the patient's internal biological clock and the external environment. However, although the effects are similar to those of jet lag, the desynchronisation isn't caused by travel or a change in external zeitgebers. Instead, DSPS is caused by a person having an internal biological rhythm that's out of phase with their environment. Typically, sufferers find it hard to go to bed before 2 am and then have difficulty waking until 10 am. Patients who suffer from DSPS are able to get plentiful sleep; it's just postponed. Unfortunately, such a sleep–wake cycle affects various aspects of their lives, such as work and family commitments. Such 'night owls' often find it difficult to meet the expectations of society, and struggle to maintain jobs and social friendships. DSPS is estimated to affect 7 per cent of teenagers and to be the cause in 10 per cent of chronic insomnia cases.

How Science Works

Practical Learning Activity 1.1

Research publications and the media representation of research
Below is a copy of an abstract published in the *Journal of Occupational and Environmental Medicine*. Read it and create a newspaper article as you think the research might have been interpreted in the popular press.

Horne, J.A. and Reyner, L.A. (1999) Vehicle accidents related to sleep: a review. Occupational and Environmental Medicine, 56(5), 289–294

Falling asleep while driving accounts for a considerable proportion of vehicle accidents under monotonous driving conditions. Many of these accidents are related to work – for example, drivers of lorries, goods vehicles, and company cars. Time of day (circadian) effects are profound, with sleepiness being particularly evident during night shift work, and driving home afterwards. Circadian factors are as important in determining driver sleepiness as is the duration of the drive, but only duration of the drive is built into legislation protecting professional drivers. Older drivers are also vulnerable to sleepiness in the mid-afternoon. Possible pathological causes of driver sleepiness are discussed, but there is little evidence that this factor contributes greatly to the accident statistics. Sleep does not occur spontaneously without warning. Drivers falling asleep are unlikely to recollect having done so, but will be aware of the precursory state of increasing sleepiness; probably reaching a state of fighting off sleep before an accident. Self awareness of sleepiness is a better method for alerting the driver than automatic sleepiness detectors in the vehicle. None of these have proved to be reliable and most have shortcomings. Putative counter measures to sleepiness, adopted during continued driving (cold air, use of car radio) are only effective for a short time. The only safe counter measure to driver sleepiness, particularly when the driver reaches the stage of fighting sleep, is to stop driving, and – for example, take a 30 minute break encompassing a short (<15 minute) nap or coffee (about 150 mg caffeine), which are very effective particularly if taken together. Exercise is of little use. Conclusions – More education of employers and employees is needed about planning journeys, the dangers of driving while sleepy, and driving at vulnerable times of the day.

Consider the problems psychologists face when presenting their research findings to the public.

If you're asked a question on the 'consequences of disrupting biological rhythms' you could include information on SAD and state how this affects both circadian and circannual rhythms (pages 6–7); material drawn from sleep deprivation studies would also be relevant. Such studies demonstrate the consequences of disrupting ultradian rhythms (see pages 6–9).

This first subsection of this chapter, on biological rhythms, lends itself to numerous possible exam questions. Table 1.1 will help to clarify which questions might be asked and the appropriate material you could use to answer the questions.

Biological rhythms subsection: essay planner

		Content
Research into:	1. Biological rhythms	• Any from 2, 3 or 4 below
	2. Circadian rhythms	• The Underground Cave Studies (Siffre, 1975) • Seasonal Affective Disorder (Terman *et al.*, 1998)
	3. Infradian rhythms	• Menstrual Synchrony Studies (McClintock, 1971, 1988) • Seasonal Affective Disorder (Terman *et al.*, 1998)
	4. Ultradian rhythms	• REM and Dreaming (Dement and Kleitman, 1957) • Characteristics of Dreams (Dement and Wolpert, 1958)
Endogenous pacemakers and exogenous zeitgebers (*Warning!* You *could* be asked a question about either endogenous or exogenous factors on their own)	5. Biological rhythms	• Any from 6, 7 or 8 below
	6. Circadian rhythms	• SCN, pineal gland, melatonin, molecular genes (endogenous) • Light, SAD (exogenous)
	7. Infradian rhythms	• Melatonin seasonal variations • Light and breeding (hamsters) (endogenous) • SAD, pheromones on menstrual cycle (exogenous)
	8. Ultradian rhythms	• Hormones, locus coeruleus, age factors (endogenous) • Total and partial sleep deprivation, shift work, jet lag (exogenous)
Consequences of disrupting biological rhythms	9. Biological rhythms	• Shift work • Jet lag • SAD • Delayed sleep phase syndrome • Sleep deprivation studies

Table 1.1 Summary table of potential essay questions

The nature of sleep

If the many hours of sleep accomplish nothing, it is the greatest mistake man has ever made – Rechtshaffen

Sleep is one of the last complex behaviours of which the exact purpose remains unclear. All mammals and birds sleep, and fish, reptiles and amphibians exhibit periods of quiet restfulness that we might call sleep. Since sleep is so common in the animal kingdom it strongly suggests that it must perform some critical function. Unfortunately, scientists do not agree what that function is and the exact purpose of sleep remains an enigma. There are countless theories proposed but the two best-known ones are the restoration (or repair) theory and the ecological (or evolutionary) theory.

✔ Specification Hint

You need to know about the nature of sleep. This could potentially cover a vast amount of information. It is probably best to concentrate on the stages of sleep, and the content and duration of sleep. Since dreaming (REM) is a sleep stage it is also appropriate to write about REM sleep. Much of this material has already been covered in the section on circadian rhythm (involving stages of sleep) above, and other material from the section on 'Lifespan changes in sleep' (below) could also be incorporated. After all, lifespan changes do relate to the nature of sleep at different ages. It is even possible that you could include sleep disorder research as a way of understanding the nature of sleep. In this section we are going to concentrate mainly on dreams in sleep.

Functions of sleep, including evolutionary explanations and restoration theory

Evolutionary explanation of sleep

According to the evolutionary explanation of sleep, the function of sleep is similar to that of hibernation. The purpose of hibernation is to conserve energy when the environment is hostile. Similarly, the purpose of sleep is to force us to conserve energy when we would not be very efficient, and to protect us at night when we might be vulnerable to predators. Sleep is thus an evolutionary stable strategy, which increases individual and, in turn, species survival. The evolutionary explanation predicts that animal species should vary in their sleep needs depending on how much time they need to search for food each day and how safe they are from predators when they sleep (see Figure 1.11).

Therefore animals preyed upon, such as herbivores, should sleep more than carnivores since sleep would protect them from predation. However, in reality, herbivores tend to sleep much less (Oswald, 1980). The theory accounts for this seeming discrepancy with the suggestion that metabolic differences affect sleep levels. Predators or carnivores eat occasional large meals, whereas herbivores have to graze for long periods to gain sufficient energy, and therefore sleep for less time. However, it still makes ecological sense for herbivores to sleep and remain inconspicuous when grazing is difficult (e.g. at night) (Green, 1987).

Another aspect of the ecological theory suggests that the size of an animal is also related to total sleep time. Animals with high metabolic rates (e.g. squirrels) expend a lot of energy; this means that they need more time for energy conservation and hence sleep for relatively long periods each day. Larger animals, with slower metabolic rates (e.g. cows, goats), therefore sleep less. Horne (1978) proposed that energy conservation is a major function of sleep in smaller mammals such as rodents.

For humans, in our evolutionary history, it was sensible to sleep at night when we weren't able to see to gather food and possibly become prey for other animals. Those humans who slept in caves during the dark also conserved their energies for hunting during the day. Thus sleep is an evolutionary hangover that no longer serves much purpose.

Sloth: 20 hours   Tree Shrew: 15 hours   Jaguar: 10 hours

Fox: 9 hours   Goat: 3 hours   Horse: 2 hours

Figure 1.11 *The average number of hours slept per day for various mammals*

Evaluation

✔ **Animal evidence:** the evolutionary explanation correctly predicts that the daily sleep time of many species is related to how vulnerable they are while asleep, how much time they must spend to feed themselves, and their metabolic rates. For example, zebras sleep for only two or three hours per day and graze almost continuously, whereas lions can sleep for as long as 20 hours after a kill.

✔ **Sleep deprivation studies:** these suggest that we can cope with very little sleep (see, for example, the study of Randy Gardner, described below). There are case studies of individuals who sleep for as little as one or two hours per night, seemingly with no adverse effects. Studies such as these tend to support the 'evolutionary hangover' theory of sleep.

✔/✗ **Cognitive sense?** It makes sense to suggest that sleep may have evolved to reduce the danger of predation for prey animals. However, it's not clear why so complex a behaviour as sleep should have evolved to do this; simple behavioural inactivity would serve the same purpose. Indeed, many animals freeze and 'play dead' when confronted by predators.

✗ **More vulnerable in sleep?** Some scientists have suggested that animals that are preyed upon may be more vulnerable to predators when asleep given their decreased sensitivity to external stimuli. According to this view, sleep would not be an adaptive response to avoid predation. Snoring is also a difficult phenomenon to explain with this theory since it's likely to make us more vulnerable to predation by drawing attention to ourselves sleeping (Bentley, 2000).

Restoration (and repair) theory of sleep

One theory of sleep is that it helps to reverse and/or restore biochemical and/or physiological processes that are progressively degraded during the day. In essence, it is suggested that being awake disrupts the homeostasis of the body in some way and sleep is required to restore it. Oswald (1980) suggested that:

- REM sleep helps the brain to recover, hence the high levels of brain activity during REM sleep

- slow-wave sleep (mainly stage 4) helps with body repair. There are increased levels of growth hormone during SWS.

Many restorative processes – such as digestion, removal of waste products and protein synthesis – do indeed occur during sleep (Adam, 1980). However, many of these processes also occur during waking and some occur more so during the day. Horne (1988) concluded that sleep does not provide any repair process in humans, except for the brain. Horne referred to core sleep, which he believed is essential for restoration, whereas other types of sleep he called optional sleep whose main purpose is for energy conservation. Stern and Morgane (1974) believe that REM sleep serves the function of allowing the brain to replenish neurotransmitters that have been used during the day. Hartmann (1973) has also suggested that REM sleep is a time for synthesising noradrenaline and dopamine to compensate for the amount used during the day.

Specification Hint

Some of the following material on sleep deprivation studies could also be used in an essay on the 'nature of sleep'.

Research studies

One way to find out how important sleep is for both brain and body restoration is to examine the effects of sleep deprivation. You could use any of the human or animal studies of total or partial sleep deprivation in the section on pages 18–22.

Everyone at some time will have experienced a certain degree of sleep deprivation and will therefore know some of its effects. Studies of sleep deprivation are helpful in order to understand the function(s) of sleep, and a greater understanding might benefit professionals who operate in sleep-deprived situations, such as shift workers, airline pilots, medics, long-distance lorry drivers and personnel in the Armed Forces. For example, research might identify how much sleep is needed and what kinds of sleep are most important.

Many questions arise when studying the effects of sleep deprivation. Total sleep deprivation refers to the situation where animals and humans are deprived of all sleep, whereas partial sleep deprivation refers to the situation where humans and animals are deprived of certain types of sleep, typically REM sleep.

Total sleep deprivation studies
Randy Gardner (Gulevich, Dement and Johnson, 1966)

In 1965, as part of a science project, a schoolboy called Randy Gardner decided to try and break the then world record of 260 hours of wakefulness. Dement read about this in the newspaper and decided to collect some useful data during the attempt. Without the use of any stimulants (even coffee), Gardner stayed awake for exactly 264 hours, 12 minutes. He did suffer the occasional hallucination, some ataxia (inability to perform coordinated movements), speech difficulty, visual deficits and some irritability. He was monitored closely by doctors after his ordeal and was very soon back to normal. After his sleep deprivation, Randy slept for 14 hours and soon returned to his normal 8-hour pattern. In all, there were 67 hours of sleep that he did not 'make up'. However, the percentage of recovery sleep varied across the stages. He made up only about 7 per cent of stages 1 and 2, in contrast to 68 per cent of stage 4 sleep and 53 per cent of REM sleep. The phenomenon whereby 'lost' REM sleep is recovered on subsequent nights is called 'REM rebound'. All in all, only 24 per cent of total sleep loss was recovered. These findings suggest that stage 4 and REM sleep are more important than the other stages (Carlson, 1994).

Synoptic Material: Problems with case studies?

Every research method has its advantages and disadvantages. Case studies have been open to the most criticism over claims that this is the least scientific method available to psychologists.

Try to put forward an argument for and against the use of case studies in psychology.

Partial sleep deprivation studies
REM sleep deprivation studies (Dement, 1960)

Eight volunteers agreed to spend a week in a sleep laboratory being deprived of REM sleep. Whenever their EEG and eye movements indicated they were entering REM sleep they were woken up and kept awake for a few minutes. The volunteers were then allowed to go

Evaluation of sleep deprivation studies

✔ **Similar findings:** many other studies involving human participants have found similar results. Horne (1978) reviewed many studies and found little evidence that sleep deprivation interferes either with physical exercise or causes physical illness or stress. Such findings don't comprehensively support the restoration and repair theory of sleep.

✗ **Case studies:** many sleep deprivation studies involve very small sample sizes and, in the case of Randy Gardner, just one participant. It's difficult to generalise findings from individual case studies, although many psychologists would nevertheless support these findings.

✗ **Confounding variables:** there are a number of problems and confounding factors in sleep deprivation experiments. First, an understanding of what occurs during sleep deprivation doesn't mean we can imply the functions of sleep. For example, there may be some important compensatory mechanism that obscures the effect of sleep deprivation.

✗ **Methodology?** Sleep deprivation experiments are not double blind. Participants are always aware that they're taking part in a study and this may bias results in terms of demand characteristics. Bentley (2000) reports that Dement (1960) accepted that some of his observations may have been the result of experimenter effects – he expected to see disturbances of behaviour due to lack of REM sleep and was biased in his observations. A double-blind technique could have overcome such problems. In addition, being constantly monitored may lead to an increase in stress for sleep-deprived participants. Furthermore, motivation is likely to be an important factor in people's ability to cope with a lack of sleep, and participants in such experiments are likely to be highly motivated. It should also be noted that deprivation experiments typically involve more than just a loss of sleep. Usual daily routines, such as work and free time, are suspended and this may make results difficult to generalise to a more realistic situation.

✗ **Future research:** molecular biologists also study the effects of over-expressing specific genes. In the sleep research field, very few studies have been carried out on the effects of an excess of sleep, but if you hear about one, please let the authors know so we can volunteer!

back to sleep until they entered REM sleep again. Over the course of the nights, the participants had to be woken more and more frequently. On the first night, they were woken an average of 12 times but by the last night this figure had increased to 26. During this period, participants reported mild personality changes such as irritability, anxiety and impaired concentration. When the participants were allowed to sleep normally, there was a 10 per cent increase in the amount of time spent in REM sleep. Again, this study suggests that REM sleep is a particularly important stage of sleep.

Animal studies

Total sleep deprivation study

Alan Rechtschaffen's Rat Experiments (1989)

Rechtschaffen and colleagues devised a procedure whereby a rat was placed on a turntable that rotated whenever its EEG record indicated that it was falling asleep. The turntable was placed above water, which ensured that the rat had to keep walking in order to stop itself falling in the water. This was the experimental rat. The second rat was a 'yoked-control' rat, which was forced to do the same exercise as the experimental rat but could fall asleep on its own

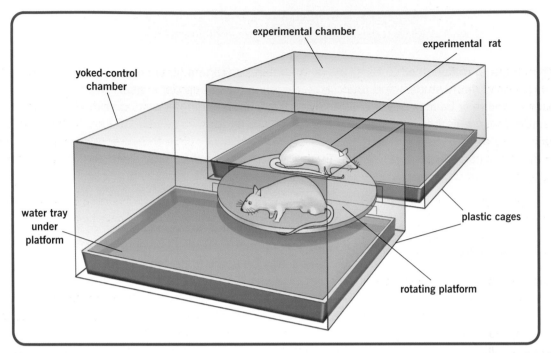

Figure 1.12 The apparatus used to deprive rats of sleep. Whenever the experimental rat fell asleep, the turntable rotated. The rat had to stay awake to avoid falling in the water

when the experimental rat was awake (the turntable did not revolve when the experimental rat was awake). (see Figure 1.12). This procedure ensured that both rats did the same exercise but that the experimental rat slept for only 13 per cent of its usual sleep time and the control slept for 69 per cent of its usual sleep time.

The experimental rats showed an immediate decline. They appeared weak, stopped grooming and became uncoordinated. Although they continued to eat, they lost weight due to a marked increase in metabolic rate. Most of the experimental rats died between 21 and 33 days. In contrast, the control rats, although they had lost some weight, appeared to be generally healthy. Sleep appears essential for physical health in rats at least!

Partial sleep deprivation study
Flowerpot Cat Studies (Dement, 1960; Jouvet, 1967)
Cats have been used to examine the effects of partial sleep deprivation specifically when the animals are deprived of REM sleep. This was done using an ingenious but cruel method whereby cats were placed on tiny islands (upturned flowerpots) surrounded by water. When a cat enters REM sleep its postural muscles relax. This meant that the cats lost their balance and fell into the water. This woke them up and they climbed back onto the flowerpots and started the sleep stage process all over again. The cats could go through all the stages of sleep except REM sleep. Interestingly, the cats became conditioned even while asleep to wake up when they went into REM sleep and didn't have to fall into the water each time. The cats become disturbed very quickly and died after an average of about 35 days.

Synoptic Material: Animals are humans ...

It is worth mentioning the problems of generalising from animal research to human behaviour. Consider in what ways humans may be similar to or different from animals.

Evaluation of animal studies

✗ **Unethical:** the methods used to keep the animals awake are unethical. Many animal studies continue until the animal dies. The use of animals in research is a controversial area. The main area of contention stems from the relative moral value that individual human beings place on animals. Individuals' attitudes range from those who attribute all animals with the same moral value as a human, to those who see animals solely as a resource for human use. Another ethical principle that affects human attitudes towards animal use is that of minimising the harm done to animals. In general the following concepts are adopted in our society:

- It is acceptable to use animals for human ends, but there must be a clear benefit of purpose and the research should be of high quality. There must be no other suitable alternative to the use of animals.
- The use of animals should be minimised.
- Any pain and distress caused to any animals should be minimised.

✗ **Results cannot be generalised to humans:** because animals cannot be persuaded to stay awake voluntarily, various methods have to be used to keep the animals awake. These methods usually involve causing some distress to the animal and it is claimed that it is this stress that leads to the results shown, not the effect of sleep deprivation alone. In addition, human volunteers know that the experiment will end and they will soon be allowed to sleep. In contrast, animals only know that they're in an unfriendly, stressful situation and have no knowledge that the ordeal will end (Carlson, 1994). In addition, the physiological characteristics of animals (e.g. metabolic requirements) make them more susceptible to the damaging effects of a lack of sleep. Despite these criticisms, such studies appear to support the restoration and repair explanation of sleep.

How Science Works

Practical Learning Activity 1.2: For and against the use of animals in research

- Using the internet:
    - try to find FOUR arguments for and against the use of animals in psychological research
    - present a poster outlining these arguments and include examples of some research studies in psychology that have involved the use of animals.

Evaluation of restoration explanation

✓ **Cognitive sense:** this restorative view of sleep function seems to make sense, especially in light of the widespread detrimental psychological and behavioural effects that we all experience with a loss of sleep.

✓ **Infant REM sleep:** babies and infants spend a far higher proportion of the day sleeping (newborns up to 18 hours), and up to 50 per cent of this time is spent in REM sleep. It has been suggested that they need this sleep to help with synaptic (brain) growth.

✔/✗ **Increased growth hormone:** Oswald (1980) proposed that protein synthesis is dependent on growth hormones that are secreted during the delta waves of slow-wave sleep. However, this is not supported by the finding of a decrease rather than increase in protein synthesis of the whole body during sleep in humans. This decrease in protein synthesis is attributed to sleep being a period of overnight fasting, since protein synthesis remains constant when subjects are fed continuously via intragastric tubes throughout the 24-hour period.

✔ **Brain trauma:** patients who have suffered brain trauma, either through injury or electro-convulsive therapy, spend an increased amount of time in REM sleep. Again, it's suggested that this is because the increased blood flow during REM sleep might help in brain repair and restoration.

✔/✗ **REM rebound and length of sleep:** sleep deprivation studies have shown that participants do make up a small proportion of the hours that they have lost on previous nights. However, they do not make up all the hours they have lost. If sleep was so vital for repair and restoration, a far greater proportion might be expected on subsequent nights (see the section on 'Total and partial sleep deprivation studies', below). The REM rebound effect whereby participants in sleep deprivation studies spend longer in REM sleep on subsequent nights also suggests that REM sleep is particularly important to restore the brain processes. REM may help the recovery and manufacture of chemicals necessary for brain restoration.

✗ **Exercise studies:** studies on the effects of exercise on subsequent sleep tend not to support the restoration theory. According to the theory, increased amounts of sleep would be predicted after sustained, intense physical exercise. Shapiro *et al.* (1981) examined runners who had completed a 57-mile race and found that they slept an average of only 90 minutes longer on two subsequent nights, with slightly increased levels of SWS. However, most studies of this type showed no effects on post-exercise sleep. In those studies that did show an enhancement of NREM sleep, it was concluded that the NREM sleep was a consequence of increased body temperature produced by the heating effects of the exercise. Moreover, physically fit individuals do not have longer sleep durations or more NREM sleep than the unfit.

✗ **Animal evidence:** the restorative theory suggests that animals should differ in their sleep needs depending on the amount of energy they expend during the day. Evidence does not support this and there appears to be no correlation between a species' sleep time and energy levels. For example, giant sloths appear to expend little energy each day and spend roughly 20 hours per day sleeping.

Lifespan changes in sleep

Lifespan changes are a crucial determinant of the amount of sleep a person needs each night. Sleep needs vary by age, both qualitatively (different stages of sleep) and quantitatively (how much sleep).

Newborns sleep an average of 16 to 18 hours a day. In the early months, an infant's sleep is divided equally between REM and non-REM sleep. The EEG of an infant in REM sleep is not noticeably different from its waking EEG; indeed, in contrast to adults, an infant in REM sleep is often quite restless, with its arms and legs and the muscles of the face moving almost constantly. This is also the case with foetuses, hence mothers-to-be can feel kicking at any hour. Newborns also have a different sequence of sleep to adults. A newborn baby will often enter REM sleep immediately and it is not until they are three months old that the sequence of REM/NREM sleep is established. Over these first few months the proportion of REM sleep decreases rapidly. A regular pattern of sleeping and waking is rarely established in newborns, but by 20 weeks, infants are mainly awake between 10 am and 8 pm. By the age of one, children usually sleep 13–14 hours, with the entire sleep stage cycle occurring every 45–60 minutes. Toddlers usually take only one daytime nap at this time. By the ages of five to ten years, the sleep stage cycle increases to approximately 70 minutes (Borbely, 1986).

Between the ages of five and twelve, total nocturnal sleep drops to about nine to ten hours. Children of this age sleep deeply, particularly in the first half of the night, indicating that thalamocortical systems are maturing. REM sleep drops to about 25 per cent of a night's sleep – this increase in NREM sleep drive is hardly surprising since this is also associated with brain maturation and increases in activities such as exercise. Pre-teens seem to experience sleep–wake utopia. During the day they are bursting with energy, at night they sleep soundly and they are wide awake and fully rested from the moment they open their eyes in the morning (Dement, 1999).

Puberty marks the onset of adolescence, and sexual and pituitary growth hormones are released in pulses during slow-wave sleep. Melatonin is the hormone that determines the biological clock in every cell in the

How Science Works

Practical Learning Activity 1.3: Sleep diary

Try designing a sleep diary for participants to record the number of hours' sleep they get each night. Include background demographic details and ask them to record any qualitative comments about each night.

You could give the diary to participants of different ages and see if you can find any changes in sleep quality as a result of lifespan changes.

What methodological problems occur with the use of self-reported dream diaries?

body, but a decrease in melatonin signals the body to begin puberty. Although sleep quantity or quality does not change a great deal, various external pressures on teenagers (e.g. school work, friendships) may lead to some having a less regular weekly sleep cycle. Many

STRETCH AND CHALLENGE

The following extract is the abstract of an academic paper on the application of the Multiple Sleep Latency Test (MSLT). Read the article and then try to answer the questions that follow it.

Aldrich, M.S., Chervin, R.D. and Malow, B.A. (1997) Value of the multiple sleep latency test (MSLT) for the diagnosis of narcolepsy. Sleep, 20(8), 620–629, University of Michigan Department of Neurology, Ann Arbor 48109, USA

Since its introduction, the multiple sleep latency test (MSLT) has played a major role in the diagnosis of narcolepsy. We assessed its diagnostic value in a series of 2,083 subjects of whom 170 (8.2%) were diagnosed with narcolepsy. The sensitivity of the combination of two or more sleep onset rapid eye movement (REM) periods (SOREMPs) with a mean sleep latency of < 5 minutes on an initial MSLT was 70% with a specificity of 97%, but 30% of all subjects with this combination of findings did not have narcolepsy. In some narcoleptics who had more than one MSLT, the proportion of naps with SOREMPs varied substantially from the initial MSLT to the follow-up test. The highest specificity (99.2%) and positive predictive value (PPV) (87%) for MSLT findings was obtained with the criteria of three or more SOREMPs combined with a mean sleep latency of < 5 minutes, but the sensitivity of this combination was only 46%. The combination of a SOREMP with a sleep latency < 10 minutes on polysomnography yielded a specificity (98.9%) and PPV (73%) almost equal to those obtained from combinations of MSLT findings, but the sensitivity was much lower. Our results suggest that the MSLT cannot be used in isolation to confirm or exclude narcolepsy, is indicated only in selected patients with excessive daytime sleepiness, and is most valuable when interpreted in conjunction with clinical findings.

- Summarise what this abstract says.
- Does it provide support for or question the usefulness of the MSLT as a diagnostic tool? In what way?
- Can you find any other articles on the internet about the MSLT?

teenagers stay up well into the evening at weekends and also get up later in the mornings. It is at this time of life that males may experience wet dreams. The finding that ejaculation can occur without any external stimulation is perhaps proof of the vividness of some REM dreams. Both sexes may start to experience erotic dreams at this time.

Young adults (18–30 years) tend to start sleeping less than during adolescence and do not experience such deep sleep. This is not particularly marked, however, and thus the majority of people would not notice any real changes. However, questionnaire research suggests that 53 per cent of 18–29-year-olds suffer from daytime sleepiness. Dement argues that people of this age require as much sleep as teens but that external factors work to prevent this. There is a whole host of external factors that can affect sleep patterns at this age, such as crying babies, work problems and snoring spouses. In middle age (30–45 years), people may start to notice a shallowing and shortening of sleep. Increasing signs of fatigue are an indication of middle age. There is a decrease in the amount of deep stage 4 sleep, and adults of this age find it harder to stay awake and feel less refreshed on waking. There are other factors that can contribute to this. Middle-aged people tend to adopt a more sedentary lifestyle with less exercise (both genders often 'retire' from competitive sport at this age), and more caffeine and alcohol is consumed on a regular basis. In addition, many adults of this age have teenage children, and they also tend to put on weight. Weight issues can also lead to respiratory problems (including snoring) which can, in turn, affect sleep (see the section on 'Narcolepsy', pages 35–37).

Sleep changes as we age. By the time people reach late middle age (45–60 years), women suffer a loss of hormones due to the menopause and men, less noticeably, through the andropause, which means that people of this age want to go to bed earlier, suffer more from the effects of sleep deprivation and also experience a poorer quality of sleep. Sleep duration drops to about seven hours and stage 4 sleep virtually disappears. There is a corresponding increase in lighter stages of sleep such as stage 1. The percentage of REM sleep remains fairly constant. Age-related effects on the prostate gland also ensure that many men have to get up in the night to urinate, thus affecting the quality of sleep.

By the age of 60-plus, many people have retired and experienced a major change in their social role. They often have fewer responsibilities and therefore have more time during the day to perform fewer activities.

How Science Works

Practical Learning Activity 1.4: Multiple Sleep Latency Test (MSLT) (Dement, 1999)

The Multiple Sleep Latency Test (MSLT) is used to see how quickly you fall asleep in quiet situations during the day. The MSLT is the standard way to measure your level of daytime sleepiness. Excessive sleepiness is when you are sleepy at a time and place when you should be awake and alert. It affects about 5 per cent of the general population.

The study is based on the idea that you should fall asleep in a shorter amount of time as your feeling of sleepiness increases. The MSLT charts your brain waves and heartbeat, and records your eye and chin movements. The study also measures how quickly and how often you enter the rapid eye movement (REM) stage of sleep. Results of this 'nap study' are routinely used to detect sleep disorders.

The MSLT scores for falling asleep are as follows.

MSLT scores Minutes to sleep onset	Description of sleepiness
0–5	Severe
5–10	Troublesome
10–15	Manageable
15–20	Excellent

The study isolates you from outside factors that can affect your ability to fall asleep.

What external factors do you think might affect your ability to fall asleep?

Source: Carskadon and Dement, 1977

Detailed guidelines on the use of the MLST in the USA can be found at: http://www.guideline.gov/summary/summary.aspx?ss=15anddoc_id=6832andnbr=4199

Again, sleep at this age is characterised by frequent interruptions and periods of wakefulness during the night. Dement (1999) reports that over 40 per cent of a group of healthy men and women aged 65 to 88 had some form of sleep apnoea, the majority being frequent 'microarousals', which are unremembered brief awakenings lasting three seconds or less, but that occur between 200 and 1,000 times per night! Stage 3 and stage 4 sleep are experienced less, possibly because of a reduced need for growth hormones. It is one of nature's cruel ironies that just when we have the opportunity to sleep more, we seem to sleep less and have poorer-quality sleep. Elderly people seem to rise earlier because their circadian dip isn't as pronounced as that of younger people, and they seem to require about an hour or two less sleep than middle-aged sleepers.

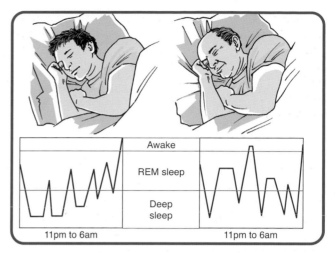

Figure 1.13 The differing sleep patterns of younger and older sleepers

Evaluation of lifespan changes

✔ **Objective measurements:** research into lifespan changes in sleep has been conducted in numerous sleep laboratories throughout the world, and the changes noted in the different stages of sleep involving both the quantity and quality of sleep have been replicated and are reasonably well established. This is particularly true with respect to normal infant sleep because since the 1970s the US National Institute of Health has conducted exhaustive research into this topic in the hope of discovering the cause of Sudden Infant Death Syndrome (SIDS), often referred to as 'cot death' (Dement, 1999). Dement (1999) himself carried out a detailed seven-year longitudinal study called the Stanford Summer Sleep Camp, where 24 10-, 11- and 12-year olds spent their summers going to a US summer camp where Dement and his research team recorded their sleep patterns each night.

✗ **Reporting difficulties:** as noted, there are questions as to the external validity of laboratory-based research into sleep. Borbely *et al.* (1981) questioned adults aged 65 to 83 years of age on their sleeping habits. They found that as many as 60 per cent of them reported taking frequent daily naps. While the elderly do find that their sleep becomes more interrupted, they continue to need about the same amount of sleep as they did in early adulthood, hence the need for daytime naps. These naps may account for the reduced sleep times recorded at night and it remains unclear whether total sleeping time always decreases in elderly people. There has also been a paucity of research into normal sleep among the middle-aged. Dement (1999) believes that this is because they are so busy trying to raise families, succeed at work, and so on, that they find less time to volunteer for sleep laboratory research. Ironically, their busy lives suggest that they are precisely the group that should be researched since it is also the time when the greatest number of sleep problems occur (see the section on 'Disorders of sleep', below).

✗ **Methodological problems:** a major problem with all sleep research involves the measurement of sleep (see the paragraph on 'Operationalisation of sleep', below). In order to measure the physiology of sleep in a laboratory, willing participants have to be connected to a number of electrodes. This must affect the quality and quantity of the sleep that they experience. For this reason, it is often preferred if participants can spend more than one night in the sleep laboratory so that they may get more used to sleeping with the equipment and wires in place.

Evaluation of lifespan changes continued...

✗ **External factors and co-sleep:** there are numerous factors that affect the quality and quantity of sleep experienced. Work patterns, children, aches and pains, and medication can all affect sleep patterns. One factor that is under-researched is the effect of sleeping with a partner. For many people the majority of their sleeping lives are spent sharing a bed with a partner and yet the effects of co-sleep are under-researched. This area of research would have practical difficulties in a laboratory but co-sleep patterns may be both qualitatively and quantitatively different from sleeping alone.

✗ **Individual differences:** Borbely (1986) warns against the use of generalisations about sleep patterns for different age groups. He reports that Wilse Webb from the University of Florida found marked differences between different participants in his sleep studies. Webb found consistent data from the same participant on different nights but not across participants, even when drawn from the same age range. This suggests that sleep patterns may be determined more by an individual person's constitution rather than a cruder measure such as age.

✗ **Operationalisation of sleep:** one difficulty with sleep research is to agree on when sleep occurs. Sleep onset is gradual and entails a predictable sequence of events rather than a discrete event. Three phases of sleep can be identified:

- phase 1 – characterised by calmness and immobility
- phase 2 – characterised by decreased muscle tone and electroencephalogram changes, and
- phase 3 – characterised by an auditory threshold increase and perceived sleep onset (Tryon, 2004).

Many researchers use EEG measures as the sole basis for defining sleep, but as Allan Rechtschaffen (1994) states:

> *Physiological measures derive their value as indicators of sleep from their correlations with the behavioural criteria, not from any intrinsic ontological or explanatory superiority. Any scientific definition of sleep that ignores the behaviours by which sleep is generally known unnecessarily violates common understanding and invites confusion.*

It is argued that restricting the definition of sleep to one measure (such as EEG) is akin to defining intelligence as what an IQ test measures. As long ago as 1963, Kleitman cited a dozen studies showing discrepancies between behavioural and EEG sleep criteria, and questioned using EEG as the sole basis for defining sleep. Although some of these issues have been resolved through newer criteria, the debate continues, particularly with the use of new mobile sleep measure recording devices, such as the wrist Actigraph, which, although easier to use, have question marks concerning their validity.

Synoptic Material: Cultural issues

✗ **Cultural traditions:** in Northern and Central Europe and North America, adults tend to adopt a so-called monophasic pattern of sleep (that is, they sleep for one long period during the night) and much of the research outlined would be applicable to these countries. However, in a significant number of countries (around the Mediterranean, Central and South America), adults take naps during the afternoon. These siestas enable people to avoid working in the hottest parts of the afternoon. Night-time sleep is thus delayed until later in the evening. Borbely (1986) reports that only 42 per cent of Greeks adopt this polyphasic sleeping pattern, and that the practice of taking a siesta is on the decrease. However, in China, the custom of an afternoon nap (called *xiu-xi*) is still widely observed.

DISORDERS OF SLEEP

This section covers explanations of insomnia, including primary and secondary insomnia, and factors influencing insomnia, for example, apnoea and personality.

Insomnia

Insomnia is simply 'the inability to sleep' and is extremely widespread. Indeed, Dement estimates that at least half of all humans acknowledge that they sometimes have difficulty sleeping, but that only 5–10 per cent of sufferers actually get diagnosed with insomnia. Furthermore, Dement argues that insomnia is not a sleep disorder but rather a symptom that can have many different causes. This stance is often promoted in order to encourage people to examine the cause(s), which may be another illness. Nevertheless, Dement concedes that it is often easier to refer to insomnia as if it were a single disorder and, in practice, doctors often attack insomnia directly rather than some unknown underlying cause in order to try to make the patient better. When the insomnia is regarded as an illness in itself and not the effect of some cause or etiology it is called *primary insomnia*. If the insomnia is a direct result of some other illness, then it is called *secondary insomnia*. General symptoms of insomnia include sleepiness, fatigue, decreased alertness, poor concentration, decreased performance, depression during the day and night, muscle aches and an overly emotional state.

Primary insomnia

Primary insomnia is sleeplessness that is not attributable to a medical, psychiatric or environmental cause. The diagnostic criteria for primary insomnia from the *Diagnostic and Statistical Manual of Mental Disorders, Fourth Edition, Text Revision* (*DSM-IV-TR*) are as follows.

- The predominant symptom is difficulty initiating or maintaining sleep, or non-restorative sleep, for at least 1 month (often called chronic insomnia if it persists for longer than 1 month).

- The sleep disturbance (or associated daytime fatigue) causes clinically significant distress or impairment in social, occupational or other important areas of functioning.

- The sleep disturbance does not occur exclusively

How Science Works

Practical Learning Activity 1.5: The nature of sleep on the web

There are some superb interactive resources available on the BBC Science website: http://www.bbc.co.uk/science/humanbody/sleep/

Activities include:

- Sheep dash: testing your reaction times when tired or after having had a coffee
- Testing your daily rhythm
- A sleep quiz
- Why do we sleep?

All the articles are well worth having a look at.

How Science Works

Practical Learning Activity 1.6

If you visit http://www.talkaboutsleep.com/sleepbasics/viewasleepstudy.htm, you can view details of how a sleep study takes place at Stanford University Sleep Disorders Clinic.

during the course of narcolepsy, breathing-related sleep disorder, circadian rhythm sleep disorder or a parasomnia.

- The disturbance does not occur exclusively during the course of another mental disorder (e.g. major depressive disorder, generalised anxiety disorder, a delirium).

- The disturbance is not due to the direct physiological effects of a substance (e.g. drug abuse, medication) or a general medical condition. These last two criteria have other causes and would therefore count as secondary insomnia.

There are numerous primary insomnia sub-types, such as those described below.

Psychophysiological insomnia

This is a form of anxiety-induced insomnia and is sometimes known as learned insomnia or behavioural insomnia. The primary components involved are intermittent periods of stress, which result in poor sleep

Figure 1.14 Insomnia can be thought of as a symptom rather than a disorder in itself

and generate two maladaptive behaviours, including (1) a vicious cycle of trying harder to sleep and becoming tenser, expressed by patients as 'trying too hard to sleep', and (2) bedroom habits and routines, and other sleep-related activities (e.g. brushing teeth), conditioning the patient to frustration and arousal.

People who sleep badly may worry about not being able to function well during the day. They therefore try even harder to sleep at night, but unfortunately this determined effort can make them more alert and thus start any number of worried thoughts, which cause even more sleep loss. Through a process of classical conditioning, some activities associated with sleep, such as changing into pyjamas, turning off the lights or drawing the curtains, can become linked with the sleep

Key Study 1.2: Stress and the effect on sleep (Morin, Rodrigue and Ivers, 2003)

Aims/hypothesis (A01)

Morin, Rodrigue and Ivers (2003) examined the role of stressful life events in the causation of primary insomnia. They examined the relationship of stress and coping skills, and the role of pre-sleep arousal (doing activities late in the evening that heighten arousal) to sleep patterns in good sleepers and insomnia sufferers.

Method/design (A01)

Their sample was composed of 67 participants (38 women, 29 men, mean age 39.6 years): 40 individuals with insomnia and 27 good sleepers. Participants were asked to complete prospective daily measures of stressful events, pre-sleep arousal and sleep for 21 consecutive days. In addition, they completed several retrospective measures of depression, anxiety, stressful life events and coping skills.

Results (A01)

They found that both poor and good sleepers reported equivalent numbers of minor stressful life events. However, insomniacs rated both the impact of daily minor stressors and the intensity of major negative life events higher than did good sleepers. In addition, insomniacs perceived their lives as more stressful, relied more on emotion-orientated coping strategies, and reported greater pre-sleep arousal than good sleepers. Prospective daily data showed significant relationships between daytime stress and night-time sleep, but pre-sleep arousal and coping skills played an important mediating role.

Conclusions (A01)

They concluded that the key factor in insomnia was the way people appraised stressors and the perceived lack of control over stressful events, rather than the number of stressful events per se, and that this perceived lack of control enhanced the vulnerability to insomnia. It is evident that personality factors and the way people cope with stress play a significant part in primary insomnia. The main implication of these results is that insomnia treatments should incorporate clinical methods designed to teach effective stress appraisal and stress coping skills.

Figure 1.15 Stress is a major cause of insomnia

problems that follow. Through repetition these bedtime activities can then trigger over-arousal and insomnia. Some individuals with learned insomnia have trouble sleeping in their own beds yet may fall asleep quickly when they don't intend to – for example, while reading the newspaper, sleeping away from home or watching TV. It is suggested that this occurs because the learned associations are not present in the new or unfamiliar sleep environment. A few nights of inter-rupted sleep per month can be enough to produce a cycle of poor sleep and increase worry about it. Treatment for learned insomnia aims to improve sleep habits and reduce unnecessary worry.

Bad sleep habits, such as those naturally acquired during periods of stress, are occasionally reinforced and, therefore, are not resolved and become persistent. Thus, the insomnia continues for years after the stress has abated and is labelled *persistent* psychophysiolog-ical insomnia.

It is evident that there are a multitude of factors that have been put forward to explain primary insomnia. One study set out to evaluate the prevalence of insomnia among first-degree relatives of chronic primary insomniacs. Dauvilliers *et al.* (2005) asked 256 consecutive primary insomniacs to complete a clinical interview, psychometric questionnaires, a question-naire on the family history of insomnia and, when indicated, a polysomnography (a series of detailed physiological recordings of their sleep). A control group was also used to obtain an estimated base-rate incidence of insomnia in their families. Results showed that of those patients with primary insomnia (n=77), 72.7 per cent reported familial insomnia compared with 24.1 per cent in the non-insomnia control group.

These findings suggest a familial link to primary insomnia.

Idiopathic insomnia

Idiopathic insomnia was originally called childhood onset insomnia because it tends to occur at a very early age. It is thought to occur due to an abnormality in the brain mechanisms that control the sleep–wake cycle. Lifelong sleeplessness is attributed to an abnormality in the neurologic control of the sleep–wake cycle involving many areas of the brain's reticular activating system (promoting wakefulness) as well as in areas such as the solitary nuclei, raphe nuclei and medial forebrain area (promoting sleep). It is suggested that a so-called neuroanatomic, neurophysiologic or neurochemical lesion exists in the sleep system, in which patients tend to be on the extreme end of the spectrum towards arousal and thus have an inability to sleep normally.

Sleep state misperception

People with sleep-state misperception sleep adequately but feel they do not. A disparity exists between the person's subjective description of a night's sleep and the objective measurement of the same night obtained in a sleep clinic. When asked about sleep, these people underestimate their total sleep time and overestimate the time it took them to fall asleep. Dement (1999) cites a case where a patient who complained of severe insomnia was asked to sleep for ten consecutive nights in the sleep lab. Each morning he was asked to com-plete a questionnaire where he had to estimate how long he took to fall asleep each night. He reported times ranging from one to four hours to fall asleep, with a mean of 90 minutes. According to Dement's sleep laboratory recordings, he never took more than 30 minutes to fall asleep and the mean was 15 minutes. Another patient reported a total sleep time of about four hours and yet her actual recordings suggested six and a half hours of sleep on average. Sleep researchers

STRETCH AND CHALLENGE

Using the internet, find out about other persistent insomnia disorders such as

- restless legs syndrome
- gastroesophalageal reflex.

Make brief notes on the symptoms and possible causes of each.

suggest that these discrepancies result from an unclear perception of consciousness and difficulty distinguishing sleep from waking.

Secondary insomnia

When insomnia is caused by a psychiatric disorder (most often depression) or a medical disorder (most often chronic pain), it is termed secondary insomnia. Secondary insomnia is more common than primary insomnia. Secondary insomnia is a result of other causes (not sleep related) such as illness, drugs (including caffeine and alcohol), excessive worrying, pain, and so on. In patients with secondary insomnia the underlying disorder needs to be treated appropriately. Treating the underlying cause is usually more successful than treating the insomnia directly (Monti, 2004). For example, many people suffering from depression begin to experience improved sleep after taking antidepressant pills even though these have been shown to have no effect on the sleep patterns of people who are not depressed.

There are a number of physical and psychiatric causes of secondary insomnia, including the following.

- Hormonal changes in women: these include premenstrual syndrome, menstruation, pregnancy and menopause.

- Decreased melatonin production: the levels of melatonin, the hormone that helps control sleep, decrease as a person ages. By age 60, the body produces very little melatonin.

- Medical conditions: many medical illnesses can disrupt sleep and produce insomnia. These include allergies, arthritis, asthma, heart disease, high blood pressure, hyperthyroidism and Parkinson's disease. It is hoped that treatment of the underlying cause will result in improved sleep, although sometimes treatment for the insomnia is also required.

- Psychiatric conditions: secondary insomnia, especially with awakenings earlier than desired, is one of the most frequently reported symptoms of depression; secondary insomnia is also associated with anxiety disorders, post-traumatic stress disorders, dementia (such as Alzheimer's disease) and other conditions. People who suffer from a psychiatric disorder often sleep badly. Treatment involving drugs and psychotherapy can often help to improve a person's sleep.

How Science Works

Practical Learning Activity 1.7

There are a number of techniques that are thought to alleviate primary insomnia. Try to research various techniques, such as:

- improving sleep hygiene
- relaxation techniques
- stimulus control
- cognitive techniques.

Produce a leaflet for patients suffering from primary insomnia that might help them with their sleep problem. Think what factors may have prevented you from having a good night's sleep in the past.

There are other lifestyle factors that can cause secondary insomnia. These include those described below.

- The use of stimulants: the most common stimulant is caffeine in coffee. It is always recommended that coffee intake should be restricted prior to bedtime. Even when caffeine does not appear to interfere with sleep onset, it can trigger awakenings during the night. Nicotine is also a stimulant and smokers generally take longer to get to sleep than non-smokers.

- Use of alcohol: although many people advocate that a glass of wine helps you sleep, or that a 'nightcap' promotes sleep, it may help sleep onset but usually interrupts night-time sleep.

- Shift work (see pages 12–13): many people find it hard to maintain regular sleep patterns when they are forced to work nights or rotating shift work. Establishing a regular sleep routine is the key to healthy sleep.

- Environmental factors: a whole host of other factors, such as noise, light and temperature, can also have a detrimental effect on sleep patterns.

Apnoea

Obstructive sleep apnoea (OSA) is defined as the cessation of airflow during sleep, preventing air from entering the lungs, caused by an obstruction. These periods of 'stopping breathing' become clinically significant only if the cessation lasts for more than ten seconds each time and occurs more than ten times every hour. OSA happens only during sleep, as it is a lack of muscle tone in the upper airway that causes the airway to collapse. It is not a problem that occurs during waking hours because people have sufficient muscle tone to keep the airway open, allowing for normal breathing. When people experience an episode of apnoea during sleep the brain automatically wakes the person up in order to breathe again. This waking up is usually accompanied by a very loud snore or snort. People with OSA will experience these wakening episodes many times during the night and consequently feel very sleepy during the day (Sleep Apnoea Trust, 2008).

OSA can range from very mild to very severe. The severity is often established using the apnoea/hypopnoea index (AHI), which is the number of apnoeas plus the number of hypopnoeas per hour of sleep – (hypopnoea being a reduction in airflow). An AHI of less than ten is not likely to be associated with clinical problems. To determine whether someone is suffering from sleep apnoea they must first undergo a specialist 'sleep study'. This usually involves a night in hospital where equipment will be used to monitor the quality of their sleep. The definitive investigation is polysomnography, which uses numerous measures of sleep patterns, including:

- electroencephalography (EEG) – brain wave monitoring

- electromyography (EMG) – muscle tone monitoring

- recording thoracic-abdominal movements – chest and abdomen movements

- recording oro-nasal airflow – mouth and nose airflow

- pulse oximetry – heart rate and blood oxygen level monitoring

- electrocardiography (ECG) – heart monitoring

- sound and video recording.

Sleep apnoea is caused by factors that make the throat narrow more than usual during sleep. If the throat is narrower to start with – for example, because the tonsils are enlarged – it is easier for the throat muscles to close and block the airway. Other causes of a narrowed throat include:

- set-back lower jaw

- partially blocked nose – for example, caused by rhinitis (inflammation of the nose lining) or nasal polyps (benign growths, often occurring as a result of allergic conditions such as hay fever)

- being overweight, particularly with a short, thick neck (fat in the neck squashes the throat from outside)

- enlarged adenoids or tonsils (the most common reason in children)

- physiological features inside the mouth, such as a particularly large tongue or small opening to the pharynx

- excessive alcohol, sedative drugs or strong painkillers; OSA becomes more likely as people get older; being overweight, smoking and drinking more than the safe recommended amount of alcohol increases the risk (Sleep Apnoea Trust, 2008).

There is a minority of patients who suffer from apnoea where the cause of the apnoea is not determined. Treatment for sleep apnoea includes weight loss and the use of jaw or nasal devices that allow continuous airway pressure.

Evaluation of insomnia

✗ **Difficulty in generalisations:** one of the world's leading sleep researchers, William Dement, wrote in 1999 that 'there are so many different types of insomnia attributable to so many different causes, that it is nearly impossible to make generalisations that will describe all cases of insomnia in a meaningful way' (1999: 129). One example of this concerns the use of melatonin as a sleep-inducing agent. Melatonin does appear to be effective in a small group of elderly patients with insomnia who have low melatonin levels (Zisapel, 2000). However, it is considered ineffective in the general treatment of insomnia, and the precise role of melatonin in sleep still needs to be clarified (van den Heuvel *et al.*, 1998).

✔ **Physiological support:** Smith *et al.* (2002) conducted a study into the neuro-imaging of NREM sleep in insomnia and found clear evidence for physiological abnormalities in insomniacs. This involved patients with insomnia and 'normal' sleeper controls, who were studied polysomnographically for three nights with whole-brain scans conducted on the third night. Nine females were investigated in total, five patients with insomnia and four normal controls. Patients with insomnia showed consistent and significant decreases in blood flow compared to good sleepers in the frontal medial, occipital and parietal cortices. Such results provide evidence that insomnia may be associated with abnormal central nervous system activity during NREM sleep that is particularly linked to basal ganglia dysfunction.

✗ **Not a sleep disorder at all!** You may be interested to know that Dement (1999) also states that insomnia is not a sleep disorder at all (should we tell the Chief Examiner?), but a symptom that occurs as a result of numerous causes. Dement accepts that many people do regard it as a disorder in itself simply because it is easier to talk about it in this way, but that it should always be dealt with as a symptom, and doctors should search for the cause of the symptom.

✔ **External validity of sleep studies:** studies have examined whether findings from sleep laboratories relate to reported sleep disorders from patients. Garcia-Borreguero *et al.* (2004) found a positive correlation between rating scales and laboratory measures of the sleep disorder called restless leg syndrome, providing some evidence that sleep laboratory measures are good indicators of certain sleep disorders.

✗ **Reliability and validity of sleep insomnia measures:** one major obstacle to explaining the cause of insomnia is that there is controversy over the identification of insomnia in the first place! Schramm *et al.* (1993) examined the test–retest reliability of the Structured Sleep Interview for Sleep Disorders when compared to sleep laboratory recordings. They found excellent reliabilities for almost all current main diagnostic categories and good agreement levels made on the basis of the structured interview and polysomnographic (or EEG sleep laboratory) data. The main source of disagreement between interviewers was found in the symptom information given by the patient, suggesting that subjective self-report should not be overly relied upon (see the section on 'Sleep state misperception', above). However, Vgontzas *et al.* (1994) argue that using a number of sleep laboratory criteria is an unsatisfactory way of diagnosing insomnia. Indeed, a study involving 375 insomniacs and 150 non-insomniac controls found that 'sleep laboratory recordings provide little relevant information for confirming or excluding the presence of insomnia'.

Explanations for other sleep disorders

Sleepwalking

Sleepwalking is a very common type of parasomnia (Latin for 'near sleep') – that is, a condition that occurs during sleep and creates a disruptive event. Sleepwalking affects approximately 1–17 per cent of children (although some estimates are as high as 50 per cent) and is more frequently seen in boys. The incidence of sleepwalking decreases with age. Although the exact prevalence of sleepwalking in adults is not known, it is estimated to be as high as 10 per cent.

The condition can cause a great deal of alarm and distress to the affected person. Sleepwalkers are usually unaware of their activity and may engage in automatic behaviour such as dressing themselves or even getting themselves something to eat. Sleepwalkers tend to be hard to wake, and even though they have their eyes open they usually appear dazed and display incoherent speech.

Sleepwalkers frequently feel embarrassment, shame, guilt, anxiety and confusion when they are told about their sleepwalking behaviour. They usually suffer from amnesia and remember little or nothing of the sleepwalking episodes.

Explanations of sleepwalking

The exact cause of sleepwalking is unknown. As mentioned above (pages 6–8), people experience several cycles of both REM and non-REM sleep each night. Sleepwalking usually occurs during deep, non-REM sleep (stage 3 or stage 4 sleep) early in the night. Sleepwalking most often occurs during childhood, perhaps because children spend more time in the 'deep sleep' phase of slumber.

Figure 1.16 Sleepwalking affects about 10 per cent of adults

How Science Works

Practical Learning Activity 1.8: British hotel chain trains workers to handle nude sleepwalkers after reporting 400 cases in one year

Workers at a chain of budget hotels are being given advice on how to deal with naked sleepwalkers. It follows an increase in the number of guests found wandering around in the night with no clothes on. A study by Travelodge found there had been more than 400 cases in the past year, almost all involving men. Sleep experts blame stress, alcohol abuse and lack of sleep for the disorder.

The research, conducted in 310 Travelodge hotels, found sleepwalkers wandered all over the building. A number had walked into the reception area asking for a newspaper or saying they wanted to check out. Travelodge said it was sending notes to its staff on how to deal with the problem.

The advice includes keeping a supply of towels in reception to help preserve a guest's dignity. Chris Idzikowski, an expert at the Edinburgh Sleep Centre, said: 'These figures are a surprise. Sleepwalking is most likely within an hour or two of going to bed, when first slipping into a deep sleep. Part of the brain switches into autopilot and can manage well-learned movements such as walking, bending or sitting.' He added: 'Sleepwalkers will awake quite unable to recall any of their actions.'

The study also found one in ten sleepwalkers had injured themselves on their travels.

Source: Sky News, 25 October 2007

Read about sleepwalking below and try to explain why guests at this hotel chain may have a higher incidence of sleepwalking than usual.

If it occurs during REM sleep, it is defined as a REM behaviour disorder and tends to happen near morning. When a person sleepwalks they are not acting out a dream, whereas in REM sleep behaviour disorder – where people might punch the bed or jump out of bed, or even injure their bed partner – they usually are.

Genetic explanation

Sleepwalking in an individual is ten times more likely if a first-degree relative has had a history of sleep-walking. Also, it occurs more frequently in identical twins. Hence, it has been concluded that sleepwalking can be inherited. Bassetti (2002) studied 74 patients who were diagnosed with adult sleepwalking and found that, of the 16 patients who underwent genetic testing, 50 per cent of them had a specific gene that was present in only 24 per cent of healthy (non-sleep-walking) people. The gene, called HLA DQB1*05, is one of a family of genes producing proteins called HLA, which are involved in regulating the immune system. The same genetic variant of the HLA gene has been found to be associated with another sleep dis-order called narcolepsy (see below).

Oliviero (2008) believes that sleep disorders such as sleepwalking arise when normal physiological systems are active at inappropriate times. Although it is not clear why the brain issues commands to the muscles during certain phases of sleep, it has been found that these commands are usually suppressed by other neu-rological mechanisms. At times this suppression can be incomplete – because of genetic or environmental factors or physical immaturity – and actions that nor-mally occur during wakefulness emerge in sleep. Oliviero (2008) proposed a possible physiological mechanism underlying sleepwalking, finding that during normal sleep the chemical messenger gamma-aminobutyric acid (GABA) acts as an inhibitor that prevents the activity of the brain's motor system. In children, the neurons involved with this suppression system are still developing and hence motor activity is not fully under control. As a result, many children have insufficient amounts of GABA, leaving their motor neurons capable of commanding the body to move even during sleep. This may explain why sleepwalking begins and is more likely in childhood. In some chil-dren, this inhibitory system may remain underdeveloped – or be rendered less effective by environmental factors – and therefore sleepwalking persists into adulthood.

Environmental factors

The environmental factors that can induce sleep-walking include stress, alcohol intoxication, sleep deprivation, chaotic sleep schedules, hypnosis, and several drugs like sedatives and antihistamines.

Zadra et al. (2008) evaluated 40 suspected sleepwalkers who had been referred to their Sleep Research Centre at a Montreal teaching hospital, between August 2003 and March 2007. They found a clear link between sleep deprivation and sleepwalking. Participants visited the laboratory and had their baseline sleep patterns moni-tored during an initial all-night assessment. During a subsequent visit, patients were kept awake for the entire evening and remained under constant super-vision. The next morning participants were allowed 'recovery' sleep, by which time they had been awake for 25 hours. Various measures were taken, including videotapes that showed the participants engaging in many different types of sleepwalking, ranging from playing with bed sheets to trying to jump over the bed rails. Subjects were evaluated on a three-point scale based on the complexity of their actions. The results were clear-cut. During the first night of basetime sleep, only half of patients exhibited some 32 sleepwalking behavioural episodes. During 'recovery' sleep, 90 per cent of patients demonstrated a total of 92 behavioural episodes. Clearly, the sleep deprivation had increased the amount of sleepwalking.

Medical conditions

Some of the conditions that can cause sleepwalking are fever, arrhythmia, asthma during the night-time, seizures during the night-time and sleep apnoea. It can also be caused by some psychiatric disorders like mul-tiple personality disorder, panic attack and stress disorder.

Evaluation of sleepwalking

✔ **Genetic research support:** Bassetti's (2002) study adopts the classic epidemiological procedure for showing a family association between sleep disorders. It was long suspected that there was a family link to sleepwalking but this study was the first to demonstrate a familial relationship in adult sleepwalking and it was also the first time that a specific genetic marker for adult sleepwalking had been found. However, it remains unclear what the exact nature of the relationship between the HLA gene and sleepwalking is. Although sleepwalkers appear to have an increased frequency of the HLA gene, it doesn't mean that the gene is entirely responsible for the sleepwalking disorder. For example, it may be that some other genes close by, that happen to be transmitted together through generations, are involved. A further problem is that not all sleepwalkers were identified as having the gene and some 25 per cent of the control group who were not sleepwalkers did have the gene. Nevertheless, it does appear that the gene may be implicated in some way with sleepwalking. An additional problem with the study is that the sample of sleepwalkers studied were not necessarily representative of the general population of sleepwalkers. Most sleepwalkers do not seek help or come to the notice of sleep researchers since they are either not aware of their problem or they don't find it causes them too many problems. Sleepwalkers who do seek help are most frequently those who have injured themselves while sleepwalking. This group of sleepwalkers may be qualitatively different to the rest of the sleepwalking population.

✔ **Objective research:** the research by Zadra *et al.* (2008) clearly demonstrated that objective methods could be used for investigating and diagnosing sleepwalking. However, in this study, sample sizes were relatively small and there still exists the possibility that sleep behaviour in a laboratory is different from that experienced at home. For instance, it may be that participants were merely becoming accustomed to the sleep laboratory during the first baseline measure of sleep and that the second night of sleep recovery was simply more indicative of their usual night of sleep and not a direct result of sleep debt.

✔ **Childhood daytime naps:** Dement (1999) also recognises the possibility that sleep deprivation plays a part in sleepwalking. He notes that sleepwalking tends to begin at around four years of age, just when children give up daytime napping, resulting in a maximum sleep debt at bedtime and also a deep, consolidated sleep throughout the night.

Narcolepsy

Narcolepsy is a malfunction of the sleep–wake regulating system in the brain, which until recently was of unknown origin. It affects approximately 1 in 2,000 individuals (Dement, 1999). Its most common manifestation is excessive daytime sleepiness and sleep attacks. The struggle to stay awake is relentless, and whenever narcoleptics relax they fall asleep. However, people with narcolepsy can also fall asleep regardless of what activity they are doing, hence people have been known to fall asleep halfway through a sentence, while eating or even while having sex. These sleep episodes typically last 10–20 minutes before the person awakes feeling refreshed, only to feel sleepy again very soon afterwards.

The other conspicuous symptom is a sudden loss of muscular control triggered by strong emotions such as amusement, anger or excitement, which is called cataplexy. Cataplexy takes the form of attacks of muscle weakness or near total paralysis that occur suddenly without warning for a few seconds or minutes and then subside. People who have cataplexy might suddenly collapse on the floor, able to see and hear but completely unable to move. As is the case in REM sleep, the muscles of the heart, eyes and breathing work normally but the arm and leg muscles become limp. After the episode, the person's muscles operate normally. Before we were aware that REM sleep caused muscle paralysis some psychoanalysts believed that such paralysis was a defence mechanism for people who were afraid to become too emotional since strong emotions often precipitated an attack.

Other symptoms of narcolepsy are:

- hallucinations – vivid images or sounds – on falling asleep or awakening (hypnagogic and hypnopompic hallucinations, respectively); many of these hallucinations are very unpleasant or terrifying in nature

- moments (but sometimes extended periods) of trance-like behaviour in which routine activities are continued on 'autopilot' (automatic behaviour)

- interruption of night-time sleep by frequent waking periods, marked by quickening of the heart rate, over-alertness, hot flushes, agitation and an intense craving for sweets.

Figure 1.17 Narcoleptic dogs have been bred to help humans understand the causes of this disorder

Narcolepsy usually begins in adolescence but instances of onset earlier, or as late as middle age, are on record. The type and severity of symptoms vary from person to person and may either improve or worsen with time.

An inheritable factor has been identified that can increase the likelihood of developing narcolepsy by up to ten times in persons with the factor compared to those without it.

Causes of narcolepsy

Narcolepsy is a neurological condition associated with a fault in the mechanisms in the brain that control wakefulness and sleep. One of the main characteristics of the condition is the intrusion of rapid eye movement (REM) sleep at inappropriate times. During REM sleep the brain is very active and the muscles of the body relaxed (paralysed). In non-narcoleptic people REM sleep does not occur until sleep has been under way for some time. However, in people with narcolepsy, REM sleep often occurs as soon as they fall asleep or even as they awake.

For over 100 years – since the condition was first described – the cause of narcolepsy was unknown. It is

Evaluation of narcolepsy

✔ **Research evidence:** it is clear that there is a genetic component to narcolepsy. In dogs, it is clear that one gene can pass on the trait, whereas in humans it does not. In humans, if one twin has narcolepsy there is only a 30 per cent chance of the other twin developing the disorder (Dement, 1999). It is equally clear that levels of orexin play an important part in narcolepsy. The absence of orexin has not been found in any other conditions that could be confused with narcolepsy, suggesting that determination of the absence of orexin in cerebro-spinal fluid is a good measure for diagnosing narcolepsy in complicated cases. However, in humans, the absence of orexin is neither necessary not sufficient to explain all cases of narcolepsy (Mahowald and Schenck, 2005).

✔ **Effective treatments and animal research:** treatments often involve stimulant drugs. The drug modafinil (Provgil) has proved useful in the treatment of narcolepsy. The drug is thought to work by activating orexin-containing nerve cells. The success of this drug lends support to the orexin deficiency explanation for narcolepsy. Systematic administration of orexin in narcoleptic dogs has also led to much reduced cataplexy and more normal sleep and waking durations (Mahowald and Schenck, 2005).

only since the late 1990s that huge steps have been made in understanding the causes of the condition.

The newly discovered neurotransmitter ('chemical messenger') orexin (also known as hypocretin) is thought to be involved in the control of wakefulness and sleep. Dement (1999) reports that a sleep research team in Texas found that mice that could not make orexin in their brains developed the symptoms of narcolepsy, including sleep attacks and cataplexy. Understanding of narcolepsy stems primarily from research involving narcoleptic dogs (for example, special laboratory-bred Dobermans and Labradors). At the same time, a group in California found that dogs with narcolepsy have a faulty receptor for orexin. Immediately afterwards, research concentrated on investigating whether there was a problem with orexin in humans with narcolepsy. It was soon discovered that, in narcoleptics, levels of orexin in the cerebrospinal fluid (the liquid that bathes the brain and spinal cord) were very low or even undetectable. These results have since been confirmed in several studies. Other scientists have found that the brains of narcoleptic patients have very little orexin in them and that the nerves containing orexin have degenerated (Narcolepsy Association UK, 2008).

STRETCH AND CHALLENGE

Read the following article, which appeared in the *Guardian* on 6 August 2005.

Ryder, R. (2005) All beings that feel pain deserve human rights: equality of the species is the logical conclusion of post-Darwin morality, available at: http://www.guardian.co.uk/uk/2005/aug/06/animalwelfare

The word speciesism came to me while I was lying in a bath in Oxford some 35 years ago. It was like racism or sexism – a prejudice based upon morally irrelevant physical differences. Since Darwin we have known we are human animals related to all the other animals through evolution; how, then, can we justify our almost total oppression of all the other species? All animal species can suffer pain and distress. Animals scream and writhe like us; their nervous systems are similar and contain the same biochemicals that we know are associated with the experience of pain in ourselves.

Our concern for the pain and distress of others should be extended to any 'painient' – pain-feeling – being regardless of his or her sex, class, race, religion, nationality or species. Indeed, if aliens from outer space turn out to be painient, or if we ever manufacture machines who are painient, then we must widen the moral circle to include them. Painience is the only convincing basis for attributing rights or, indeed, interests to others.

Many other qualities, such as 'inherent value', have been suggested. But value cannot exist in the absence of consciousness or potential consciousness. Thus, rocks and rivers and houses have no interests and no rights of their own. This does not mean, of course, that they are not of value to us, and to many other painients, including those who need them as habitats and who would suffer without them.

Many moral principles and ideals have been proposed over the centuries – justice, freedom, equality, brotherhood, for example. But these are mere stepping stones to the ultimate good, which is happiness; and happiness is made easier by freedom from all forms of pain and suffering (using the words 'pain' and 'suffering' interchangeably). Indeed, if you think about it carefully you can see that the reason why these other ideals are considered important is that people have believed that they are essential to the banishment of suffering. In fact they do sometimes have this result, but not always.

Why emphasise pain and other forms of suffering rather than pleasure and happiness? One answer is that pain is much more powerful than pleasure. Would you not rather avoid an hour's torture than gain an hour's bliss? Pain is the one and only true evil. What, then, about the masochist? The answer is that pain gives him pleasure that is greater than his pain!

STRETCH AND CHALLENGE CONTINUED...

One of the important tenets of painism (the name I give to my moral approach) is that we should concentrate upon the individual because it is the individual – not the race, the nation or the species – who does the actual suffering. For this reason, the pains and pleasures of several individuals cannot meaningfully be aggregated, as occurs in utilitarianism and most moral theories. One of the problems with the utilitarian view is that, for example, the sufferings of a gang-rape victim can be justified if the rape gives a greater sum total of pleasure to the rapists. But consciousness, surely, is bounded by the boundaries of the individual. My pain and the pain of others are thus in separate categories; you cannot add or subtract them from each other. They are worlds apart.

Without directly experiencing pains and pleasures they are not really there – we are counting merely their husks. Thus, for example, inflicting 100 units of pain on one individual is, I would argue, far worse than inflicting a single unit of pain on a thousand or a million individuals, even though the total of pain in the latter case is far greater. In any situation we should thus concern ourselves primarily with the pain of the individual who is the maximum sufferer. It does not matter, morally speaking, who or what the maximum sufferer is – whether human, non-human or machine. Pain is pain regardless of its host.

Of course, each species is different in its needs and in its reactions. What is painful for some is not necessarily so for others. So we can treat different species differently, but we should always treat equal suffering equally. In the case of non-humans, we see them mercilessly exploited in factory farms, in laboratories and in the wild. A whale may take 20 minutes to die after being harpooned. A lynx may suffer for a week with her broken leg held in a steel-toothed trap. A battery hen lives all her life unable to even stretch her wings. An animal in a toxicity test, poisoned with a household product, may linger in agony for hours or days before dying.

These are major abuses causing great suffering. Yet they are still justified on the grounds that these painients are not of the same species as ourselves. It is almost as if some people had not heard of Darwin! We treat the other animals not as relatives but as unfeeling things. We would not dream of treating our babies, or mentally handicapped adults, in these ways – yet these humans are sometimes less intelligent and less able to communicate with us than are some exploited non-humans.

The simple truth is that we exploit the other animals and cause them suffering because we are more powerful than they are. Does this mean that if those aforementioned aliens landed on Earth and turned out to be far more powerful than us we would let them – without argument – chase and kill us for sport, experiment on us or breed us in factory farms, and turn us into tasty humanburgers? Would we accept their explanation that it was perfectly moral for them to do all these things as we were not of their species?

Basically, it boils down to cold logic. If we are going to care about the suffering of other humans then logically we should care about the suffering of non-humans too. It is the heartless exploiter of animals, not the animal protectionist, who is being irrational, showing a sentimental tendency to put his own species on a pedestal. We all, thank goodness, feel a natural spark of sympathy for the sufferings of others. We need to catch that spark and fan it into a fire of rational and universal compassion.

All of this has implications, of course. If we gradually bring non-humans into the same moral and legal circle as ourselves then we will not be able to exploit them as our slaves. Much progress has been made with sensible new European legislation in recent decades, but there is still a very long way to go. Some international recognition of the moral status of animals is long overdue. There are various conservation treaties, but nothing at UN level, for example, that recognises the rights, interests or welfare of the animals themselves. That must, and I believe will, change.

Dr Richard Ryder was Mellon Professor at Tulane University, New Orleans, and has been chairman of the RSPCA council; he is the author of Painism: A Modern Morality, *and his new book,* Putting Morality Back into Politics, *will be published by Academic Imprint in 2006.*

- Summarise this article.
- Take a look at a BBC article on speciesism, available at: http://www.bbc.co.uk/religion/ ethics/animals/rights/speciesism.shtml.
- Having read both articles, can you outline some counter-arguments to the views of Richard Ryder.

Synoptic Material

✔/✘ **Animal research:** one problem with research into measures involving the measurement of spinal fluid levels in human patients is that understandably people are fairly reluctant to volunteer for such research. Dement (1999) reports that it was discovered that dogs seem to suffer a very similar form of narcolepsy (and indeed cataplexy) and thus breeding programmes were developed to breed groups of narcoleptic dogs. Through selective breeding and genetic analysis there are now a number of Doberman and Labrador narcoleptic dogs used in the research. Questions still exist as to the generalisability of non-human animal research of this type. Although many would argue that important research findings have been discovered from animal research, others claim that there is a qualitative difference between humans and other animals. For example, the inherited nature of narcolepsy has been shown to be qualitatively different in humans compared to dogs (see above). Nevertheless, it is difficult to deny the value of much of this animal research in respect to humans. Whether humans should use animals in this way for the benefit of humans remains open to question. It has been claimed that using animals in this way is an example of 'speciesism'.

CONCLUSION

The sheer number of hypotheses put forward to explain the function of sleep and the causes of sleep disorders illustrates the degree of our ignorance. From studies such as those outlined above, sleep does appear to be necessary and widespread in all animals. Psychologists have tried to identify the correct amount of sleep required for normal functioning. However, no clear pattern has emerged. There's a considerable variation in the amount of sleep reported by individuals. There appears to be no correlation between the amount of sleep and performance or intelligence.

Thomas Edison and Margaret Thatcher were both said to sleep for short periods each night, whereas Albert Einstein was a long sleeper. Take your pick!

Sleep tends to be devalued by the values inherent in a capitalist society. Why make money only from 9 to 5 when we can keep going all day and all night? The invention of the electric light led to an increasing emphasis on a 24/7 society. Perhaps sleep disorders are an unavoidable consequence of this. Society still recognises the importance of regular sleep patterns for children, but perhaps it's time to re-emphasise the importance of regular sleep patterns for adults as well.

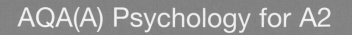

CHAPTER

SUMMARY
Biological rhythms

- **A bodily rhythm** is 'a cyclical variation over some period of time in physiological or psychological processes' (Gross *et al.*, 2000).

- **Circadian rhythms** have a cycle of approximately one day (24 hours). Research studies into circadian rhythms include The Underground Cave Studies (Aschoff and Weaver, 1962; Siffre, 1975).

- Rhythms that have a cycle longer than 24 hours are called **infradian rhythms** (e.g. the human menstrual cycle). Research studies into infradian rhythms include The Menstrual Synchrony Studies (McClintock, 1971; McClintock and Stern, 1998).

- **SAD** can be categorised as a disorder of either infradian and/or circadian rhythms (Terman *et al.*, 1998).

- Cycles of less than 24 hours are called **ultradian rhythms** (e.g. the 90–120-minute human sleep cycle). There are four stages of sleep plus REM sleep. Research studies into ultradian rhythms include the REM and Dreaming Study (Dement and Kleitman, 1957) and the Characteristics of Dreams Study (Dement and Wolpert, 1958).

- **Endogenous rhythms** are rhythms generated from within the organism. The main human internal biological clock is the **SCN**. Animal studies have shown the importance of the role of the SCN in bodily rhythms. Melatonin and the locus coeruleus also play an important role.

- Environmental factors such as light–dark cycles, noise, clocks and so on give clues as to external cycles and are called **exogenous zeitgebers**. Research into exogenous zeitgebers includes that of Campbell and Murphy (1998), and studies into SAD and menstrual synchronisation.

- **Shift work, jet lag and delayed sleep phase syndrome (DSPS)** all involve disruption to biological rhythms. Effects include health, task performance and memory deficits.

Sleep states

- The nature of sleep includes the stages of sleep, and the content and duration of sleep.

- It's still unclear exactly why we sleep. Two explanations into the function of sleep are the **evolutionary explanation and the restoration theory**.

- **The evolutionary explanation of sleep** suggests that the function of sleep is similar to hibernation. The purpose is to conserve energy when the environment is hostile. Sleep protects us from predators in the dark. Sleep is an 'evolutionary hangover'.

- The **evolutionary explanation** also takes into account metabolic differences that affect sleep levels. The size of the animal is also important and related to total sleep time.

- **Sleep deprivation studies**, like that of Randy Gardner (Gulevich, Dement and Johnson, 1966), suggest that humans can cope with very little sleep.

- **Total and partial sleep deprivation animal studies** include Rechtschaffen's Rat Experiments (Rechtschaffen *et al.*, 1989) and Flowerpot Cat Study (Jouvet, 1967).

- **The restoration theory** suggests that sleep helps to reverse and/or restore biochemical and/or physiological processes that are progressively degraded during the day (Oswald, 1980).

- Horne (1988) distinguished between **'core'** and **'optional' sleep**. Some have suggested that REM sleep serves the function of allowing the brain to replenish the neurotransmitters used during the day. Human or animal studies of total or partial sleep deprivation are used to evaluate the restoration and repair theory.

- Brain trauma patients also seems to have a higher proportion of REM sleep, again suggesting that this may be a restorative process.

Disorders of sleep

- **Insomnia** is simply 'the inability to sleep' and is extremely widespread. General symptoms include sleepiness, fatigue, decreased alertness, concentration and performance.

- When the insomnia is regarded as an illness in itself and not the effect of some other cause it is termed primary insomnia. There are many sub-types, including: **psychophysiological insomnia and idiopathic insomnia**.

- **Secondary insomnia** is more common than primary insomnia and is typically caused by a psychiatric disorder (often depression) or a medical disorder (often chronic pain).

- **Obstructive sleep apnoea** is the cessation of airflow during sleep, preventing air from entering the lungs. It is usually caused because of a narrowing of the throat. This can occur as a result of factors such as jaw structure, blocked nose, tonsil problems, obesity, age, alcohol or medication issues.

- There is a great deal of physiological research support on the causes of insomnia, but the **external validity of laboratory sleep studies** has been questioned.

- **Sleepwalking** is a disruptive event that occurs more in children than adults. The incidence in adults is approximately 10 per cent. Although the exact cause is unknown, the best explanation centres on a genetic cause. Sleep debt, alcohol and drugs have also been implicated in sleepwalking.

- **Narcolepsy** affects approximately 1 in 2,000 people, and involves excessive daytime sleepiness and sleep attacks. In the latter case, the sudden loss of muscle control is called cataplexy. The major cause of narcolepsy is believed to be the neurotransmitter orexin (also called hypocretin). Much of the research conducted has involved animal research and it is questionable whether such findings can be generalised to humans.

Essay Questions

Biological rhythms
1. Describe and evaluate research studies into infradian rhythms. (25 marks)
2. Discuss the role of endogenous pacemakers and exogenous zeitgebers in the sleep–waking cycle, and at least one other biological rhythm. (25 marks)
3. Outline and evaluate the consequences of disrupting biological rhythms (for example, shift work, jet lag). (25 marks)

Sleep states
4. Outline and evaluate the nature of sleep. (25 marks)
5. Describe and evaluate any TWO theories of the function of sleep. (25 marks)
6. Discuss lifespan changes in sleep. (25 marks)

Disorders of sleep
7. Outline and evaluate explanations of primary and secondary insomnia. (25 marks)
8. Describe and evaluate factors that influence insomnia – for example, apnoea and personality. (25 marks)
9. Discuss explanations for sleepwalking and/or narcolepsy. (25 marks)

It should take you 30 minutes to answer each question.

Relationships

What's covered in this chapter?

You need to know about:

The formation, maintenance and breakdown of romantic relationships
- Theories of the formation, maintenance and breakdown of romantic relationships – for example, reward/need satisfaction, Social Exchange Theory

Human reproductive behaviour
- The relationship between sexual selection and human reproductive behaviour
- Evolutionary explanations of parental investment – for example, sex differences, parent–offspring conflict

Effects of early experience and culture on adult relationships
- The influence of childhood and adolescent experiences on adult relationships, including parent–child relationships and interaction with peers
- The nature of relationships in different cultures

THE FORMATION, MAINTENANCE AND BREAKDOWN OF ROMANTIC RELATIONSHIPS

✔ Specification Hint

- The two examples of theories given in the specification – namely, reward/need satisfaction and Social Exchange Theory – are usually discussed in relation to the formation and maintenance of relationships (as distinct from relationship breakdown). Therefore this is how they'll be treated here, with one or two additional explanations of breakdown being offered (such as Duck's Theory of Relationship Dissolution).

- As they are only given as examples, you cannot be asked specifically about either theory. However, you need to know about *at least two* theories, and these two will do as far as the formation and maintenance of relationships are concerned. The chapter will also include other theories (e.g. stage theories), which could be referred to instead of these two named theories or in addition to them (as AO2 material, for example).

- It's also worth noting that any one or all of these theories may help to explain the breakdown of relationships (i.e. if factors required for maintaining a relationship change in a particular way, or cease to apply, that relationship might be threatened and break down).

- Note also that the specification refers to 'romantic relationships'. While most theories – and research studies – are relevant to both romantic and non-romantic relationships (such as friendships), you need to emphasise those that focus on romantic relationships (or *how* they apply to romantic relationships).

Theories of formation and maintenance of relationships

A fundamental human need is to belong and to be accepted by other human beings (the need for *affiliation*). This is one of Maslow's (1954) basic survival needs, and is also a major motive underlying conformity, namely *normative social influence* (NSI) (Deutsch and Gerard, 1955; see Gross and Rolls, 2008).

Complementing this general need for others is the preference for certain other people (*attraction*), which is often (but not always) what 'gets a relationship going'; sometimes, 'friends may become lovers', but, typically, a romantic relationship begins with a physical/sexual attraction (preferably mutual). But are there factors that affect the chances that two people will start dating, other than physical attractiveness?

Reward theory

A general theoretical framework for explaining initial attraction (and the formation/maintenance of relationships) is *reward theory* (Clore and Byrne, 1974; Lott and Lott, 1974). The basic idea is that we're attracted to individuals whose presence is rewarding for us. The more rewards someone provides, the more we should be attracted to them. Research has shown that a number of factors influence initial attraction through their reward value, including:

- proximity

- exposure and familiarity

- similarity

- physical attractiveness.

The first three don't refer to personal qualities but to situational factors, over which we often have little (conscious) control. As for the fourth, 'beauty is in the eye of the beholder' and so is as much about the person who is attracted as it is about the person s/he is attracted to. Who we find attractive is influenced by our gender, culture and our evolutionary history as a species, as well as by more individual factors (see pages 45–46).

Proximity

Proximity (physical or geographical closeness) represents a minimum requirement for attraction: the further apart two people live, the less likely it is they'll meet – let alone date and get married. However, this 'rule' only applies to the 'real' world – in the virtual world of the internet, distance is no barrier to the formation of romantic attachments.

Related to proximity is the concept of *personal space* (Hall, 1959, 1966), which describes the human version of the 'individual distance' of zoo animals (see Box 2.1).

Exposure and familiarity

Proximity increases the opportunity for interaction (*exposure*), which, in turn, increases *familiarity*. There's considerable evidence that familiarity breeds fondness (not contempt) – that is, the better we know someone, the more likely we are to like them (see below). According to Argyle (1983), the more two people interact, the more *polarised* (extreme) their attitudes towards each other become – usually in the direction of greater liking. This, in turn, increases the likelihood of further interaction – but only if the people involved are peers ('equals') (see Key Study 2.2, page 49).

Similarity

Evidence suggests that 'birds of a feather flock together'. The key similarities are those concerning *beliefs, attitudes* and *values*. According to Rubin (1973), similarity is rewarding because:

- agreement may provide a basis for engaging in joint activity

- a person who agrees with us helps us feel more confident about our own opinions; this boosts our self-esteem

- most of us are vain enough to believe that anyone who shares our views must be sensitive and praiseworthy

- people who agree about things that matter to them usually find it easier to communicate with each other

- we assume that people with similar attitudes to ourselves are going to like us, so we like them in turn (*reciprocal liking*).

Box 2.1: Personal space

Personal space is like an invisible bubble that surrounds us. According to Hall, we learn *proxemic rules*, which prescribe:

- the amount of physical distance that's appropriate in daily interactions, and
- the kind of situations in which closeness or distance is proper.

Hall identifies four main regions, or zones, of personal space (see Figure 2.1).

There are important *cultural differences* regarding proxemic rules. Each zone of personal space allows the use of different cues of touch, smell, hearing and seeing, which are more important in some cultures than others. The *caste system* in India represents a highly formalised, institutionalised set of proxemic rules.

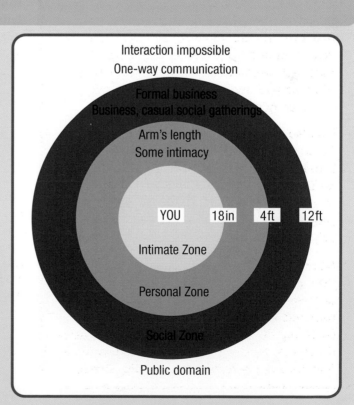

Figure 2.1 Hall's four zones of personal space (from Nicholson, J., 1977)

According to Griffiths (2000), probably one of the most unexpected uses of the internet is the development of *online relationships* (or *cyber affairs*). In the UK, one newspaper reported that there have been over 1,000 weddings resulting from internet meetings.

Cyberspace is becoming another 'singles bar', with many sites aimed at those looking for romance or a sexual liaison; some are directed at singles, while others seem to encourage or facilitate virtual adultery. Online relationships can proceed through chat rooms, interactive games or newsgroups. What may begin as a simple email exchange or innocent chat-room encounter can escalate into an intense and passionate cyber affair – and eventually into face-to-face sexual encounters. Griffiths (2000) claims that 'electronic communication is the easiest, most disinhibiting and most accessible way to meet potential new partners'.

Griffiths (1999a) identifies three basic types of online relationship.

1. *Purely virtual:* while these are usually sexually very explicit, the 'correspondents' never meet, just want sexual kicks, and don't consider they're being unfaithful to their actual partners.
2. Increasingly sexually intense *online* contact may eventually lead to the exchange of photographs, secret telephone calls, letters and meetings. Once the individuals have met, and if practically possible, actual time spent together largely replaces online contact.
3. An initial *offline* meeting will be maintained largely by an online relationship. This usually involves people living in different countries.

Physical attractiveness

It often takes time to find out about other people's attitudes and values, but their physical appearance, including their attractiveness, is immediate. *Physical attractiveness* has been studied in its own right, as well as one aspect of similarity.

According to the *attractiveness stereotype* (e.g. Dion *et al.*, 1972), we tend to perceive attractive-looking people as also having more attractive personalities. But what makes someone attractive? Different cultures have different criteria for judging physical beauty. For example, chipped teeth, body scars, artificially elongated heads and bound feet have all been regarded as signs of beauty in various non-western cultures. Definitions of beauty also change over time, as in western culture's 'ideal' figure for women.

Traditionally, facial beauty has been regarded as more important in women than in men. In contrast, men's stature – especially height – plus a muscular body and (in recent years) a firm, round 'bum', influence how attractive they are to women (and some other men). There are exceptions to these 'rules', of course, and some of the most beautiful people – both male and female – combine facial and bodily beauty (see page 47).

Figure 2.2 Size zero: the epitome of western female beauty?

Figure 2.3 *Ideas about what constitutes female beauty have changed over the centuries*

Figure 2.4 *Brad Pitt and Angelina Jolie: beautiful faces and beautiful bodies*

How Science Works

Practical Learning Activity 2.1

- Without actually carrying it through, discuss in small groups how you would design a study of people's online relationships. Consider both the methodological and ethical issues that would be raised by such a study.
- In your groups you could also discuss concerns raised by online relationships – what (potential) problems do they create for internet users? How does the formation of an online relationship differ from the formation of an actual relationship, and how might these differences be potentially harmful?

How Science Works

Practical Learning Activity 2.2

- Another interesting exception to the 'rule' that we tend to become involved with those who are 'accessible' is the not uncommon report of women falling in love with high-profile prisoners, such as the 'Yorkshire Ripper'.
- Try to find newspaper/magazine articles describing such relationships.
- How might you account for such relationships in terms of psychological theory?

Key Study 2.1: Space Invaders in the Library (SIL) (Felipe and Sommer, 1966)

Aim/hypothesis (AO1)

This was a direct test of Hall's concept of personal space, focusing on the intimate zone. The prediction was that when participants' intimate zone is invaded by a stranger, they are more likely to take evasive action of some kind than when the stranger remains outside the zone.

Method/design (AO1)

This was a naturalistic (or field) experiment, which also used observation, in which naive participants (unsuspecting female university students studying at a large table, 1 m × 5 m) were unexpectedly 'joined' by the female experimenter. There were six chairs evenly spaced on either side of the table, with at least two empty chairs on either side of each student, and one opposite.

There were five experimental conditions in which the female experimenter:

1. sat next to the student and moved her chair to within about 8 cm of the student (about as close as you can get without actually touching); if the student moved her chair away, the experimenter would move her chair nearer

2. sat in the chair next to the student at a normal, acceptable distance (about half a metre)

3. sat two seats away from her (leaving one chair between them)

4. sat three seats way

5. sat immediately opposite her (about a metre apart).

Results (AO1)

About 55 per cent of the participants in condition 1 stayed in the library for longer than 10 minutes, compared with 90 per cent in conditions 2–5 combined. A total of 100 per cent of participants in a control condition (who sat at the same-sized table, with the same number and arrangement of empty chairs, but weren't 'invaded' by the experimenter) stayed longer than 10 minutes.

After 20 minutes, these percentages reduced to 45 in condition 1, 80 in 2–5, and just below 100 in the control condition. By the end of the 30-minute experiment, the figures were 30, 73 and 87 respectively.

Students were more likely to leave, move away, adjust their chair or erect barriers (such as putting a bag on the table between themselves and the experimenter) in condition 1.

Conclusions (AO1)

The experiment showed that, in Hall's terms, a stranger who invades the intimate zone of our personal space is likely to make us feel uncomfortable, such that we either leave the situation or in some other way increase the distance from the stranger.

Evaluation (AO1/AO2)

As a naturalistic/field experiment, the study had *high ecological validity.* The students didn't realise they were involved in an experiment, so their behaviour was entirely 'natural'. But, by the same token, they weren't in a position to give their consent – let alone their informed consent. So, a fundamental ethical principle was being breached.

The participants were all female university students, so we cannot be sure that male students, or non-students, would necessarily react to the 'invasion' in a similar way. However, similar results were found for male psychiatric patients and for people sitting on park benches (Sommer, 1969).

Social Exchange Theory

While there are different versions of Social Exchange Theory (SET), underlying all of them is the view of people as fundamentally selfish.

According to Homans (1974), we view our feelings for others in terms of *profits* (the amount of reward obtained from a relationship minus the cost). The greater the reward and lower the cost, the greater the profit, and, therefore, the initial attraction and the longer-term wish to stay in the relationship.

Blau (1964) argues that interactions are 'expensive': they take time, energy and commitment, and may involve unpleasant emotions and experiences. Because of this, what we get out of a relationship must exceed what we put in.

According to Berscheid and Walster (1978), all social interactions involve an exchange of rewards (such as affection, information and status). The degree of attraction or liking will reflect how people evaluate the rewards they receive relative to those they give.

Key Study 2.2: The Taste of Strangers Experiment (TOSE) (Saegert *et al.*, 1973)

Aim/hypothesis (AO1)

According to the *mere exposure effect* (Zajonc, 1968), we like 'things' that are more familiar to us (that we've been exposed to) purely because they are familiar. Zajonc is one of the researchers involved in this experiment, which predicted that the more often a participant came into contact with another, the more she would like her compared with those she encountered less often.

Method/design (AO1)

Female students were invited to take part in an experiment supposedly to do with the sense of taste. This involved tasting and rating various liquids. The experiment was designed such that each student would find herself in a closed cubicle with another student once, twice, five times, ten times – or alone.

At the end of the experiment, each student was asked to complete a questionnaire relating to details of the experiment. In fact, the only item of interest to the researchers was the one that asked participants to assess their attraction to the person who'd shared the cubicle.

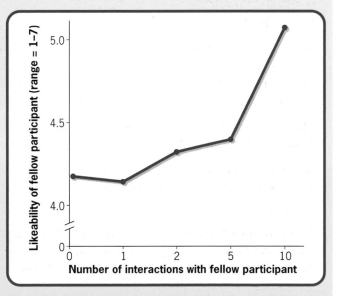

Results (AO1)

As shown in Figure 2.5, the participants' attraction to the other student was directly related to how many interactions they'd had: the more interactions, the greater the attraction.

Conclusions (AO1)

Consistent with the mere exposure effect, and as predicted by Saegert *et al.* (1973), participants' degree of familiarity with another

Figure 2.5 Familiarity, exposure and attraction: the rated likeability of a fellow participant as a function of a number of interactions (based on Saegert et al., 1973, adapted with permission)

participant determined their degree of attraction towards her. Far from breeding contempt, familiarity seems to breed
liking.

Evaluation (AO1/AO2)

As with SIL, the participants were female students, hardly representative of people in general. Unlike SIL, this was a highly contrived, artificial situation: people aren't usually asked to taste a number of different liquids – except as part of a market research exercise.

Related to the artificiality of the experiment is the use of deception. Participants believed this was a study concerned with the sense of taste, whereas it was really about how attraction is influenced by familiarity.

As with other experiments conducted by Zajonc and his colleagues, familiarity is operationalised as the *number of times* something has occurred (a *quantitative* definition). However, this overlooks the importance of *qualitative* definitions. For example, how familiar we are with another person could be judged in terms of what we've learned about them (such as their attitudes and beliefs) or how well we could predict their behaviour.

How Science Works

Practical Learning Activity 2.3

● Conduct a survey of (a) other A-level students and/or your friends, and (b) a sample of older people, asking them to list – in order of importance – the qualities that make other people attractive to them.
● Do you expect their responses to be basically similar?
● What qualities are common to both groups?
● Are there any qualities that distinguish between them?
● Do you expect that responses will include reference to proximity, exposure and familiarity, and similarity? Explain your reasons.

Synoptic Material

In the context of personal ads and commercial dating services, the primary 'resource' (or reward) offered by females seeking a male partner is still physical attractiveness (Brehm, 1992). This matches what men actually want from a female partner. According to Buss (1989), this isn't confined to western culture, but is a universal male preference.

From a *sociobiological* perspective, attractive facial features may signal sexual maturity or fertility. According to Darwinian theories of human mate selection, both men and women select partners who should increase their chances of *reproductive success* – that is, our mates help to ensure that our genes survive into the next generation. This is also consistent with the tendency to equate beauty with youthfulness) (see the section on 'Human reproductive behaviour', below, pages 61–70).

Evaluation of reward theory

✔ **Supporting evidence:** as we've seen above, there are several studies that support the different components of reward theory.

✔/✘ **Lack of a coherent theory:** the basic idea of people being more or less rewarding is very simple, which is a positive aspect of the theory. However, the theory is tested by investigating several unrelated factors (proximity, familiarity etc.), giving the theory a lack of coherence; in other words, there's no attempt to integrate the different factors.

✘ **The 'magnetic metaphor':** according to Duck (1999), the 'magnetic metaphor' of attraction implies that people are unwittingly – and almost against their will – pulled towards one another's inherent, pre-existing characteristics. This is a caricature of social and personal relationships as 'the unthinking domain of reactive magnetism'. More recent research has looked at the *dynamics* of relationships (how they develop and unfold over time) and how they're conducted in real life (such as their inherent tensions). This shift involves fewer controlled experiments (such as SIL and TOSE) and increasing interest in previously 'under-studied' relationships, such as gay and lesbian (see below) and 'electronic' or virtual (see above).

The matching hypothesis

According to SET, people are more likely to become romantically involved if they're fairly closely matched in their ability to reward one another. This is the *matching hypothesis* (MH).

Ideally, we'd all have the 'perfect' partner because, the theory says, we're all fundamentally selfish. But since this is impossible, we try to find a compromise, which takes the form of a *value-match* – that is, the best general 'bargain' that can be struck, a subjective belief that our partner is the most rewarding we could realistically hope to find.

The findings from various tests of the MH (see below) imply that the kind of partner we'd be satisfied with is one we feel won't reject us, rather than one we positively desire. But Brown (1986) argues that the matching phenomenon results from a well-learned sense of what's 'fitting', rather than a fear of rejection. We learn to adjust our expectations of rewards in line with what we believe we have to offer others.

A common early way of investigating the MH was the 'computer dance', such as Walster *et al.*'s 1966 study, described in Key Study 2.3 (see pages 52–53).

How Science Works

Practical Learning Activity 2.4

- As in Practical Learning Activity 2.3, ask a sample of A-level students and/or friends, and a sample of older people, what it is they obtain from their relationships with boy/girlfriends, partners, husbands/wives, as well as what it is they give.
- Compare the responses of the two samples: what responses were common to both and how were they different? Were you surprised by any of these responses – shared or different? Are they consistent with SET's underlying view of people as fundamentally selfish?
- As a kind of 'control' condition, you could present two different samples with a summary of SET and ask participants whether they think this is an appropriate way of thinking about romantic relationships (why / why not?). (A word of warning: *social desirability* might dictate that participants will reject this view of relationships and so their responses may not reflect their true beliefs.)

Evaluation of SET

✔/✘ Are relationships really like this? Although the view of people as fundamentally selfish shouldn't be taken too literally, our attitudes towards others are determined to a large extent by how rewarding we think they are for us (Rubin, 1973). Sedikides (2005) claims that thinking about close relationships helps fight off life's adversities, such as being confronted with failure or unfavourable evaluations: 'They [close relationships] bolster the self-system to the point where failure is taken more lightly and may even be seen as a challenge rather than a threat.' But we're also capable of being *altruistic* – that is, doing things for others without expecting anything in return (the opposite of selfish); this is most evident in our relationships with those who are emotionally closest to us. In Sedikides's terms, we can bolster our partners' self-systems when they are faced with failure and other stressful life events.

✘ Alternative views of relationships: some psychologists distinguish between 'true' love (and friendship), which are altruistic, and less admirable forms based on considerations of exchange (Brown, 1986). Fromm (1962) defines true love as giving, as opposed to the false love of the 'marketing character' (expecting to have favours returned).

✘ Empirical support for these alternative views: Mills and Clark (1980, in Brown, 1986) found support for this distinction, thus contradicting SET. They identified two kinds of intimate relationship: (a) the *communal couple*, in which each partner gives out of concern for the other; and (b) the *exchange couple*, in which each keeps mental records of who's 'ahead' and who's 'behind'.

✔/✘ Coherent but over-simple: the different versions of SET share a few basic ideas, such as profit and reward. The obvious overlap between SET and reward theory (see above) is useful as a bridge between (a) explanations of initial attraction/relationship formation and (b) the maintenance of relationships. However, the underlying view of human beings as just out for what they can get is, as we've seen, simplistic and, probably, inaccurate.

Key Study 2.3: The Computer Dance (CD) Study (Walster *et al.,* 1966)

Aim/hypothesis (AO1)

The aim was to test the MH, specifically the prediction that the more physically attractive one's partner, with whom one had, supposedly, been matched by a computer, the more rewarding s/he would be, and therefore the more likely one would be to want to date them again.

Method/design (AO1)

A total of 752 male and female fresher (first year) students bought tickets for a 'Welcome Week' computer dance at the University of Minnesota at the start of the new academic year. When they bought their ticket, they were asked to complete a detailed questionnaire about themselves; they were told that the information provided would be fed into a computer, which would then match them with their ideal date. In fact, they were assigned a partner purely *randomly*.

As they completed the questionnaire, an unseen observer rated each student for physical attractiveness. During the intermission, the students were asked to indicate how much they liked their partner (having spent two and half hours with them).

Results (AO1)

Physical attractiveness proved to be the single most important factor that determined how much students liked their partner – for both males and females. It was also the best single predictor of how likely the male students were to ask the female students out on a(nother) date – *regardless* of the male's own attractiveness rating.

Conclusions (AO1)

As predicted, the more physically attractive the partner (as rated by the observer), the more s/he was liked (the more rewarding s/he was) and the more desirable s/he was as a future dating partner. This strong evidence for the impact of physical attractiveness in initial attraction is consistent with reward theory: an attractive partner is very rewarding, and the more attractive the better! (This could also be seen as the common-sense view.) However, this is actually *contrary* to what the MH predicts: if we settle for a value match, then only those males who happened to be paired (by chance) with a date whose attractiveness closely matched their own would have asked their female partner for a date.

Evaluation (AO1/AO2)

The study took place in a naturalistic setting: the context was an expected – and desirable – event (the 'Freshers' Ball'); this means it had high ecological validity. However, students were already guaranteed a date prior to meeting and interacting with their partner. According to Berscheid *et al*. (1971), a more valid test of the MH would involve having to *choose* a dating partner – that is, specifying in advance the kind of partner we'd like, including how attractive we'd like them to be. Later computer dance studies (e.g. Berscheid and Walster, 1974) used this improved methodology and the results tended to support the MH.

The students were told that the questionnaire information would be used to match them with their ideal date, but the matching was purely random. Also, they didn't know that their attractiveness was being assessed, or that they were taking part in a study at all, so there was a lack of both consent and informed consent.

How Science Works

Practical Learning Activity 2.5

Either in pairs or small groups, consider the following questions.

- Try to identify one other crucial methodological weakness of the Walster *et al*. (1966) study.
- How were the couples created/what kind of couples were they?
- How might other kinds of couples be studied as a way of testing the MH?

As an alternative to the computer dance method, Murstein (1972) took photographs of 99 engaged couples, then of a separate sample of 98 engaged couples. So, in both cases the couples were in 'natural' (not artificially created), real relationships that existed prior to the study.

Independent judges then rated the photographs for physical attractiveness on a five-point scale without knowing who the couples were ('who belonged to whom'). The couples had to rate their own and their partner's attractiveness.

Partners received very similar ratings, and these were significantly more alike than those given to a control group (created by the real couples' photographs being

Evaluation of the MH

✗ **The magnetic metaphor again:** Duck's 'magnetic metaphor' criticism (see above) applies here (as well as to attraction research in general).

✔/✗ **Supporting evidence and methodological weaknesses:** again as we saw above, the later computer dance studies tended to support the MH. When people are asked in advance what kinds of partner they'd like, those rated as high, low or of average attractiveness tend to ask for dates of a similar attractiveness level. Other methodologies, such as Murstein's, also lend support to the MH. While Murstein's study tried to correct a major methodological weakness of the computer dance studies, it has limitations of its own (see above).

randomly sorted into 'random couples'). How partners rated themselves (self-concept for attractiveness) was significantly more similar than self-ratings for the random couples, although real partners' ratings of each other weren't significantly correlated. Murstein's findings applied more or less equally to both samples.

In common with other similar studies, Murstein restricted his definition of physical attractiveness to facial appearance ('good-looking' and 'looks' were terms used in the rating scale). But, as we saw above, in western culture facial beauty has traditionally been a more important criterion of attractiveness in men's perception of women than vice versa, as well as different cultures defining facial beauty in different ways. Also, 'physical attractiveness' isn't confined to facial appearance, at least in western culture; having a 'good body' is important in both men's and women's judgements of attractiveness (perhaps much more recently in the case of women).

Equity theory

SET is really a special case of a more general account of human relationships called *equity theory* (ET). The extra component in ET that's added to reward, cost and profit is *investment*. According to Brown (1986), 'A person's investments are not just financial; they are anything at all that is believed to entitle him to his rewards, costs and profits. An investment is any factor to be weighed in determining fair profits or losses.'

Equity *doesn't* mean equality. Rather, it means a *constant ratio* of rewards to cost, or profit to investment. So, ET involves a concern with *fairness:* it is *changes* in the ratio of what you put in and what you get out of a relationship that are likely to cause changes in how you feel about it, rather than the initial ratio. You may believe it's fair and just that you give more than you get

– but if you start giving very much more than you did, and receive proportionately less, then you're likely to become dissatisfied.

✔ Specification Hint

This is a good example of how an account of the maintenance of relationships can be used to help explain relationship breakdown.

Box 2.2: The concepts of comparison level and comparison level for alternatives (Thibaut and Kelley, 1959)

- *Comparison level* (CL) is basically the average level of rewards and costs you're used to in relationships, and is the minimum level you expect in any future relationship. So, (a) if your current reward–cost ratio (RCR) falls below your CL, the relationship will be unsatisfying; (b) if it's above your CL, you'll be satisfied with it.
- *Comparison level for alternatives* (CL alt.) is basically your expectation about the RCR that *could* be obtained in other relationships. So, (a) if your current RCR exceeds the CL alt., then you're doing better in the relationship than you could elsewhere. This is likely to make the relationship satisfying for you, and you'll want it to continue; (b) if the CL alt. exceeds your current RCR, then you're doing worse than you could elsewhere, the relationship is likely to be unsatisfying, and you'll not want it to continue.

Evaluation of ET

✔ **Improvement on SET:** according to Duck (1988), the concept of CL alt. implies that whether or not a relationship lasts (from the perspective of one of the partners) could be due to the qualities of the other partner and the relationship, the negative features of the perceived alternatives, or the perceived costs of leaving.

✔ **Usefulness of the concepts of equity/exchange:** concern with either exchange or equity is negatively correlated with marital adjustment (Murstein *et al.,* 1977). People in close relationships don't think in terms of rewards and costs at all – unless they start to feel dissatisfied (Argyle, 1987). A conscious concern with 'getting a fair deal', especially in the short term, makes *compatibility* very hard to achieve – especially among married couples (Murstein and MacDonald, 1983). This corresponds to Mills and Clark's *exchange couple* (see above).

✗ **Still theoretically limited:** ET still portrays people as fundamentally selfish. Many researchers (e.g. Walster *et al.,* 1978; Duck, 1988) prefer to see people as concerned with an equitable distribution of rewards and costs for both themselves *and* their partners.

✗ **Is equity all there is to relationships?** According to *interdependence theory* (IT) (Kelley and Thibaut, 1978), not all social interactions reflect a mutual desire for equity and fair exchange. Intimate relationships are both diverse and complex, and partners' motives can clash as well as converge. This can produce a variety of outcomes, including aggression, altruism, competition, capitulation, cooperation and intransigence ('digging your heels in'). So, IT goes beyond individual partners, and considers the *intersubjective* harmony or conflict between the attitudes, motives, values or goals of people in various social relationships (Ickes and Duck, 2000).

Some versions of ET (e.g. Thibaut and Kelley, 1959; see Box 2.2) actually take account of factors other than the simple and crude profit motives of SET.

Stage theories of relationships

The filter model (Kerckhoff and Davis, 1962)

This was based on a comparison of 'short-term couples' (together for less than 18 months) and 'long-term couples' (18 months or more) over a seven-month period.

- *Similarity of sociological* (or *demographic*) *variables* determines the likelihood that individuals will meet in the first place (the first filter). Social circumstances reduce the '*field of availables*' (Kerckhoff, 1974) – that is, the range of people who are *realistically* available for us to meet (as opposed to those who are *theoretically* available). We're most likely to come into contact with people from our own ethnic, racial, religious, social class and educational groups. We tend to find these types of people most attractive initially, because similarity makes communication easier and we've something immediately in common. At this point, attraction has little to do with people's individual characteristics.

- The second filter involves individuals' *psychological characteristics*, specifically *agreement on basic values*. Kerckhoff and Davis found this to be the best predictor of the relationship becoming more stable and permanent. For the short-term couples, the more similar their values, the stronger the relationship.

- For the long-term couples, *complementarity of emotional needs* was the best predictor of a longer-term commitment (the third filter). Complementary behaviours take account of each other's needs, helping to make a perfect whole and the relationship feel less superficial (Duck, 1999).

According to Winch (1958), happy marriages are often based on each partner's ability to fulfil the other's needs. For example, a domineering person could more easily satisfy a partner who needs to be dominated than one who's equally domineering. However, the evidence – apart from Winch's – is sparse, and we're more likely to marry others whose needs and personalities are *similar* to ours (the *matching phenomenon*: e.g. Berscheid and Walster, 1978). In other words, 'birds of a feather flock together' (rather than 'opposites attract'). According to Buss (1985, in Myers, 1994), 'The tendency of opposites to marry or mate … has never been reliably demonstrated, with the single exception of sex.'

Instead of complementary needs, what about complementarity of *resources* (Brehm, 1992)? Men seem to give a universally higher priority to 'good looks' in their female partners than do women in their male partners. The reverse is true when it comes to 'good financial prospect' and 'good earning capacity'.

Buss (1989) studied 37 cultures (including Nigeria, South Africa, Japan, Estonia, Zambia, Colombia, Poland, Germany, Spain, France, China, Palestinian Arabs, Italy and the Netherlands), involving over 10,000 people. He concluded that these sex differences 'appear to be deeply rooted in the evolutionary history of our species'. (This is discussed further in relation to human reproductive behaviour, on pages 67–68.)

Stimulus-Value-Role (SVR) Theory (Murstein, 1976, 1987)

According to Murstein, intimate relationships begin with a *stimulus stage*, in which attraction is based on external attributes (such as physical attractiveness). In the *value stage*, similarity of values and beliefs becomes much more important, and, finally, the *role stage* involves a commitment based on the successful performance of relationship roles (such as husband and wife).

All three factors play a part throughout a relationship. But each one assumes greatest significance during one particular stage (see Figure 2.6).

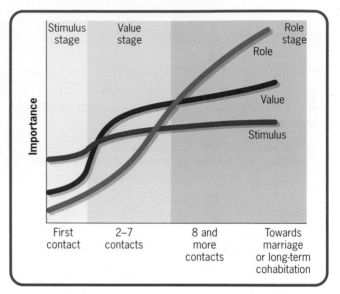

Figure 2.6 *States of courtship in SVR theory (Murstein, 1976, 1987; based on Brehm, 1992)*

Synoptic Material

Throughout the preceding discussion of the formation and maintenance of relationships, there has been an implicit assumption that 'romantic'/'intimate' relationships involve opposite-sex partners – in other words, they are *heterosexual*. Sometimes, the research has explicitly referred to married or engaged couples, again based on the assumption that the institution of marriage is, by definition, restricted to heterosexual couples. So, relationship research has been dominated by this *heterosexist bias*, which, in turn, reflects heterosexism in society: any deviation from the norm of heterosexuality (homosexuality or bisexuality) is judged to be abnormal and these deviant groups should be excluded from social institutions such as marriage (see Gross and Rolls, 2008).

Box 2.3: Same-sex marriage and equality (based on Wilkinson and Kitzinger, 2005)

As of January 2005, same-sex couples can legally marry in:

- the Netherlands (since 2001)
- Belgium (since 2003)
- Canada – in Ontario and British Columbia (since 2003); Quebec, Saskatchewan, Nova Scotia, Manitoba, Newfoundland and the Yukon (since 2004); federal legislation pending for 2005
- the USA – in Massachusetts (since 2004).

Other countries (such as New Zealand, Norway and the UK) grant same-sex couples civil partnerships. In the UK, the Civil Partnership Act became law in 2004; from late 2005 same-sex couples have been able to register their relationships and have these legally recognised as conferring a range of rights and benefits. However, civil partnerships offer far fewer legal benefits than legal marriage.

The UK version is one of the most extensive, covering virtually all the rights and responsibilities of marriage, and its introduction is an important advance for lesbians and gay men in the UK. However:

Marriage is universally understood to be the fundamental social institution for recognition of the couple relationship: and civil partnerships are generally seen as something 'less than' marriage. Indeed, this is precisely why they are sometimes favoured by those who oppose same-sex marriage. Historically, exclusion from marriage – on grounds of the partners' gender, sexual orientation, 'race', ethnicity or religion – has always been used as a tool of oppression . . . (Wilkinson and Kitzinger, 2005).

And again:

By continuing to exclude same-sex couples from marriage . . . the new civil partnerships send the inescapable message that lesbians and gay men are second-class citizens. Separate is still not equal.

How Science Works

Practical Learning Activity 2.6

- Research historical examples of how exclusion from marriage has been used as a tool of oppression. Perhaps the most 'obvious' places to start are Nazi Germany and the apartheid regime in South Africa.

STRETCH AND CHALLENGE

According to Duck (1999), the focus on long-term heterosexual relationships has now been supplemented with discussion of gay and lesbian ('under-studied') relationships. This includes studies of their stability and dissolution or breakdown (Kurdeck, 1991).

According to Kitzinger and Coyle (1995), psychological research into homosexuality since the mid-1970s has moved away from a 'pathology model' towards one comprising four overlapping themes:

1. belief in a basic, underlying similarity between homosexuals and heterosexuals
2. rejection of the concept of homosexuality as a central organising principle of the personality in favour of recognising the diversity and variety of homosexuals as individuals
3. an assertion that homosexuality is as natural, normal and healthy as heterosexuality
4. denial of the idea that homosexuals pose any threat to children, the nuclear family or the future of society as we know it.

This last theme is perhaps the most relevant and directly related to the debate concerning same-sex marriage. According to Wilkinson and Kitzinger (2005), the findings of psychological research into mental health factors associated with being lesbian or gay are a cornerstone of the arguments presented in support of legal recognition of same-sex relationships. Two kinds of evidence predominate.

57

1. There's a frequently cited collection of findings of 'no difference' between the children of same-sex and different-sex couples. More generally, there are no mental health differences between gays/lesbians and heterosexuals, or between the quality of same-sex and different-sex relationships.
2. There are findings of psychological damage caused by social exclusion and suffered by lesbian and gay individuals (and families) as the 'mark of oppression'. For example, Weston (1991) argues that 'blood-family' is often replaced for homosexuals by 'families of choice'. Gays and lesbians often aren't 'out' to blood-family, or may be estranged from their blood-families specifically because of their homosexuality. As a result, the blood-family can function very differently for gays and lesbians: not only are they less likely to tell their parents and siblings of developing relationships, they're less likely to talk about developed intimate relationships (Huston and Schwartz, 1995).

According to Bee (1994), homosexual partnerships are far more like heterosexual ones than they are different. In terms of sexual behaviour, apart from their sexual preferences, gays and lesbians don't look massively different from their heterosexual counterparts (Fletcher, 2002). Researchers have repeatedly found that many of the same gender differences between heterosexual men and women occur when comparing gays and lesbians. For example, both straight and gay men have higher sex drives than straight women and lesbians, and females (straight or lesbian) are more relationship-focused than males (straight or gay). In other words:

many central patterns of sexual attitudes and behaviour are more closely linked to gender than to sexual orientation. If one wants to understand gays and lesbians, a good place to start is by looking at heterosexual men and women respectively (Fletcher, 2002).

However, Kitzinger and Coyle (1995) argue that certain factors are omitted or distorted when homosexual relationships are assessed in terms derived from heterosexual relationships. Some of these are described in Box 2.4.

Theories of the breakdown of romantic relationships

Why do relationships go wrong?

According to Duck (2001), there's an almost infinite number of reasons why relationships break up. But they can be put into three broad categories.

1. *Pre-existing doom:* incompatibility and failure are almost pre-destined (for example, 'Schoolgirl, 17, marries her 50-year-old teacher who's already a grandfather').

2. *Mechanical failure:* two suitable people of goodwill and good nature nevertheless find they cannot live together (this is the most common cause).

3. *Sudden death:* the discovery of a betrayal or infidelity can lead to the immediate termination of a romantic relationship.

Duck believes that the 'official' reasons given to others (including the partner) to justify the break-up are far more interesting psychologically than the real reasons. The psychology of break-up involves a whole layer of individual psychological processes, group processes, cultural rules and self-presentation. But this applies mainly to romantic relationships, rather than friendships. When you fall out with a friend, there's usually no formal or public 'announcement'. There's no need for this, because friendships aren't exclusive relationships in the way that most sexual relationships are (it's 'normal' to have several friends at once, but not several partners). (However, see Box 2.4.) As Duck (2001) says, 'Truly committed romantic relationships necessarily involve the foregoing of other romantic relationships and commitment to only one partner ("forsaking all others", as it says in the marriage ceremony) …'.

So, the ending of a romantic relationship indicates that the two people are now legitimately available as part-

Box 2.4: Some key differences between homosexual and heterosexual relationships

- *Cohabitation* (living together) is much less common for homosexuals than heterosexuals.
- *Sexual exclusivity* (having only one sexual partner at a time) is less common in lesbian relationships and *much* less common in gay relationships (Peplau, 1982). But the ideal of sexual exclusivity is based on an assumed heterosexual norm or 'blueprint' (Yip, 1999), which many gays and lesbians reject. Sexual infidelity may cause heterosexual couples to break up, largely because it's 'secretive'. But homosexual couples are more likely to have open relationships, and so are 'less likely to experience their own, or their partners' sexual affairs as signalling the end of the couple relationship' (Kitzinger and Coyle, 1995).
- Most gays and lesbians actively reject traditional (i.e. heterosexual) husband/wife or masculine/feminine sex roles as a model for enduring relationships (Peplau, 1991). Gay and lesbian couples tend to adopt 'the ethic of equality and reciprocity'. This is especially true for lesbians, who've previously been in 'unequal' relationships (Yip, 1999).

- is aware of others' deficiencies but isn't overly critical

- is willing to work to improve a relationship or take decisive action when partners turn nasty or break the rules of relating

- is rational and sensible, and brings closure to relationships only after trauma, hard work, or on reasonable grounds after real effort to make things work.

Duck's Theory of Relationship Dissolution (ToRD) (1982)

According to Duck, breaking up (dissolution) is a personal process, but one in which partners have an eye on how things will look to their friends and social networks. This suggests an account of dissolution comprising several parts. ToRD begins at the point where one of the partners has become sufficiently dissatisfied with the relationship over a long enough period of time to be seriously considering ending it.

The four phases (*intrapsychic, dyadic, social* and *gravedressing*) and the related thresholds are shown in Table 2.1.

ners for other relationships. This requires them to create a story for the end of the relationship that leaves them in a favourable light as potential partners. Romantic relationships are, therefore, typically ended publicly in a way that announces the ex-partners' freedom from the expectations of exclusive commitment.

Duck (2001) identifies a number of classic formats for a break-up story (such as 'X suddenly changed and I had to get out'; 'X betrayed me'; and 'We grew apart'). The crucial ingredients of such stories are those that show the speaker:

- is open to relationships but doesn't enter them thoughtlessly

Figure 2.7 Charles Darwin (1809–1882)

Breakdown – dissatisfaction with relationship

Threshold: 'I can't stand this any more'

INTRAPSYCHIC PHASE

- Personal focus on partner's behaviour
- Assess adequacy of partner's role performance
- Depict and evaluate negative aspects of being in the relationship
- Consider costs of withdrawal
- Assess positive aspects of alternative relationships
- Face 'express/repress dilemma'

Threshold: *'I'd be justified in withdrawing'*

DYADIC PHASE

- Face 'confrontation/avoidance dilemma'
- Confront partner
- Negotiate in 'our relationship talks'
- Attempt repair and reconciliation?
- Assess joint costs of withdrawal or reduced intimacy

Threshold: *'I mean it'*

SOCIAL PHASE

- Negotiate post-dissolution state with partner
- Initiate gossip/discussion in social network
- Create publicly negotiable face-saving/blame-placing stories and accounts
- Consider and face up to implied social network effect, if any
- Call intervention team

Threshold: *'It's now inevitable'*

GRAVE-DRESSING PHASE

- 'Getting over' activity
- Retrospective; reformative post-mortem attribution
- Public distribution of own version of break-up

Table 2.1: A sketch of the main phases of dissolving personal relationships (based on Duck, 1982; from Duck, 1988)

Evaluation of ToRD

✔ **Intuitively appealing:** it makes good common sense, and it's an account of relationship breakdown that we can relate to our own and/or others' experiences.

✔ **Theoretically important:** the view of relationship dissolution as a *process* (rather than an event) that underlies ToRD is an important insight, which is now widely accepted. This view applies to the breakdown of friendships as well as sexual relationships (including marriages). The common and crucial factor is that the relationship is long term and has embraced many parts of the person's emotional, communicative, leisure and everyday life (Duck, 1988). However, ToRD applies mainly to romantic relationships, because these are usually seen as exclusive in a way that friendships aren't (see above).

Evaluation of ToRD continued...

✔ **Taking the broader picture:** ToRD doesn't focus exclusively on the individual partner, but takes his/her social context into account. As Duck (2001) says, 'Break-up involves not only the individual who creates the break-up but the psychological sense of integrity of the person to whom it all happens ... But a lot that happens is done with an eye on the group that surrounds the person.'

✗ **Theoretical limitations:** ToRD takes no account of why the dissatisfaction has arisen in the first place – its starting point is where the dissatisfaction has already set in. To this extent, it fails to provide a complete picture of dissolution.

✗ **The trouble with phases/stages:** as with all such theories, ToRD's four phases may not apply in every (or even most) cases of relationship breakdown; nor may they occur in the order described.

HUMAN REPRODUCTIVE BEHAVIOUR

The relationship between sexual selection and human reproductive behaviour

✔ Specification Hint

While the specification refers to *human* reproductive behaviour, this doesn't mean that you cannot include studies and examples that involve non-human animals. However, these should only be used to help illustrate important points relating to human behaviour, which should remain the focus. Always try to make the link *explicit*.

How Science Works

Practical Learning Activity 2.7

In order to understand human reproductive behaviour, it's necessary to have a working knowledge of the *theory of evolution* (as it first appeared in Darwin's *The Origin of Species By Means of Natural Selection,* 1859). He published *The Descent of Man and Selection in Relation to Sex* in 1871. About 100 years later, *sociobiology* extended some of Darwin's basic ideas, applying them to social behaviour in general (e.g. Wilson, 1975). More recently still, *evolutionary psychology* (e.g. Buss, 1995) developed from sociobiology (and is often referred to as *neo-* or *modern Darwinism*) and, representing 'a marriage of sociobiology and cognitive psychology' (Dennett, 1996), claims that human behaviour and the human mind have evolved to solve problems faced by our hunter-gatherer ancestors.

Try to find definitions of the following terms:

● evolution
● natural selection
● 'survival of the fittest'
● fitness

- reproductive fitness
- kin selection theory
- inclusive fitness
- selfish gene theory
- sexual selection
- sexual dimorphism

- kin selection
- apparent altruism
- reciprocal altruism
- parental investment
- parent–offspring conflict.

A brief account of evolution theory

Animals are grouped into species (for example, humans belong to the species *Homo sapiens*), and within each species there is *variation*: people aren't all identical, either in appearance or behaviour. Part of that variation is caused by differences in individuals' genetic make-up (*genetic variation*), 50 per cent inherited from each parent. Genes (strands of DNA) may not always be 'switched on', some are expressed only if they are combined with other genes (e.g. recessive genes), and some may undergo *mutation* (a random change that affects the animal's anatomy and, hence, some aspect of its behaviour).

Most mutations are harmful and the individuals concerned are unlikely to reproduce and pass that mutated gene on to their offspring. But sometimes a mutation confers some benefit on the individual. All animals require resources (such as food and water for survival), which are often limited. Mates and territories are also limited. Hence, individuals compete and those who survive may have benefited from a mutated gene, which helps them *adapt* to their particular environment; if they survive until adulthood, they will breed more and leave more offspring with this mutated gene. Over a sufficiently long period of time (many thousands of years, usually), the characteristic determined by that mutation (if sufficiently distinctive) becomes a permanent feature of particular groups of animals – and marks the emergence of a new species. *Evolution*, then, can be defined as the process of *natural selection* by which new species arise as the result of gradual changes to the genetic make-up of existing species over long periods of time.

Darwin's theory of evolution by natural selection has often been popularly portrayed as the 'survival of the fittest'. However, this isn't only an oversimplification – it's an inaccurate representation of Darwin's theory. *Fitness* isn't a quality of an individual (such as strength or speed) but refers to the capacity to reproduce one's genetic material. Of course, survival is a necessary prerequisite to successful reproduction (if individuals don't survive to sexual maturity, then they cannot reproduce). But of those that do reach sexual maturity, some will have a better chance of reproducing than others (see below); so, 'fitness' here actually means *reproductive fitness*.

If survival is necessary for reproductive fitness, then Darwin's original theory faced a major difficulty when trying to explain *altruistic behaviour*. This is commonly observed in many non-human species (including blackbirds, rabbits and lions), as well as human, and refers to behaviour that enhances the fitness of another animal (the recipient or 'beneficiary') at the cost of the performer's own fitness. For example, when a rabbit bangs on the ground as a warning to others of a potential predator, it increases the chances of the others escaping but draws attention to itself and so puts itself at greater risk. Natural selection would predict that, in a competitive world, the altruist would quickly lose the evolutionary 'race' – and this trait wouldn't survive (altruists would have very low reproductive fitness). So, how can altruism be explained in evolutionary terms?

The contribution of sociobiology

Two major *sociobiological* explanations share the view of altruism as only *apparent*, such that there *is* an inherent gain for the altruist.

1. According to *kin selection theory* (Hamilton, 1964), traits that directed an individual's altruism towards its relatives – but not to non-relatives – would evolve. By increasing the reproductive fitness of relatives, the altruist is indirectly enhancing its own relatives who, by definition, share some of the altruist's genes and these will be reproduced via the surviving relatives. This is called *inclusive fitness*. These relatives are likely to be genetically predisposed to be altruistic. Also, the closer the genetic tie, the greater the altruistic sacrifices.

2. Where the altruist and the beneficiary aren't related, a different explanation is needed. According to Trivers (1971), the altruist is later 'repaid' by help from the unrelated recipient: short-term reduction in individual fitness is followed by a gain in fitness for both individuals. This is called *reciprocal altruism theory* ('you scratch my back and I'll scratch yours').

What makes sociobiological explanations different from a 'classical' Darwinian one is the formers' emphasis on the *set of genes* in contrast with the latter's 'individual animal' as the basic unit of evolution. In other words, it's not as important for individuals to survive as it is for their genes to do so. According to *selfish gene theory* (e.g. Dawkins, 1976, 1989), what appears as an altruistic act at the individual level (a rabbit calls attention to itself when warning other rabbits) turns out to be a *selfish* act at the gene level (the rabbit helps its relatives to escape, increasing their reproductive fitness and hence the survival of its genes). Any behaviour of an organism is specifically 'designed' to maximise the survival of its genes; from the 'gene's point of view', the body is a sort of survival machine created to enhance the gene's chances of continued replication.

Evolutionary psychology

Evolutionary psychology (EP) uses Darwinian concepts to generate testable hypotheses about human behaviour – based on the assumption that individuals will act in a way that will increase the survival of their genes.

According to Miller (1998), the application of *sexual selection* theory to human behaviour has been EP's greatest contribution to understanding human behaviour. While Darwin emphasised the role of natural selection, he recognised that natural selection couldn't explain *all* evolutionary processes. One problem for a theory based solely on natural selection is to explain the evolution of certain behaviours or anatomical structures that appear to *reduce* the individual animal's chances of survival. As Darwin (1871) put it:

> *Thus it is, as I believe, that when the males and females of any animal have the same general habits of life, but differ in structure, colour, or ornament, such differences have been mainly caused by sexual selection; that is, individual males have had, in successive generations, some slight advantage over other males, in their weapons, means of defence, or charms; and have transmitted these advantages to their male offspring.*

A much-cited example of such an ornament or charm is the peacock's tail (as described in Box 2.5).

The peacock's tail illustrates *sexual dimorphism*: the different characteristics of females and males of the same species. For example, male humans tend to be larger and stronger than females. It's easy to guess that

these features may have been beneficial in the past if males went out and hunted for food while women stayed at home and looked after the children, since

Box 2.5: Sexual selection and the peacock's tail

The peacock's tail seems to be doubly disadvantageous – it both attracts predators (tigers especially catch it by grabbing the tail) and makes efficient flight – and hence escape – much more difficult. So, surely a shorter tail – or no tail – would have been of greater benefit to peacocks? If possessing such a tail really increased fitness (in some non-obvious way), we'd expect females to have one too.

So, why has natural selection resulted in such a long tail? It all comes down to sex! For Darwin, *sexual selection* confers advantages to certain individuals over others of the same sex and species only in relation to reproduction. In the case of the peacock, peahens seem to prefer males with the longest and most brightly coloured tails. The effects of sexual selection, therefore, outweigh the disadvantage of owning such a cumbersome appendage (Clamp and Russell, 1998). Being eaten is an affordable risk. Can a comparison be made with young male drivers and their 'souped-up' cars with lots of unnecessary refinements (such as spoilers and alloy wheels)?

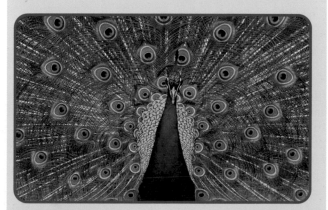

Figure 2.8 Can natural selection explain the peacock's tail?

only females can breastfeed their babies. Thus, these features may have developed through natural selection.

Strictly, sexual dimorphism is defined in terms of different-sized *gametes* (sex cells): males produce very large numbers of small, mobile gametes (*sperm*), while females produce much smaller numbers of *ova* (egg cells) that have a store of energy that aids the embryo's development.

A human female can produce fertile gametes for only a small proportion of her lifespan, during which she's fertile for only about two days in every month. Once she has become pregnant, no further eggs will be released. Men, by contrast, are fertile for decades and sperm are being constantly produced in vast numbers. It's this key biological difference that underpins human reproductive behaviour and subsequent parental investment (see below).

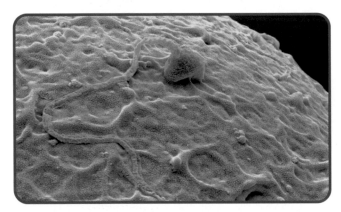

Figure 2.9 For any species, each gamete (sperm or egg) contains the same amount of genetic information; eggs, however, are very much bigger, so require greater investment; hence females can afford to produce fewer gametes than males

There are actually two kinds of sexual selection.

1. *Intrasexual selection ('intra' = 'within'):* individuals of one sex (usually males) compete with others of the same sex for access to, and matings with, individuals of the opposite sex (usually females). This tends to take place prior to mating, as when stags fight for access to females in the rutting season. The winner takes the territory and the access to females within it, while the loser goes home with a broken antler!

2. *Intersexual selection ('inter' = 'between'):* individuals of one sex (usually females) are very choosy in selecting a sexual partner (usually male). This leads to

the development of traits that enable animals to attract members of the opposite sex, as in the peacock's tail.

Both intra- and intersexual selection can also be related to human sexual behaviour.

Sex differences and sexual selection: what do males and females find attractive?

Evidence suggests that humans are a *mutually* sexually selected species – that is, both males and females have evolved preferences for certain behavioural and/or anatomical features in the opposite sex. According to Ridley (1993), 'People are attracted to people of high reproductive and genetic potential – the healthy, the fit and the powerful.' So, how exactly do we choose our mates?

While the stage theories of Kerckhoff and Davis, and Murstein, that we discussed earlier, put physical (sexual) attractiveness into a social and also a temporal (time-related) context, evolutionary psychologists try to explain mate choice in terms of 'built-in' preferences that have developed through the course of human evolution.

How Science Works

Practical Learning Activity 2.8

- Look back at the earlier discussion of physical attractiveness (see page 46). Some examples were given there of differences between males and females in what they 'typically' find attractive in the opposite sex.
- Thinking just about the face, what different characteristics of the male and female face might make it more attractive to the opposite sex?
- Are there any general characteristics that might make it equally attractive for males and females?
- Repeat the exercise for the body. (Here, the role of evolutionary forces in relation to reproductive behaviour might be a more obvious influence on sexually dimorphic preferences.)

The importance of facial symmetry

Although two individuals can vary widely in what they consider facially attractive, these differences actually vary around an underlying norm, which is surprisingly consistent across cultures (Langlois and Roggman, 1990; Berry, 2000). Langlois *et al.* (1987) found that when babies under 12 months are shown faces that adults consider attractive or unattractive, they spend longer looking at the former (implying that they prefer them). Clearly, they're too young to have learned cultural standards of beauty.

Langlois and Roggman (1990) took photographs of faces with standard poses, expressions and lighting, and then scanned them into a computer. Each image was then divided into a very large number of tiny squares (or *pixels*), and the brightness of corresponding pixels in different same-sex faces were *averaged* to produce *computer-composite images* (see the photographs in Figure 2.5). When people were asked to judge the attractiveness of these composite faces (made from four, eight, sixteen or thirty-two faces), they rated them as increasingly attractive the more faces that went into each image. This applied to both male and female faces.

The greater the number of faces making up a composite image, the more the peculiarities of particular faces become ironed out – that is, the more *symmetrical* they become. Most faces, are (to varying degrees) asymmetrical around the vertical midline, and even those that are slightly asymmetrical can be made more attractive. Hence, as Bruce and Young (1998) observe, 'It seems that moving a facial image closer to the average … increases its perceived attractiveness.'

Studies have shown men prefer photographs of women with symmetrical faces – and vice versa (Cartwright, 2000). It seems likely that symmetry (which shows a tendency to be inherited) equates with fitness. Development may be disrupted by parasites or other infectious agents, and only individuals with the best genes and food supplies will develop perfectly symmetrical faces. For example, the male jawline lengthens and broadens during puberty in response to increases in testosterone levels. But testosterone also suppresses the immune system. So, perhaps only the fittest males will develop perfectly sculpted jaws at the same time as their immune system is compromised.

If facial symmetry is a genuine phenomenon, how can we explain it? According to Langlois and Roggman

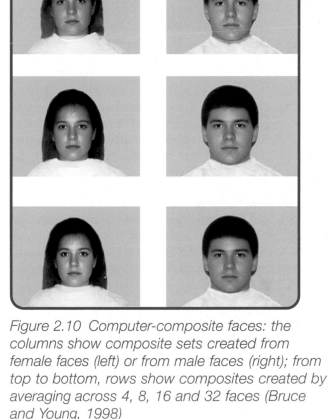

Figure 2.10 Computer-composite faces: the columns show composite sets created from female faces (left) or from male faces (right); from top to bottom, rows show composites created by averaging across 4, 8, 16 and 32 faces (Bruce and Young, 1998)

(1990), individuals whose characteristics are close to the average of the population might be preferred because they're less likely to carry harmful genetic mutations.

Is attractiveness really no more than averageness?

This seems unlikely. For example, if we describe someone as 'average looking', we usually mean that s/he is neither 'good-looking' nor 'ugly', and movie stars and sex symbols *aren't* obviously average (otherwise most of us would be sex symbols!).

Figure 2.11 Joan Van Ark – the after photo

According to Perret *et al.* (1994), the average derived from highly attractive faces is consistently preferred to the average of the entire set of photographs they were taken from. This wouldn't happen if 'attractive' equalled 'average'. When the difference between the average shape of attractive faces and the average shape of the entire set was increased, perceived attractiveness of the former also increased. But the effect of this was to make the resulting faces *more different* from the average. Perret *et al.* found exactly the same pattern of results for European and Japanese faces, regardless of whether they were judged by European or Japanese people.

These findings imply that there's more to attractiveness than averageness. Other research suggests that having younger-looking features, for both sexes, seems to be an advantage. For women, 'favourites' included child-like features (large eyes, spaced far apart, small chin and nose), narrow face and prominent cheekbones, expressive features (high eyebrows and large smile), and sexual cues (larger lower lip and well-groomed, full hair). The recent trend in cosmetic surgery for full lips has resulted, for some, in a bizarre change of appearance.

Facial attractiveness in men is less often studied, but high cheekbones and a rugged jaw seem to be favoured (see above) (Berry, 2000).

These other explanations aren't necessarily opposed to evolutionary accounts; indeed, they may complement each other. But because of EP's emphasis on 'human nature', it claims to have discovered fundamental 'truths' about human behaviour and cognition that many other researchers simply do not accept. (See the evaluation of EP below, pages 68–70.)

How Science Works

Practical Learning Activity 2.9

How would the following account for individual differences in perceived attractiveness?

- Social Exchange Theory, specifically the matching hypothesis (see above, pages 49–54).
- Psychoanalytic Theory (see Gross and Rolls, 2008; and Chapter 5).
- Imprinting (see Gross, 2005).
- Cultural relativism (see Chapter 5).

Body symmetry and waist-to-hip ratio (WHR)

Facial symmetry is also the best predictor of *body symmetry*. Research indicates that women with symmetrical male partners have the most orgasms, and women with symmetrical breasts are more fertile than more asymmetrically-breasted women (Cartwright, 2000). Males and females with near-perfect body symmetry report two to three times as many sexual partners as those with the most asymmetrical bodies. But it may not be symmetry itself that is directly attractive: other characteristics that are correlated with body symmetry, such as being more dominant, or having higher self-esteem, might be crucial.

Another physical characteristic shown to be a universally major determinant of attractiveness concerns *body shape*. In a series of studies conducted in the early 1990s, Singh (e.g. 1993) identified *waist-to-hip ratio* (WHR) as reliably conveying information about female mate value.

WHR refers to fat distribution (regulated by sex hormones) that sculpts typical male/female body shape differences: after puberty, females have greater amounts of body fat deposited in the lower part of the body, such that their WHR is greater than men's, giving them their 'curves', or hourglass figure.

Singh (1993) used archival data from the previous 50 years to examine the WHR of beauty contest winners and *Playboy* centrefolds. He found that a small waist set against full hips was a consistent feature of female attractiveness, while bust line, overall body weight and physique varied over the years. He concluded that a larger WHR was associated with better health status and greater reproductive capacity (i.e. fertility). The optimum WHR is 0.7, which happens to correspond closely to the measurements of supermodels like Anna Nicole Smith (0.69), Kate Moss (0.66) and Cindy Crawford (0.69) (Swami and Furnham, 2006).

However, cross-cultural replications haven't generally supported the claim that there's a universal preference for a low WHR (such as 0.7). Singh himself argued that the WHR acts as an initial 'filter' (screening out those who are unhealthy or have low reproductive capacity), after which the face and/or *body weight* (which may vary between cultures) are used in final mate selection (Swami and Furnham, 2006).

Is physical attractiveness more important to men?

A very general example of sexual dimorphism is that the physical attractiveness of females is central to male mate preferences; in other words, males use physical attractiveness as an indicator of reproductive fitness to a much greater extent than women do. As already noted above, this was demonstrated in a much-cited study by Buss (1989) of 37 cultures (including Nigeria, South Africa, Japan, Estonia, Zambia, Colombia, Poland, Germany, Spain, France, China, Palestinian Arabs, Italy and the Netherlands) involving over 10,000 people. Men seem to give a universally higher priority to 'good looks' in their female partners, while the situation is reversed when it comes to 'good financial prospect' and good earning capacity'. According to Buss, these sex differences 'appear to be deeply rooted in the evolutionary history of our species'. Why should they have evolved?

Men value female partners in terms of *fecundity* – that is, the ability to produce and care for children. Men often have to rely on a woman's physical appearance in order to estimate her age and health, with younger, healthier women being perceived as more attractive ('fitter'). The preference for the large eyes and lips etc. (see above) is also related to the need to estimate a woman's age, and hence her reproductive fitness.

Women's reproductive success is less dependent on finding fertile males, for whom age is a much less reliable indicator of fertility. Also, male fertility cannot be assessed as accurately from their physical appearance as can females' (Buss, 1995). Consequently, women's mate selection depends on their need for a provider to take care of them during pregnancy and nursing: men seen as powerful and controlling resources that contribute to the mother and child's welfare will be seen as especially attractive. However, although physical attractiveness may be less important to females, they tend to be much more choosy in selecting a mate since they have greater *investment* in their offspring (Buss and Malamuth, 1996; see below).

Sexual enthusiasm

Another factor involved in sexual selection is *sexual enthusiasm* – that is, the capacity to be sexually aroused (Cartwright, 2001). Males appear to have a lower arousal threshold than females; indeed, some male frog species will mate with anything that vaguely resembles a female frog. It seems that males can be sexually aroused for long periods of time with the continued introduction of different females. It makes evolutionary sense for a male to have multiple partners, each of whom can produce a baby for him. A female, having selected the best 'mate', gains nothing from the sperm of other males.

The 'Good Taste' or 'Runaway Effect' Hypothesis (Fisher, 1930)

This represents one of two specific explanations of intersexual selection, as seen from the perspective of the choosy partner (typically the female); the other is the 'Good Genes' or 'Handicap Process' Hypothesis (Zahavi, 1975; see below). In animal behaviour, females may choose males with exaggerated features simply because such signals indicate the presence of direct fitness benefits that enhance reproductive success. Males may be able to offer females some *direct* benefits such as high-quality territory, food, protection, no diseases and healthy sperm. Some male displays may also signal *indirect* benefits that appear only in the next generation through the success of the offspring. If the male signal and the female preference both have a genetic basis, then these characteristics could become genetically linked over the generations and their offspring could inherit these genes.

A so-called 'runaway effect' will occur where the male trait and the female preference will co-evolve in increasingly extreme ways. The peacock's tail is a good example. The runaway effect will stop only when balanced by a natural selection pressure whereby the disadvantages of the trait outweigh the benefits. The tail represents a secondary characteristic that has no direct genetic benefit; it's valued simply because it has become the fashionable trend, or a mark of 'good taste'. A human example might be when a woman selects a man with a fine, deep voice because her sons will be more successful at breeding if they possess this characteristic.

The 'Good Genes' or 'Handicap Process' (Zahavi, 1975)

This suggests that only individuals in prime physical condition can afford to develop costly, secondary characteristics. For example, the peacock's long tail is actually a handicap in relation to survival since it makes movement and escape from predators more difficult. The peacock that can escape the tiger despite having a huge tail must be worth mating with: only particularly strong and robust individuals with a healthy genetic constitution would survive in the face of such serious handicapping and costly traits. Thus females choose those individuals who thrive with the greatest handicap.

For example, a woman will select a man not because he has a Porsche or BMW, but because he has still managed to feed and clothe himself despite having the financial handicap of paying for an expensive car.

Evaluation of the evolutionary account of sexual selection

✔ **Great explanatory power:** according to Miller (1998), 'The application of sexual selection theory to human behaviour has been the greatest success story in evolutionary psychology, and one of the most fruitful and fascinating developments in the human sciences over the last two decades.'

✔/✗ **Mixed research support:** Regan et al. (2000) investigated what characteristics American university students look for in a partner. Distinctive differences between the sexes were found. Men disliked females with a low sex drive and also attached greater value to a female's sexual desirability than the women did. Women placed greater importance on a partner's social position and socio-economic status. Regan et al. concluded that this was partly because women want a man who can provide for their family in terms of food, protection and material possessions. Clark and Hatfield (1989) report the findings of two experiments that tested the hypothesis that men are more eager for sex than women. Again using American university students, male and female confederates of average attractiveness approached a potential partner and asked them one of three questions: (i) 'Would you go out with me tonight?' (ii) 'Will you come over to my apartment?' (iii) 'Would you go to bed with me?' Results were almost identical for both experiments: (i) both men and women were equally willing to go on a date with a person they'd just met; (ii) men were 11 times more likely than women to agree to visit the person's apartment; (iii) while no women agreed to sex, 75 per cent of the men did so!

Both these studies support the hypothesis that men and women, through intersexual selection, have different strategies when it comes to mate choice. They help to provide answers to the 'who', 'when' and 'how many' questions of sexual behaviour. However, the findings of an experiment conducted on the internet by Strassberg and Holty (2003) run counter to the evolutionary argument – and to previous research. The researchers argued that personal ads provide a rich source of information on relationships, particularly mating strategies. While other studies have concentrated on content analysis of naturally-occurring ads, Strassberg and Holty placed four 'female seeking

Evaluation of the evolutionary account of sexual selection continued...

male' ads on two large internet dating bulletin boards. The four ads, each with different key words, were the manipulated independent variable; the 500 email responses during the next six weeks were the dependent variable. Contrary to what was predicted by previous research findings based on personal ads (e.g. Dunbar's 1995 study of newspapers and magazines; see below) – and evolutionary theory – the most popular ad was the one in which the woman described herself as 'financially independent . . . successful [and] ambitious'; this produced over 50 per cent more responses than the next most popular ad (in which she described herself as 'lovely . . . very attractive and slim'.

✔/✗ **Ability to make specific predictions about deception and age preference:** according to Buss (1995), this account of sexual selection pressures provides specific predictions about the nature of male and female deception. Females would be expected to lie about their age, alter their appearance and conceal prior sexual encounters. Males would be expected to exaggerate their resources and their willingness to commit, and feign love in order to induce a female to mate with them. This is consistent with Dunbar's (1995) study of 'lonely hearts' columns. While women are predicted to prefer higher-status mates, men should prefer younger, highly fertile women. This does indeed appear to be the case across different cultures. Men in all cultures tend to seek mates near their own age when they themselves are young, and seek to find progressively younger women as they age. However, contrary to these predictions, teenage males are sometimes attracted to substantially older women (Kenrick and Simpson, 1997). Echoes of this can be seen in the film *The Graduate* starring Dustin Hoffman. Such behaviour is difficult for evolutionary theories of sexual selection to explain.

✗ **Reducing human relationships to 'animal' relationships:** the evolutionary account removes male–female relationships from their cultural or historical context (*de-contextualisation*). For example, women may have been forced to obtain desirable resources through men because they've been denied direct access to political and economic power. Traditionally, a woman has been regarded as the man's property, whereby her beauty increases his status and respect in others' eyes. This de-contextualisation is captured in the use of the term 'mate selection', which is normally reserved for describing non-human animals. This is a form of *reductionism*: by removing them from any 'man-made' context, human relationships are treated as if they are no different from those of non-humans. (See the evaluation of evolutionary psychology in the Synoptic Material section, below.)

✗ **Selective reporting of results:** Buss conveniently seems to overlook a major finding from his (1989) cross-cultural study: 'kind' and 'intelligent' were universally ranked as *more important* than either 'physically attractive' or 'good earning power' by both men and women!

✗ **Do women need men as mates as much as they used to?** When Kephart (1967) asked Americans, 'If someone had all the other qualities you desired in a marriage partner, would you marry this person if you were not in love?', well over twice as many men replied 'no' as did women. But when Simpson *et al.* (1986) repeated the study 20 years later, more than 80 per cent of both men and women said 'no'. This can be explained at least partly by the fact that, 20 years later, financial independence has allowed women to choose marriage partners for reasons other than material necessity. But this doesn't explain why romantic love has become so central for both American men and women (Moghaddam, 1998). As

Evaluation of the evolutionary account of sexual selection continued...

non-western societies become westernised, there's a greater tendency for young people to say 'no' to the question asked by Kephart and Simpson *et al*. Even in collectivist cultures (such as India and Pakistan; see below, pages 83–84), about 50 per cent of young people said 'no', and the indications are that this figure is rising (Moghaddam, 2002).

About 82,000 single women over 30 had a baby in the UK in 2006, and nearly 2,000 children are born every year in the UK using donated eggs, sperm or embryos. More than 25 per cent of British families are classed as single-parent; teenage mothers make up 3 per cent of single parents at any one time, while 60 per cent of single mothers have previously been married to their children's fathers. Finally, the number of women in England and Wales not registering the father's name on the birth certificate rose from 28,000 in 1988 to nearly 50,000 in 2006. In addition, an increasing number of women are choosing not to have children. These statistics are hardly consistent with a view of women needing male partners to provide for them and their offspring.

✗ **What about unfaithful women?** According to both sexual selection and parental investment (see below) explanations, a woman's mate choice is largely influenced by the resources he brings to the relationship. A woman who is unfaithful risks losing these resources for her (future) offspring. These explanations suggest that a woman will take this risk only if the new partner could offer even greater resources. An important distinction here is between life partners and one-night stands. From an evolutionary perspective, the ideal situation for the unfaithful woman is to have a caring partner who will look after the young (thrifty, stay-at-home type), freeing her to mate with someone who has characteristics that will promote their children's reproductive success (perhaps an extroverted, good-looking, rich man). According to Ridley (1993), 20 per cent of UK children are the offspring of males other than their presumed father.

✗ **The tricky case of homosexuality:** how can Buss's argument account for homosexual relationships, which clearly don't contribute to the survival of the species, but are subject to many of the same socio-psychological influences involved in heterosexual relationships (Brehm, 1992)? (See the discussion of homosexuality in 'Stretch and Challenge', below, pages 74–75.)

Evolutionary explanations of parental investment

Parental investment (PI)

Trivers (1972) introduced the idea of *parental investment*, defining it as 'any investment by the parent in an individual offspring that increases the offspring's chance of surviving (and hence reproductive success) at the cost of the parent's ability to invest in other offspring'.

PI includes the provision of resources (such as food, energy and time used in obtaining food and maintaining the home or territory), time spent teaching offspring, and risks taken to protect young. As regards human PI, there's a fundamental asymmetry between the sexes: females have an initial investment in their offspring that's far greater than the male's, because the female gamete (egg cell) is much more costly to produce than male sperm (see above). Females also nourish the embryo for nine months prior to giving birth, which means that they have only a limited number of offspring. Breastfeeding may last for up to four years in some societies (Shostak, 1981), but on average 3–12 months in the UK and most western cultures. By contrast, a male can have a virtually unlimited number – provided he can find females willing to mate with him. But we should note that, in certain species, males provide a great deal of parental care; for example, a male seahorse has a pouch where it keeps the infant until maturity, and the females compete with each other for the male's attention. It is the females that are brightly coloured (in contrast with the dull-looking males). Competition seems to be for the sex with the greater PI.

How Science Works

Practical Learning Activity 2.10

- Try to find evidence of how the role of fathers (a) traditionally differs between different cultures; and (b) has changed within western societies (such as the UK and USA) during the last 30–40 years.
- What implications do your findings have for parental investment theory?

Trivers (1972) argued that there's an optimum (or ideal) number of offspring for each parent. A low-investing male could afford many offspring and might favour a 'quantity rather than quality' approach. Females, on the other hand, would prefer quality rather than quantity. Consequently, females generally need to be much more choosy about whom they mate with (although the criteria for what constitutes a good choice of male will vary considerably from species to species).

One way to understand human reproduction is simply to measure the potential offspring of males and females. The world record for the number of children is 888, fathered by Ismail the Bloodthirsty (1672–1727), an Emperor of Morocco; a Russian woman gave birth to 69 children! Clearly, women are the limiting factor in human reproduction, which suggests some male–male intrasexual competition and some male–female intersexual competition.

To be successful, you must pass on your genes. This means, in most cases, that you must have more than two babies who grow up to do the same. There's no necessity to live a long time, especially if you're male: he can be promiscuous during the period of pregnancy and impregnate (many) other women, while the woman cannot be impregnated once she's pregnant. However, while women usually know who the father is, men cannot be certain that any particular child is theirs. So, does it make more sense to 'sow your wild oats' with lots of women, in the hope that at least *some* of them mother your children, *or* to stick to one woman and watch her like a hawk so you can be sure she's mothering only *your* children?

Evaluation of PI theory

✔/✗ **Inconclusive empirical support:** according to Daly and Wilson (1988b), children under the age of two are at least 60 times more likely to be killed by a step-parent – almost always a stepfather – than by a natural parent. This is exactly what evolutionary theory would predict, since step-parents and stepchildren are genetically unrelated, whereas a child inherits half its genes from each biological parent. However, most stepfathers *don't* kill or abuse, and a minority of biological fathers *do*: these findings are difficult to square with any explanation based on shared/non-shared genes.

✗ **How do evolutionary psychologists explain maternal neonaticide?** More tricky still for evolutionary theory to explain is the case of the woman who kills her newborn baby (neonaticide). According to Pinker (1997), when such an act takes place in conditions of poverty, it could be regarded as an *adaptationist* response. The psychological module that normally induces protectiveness in mothers of their newborns is switched off by the challenge of an impoverished environment. This means that both killing *and* protecting are explained by evolutionary selection. As Hilary Rose (2000) says, this explains everything and, therefore, nothing.

Parent–offspring conflict (POC)

Trivers's *theory of parent–offspring conflict* (POC) (1974), a direct extension of Hamilton's (1964) kin selection theory, was the first to recognise that children should desire greater investment than their parents have been selected to provide. Parents endeavour to allocate resources to their offspring in order to ensure that the maximum number of offspring survive. However, conflict occurs when each child wants more resources from the parent than they're prepared to give.

As noted above, parental investment includes any actions performed by a parent for an offspring that increase the offspring's chances of survival while reducing the parent's ability to invest in other offspring – either existing or future ones. When infants are young and highly dependent on their parents for care and resources, the costs of investment to parents are relatively low and the benefits to infants quite high – from the reproductive perspective of both parents and infants. But as infants grow, consume more resources and become more self-sufficient, the costs of parental investment increase, while the benefits to the child gradually level out.

During evolutionary history, weaning typically occurred when a new baby was born: new offspring enhanced the parents' reproductive success more than continuing to invest heavily in an increasingly self-sufficient child (Simpson, 1999). At the same time, each child will regard him/herself as more important than any of his/her brothers or sisters. Competition between siblings for limited parental resources is inevitable. According to Buss (1999):

- the child wants to delay the weaning process as long as possible, often in contrast to the mother's wishes

- parents also encourage their children to value their siblings more than they naturally would

- parents punish conflict between siblings and reward cooperation, against the child's natural instincts.

Several interesting and novel predictions can be derived from the theory of POC (Simpson, 1999), as in the following examples.

- Conflict should be increased when half-siblings exist in families. Because half-siblings share only 25 per cent of their genes, four half-siblings must survive and reproduce if the genes of an infant are to be fully propagated. So, in *blended families* (where there are step-parents and two or more half-siblings plus full siblings), offspring should demand approximately four times as much investment as their parents are willing to give; this will result in particularly long and intense periods of POC.

- Conflict should be greater in families with very young mothers. Because they have more child-bearing years ahead of them (and, therefore, more and better future reproductive opportunities) than older mothers approaching menopause, younger mothers should be less tolerant of the demands of high-cost infants.

Evaluation of POC theory

✔ **Substantial empirical support:** cross-cultural research indicates that parental investment is lower in families with at least one step-parent; when fathers question their paternity; when infants are ill, weak or deformed; during periods of famine; when families are poor or lack social support; when mothers are very young; when families have too many children; when birth spacing is too short (Daly and Wilson, 1984, 1988). Also, as we saw above in relation to parental investment, step-parents (especially fathers) are many times more likely to kill their biologically unrelated stepchildren than are biological parents (Daly and Wilson, 1988). The same is true for 'mere' child abuse (Daly and Wilson, 1981, 1985, 1987, 1993), samples of children dying before age 15 (Hill and Kaplan, in Daly and Wilson, 1994), and samples of children suffering head and other injuries (Ferguson *et al.*, 1972; Wadsworth *et al.*, 1983; both cited in Daly and Wilson, 1994).

Even when financial resources and marital status are held constant, younger mothers are more likely to kill their infants than are older mothers (Daly and Wilson, 1988), and older mothers are less likely to abuse or harm their infants (Daly and Wilson, 1985).

73

Synoptic Material

Starting with the principle of natural selection, evolutionary psychologists construct a theory of *human nature* – that is, an overall view of how we should expect humans to behave. From this, they derive and test more specific theories and hypotheses (Archer, 1996).

According to Rose (S. Rose, 2000):

The declared aim of evolutionary psychology is to provide explanations for the patterns of human activity and the forms of organisation of human society which take into account the fact that humans are animals, and like all other currently living organisms, are the present-day products of some four billion years of evolution . . .

Some basic principles and assumptions of evolutionary psychology (EP)

- EP *rejects* the Standard Social Science Model (SSSM), which makes two broad assumptions about human beings: (i) there's no such thing as human nature, or if there is, it has so little effect on people's social lives that it can be ignored; (ii) explanations of social behaviour can be derived from considering only social roles, socialisation and culture.

- Human social behaviour, like that of non-humans, can be understood in terms of its past contribution to survival and reproduction. For example, instead of regarding young males' proneness to violence in terms of social learning (modelling) or frustration (Berkowitz, 1993; see Chapter 3), EP views it as the result of its past contributions to obtaining resources, status and access to women (Daly and Wilson, 1988).

- While acknowledging their debt to sociobiology, evolutionary psychologists argue that sociobiologists often ignored the role of the *mind* in mediating links between genes and behaviour. According to Barkow *et al.* (1992), the mind consists of a collection of specialised, independent mechanisms (or *modules*), designed by natural selection to solve problems faced by our hunter-gatherer ancestors (see text below). Together, these modules and related emotions (such as jealousy and anger) constitute *human nature*.

- EP is, in general, concerned with *universal* features of the mind. To the extent that individual differences exist, the default assumption is that they're expressions of the same universal human nature as it encounters different environments. *Gender* is the crucial exception to this rule (*sexual dimorphism*; see text above).

- EP *isn't* a form of *genetic determinism* (or *nativism*). Like most modern biologists and social scientists, evolutionary psychologists argue that 'nature or nurture' is a false dichotomy, and they distinguish themselves from behaviour geneticists (see Gross, 2005).

Evaluation of EP

✗ **What can we know about our hunter-gatherer past?** EP is based on the belief that the human mind is adapted to cope with life as a Pleistocene hunter-gatherer (which we were for about two million years before the Ancient Chinese, Indian, Egyptian and Sumerian civilisations; Abdulla, 1996). Forms of behaviour and social organisation that evolved adaptively over many generations in human hunter-gatherer society may or may not be adaptive in modern, industrialised society, but they have become, to a degree, fixed by humanity's evolutionary experience in the Palaeolithic *Environment of Evolutionary Adaptation* (EEA), thought to be the African savannah (S. Rose, 2000).

✗ **This account involves circular reasoning:** the story of our human hunter-gatherer ancestors is, inevitably, partly a work of fiction (Turney, 1999). According to Rose (S. Rose, 2000), the descriptions offered by EP of what hunter-gatherer societies were like read little better than 'Just so' accounts:

Evaluation of EP continued...

'There is a circularity about reading this version of the present into the past, and then claiming that this imagined past explains the present.' In other words, based on what human beings are capable of *now*, evolutionary psychologists imagine how these abilities may have evolved, then propose this *constructed past* as the cause of these current abilities.

✗ Phylogeny versus ontogeny: according to Karmiloff-Smith (2000), developmental psychologists see *plasticity* during brain growth as the rule rather than the exception or a response to brain injury (where uninjured parts take over the function of injured parts). Cosmides and Tooby (1994) compare the newborn brain to a Swiss army knife, crammed with independent functional tools, each designed for a specific problem that faced our hunter-gatherer ancestors. But even if we set aside the problem of knowing just what the problems faced by our ancestors were (and, therefore, what tools they needed), Karmiloff-Smith believes that it's just as plausible that, unlike the gross macro-structure of the brain, cortical micro-circuitry *isn't* innately specified by evolution, but is progressively constructed through postnatal experience of different kinds of input. She argues that 'Evolution has helped to guarantee human survival by raising the upper limits on complexity and avoiding too much prespecification of higher cognitive functions ...'. Development requires both evolution (*phylogeny*) and *ontogeny* (individual development). While evolution may have provided a wide range of different learning mechanisms, during an individual child's development these interact with environmental input and gradually become more domain-specific. The Swiss army knife analogy implies that most, if not all, of a child's abilities are pre-specified (through evolution of the species), leaving virtually no room for an individual's experience to influence his/her development. This seems to contradict the claim of evolutionary psychologists that they aren't genetic determinists/nativists (see above).

STRETCH AND CHALLENGE How can EP explain same-sex romantic relationships?

Same-sex romantic relationships seem to have existed in most cultures throughout recorded history regardless of prevailing attitudes towards homosexuality and bisexuality.

As we saw earlier in the chapter, attraction research has traditionally been heavily biased towards heterosexual relationships; this also applies to both evolutionary accounts of mating and research into adult romantic relationships in terms of attachment theory (see Gross and Rolls, 2008). Indeed, Bowlby's theory is usually described as an evolutionary theory (see the next main section in this chapter, pages 76–77).

According to McKnight (1997, in Mohr, 1999):

Perhaps one of the cleverest challenges to confront evolutionary theory is homosexuality. Homosexuality seems to be a tailor-made rebuttal of the great evolutionary credo – survival of the fittest. How do we explain what is often a life-long preference for non-reproductive sex?

At the core of Bowlby's theory (1969) is the idea that the human tendency to establish affectional bonds is adaptive from an evolutionary perspective: the infant–caregiver bond and the romantic

STRETCH AND CHALLENGE CONTINUED...

partnership (as well as the close friendship) ultimately serve to enhance reproductive success. In evolutionary terms, the survival of the infant is in the best interests of both the infant and his/her parents, because they all have a stake in passing on their genes.

But how do same-sex relationships fit into this reproductive scenario? McKnight (1997, in Mohr, 1999) asks why homosexuality hasn't died out as a less reproductive strain of humanity? For Bowlby, the sexual behavioural system of homosexuals isn't serving its functional goal of reproduction. But at the same time he never denied that legitimate, psychologically healthy same-sex romantic attachments exist. Similarly, Ainsworth (1985) maintained that same-sex romantic attachments are likely to function in the same way as opposite-sex attachments: the main difference between them is that only the latter are socially acceptable.

Evolutionary theorists have assumed that there's a genetic component to homosexuality and bisexuality; further, 'gay genes' offer a direct reproductive advantage – such as homosexuals possessing traits such as charm, empathy and intelligence that are attractive to females (McKnight, 1997, in Mohr, 1999). Alternatively, one version of the *kin-selective altruism hypothesis* claims that males with gay genes instinctively feel at a reproductive disadvantage and decide to divert their energies into supporting the reproductive fitness of close relatives (e.g. Wilson, 1975).

However, the great variability in sexual behaviour among lesbian, gay and bisexual (LGB) individuals, as well as recent developments in artificial insemination and family structures, means that significant numbers of LGB people do have children (Patterson, 1995). Thus, same-sex romantic relationships may also increase individuals' ability to provide for their children, as appears to be the case for opposite-sex couples (Weiss, 1982).

Arguably, the most viable explanation of same-sex relationships derives from the model proposed originally by Hazan and Shaver (1987) in their groundbreaking study of *heterosexual* romantic relationships in terms of attachment theory (see Key Study 2.4, pages 77–8). A key component of their theoretical model was the distinction between the evolved social-behavioural systems of *attachment, caregiving* and *sexuality.* Although romantic adult attachments typically integrate all three systems, they in fact have distinct origins, functions and underpinnings. Research into the brain substrates of both human and non-human sexuality and pair bonding has confirmed this view (e.g. Bartels and Zeki, 2000, in Diamond, 2006).

This view of romantic love and sexual desire as fundamentally distinct has profound implications for our understanding of the nature and development of same-sex relationships. Specifically, if love and desire are based in independent social-behavioural systems, then one's *sexual orientation* towards same-sex or opposite-sex partners needn't correspond with experiences of *romantic attachment* to same-sex or opposite-sex partners.

This, of course, runs directly counter to the implicit presumption among both scientists and lay people that heterosexual individuals fall in love only with other-sex partners and lesbian and gay individuals fall in love only with same-sex partners (Diamond, 2006).

Diamond (2006) reports on a study of 79 women (aged 18–23), most describing themselves as either lesbian or bisexual. One important finding was that the experience of being attracted to 'the person and not the gender' is appreciably distinct from that of needing an emotional bond with another person in order to experience physical attraction to them. Unsurprisingly, non-gendered attraction was strongly associated with bisexuality.

75

The influence of childhood and adolescent experiences on adult relationships

The influence of attachment theory

Attachment theory represents a major way of trying to understand the influence of childhood and adolescent experiences on adult relationships (including parent–child relationships and interaction with peers). As mentioned earlier, Hazan and Shaver's (1987) study of adult romantic relationships for the first time depicted them in terms of attachment theory, specifically Ainsworth *et al.*'s (1971, 1978) categorisation of infants into three attachment styles.

Attachment theory as an evolutionary theory

Given the critical influence of attachment theory in our understanding of the influences of early relationship experiences on later relationships, and given the fact that attachment theory is an evolutionary theory, it's useful to point out some of the limitations and reinterpretations of attachment theory in the light of evolutionary psychology.

- Bowlby's (1969) original formulation of his theory maintained that attachment behaviour had evolved in order to promote the *survival of the species*. But, as Belsky (1999) observes, attachment behaviour wouldn't have evolved if it had functioned only to protect the individual child and thereby to promote survival, because survival as such clearly isn't the goal of natural selection. Thus, unless survival enhanced the reproductive fitness of ancestral human infants, there wouldn't have been sufficient evolutionary pressure for attachment behaviour to evolve. So, human attachment evolved because the protection and survival it promoted increased the chances of successful reproduction of those individuals who tended to maintain proximity and/or seek contact with their caregivers.

- Bowlby later recognised his mistake and acknowledged that evolution works at the levels of the gene and the individual – not the species (reproductive fitness, not just survival) (Belsky, 1999).

How Science Works

Practical Learning Activity 2.11

- Remind yourself of the three attachment styles identified by Ainsworth *et al.* in 12-month-olds using the Strange Situation (see Gross and Rolls, 2008).
- How are these styles related to the mother's behaviour?
- Think about how these attachment styles might be 'translated' in a way that would make it possible to assess them in adults.
- If you asked adults to remember the way their parents treated them, how would you expect their recollections to be related to their attachment style within their romantic relationships?

- It's widely believed that the environment of evolutionary adaptedness (EEA) was neither as uniform nor as benign as Bowlby seems to have imagined (Chisholm, 1996, in Belsky, 1999). It's very likely that in some ecological niches food was abundant and maternal care was sensitively responsive (as it appears to be in certain present-day hunter-gatherer societies); but it's more than likely that in others (or at least at certain times) resources were scarce or of poor quality, making care mostly insensitive. Assuming that there were many different EEAs and that attachment behaviour probably evolved within these different contexts, it becomes very difficult to believe that one single pattern of attachment (namely, secure) was or is 'species-typical' or normative. As Belsky (1999) says:

Under the diverse conditions in which hominids evolved, it seems more reasonable to presume that no pattern of attachment was primary and others secondary, but rather that what evolved was a repertoire of attachment behaviours that could be flexibly organised into different patterns contingent on ecological and caregiving conditions . . .

- By the same token, there's no reason to believe that sensitive maternal responsiveness is any more species-typical, normative or characteristic of ancestral humans (i.e. 'natural') than insensitivity (Belsky, 1999).

We cannot simply claim that insecure attachments are 'maladaptations' because they compromise the capacity for dealing with later developmental issues, especially those surrounding intimate social relationships and parenting (Sroufe, 1988). It makes just as much sense to regard them as *evolved* responses to contextual demands (i.e. mothering practices) that *enable* the individual to reproduce 'successfully' (or at least once did so in some EEAs). While many developmental psychologists regard insecure attachments as 'secondary', less optimal in some basic developmental sense, from an evolutionary perspective they're *not*: they're just as 'natural' as secure attachments (Belsky, 1999) (see Table 2.2, page 78).

Attachment as a lifelong phenomenon

Ainsworth was originally a student of Bowlby's, and both are best known for their study of attachment in young children. However, Bowlby made repeated references to attachment as a lifespan phenomenon (for example, 'attachment behaviour is held to characterise human beings from the cradle to the grave' (Bowlby, 1977)). Attachment theory, which Ainsworth and Bowlby developed both independently and together, leads to two very significant hypotheses (Bartholomew, 1993).

1. Attachment behaviour characterises human beings throughout life.

2. Patterns established in childhood parent–child relationships tend to structure the quality of later bonds in their adult relationships and may account for why some people even seem to avoid this presumably 'natural' inclination.

Hazan and Shaver's (1987) groundbreaking study addressed both these hypotheses, as well as other aspects of attachment theory.

Key Study 2.4: Romantic love conceptualised as an attachment process (Hazan and Shaver, 1987)

Aims/hypotheses (AO1)

The aims of the study were: (a) to explore the possibility that attachment theory offers a valuable perspective on adult romantic love; and (b) to create a coherent framework for understanding love, loneliness and grief at different points in the life cycle.

Hazan and Shaver argued that attachment theory can help explain both healthy and unhealthy forms of love, encompassing both positive emotions (caring, intimacy and trust) and negative emotions (fear of intimacy, jealousy, and emotional ups and downs).

More specifically, they predicted that:

- about 60 per cent of adults will classify themselves as securely attached, with the other two (insecure) attachment styles (anxious-avoidant/anxious-ambivalent) being fairly evenly split (but a few more anxious-avoidant) (this is in line with Ainsworth *et al.*'s findings with one-year-olds using the Strange Situation)

- there will be a correlation between (a) adults' attachment styles and (b) the type of parenting they received as children (also consistent with Ainsworth *et al.*'s findings)

- adults with different attachment styles will display different characteristic *mental models* (internal representations) of themselves and their major social-interaction partners (this relates to the child's *expectations* regarding the mother's accessibility and responsiveness (Ainsworth *et al.*, 1978) and to Bowlby's (e.g. 1969) concept of *inner working models* (IWMs)).

Method/design

The three attachment styles identified by Ainsworth *et al.* had to be 'translated' in a way that would make them suitable for the study of adult attachments. This was done as shown in Table 2.2, where respondents to a 'love quiz' in a local newspaper were asked to indicate which of three descriptions best applied to their inner feelings about romantic relationships. (This relates to hypotheses 1 and 3.)

The participants were also asked to complete a simple adjective checklist describing their childhood relationships with their parents. (This relates to hypothesis 2.) (See Table 2.3.)

Hazan and Shaver tested two separate samples.

1. *Sample one* comprised 205 men and 415 women, aged 14–82 (mean age 36), 91 per cent of whom described themselves as 'primarily heterosexual'. At the time of the survey, 42 per cent were married, 28 per cent were divorced or widowed, 9 per cent were 'living with a lover' and 31 per cent were dating. (Some checked more than one category.)

2. *Sample two* comprised 108 undergraduate students – 38 men and 70 women (mean age 18). They completed the questionnaire as a class exercise. They also answered items that focused more on the *self* side of the mental model (as opposed to the partner), as well as additional items measuring loneliness. (These extra items relate to hypothesis 3.)

(Strictly, the use of two different samples represents two separate studies, both reported in the same journal article. But here the findings are described as if for a single study.)

Results/findings

Hypothesis 1

Classification	Percentage of respondents	Response
Securely attached	56	I find it relatively easy to get close to others and am comfortable depending on them and having them depend on me. I don't often worry about being abandoned or about someone getting too close to me.
Anxious-avoidant	23–25	I am somewhat uncomfortable being close to others; I find it difficult to trust them completely, difficult to allow myself to depend on them. I am nervous when anyone gets too close, and often, love partners want me to be more intimate than I feel comfortable being.
Anxious-ambivalent	19–20	I find that others are reluctant to get as close as I would like. I often worry that my partner doesn't really love me or won't want to stay with me. I want to merge completely with another person, and this desire sometimes scares people away.

Table 2.2: Responses to the question 'Which of the following best describes your feelings about romantic relationships?'

Table 2.2 shows the percentage of respondents, classified as either securely attached (56 per cent in both samples), anxious-avoidant (23 per cent in sample one and 25 per cent in sample two), or anxious-ambivalent (19 per cent in sample one and 20 per cent in sample two). The classification is based on which of three descriptions respondents chose.

Both samples were also asked to describe 'the most important love relationship you have ever had, why you got involved in it, and why it turned out the way it did ... it may be a past or a current relationship, but choose only the most important one'.

The responses from both samples were very similar. Those classified as securely attached described this special relationship as especially happy, friendly and trusting, being able to accept and support their partner despite his/her faults. Their relationships also tended to last longer and, if married, were less likely to end in divorce.

Hypothesis 2

Attachment style	Type of parenting
Securely attached	Readily available, attentive, responsive
Anxious-avoidant	Unresponsive, rejecting, inattentive
Anxious-ambivalent	Anxious, fussy, out-of-step with child's needs, only available/responsive some of the time

Table 2.3: Correlation between adult attachment style and type of parenting respondents received as children

Hypothesis 3

Questions designed to measure the mental model of self and relationships were answered in line with the prediction only in sample one, whose items were more focused on the partner or relationship than on the self.

● The *securely attached* expressed belief in lasting love. Even though romantic feelings wax and wane, only sometimes reaching the intensity experienced at the start of the relationship, genuine love is enduring. They also generally find others trustworthy and have confidence in themselves as likeable.

● The *anxious-avoidant* are much more doubtful about the existence or durability of romantic love: the kind of head-over-heels love portrayed in fiction doesn't happen in real life, and it's rare to find a person you can really fall in love with. They also maintain that they don't need a love partner in order to be happy.

● They also express more self-doubts (compared with both the other types), but compared with the anxious-avoidants, they don't repress or try to hide their feelings of insecurity.

The two insecure types, compared with the secure, were found to be the most vulnerable to loneliness; the anxious-ambivalent (sample two) were the most vulnerable of all.

Conclusions (AO1)

Support was found for all three hypotheses.

● Based on Ainsworth *et al.*'s original studies and later studies involving young children, the percentages falling within each of the three attachment style categories were closely matched by the percentages of adults in the present study.

- The correlation between adults' attachment style and their recollections of the kind of parenting they received was remarkably similar to Ainsworth *et al.*'s findings. (In the latter, the child's attachment style was correlated with the degree of *sensitivity* shown by mothers.)

- The mental models of adults differed according to their attachment styles. The securely attached were far more positive and optimistic about both themselves and (potential) love partners, compared with either of the insecurely attached.

Activity

- The two insecure groups, compared with the secure, were the most vulnerable to loneliness.

- Try to identify some methodological and theoretical limitations of Hazan and Shaver's study.

- For example, correlations between current attachment style and parent variables (see Table 2.3) were higher for sample two, who were much younger than sample one. What does this suggest about the *continuity* between early childhood and adult experience?

- Were the measures (of attachment styles, relationship with parents, mental models etc.) adequate?

Evaluation (AO1/AO2)

✔ **Theoretical importance and inspiration for later research:** despite the study's limitations (see below), Hazan and Shaver succeeded in providing both a *normative* account of romantic love (i.e. an account of typical processes of romantic attachment) and an understanding of *individual differences* in adult relationship styles (Feeney, 1999). They provided a bridge between infant attachment theory and theories of romantic love, which generated intense interest among relationship researchers.

✗ **The issue of *continuity* between early childhood and adult experience:** at least from the point of view of the insecurely attached person, it would be overly pessimistic if continuity were the rule rather than the exception – that is, if an insecurely attached child inevitably became an insecurely attached adult. The finding that the correlations between current attachment style and parent variables were higher for the younger sample two suggests that continuity *decreases* as one goes further into adulthood. The average person participates in several important friendships and love relationships, which provide opportunities for revising mental models of self and others.

A study by Main *et al.* (1985) lends support for this more optimistic view. They found a strong association between adults' attachment history and the attachment styles of their own young children. However, some adults who reported being insecure in their relationships with their parents managed to produce securely attached children (assessed at ages one and six). These adults had mentally worked through their unpleasant experiences with their parents, and now had mental models of relationships more typical of the securely attached.

✗ **Problems with the measurements used:** just as attachment patterns derived from the Strange Situation reflect qualities of unique relationships (rather than characteristics of the child; see Gross and Rolls, 2008), so adults' choice of paragraphs describing attachment styles might reflect the state of a current relationship (or lack of one). For example, if you've just got out of a relationship that ended badly, you're more likely to perceive relationships *in general* in a negative way. Hazan and Shaver recognise that their measures (of attachment styles, relationships with parents, mental models etc.) were brief and simple. In the case of the paragraphs describing attachment styles, participants had to choose just one (a forced-choice, self-report measure). Is this a valid way of measuring such a complex aspect of behaviour? According to Parkes (2006), although these three categories appear clear-cut (i.e. distinct from each other), one of the weaknesses of the Strange Situation (and, by extension, the paragraphs) is its failure to measure the *strength* of the attachment styles. Common sense suggests that, both in infants and adults, there must be degrees of attachment security/insecurity: the use of graded measures would provide more subtle results.

How Science Works

Practical Learning Activity 2.12

- Try the Hazan and Shaver 'love quiz' yourself.
- Consider what improvements you might make to their measures of attachment styles and parental behaviours.
- Consider any ethical issues that may be raised by such studies.

Intergenerational continuity and the Adult Attachment Interview (AAI)

The study by Main *et al.* (1985) described in Box 2.6, together with many others stimulated by Hazan and Shaver, used the *Adult Attachment Interview* in the context of *intergenerational continuity* (or *intergenerational transfer* of attachment patterns; Meins, 2003) – that is, the relationship between *parents'* attachment style and their *children's*; in other words, do people parent their children as they themselves were parented?

Apart from the Strange Situation, the AAI is probably the most widely used and best-developed measure of attachment. It's based on the assumption that what's crucial for predicting parenting behaviour isn't so much the objective facts about our early attachments, but rather how we *construe* these facts – that is, the nature of our inner working models (IWMs; see Gross, 2005) (see Box 2.6).

So, the AAI may predict how the mother's child will be attached to her as determined by the Strange Situation (Main, 1995; Heard and Lake, 1997). However, it's possible that these findings are affected by the mother's *selective recall*: how she remembers her childhood might be influenced by her *current* experiences with her own child.

Fonagy *et al.* (1991) gave the AAI to 96 women *before* the birth of their children (i.e. during pregnancy), then classified the children (using the Strange Situation) when they were 12 and 18 months old. As Table 2.4 shows, Main *et al.*'s (1985) results (see Box 2.6) were largely replicated (with the exception of the preoccupied mothers). The correlation was especially strong for the autonomous mother/secure child pairing.

These basic findings have been replicated by several other studies. A meta-analysis ('study of studies') by van Ijzendoorn (1995) confirmed that mothers and fathers classified as autonomous/secure are disproportionately

	Classification of the mother		
Classification of the child	Dismissing	Autonomous	Preoccupied
Anxious-avoidant	15	8	7
Secure	5	45	5
Anxious-ambivalent	2	6	3

Table 2.4: Mothers' prenatal AAI classification and children's Strange Situation classification (based on Fonagy et al., 1991)

Box 2.6: The Adult Attachment Interview (AAI) (Main *et al.*, 1985)

- The AAI is a structured interview, comprising 15 questions designed to tap an individual's experience of attachment relationships in childhood, and how s/he considers those experiences to have influenced later development and present functioning.
- More specifically, for each parent, the person is asked to choose five adjectives that best describe that relationship during childhood. The person then has to illustrate each of these choices by drawing on childhood memories.
- Later, the person is asked how they reacted when upset, to which parent they felt closest and why, whether they ever felt rejected or threatened, why parents may have acted as they did, how these relationships may have changed, and how these earlier experiences (including major loss up to the present time) may have affected their adult functioning and personality.
- Each interview (which lasts about 90 minutes) is classified as a whole, giving an overall 'state of mind' regarding attachment. Four attachment styles are possible, as follows. *Secure/autonomous (F):* people with this style discuss their childhood experiences openly, coherently and consistently, acknowledging both positive and negative events and emotions. This is the most common style among parents of *securely attached* infants. *Dismissing (D):* these individuals seem cut off from the emotional nature of their childhood, denying especially their negative experiences and dismissing their significance. The importance of attachment experiences is minimised. They appear cooperative, but contradictions make them seem dishonest. This is the most common style among parents of *anxious-avoidant* infants. *Preoccupied/entangled (E):* such

people are over-involved with what they recollect, appearing so overwhelmed that they become incoherent, confused, even angry. They're still actively trying to please their parents. This is the most common style among parents of *anxious-ambivalent* infants. *Unresolved/disorganised (U):* this style describes mainly those who've experienced a trauma (which may include physical or sexual abuse), or the early death of an attachment figure, and who haven't come to terms with it or worked through the grieving process. This is the most common style among parents of *disorganised* infants (those who don't fit neatly into the other categories and who act as if afraid of the attachment figure: Main and Hesse, 1990).

Source: based on Main *et al.* (1985), Schaffer (1996), Heard and Lake (1997), Goldberg (2000)

How Science Works
Practical Learning Activity 2.13

- How might you try to control this potential confounding variable? (In other words, how could you separate the mother's memories of her own childhood from her current experiences with her own child?)

likely to have offspring who are themselves classified as secure when observed in the Strange Situation with their mothers. Van Ijzendoorn also found that mothers classified as dismissing provide consistently less sensitively responsive care than mothers of secure infants.

Attachment styles and mate choice

Having discussed evidence regarding the relationship between adults' attachment styles and those of their children (intergenerational continuity), we need to take a step backwards, as it were, and ask about the relationship between adults' attachment styles and their choice of romantic partner.

Securely attached

Observational studies of couple interaction during problem-solving and self-disclosure tasks indicate that secure men engage in more positive and supportive interactions with their partner than do insecure men (Belsky, 1999). When female members of college dating couples were confronted with a stressful situation, securely attached women sought more emotional support and accepted more physical contact from their male partners than did insecure women (Simpson *et al.*, 1992). Secure men (who are disproportionately likely to partner secure women; van Ijzendoorn and Bakermans-Kranenburg, 1996) provided more emotional support, made more reassuring comments and showed greater concern for their partners' well-being, compared with insecure men.

Belsky (1999) cites studies which show that secure women experienced less conflict with their husbands on topics related to time spent together and household division of labour than did insecure women. They're also more likely to manage conflict in mutually focused ways, which helps explain why they experience less conflict in the first place and why their relationships are likely to be mutually rewarding. This applies to both dating and married couples. Secure individuals also are more committed to their relationships and feel greater love for their partners. This is consistent with Hazan and Shaver's 'secure' description of feelings about romantic relationships.

Kirkpatrick and Davis (1994) followed a sample of over 300 dating couples for three years and observed that secure males and females were most likely to have stable and satisfying relationships. According to Collins and Read (1990), when *both* members of dating couples are asked about their mental models, the securely attached tend to choose partners who are also securely attached.

Anxious-avoidant

Brennan and Shaver (1995) found that individuals classified as avoidant were most uninhibited in their sexual behaviour – that is, they were most willing to engage in sex in the absence of strong feelings of love or an enduring relationship. Similarly, Hazan *et al.* (1994) found that such individuals were most likely to report involvement in one-night stands and sex outside established relationships: they preferred purely sexual contact (e.g. oral and anal sex) to more emotionally intimate sexual contact (such as kissing and cuddling).

Miller and Fishkin (1997) reported that insecure men desired a greater number of sexual partners over the next 30 years of their lives, and Kirkpatrick and Hazan (1994) observed that, over a four-year period, avoidant individuals were most likely to be dating more than one person simultaneously.

All these data are consistent with Simpson's (1990) findings that dating college students who scored high on avoidance scored lowest on commitment and trust; they also tended to be attracted to avoidant partners. Avoidant college students were most likely to have experienced a relationship break-up (Feeney and Noller, 1992). When the woman in college dating couples was stressed, the man withdrew support from his anxious partner, and the avoidant woman tended to stop looking for support (Simpson *et al.*, 1992).

These relationships tend to be opportunistic and self-serving, rather than mutually rewarding; they're likely to be short-lived (Belsky, 1999).

Anxious-ambivalent

The evidence here is much less plentiful than for the other two attachment styles. However, one important finding (Kunce and Shaver, 1994) is that ambivalent women reported the highest levels of 'compulsive caregiving' – that is, they were most likely to agree with statements such as 'I can't seem to stop from "mothering" my partner too much.'

The nature of relationships in different cultures

How Science Works

Practical Learning Activity 2.14

- What do you understand by the term 'culture'?
- What features of cultural difference might be relevant for understanding the nature of adult relationships? (See Gross, 2005.)

Individualism/collectivism

Hofstede (1980) defined culture as 'the collective programming of the mind which distinguishes the members of one group from another'. He identified four dimensions of culture, two of which are:

1. *power distance* – the amount of respect shown by those in both superior and subordinate positions

2. *individualism-collectivism* – whether one's identity is defined by personal choices and achievements (individualism) or by characteristics of the collective group one is, more or less, permanently attached to (collectivism).

Individualism-collectivism is one of four *cultural syndromes* that define culture, according to Triandis (1990). Triandis *et al.* (1986) identified four factors related to this syndrome. These are:

1. *family integrity* ('Children should live at home with their parents until they get married')

2. *interdependence* ('I like to live close to my good friends').

These are both features of *collectivism*. And:

3. *self-reliance with hedonism* ('If the group is slowing me down, it's better to leave and work alone; the most important thing in my life is to make myself happy')

4. *separation from ingroups* (indicated by agreement with items showing that what happens to extended family members is of little concern).

These are both features of *individualism*. Other 'defining attributes' are described in Box 2.7.

Voluntary/involuntary relationships

According to Moghaddam *et al.* (1993), interpersonal relationships in western cultures tend to be *individualistic, voluntary* and *temporary*. Those in non-western cultures are more *collectivist, involuntary* and *permanent*. As they say:

> The cultural values and environmental conditions in North America have led North American social psychologists to be primarily concerned with first-time acquaintances, friendships and intimate relationships, primarily because these appear to be the relationships most relevant to the North American urban cultural experience.

In other words, western psychologists tend to equate 'relationships' with 'western relationships' – a form of *ethnocentrism*.

According to Duck (1999), the *choice to marry* is voluntary, presumably. But once the marriage is a few years old, it's much less voluntary than it was, since getting out of it is accompanied by a great deal of 'social and legal baggage':

Box 2.7: Some defining attributes of individualism-collectivism (Triandis, 1990)

- Collectivists pay much more attention to an identifiable ingroup, and behave differently towards ingroup compared to outgroup members. The ingroup is best defined in terms of the *common fate* of its members. Often it is the unit of survival, or the food community. In most cultures, the family is the main ingroup, but in some the tribal groups or work groups (in Japan) can be just as important.
- Collectivists emphasise social hierarchy much more than individualists. Usually, the father is 'head of the household' and women are generally subordinate to men.
- For collectivists, the *self* is an extension of the ingroup, whereas for individualists it is separate and distinct. In collectivist cultures, people usually belong to a small number of ingroups, which influence their behaviour greatly. This is unusual in individualist cultures, where people belong to so many groups that often make conflicting demands on the individual.
- In collectivist cultures, *vertical relationships* (such as parent–child) take priority over *horizontal relationships* (such as spouse–spouse) when there's a conflict between them. The reverse is true in individualist cultures.
- Collectivists stress family integrity, security, obedience and conformity, while individualists stress achievement, pleasure and competition.

Thus when we talk about 'voluntary relationships', we need to recognise not only that the exercise of apparently free choice is always tempered by the social realities and constraints that surround us, but also that, once exercised, some choices are then disabled, and cannot be easily or straightforwardly remade. To that extent, therefore, their consequences become non-voluntary.

Synoptic Material

According to Smith and Bond (1998), *cross-cultural psychology* (CCP) studies *variability* in behaviour among the various societies and social groups around the world. For Jahoda (1978), an additional goal is to identify what's *similar* across different cultures, and thus likely to be our common human heritage (the *universals* of human behaviour).

CCP is important because it helps to correct *ethnocentrism* – the strong human tendency to use our own ethnic or cultural groups' norms and values to define what's 'natural' and 'correct' for everyone (that is, 'reality'; Triandis, 1990). Historically, psychology has been dominated by white, middle-class males in the USA; over the last century, they've enjoyed a monopoly as both the researchers and the 'subjects' of the discipline (Moghaddam and Studer, 1997) and constitute the core of psychology's *First World* (Moghaddam, 1987).

According to Moghaddam *et al.* (1993), American researchers and participants 'have shared a lifestyle and value system that differs not only from that of most other people in North America, such as ethnic minorities and women, but also the vast majority of people in the rest of the world'. Yet the findings from this research – and the theories based upon it – have been applied to *people in general*, as if culture makes no difference. An implicit equation is made between 'human being' and 'human being from western culture' (the *Anglocentric* or *Eurocentric bias*).

When members of other cultural groups have been studied, they've usually been *compared* with western samples, using the behaviour and experience of the latter as the 'standard'. It's the failure to acknowledge this bias that creates the misleading – and false – impression that what's being said about behaviour can be generalised without qualification. Cross-cultural psychologists *don't* equate 'human being' with 'member of western culture', because cultural background is the crucial *independent variable.* (For a further discussion of CCP and related issues, see Gross, 2005.)

The examples of relationships given in the quote above from Moghaddam *et al.* are all *voluntary.* But western psychologists have studied a wide range of such relationships during the last 20 years or so, some of which may seem more voluntary than others. Duck (1999) gives the following examples: relationships of blended families, cross-sex non-romantic friendship, romantic or friendly relationships in the workplace, relationships between cooperative neighbours, relationships between prisoners and guards, sibling relationships, children relating to other children, and adults' relationships with parents.

Marriage is found in all known cultures (Fletcher, 2002), and is usually taken to be a voluntary relationship. But there are several reasons for asking if it really is. For example, there are wide and important cultural variations in marital arrangements. From a western perspective, the 'natural' form of marriage is *monogamy* (marriage to one spouse at any one time). This belief is enshrined in the law (bigamy is a criminal offence) and reflects basic Judeo-Christian doctrine. But monogamy is only one form that marriage can take; others are described in Box 2.8.

When discussing Kerckhoff and Davis's (1962) *filter model* (see page 55–56), we noted that our choice of potential (realistic) marriage partners is limited by *demographic variables*. To this extent, most relationships are 'arranged'. As Duck (1999) says, 'Many of us would perhaps not recognise – or accept – that marriages are actually "arranged" by religion, social position, wealth, class, opportunity and other things over which we have little control, even within our own culture ...'. Conversely, parentally-arranged marriages in some cultures are gladly entered into, and are considered perfectly normal, natural relationships that are anticipated with pleasure.

Box 2.8: Culture and marriage

- *Polygamy* refers to having two or more spouses at once.
- It can take the form of *polygyny* (one man having two or more wives) or (less commonly) *polyandry* (one woman with two or more husbands).
- Another arrangement is *mandatory marriage to specific relatives*, as when a son marries the daughter of his father's brother (his first cousin; Triandis, 1994).
- 84 per cent of known cultures allow polygyny, but only 5–10 per cent of men in such cultures actually have more than one wife (Fletcher, 2002).
- Probably fewer than 0.5 per cent of human societies have practised polyandry as a common or preferred form of marriage (Price and Crapo, 1999). But throughout Tibet and the neighbouring Himalayan areas of India, Nepal and Bhutan, it's been common for generations. Usually, a woman marries two or more brothers (*fraternal polyandry*). This helps to keep family numbers down in order to cope with scarce resources; it also keeps brothers together. Land doesn't need to be divided between the brothers, and a single family is preserved as an economic unit.

Research studies of arranged marriages

Gupta and Singh (1982) found that couples in Jaipur, India, who married for love reported *diminished* feelings of love if they'd been married for more than five years. By contrast, those who'd undertaken arranged marriages reported *more* love if they weren't newly-weds. These findings reveal that passionate love 'cools' over time, and that there's scope for love to flourish within an arranged marriage.

In cultures where arranged marriages occur, courtship is accepted to a certain degree. But love is left to be defined, and discovered, *after* marriage (Bellur, 1995). This, of course, is the reverse of the 'Hollywood' picture, where love is supposed to *precede* marriage and be what marriage is all about.

However, even in traditional cultures that practise arranged marriages, brides (and grooms) are typically given some choice in the matter (Fletcher, 2002). For example, in Sri Lanka men and women who like one another (or fall in love) usually let their parents know their choices in advance through indirect channels (de Munck, 1998). Families often use similar criteria that the individuals themselves might use if they had a free choice (including matching on attractiveness; see above). The classic example is the Jewish tradition of having a *matchmaker* arrange a suitable match (Rockman, 1994).

Arranged marriages are far more common in collectivist cultures, where the whole extended family 'marries' the other extended family. This is in contrast with individualistic cultures, in which the individuals marry one another (Triandis, 1994). In Japan, almost 25 per cent of marriages are arranged (Iwao, 1993).

In general, *divorce rates* among those who marry according to parents' wishes are much *lower* than among those who marry for love. This is an argument in favour of arranged marriages. But divorce rates among 'arranged couples' are rising, indicating that personal freedom is gaining importance and that traditional structures that define set roles for family members are becoming less valid (Bellur, 1995).

Figure 2.12 Polygamy in Nevada, USA, is alive and well!

SUMMARY

The formation, maintenance and breakdown of romantic relationships

- **Affiliation** is one of Maslow's basic survival needs and is also a major motive underlying conformity, namely **normative social influence** (**NSI**) (Deutsch and Gerard). **Attraction** complements these basic needs.

- **Reward theory** represents a general theoretical framework for explaining initial attraction and the formation/maintenance of relationships. Factors that influence initial attraction through their reward value include proximity, exposure and familiarity, similarity and physical attractiveness.

- In the 'real' world, **proximity** represents a minimum requirement for attraction. But in the virtual world of the internet, distance is no barrier to the formation of romantic attachments.

- **Online relationships** (or **cyber affairs**) can take place though chat rooms, interactive games or newsgroups, and can escalate from purely online into face-to-face sexual encounters.

- Related to proximity is Hall's concept of **personal space**. There are important **cultural differences** regarding **proxemic rules** (an extreme example being the **caste system** in India). People's response to invasion of their personal space is well illustrated by Felipe and Sommer's library study.

- Proximity increases the opportunity for interaction (**exposure**), which, in turn, increases **familiarity**. Increased interaction produces more **polarised** attitudes, usually towards greater liking.

- Zajonc's **mere exposure effect** was demonstrated by Saegert *et al*.'s TOSE.

- **Similarity** seems to be most important in relation to **beliefs**, **attitudes** and **values**. Assumed similarity of attitudes produces **reciprocal liking**.

- **Physical attractiveness** has been studied in its own right, as well as one aspect of similarity.

- According to the **attractiveness stereotype**, attractive-looking people are perceived as also having attractive personalities. But different cultures define physical attractiveness differently, and males and females within cultures use different criteria for assessing attractiveness.

- Underlying different versions of **Social Exchange Theory** (**SET**) is the view of people as fundamentally selfish. An important distinction that challenges this assumption is that between **communal** and **exchange couples**.

- Related to SET is the **matching hypothesis** (**MH**). But since it's impossible for us to all have the 'perfect' partner, we compromise in the form of a **value match**.

- The MH has been tested through the 'computer dance' (such as Walster *et al*.'s study). While the study found evidence consistent with reward theory, the findings were contrary to what the MH predicts.

- Subsequent computer dance studies, together with other methodologies (such as Murstein's) tend to support the MH.

- SET is really a special case of a more general account of human relationships called **equity theory (ET)**; the extra component is **investment**. Equity denotes **fairness**, a **constant ratio** of rewards to costs / profit to investment.

- Thibaut and Kelley's ET distinguishes between **comparison level (CL)** and **comparison level for alternatives (CL alt.)**. Depending on whether your current reward–cost ratio (RCR) exceeds or falls below your CL / CL alt., you'll either find the relationship satisfying or not want it to last.

- Concern with either exchange or equity is negatively correlated with marital adjustment, making compatibility difficult to achieve.

- Kelley and Thibaut's **interdependence theory (IT)** goes beyond individual partners and considers the **intersubjective** harmony or conflict between the attitudes, motives etc. of people in various types of relationship.

- The three filters in Kerckhoff and Davis's **filter model** are (i) **similarity of sociological** (or **demographic) variables**; (ii) similarity of **psychological characteristics**, specifically, agreement on basic values; and (iii) **complementarity of emotional needs**.

- An alternative to complementary needs is complementarity of **resources**, as demonstrated in Buss's cross-cultural study.

- According to Murstein's **stimulus-value-role (SVR) theory**, each of these three factors (in this order) assumes greatest significance during one particular stage.

- Relationship research has been dominated by a **heterosexist bias**, reflecting heterosexism in society. More recently, gay and lesbian ('under-studied') relationships have assumed prominence.

- One major theme of this research has been the fundamental similarity between homosexuals and heterosexuals, including mental health and quality of their relationships. These findings are cited in arguments supporting legal recognition of same-sex relationships.

- Kitzinger and Coyle point out some important **differences** between homosexual and heterosexual relationships, in terms of **cohabitation, sexual exclusivity** and the adoption of **traditional (heterosexual) sex roles**.

- Duck identifies three broad categories of reasons for relationship break-up, namely **pre-existing doom, mechanical failure** and **sudden death**.

- Romantic relationships (unlike friendships) are (mostly) **exclusive**, making it necessary to provide an 'official' (public) account of what went wrong that will show the partners in a favourable light and free to enter a new relationship.

- Duck's **Theory of Relationship Dissolution** (**ToRD**) identifies four phases (**intrapsychic, dyadic, social** and **grave-dressing**), each with its related threshold. Relationship dissolution is seen as a **process** (rather than an event).

Human reproductive behaviour

- **Evolution** is the process of **natural selection**, by which new **species** arise as the result of gradual changes to the **genetic make-up** of existing species over long periods of time.

- **Reproductive fitness** refers to the capacity to reproduce one's genetic material. Since survival is a necessary prerequisite for reproductive fitness, Darwin's original theory of evolution by natural selection couldn't account for **altruistic behaviour**.

- Two major **sociobiological** explanations – Hamilton's **kin selection theory** and Trivers's **reciprocal altruism theory** – regard altruism as only **apparent**.

- According to Dawkins's **selfish gene theory**, any behaviour (including apparent altruism) is designed to maximise the survival of the organism's genes: the body is a survival machine for enhancing the gene's chances of replication.

- **Evolutionary psychology** (**EP**) uses Darwinian concepts to generate testable hypotheses about human behaviour; it assumes that individuals will act to increase the survival of their genes.

- Arguably, EP's greatest contribution to understanding human behaviour has been the application of **sexual selection** theory. There are two kinds: **intrasexual** (**within** one sex, usually males) and **intersexual** (**between** the sexes).

- A classic example of sexual selection is the (male) peacock's tail, which also illustrates **sexual dimorphism**.

- Humans appear to be a **mutually** sexually selected species. According to EP, **mate choice** is determined by 'built-in' preferences that have developed through the course of human evolution.

- The **symmetry** of the face around the vertical midline (its '**averageness**') appears to be an important determinant of attractiveness and is quite consistent across cultures. Symmetry equates with fitness.

- There's more to facial attractiveness than averageness, and younger-looking features in women seem to be an advantage.

- As far as bodily attractiveness is concerned, symmetry is again important (for both sexes), as is **waist-to-hip ratio** (**WHR**) (for females). This filters out unhealthy females and those with low reproductive capacity, after which face and/or **body weight** are used to select a mate; this allows for cultural differences.

- Another factor involved in sexual selection is **sexual enthusiasm** – the capacity to become sexually aroused.

- Two specific explanations of intersexual selection are Fisher's **'good taste' / 'runaway effect' hypothesis** and Zahavi's **'good genes' / 'handicap process' hypothesis**.

- Trivers's concept of **parental investment** (**PI**) refers to any investment (food, energy, time) by the parent in an individual offspring that increases the offspring's chances of survival (and reproductive success) at the expense of the parent's ability to invest in other offspring.

- There's a fundamental asymmetry between the sexes, with females' investment being far greater than that of males, both pre- and post-natally.

- The **theory of parent–offspring conflict** (**POC**), a direct extension of Hamilton's kin selection theory, claims that conflict occurs when each child wants more resources from the parent than they're prepared to give.

- POC predicts that conflict should be greater (a) when half-siblings live together (as in **blended families**); and (b) in families with very young mothers. Both predictions have received empirical support.

- Unlike sociobiologists, evolutionary psychologists see the **mind** as linking genes and behaviour; the mind comprises several specialised, independent **modules**, designed by natural selection to solve problems faced by our hunter-gatherer ancestors.

- EP rejects the Standard Social Science Model (SSSM) and argues firmly in favour of **human nature**; this consists of modules together with related emotions (such as jealousy and anger).

- EP in general is concerned with **universal** features of the mind. **Gender** is the crucial exception to this rule.

- A major difficulty with EP is its **assumptions** about the nature of our hunter-gatherer past in the Palaeolithic **Environment of Evolutionary Adaptation** (**EEA**).

- Another problem for EP (including Bowlby's attachment theory) is its inability to explain same-sex (non-reproductive) romantic relationships. These are better explained by a distinction between **sexual orientation** and **romantic attachment**.

Effects of early experience and culture on adult relationships

- **Attachment theory** represents a major way of trying to understand the influence of childhood and adolescent experiences on adult relationships.

- Human attachment **evolved** because, through the protection and survival it promoted, it increased the chances of successful reproduction of those who stayed close to their caregivers.

- Given that the EEA was highly variable, it's unlikely that any one pattern of attachment (i.e. secure) was or is 'species-typical' or normative ('natural'). By the same token, maternal sensitivity may be no more natural than insensitivity.

- Attachment is a **lifelong phenomenon**, and patterns established in childhood parent–child relationships tend to structure the quality of later bonds in their adult relationships. This hypothesis was tested in Hazan and Shaver's groundbreaking study of adult romantic relationships.

- Hazan and Shaver translated Ainsworth *et al.*'s three **attachment styles** into a 'love quiz' with adult samples and found a similar distribution as that found for young children. They also found a correlation between adult attachment style and the **type of parenting** they received as children.

- Hazan and Shaver also found evidence that adults with different attachment styles display different characteristic **mental models** of themselves and their closest relationships. This is related to Bowlby's **inner working models (IWMs)**.

- The **Adult Attachment Interview (AAI)** is a structured interview designed to tap an individual's experience of attachment relationships in childhood and how s/he considers those experiences to have influenced later development and present functioning.

- According to the AAI, four attachment styles are possible: **secure/autonomous (F)**, **dismissing (D)**, **preoccupied/entangled (E)** – corresponding to the three identified by Ainsworth *et al.* – and **unresolved/disorganised (U)**.

- Many studies have used the AAI in the context of **intergenerational continuity** or **intergenerational transfer of attachment patterns**. Several studies have considered the relationship between attachment style and **mate choice**.

- **Individualist** and **collectivist cultures** define and organise the self and social relationships in very different ways. For example, collectivists stress family integrity, security, obedience and conformity, the common fate of ingroup members, and hierarchy, while individualists stress achievement, pleasure and competition.

- Interpersonal relationships in western cultures tend to be **individualistic**, **voluntary** and **temporary**, while those in non-western cultures are more **collectivist**, **involuntary** and **permanent**.

- **Marriage** is found in all cultures, but there are wide variations in marital arrangements. These include **monogamy** and **polygamy** (**polygyny** or **polyandry**).

- **Arranged** marriages are much more common in collectivist cultures.

- Western psychologists tend to equate 'relationships' with 'western relationships' – a form of **ethnocentrism**.

- **Cross-cultural psychology (CCP)** helps to correct ethnocentrism, challenging the **Anglocentric/Eurocentric bias** by taking cultural background as the key **independent variable**.

Essay Questions

The formation, maintenance and breakdown of relationships

1. Outline TWO OR MORE theories relating to the formation and/or maintenance of relationships. (25 marks)
2. Outline and evaluate research into the breakdown of relationships. (25 marks)

Human reproductive behaviour

3. Critically consider the relationship between sexual selection and human reproductive behaviour. (25 marks)
4. Describe and evaluate evolutionary explanations of parental investment (for example, sex differences, parent–offspring conflict). (25 marks)

Effects of early experience and culture on adult relationships

5. 'Attachment is a lifelong process; the same basic mechanisms are involved in both childhood and adulthood.' Discuss research into the influence of childhood and adolescent experiences on adult relationships. (25 marks)
6. Discuss the extent to which relationships have been shown to differ in different cultures. (25 marks)

It should take you 30 minutes to answer each question.

Eating behaviour

What's covered in this chapter?

You need to know about:

Eating behaviour
- Factors influencing attitudes to food and eating behaviour – for example, cultural influences, mood and health concerns
- Explanations for the success and failure of dieting

Biological explanations of eating behaviour
- The role of the neural mechanisms involved in controlled eating and satiation
- Evolutionary explanations of food preference

Eating disorders
- Psychological explanations of one eating disorder – for example, anorexia nervosa, bulimia nervosa, obesity
- Biological explanations of one eating disorder – for example, anorexia nervosa, bulimia nervosa, obesity

> ✔ **Specification Hint: Warning!**
>
> Eating behaviour is an extremely complex psychological topic to study. The factors that explain attitudes to eating behaviour are very wide ranging, and biological explanations of eating behaviour are very involved and still not clearly understood. Furthermore, there are ethical considerations concerned with the study of eating disorders among a group of young people many of whom may be suffering from or know someone who suffers from an eating disorder. The eating disorders section was included as a compulsory element in the previous AQA spec A so may be a popular topic, but we would urge you to review the details of the chapter and consider carefully your choice of topic.

Factors influencing attitudes to food and eating behaviour – for example, cultural influences, mood, health concerns (parents/peers)

The key factor influencing our eating behaviour is of course hunger, but what we choose to eat is not determined solely by physiological or nutritional needs. There are numerous other factors that influence food choice, including our attitudes, beliefs and knowledge about food, the social context in which we live and eat, and the influence of our parents and peers. Many cultural and socio-economic factors also influence our attitudes to food and our eating behaviour, as does our mood, as we gain comfort from it and experience cravings for it.

Attitudes to food

Food choice is influenced by a large number of factors, including social and cultural factors. One method for trying to understand the impact of these factors is through the study of attitudes.

The attitude–behaviour relationship

Eagly and Chaiken (1993) define an attitude as 'a psychological tendency that is expressed by evaluating a particular entity with some degree of favour or disfavour'. Therefore we can assume that attitudes are an important determinant of behaviour, and therefore important to study in relation to food choice and eating behaviour. It can be assumed that an individual who has a positive attitude towards a certain food (e.g. chocolate) is more likely to consume that food. Indeed, Conner (2000) found that the correlation between food choice attitudes and behaviour were moderate to large. However, Wicker's (1969) review of the attitude–behaviour link concluded that, at best, only a weak correlation connected expressed attitudes and behaviour.

The Theory of Reasoned Action (TRA) and the Theory of Planned Behaviour (TPB)

The Theory of Reasoned Action (TRA), of Ajzen and Fishbein (1980), has been used along with its progression, the Theory of Planned Behaviour (TPB) (Ajzen, 1985, 1988; Ajzen and Madden, 1986) to explain as well as to predict the intention of certain health behaviours. The TRA placed its emphasis on the role of social cognition in the form of subjective norms (the individual's beliefs about their social world), and included both beliefs and evaluations of these beliefs (both factors constituting their attitudes). The TPB is an extension of the TRA.

The TPB proposes that an individual's behavioural intention is jointly derived from three components, as follows.

1. *Attitude towards behaviour:* this is a composition of both an individual's positive and negative evaluation of a particular behaviour and beliefs about the outcome of the behaviour (e.g. exercising is fun and will improve my health).

2. *Subjective norms:* this is an individual's perception of social norms and pressures to perform a behaviour and an evaluation of whether the individual is motivated to comply with this pressure (e.g. people who are important to me will approve if I lose weight, and I want their approval).

3. *Perceived behavioural control (PBC):* an individual's belief that they can carry out a particular behaviour, based upon a consideration of internal control factors (e.g. skills, ability, information) and external factors

(e.g. obstacles, opportunities), both relating to past behaviour.

Supporting research

The use of the TPB enables us to understand the strength of the influence of attitude upon individuals' eating behaviour, and can help us recognise the determinants of food choice.

The use of the TPB has, in the main, focused on *predicting the intentions* of an individual to consume specific foods. For example, Sparks *et al.* (1992) investigated the extent to which cognitions relate to the intentions to eat cookies and wholemeal bread, while Raats *et al.* (1995) studied the intentions of drinking skimmed milk, and Sparks and Shepherd (1992) the intention to eat organic vegetables.

Cox *et al.* (1998) assessed attitudes and predictors of intention, and identified perceived barriers to increasing fruit and vegetable consumption among UK consumers. Factors such as health, cost and taste were strongly associated with overall attitudes, which were reported as being largely positive towards fruits and vegetables. However, consumers' intention to increase consumption was found to be weak. It was suggested that social pressure was strongly associated with reported intention to increase consumption; however, perceived social pressure to do this was low.

However, behavioural intentions are not particularly good predictors of *actual* behaviour. Therefore researchers have also used both the TRA and the TPB to investigate predictors of actual behaviour, rather than simply intended behaviour. For example, Shepherd and Stockley (1985) used the TRA to predict fat intake and reported that attitude was a better predictor than subjective norms. Similarly, attitude has also been found to be the best predictor of table salt use (Shepherd and Farleigh, 1986).

A more useful application of the TPB would be to see whether it could predict actual behaviour over a period of time. Povey *et al.* (2000) found that the TPB explained 57 per cent of the variance in intentions to eat five portions of fruit and vegetables. Participants were assessed on their actual behaviour one month later, finding that the TPB accounted for 32 per cent of the variance in actual fruit and vegetable consumption. In a similar study, Armitage and Conner (1999) asked participants about their attitudes and intentions towards eating a low-fat diet. These participants were contacted again after a month and asked whether or not they had eaten a low-fat diet in the intervening period. Analyses of these responses revealed that the TPB accounted for 39 per cent of the variance in behaviour.

However, unlike fruit and vegetable consumption, where it is possible to count portions, it is harder for people to assess how much fat they have actually eaten in the past months.

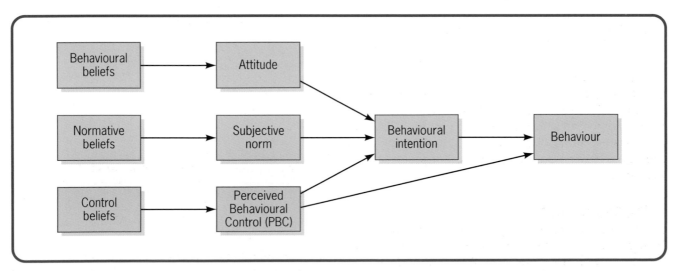

Figure 3.1 The theory of planned behaviour (from Conner and Armitage, 2002)

Evaluation of TPB

✗ Schwarzer (1992) has criticised the TPB as it does not describe either the order of the different beliefs or any direction of causality. The TRA/TPB assume that behaviour is a consequence of a series of rational stages: a weighing-up of the pros and cons before deciding how to act. This may not be the cause of all behaviour. Although the TRA/TPB have been applied extensively to eating behaviour, their ability to predict actual behaviour remains poor, leaving a large amount of variance to be explained by undefined factors.

✔/✗ However, the model does attempt to address the problem of social and environmental factors (normative beliefs) and also includes the role of past behaviour (perceived behavioural control). This approach has shown good prediction of behaviour, but there are a number of possible extensions to this basic model that might improve its utility. One such extension is the inclusion of measures of moral concern, which have been found to be important both for the choice of genetically modified foods and also for foods to be eaten by others (Shepherd, 1999).

Attitudinal ambivalence

In the main, attitudes are thought to be either positive or negative; however, individuals can simultaneously hold both positive and negative attitudes. For example, the positive attitude towards the taste of a delicious cream cake can simultaneously be held with a negative attitude towards the amount of fat it contains and therefore the possibility of putting on weight. This view is known as attitudinal ambivalence. The consequence of attitudinal ambivalence is that is moderates our behaviour – ambivalent individuals are less likely to carry out the behaviour. Ambivalence undermines the attitude–intention correlation.

Conner *et al.* (2003) examined the moderating role of attitudinal ambivalence within the TPB, finding attitude–behaviour and perceived behavioural control–behaviour relationships to be weaker in individuals with higher ambivalence.

Sparks *et al.* (2001) examined ambivalence with respect to eating meat and chocolate, and found that greater ambivalence was associated with weaker intention to carry out the behaviour. Similarly, Povey *et al.* (2001) examined the determinants of eating meat, vegetarian and vegan diets; in each case more ambivalent attitudes were associated with weaker attitude–intention correlations.

🔍 How Science Works

Practical Learning Activity 3.1: Factors affecting food choice

- Make a list of all factors that might affect eating behaviour and subsequent food choice.
- Discuss with friends and family what factors affect their daily food choices. You could discuss with an elderly relative what food choices they had when they were children and see if they are different to the food choices available nowadays. Which generation had the healthier diet?

Synoptic Material: Research methods

Most of the research carried out in this area of attitudinal research uses questionnaires and interviews. Review the research methods chapter (Chapter 11) in order to understand the advantages and disadvantages of using such methods. Often, rating scales are used in questionnaires to show the degree of agreement with a particular measure. Consider the strengths and weaknesses of using quantitative measures in the measurement of attitudes and behaviours.

Social context

Influence on children's attitudes to food and eating

By the time a child reaches the age of three or four years old, their eating behaviour is no longer driven by a biological need, but is influenced instead by their responsiveness to environmental cues about food intake. Indeed, children's food-related knowledge, preferences and consumption are related to their parents' preferences, beliefs and attitudes towards food (Birch and Fisher, 1998). The development of an individual's attitude towards food and eating can therefore be explained by the experiences of childhood.

Research has shown that the family strongly influences childhood behaviour, including children's attitudes towards food (Nicklas *et al.*, 2001). Parental attitudes to food, food choices and eating are central in determining a child's attitude towards food. In line with this, Wardle (1995) suggested that 'parental attitudes must certainly affect their children indirectly through the foods purchased for and served in the household … influencing the children's exposure and … their habits and preference'.

Research has demonstrated that in children as young as two years old, food preferences were associated with their mothers' food preferences (Skinner *et al.*, 2002). This may be due, in part, to the fact that parents tend to have food in the home that they like and eat (Birch and Fisher, 1998).

Exposure

Food preferences that develop during infancy remain relatively stable and are reflected in food choices made later in life (Skinner *et al.*, 2002). Rozin's (1976) concept of food neophobia (fear of trying new food), can go some way to explaining how food preferences develop in children. Research has demonstrated that food neophobia is an important predictor of fruit and vegetable intake. Children who are reluctant to try new foods generally have lower intakes of fruit and vegetables (Wardle *et al.*, 2003). Research has suggested that repeated exposure to novel foods can change a child's preference to favour that food (Patrick and Nicklas, 2005). For example, Birch and Marlin (1982) gave two-year-old children novel foods over a six-week period. One food was presented twenty times, one ten times and one five times, while one remained novel. The results showed a direct relationship between exposure and food preference, and indicated that a minimum of about eight to ten exposures was necessary before preference began to shift significantly.

Modelling

Social Learning Theory describes the impact of observing other people's behaviour on one's own behaviour and is sometimes referred to as 'modelling' or 'observational learning'. Children learn about eating not only through their own experience but also by watching others.

The family is widely recognised as being significant in food decisions. Research shows the shaping of food choices taking place in the home. Because family and friends can be a source of encouragement in making and sustaining dietary change, adopting dietary strategies that are acceptable to them may benefit the individual, while also having an effect on the eating habits of others (Anderson *et al.*, 1998).

Parents

Duncker (1938) conducted an early study that explored the impact of 'social suggestion' on children's food choices. Children observed a series of role models making food choices different from their own. The models chosen were other children, a friend, their mother, an unknown adult and a fictional hero. The results showed a greater change in the child's food preference if the model was an older child, a friend, their mother or the fictional hero. The unknown adult had no impact on food preferences. Therefore children are more likely to sample unfamiliar food after they have seen an adult eat the food, and are even more likely to do this after seeing their mother rather than a stranger eating that food. Parental behaviour and attitudes can therefore be viewed as an essential part of the process of social learning with regard to the acquisition of eating behaviours. Children and parents show similar patterns of food preference and acceptance (Patrick and Nicklas, 2005).

Both Fisher *et al.* (2002) and Gibson *et al.* (1998) have shown that children's intake of fruit and vegetables is positively related to parents' intake of fruit and vegetables. Tibbs *et al.* (2001) have also demonstrated a similar effect of parental modelling of healthful dietary behaviours, with low-fat eating patterns and lower dietary fat intake. Olivera *et al.* (1992) reported a correlation between mothers' and children's food intakes for most nutrients in preschool children, and suggested targeting parents to try to improve children's diets, whereas Contento *et al.* (1993) found a relationship

How Science Works

Practical Learning Activity 3.2: A chip off the old block? Like father like son, like mother like daughter . . .

Devise a self-completion questionnaire that lists a number of different foodstuffs and includes a rating measure of how much the respondent enjoys eating them. Administer the questionnaire to fathers and sons and mothers and daughters. Test to see if there is a degree of correlation between the father-and-son and mother-and-daughter scores. Did you find that parents and their children prefer similar types of food?

● What kind of correlational test would you conduct on the data?
● What significance level would you hope to achieve?
● What is the experimental hypothesis you are testing?

Figure 3.2 Children's intake of fruit and veg mirrors that of their parents

between mothers' health motivation and the quality of children's diets.

Peers

Although parents are the major influence on a child's attitudes to food, they are not the only influence. As seen in Duncker (1938), children are also likely to model both an older child and a friend. It is therefore important to look at research into the influence that peers have on eating behaviour. Birch (1980) studied how peer modelling could be used to change children's preference for vegetables. The target children were placed at lunch for four consecutive days next to other children who preferred a different vegetable (peas vs carrots). By the end of the study the children showed a shift in their vegetable preference that persisted at a follow-up assessment several weeks later.

Peers are also considered to be particularly influential in adolescent eating behaviour. Feunekes *et al.* (1998) found that 19 per cent of food consumed by adolescents was similar to that consumed by their friends. More specifically, associations with peer intake were found for the type of milk used in coffee, alcoholic drinks and several snack foods, including French fries. Another study on adolescent girls' eating behaviours found that peer pressure was a strong predictor of eating behaviour, even after controlling for other interpersonal variables (Monge-Rojas *et al.*, 2002).

Social support can have a beneficial effect on food choices and healthful dietary change (Devine *et al.*, 2003). Social support from within the household and from co-workers was positively associated with improvements in fruit and vegetable consumption (Sorensen *et al.*, 1998a) and with the preparative stage of improving eating habits, respectively (Sorensen *et al.*, 1998b). Social support may enhance health promotion through fostering a sense of group belonging and helping people to be more competent and self-efficacious (Berkman, 1995).

Food as a reward

Children often learn to associate food with a reward; parents can be heard to say things like 'If you eat all your vegetables, I will be very pleased with you', and this can obviously impact on both their attitude to food and their future eating behaviour. Birch *et al.* (1980) found increased preferences towards food when associated with positive adult attention. They also explored the impact of using food as a reward by presenting children with a snack as a reward. The results showed that food acceptance increased if the foods were presented as a reward, compared with a non-social control condition, thus suggesting that using food as a reward increases preference for that food. So maybe parents should be saying 'If you behave well you can have a carrot', rather than a biscuit, if they want to encourage their child to eat more vegetables!

However, the relationship between food and rewards

appears to be more complex and often confusing to the child. So although parents might say 'Eat all your vegetables and you can have a pudding', in an attempt to encourage the child to eat their vegetables, this approach often fails, as it just increases the child's liking for the pudding rather than the vegetables they are trying to encourage them to eat (Birch, 1999)! Birch concluded that restricting children's access to snack foods actually makes the restricted foods more attractive to the child. Fisher and Birch (1999) found that when food was freely available, children will choose more of the restricted than the unrestricted foods, particularly when the mother is not present.

Cultural influence

What people eat is influenced by social and cultural circumstances. Cultural influences lead to the differences in the consumption of certain foods and in traditions of preparation, and in certain cases can lead to restrictions such as the exclusion of meat and milk from the diet. Cultural influences are, however, flexible. For example, when moving to a new country, individuals often adopt particular food habits of the local culture.

Mealtimes

Whether a family eats together can have an important impact on the development of a child's attitude towards food. Research has demonstrated that children who eat meals with other family members and have companionship at mealtimes consume more healthy foods and nutrients, and eat more servings of the basic food groups (Stanek *et al.*, 1990). In adolescents, the presence of the family at the dinner meal has been positively associated with consumption of fruit, vegetables and dairy foods, and lower likelihood of skipping breakfast (Videon and Manning, 2003). Finally, Neumark-Sztainer *et al.* (2003) found that frequency of eating meals as a family was positively associated with intake of fruit, vegetables, grains and calcium-rich foods, and with the general intake of vitamins and minerals.

Eating at home, at school or at work

Although the majority of food is eaten in the home, an increasing proportion is eaten outside the home (e.g. in schools, at work and in restaurants). In 1970, only 34 per cent of a family's food budget was accounted for by foods consumed outside the home (Kant and Graubard, 2004), but by the late 1990s this had risen to more than 47 per cent.

However, access to healthy food options is sometimes limited; this is particularly so in many work and school environments, and especially true for those with particular dietary requirements, such as vegetarians, or those who work irregular hours or shift patterns.

While campaigns – such as that of TV chef Jamie Oliver, which aimed to improve the standard of food in UK schools – have experienced some success, this is often undermined by competition from the presence of vending machines. Most secondary schools (78 per cent) have student-accessible vending machines. Foods from these are typically higher in fat and lower in

Evaluation of food as a reward

✗ Much research in this area has been carried out in a laboratory setting, thus making it harder to generalise results to a more naturalistic setting (e.g. the child's family home). Dowey (1996) reviewed the literature examining food and rewards, argued that results may be due to methodological differences, and suggested that studies should be conducted in real-life situations and the outcomes measured over time. The majority of the research measures children's preferences and not actual food intake – the relationship between the two is often assumed. This approach ignores the 'body' – both the biological need for food and the influence of body image.

✔/✗ This approval emphasises the importance of learning in the development of attitudes towards food, as well as the influence of parental attitudes to food preference. Cognitions are often included as influencing factors, being used to explain such phenomena as neophobia of food. However, these cognitions remain implicit and are not explicitly described.

overall nutritional value. Additionally, research has now demonstrated how these alternative sources of food choice can have an adverse effect on the quality of foods schoolchildren and adolescents consume. As vending machine availability has increased, fruit consumption has decreased. Thus the types of foods available to children at school can also impact the types of quality of foods consumed (Kubik *et al.*, 2003), although French *et al.* (2001) found that price reductions for healthier snacks in vending machines increased sales.

The majority of families in the UK consist of only one parent or of two parents who are both working outside the home. Therefore convenience foods are increasingly being relied upon to provide the family meal (Hart, 1997). In a nationally representative survey, the NPD Group reported that time spent preparing meals declined more than 10 per cent from 1994 to 1999, while home meal replacement such as restaurants and pre-packaged foods have become increasingly popular.

Portion size

An increasing trend worldwide, and particularly in the UK, started in the USA and has been termed 'the supersizing of America'. In the United States and elsewhere it is clear that portion sizes are getting bigger. Many fast-food restaurants now have 'big kids' meals', which are in essence adult-sized portions, and a number of international chain restaurants have stopped offering 'small' sizes. Accompanying this is the realisation that people's attitudes to portion size are changing. They seem increasingly unaware of what an appropriate healthy portion size is and thus many people are beginning to inadvertently consume excess energy (Patrick and Nicklas, 2005)

Figure 3.3 Portion sizes are gradually getting larger

A survey of take-away foods sold by chain restaurants, published in 2002, found that portion sizes had increased substantially from those served in the recent past. For example, current sizes of common fast-food items such as French fries, hamburgers and soft drinks were two to five times larger than when the items were originally marketed (Young and Nestle, 2002). Between 1977 and 1998, energy intake for soft drinks increased by 49 kcal, for hamburgers by 97 kcal and for French fries by 68 kcal. Thus larger portions not only contain more energy, but also encourage people to eat more (Patrick and Nicklas, 2005).

Rolls *et al.* (2000) found a positive linear relationship between larger portion sizes and intake in children aged between four and six years. Additionally, Orlet *et al.* (2003) found that doubling an age-appropriate portion of a starter increased intake by 25 per cent, and those children who were served larger portions tended to take larger bites. Therefore together these findings suggest that larger portions influence children's eating behaviour by promoting intake of food.

Socio-economic factors

In addition to the more direct influences on our eating behaviour, various other factors influence our attitudes to food and eating. These include socio-economic factors such as income, level of education and knowledge of food.

Education

The level of education a parent has is thought to directly influence the eating behaviour of their children. For example, higher-level parental education has been associated with health consciousness in food choice (North and Emmett, 2000), and adolescents whose parents were relatively more educated had higher intakes of carbohydrates, protein, fibre, foliate, vitamin A and calcium, and were more likely to consume more servings of vegetables and dairy products compared with their peers (Xie *et al.*, 2003). Also, the use of reduced-fat milk was higher in families where the parents were of college education level, whereas those families whose parents had less than a college education tended to use full-fat milk exclusively (Dennison *et al.*, 2001).

Studies indicate that level of education can influence dietary behaviour during adulthood (Kearney *et al.*, 2000). In contrast, nutrition knowledge and good dietary habits are not strongly correlated. This is because knowledge about health does not lead to direct action when individuals are unsure how to apply their knowledge. Furthermore, information disseminated on nutrition comes from a variety of sources and is viewed as conflicting or is mistrusted, which discourages motivation to change (De Almeida *et al.*, 1997). Thus it is important to convey accurate and consistent messages through various media, on food packages and of course via health professionals.

Income

Income is also an important predictor of eating behaviour. Children and adolescents from higher-income families have been found to have a greater intake of polyunsaturated fats, protein, folate, calcium and iron than those from a lower-income family, and were more likely to meet the recommended number of daily servings for dairy products (Xie *et al.*, 2003) compared with their peers in lower socio-economic groups whose diets consisted of a higher intake of foods such as meat, full-fat milk, fats, sugars, preserves, potatoes and cereals, and relatively low intake of vegetables, fruit and brown bread. Neumark-Sztainer *et al.* (1998) found that as many as 40 per cent of lower-income adolescents do not meet the recommended level of daily consumption of fruit and vegetables. British children in lower socio-economic groups had significantly lower daily intakes of many micronutrients, a higher percentage of energy from fat, and a tendency to receive a greater proportion of energy and nutrients from snacks than children in higher socio-economic groups (Patrick and Nicklas, 2005).

Cost and accessibility

There is no doubt that the cost of food is a primary determinant of food choice. Whether cost is prohibitive depends fundamentally on a person's income and socio-economic status. Low-income groups have a greater tendency to consume unbalanced diets and in particular have low intakes of fruit and vegetables (De Irala-Estevez *et al.*, 2000). However, access to more money does not automatically equate to a better-quality diet, but the range of foods from which one can choose should increase.

Accessibility to shops is another important physical factor influencing food choice, which is dependent on resources such as transport and geographical location. Healthy food tends to be more expensive when avail-

How Science Works

Practical Learning Activity 3.3: Know your meat and veg!

- Conduct a study that determines the relationship, if any, between healthy knowledge of food and actual food consumption. Devise a questionnaire that tests people's knowledge of healthy eating. You could ask about healthy food types, the number of recommended calories per day and how many calories each food type has. Then ask the participants to keep a food diary detailing everything they eat over a weekend.
- Give each participant a healthy eating knowledge score and a healthy eating behaviour score. Correlate the two scores and see if there is a positive correlation. You could create bar graphs and use some descriptive statistics to analyse the data collected.

able within towns and cities compared to supermarkets on the outskirts (Donkin *et al.*, 2000). However, improving access alone does not increase purchase of additional fruit and vegetables, which are still regarded as prohibitively expensive (Dibsdall *et al.*, 2003).

Ethnic groups and religion

Cultural influences lead to differences in the habitual consumption of certain foods and in traditions of preparation – and, in certain cases, can lead to restrictions such as exclusion of meat and milk from the diet.

Minority ethnic groups are disproportionately represented in lower-income areas within the UK; evidence suggests that those living in households with a lower income have a poor-quality diet, and often lack confidence and experience in cooking skills (Stead *et al.*, 2004). What factors influence the eating behaviour and food choices of these individuals?

Key Study 3.1: Factors that affect the food choices made by girls and young women, from minority ethnic groups, living in the UK (Lawrance *et al.*, 2007)

Aim/hypothesis (A01)

Lawrance *et al.* (2007) wanted to investigate factors that might influence food choice and the nutritional intake of girls and young women from minority ethnic groups.

Method/design (A01)

Discussion groups were set up across the UK to explore factors that might affect the food choices of girls and young women of African and South Asian descent. The discussions centered around buying and preparing food, eating food, and dietary changes. The results of their discussions were analysed using content analysis.

Results (A01)

A number of common concerns were voiced by the women. Food choices were indeed influenced by culture, time, availability, cost, health and price.

- Pakistani/Bangladeshi women's cooking skills appeared to have been learnt from the older generation of females in the family, and they also took pride in their traditional cooking.

- All the women surveyed appeared to have low levels of western food in their diets. However, they appeared to adopt the less healthy aspects of the western diet including fried fish, pizza, chips and fatty snack foods. However, these were mainly chosen to give people a change or when preparation time available was short.

- The Pakistani/Bangladeshi women expressed the opinion that their diet had become less healthy following the adoption of the worst of the British diet!

- The women did make a link between food and health; however, cultural background and knowledge influenced this.

- Pakistani/Bangladeshi women generally appeared to have quite a good understanding of what food and methods of cooking are healthy and unhealthy. However, this knowledge did not appear to translate consistently into dietary choices.

- Zimbabwean women noted that in Zimbabwe nobody worried about being slim, but now that they were in the UK there was more pressure to be slim.

Conclusions (A01)

Many issues that affect the food choice of people who move to the UK are common within different ethnic groups.

Mood and food

It is recognised that food influences our mood and that mood has a strong influence over our choice of food. Comfort is gained through the consumption of certain foods and we crave others.

Comfort eating

Comfort foods are foods whose consumption evokes a psychologically comfortable and pleasurable state for a person; we are attracted to them by a combination of our physiological and psychological needs. These

STRETCH AND CHALLENGE: Eating behaviour and obesity at Chinese buffets (Wansink and Payne, 2008)

- *Objective:* the aim of this study was to investigate whether the eating behaviours of people at all-you-can-eat Chinese buffets differ depending upon their body mass. The resulting findings could confirm or disconfirm previous laboratory research that has been criticised for being artificial.
- *Methods and procedures:* trained observers recorded the height, weight, sex, age and behaviour of 213 patrons at Chinese all-you-can-eat restaurants. Various seating, serving and eating behaviours were then compared across BMI levels.
- *Results:* patrons with higher levels of BMI were more likely to be associated with using larger plates vs smaller plates (OR 1.16, $p < 0.01$) and facing the buffet vs side or back (OR 1.10, $p < 0.001$). Patrons with higher levels of BMI were less likely to be associated with using chopsticks vs forks (OR 0.90, $p < 0.05$), browsing the buffet before eating vs serving themselves immediately (OR 0.92, $p < 0.001$), and having a napkin on their lap vs not having a napkin on their lap (OR 0.92, $p < 0.01$). Patrons with lower BMIs left more food on their plates (10.6 per cent vs 6.0 per cent, $p < 0.05$) and chewed more per bite of food (14.8 vs 11.9, $p < 0.001$).
- *Discussion:* these observational findings of real-world behaviour provide support for laboratory studies that have otherwise been dismissed as artificial.
  1. Why are such real-life studies important?
  2. What does a probability level of $p = >0.05$ mean?
  3. What criticisms might be made of this study?

Figure 3.4 All-you-can-eat buffets: good value but bad for your health?

needs for food can influence taste and preferences towards specific types of comfort-giving foods.

Psychological motivations

Our psychological motivations towards consuming comfort foods can be related to factors such as social context, social identification and conditioned responses that have influenced our attitudes towards food. Cowart and Beauchamp (1986) suggested that the social and psychological context of the taste experience is important in determining food preferences, and went on to suggest that this is an explanation of why some favour the taste of foods such as liver and onions, while others find it aversive. Chocolate is considered pleasurable by most people, for instance, because it combines favourable sensory qualities with the positive connotations of gift and reward that were developed through childhood experience.

Food cravings

The choice of comfort food relates to the fact that when foods we like the taste of are consumed, the body releases trace amounts of opiates, which both elevate mood and increase our satisfaction with that food. Although released in small amounts, opiate-related food can cause discomforting or distracting cravings (Le Magnen, 1985). One suggested explanation for food cravings is the need for variety in our diets. These cravings reflect the body's need for nutrients or calories, which in turn influences our eating behaviour (Pelchat and Schaeffer, 2000). However, Pliner and Melo (1997) suggested that nutritional deprivation is not necessary for cravings to occur and that other factors – for example, stress – can cause this type of eating behaviour.

Figure 3.5 Chocolate: the classic 'comfort food'

More importantly, do food cravings increase food intake? Martin *et al.* (2008) conducted a laboratory study into the relationship between food cravings and food intake. Participants' cravings were measured for sweets, fats, carbohydrates and fast foods; they were then allowed to freely eat the items. The findings show that specific food cravings were significantly correlated with consumption of the corresponding food types, thus suggesting that cravings do indeed increase our food intake.

A final physiological link between cravings and comfort eating comes from the fact that women more commonly report food cravings than men. Food cravings are commonly reported in the premenstrual phase, a time when total food intake increases and a parallel change in basal metabolic rate occurs (Dye and Blundell, 1997).

Which foods are comfort foods?

While the popular press often refers to comfort foods as snack foods and desserts, the physiological and psychological motivations fulfilled by comfort foods suggest that a wide range of comfort foods exists. For instance, chocolate or ice cream may be a comfort food for one person, while steak or soup may be a comfort food for another. Our childhood influences can have a strong effect on our attitudes and eating behaviours. For example, social context has been found to have a significant influence on a person's food preferences (Azar, 1998). An adult male may have become accustomed to having meals prepared for him; he may have developed stronger preferences for hot or prepared foods as comfort foods. On the other hand, adult females may not be accustomed to have food prepared for them, perhaps because they may have been encouraged to be the food preparers. Therefore females may

have fewer comfort-related associations with hot foods and may instead prefer more convenient and less preparation-intensive foods, which include convenience and comfort foods.

Affective states

Garg *et al.* (2007) have examined how different discrete affective sates (sad vs happy) influence food consumption, and whether this relationship is influenced by nutritional information and product type. Their findings suggest that happy people treat pleasurable products, such as buttered popcorn and M&M's, as mood-threatening and avoid them, whereas sad people consider them mood-uplifting and over-consume them (relative to a control group).

Tice *et al.* (2001) put forward a similar argument; they found that people respond to distress by eating more fattening, unhealthy snack foods, but that this tendency is reversed if they believe that eating will not change their mood state.

Stress

In today's world people are increasingly experiencing stress; it therefore must be of importance to investigate its influence on our eating behaviour. Greeno and Wing (1994) suggested that two general hypotheses exist in this area: first, a general effect hypothesis that stress changes consumption of food generally; second, an individual difference hypothesis that stress leads to changes in eating in particular groups (e.g. the obese, dieters and women).

The general effect of stress on eating

The majority of work on the stress–eating relationship focuses on the so-called 'general effect model', which assumes that stress produces a general response to eating. Such a model is particularly consistent with stress producing physiological changes in the organism and these changes explaining changes in eating behaviour.

The majority of research in this area has been done on animals. For example, Antelman *et al.* (1975) induced stress in rats by pinching their tails, and observed significant increases in gnawing, eating and licking food. With humans, Bellisle *et al.* (1990) compared the amount and types of food eaten by a group of men on the morning before they were to undergo surgery with a later day when they were not due to undergo surgery. No evidence was found that an acute stressor changed

Key Study 3.2: *Sweet Home Alabama* study (Garg *et al.*, 2007)

Aim/hypothesis (A01)

To examine how manipulating happiness and sadness through the content of a movie can influence the consumption of hedonistic foods such as buttered popcorn. It is expected that sad people will attempt to repair their negative state, leading them to consume more than happy people.

Method/design (A01)

To induce the relevant affective state, participants watched full-length movies that evoked positive or negative effects. They were recruited for the two-hour, two-day study and were told that researchers were interested in their evaluations of the movies. They were not told which movies they would be watching. The 'sad state' was induced by watching *Love Story*, and the happy state by watching *Sweet Home Alabama*. These films were selected because they could be matched on several key variables, such as running time, quality (critic rating), box office success and broad content area.

Participation involved taking part in both days of the study. On arriving for the study, participants were randomly assigned to one of two viewing rooms. The viewing rooms were designed to look like living rooms and five to eight participants watched the movie together. Participants were given popcorn and calorie-free drinks, which had been weighed before the movie began. Each portion contained an average of 180 grams of popcorn.

At the end of the movie, participants were asked to indicate their assessment of the movie (1 = sad to 9 = happy). They were also asked to rate their mood and say what it was about the film that made them feel happy or sad. The popcorn container was weighed again and the amount consumed was calculated.

Results (A01) and Conclusions (A01)

First, the results showed that the movies were successful in manipulating the desired emotions. Second, as was predicted, participants consumed significantly more (28 per cent more) while watching the sad movie than while watching the happy movie. The mean popcorn consumed for the sad conditions was 124.97 grams verses the 97.97 grams consumed in the happy condition.

Evaluation (A01/A02)

- Using a full-length film enabled the researchers to mimic the natural environment (e.g. a movie-going experience) in the laboratory.

- By using a laboratory, the researchers could investigate the cause-and-effect relationship of 'happy' and 'sad' rather than a more global effect.

- Participants might have known the content of *Love Story* and *Sweet Home Alabama*, therefore it could be argued that mere anticipation could have influenced consumption.

This study has important practical implications as it shows how the content of a movie, TV programme or perhaps even reading material can induce changes in our eating behaviour.

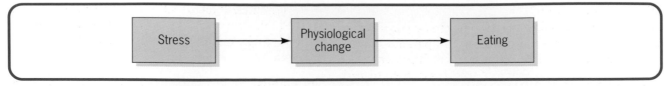

Figure 3.6 The general effect model of the stress–eating relationship (from Conner and Armitage, 2002)

the amount or types of food eaten in a group of men. However, Michaud *et al.* (1990) found the stress of an upcoming examination increased calorie intake of fatty foods such as snacks in a sample of school-children.

Synoptic Material: Animal research generalisation

Much of this research has been conducted on animals (mainly rats). My friends tell me that the only difference between me and a rat is that some people like rats! However, other people believe there are essential qualitative differences between humans and rats and, as such, research findings using animals are limited in their application to human behaviour. This might be especially true in the case of food choice, which is subject to many different factors in humans in particular.

The individual difference approach to stress–eating relationships

The individual difference model of stress–eating relationships suggests that differences in childhood experience of food, attitudes towards eating or variations in biology cause dissimilarities in vulnerability to the effects of stress. Those exhibiting high vulnerability respond to stress with an environmental or psychological change that promotes eating. In contrast, those with low vulnerability exhibit a different environmental or psychological change that does not promote eating (Connor and Armitage, 2002). Therefore differing groups, with different levels of vulnerability, will differ in their eating behaviour when under stress. One such group is emotional eaters. The individual differences model of stress–eating relationships can also go some way to explaining the differences in eating behaviour that occur between the two genders as a response to stress.

Evaluation of the general effect model

✔/✗ **Mixed research support:** in general this research provides some support for the general effect model of stress, although the effects are not wholly consistent. While tail pinching in rats does appear generally to increase oral behaviours, including eating, it is not clear that this represents stress-induced eating.

✗ **The precise effects of stress:** it is not yet clear whether the type of stressor (acute vs chronic) is important. The mechanisms by which stress influences eating in the general effect model remain under-investigated.

The emotional eater

Emotional eating refers to a tendency to eat more when anxious or emotionally aroused compared to non-emotional eaters, who do not show such reactivity to emotion in their eating habits. Stress is assumed to lead to increased eating in emotional eaters because they fail to distinguish between anxiety and hunger (i.e. they respond to stress as if it were hunger), while not affecting those low in emotional eating (Connor and Armitage, 2002). Van Strien *et al.* (1986) found that stressful life events predicted weight gain in men over a period of 18 months, but only among those who were emotional eaters. However, similar studies have reported limited impact of stress on the eating behaviour of those classed as 'emotional eaters' (Schlundt *et al.*, 1991; Conner *et al.*, 1999). Research in this area is, however, limited and future investigation is required.

Men and women

The possible differences between men and women's vulnerability to 'stress-induced eating' have been investigated by Grundberg and Straub (1992). They provided their participants with sweet, salty and bland foods while they watched a video; half watched an unpleasant, stress-inducing video. Their results showed that men in the unstressed condition consumed considerably more than those in any other condition. Of the women, those who were in the stressed condition consumed more sweet food than those in the unstressed condition, suggesting that stress goes some way to influencing our food preference as well as our overall eating behaviour. However, Stone and Brownall (1994) examined the relationship between stress and eating for married couples, who completed daily records of stress and eating. Their results showed that both men and women were likely to eat less than their usual amount in response to a stressful event; women were particularly less likely to increase their eating as the severity of the stress increased.

The findings in this area are therefore contradictory; however, the impact of stress does seem to have a greater effect on the eating behaviour of women than on that of men. There does, however, seem to be a commonality in the type of food that is eaten in response to stress, with sweet foods being favoured (Connor and Armitage, 2002).

Figure 3.8 Stress levels can affect food choices

Social context

Social influences on food intake refer to the impact that one or more persons have on the eating behaviour of others, either direct (buying food) or indirect (learn from peers' behaviour), either conscious (transfer of beliefs) or subconscious. Even when eating alone, food choice is influenced by social factors because attitudes and habits develop through the interaction with others. However, quantifying the social influences on food

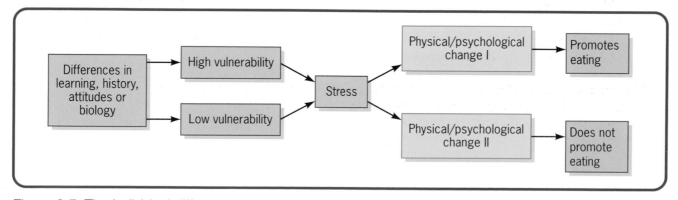

Figure 3.7 The individual difference model of the stress–eating relationship (adapted from Conner and Armitage, 2002)

intake is difficult because the influences that people have on the eating behaviour of others are not limited to one type and people are not necessarily aware of the social influences that are exerted on their eating behaviour (Feunekes *et al.*, 1998).

Conclusion

It is obvious from the material presented above that an amazing array of factors influences food and eating behaviour. The influence of one factor will vary from one individual or group of people to the next. Thus it is difficult to ascertain exactly how important each factor is in affecting eating behaviour. Indeed, it is likely that the individuals themselves do not know all the factors that influence their attitude to food and eating behaviour, and that these influences vary across time and context as well.

Explanations for the success and failure of dieting

Dieting is the main consequence of body dissatisfaction. The majority of dieters are women, and as many as 87 per cent of all women have dieted at some time in their lives (Furnham and Greaves, 1994). One of the best-known explanations of dieting is offered by Restraint Theory.

Restraint Theory

Restraint Theory has become synonymous with dieting and suggests that attempting to eat less might be a better predictor of food intake than weight per se (Ogden, 2003). Restrained eating is measured using various different questionnaires involving self-report measures. It would seem obvious that restrained eating would lead to successful dieting, but Restraint Theory argues that restrained eating can lead to both under- and overeating.

Various research studies have investigated Restraint Theory. One classic way to do this involves the so-called pre-load/taste-test paradigm (Herman and Mack, 1975). This involves giving participants either a high-calorie food (the 'pre-load'), such as chocolate, or a low-calorie food such as crackers. After eating this, participants are told they are going to take part in a taste preference test. They are given a number of different foods to taste, such as biscuits, snacks and ice cream, with different taste qualities such as saltiness, sweetness and so on. The participants are left alone to do the taste test in their own time. The key factor in the study is how much of the taste test food they eat. The

participants are not aware of this but the amount of food they eat is measured. The results are shown below and demonstrate that non-dieters compensate their food intake in response to the high-calorie pre-load food, whereas the dieters ate more in the taste test if they had had the high-calorie pre-load. However, the dieters did eat less after the low calorie pre-load. The results suggest that although dieters may eat less at some times, restrained eating is also associated with eating more at other times and this factor may explain why dieters are often unsuccessful (Ogden, 2003).

Other studies have also found that dieters actually end up eating more food than non-dieters (Ruderman and Wilson, 1979). Klesges *et al.* (1992) studied 141 men and 146 women, and found that dieters consumed fewer calories than non-dieters but consumed a higher amount of fat. Overeating in dieters has been termed counter-regulation (where people eat more after high calorie intake), disinhibition (eating more as a result of the loosening of restraints on eating) or the 'what the hell' effect (eating more after a period of undereating) (Herman and Polivy, 1984).

Herman and Polivy (1988) came to the somewhat surprising conclusion that many diets fail because 'restraint not only precedes overeating but contributes to it causally'. Wardle and Beale (1988) tested the causal analysis of overeating by assigning 27 women to one of three groups (diet group, exercise group and control

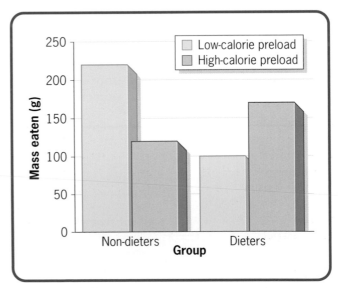

Figure 3.9 Dieting and overeating (Source: P. Herman and D. Mack, Restrained and unrestrained eating, Journal of Personality, 43 (1975), *pp. 646–60)*

How Science Works

Practical Learning Activity 3.4: Testing Restraint Theory

It is possible to conduct your own pre-load/taste-test paradigm. Re-read the details of the study by Herman and Mack (1975), above, carefully and try to devise your own detailed procedure to conduct such a study. You could test it out on naive classmates or members of your family. Always remember the importance of ethics in any psychological study.

group) for seven weeks. At various points during the study, participants took part in a laboratory experiment designed to assess their food intake. Results illustrated the fact that those in the diet condition ate more than those in the exercise and control groups. Thus it was concluded that the over-eating by dieters is caused by the dieting process itself (Ogden, 2003).

Herman and Polivy (1984) presented the boundary model of overeating as an attempt to explain how dieting may cause overeating. The model suggests that dieters set a 'diet boundary' and try to eat within this self-imposed limit. However, on occasions they may cross the diet boundary (i.e. eat something not allowed, such as chocolate) and will binge until they are full.

Cognitive shifts

Overeating in dieters has been explained as a shift in the dieter's cognitions or thoughts. Primarily it often involves a breakdown of self-control, or 'motivational collapse' (Herman and Polivy, 1984). Interviews with dieters support this, with many dieters reporting that they could no longer be bothered to diet since it took too much effort. It is also shown that many dieters overeat as an act of rebellion. Rather than becoming resigned to failing the diet they actively decide to overeat as a form of rebellion against self-imposed food restrictions.

Mood

Dieters may also overeat because of lowered mood. Research has shown that dieters in a poor mood may overeat to cause temporary heightened mood to mask their negative mood (hence it is called the 'masking

hypothesis') (Ogden, 2003). One study that investigated this was carried out by Polivy and Herman (1999), who told participants that they had either passed or failed a cognitive task (thus manipulating their mood) and then presented them with either unlimited amounts of food or food in controlled amounts. The dieters who were given unlimited amounts of food attributed their distress to their eating rather than the task failure. The researchers suggested that dieters may overeat in order to shift responsibility for their negative mood away from other areas of their life and on to their eating behaviour.

This mood modification theory of overeating has been supported by research which suggests that dieters who are anxious are also more likely to eat more than non-dieters, regardless of the palatability of the food (Ogden, 2003).

Denial

Another paradoxical finding is that trying to suppress various thoughts can actually bring them to the fore. This is called the 'theory of ironic processes of mental control' (Wegner, 1994). In effect, the more you try not to think of something the more you think of it! Wegner *et al.* (1987) asked participants not to think of a white bear but to ring a bell if they did. They found that participants rang the bell more often than participants who were specifically asked to think about a white bear! The same process occurs with dieters. They try to deny themselves certain foods, and try to suppress thoughts about chocolate, cakes, biscuits and so on. The more they try to forget about the 'forbidden food-stuffs' the more they become preoccupied with them: something that is forbidden becomes desired (Ogden, 2003).

'All or nothing' theory of excess

There are comparisons that can be made between dieting behaviour and smoking or drinking behaviour. In many cases, the individual is seeking to reduce their eating, smoking or drinking behaviour. However, in the case of food people still need to consume food, whereas with smoking or drinking alcohol they could give up altogether. Comparisons between these three behaviours have led to a belief that the behaviour is 'all or nothing' and that this belief is why many smokers, drinkers and over-weight people fail and relapse into their old ways. It is often stated that alcoholics or smokers have to give up completely and it may be that many people on a diet also believe in the 'all or nothing' approach – that is, one minor

How Science Works

Practical Learning Activity 3.5: Test the theory of ironic processes of mental control

Get a group of participants and give them a topic heading. For example, sport, chocolate, war, ice cream, sex and so on. Take the participants individually into another room and tell half of them to think about the topic and the other half to not think about the topic for five minutes. Ask them to ring a bell every time they think about the topic.

Record the number of times each group thinks about the topic.

- Did you find any support for the idea that being told not to think about a topic makes you think about it more?
- Can you suggest some methodological criticisms of such a study?

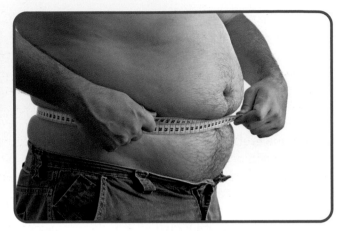

Figure 3.10 Sometimes dieting can lead to weight increases or weight fluctuations

How Science Works

Practical Learning Activity 3.6: Do diets work?

It should be easy to test whether people on diets eat more than those people who are not on diets. You will need to find two groups of people willing to take part in the study – those on a diet and those who aren't. You will need to provide the two groups of people with food diaries that they can complete on a daily basis. You will then need to compare the two groups' responses. You should seek to maintain the confidentiality of all your respondents' data.

Use both descriptive and inferential statistics to analyse your data.

- What methodological problems are there with this kind of research?
- Write up your research in the form of a poster presentation that can be displayed.

lapse in the diet routine means that the diet has failed altogether.

Cognitive state

Dieting or food restriction may lead to a change in people's cognitive state. Keys *et al.* (1950) studied 36 non-dieting conscientious objectors to the Korean War. They were given half their usual daily food intake for 12 weeks and lost 25 per cent of their normal body weight. Keys *et al.* reported that they became obsessed with food and started hoarding or stealing it. Many became depressed and couldn't concentrate. When they were later allowed to eat freely, many ate continuously and became binge eaters. Later research confirmed some of these findings, suggesting that dieting or food restriction can cause changes in thought processes and self-control, and that this can lead to later overeating problems. In effect dieting has a negative effect and may cause overeating.

It may be obvious how dieting can lead to a negative mood, and especially so when the diet fails. However, researchers have also been surprised by how willing people are to try a new diet when they have failed so many times before. Polivy and Herman (1999) have suggested that this can be explained by 'false hope syn-

Evaluation of Restraint Theory

✔ **Research support:** there is a good deal of research that supports the Restraint Theory of eating, suggesting that dieting can lead to both under- and, paradoxically, overeating. It seems that higher levels of dietary restraint can lead to greater weight fluctuations.

✗ **Unanswered questions:** however, not all individuals who diet inevitably partake in overeating sessions. Attempting not to eat does not result in overeating in anorexics, for example. Similarly if attempting not to eat something results in eating it, how do vegetarians manage to never eat meat? A proportion of dieters do manage to lose weight successfully and maintain their new body weight. Why do these individuals not overeat? A number of experimental studies have shown that restrained eating does lead to reduced food intake and that dieting is successful. Using the pre-load/taste-test methodology outlined above, dieters have been found to consume fewer calories after both low- and high-calorie pre-loads (Thompson *et al*., 1988). However, these experimental studies are very unrealistic and so studies examining more naturalistic dieting situations are often favoured. Many of these studies use dietary self-monitoring forms and these have also found that dieters frequently do eat less than non-restrained eaters. For example, Laessle *et al*. (1989) found that restrained eaters consumed 400 kcal less than unrestrained eaters and also consumed less food with a high carbohydrate and fat content.

✗ **Different measures of dietary restraint:** the apparent conflict between the findings of different research studies has led to a renewed concentration on the measures used to assess dietary restraint. There are a number of different measures used to assess restrained eating, including the Restraint Scale (Herman and Polivy, 1980) and the Three Factor Eating Questionnaire (Stunkard and Messick, 1985). Some researchers have suggested that the different findings are merely the product of the different self-report measures. It may be that some measures do not incorporate overeating measures to the same extent as the Restraint Scale, and this explains why some research has not found that dieters overeat.

✗ **Only relevant for the minority:** it has been argued that most dieters are unsuccessful. Ogden (2003) writes that dieting is best regarded as an attempt that is only rarely realised. Dieting is best understood, then, as an attempt to lose weight, which is only sometimes achieved, but most attempts to eat less result in eating more. It is argued that Restraint Theory applies to the majority of unsuccessful dieters but doesn't relate to the small minority of successful dieters.

drome'. It is believed that making a commitment to diet leads to a temporarily improved mood and self-image. However, this is not the case for all dieters. For some it leads to a deterioration in mood, but an increased hope of success outweighs this negative mood (Ogden, 2003).

Conclusion

Dieting is a more complex behaviour than sometimes thought. For most people dieting does not work. Initial weight loss may occur but more often than not the weight is put back on. The situation becomes even worse when it is noted that losing weight becomes progressively more difficult after putting weight back on. Prolonged dieting means that weight becomes easier to regain and more difficult to lose, and thus dieters never stop dieting. The goal for health professionals is to target education resources appropriately so that people eat sensibly and healthily from birth and thus do not need to attempt to diet later in life. Rising levels of obesity in the developed world suggest that this goal is not being achieved.

BIOLOGICAL EXPLANATIONS OF EATING BEHAVIOUR

The role of neural mechanisms involved in controlled eating and satiation

Hunger is activated by many different cues, both biological and environmental. All animals have a motivation to eat and this motivation increases as energy levels decrease. An imbalance occurs when the energy expended exceeds the energy consumed; this imbalance is signalled to the brain in a number of different ways.

The hypothalamus and other neural mechanisms

Originally, Walter Cannon (1927) suggested that hunger signals originated from the stomach. These 'hunger pangs' led to eating and so it was argued that the motivation to eat did not come from neural mechanisms but from a peripheral signal in the stomach. Cannon and Washburn (cited in Coon, 1995) proposed this stomach contraction theory and Washburn conducted an amazing experiment to support the idea. Washburn trained himself to swallow a balloon that was attached to a tube. Once the balloon was in his stomach he inflated it to see if a full stomach would mean that he did not feel hungry. Washburn reported that with a fully inflated balloon in his stomach he did not feel hungry! However, this theory was later refuted by evidence showing that people who had to have their stomach surgically removed (due to medical reasons) still feel hunger. Although stomach contractions are a strong incentive to eat they are not the most significant indication of hunger. Karl Lashley (1938) was the first psychologist to suggest that hunger is not just a reflex to an empty stomach. Lashley argued that neural mechanisms are involved in making decisions about when and when not to eat. Lashley set out to discover which areas of the brain were responsible for this behaviour by training rats to negotiate a maze in order to gain food. Using hungry rats, he cut out different areas of the brain to see the effect of these lesions on behaviour. This technique led him to recognise the vital role that the hypothalamus plays in regulating food intake. More specifically, the lateral hypothalamus was identified as the main 'hunger centre' and the ventromedial hypothalamus as the main 'satiety centre' (satiation is the feeling of fullness and disap-

Figure 3.11 Rats who have different parts of their hypothalamus destroyed either stop eating (aphagia) or overeat (hyperphagia)

pearance of appetite). Lashley found that after lesions to the lateral hypothalamus, animals stop eating spontaneously and that the reverse occurred after lesions to the ventromedial hypothalamus – that is, lesions in the ventromedial hypothalamus caused the rats to overeat to excess.

It has become increasingly clear that the hypothalamus is the body's control centre, playing a vital role in many physiological functions such as emotions, endocrine functions and food/water intake. In much the same way that a thermostat maintains temperature, the hypothalamus maintains the body's homeostasis by receiving messages from different parts of the body and making changes in response. For example, when the level of glucose (blood sugar) in the blood is low, the liver sends signals to the lateral hypothalamus that more food is required. The hypothalamus thus helps to maintain a constant internal environment. The particular food that is then consumed in response to these low glucose levels depends on numerous factors such as usual diet, culture, availability, habits and so on.

As research has progressed, it is evident that the hypothalamus is an extremely complex part of the brain, which contains many different types of specialised nerve cell and controls many different physiological functions. Apart from the lateral and ventromedial hypothalamus, the arcuate nucleus of the hypothalamus plays a vital role. This region contains several different types of nerve cells, one of which makes a neuropeptide (called neuropeptide Y, or NPY), which is a very potent orexigen (something that stimulates the appetite). Neuropeptides are very small proteins that are encoded by genes. Neuropeptides are small enough to serve as chemical messengers between neurons, or between the fat depots of the body and the brain. The fat hormone leptin is an example of a neuropeptide that is secreted from fat cells into the blood, and signals the brain (via the hypothalamus) that caloric storage is high. When people do not eat enough food, fat is used up, the fat cells cease to secrete leptin, and leptin levels in the blood fall. The hypothalamus detects this drop in leptin, interprets the low leptin as a lack of calories, and generates the sensation of hunger (feelings of hunger are assumed in rats when they start eating). Evidence to support the influence of leptin in affecting eating behaviour has been found in rare cases of people born with leptin deficiency. Such individuals cannot control their eating and frequently become obese, but leptin injections can help them return to their normal weight.

Advanced research has shown that there are many different neuropeptides used as chemical signals in the circuits of the hypothalamus, and each may play a subtly different role in the response to caloric deficiency. Not only neuropeptide Y (NPY), but also agouti-gene-related peptide (AGRP) appears to signal hunger. When a rat is food-deprived, levels of NPY and AGRP are increased in the brain. If NPY or AGRP is injected into a satiated rat, the rat becomes ravenously hungry. However, NPY and AGRP have different temporal characteristics. NPY levels increase rapidly with food deprivation, and NPY injections induce feeding for only a few minutes. AGRP, on the other hand, is slow to rise during fasting and slow to fall upon refeeding; a single injection of AGRP will cause a rat to over-eat for several days. NPY neurons are also activated by ghrelin, a hormone that is secreted from the empty stomach, and whose concentration in the blood falls after each meal and rises progressively until the next.

Leptin and ghrelin are not the only signals that reach the hypothalamus; cells in the ventromedial nucleus and some in the lateral hypothalamus are directly sensitive to glucose concentrations – some are inhibited when glucose concentrations are high, others are facilitated. The hypothalamus also contains neurons that are sensitive to insulin; insulin is secreted overall in amounts proportional to the size of the body-fat stores, so is another signal that the brain can use to evaluate its energy reserves. Other hormones are also produced by the stomach, pancreas and gastrointestinal tract, including pancreatic polypeptide and the products of the gastrointestinal L cells, glucagon-like peptide 1 (GLP-1), oxyntomodulin and peptide YY (PYY 3-36), which appear to act as satiety signals.

Satiation

Satiety, or the feeling of fullness and disappearance of appetite after a meal, is mediated by signals that arise from the stomach and gastrointestinal tract. These signals, which include signals arising from stretch receptors as the stomach is distended by food, and chemical signals arising in the stomach as the result of secretion from cells regulating digestion, activate afferent fibres of the vagus nerve. For example, the gut hormone cholecystokinin (CCK) is secreted in the stomach during a meal, and activates specific receptors (CCK-A receptors) on the nerve endings of the gastric vagus nerve. The vagally mediated signals reach the hypothalamus via nuclei in the caudal brainstem – notably the nucleus of the solitary tract. Noradrenergic neurons in this area play a particularly important role in carrying these signals; these neurons project to many different parts of the hypothalamus.

Eating appears to stop when the satiety signals reaching the hypothalamus are sufficiently strong to activate particular populations of neurons that make 'anorexigenic' (loss of appetite) peptides – peptides that when injected into the brain are potent at suppressing hunger. There are many different anorexigenic peptides just as there are many different orexigenic peptides (appetite stimulants); the neural circuitry that regulates appetite is extremely complex. However, one of the most important anorexigenic peptides is alpha melanocyte-stimulating hormone (alpha-MSH), which is made in another population of neurons in the arcuate nucleus. These neurons project to many different parts of the hypothalamus where alpha-MSH is released and acts on other neurons via specific melanocortin receptors.

Support for the effect of alpha-MSH hormones and their effect on eating behaviour comes from evidence showing that genetic disorders that prevent alpha-MSH being made, or that prevent its normal actions, result in individuals who are grossly obese as a result of chronic overeating.

One hypothesis that relates to controlled eating and satiation is called the 'set point' hypothesis. This suggests that everyone has a certain metabolic set point, a certain weight that their body is geared towards, which is determined by their hypothalamus, metabolism or the rate at which they burn calories. Different people have different set points, and it is believed that these set points can change depending on a number of factors, including eating patterns and exercise. When people try to diet, their leptin levels decrease and this causes the hypothalamus to trigger 'hunger pangs'. The set point for obese people may be higher than for healthy individuals, and may be lower for underweight individuals. Thus neural mechanisms in the hypothalamus may be involved in many different aspects of eating behaviour.

Techniques used to study controlled eating and satiation

A number of different techniques are used to investigate neural effects on eating behaviour. These include those described below.

Central micro-injection

This involves injecting minute quantities of certain neurotransmitters into the specific brain areas of animals. These injections may cause animals to perform complex behaviours similar to those that occur naturally. For example, Lee and Stanley (2005) have shown that microinjections of neuropeptide Y into specific areas of the hypothalamus can cause animals to eat and, with chronic stimulation, to develop massive obesity. By determining which neurotransmitters act similarly and the brain areas where they are effective, psychologists can begin to reveal the specific neurochemicals and brain sites involved in controlling eating behaviour (Stanley, 2008).

Measurement of neurotransmitter release

A different method involves manipulating an animal's behaviour and then using various biochemical techniques to try to measure any corresponding changes in brain chemistry. For example, Stanley (2008) also reports that noradrenaline, another neurotransmitter that causes eating when injected into a certain brain area, is also released from this same brain area during natural eating behaviour.

Imaging brain activity

This technique exploits the fact that more active brain areas have higher metabolic rates. Using brain imaging techniques, it is possible to see which areas of the brain are activated during eating behaviour. Using this approach, researchers are identifying the neuronal sites and brain pathways that are activated by central neurotransmitter injections that produce eating, as well as those naturally activated during this behaviour (Duva *et al.*, 2001; Stanley, 2008).

Evaluation of neural mechanisms and eating

✗ **Neural mechanisms still unclear:** although the hypothalamic centres outlined above are clearly very important in controlling hunger and satiety, they don't explain the whole story. Exactly how ghrelin and leptin reach their targets in the brain is not wholly clear; both are large peptides that do not cross the blood–brain barrier readily. It is thought that there is a specific mechanism for transporting leptin into the brain in the choroid plexus, but whether something similar exists for ghrelin is unclear. The arcuate nucleus is adjacent to the median eminence, an area of the brain that lacks a blood–brain barrier, so it is also possible that ghrelin and leptin gain direct entry into the brain at this site.

✗ **The influence of biological rhythms:** the various signals that send information to the hypothalamus are only part of the complex systems regulating when and how much we eat. Neural mechanisms are important in controlled eating and satiation but other factors play a part as well. Some of these relate to environmental factors outlined in more detail below. However, biological rhythms also affect our eating behaviour. For example, rats become most active and start to eat soon after darkness descends. This and similar rhythms are controlled by another area in the hypothalamus called the suprachiasmatic nucleus (see Chapter 1, pages 9–11).

Evaluation of neural mechanisms and eating continued...

✗ **Evidence for other biological theories about controlled eating and satiation:** glucose theory states that we feel hungry when our blood glucose level is low. Bash (cited in Franken, 1994) conducted an experiment transfusing blood from a satiated dog to a starved dog. The transfusion resulted in termination of stomach contraction in the starved dog and supported the glucose theory. But Le Magnen (cited in Kalat, 1995) suggests that blood glucose level does not change much under normal conditions. Insulin theory states that we feel hungry when the insulin level increases suddenly in our bodies (Heller and Heller, 1991). However, this theory seems to indicate that we have to eat to increase our insulin level in order to feel hungry. Fatty acid theory states that our bodies have receptors that detect an increase in the level of fatty acid. Activation of the receptor for fatty acid triggers hunger (Dole, 1956, and Klein *et al.*, 1960, both cited in Franken, 1994). Heat Production Theory, suggested by Brobeck (cited in Franken, 1994), states that we feel hungry when our body temperature drops, and when it rises the hunger decreases. This might explain why we tend to eat more during winter (Hara, 1987).

✗ **Set point theory:** set point theory suggests that the set point is maintained by energy consumption and expenditure. However, it is also set by an individual's metabolic rate, which is genetically determined. Some researchers argue that the set point can be altered by individuals who lose or gain weight. It has also been pointed out that many people easily gain weight when they have ready access to high-fat foods.

✗ **Psychological hunger:** there is a difference between physical hunger (where the body requires energy to function) and psychological hunger (where an individual thinks they need food but it is not biologically required). There are various learned and cognitive components to eating. These include those listed below.

- *Availability of rich foods:* people tend to gain weight when rich foods are plentiful.
- *Taste preferences:* eating is also affected by taste preferences acquired through conditioning or observational learning.
- *Smell:* some food smells are so attractive that people cannot resist feeling hungry even if they have just eaten a meal. Again, these preferences affect eating behaviour and are culturally learned preferences.
- *Habits:* people learn habits, such as when and how much they eat. Time of day can affect feelings of hunger beyond any physiological requirements. These habits also influence hunger and food intake. Schachter (1971) proposed the internal–external theory of hunger and eating of the obese. He devised an experiment where participants were measured by the amount of crackers eaten during a period when the real time was manipulated by a faster clock or a slower clock. It was hypothesised that if the obese person is more affected by the clock time than the real time, then he or she should eat more when the clock shows it is close to dinner time. The results were consistent with the hypothesis. Schachter concluded that obese people respond to external cues of hunger, such as time, more than non-obese people, who tend to respond more to internal cues of hunger (Hara, 1987).
- *Stress:* the increased physiological arousal associated with stressful situations can stimulate hunger in some people, whereas in others stress can decrease hunger. Some people 'comfort eat' and use food as a way to suppress an emotional problem in order to avoid dealing with the actual problem. High-fat, sweet foods are most often consumed.
- *Cultural attitudes:* different cultures have different expectations and ideals concerning food intake and body ideals. These factors can also affect controlled eating and satiation in any particular society.

115

All these external stimuli provide other ways to signal the hypothalamus to make us feel hungry even though the signals are not physiological (Hara, 1987).

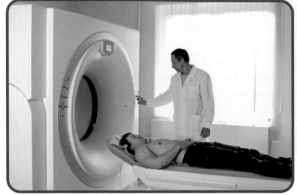

Figure 3.12 Advanced brain imaging techniques allow us to see the internal workings of the brain

How Science Works

Practical Learning Activity 3.7: Techniques used to study eating behaviour

Read the section above regarding the techniques used to study controlled eating and satiation. Try to evaluate the use of these techniques. Think particularly about the ethics of using animals in such research and the applicability to human studies.

Conclusion

There is no doubt that neural mechanisms play a vital part in controlled eating and satiation. The hypothalamus is the key area of the brain involved in eating behaviour. However, the precise mechanisms are extremely complicated and new fields of investigation are still being explored to better understand the complex central nervous system network involved in eating behaviour. There are also other external influences that play an influential role in eating behaviour.

Evolutionary explanations of food preference

Evolutionary theory suggests that organisms should behave so as to maximise the survival of their genes or their inclusive fitness (the probability that their bio-

Figure 3.13 'The mind is a Swiss army knife, crammed with tools designed for specific problems that faced our hunter-gatherer ancestors' (Horgan, 1995)

logical relatives will survive (Barash, 1977). In this way, natural selection – survival and reproduction of the fittest individuals – occurs. Survival depends on any number of things, one of which involves remaining healthy by managing to obtain sufficient nutrients to meet the demands of the body.

In pre-agricultural societies, food supplies were almost certainly limited or erratic. There would not have been constant, regular and adequate food for the daily needs of all the hunter-gatherer population throughout the year. Given this perspective, it is clear that humans evolved in an environment that encouraged the maximisation of stored energy. In other words, binge eating would have been an adaptive behaviour. 'Eat, drink and be merry, for tomorrow we die' would have been an apt maxim for life (Stevens and Price, 2000). Sweet, fatty or salty foods would have been particularly valued since they are vital requirements and were relatively rare in the ancestral environment. Thus in these situations it was advantageous to overeat in times of plenty, and those that did adopt this strategy were probably more likely to survive and pass on their genes to the next generation. It was a good idea to retain as many calories as possible and expend as few as possible, as an insurance against future times of food scarcity. In much of the current world, such strategies are obsolete (except in some extreme poverty situations) and yet people may find it hard to escape the evolutionary pressures on them for particular food preferences (Stevens and Price, 2000). Hence, nowadays many people have a problem with overeating and gaining weight. Furthermore, although exercise could help alleviate these evolutionarily led behaviours, the evolutionary hangover is also to conserve energy, and people do this by not exercising and using labour-saving devices such as escalators, lifts, cars and so on.

Evaluation of preference for high fat foods

✔ **Experimental support:** the increased levels of obesity in the developed world suggest that people as predicted by evolutionary theory find it very hard to ignore high-fat food offerings when they are readily and cheaply available. Experimental studies also support the development of such food preferences. Birch and Deysher (1985) provided evidence for the self-regulation of food intake in preschool children by demonstrating that children learn to eat smaller meals following a taste that has previously been associated with a high-calorie snack, and larger meals following a taste that has previously been associated with a low-calorie snack.

Preference for high-fat foods

It is adaptive for animals to learn which foods have high nutritional value. Calories are essential to provide energy for the body to function. Humans are not born with knowledge of every high-calorie food type and thus they have to learn about them, and it would be most adaptive for humans to have the ability to learn to prefer, after brief exposure to them, foods that contain substantial amounts of calories; those humans who learnt quickest which foods would provide the most nutrition were the most likely to survive. Fat contains twice as many calories as the same amount of protein or carbohydrate. Thus it is easy to comprehend how humans (and other animals) would learn at an early age to prefer high-fat foods. High-fat foods were not easily available in our ancestral environment, so

when they were found it was sensible to binge on such ready sources of energy. Nowadays, however, in many countries high-fat foods are readily available and people find it difficult to keep their fat consumption levels low. By eating high-fat foods to excess, humans are now behaving in a way that is not adaptive to their current environment but more suited to the environment in which we evolved.

Preference for sweet foods

Although it is impossible for humans (or animals) to have innate preferences for all high-calorie foods, it might be possible for humans to have some innate preferences for certain specific tastes. A sweet taste is often associated with ripeness (in fruit, for example), a

How Science Works

Practical Learning Activity 3.8: Psychological factors that affect taste

Colour is an important part of taste perception. DuBose (1980) tested the effects of colorants on identification of carbonated fruit drinks. Participants tasted grape, lemon-lime, cherry and orange drinks with different colours:

When participants tasted the drinks and were able to see the 'correct' colours of the drinks, they were always able to identify the taste of the drink correctly. However, when they could not see the colour of the drink, they made mistakes. For example, 70 per cent of the people who tasted the grape drink said it was grape. However, 15 per cent of the people thought it tasted of lemon-lime. Only 30 per cent of the people who tasted the cherry drink thought it was cherry. A high proportion of people thought the cherry drink was lemon-lime (40 per cent).

Devise and conduct your own experiment that tests the accuracy of taste perception and how it is affected by colour.

Source: adapted from: http://faculty.washington. edu/chudler/coltaste.html

Figure 3.14

Evaluation of preference for sweet foods

✔ **Research support:** there is considerable evidence to show that people do have an innate preference for sweet-tasting foods. People of any age seem to prefer sweet foods over other tastes. First, people of any age are likely to pick sweet foods over others (Meiselman, 1977); this is equally true for many other species such as horses, bears and ants (Capaldi *et al.*, 1989).

Infants seem to have an innate preference for the taste of sweet. Desor *et al.* (1973) found that one- to three-day-old human infants prefer sweet over non-sweet fluids. An interesting study was conducted by Bell *et al.* (1973). They gave sweet, sugar-containing foods to Eskimos of northern Alaska who had previously lacked sweet foods and drinks (with the exception of milk, which is slightly sweet). They found that, in all these cases, cultures previously without sugar did not reject the sugar-containing foods and drinks of the other culture, suggesting that a preference for sweet taste is not culturally learned. Furthermore, newborn infants who have never been bottle- or breastfed show an acceptance of sweet tastes the very first time they come across them. This acceptance response appears to be an innate, reflexive response, which has also been demonstrated in rats (Grill and Norgren, 1978).

✔ **Physiological support:** the human tongue seems to have specific receptors for detecting sweetness. This is not the case with other tastes, which are detected by non-specific receptors. There also appear to be more receptors for detecting sweetness than other tastes. All this evidence suggests that the taste of sweet is more important to the body than is any other taste, again suggesting that the preference for sweet has a substantial genetic component (Logue, 1991).

As with the tendency to learn a preference for high-calorie foods, the preference for sweet foods would have been adaptive in the environment in which humans evolved. However, it is not adaptive now, when so many sweet foods are easily and cheaply available. Perhaps we all ought to think of our evolutionary past next time we are tempted to eat another cream cake!

Figure 3.15 A preference for ripe fruit was advantageous to early man

high concentration of sugar and a quick fix of calories. A preference for sweet foods and drinks that would encourage consumption of ripe fruit was probably advantageous to our early ancestors (Rozin, 1982). Thus it would have been adaptive for humans to have evolved with an innate preference for the taste of sweet (Logue, 1998a).

Preference for salty foods

Salt is also essential for the body to function properly. For example, the concentration of salt in the blood must be kept at a specific level. We all lose small amounts of salt through sweat and through the action of the kidneys. We need to keep salt at a constant level. Again, nowadays it is relatively easy to get access to salt. However, it is not easy to get salt in the wild. Before industrial processing humans found it quite difficult to get enough salt. As with some of the other food preferences, it may be the case that natural selection has resulted in an innate preference for salt and that this preference is present in a number of species (Denton, 1982).

✔**Universal facet of human behaviour:** humans are not born with an innate preference for salt. Indeed, humans cannot taste salt very well until they are about four months old, when infants do seem to show a marked preference for salty foods over non-salty foods. At the age of two years, children reject foods that do not contain the expected amount of saltiness (Beauchamp, 1987). This preference for salt appears to be universal and not restricted to cultural experiences. Although this preference for salt was adaptive in the environment in which our ancestors lived, it is no longer adaptive and indeed causes serious problems for many people who consume too much salt. It is argued that major food companies exploit our evolutionary inheritance by producing over-salty food, which makes us unhealthy.

Self-control and food preferences

Every day we are faced by food choices. Chips or a salad? Pudding or an apple? We all ought to watch what we eat, and self-control is an important element of this. Self-control seems to be particularly difficult for many people. This lack of self-control may also be due to our evolutionary past. Living 1.4 million years ago on the African savannah, times were relatively good. Food was fairly easy to source and adequate shelter was easily obtained (Zihlman, 1982). Hunter-gatherer groups moved around to exploit different food sources as they became available. Although food was readily available, life expectancy was still short due to a combination of disease and accidents. However, one million years ago groups of people started to migrate northwards and encounter harsher weather conditions and less readily available food access. In the face of this, it made evolutionary sense to take food and resources whenever they were available and not wait for a later, delayed benefit. In essence, impulsiveness, not self-control, is encouraged: don't wait for the fruit to grow bigger, eat it

immediately. After all, it may go rotten, be eaten by another or you may meet an accident in the meantime while you wait. The successful ancestor was the one

Evaluation of self-control and food preferences

✔**Metabolic rate support:** if evolutionary theory is correct, then animals that live in environments where it is difficult to obtain food should be more impulsive with regard to eating and less willing to delay for a larger amount of food later over a smaller amount of food immediately. Forzano and Logue (1992) have found a correlation between increasing deprivation and decreasing levels of self-control in humans. It has also been demonstrated that animals with higher metabolic rates (who therefore have a greater cost associated with not eating) show less self-control for food than animals who have lower metabolic rates. Tobin and Logue (1994) found that pigeons have the highest metabolic rates and are the most impulsive compared to rats and then humans, who have the lowest metabolic rates and are the least impulsive when it comes to food choices. Findings have generally supported the argument, with the exception of macaque monkeys who showed remarkable levels of self-control over food. It was hypothesised that this is because the natural environment they live in has a constant year-round abundance of food (Tobin and Logue, 1994; Logue, 1998a).

Figure 3.16 Salt is vital for human functioning but is difficult to source in the wild

Evaluation of evolutionary theory

✔ **Explanatory theory:** evolutionary theory does appear to be a valuable framework to explain many different human behaviours under one unifying theory. Not only does it seem able to explain food preferences concerned with sweet, high-fat and salty foods, but it can also help to explain apparent anomalies in learning theory such as the results of taste aversion studies. It seems that evolutionary theory can help to explain many aspects of psychology concerned with eating behaviour, and also bridge the gap between psychology and other fields such as biology (Zeiler, 1992).

who took whatever food was available whenever it was available (Logue, 1998).

It is apparent that our evolutionary heritage again causes us problems with our modern-day food preferences. In many societies nowadays, food is readily available and there is far less uncertainty over death and disease. In many cases, it would be advantageous for people to adopt food preferences that place the emphasis on self-control. For example, eating a burger as a snack on the high street will give us a short burst of energy but might have longer-term adverse health consequences. Far better to wait and have a salad at the normal mealtime. Our evolutionary inheritance persists, however, and we engage in behaviours that are unadaptive and impulsive.

Taste aversion learning

It is obviously adaptive to learn which foods will lead to good health, but it is equally beneficial to learn which foods will cause illness. Virtually all of us at one time or another must have eaten some food that didn't agree with us and then not eaten that particular food again. This is known as taste aversion learning, or illness-induced food aversion learning. The classic study into this type of learning was conducted by Garcia and Koelling (1966), who found that rats more easily learned to avoid drinking flavoured water when that licking was followed by illness (nausea) than by electric shock, and they more easily learned to avoid drinking water accompanied by clicks and light flashes when that drinking was followed by electric shock than by illness. They concluded that it is easier for rats to associate tastes with illness and audiovisual events with shock than vice versa. This study seems to violate traditional learning theory suggesting that it is easier to learn an association between two events (e.g. drinking and nausea) than two other events (e.g. light and nausea). Furthermore, it was found that taste aversions could be acquired in a single trial with delays of up to

24 hours between consumption of the food and illness. Again these findings seemed at odds with learning theory, which suggests that a short gap between two events is required for learning to take place and often more than one trial is required (Garcia et al., 1972).

Again, maybe our evolutionary heritage has played a part in developing these tastes. After all, animals with taste aversion learning are more likely to survive and avoid illness-causing foods. Evolutionary psychologists have suggested that the rules governing taste aversion learning have been shaped by evolution (Bolles, 1973).

Conclusion

Many aspects of eating that benefited our ancestors living millions of years ago do not appear to be beneficial in our current environment. Many of these eating behaviours, developed through evolution, cause our population to make unhealthy food choices. Nevertheless, we are not doomed to slavishly follow our evolutionary desires: self-control means that evolutionarily developed behaviours can be overcome.

EATING DISORDERS

Biological explanations of one eating disorder – for example, anorexia nervosa, bulimia nervosa, obesity

Eating disorders have attracted more and more attention over the last few years. Anorexia nervosa and bulimia nervosa are perhaps the best-known eating disorders, although obesity as an eating disorder is a growing worldwide problem.

The aetiology of eating disorders is usually a combination of factors including biological, psychological, familial and socio-cultural. Increasing numbers of sufferers from eating disorders have been reported in the

✔ Specification Hint

You only need to learn about any one eating disorder from the three mentioned in the spec, namely anorexia nervosa, bulimia nervosa or obesity. The best known and best researched is anorexia nervosa, thus we look at this eating disorder in detail. Indeed, while most psychologists agree that anorexia and bulimia nervosa are psychiatric disorders, there is far less agreement about obesity. Obesity is included in the European ICD 10 (International Classification of Diseases) as a general medical condition, but excluded from the American DSM IV because it is not established that it is consistently a psychological or behavioural syndrome (Stevens and Price, 2000).

last 20 years. The best-known eating disorder is anorexia nervosa (AN).

Clinical characteristics of anorexia nervosa

There are estimated to be 70,000 people with AN in Britain. AN literally means 'nervous loss of appetite'. AN is primarily a female disorder, which usually (but not exclusively) occurs during adolescence. There is a refusal to maintain normal body weight. Individuals have to weigh less than 85 per cent of their normal body weight to be diagnosed as anorexics. Anorexics have an intense fear of being overweight. This continues even when their actual body weight is extremely low. This distorted body image is not evident to anorexics themselves. Anorexia nervosa causes a general physical decline. This can include cessation of menstruation (amenorrhoea), low blood pressure, dry, cracking skin, constipation and insufficient sleep. Depression and low self-esteem are also common, and up to 20 per cent of AN cases are fatal. Many more individuals cause themselves long-term lasting harm.

Biological explanations of anorexia nervosa

There are a number of different biological or physiological explanations for eating disorders, specifically anorexia nervosa. One focuses on the idea that

anorexia nervosa may have a genetic origin. Family studies have shown that first-degree relatives (e.g. siblings) of bulimics and anorexics have an increased risk of developing an eating disorder (see Key Study 3.3, below).

Another hypothesis places the blame on hypothalamic dysfunction. The hypothalamus contains an 'on' and 'off' command for eating. The lateral zone of the hypothalamus functions as a 'hunger centre' while the ventromedial region operates as a 'satiety centre' (see pages 112–114). Humans (and other animals) have a 'set weight' that is 'correct' for them. Anyone who falls below this weight will feel hungry and anyone who goes above it will eat less in order to regain their 'normal' weight. It's suggested that dysfunction of these hypothalamic brain regions can lead to eating disorders. However, much of this research has occurred in laboratory animals. It's unclear whether the influences are the same for humans, although tumours in these regions have been shown to lead to excessive bingeing. There is evidence that neurotransmitter imbalance contributes to anorexia nervosa. For example, noradrenaline has been shown to increase appetite in animals, and bulimics have been found to have low levels of serotonin. This evidence supports the finding that serotonin acts to suppress appetite. Indeed, drugs that affect serotonin have been helpful with eating disorders. It has also been found that additional abnormalities in serotonin (5-HT), noradrenaline and corticotropic-releasing hormone (CRH) function have been observed in patients who have recovered from anorexia. It's unclear whether neuro-

Figure 3.17 Body dysmorphia: individuals can be overly concerned by imagined bodily defects

transmitter levels are a cause or effect of eating disorders, although it's most likely that they are the effect of continued starvation (Fichter and Pirke, 1995).

Hormonal imbalances have also been implicated in eating disorders. Leptin is a hormone secreted by fat cells that plays a role in the regulation of body-fat

Key Study 3.3: Biological explanations of anorexia nervosa: study of AN twins (Holland *et al.*, 1988)

Aim/hypothesis (A01)

To investigate genetic factors as an explanation for AN.

Method/design (A01)

The sample comprised identical (monozygotic – MZ) twins and non-identical (dizygotic – DZ) twins, where one twin (at least) had AN. All the twins had been brought up in the same environment. Holland *et al.* measured the concordance rate for AN. This is a percentage measure of the extent to which a trait in two people is in agreement, or 'concord'. The higher the concordance rate in MZ twins, the higher the likelihood that AN is influenced by genetic factors (since MZ twins have identical genes).

Results (A01)

They found a 56 per cent concordance rate in MZ twins, and 7 per cent in DZ twins brought up in the same environment.

Conclusions (A01)

There is a large genetic component to AN. Genetic inheritance can identify a predisposition to AN. Nevertheless, other environmental factors must play a role in the development of the disorder.

Evaluation (A01/A02)

✔ **Statistically significant:** the significantly higher rate found in MZs compared to DZs provides good evidence for genetic factors influencing the development of AN. But, if the disorder were entirely genetic, then the MZ rate should be nearer 100 per cent.

✗ **Twins don't just share the same genes:** they also share similar cultural and family values, and the environment for MZ twins is more similar than for DZ twins. Therefore physiological and environmental factors are confounded. Indeed, the 56 per cent concordance rate in MZs *might* be *entirely* due to their more similar upbringing than DZs.

✗ **Small samples:** in addition, many twin studies involve a small sample size. Holland *et al.*'s study involved only 30 pairs of twins, and Holland estimated that 15,000 pairs would be needed for a definitive, genetic study. The low occurrence of both twin births and eating disorders make this unlikely.

✗ **Immigrant data:** immigrants into western society can develop eating disorders. Their relatives in non-western societies don't suffer from eating disorders. This evidence doesn't suggest a genetic, family-based explanation for AN.

✗ **Social class:** McClelland and Crisp (2001) found a higher incidence of AN in social classes 1 and 2. They reject the idea that this is due to higher referral levels and suggest it is due to an avoidance response to adolescent conflict within such families. The biological approach cannot account for such findings.

Evaluation of biological explantation of AN

✗ **Family genetic influence:** families do pass on their genes to the next generation but they also transmit social and cultural values. Evidence that anorexia nervosa appears to run in families therefore does not preclude the possibility that social and cultural values that have been learnt from family members have contributed to the illness rather than simply being a straightforward genetic inheritance. The environment of identical twins is also probably more similar than that of non-identical twins, so a higher concordance rate for identical twins could be explained by the shared environment rather than a genetic argument. The fact that people from families who have immigrated into western cultures from cultures that do not have eating disorders go on to develop anorexia nervosa at the same rate as people from families who have always lived in the west also weakens the genetic argument.

✗ **Set weight theory:** experiments using laboratory rats do seem to support the 'set weight' theory of food regulation. However, the set weight theory may apply to 'normal' food behaviour in non-human animals but not to more abnormal undereating by humans. This theory seems to ignore any social factors that affect human behaviour. We have previously seen, above, that many factors influence food choice, and advertising, health messages, peer behaviour, ideas about ideal body shapes, and eating habits may well play a part in overriding any physiological mechanisms that may be regulating our body weight.

stores. Underweight individuals with anorexia have low serum levels of leptin, which increase with weight gain. Alterations in leptin regulation may play a role in the persistence of anorexia, contributing to difficulties in attaining and maintaining normal weight (Walsh and Devlin, 1998).

A blood flow deficiency in the area of the brain responsible for perception and appetite could cause AN. This might explain the mismatch between anorexics' actual and perceived appearance. However, post-mortems

have failed to record clear evidence for the brain damage hypothesis. Eagles *et al.* (2001) report that a high proportion of anorexics are born in late spring and early summer. It's suggested that an intrauterine infection during the winter months is a causative factor.

Psychological explanations of anorexia nervosa

Although there are numerous psychological explanations for eating disorders, only two *need* be dealt with, namely behavioural and psychodynamic.

Behaviourist explanations and research studies

According to the behavioural approach, AN can be viewed as a learnt behaviour. Using classical conditioning principles, eating is associated with anxiety since it can make people overweight. Losing weight ensures that the individual reduces these feelings of anxiety.

Using operant conditioning principles, the individual avoids food to gain a reward such as feeling positive about themselves. In the early stages of the illness, indi-

✔ Specification Hint

Many of the criticisms that were made of the biological approach to abnormality at AS are also applicable to the biological explanation of eating disorders (more specifically anorexia nervosa). You should have a look at many of the criticisms of the biological approach that were made then (see Gross and Rolls, 2008: 186–187). After all, anorexia is an abnormality – indeed it is classified as a neurotic disorder in DSM IV.

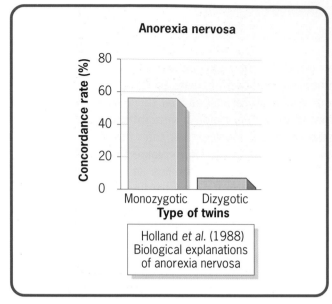

Anorexia nervosa

Holland *et al.* (1988)
Biological explanations
of anorexia nervosa

Figure 3.18 Biological explanations for anorexia nervosa. Reprinted from Journal of Psychosomatic Research, 32, Holland et al. (1988), Anorexia Nervosa, 516–572, with permission from Elsevier.

viduals may even be admired or congratulated for losing weight and looking slim and 'healthy'. The refusal to eat is reinforcing and becomes a dangerous habit. In addition, the misperception of body image means that an anorexic continues to feel that they're overweight, despite physical evidence to the contrary. The anorexic may also gain the reward or satisfaction of being in control of their food intake.

Social Learning Theory (an adaptation of Behaviourist Theory) suggests that people imitate and copy people they admire. Young women see female role models rewarded for being slim and attractive. Today's society tends to associate being slim with being successful, fit and healthy. Some studies have blamed various media for this. Fashion supermodels are increasingly thin, magazine centrefolds are consistently below the average weight and even the Sindy doll has slimmed down. Impressionable adolescent women may try to copy such models in the hope of gaining *vicarious rein-forcement*. This is defined as reward received indirectly, by observing another person being rewarded. Indeed, if they do slim, the reinforcement will be direct!

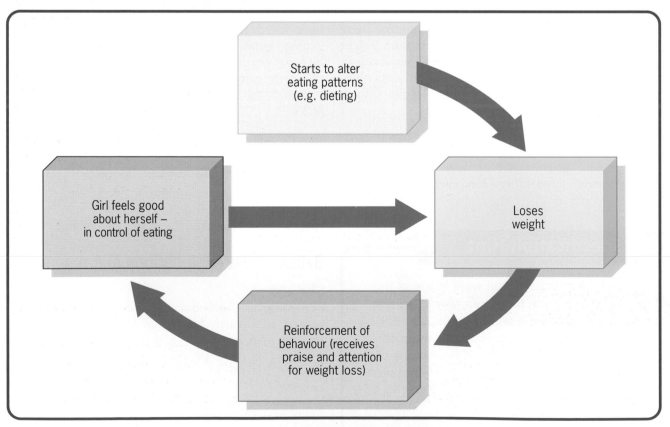

Figure 3.19 The behaviourist explanation of eating disorders

How Science Works

Practical Learning Activity 3.9: Adverts may be hazardous to your health!

- Go to the following website and read the research report outlined there: http://clearinghouse.missouriwestern.edu/manuscripts/355.asp
- Summarise the findings in fewer than 500 words.

Figure 3.20 The fashion industry has been accused of using inappropriate role models

Groesz *et al.* (2001) support the view that the mass media portray a slender beauty ideal. A review of 25 studies showed that this ideal causes body dissatisfaction and contributes to the development of eating disorders. The effect was most marked in girls under 19 years. It does seem to be the case that the media have a preoccupation with a thin body shape, particularly in the case of girls and younger women (Hofschire, 2002). This pressure encourages women to become more and more dissatisfied with their own body shape and physical appearance (Thompson, 1999). Although this is often done in an explicit way with slim models and articles on achieving the ideal (thin) body shape, it is also done implicitly or indirectly whereby peers voice admiration of certain role models they see being successful in the media. The slim ideal becomes equated with success and health, whereas average weight or overweight becomes synonymous with failure, and this view slowly becomes the dominant belief in society (Harrison, 2001). Forehand (2001) found that women feel undue pressure on their appearance and reported that 27 per cent of girls felt that the media pressure them to strive to have a perfect body.

Thus anorexia nervosa becomes a learned behaviour through observation, and this is maintained by posi-tive reinforcement. An individual who diets and loses weight is encouraged by peers and society. Those that remain overweight get criticised and are disapproved of, and sometimes even face ridicule because of their bodily appearance. Positive reinforcement for weight loss can become so powerful that the individual main-tains the anorexic behaviour despite threats to health, and in some cases this can result in death.

Studies have shown a high incidence of AN in occupations such as ballet dancing and modelling, where there's great pressure about appearance and a desire to remain thin (Alberge, 1999). Further support comes from the fact that eating disorders aren't so prevalent in non-western societies (e.g. China), where fewer such role models exist. Here, pressures on women to be thin are rare. Fearn (1999) reported an increase in eating disorders in Fiji with the introduction of American television programmes, which emphasise a westernised idealised body shape.

✔ Specification Hint

Many of the criticisms that were made of the psychological approaches to abnormality at AS are also applicable to the biological explanation of eating disorders (more specifically anorexia nervosa). You should have a look at many of the criticisms of the biological approach that were made then (see Gross and Rolls, 2008: pages 193–194 for the behavioural approach, and pages 188–189 for the psychodynamic approach).

Key Study 3.4: Psychological explanations of AN/BN: predictors of anorexic and bulimic syndromes (Tyrka *et al.*, 2002)

Aim/hypothesis (AO1)

To investigate future predictors of both AN and BN.

Method/design (A01)

A total of 157 white, 'middle-class or upper-middle-class' females were studied from adolescence (12–16 years) (Time 1) and followed up two (Time 2) and eight years later at young adulthood (Time 3). Questionnaire and semi-structured telephone interviews were used. Diagnoses of AN and BN were made according to DSM-IV criteria.

Results (A01)

- Perfectionism at either Time 1 or Time 2 was a significant predictor of the onset of AN.

- Low body weight was also a significant predictor of AN – this was not due to excessive dieting *prior* to the development of AN.

- Negative emotion or depressed mood was a significant predictor of BN.

- No other psychosocial characteristics were significant.

Conclusion (A01)

- Psychosocial factors can be used to predict the onset of both AN and BN.

- A simple measure of body weight can help to identify girls at higher risk of developing AN.

- The measure of perfectionism provides some support for the psychodynamic approach. Girls with such standards may shrink from the demands of adolescence.

Evaluation (A01/A02)

✔ **Experimental support:** other studies (e.g. Garner *et al.*, 1980) have found high levels of perfectionism in anorexics.

✗ **Prospective study:** tracking participants over time means that there is no reliance on memory. Psychological functioning has been shown to be affected by semi-starvation or malnutrition (Keys *et al.*, 1950). Therefore asking anorexics about their past may not be reliable. This study avoids such problems.

✗ **Over-simplistic:** the study doesn't take into account any number of other factors that might contribute to eating disorders. For example, the biological basis of eating disorders is ignored.

✗ **Sample size and characteristics:** the sample was relatively small and selective (white, 'middle class'). In addition, many of the cases of AN in the sample were 'relatively mild and short-lived'.

STRETCH AND CHALLENGE

A study reported in the *British Journal of Psychiatry*, in an article entitled 'Media influences on body size estimation in anorexia and bulimia. An experimental study' (Hamilton and Waller, 1993), found that anorexic and bulimic women overestimate their body sizes substantially more than comparison women, but little is known about the factors that influence this overestimation. This study examined the influence of the media portrayal of idealised female bodies in women's fashion magazines. Comparison women were not affected by the nature of the photographs that they saw, but eating-disordered women were: they overestimated more when they had seen the pictures of women than when they saw photographs of neutral objects.

- Evaluate the methodology of this study.
- Are there any problems with this type of study?
- Do the media have a responsibility for the increase in eating disorders over the last 20 years?
- Are there any dangers in blaming the media for this increase?
- In what way do parents and peers have a role to play?

Evaluation of behavioural explanation of AN

✗ **Unanswered questions:** why don't all dieters carry on and become anorexic? Are anorexics really conditioned in different ways to dieters? Why do anorexics continue to starve themselves when they no longer receive praise and compliments about their size? It's possible that it is the attention they receive that's reinforcing.

✗ **Binge eating:** the behavioural model is supposed to be a model that can explain all behaviours and all eating disorders. However, it is less successful in its explanation of bulimia nervosa. The reward for purging is explained as the lessening of anxiety from the initial binge. But why do bulimics binge in the first place? What reward do they get from bingeing? Some suggest that bingeing represents 'comfort eating'. Bulimics binge in order to compensate for their feelings of loneliness and social inadequacy. Some bulimics may use the disorder as a way to remain the centre of attention in the family and not grow up and become independent.

✗ **Cognitive aspects of behaviour:** the behavioural approach tends to underplay the cognitive aspects of anorexia nervosa. For example, it doesn't really deal with the faulty perceptions of body image that play such a large part in eating disorders.

Psychodynamic explanations of anorexia nervosa

Psychodynamic explanations of eating disorders suggest that adolescents don't want to grow up and separate from their parents. They become fixated at the oral stage when they were completely dependent on their parents. AN is an unconscious desire to remain dependent on their parents. In reality, this is often what happens. The adolescent struggling to cope with the disorder relies more and more on parental support. Geist (1989) proposed that the mother of a child with anorexia allowed identification by the daughter but the daughter is then unable to express any thoughts or feelings different from those of her mother. Subordinating her self-needs to her mother's needs, the child turns to the father for empathy. This bond becomes threatened by sexual maturation, so in order to maintain the father/daughter bond, the child stops eating. This explains why anorexia typically arises during adolescence.

In Freudian terms, eating and sex are symbolically related. A refusal to eat represents a refusal of sexuality. Adolescents may be unconsciously trying to prevent sexual maturity. Again, this often occurs in reality since menstruation can cease, breasts stop developing and the link to a pre-puberty age is obvious. It is also suggested that pregnancy and a fat stomach are unconsciously linked in the anorexic mind. Thus avoidance of food can be seen as an attempt to avoid pregnancy and adult responsibilities.

Evaluation of the psychodynamic approach

✗ **Lack of evidence:** criticisms of the psychodynamic approach focus on the lack of objective evidence. The unconscious cannot be observed or measured, and most of the claims cannot be tested or proved. However, there are cases reported where people with AN or BN were sexually abused as children. Their desire to destroy their sexually maturing bodies may be a reaction to this.

✔ **Childhood sexual abuse?** Romans *et al.* (2001) found evidence for a link between childhood sexual abuse and the development of eating disorders. They found that early maturation and paternal over-control were risk factors for AN and BN, and that these factors are a specific concern after the experience of childhood sexual abuse.

✗ **Demand characteristics:** it has also been claimed that patients who've accepted a psychodynamic explanation for their eating disorder do so due to demand characteristics. From a desire to please their therapist, patients accept this explanation for their disorder.

✗ **Doesn't explain AN increase:** finally, psychodynamic explanations cannot account for the increase in eating disorders in recent years. Surely adolescent unconscious desires couldn't have changed substantially in the last 20 years?

Stretch and Challenge: 'Validity of retrospective reports of eating behavior from the eating disorder examination' (Stone, 1999)

Abstract

The Eating Disorder Examination (EDE – Cooper and Fairburn, 1987) is the most widely used instrument for the diagnosis of eating disorders. The EDE relies on retrospective self-report to obtain eating behaviour information. However, there is growing evidence that retrospective self-reports are prone to errors arising from autobiographical memory. Stone and Shiffman (1994) adopted a method for collecting moment-by-moment data to address these concerns. The present study examined the accuracy of these estimates by comparing retrospective reports from questions on the EDE with data recorded in hand-held computerised eating diaries by obese and normal-weight women. The results suggest some lack of correspondence between the diary data and the EDE for a frequency count of most meal types and for overeating days and episodes, as well as for most cognitive-affective states. Many responses on the EDE appeared anchored at either end, reflecting endorsements of daily or never. However, moment-by-moment recording in the eating diary reflected a range of responses.

- What does this study mean in terms of the validity of research that uses EDE measures?
- Evaluate the respective advantages and disadvantages of EDE and 'moment-by-moment' data collection.

How Science Works

Practical Leaning Activity 3.10: Anorexia nervosa booklet

Develop a self-help brochure on anorexia nervosa. Give brief details on the symptoms, possible causes and treatments. Include a list of resources for additional information that includes recommendations for those seeking help.

SUMMARY

CHAPTER

Eating behaviour

Factors influencing attitudes to food and eating behaviour, for example, cultural influences, mood and health concerns

- **Hunger** is not the only factor that influences eating behaviour. Many cultural and socio-economic factors also influence our attitudes to food. An **attitude** is 'a psychological tendency that is expressed by evaluating a particular entity with some degree of favour or disfavour' (Eagly and Chaiken, 1993). Attitudes are an important determinant of behaviour.

- **The Theory of Reasoned Action** (Ajzen and Fishbein, 1980) and the **Theory of Planned Behaviour** (Ajzen, 1985, 1988) can be used to explain and predict the intention of certain health behaviours. The three key components are **attitude towards behaviour, subjective norms and perceived behavioural control**.

- By the age of three or four, children are no longer driven purely by a biological need when it comes to eating. **Children's eating choices** and behaviour are closely related to their parents' preferences, beliefs and attitudes towards food. Children learn about food from their own experiences and observing parents and peers. **Repeated exposure to new food tastes** is needed for food preferences to change.

- There are various **cultural influences on eating behaviour**. These include factors such as whether people eat meals together as a family, food choice availability at school or work, portion size, education, income, cost and accessibility. Ethnicity and religious practices can also affect eating behaviour.

- **Mood** can play a part in eating behaviour and food can also affect mood. A study by Garg *et al*. (2007) showed that the content of a movie (happy vs sad) can affect the amount of food eaten. **Stress** also has an effect on eating behaviour. The so-called **'general effect' model** assumes that stress produces a general response to eating. Much of the research here has been done on animals but there is some evidence that the stress of an upcoming exam increased the calorie intake of fatty food in schoolchildren. There do appear to be individual and gender differences with regard to the complex relationship between stress and eating, with women more likely to eat more (particularly sweet foods) than men as a result of stress.

Explanations for the success and failure of dieting

- As many as 87 per cent of all women have dieted at some point in their lives. **Restraint Theory** suggests that restrained eating can lead to both under- and overeating. A classic test of Restraint Theory uses the **pre-load/taste-test paradigm**. Research studies suggest that, paradoxically, dieters often eat more rather than less when they are dieting. **Overeating in dieters** is called **'counter-regulation', 'disinhibition'** or the 'what the hell' effect. **The diet boundary theory** suggests that dieters try to eat within a self-imposed limit. However, once they cross this boundary they will often binge until they are full, thus leading to diet failure. Cognitive shifts ('motivational collapse'), mood and denial also contribute to diet failure.

Biological explanations of eating behaviour

The role of neural mechanisms involved in controlled eating and satiation

- Hunger is activated by many different cues, both biological and environmental. Originally, it was thought that hunger signals were controlled by the stomach but it is evident that these are peripheral signals and the key signals are determined by neural mechanisms, specifically the **hypothalamus. The lateral hypothalamus** was identified as the main **'hunger centre'** and the **ventromedial hypothalamus** as the main **'satiety centre'** (satiation is the feeling of fullness and disappearance of appetite). It is clear that other brain areas, such as the arcuate nucleus, also play a role. **Neuropeptides** such as NPY and leptin also send messages to the brain about eating and satiation.

- **The 'set point' hypothesis** suggests that everyone has a certain metabolic set point – a certain weight that their body is geared towards, which is determined by their hypothalamus, metabolism, or the rate at which they burn calories. Techniques used to investigate neural effects on eating behaviour include central micro-injection, measurement of neural transmitter release and brain imaging.

- There is continuing research into the exact neural mechanisms that affect eating behaviour. There is evidence for other biological theories, such as **Glucose Theory** and **Fatty Acid Theory**, which explain much eating behaviour. Biological rhythms and other psychological factors also appear to be implicated in much eating behaviour.

Evolutionary explanations of food preference

- **Evolutionary theory** suggests that organisms should behave so as to maximise the survival of their genes or their inclusive fitness (the probability that their biological relatives will survive) (Barash, 1977). Survival depends on any number of things, one of which involves remaining healthy by managing to obtain sufficient nutrients to meet the demands of the body.

- In pre-agricultural societies, food supplies were almost certainly limited or erratic. Thus the hunter-gatherer evolved in an environment that encouraged the maximisation of stored energy. In other words, **binge eating** would have been an **adaptive behaviour. Sweet, fatty or salty**

foods would have been particularly valued and advantageous since they are vital requirements and were relatively rare in the ancestral environment.

- Nowadays such strategies are obsolete (except in some extreme poverty situations) and people may find it hard to escape the evolutionary pressures on them for particular food preferences (Stevens and Price, 2000). There is a good deal of evidence that supports human food preferences for sweet, salty and high-fat foods. **Taste aversion studies** (Garcia and Koelling, 1966) also suggest that our evolutionary heritage has shaped our food preferences.

Eating disorders

- **Anorexia nervosa (AN)** is characterised by a fear of being overweight. Anorexics weigh less than 85 per cent of their normal body weight. Other physical symptoms include amenorrhoea and constipation.

Biological explanations of one eating disorder – for example, anorexia nervosa, bulimia nervosa, obesity

- **The biological (medical) model of abnormality** assumes an underlying physical cause. Studies involving genetics and brain damage and biochemistry support this. A key study by **Holland et al. (1988)** on anorexia found a 56 per cent concordance rate in monozygotic twins and 7 per cent in dizygotic twins who had been brought up in the same environment Other biological explanations concentrate on hypothalamic dysfunction, neurotransmitter imbalance, hormonal imbalance and intrauterine infection.

Psychological explanations of one eating disorder – for example, anorexia nervosa, bulimia nervosa, obesity

- **The behavioural model** isn't associated with mental disorders but maladaptive behaviour. It assumes that all behaviour is learnt through the process of **classical and operant conditioning**, and thus can be unlearnt using the same principles. Thus anorexia nervosa is a learnt behaviour. Classical conditioning principles suggest that eating is associated with anxiety since it can make people overweight. Losing weight ensures that the individual reduces these feelings of anxiety. Operant conditioning principles suggest that the individual avoids food to gain a reward such as feeling positive about themselves. In the early stages of the illness, individuals may even be admired or congratulated for losing weight and looking slim and 'healthy'. The refusal to eat is reinforcing and becomes dangerous. **Social Learning Theory** suggests that observational learning plays a part in anorexia nervosa. The media have a preoccupation with a thin body shape in women and this puts pressure on women to conform to this shape. In this way women become more and more dissatisfied with their own body shape and physical appearance, and this can lead to AN.

- **Psychodynamic explanations of eating disorders** suggest that adolescents don't want to grow up and they become fixated at the oral stage when they were completely dependent on their parents. AN is an unconscious desire to remain dependent on their parents. In Freudian terms, eating and sex are symbolically related: a refusal to eat represents a refusal of sexuality.

Essay Questions

Eating behaviour

1. Discuss factors that influence attitudes to food and eating behaviour – for example, cultural influences, mood and health concerns.   (25 marks)
2. Critically consider explanations for the success and failure of dieting.   (25 marks)

Biological explanations of eating behaviour

3. Discuss the role of neural mechanisms involved in controlled eating and satiation.   (25 marks)
4. Outline and evaluate evolutionary explanations of food preference.   (25 marks)

Eating disorders

5. Outline and evaluate psychological approaches as explanations of any one eating disorder (anorexia nervosa, bulimia nervosa or obesity).   (25 marks)
6. 'Eating disorders tend to be biological rather than psychological disorders.' Assess to what extent research supports the view that any ONE eating disorder is caused by biological factors.   (25 marks)

It should take you 30 minutes to answer each question.

A2 Unit 3

Aggression

What's covered in this chapter?

You need to know about:

Social psychological approaches to aggression
- Social psychological theories of aggression – for example, Social Learning Theory, deindividuation
- Explanations of institutional aggression

Biological explanations of aggression
- The role of neural and hormonal mechanisms in aggression
- The role of genetic factors in aggressive behaviour

Aggression as an adaptive response
- Evolutionary explanations of human aggression, including infidelity and jealousy
- Explanations of group display in humans – for example, sports events and lynch mobs

DEFINITIONS OF AGGRESSION

Aggression is defined as behaviour that is intended to harm or injure, directed towards another living being. This applies primarily to human behaviour, and can include psychological as well as physical injury (Lippa, 1994).

Several types of aggression are identified by psychologists, including those listed below.

- **Hostile aggression:** this is generally caused by being provoked or upset and the primary purpose is to harm someone.

- **Instrumental aggression:** the primary goal here is to gain some kind of reward, such as money. Aggression is used as a means to an end. It is not usually provoked by anger or emotion.

- **Pro-social aggression:** this is aggression that is performed to prevent greater harm (e.g. a police officer who shoots a terrorist).

Figure 4.1 Norfolk farmer Tony Martin, who shot a burglar in his home: an example of hostile and/or sanctioned aggression

SOCIAL PSYCHOLOGICAL APPROACHES TO AGGRESSION

Social Learning Theory (SLT) of aggression

Of the many cues that influence behaviour, at any point in time, none is more common than the actions of others – Bandura (1986)

Figure 4.2 Albert Bandura: the psychologist most closely associated with Social Learning Theory (SLT)

Definition of SLT

Social Learning Theory (SLT) is defined as learning behaviour that is controlled by environmental influences rather than by innate or internal forces. SLT is often called modelling or observational learning.

SLT emphasises the importance of observing and modelling the behaviours, attitudes and emotional reactions of others. The theory suggests that aggression, like other forms of behaviour, is primarily learned (Bandura, 1973). Humans are not born as aggressive individuals but acquire these behaviours in the same way as other forms of social behaviour: through direct experience or by observing the actions of others.

SLT developed from Learning Theory (the behaviourists). According to behaviourists:

- behaviour that is reinforced (rewarded) will be repeated and learned

- aggression that is associated with a reward (e.g. praise, increased self-esteem) is likely to be learned.

However, learning doesn't only occur directly, it can also occur indirectly, through observing other people. This is called learning by vicarious experience, or observational learning. Bandura (1977a) sums this up thus:

Learning would be exceedingly laborious, not to mention hazardous, if people had to rely solely on the effects of their own actions to inform them what to do. Fortunately, most human behaviour is learned observa-

tionally through modelling: from observing others one forms an idea of how new behaviours are performed, and on later occasions this coded information serves as a guide for action.

So, observational learning occurs when individuals observe and imitate others' behaviour. There are four component processes in the theory: Attention, Retention, Production and Motivation/Reinforcement (ARPM), as described below.

1. **Attention:** someone can learn through observation only if they attend to the model's behaviour. For example, children must attend to what the aggressor is doing and saying in order to reproduce the model's behaviour accurately (Allen and Santrock, 1993) (see the section on the bobo doll experiment, below).

2. **Retention:** in order to reproduce the modelled behaviour, an individual must code and remember the behaviour by placing it into long-term memory (LTM). This enables the behaviour to be retrieved. In the bobo doll experiment, the children were only able to act aggressively since this information had been stored in LTM.

3. **Production:** an individual must be capable of reproducing the model's behaviour; the observer must possess the physical capabilities of the modelled behaviour. In the bobo doll study, the children possessed the physical capabilities of hitting and punching the doll.

4. **Motivation or reinforcements:** an individual expects to receive positive reinforcements (rewards) for the modelled behaviour. This will help to motivate their behaviour. In the bobo doll experiment, the children witnessed the adults gaining a reward for their aggression. Therefore the children performed the same act to achieve the same reward.

There are a number of factors that influence imitative behaviour. Individuals are more likely to copy modelled behaviour if:

- it results in outcomes (rewards) that they value

- the model is similar to the observer, and is a powerful and admired role model

- the model is seen as similar to the learner (e.g. the same sex, age and with similar interests)

- the task to be imitated is neither too easy nor too difficult

Figure 4.3 Although amateur footballers spend many years observing Premiership footballers, they're still not as good as David Beckham – perhaps they should accept that they don't possess the physical capability!

- they have low self-esteem or are unconfident in their own abilities.

Bandura believed aggression reinforced by family members was the most prominent source of behaviour modelling. For example, the boy who watches his father attack his mother is more likely to become an abusive parent and husband (Siegel, 1992).

Research studies

✔ **Specification Hint**

Research studies can be used as AO1 (descriptive), AO2 (analysis and evaluation) and AO3 (evaluation of the methodology of the studies) and, as such, the research studies are extremely important. Do not get too preoccupied with AO1, AO2 and AO3 criteria – it is actually quite difficult to work out which is which. Just answer the exam question and you will automatically gain the marks without even knowing how AO1, AO2 and AO3 marks are allocated.

Evaluation of SLT

✔ **Useful applications:** Social Learning Theory has numerous implications for classroom use. A discussion of the consequences of behaviour in terms of rewards and consequences can be effective in increasing appropriate behaviours and decreasing inappropriate behaviours. SLT can also be applied in other social and cultural settings.

✔ **Experimental support:** studies such as those above (e.g. bobo doll) provide support for SLT. Bandura *et al*. (1963) also demonstrated that viewing aggression by cartoon characters produces as much aggression as viewing live or filmed aggressive behaviour by adults. Additionally, they demonstrated that having children view pro-social behaviour can reduce displays of aggressive behaviour.

✔ **Cognitive sense:** it seems obvious that environmental experiences must have an influence on the social learning of violence in children. Bandura (1977b) reported that individuals who live in areas with high crime rates are more likely to act violently than those who dwell in low-crime areas. However, there may be other factors that might explain this finding (e.g. unemployment, lack of educational opportunity, the fact that you are constantly getting burgled!). A straightforward observational learning explanation appears too simplistic.

✔ **Successful applications:** SLT has been applied to the development of psychological disorders (particularly phobias) and therapies associated with these disorders, such as behaviour modification programmes. SLT can also be used to explain the success of television commercials. Adverts suggest that buying a particular product will help us to identify with the people that are used to advertise the product.

✘ **Ignores biological factors:** biological theorists argue that SLT completely ignores individuals' biological factors and the differences of individuals due to genetic, brain and learning differences (Jeffery, 1990). SLT ignores any evidence that might suggest a biological or genetic component to human aggression (Miles and Carrey, 1997).

Figure 4.4 Do consumers identify with the personality used to advertise the brand?

Key Study 4.1: Transmission of Aggression Through Imitation (TATI) study (Bandura, Ross and Ross, 1961)

Aim/hypothesis (A01)

Can aggressive behaviour be learned through observation

Method/design (A01)

A total of 36 boys and 36 girls (aged between three and five years) were divided into eight experimental groups of six children. The remaining children acted as a control group. The children were brought individually to the experimental room, where they were invited by an experimenter to play a game. In the room, there were a number of toys, such as potato prints, picture stickers, a tinker toy set, a mallet and a five-foot inflatable bobo doll (this bounces back upright when hit). The children were guided to start playing with the picture sticker sets. An adult 'model' then entered the room and started assembling the tinker toys.

In the non-aggressive condition, the model continued to assemble the tinker toys in a quiet manner and ignored the bobo doll. In the aggressive condition, after a minute, the model started acting aggressively towards the bobo doll. The model performed novel aggressive behaviours that might not be expected of children unless they were influenced by the model's behaviour. These included pummelling it on the head with a mallet, hurling it down, sitting on it and punching it on the nose repeatedly, kicking it across the room and flinging it in the air. It also included verbal aggression such as shouting: 'Sock him in the nose ...', Pow, 'He keeps coming back for more ...' and 'He sure is a tough fella.' It was proposed that identical actions performed by the children would provide good evidence for observational learning. Merely hitting the bobo doll might not be so convincing since that is what a bobo doll is designed for.

Prior to the subsequent test for imitation, all the children were subjected to 'mild aggression arousal'; this involved taking them to a room that contained a number of attractive toys that they were told they could play with. After two minutes of playing they were told that they couldn't play with them after all! They were then taken to a further room where there were a number of aggressive (e.g. mallet, darts) and non-aggressive toys (e.g. crayons, dolls) for the children to play with. Of course, there was also a bobo doll. The children spent 20 minutes in this room, observed through a one-way mirror. An experimenter rated the different levels of aggression (and non-aggression) shown by the children. This experimenter had no knowledge as to which group the children had been pre-assigned to.

Figure 4.5 Original stills from the Bobo doll studies

Results

Children in the aggressive condition showed a good deal of physical and verbal aggression. Their scores were significantly higher than those of the children in the non-aggressive and control groups. Indeed, 70 per cent of children in the non-aggressive or control groups had zero ratings of aggression. Bandura *et al.* also ensured that both male and female models were used. Their findings indicated that both boys and girls were more influenced by the male model. The tentative explanation for this was that physical aggression is typically seen as a more male sex-appropriate behaviour.

Conclusion (A01)

The conclusion from the study was that observation of the behaviour of others does lead to imitative learning.

Imitation of Film-mediated Aggressive Models (IF-MAM) (Bandura, Ross and Ross, 1963)

A similar method to the one above was used in this study. This time the children watched a short film in which the 'model' behaved aggressively (physically and verbally) towards the bobo doll. There were three experimental conditions, as follows.

1. 'Model-reward' condition: here the model was rewarded for abusing the doll. The model was given sweets and drinks, and called a 'strong champion'.

2. 'Model-punished' condition: here the model was punished for abusing the doll. The model was told off for 'picking on the clown'.

3. 'No consequences' (control) condition: here no reinforcement was given.

After the video, the children were again placed in a room with attractive toys, but they could not touch them, making them angry and frustrated. After this, the children went to a playroom containing a bobo doll and a number of other toys. Each child was observed for ten minutes in the playroom. Children who were in the model-punished group produced significantly fewer imitative aggressive behaviours than children in either of the other two groups. There was no significant difference between the 'model-reward' and 'no consequences' groups. An experimenter then offered all the children a reward if they could imitate the behaviours they had earlier seen the model performing.

Children in all three groups then performed the aggressive behaviours to the same extent. All the children had learnt the model's aggressive behaviours. Bandura concluded that reinforcement (reward or punishment) is not necessary for the *learning* of new behaviours through observation – but that the expectancy of reinforcement (reward or punishment) is essential for the *performance* of these new behaviours. Other studies conducted by Bandura *et al.* demonstrated that children are more likely to model behaviour if they identify with and admire the model.

Conclusion

Such studies provide clear evidence for SLT and the modelling influence of both real-life and filmed aggression.

Conclusion

Despite criticisms, SLT has maintained an important place in the study of aggression. In order to control aggression, Bandura believed that both the family and the mass media should provide positive role models for children and the general public.

Evaluation of research studies

✔ **Well-controlled experiments:** the experiments were well planned and executed. The inclusion of other toys in the room and the copying of specific aggressive responses clearly showed that the children had indeed learned behaviour from the model.

✘ **Sample characteristics:** the nursery children used were from the Stanford University nursery. This is unlikely to be a very representative sample. In addition, these experiments only involved children as participants. Would adult learners behave in the same way? Stack (1987) reports that the highest number of suicides in New York City was recorded a few days after Marilyn Monroe's death. This suggests that adults may also learn from modelling.

✘ **Lacks ecological validity:** the artificial laboratory situation ensures that it is difficult to generalise the findings to a more realistic setting. For example, the films were only four minutes long and included no justification for the violence portrayed.

✘ **Not real aggression:** aggression was limited to a bobo doll. Would the children have imitated

Evaluation of research studies continued...

aggressive acts towards a real person? Johnston *et al.* (1977) found that play aggression correlated with ratings of aggression by peers (0.76) and teachers (0.57). This suggests that play aggression is a worthwhile measure of real aggression.

✗ **Only adult models:** Bandura *et al.* used only adult models with children. Would the same results have been found with children as models?

✗ **Demand characteristics:** some of the children said that they felt they were expected to perform aggressively towards the doll. However, the very specific nature of the imitative aggression suggests that modelling had occurred.

✗ **Short-term effects:** it has been claimed that these studies merely demonstrated short-term effects of modelling. However, Hicks (1965) found that 40 per cent of a model's acts could be reproduced up to eight months after one showing of a ten-minute film.

✗ **Manipulation of participants:** in the bobo doll experiment, the children were manipulated into responding to the aggressive behaviours in the film. For example, they became frustrated because they could not play with the toys when taken into the room immediately after the film.

✗ **Unethical and morally questionable:** the experiment conducted was unethical and morally wrong because the children were encouraged to be aggressive.

✗ **Questionable operationalisation of the dependent variable**: is the number of times a child punches a bobo doll a valid measure of aggression? Since a bobo doll is designed to be punched, the number of punches is not really an adequate measure of aggression.

STRETCH AND CHALLENGE: The bobo doll studies

Although textbooks try to be as accurate as possible, there is no substitute for actually reading the original research paper. 'The Transmission of Aggression through Imitation' study is available at: http://psychclassics.yorku.ca/Bandura/bobo.htm.

Read the original paper and try to outline some more ethical arguments for and against the study.

Consider if any behavioural change induced in the children might have been permanent, whether there might have been any personal distress or psychological harm caused to the children, and to what extent the deception in the study was justified.

✓ Specification Hint

If the question asks for ONE social psychological theory of aggression, then it's probably best to use SLT and the research studies that support it. We've provided most information on this theory.

Deindividuation

Definition of deindividuation

Deindividuation is defined as the loss of a sense of individual identity, and a loosening of normal inhibitions against engaging in behaviour that is inconsistent with internal standards.

Figure 4.6 Le Bon suggested that in large crowds people act as one!

Deindividuation theory of aggression

Deindividuation theory is a social psychological account of the individual in a group or crowd. It can be applied to aggression since the theory helps to explain how rational individuals can become aggressive hooligans in an unruly mob or crowd. Festinger (Festinger *et al.*, 1952) suggested that there is a reduction of inner restraints or self-awareness when individuals are 'submerged in a group'. Individuals in groups fail to see the consequences of their actions, and the social norms they would usually follow are forgotten.

Although Festinger *et al.* (1952) were the first to coin the phrase 'deindividuation', Le Bon (1995, originally published 1895) was the first to recognise how an individual's behaviour changes when in a crowd. Le Bon wrote that an individual in a crowd 'descends several rungs of the ladder of civilisation'. Le Bon proposed that there are a number of factors that lead an individual to become psychologically transformed in a crowd; the most important of these is anonymity. Le Bon proposed that the more anonymous the crowd, the greater the threat of extreme action. In short, a 'collective mindset' takes over and the crowd acts as one. The person becomes submerged into the crowd and loses self-control.

Le Bon's idea of a collective mindset was criticised and it was proposed that anonymity leads to a release from internal restraints to produce emotional, impulsive and irrational behaviour. Zimbardo (1970) also argued that there was more to deindividuation than just anonymity in a group, and suggested that reduced responsibility, increased arousal, sensory overload and altered consciousness due to drugs or alcohol play an important part.

In the 1980s, new adaptations of deindividuation theory were proposed, as outlined below.

- Diener (1980) suggested that people often behave in well-scripted ways and do so without conscious awareness (this is certainly true of my teaching!). When an individual is evaluated by others or when their behaviour does not follow the script, then the individual becomes self-aware (this might occur when a student asks me a difficult question). Diener believed that crowds block the individual's capacity for self-awareness and thus the individual becomes deindividuated. However, a key factor in behaviour is social arousal. This is particularly noticeable at major sports events when fans become so involved in focusing on the game that they are no longer self-aware.

Figure 4.7 Anonymous group behaviour ensures a reduced capability to engage in rational thinking

- Prentice-Dunn and Rogers (1982) suggested that there are two types of self-awareness.

1. **Public self-awareness:** a concern about the impression presented to other people knowing that you'll be evaluated by them on this basis. Public self-awareness can be reduced by anonymity (in a crowd), diffusion of responsibility (see pages 170–171) – a decrease in individual responsibility when in a group – and the fact that other members act as role models in a group to set the social norms or standards of behaviour that you're likely to copy. In essence, loss of public self-awareness leads to a loss of public standards of behaviour or a lowering of inhibitions.

2. **Private self-awareness:** this is the concern we have for our own thoughts and feelings. This can be reduced by becoming so involved in an activity that we 'forget' ourselves. Dancing and singing (often accompanied by alcohol) at a club would be an example of this. In essence, loss of private awareness leads to a loss of internal standards and hence an over-reliance on environmental cues (others in the crowd) as to how to behave (i.e. people forget how to think for themselves).

The loss of both private and public awareness is caused by becoming immersed in a group or crowd.

Figure 4.8 An example of reduced private self-awareness

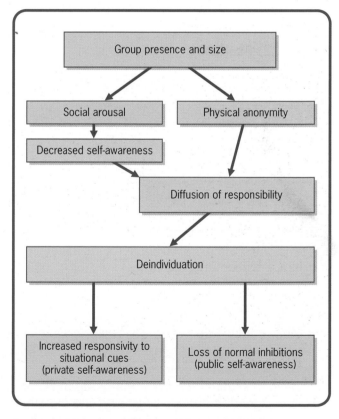

Figure 4.9 Factors that interact to cause deindividuation: several influences converge to create a sense of diffused responsibility and this decreases the burden of accountability that an individual would normally assume for his/her actions (adapted from Myers, 1998)

Most psychologists agree that deindividuation results in disinhibited behaviour that does not follow the usual social norms (e.g. Postmes and Spears, 1998). The only difference is whether in a crowd we are controlled by someone else or whether we simply can't control our own anti-social tendencies.

How Science Works

Practical Learning Activity 4.1: Anonymity and antisocial behaviour

A clever test of our antisocial tendencies was suggested by Dodd (1985) when he asked students to respond anonymously to the following question: 'If you could be totally invisible for 24 hours and were completely assured that you would not be detected or held responsible for your actions, what would you do?'

Students wrote their answers on blank sheets, which were then collected and read out anonymously.

The average number of antisocial responses was 36 per cent – the same figure given by inmates at a maximum security prison where Dodd once taught!

You could try this activity with friends, but you need to be able to guarantee their anonymity and the group would have to be sufficiently large so that people could not guess who wrote what. You also need to ensure that you have gained fully informed consent.

Think of some problems with this research.

Research studies

Key Study 4.2: Zimbardo *et al.*'s Prison Experiment (PE) (1973)

Aim/hypothesis (A01)

Deindividuation may be particularly marked in 'total institutions' (e.g. mental hospitals, prisons) where people are removed from their normal environment and stripped of their individuality. Zimbardo *et al.* investigated such a process in their simulation of a prison environment (see Gross and Rolls, 2008: 149–52). Briefly, the details were as follows.

Method/design (A01)

A mock (simulated) prison was deliberately created (in the basement of the Stanford University psychology department) and 24 emotionally stable, male participants were recruited. One group of students was assigned to the role of guards and the others were prisoners. Both the guards and prisoners were deindividuated and became anonymous members of their groups.

Figure 4.10 Original photo from the Prison Experiment

On arrival, the prisoners were stripped naked and issued with a loose-fitting smock. Their ID number was printed on the front and back, and they had a chain bolted around one ankle. They wore a nylon stocking to cover their hair, and were referred to by number only. The guards wore military-style khaki uniforms and silver reflector sunglasses (making eye contact impossible). They carried clubs, whistles, handcuffs and keys to the cells. The guards had almost complete control over the prisoners, who were confined to their cells around the clock – except for meals, toilet privileges, headcounts and work.

Results (A01)

Despite it being a simulation, the guards created a brutal atmosphere. The prisoners soon began to react passively as the guards stepped up their aggression. They began to feel helpless and no longer in control of their lives. Every guard at some time or another behaved in an abusive, authoritarian way. Many seemed to really enjoy the new-found power and control that went with the uniform.

Conclusions (A01)

In sum, both sets of participants showed some of the classic signs of deindividuation: 'a lowered sense of personal identity, an altered state of subjective consciousness, and a host of disinhibited anti-social behaviours' (Lippa, 1994).

Evaluation of the Prison Experiment

✔ **High ecological validity:** both the environment and the behaviour (of guards and prisoners) were 'realistic', and the findings can be applied to real prisons. The results were especially surprising given that everyone knew it to be a 'simulation'.

✔ **Realistic measures of aggression:** both verbal and physical aggression were measured. The guards placed 'prisoners' in physical discomfort (stood on them doing press-ups, pushed them in urinals) and verbally abused them.

✘ **Unethical?** Even Zimbardo accepted that certain aspects of the study were unethical (protection from harm, informed consent) and admitted that he became over-involved in the study.

✘ **Sample characteristics:** the sample was unrepresentative in that it included only young males.

How Science Works

Practical Learning Activity 4.2: Zimbardo's prison simulation study

There is an excellent web resource about this study, which can be found at:
http://www.holah.karoo.net/zimbardostudy.htm.

Make brief notes on the strengths and weaknesses of the study.

There is a wealth of other material on the internet about this (in)famous study, including footage of the original study on many file-sharing websites.

Trick or Treater Study (TOTS) (Diener *et al.*, 1976)

This study tested the effects of disguise, anonymity and group membership on the anti-social behaviour of young 'trick or treaters' in Seattle, USA. A total of 27 women were asked to give out sweets to 1,000 'trick or treaters' during Halloween night. Half of the children who knocked at their doors were asked for their names and addresses (identifiable), whereas the others remained anonymous. Some of the children were on their own, while others were in groups (crowds). While chatting to the children, the women had to go and answer their phone and so left the children at the front door with the strict instruction to take one sweet each. A hidden observer recorded whether the children stole any additional sweets. The results are shown in Figure 4.12. Children were more likely to steal in groups when they were anonymous.

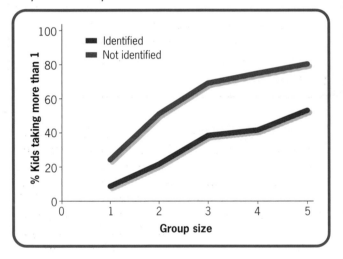

Figure 4.11 *Effects of group membership and deindividuation on children's likelihood of stealing (Diener et al. 1976, adapted with permission)*

Anonymous Laboratory Coat (ALC) Study (Zimbardo, 1970)

Women were dressed in white laboratory coats and hoods in order to render them anonymous. A control group wore their ordinary clothes and had name tags prominently displayed. In an experimental situation similar to Milgram's (1963) study of destructive obedience, participants had to shock a victim (actually a confederate). The anonymous participants shocked longer (and therefore more painfully) than the identifiable participants. Anonymity would appear to contribute to aggressive behaviour.

Evaluation of the Anonymous Laboratory Coat Study

✗ **Ku Klux Klan effect:** it was suggested that the wearing of white hoods and the subsequent association with the Ku Klux Klan may have affected the intensity of the shocks given, rather than the anonymity of the participants.

✗ **Sample:** the sample was composed entirely of women and the study thus may not be generalised to men.

✗ **Unethical?** Ethical criticisms of Milgram's (1963) study are relevant here as well. These include lack of informed consent and protection from harm (i.e. stress).

Evaluation of the Trick or Treater Study

✓ **High ecological validity:** the experiment took place in a real-life setting with a substantial number of children taking part.

✗ **Sample:** despite the large sample, only children were used. Would the same findings be applicable to adults?

✗ **Operationalisation of aggression?** The study examined anti-social behaviour (stealing sweets) rather than aggression per se.

The Costume Experiment (CE) (Johnson and Downing, 1979)

This involved a variation of the Anonymous Laboratory Coat Study, described above. Participants were made anonymous by the wearing of masks and overalls, similar to those worn by the Ku Klux Klan, or by means of nurses' uniforms. Compared to the control condition, participants shocked more when dressed in the Ku Klux Klan uniforms, but they actually shocked less when dressed as nurses.

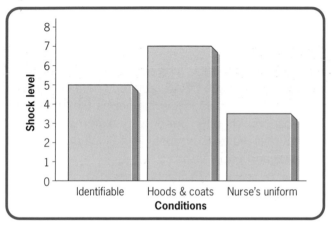

Figure 4.12 Results from the Costume Experiment (from Johnson and Downing, 1979, reprinted with permission)

Evaluation of the Costume Experiment

✔ **Criticism of the Costume Experiment:** the experiment demonstrated that it is not anonymity per se that leads to aggression but the norms associated with the social context that affect behaviour.

✘ **Artificial situation:** the study adopts a very artificial methodology and could be subject to demand characteristics.

Darkened Room Arousal Study (DRAS) (Gergen, Gergen and Barton, 1973)

This study also showed the effects of anonymity on deindividuation. Both male and female students were asked to interact for an hour in an environmental chamber (a padded room). The only instruction was that there 'are no rules ... as to what you should do together'. After the experiment, they were told that they would not interact with the other participants and would leave alone. In effect, the participants could do what they liked.

Evaluation of the Darkened Room Arousal Study

✔ **Evidence against the deindividuation theory of aggression:** the study demonstrated that anonymity does not always lead to aggression. Indeed, this might be an example of anonymity leading to pro-social acts. Since most participants were willing to volunteer again, they must have enjoyed the feelings of intimacy!

✘ **Low ecological validity:** although a well-controlled study, the situation was rather artificial and involved only a small number of participants.

There were two conditions: in one the lights were left on; in the other the participants were left in total darkness! This meant that participants in the dark room were anonymous, in a strange environment and deindividuated. Participants in the lit room found the study rather boring – no one hugged another person. In contrast, half of those in the dark room hugged another person, 89 per cent intentionally touched others, and they reported the experience to be sensuous and fun. Indeed, many volunteered to take part again.

This study shows that deindividuation leads to the freeing of inhibitions, not necessarily aggression.

Conclusion: research studies

Evidence for deindividuation theory is mixed. A meta-analysis of 60 research studies testing deindividuation theory concluded that there was insufficient support for the theory (Postmes and Spears, 1998). Both disinhibition and anti-normative behaviour are not more common in large groups and crowded anonymous settings.

Evaluation of deindividuation theory

✔ **Experimental support:** there is certainly some experimental support for the theory of deindividuation (see above).

✘ **Other theories:** there are other theories that can explain some aspects of human aggression (see below).

✘ **Recent analysis:** more recent social psychological research suggests that a norm-based analysis of collective behaviour is supported (i.e. people are more likely to follow local group norms if they are deindividuated).

✘ **Deindividuation does not always lead to aggression:** sometimes there is increased conformity within a crowd and deindividuation causes increased pro-social behaviour (see DRAS, above). There is a strong feeling of belonging to the crowd (a social identity) and individuals follow the norms that may occur within the crowd (Reicher, 1987). This can explain how crowds often act on very high moral principles and do not always result in unrestrained and irrational ways. Examples would include crowd (helping) behaviour during disasters (e.g. Turkish earthquake) and papal visits.

✘ **Analysis of football supporters' behaviour:** Ingham (1978) has shown that football supporters follow strictly ritualised rules of behaviour on the terraces, and acts of violence are not the result of 'mob rule'.

✘ **Other theories:** there are other theories that can explain human aggression. These include the following.

- **Instinct theory:** the view that aggression stems from innate tendencies that are universal among members of a given species.
- **Biological theories:** the view that biological processes (sex hormones, neurotransmitters) influence aggression (see pages 152–163).
- **Drive theories:** the view that aggression stems from external conditions that arouse the motive to harm others. The frustration-aggression hypothesis is one of these.

✔ Specification Hint

A sentence or so on competing theoretical explanations of aggression could be included as evaluation (AO2) but you *mustn't* describe them in detail. Indeed, many of them are not social psychological explanations and therefore cannot gain any descriptive (AO1) marks.

Explanations of institutional aggression

Aggression in institutions is a significant problem. In the UK the most obvious examples of institutional aggression occur in prisons and the National Health Service. There were as many as 84,272 reported violent or abusive incidents against NHS staff in 2000/2001 (Department of Health, 2002). In the USA, Wortley (2002) reports that there were 26,000 prisoner–prisoner assaults during 1995. These figures should be set against the fact that recorded incidents are believed to grossly underestimate the actual level of institutional violence, with the actual levels estimated at five times as high (Wortley, 2002).

The impact of violence on institutions is not hard to discern: staff and patients are physically injured and may become psychologically disturbed, property is destroyed, and regimes and programs are disrupted and thereby impoverished. Furthermore, violent individuals are not only incarcerated for longer but are held in more expensive and more restrictive conditions. (Gadon et al., 2006)

In order to try to reduce institutional aggression, risk factors need to be identified and various explanations for institutional aggression have been proposed.

✔ Specification Hint: Zimbardo and deindividuation

Aggression committed by prisoners or prison officers can be covered in this section, as long as the explanation focuses on the group's behaviour and doesn't focus on the individual. Zimbardo's Prison Experiment and the findings of this can also be included here (see page 143).

✔ Specification Hint

The Spec mentions that you must know 'explanations of institutional aggression'. This means that you must know at least TWO explanations of any institutional aggression. We will concentrate primarily on two explanations of aggression that occur in prisons.

Many explanations of prison aggression tend to focus on two broad explanations: one suggests that aggression occurs as a result of individual characteristics that the prisoner brings into the prison (the Importation Model) and the other suggests that aggression occurs as a result of internal factors within the prison setting (situational models, including the Deprivation Model).

The Importation Model

The importation model suggests that prisoners bring their own social histories and traits with them to the prison environment, and such aspects influence their subsequent behaviour in prison (Irwin and Cressey, 1962). Much of the aggressive behaviour acted out in the prison institution is not peculiar to that institution and was acted out in wider society by these same individuals; indeed, for many of them, that is precisely why they have ended up in prison. Such men (they are predominantly men) bring with them into prison a ready-made way of behaving, which they simply apply to their new institutional setting (Cheeseman, 2003). As Toch (1977) puts it: 'All prisons inherit their subcultural sediments from the street corners that supply them with clients', suggesting that similar influences drive aggression among young people both in prison and on the street (1977: 56). Irwin and Cressey (1962) argued that it was wrong to look solely at the 'inmate culture' in isolation, and that it was necessary to examine how it is influenced by elements and experiences outside it.

Many pre-existing personal and psychological factors of incarcerated individuals have been shown to affect the levels of aggressive behaviour exhibited in prison. One such factor is alcohol addiction. Mills, Kroner and Weekes (1998) surveyed 202 inmates newly admitted to a Canadian prison, using the Alcohol Dependence Scale (ADS). They found that higher levels of 'serious institutional misconduct' were associated with more severe levels of alcohol dependence. Other factors that have been seen to be important include previous employment record, level of education and extent of criminal history prior to imprisonment. Not surprisingly, greater periods of unemployment, a lower level of education and a more serious criminal record were correlated with a greater likelihood of aggression while imprisoned (Kane and Janus, 1981, cited in Brooks, 2004). Two extremely important demographic variables influencing aggression in prison are race and age. Evidence from the USA shows that non-whites and younger inmates are far more likely to be aggressive while in prison. Kane and Janus (1981, cited in Brooks, 2004) suggest that this is because these groups are more likely to be 'disenfranchised' and separated from the mainstream society's norms and values that promote pro-social methods of meeting basic needs

147

and solving interpersonal conflict. In contrast, many of these individuals live in a subculture where aggression is valued, respected and reinforced. These subcultural forces have influenced them to be aggressive in many contexts – in their home, in their neighbourhood and in the prison institution.

Figure 4.14 Violence often occurs in an institutional setting such as a prison

Irwin and Cressey (1962) recognised the importance of different prisoner subcultures and identified three different categories.

1. **The Criminal or Thief Subculture:** such inmates follow the norms and values that are inherent within the professional thief or career criminal. Values such as not betraying one another and being trustworthy and reliable among fellow criminals are adopted. Such prisoners refer to their fellow thieves in the prison as their primary reference group.

2. **The Convict Subculture:** convicts are inmates who have been raised in the prison system. These inmates seek positions of power, influence and information within the prison institution. The convicts' primary reference group in prison is fellow convicts. It is those in this particular group that are most likely to turn to aggression or other maladaptive forms of coping. This group of inmates are influenced by deprivation prior to imprisonment, and the values of this subculture are imported from outside the walls of the institution (Blomberg and Lucken, 2000).

Evaluation of the Importation Model

✔ **Detailed explanation:** instead of viewing all inmates as solely influenced by one shared, common set of values, the Importation Model proposed by Irwin and Cressey (1962) has merit in looking at subcultures within prison institutions. Early theories of prison culture, such as those proposed by Clemmer (1940) or McKorkle and Korn (1954), tended to suggest that inmates imported one 'holistic' criminal subculture into the institution. Irwin and Cressey (1962) suggested that there were different subcultures within prison, and their attempt to identify a typology of conflicting inmate subcultures has some support (Blomberg and Lucken, 2000).

✘ **Little practical use:** it has been suggested that the Importation Model fails to provide suggestions for how best to manage aggressive prisoners and/or policy suggestions for reducing prison violence in general (McCorkle *et al.* 1995).

✔ **Gang support:** DeLisi *et al.* (2004) studied the prison records of 831 male inmates sampled from the south-western USA in order to explore the prison violence records of inmates involved in street gangs and prison gangs. There was a small but significant relationship between gang membership and prison aggression, suggesting that subcultural values had been imported into prisons by gang members. However, other factors, such as race, were also of great importance.

✔ **Juvenile delinquent support:** Poole and Regoli (1983) assessed the relative impact of several deprivational and importational variables on inmate violence in four juvenile correctional institutions. While both sets of variables were shown to exert some effects on inmate aggression, pre-institutional violence emerged as the best predictor of inmate aggression, lending greater support to the importation explanation. However, this study examined only juvenile institutions, so results may be different in adult settings.

3. **The Conventional or 'Straight' Subculture:** these individuals tend to be one-time offenders and are characterised as 'straights' by Irwin and Cressey (1962). They were not part of a criminal or thief subculture before entering prison. These one-time offenders reject both the other subcultural groups while in prison, and identify more with the prison officers and staff. Such prisoners do not tend to be very aggressive while in prison.

Situational models

Individual factors, such as personality and the subcultural norms and values that a prisoner brings into prison, are important but it also has to be recognised that the prison environment or institution must play a part in the level of aggression exhibited by prisoners. Behaviour in prison does not take place in a social vacuum and thus situational factors must influence prisoner behaviour. Situational factors can be thought of as:

● organisational – leadership, management, policies and procedures

● physical – security level, level of available resources

● staff characteristics – gender, level of experience, relationship to and interactions with prisoners.

The role of these situational factors is perhaps best demonstrated in the Deprivation Model.

The Deprivation Model

Early explanations of prison aggression concentrated on what went on within the walls of the institutions. The aggressive behaviour of many inmates was said to originate in the deprivations that they experienced on a daily basis. These deprivations were such that prisoners could not maintain or form healthy relationships with people outside the prison. A classic study by Sykes (1958) outlined the pains of imprisonment that inmates experience during their sentence. Sykes argued that the origin of the prison subculture emanates from within the institution, not from outside. Sykes outlined five deprivations that arise 'from the indignities and degradations suffered by becoming an inmate' (Massey, 1986). These deprivations are as follows.

1. **Deprivation of liberty:** through imprisonment, society is informing the prisoner that he (or she) is no longer a person who can be trusted to live in a free world. Prisoners are morally rejected by society and this loss of liberty is emphasised by other symbols, such as the use of numbers and uniforms. Many civil rights are lost. Overcrowding may be an important factor. For example, prisoners have to obtain permission to eat, sleep, shower and interact, the last of which restricts the ability to maintain relations with family and friends (Blomberg and Lucken, 2000).

2. **Deprivation of autonomy:** prisoners realise they have no power and that they have very few choices to make on a daily basis. Prison officials have almost complete control over prisoners' behaviour, which leads to a feeling of almost total helplessness among inmates. This situation can lead to frustration and in turn aggression. Prisoners are often informed as to what will be happening (e.g. 'no exercise today') but not given the reasons why. This deprivation of autonomy can have unfortunate effects upon release, with prisoners unable to make decisions for themselves.

3. **Deprivation of goods and services:** prisoners are deprived of many of the goods and commodities that they would expect to experience if they weren't in prison. The western emphasis on possessions may make this deprivation particularly hard to bear. Some prisoners believe that the prison environment is structured in order to force prisoners to live in near poverty conditions. This deprivation of goods and services brings about a sense of failure to most people serving time in prison (Sykes, 1958).

4. **Deprivation of heterosexual relationships:** for many heterosexual men, female companionship is an important part of their self-identity. The denial of heterosexual relationships reduces many men's sense of self-worth. In addition, the greater opportunity for homosexual behaviour in prison may lead to greater anxieties for prisoners.

5. **Deprivation of security:** although security in many institutions is well controlled, prisoners do report fears for their own security. Many inmates describe other prisoners as violent and aggressive, and this can lead to a heightened sense of physical threat.

All these deprivations lead to increased stress for prisoners. It is believed that, as a consequence of suffering these deprivations, some inmates act aggressively towards others in order to both reduce stress and obtain desired resources. Thus aggression in prisons is seen as a way that prisoners can gain some control over the social order imposed on them in prison. Although some aggression may be goal-motivated, it is suggested that, with much aggression, there is a lack of real purpose or goals other than the reduction of stress (Cheeseman, 2003).

Other situational models

There are so many models that seek to explain situational factors that lead to aggression in prisons that perhaps the value of each is diminished. Other models proposed include the following.

The Popcorn Model (Folger and Skarlicki, 1995)

This suggests that the first individual to become aggressive is like the first piece of corn to pop when the saucepan is heated. Although it might be worth examining what factors lead that individual to explode into violence, it is better to seek to understand what factors lead to the 'heat' being applied in the first place. After all, no corn 'pops' without heat. In other words, sort out the prison environment and inmates will not become aggressive. Notice that this model also suggests that prisoners who do not bring values of aggression into prison can become aggressive if enough 'heat' is applied.

The Management Model (Dilulio, 1987)

This suggests that aggression in prisons occurs as a result of failed management, high staff turnover and a lack of discipline among staff. McCorkle et al. (1995) conducted a study investigating the relative strength of the deprivation and management models to explain prison aggression. Their sample included 371 US state prisons, and measures of both individual and collective violence were included. They concluded that the deprivation models were less useful in explaining rates of prison violence. There was a lack of evidence to support the connection between deprivation measures such as overcrowding and/or inadequate living conditions. They suggested a stronger link between prison administrative practices and levels of prison violence. For example, prison communities with a higher ratio of white to black staff experienced higher rates of assault on both inmates and staff. Their data also showed the benefits of educative programmes in prisons. It is believed that prisoners are less likely to engage in violence because they believe in the merits of the treatment and educational programmes that they undertake.

Evaluation of situational models

✗ **Constant levels of prison stress:** it is argued that the situational explanation does not explain why prison riots suddenly explode in the absence of any new environmental or situational factors. Levels of deprivation remain fairly constant in many institutions and yet violence can erupt suddenly, for seemingly little reason. More recent research has focused on levels of *relative* rather than *absolute* deprivation – that is, the prisoners' perceived discrepancy between what they receive and what they might expect to receive (Colvin, 1992).

✔/✗ **Research support:** Richards (2007) examined inmate-on-staff and inmate-on-inmate assaults in some 900 US state prisons operating from 1984 to 1995. Some inmate programmes increased mean rates of assaults in prisons, while others decreased levels of violence, suggesting that it is indeed the particular characteristics of the prison institution itself that account for the violence. In addition, frequent changes in governors and administrators of state prison systems increased mean rates of staff assaults. All this evidence provides support for the Deprivation Model. However, Jiang and Fisher-Giorlando (2002) reviewed 431 disciplinary reports from a men's state prison in the deep south of America. They reviewed a number of explanations for inmate aggression and concluded that the Situational Model was the most powerful in explaining overall inmate misconduct in prison, but that the Deprivation Model was the best at explaining violent incidents and incidents against correctional staff.

✗ **Conflicting findings on crowding in prisons:** empirical findings do not seem to support the hypothesis

Evaluation of situational models continued...

that there is a direct relationship between crowding and institutional aggression. Megargee (1976) found that aggressive incidents in prisons were negatively correlated to the amount of living space available for each prisoner. It is suggested that, when a prison is full or overcrowded, management strategies are put in place to compensate for this. This may involve fewer opportunities for inmates to interact with one another. Researchers have thus proposed that there should be a distinction made between social density (the amount of space available when prisoners interact) and spatial density (the amount of space each prisoner has in their cell).

✗ Unexplained motives: Light (1991, cited in Cheeseman, 2003) developed a set of categories to describe the different settings in which prisoners assault prison officers. The first category was known as 'the unexplained'. Light found that over 25 per cent of the assaults examined had no apparent reason or motive for the aggressive behaviour. This finding is supported by Goffman (1961), who previously noted that prisoners in a total institution will often attempt to hide the motives behind their aggressive actions. Of course, given such secrecy among prisoners, it makes research difficult to conduct and brings into doubt any conclusions based on such research.

✗ Female aggression in prisons: the current state of research is mixed, as support has been found for both the Deprivation and Importation Models in understanding the female inmate subculture. Scholars have reported that female offenders develop stronger bonds with the other members of their social groups rather than identify with the prisoner subculture, and thus explanations for female aggression in prisons may be qualitatively different from those for male inmates.

Interaction models

The interaction between these two models – the Importation and Situational (Deprivation) Model – has been widely accepted as providing a more convincing understanding of the impact of imprisonment on inmate violence than either model separately (Thomas and Peterson, 1977). The integration of the two models into one theoretical perspective provides the impetus for the model presented herein.

How Science Works

Practical Learning Activity 4.3: Inside prisons

Imagine you are on the Board of Governors at a local high-security prison. You have noticed a 20 per cent increase in inmate–inmate violence and a 30 per cent increase in inmate–staff assaults. Design a research programme that might investigate these increases. Try to include research methods that would test both the Importation and Situational explanations for institutional aggression.

Consider what recommendations you might make dependent on your findings.

Conclusion: explanations of institutional aggression

Violence is best viewed as the product of three interacting sets of variables:

1. the aggressor (personality, needs, concerns, perceptions)

2. the victim (personality, needs, concerns, perceptions etc.), and

3. the situation (the human and physical environment in which the incident is taking place (Gibbs, 1981).

The first two variables relate more to the Importation Model and the third to the Situational Model.

It is widely accepted that racial and ethnic tensions exist in mainstream American society and these tensions seem to play an important role in much of the aggression seen in US prisons. Indeed, 50 per cent of US state prison officials reported that racial conflicts were a problem among inmates (Knox *et al.*, 1996). Some hold these tensions responsible for creating the racial divides among inmates that have increased inmate assaults and resulted in full-scale race riots in some facilities, suggesting that aggression in prison may be a reflection of problems imported from wider society (McCorkle *et al.*, 1995).

152

BIOLOGICAL EXPLANATIONS OF AGGRESSION

The role of neural and hormonal mechanisms in aggression

There is little doubt that neural and hormonal mechanisms play a part in many human behaviours. Hormone levels have been implicated in many psychological disorders, such as depression (see pages 310–311) and eating disorders (see pages 123–129).

Studies have shown links between testosterone measures and aggression in both adolescent males (Olweus *et al.*, 1988) and women (Ehlers *et al.*, 1980). For example, Clare (2000) observes that girls suffering from congenital adrenal hyperplasia, which is implicated in high levels of testosterone, indulge in more rough-and-tumble play. Testosterone appears to be particularly influential during two separate periods of life: the 'critical time period' a few days after birth, during which sensitisation of neural circuits occurs, and in adulthood when testosterone modulates neurotransmitter pathways.

Hormones are certainly linked to behaviour since the presence or absence of hormones has been shown to have numerous effects on an organism. Testosterone has been shown to be correlated with outward displays of human and non-human animal aggression. For example, when levels of testosterone peak around the start of puberty there appears to be a corresponding peak in aggression levels among young boys.

Perhaps unsurprisingly, much of the research that has found a link between testosterone levels and aggression has involved (non-human) animals. This is because the classic methodology has involved hormone removal and replacement in animals. For example, castration leads to a marked decrease in aggression, as shown by castration experimentation on various species. Furthermore, when testosterone is replaced through hormone therapy in these castrated animals, the amount of aggression increases and is restored to its original pre-castration level (Simpson, 2001). As early as 1849, Berthold (reported by Edwards, 1969) observed marked behavioural changes in cockerels after castration and how these effects were reversed when the testes were replaced. A similar pattern has been seen in mice. Male mice who are castrated at birth show decreased levels of aggression even if given huge doses of testosterone as adults. However, if the castration occurs ten days after birth, the difference in aggression compared to controls is much less marked. It is suggested that androgen stimulation in the early days after birth (up to ten days) causes changes in the neural system, which affects aggression levels into adulthood (Motelica-Heino *et al.*, 1993).

So how might testosterone exert its hormonal and behavioural effects? It is thought that testosterone interacts with androgen or oestrogen receptors. During the critical time period soon after birth, testosterone acts to sensitise particular neural circuits in the brain. This sensitisation allows for the effects of testosterone that manifest in adulthood. A hormone such as testosterone can affect neural transmission and the amount of neurotransmitter that is released during synaptic transmission. Testosterone appears to act on serotonergic synapses and lowers the amount of serotonin (or 5-HT) available for synaptic transmission. This is important given that it is fairly well established that the presence of serotonin serves to inhibit aggression, as shown convincingly in studies done on male rhesus monkeys. Serotonin reuptake inhibitors such as Fluoxentine and several other antidepressants lead to a significant decrease in aggression in both monkeys and humans (Simpson, 2001).

The so-called 'subtraction and replacement' testosterone paradigm appears to provide convincing proof that testosterone (under the influence of genes) is implicated in aggression. Sapolsky (1997) suggests that many textbooks include phrases such as 'normal testosterone levels appear to be a prerequisite for normative levels of aggressive behaviour'. Sapolsky argues that this tells us nothing about how testosterone affects individual differences in levels of aggression, nothing about why some men are exceptionally aggressive, and

Figure 4.14 Aggression in cockerels can be reduced when they are castrated

doesn't explain why the highest testosterone levels are not found in the most aggressive individuals. He concludes that if you give four times the level of normal testosterone to castrated animals they do display aggression, but that studies such as these have little relevance for everyday animal and human functioning. Individual differences in testosterone levels do not predict aggressiveness and the relationship is not straightforward.

There are three possible explanations for the testosterone–aggression relationship (Sapolsky, 1997). These are:

1. testosterone causes aggression (if only it were that simple!)

2. aggression increases testosterone secretion

3. neither has an effect on the other.

Although many people would assume that the first answer is the correct one, it seems that the second suggestion is far more likely. Put a number of men together after measuring their testosterone levels and you cannot accurately predict the levels of aggression displayed on the basis of the testosterone measures. However, if you observe who is the most aggressive and *then* measure their testosterone levels, the most aggressive male will usually have the highest level of testosterone. Therefore it is the aggressive behaviour that appears to drive the testosterone levels, not the other way round. Sapolsky (1997) concludes that scientists have been confused as to the cause and effect order because hormones seem more important than behaviour and thus it seems reasonable to conclude that hormones regulate behaviour when it is actually the other way round. There is research to support this behaviour-regulating hormone hypothesis.

Research by Bernhardt *et al.* (1998) has shown that merely watching participants win or lose in sports competitions increases testosterone levels in interested spectators. Highly committed male fans also demonstrate a rise in testosterone just by anticipating a sporting event of their favourite team, compared to fans who are less committed to the team. The research examined two separate groups of fans. The first part measured testosterone levels of male fans attending a basketball game between US rivals Georgia Tech and the University of Georgia in 1991. The second part tracked testosterone levels among male fans watching Brazilian and Italian teams play in the football World Cup Final in 1994. Saliva samples were collected for analysis before and after each game. Bernhardt found that testosterone levels increased by about 20 per cent in fans of winning teams and decreased by about 20 per cent in fans of losing teams. Both games had very close finishes and thus the testosterone effect was probably extremely sudden given that the outcome was not determined until the last few seconds (the World Cup Final went to sudden-death penalties). Looking at a less physical game, Mazur *et al.* (1992) found evidence that losing a chess match also depresses testosterone levels in competitive chess players. According to Dabbs (1998), the evidence is so clear-cut that 'identifying testosterone with aggression is an idea whose time has come and gone'.

Klinesmith *et al.* (2006) also showed how testosterone levels change as a result of behaving aggressively. The study involved male students aged 18–22. They told the men they'd be taking part in a study of the effect of attention to detail on taste sensitivity. A saliva sample was collected for testosterone testing prior to the study commencing. Next, each participant was led into a room where he had to take an object apart and then put it back together again. There were two conditions: half the participants had to dismantle and reassemble a pellet gun, which looked like a Desert Automatic handgun, while the other half were given the board game Mouse Trap to assemble. Fifteen minutes later the men gave another saliva sample. Next, they were given a drink of water with a small drop of chilli sauce in it. They were then given another cup of water and a bottle of chilli sauce. They were told that the 'spiked' water would be given to the next man in the study and they could put as much or as little chilli in as they liked. It was assumed that the more aggressive a man was feeling, the more chilli he would put in. Results showed that testosterone went up about 100 times more in the men who handled the gun than in the men who handled the children's toy. Those participants who handled the gun put three times more hot chilli sauce in the water than those who handled the toy. Indeed many of the gun-handling group were disappointed that the drink wasn't actually going to be given to the next man! The conclusion from the research was that environmental stimuli such as guns may increase aggressiveness partially via increases in the hormone testosterone.

It has been shown that social status also greatly influences the presence/degree of aggressive behaviour in both animals and humans. Higher levels of social status correspond to higher levels of testosterone, although the question of cause and effect remains: is this elevated status a result of elevated testosterone levels and the consequence of some evolutionarily advantageous aggressive behaviour, or is the testosterone level a result of the heightened social status (i.e. building on the well-supported idea that 'winning' social competition leads to an increase in testosterone levels)? Given the findings of Klinesmith *et al.* (2006) and Bernhardt *et al.* (1998) – albeit in different areas – it may be more likely to be the latter.

Sapolsky (1997) has put forward some impressive arguments as to the real role of testosterone in aggression. The first argument involves the 'passive effect' of a hormone. Remove all testosterone and aggression levels plummet; increase to the norm and aggressive levels return to the norm. However, if testosterone is removed and then only 20 per cent of normal levels are reintroduced, levels of aggression revert back to pre-castration levels. It seems you need some testosterone (approximately 20 per cent to 200 per cent normal levels) but that levels only matter when it comes to the extreme. In other words, testosterone is needed but the amount of testosterone doesn't seem to affect aggression levels unless it almost zero or well above normal levels.

Another fascinating argument involves what we'll call the 'middle-ranking monkey' study. Sapolsky (1997) states that if you have five monkeys and you put them together they quickly sort out a dominance hierarchy based on aggressive levels and so forth. Then you take the third-ranking monkey and give him lots and lots of testosterone – enough to supersede the levels of the leader and second-placed monkey. Then you put the testosterone-fuelled third-ranked monkey back in the cage, perhaps with the expectation that he will be aggressive enough to become the most dominant monkey. Indeed, the third-placed monkey does show increased levels of aggression (presumably caused by the testosterone injections), but he remains the third-placed monkey in the hierarchy. The increase in aggression is entirely directed at the unfortunate fourth- and fifth-placed monkeys, whereas the leader and second-placed monkeys still have no problem with the now testosterone-fuelled number three monkey. It seems that testosterone doesn't cause aggression, but it may exaggerate the aggression that is already there as a result of other factors.

Hyenas are amazing animals when it comes to the study of hormones because of their sex-reversal system. Female hyenas in the wild are more aggressive and more socially dominant than their male counterparts. This is quite unusual among mammals, and support for the testosterone causes aggression argument comes from the fact that female hyenas secrete more testosterone-related hormones than males. Indeed, the females produce so much testosterone that their genitalia look so masculinised that it is extremely difficult to tell the sex of a wild hyena. However, Sapolsky (1997) quotes Laurence Frank who runs the University of California at Berkeley's hyena colony, who found that the female hyenas in the colony did not display the same levels of aggression as wild hyenas despite having the same levels of testosterone and elevated androgen levels. It was concluded that this was because the social system was significantly delayed when the animals were transferred from the wild to the university, so the females were not brought up in a social system where females dominated males. Thus, although they had heightened levels of testosterone and androgens, they had not learnt form the social hierarchy about how to behave. Perhaps this is another nail in the coffin of the testosterone-causes-aggression hypothesis.

Key Study 4.3: 'Clinical correlates of aggressive behavior after traumatic brain injury' (Tateno *et al.*, 2003)

Aim/Hypothesis (A01)

To investigate the effect of brain injury on subsequent aggression.

One way of investigating aggression is to examine patients who have suffered a Traumatic Brain Injury (TBI) and subsequently exhibited raised levels of aggressive behaviour. Associations between TBI and neuropsychiatric disorders have been recognised for many years, and aggressive behaviour is one of the most disruptive consequences of these neuropsychiatric disorders (Morton and Wehman, 1995). Estimates of the frequency of aggressive behaviours during the acute period after TBI have ranged from 11 per cent to 96 per cent. This high variability is related to:

- the use of different operational definitions of aggressive behaviour

- different assessment measures of aggressive behaviour (the Overt Aggression Scale is most commonly used)

- the difficulties in obtaining suitable case study patients.

This study examined 89 male Caucasian patients with closed head injury, admitted to two different hospitals in Iowa. A diagnosis of TBI was substantiated by history of post-traumatic amnesia that lasted at least 30 minutes after the traumatic event. Patients with penetrating head injuries, associated spinal cord injury or severe comprehension deficits were excluded from the study. The control group consisted of 26 patients with clinical traumas but without primary or secondary brain damage or spinal cord injury. The majority of patients had been injured in car accidents.

Method/design (A01)

All patients were assessed by psychiatrists using semi-structured interviews. The research team recognised that the measure of aggression of patients prior to the TBI is adversely affected by retrospective bias, so they used aggression measures from many different sources including the police, relatives and friends. Brain scans of all patients were undertaken by a neurologist who was 'blind' to the records of the patients in terms of their psychiatric examinations and their aggressiveness measures.

Results (A01)

There were no significant differences between the two patient groups in terms of age, gender, race and various other socio-economic measures. However, a history of alcohol and substance abuse was reported more in the aggressive patients than non-aggressive patients. A total of 33.7 per cent of the 89 TBI patients met the criteria for being classified as having significant aggressive behaviour during the six months after the head injury. The remaining 59 patients (66.3 per cent) were classified in the non-aggressive group. The non-aggressive group had a greater frequency of diffuse brain injury than aggressive patients, and the frequency of frontal lobe lesions was significantly higher among patients in the aggressive group ($p < 0.005$). In addition, patients with focal frontal lobe lesions showed significantly higher mean aggression scores.

Conclusion (A01)

The results suggest that frontal lobe lesions, including damage to the ascending serotonergic pathways, contribute to both depression and aggression. Similar findings have previously been reported in that abnormalities of the serotonergic system have consistently been implicated in violent and impulsive behaviour (Mysiw and Sandel, 1997).

- How could the researchers have improved the psychiatric assessment procedure to check that the psychiatrists were assessing the patients in a standardised way?

- Why was it important that the neurologist did not know details of the patients' psychiatric examinations?

- What does a significance level of $p < 0.005$ mean?

- Can you think of some further limitations of this research? For example, are there any problems with generalising the results of this study to the wider population? Were there any important differences between the two patient groups prior to the head injuries?

The amygdala is an area of the brain that is also frequently mentioned in relation to aggressive behaviour. When testosterone is injected into the bloodstream and makes its way to the amygdala, it only works by exaggerating the pre-existing pattern of neural firing. It doesn't turn on any neural pathways on its own; it simply increases the firing rate by shortening the resting time between bursts of electrical activity. In other words, it's not causing aggression, it is simply increasing or exaggerating the response to any pre-existing environmental triggers of aggression (Sapolsky, 1998).

Evaluation of neural and hormonal mechanisms in aggression

✗ **Types of aggression:** aggression covers many different forms including predatory, territorial, fear-induced and inter-male aggression. Testosterone appears to be implicated in only certain forms of aggression, such as inter-male aggression, but appears to play no part in, say, predatory aggression (Simpson, 2001).

✗ **Not just testosterone:** although testosterone may sensitise certain neural circuits during the critical time period soon after birth, it does so only within a range that is determined by genetic inheritance. The neural mechanisms that underlie aggression are modified by other factors. For example, many animals display different levels of aggression dependent on the time of year and breeding season, with a corresponding increase in testosterone levels (Simpson, 2001). Hormones cannot cause a particular behavioural outcome such as aggression. The mere presence of testosterone does not inevitably invoke aggression – for example, there are a significant majority of testosterone-fuelled men who are not aggressive. Studies have also shown that neurotransmitters such as serotonin, GABA, noradrenaline and dopamine are all implicated in levels of aggression. The entire endocrine system is a complicated system involving numerous hormones, none of which works independently of the others.

✗ **Human behaviour not animal behaviour:** human behaviour has been shown to be far more complicated than animal behaviour. Although there is strong evidence of a clear link between testosterone levels and aggression in animals, the correlation is less clear in humans. For example, Tomaszewski *et al.* (2003) examined 933 healthy young men and found that there was no difference in testosterone levels between the most angry and aggressive men and the least angry and aggressive. The difference they found was that the most aggressive men were obese and had lower levels of good HDL cholesterol. Other studies have clearly shown that human aggression is mediated by the outcomes of previous aggressive encounters. Chase (1982) showed that aggressive behaviour in humans is affected by learning – that is, the outcome of previous fights influenced subsequent fights. Van de Poll and van Goozen (1992) have even found evidence suggesting that aggression in animals may itself be intrinsically rewarding. In a rather bizarre study, animals with lateral hypothalamic electrodes were allowed to control the level of stimulation by pressing levers. The animals pressed the levers frequently, suggesting that they had positive feelings about the stimulation. After castration, they pressed less, only for the lever pressing level to increase again when they were given hormone replacement. Other factors linked to aggression are the Y chromosome, alcohol consumption and even smell! Indeed, 'since testosterone is present in males that are not aggressive as well as in those that are, it is obvious that another factor(s) is involved, such as cognition and environmental circumstances which have been found to affect the expression of aggression' (Simpson, 2001).

✗ **Methodological problems:** it is not always easy to accurately measure testosterone levels. Measurement of cerebrospinal fluid is thought to be more accurate but is less easy to conduct on human research participants (Higley *et al.*, 1996). The castration subtraction and replacement technique is also not without problems. Apart from ethical concerns, castration affects many hormone systems and this means that the precise effect of any one hormone, such as testosterone, is difficult to determine. Questions continue as to the value of animal studies to human behaviour. However, castration subtraction and replacement techniques cannot be conducted on humans and, as such, these studies are necessarily restricted to animals. Whether we can extrapolate findings from such animal studies remains contentious. Van de Poll and van Goozen (1992) write that 'there is a danger of triviality or even misleading simplification in many of our extrapolations and animal models'.

How Science Works

Read the following extract from Robert Sapolsky's highly readable book, *'The Trouble with Testosterone' and Other Essays on the Human Predicament* (Sapolsky, 1998, Simon & Schuster).

'Testosterone equals aggression' is inadequate for those who would offer a simple biological solution to the violent male. And 'testosterone equals aggression' is certainly inadequate for those who would offer the simple excuse that boys will be boys. Violence is more complex than a single hormone, and it is supremely rare that any of our behaviors can be reduced to genetic destiny. This is science for the bleeding-heart liberal: the genetics of behavior is usually meaningless outside the context of social factors and environment in which it occurs.

- Summarise what Sapolsky means.
- What implications are there for politicians who wish to reduce levels of aggression in our society?

The role of genetic factors in aggression

There is a huge body of research evidence that shows that all behaviour including aggression is influenced by genetic factors. Genetic factors do not work in isolation but alongside environmental factors as well (Grigorenko and Sternberg, 2003). Early research (Court Brown, 1967) concentrated on chromosomal abnormalities, specifically the XYY genotype, as being correlated with aggression. This has not proved to be the case (Milunsky, 2004).

According to Sapolsky (1997), genes are the 'hand behind the scenes', directing testosterone's actions. Genes determine how much testosterone or oestrogen is produced and how quickly it circulates around the body. Genes determine the synthesis of testosterone receptors, and how many and how sensitive such receptors are. Testosterone may affect brain function and contribute to aggression but genes regulate how much testosterone is made and how effectively it works. Genes control our behaviour via the messenger testosterone.

One method used to study aggression genetically is through heritability studies. This typically involves animals, and researchers selectively breed animals in order to see if aggression levels are inherited from parent to offspring. Turner (2007) reports that aggressiveness in pigs is a moderately heritable trait and that aggressive characteristics in pigs can therefore be passed from parents to offspring. Turner suggests that commercial pig farmers might try to selectively breed non-aggressive pigs and hypothesises that if selection pressure is placed on aggressiveness, the average aggressiveness of the herd should fall by up to 5 per cent per year during the early years of selection. Many studies have involved the genetic manipulation of mice. Using reverse genetics, scientists have managed to clone the genetic DNA, and the role of neurotransmitters has been investigated through the use of imitative drugs that mimic these effects. Mutant mice have been produced that lack a gene for the serotonin receptor. Such mice exhibit normal behaviour in most respects but appear to be twice as aggressive as 'normal' mice, as evidenced by them attacking mice who are introduced into their territory. It has also been shown that male mice that are reared alone show a stronger tendency to attack other male mice then those reared with others. It is suggested that this shows that aggression is a natural biological tendency since they could not have learnt the behaviour, having been reared in isolation. The other mice, reared with their parents, had been shown when it was necessary to be aggressive and when it wasn't (Bock and Goode, 1996).

Scientists became interested in a gene called monoamine oxidase A (MAOA) when they discovered by chance in 1995 that mice that lacked it suffered serious anger management problems. The enzyme made by the gene mops up the excess neurotransmitters (the brain's chemical messengers) so mice lacking the gene had unusually high levels of neurotransmitters like serotonin, noradrenaline and dopamine. MAOA-deficient male mice (female mice with the defective gene behaved normally) were quick to attack an intruder in a resident intruder test (when a new mouse is introduced into a cage) and failed to establish

Practical Learning Activity 4.5: Dangerous dogs and the Kennel Club

Read the following extract from the Kennel Club website (http://www.thekennelclub.org.uk/item/928).

Genetics and Behaviour

Genetics (breed) plays only a part in the temperament of an individual dog and scientific studies from around the world show that environment probably has a far greater effect. A large percentage of dog biting incidents are due to the irresponsible actions of owners, who have either not taken the time and trouble to train their dog correctly, or have indeed trained them to behave aggressively. Consequently any legislation based on genetics that ignores the influence of the dog's keeper on its behaviour is likely to be ineffective.

● Why would scientists not be impressed by such statements?
● Why do you think the powers-that-be (law enforcement agencies) have concentrated on the genetics and targeted dog breeds, not dog owners?

Figure 4.15 Aggressiveness in dogs has been selectively bred through the generations

the usual dominant-submissive relationships, which meant that these mice suffered from an increased number of injuries when confined with other male mice (Mattson, 2003). The same gene had previously been implicated in human aggression when it was found that members of a Dutch family whose men suffered from excessive bouts of aggression carried a rare MAOA gene mutation (Cases *et al.*, 1995).

Caspi *et al.* (2002) studied 1,037 children (442 boys) born in 1972 in Dunedin, New Zealand. The children were studied for 26 years, from birth to adulthood, and the researchers examined the genetic make-up of the children, concentrating on a gene that controls production of MAOA. Participants were recorded as either having high or low activity levels of MAOA. The research team also examined the upbringing of the children, noting incidences of abuse and maltreatment as children. Then the research team measured antisocial behaviour, using four criteria: diagnosis of conduct disorder during adolescence; conviction for a violent crime; tendency towards violent behaviour; and signs of an antisocial personality. In all four areas, men who had been maltreated or abused as children but who had the genotype for high MAOA activity were far less likely to show antisocial behaviour as adults. In contrast, while maltreated men without the genotype for high MAOA activity made up only 12 per cent of the group studied, they accounted for 44 per cent of the group's convictions for violent crimes. On its own, the MAOA gene variant had no effect, but if men who carried the MAOA gene were abused as children, then they were over three times more likely to commit violent crime. In adults, a gene that generated higher levels of MAOA seemed to act as a buffer or promote 'trauma resistance' against the potential negative effects of maltreatment experienced in childhood. The gene's effects were not so noticeable in girls since it is found only in the X chromosome. Girls have two X chromosomes and it is suggested that the version of the gene found in one of their X chromosomes could cancel out the effects of the other.

Later still, Newman *et al.* (2005) investigated the role of the MAOA gene in macaque monkeys. They examined 45 unrelated male monkeys raised with or without their mothers, and tested them for competitive and social group aggression. They also measured the activity of the MAOA gene and these genotypes were scored for assessing genetic and environmental influences on aggression. They concluded that aggressiveness is influenced by a variation in MAOA activity and that this is in itself

STRETCH AND CHALLENGE

Read the extract below, taken from an article at http://social.jrank.org/pages/300/Heredity-Versus-Environment.html.

Despite its nomenclature, the nature–nurture controversy in its current state is less dichotomous than commonly believed. In other words, the term 'nature–nurture controversy' suggests a polarization of nature and nurture; continuity and interaction, however, more aptly describe the central processes involved in this controversy. Therefore, it is not about whether either heredity or environment is solely responsible for observed outcomes. Rather, it is more about the extent to which these factors influence human development and the ways in which various factors influence each other.

For example, following the fifteen-person massacre committed by two boys at Columbine High School in Colorado in April 1999, the media were flooded with people offering their interpretations of what drove these high school students to commit this heinous and violent act. Some were quick to attribute the boys' actions to such environmental factors as inadequate parenting practices in their families and the violence prevalent and even glorified in the American media. Others, by contrast, were convinced that these boys were mentally ill as defined in the American Psychiatric Association's Diagnostic and Statistical Manual of Mental Disorders and that their ability to make responsible judgments had been impaired, perhaps due to a chemical imbalance to which they were genetically predisposed. Which argument is 'correct,' according to most researchers? Probably neither. Most theorists agree that both nature and nurture are intertwined and influence most aspects of human emotion, behavior, and cognition in some ways. Given the prevailing views in current psychology, most researchers would agree that the violent acts committed by these boys probably stemmed from an unfortunate interaction among various hereditary and environmental factors. Researchers, however, may disagree on (1) the extent to which heredity and environment each influences particular developmental outcomes and (2) the way in which a mixture of hereditary and environmental factors relate to each other. In other words, the controversy involves the extent of contribution as well as the nature of interaction among a variety of genetic and environmental forces.

… mental health, education, and applied psychology researchers are especially concerned about optimizing the developmental outcomes among people from all backgrounds. To this end, knowing that there is a .86 heritability estimate for IQ scores among identical twins, for example, is not particularly helpful in terms of establishing ways of maximizing the life choices and opportunities for individuals. In attaining such goals, it is crucial to understand how various factors relate to each other. Naturally, in order to do so, one must first identify which factors are involved in the development of a given trait. Unfortunately, researchers have had very limited success in identifying specific genetic patterns that influence particular psychological and behavioral characteristics.

- Consider the methodological problems with twin and adoption studies.
- Consider the problems you might face as a researcher if you concluded that aggression was almost entirely genetic. What might the general public, policy makers and the media make of such research?
- Consider the problems you might face as a researcher if you concluded that aggression was almost entirely a result of upbringing or environmental influence. What might the general public, policy makers and the media make of such research?
- Discuss whether it might be possible to identify individuals at risk prior to them committing violent acts. Would this be a good thing for society?

In the late 1800s, the criminologist Cesare Lombroso suggested that many criminals were evolutionary throwbacks who were biologically predisposed to be aggressive. The idea was based loosely on the ideas of Darwin, and suggested that criminals had primitive features such as long arms, sloped foreheads and certain facial features. This idea has been completely discredited and has tarnished later theories on the genetics of aggression.

One way to study the possible genetic influence on aggression is to use twin studies. Monozygotic (MZ), or identical, twins, because they are formed from one egg, have the same genetic make-up. Dizygotic (DZ), or non-identical, twins are formed when two eggs are fertilised at the same time, and therefore contain genetic material no more similar than that of regular brothers and sisters. The degree of similarity in a pair of twins with respect to the presence or absence of a particular genetic pattern is called concordance. By studying the concordance rates of crime between identical twins and their fraternal counterparts, one may find how much significance genetic material has in leading humans towards criminal and aggressive behaviour. Berkowitz (1993) reports that studies from the 1930s using these methods found an average concordance rate of 75 per cent for monozygotic and 24 per cent for dizygotic twins. Later studies that used more accurate methods reported 48 per cent concordance for mono- and 20 per cent for dizygotic twins. Regardless of the specific figures, the results appear to support the idea that genetics do influence crime rates, including levels of aggression.

sensitive to social experiences early in development and that its functional outcome might depend on social context. In other words, we have a genetic/environment interaction. Uncovering the nature of this genetic/environment interaction is the goal of much genetic research today.

Adoption studies

Another way that researchers have investigated genetic influences on aggression is through adoption studies. Adoption studies exploit the fact that an adopted person shares a similar genetic make-up to their parents but is brought up in a different environment. If aggression is primarily genetically determined, the adopted child will show more similar levels of aggression to their biological parents than their adopted parents.

Adoption studies have corroborated the strong genetic and the weak common family effect on adult antisocial behaviour. One Danish study conducted by Mednick *et al.* (1984) followed some 14,000 adoptees and found that boys with no criminal parents, either adoptive or biological, had a baseline rate of criminal conviction of 14 per cent. If the adoptive but not the biological parents were criminals, boys still had a conviction rate of only 15 per cent. If the biological but not adoptive parents were criminal, the rate increased to 20 per cent. If both biological and adoptive parents were criminal, the rate increased to 25 per cent. Such figures seem to suggest that biological characteristics that increase the likelihood of antisocial behaviour and aggression are in part transmitted genetically from biological parents to their offspring, and that this has a greater effect than environmental factors.

However, Miles and Carey (1997) conducted a meta-analysis on data from 24 genetically informative studies by using various personality measures of aggression. There was a strong overall genetic effect that may account for up to 50 per cent of the variance in aggression. They concluded that this effect was not attributed to methodological inadequacies in the twin or adoption designs and that the influence of genes increased but that of family environment decreased at later ages. Interestingly, they noted that observational ratings of laboratory behaviour found no evidence for heritability and a very strong family environment effect. Given that almost all substantive conclusions about the genetics of personality have been drawn from self- or parental reports, this last finding has obvious and important implications for the method-ologies employed in aggression research.

A meta-analysis of 51 twin and adoption studies was conducted by Rhee and Waldman (2002) to estimate the magnitude of genetic and environmental influence on anti-social behaviour. The best-fitting model included proportions of variance due to genetic influences (41 per cent), shared environmental influences (16 per cent) and non-shared environmental influences (43 per cent). There were no significant differences in the magnitude of genetic and environmental influences for males and females. With age, during adolescence, the importance of genetic factors grew stronger and that of common environment grew weaker.

Evaluation of the genetic basis of aggression

✗ **Methodology of twin and adoption studies:** twin studies hope to disentangle the effects of genetics and environment (upbringing). It is hypothesised that all twins probably share a similar upbringing and thus the only difference between identical and non-identical twins is that identical twins share the same genetic inheritance. However, many psychologists suggest that this idea may be false. It is argued that identical twins may form closer relationships than fraternal twins, so they influence each other to a greater extent and are more likely to copy each other's aggressive actions than is the case with non-identical twins. In addition, identical twins may be treated far more similarly than non-identical twins and they may have a more similar upbringing, suggesting that there is a stronger environmental influence on their similarities (Berkowitz, 1993). One note of caution regarding adoption studies is that environmental factors such as the stress of being adopted may in themselves have led to anti-social behaviour. This may explain *some* of the increase in the antisocial behaviour of adopted boys with criminal records in Mednick *et al.*'s (1984) study.

✗ **Operationalisation measures:** Rhee and Waldman (2002) noted in their meta-analysis that different researchers used different methods to collect data. This means that direct comparison between the research is not possible. Some of the differences included the measurement of antisocial behaviour (self-report versus criminal convictions), methods used to determine whether twins were MZ or DZ, and age of the participants and age when adopted; all were significant moderators of the magnitude of genetic and environmental influences on antisocial behaviour.

✗ **Multi-gene studies:** despite decades of research, the genetic basis of aggression has proved elusive. It appears that there are numerous genes involved, each of which, interacting with environmental stimuli, causes aggression (Tremblay *et al.*, 2005). It is likely that each genetic variant that influences antisocial behaviour will have only a small impact on an individual's overall predisposition to such behaviour (Morley and Hall, 2003). It is therefore unsurprising that individual studies of single candidate genes do not always produce the same result (Ioannidis *et al.*, 2001). Some researchers have begun to address this problem by studying multiple susceptibility genes for behavioural traits and disorders that increase the risk of engaging in antisocial behaviour. Comings (2000) and Comings *et al.* (2000a, 2000b) have simultaneously examined multiple candidate genes for their involvement in ADHD, CD and ODD. These studies suggest that some of the genes in the serotonin, dopamine and noradrenergic pathways do influence the development of these disorders. However, some of the results of these studies conflict with the results of some single-gene studies. The authors found that the noradrenergic genes had a stronger influence than other groups, but only single-gene studies of DBH have produced relatively consistent positive results. It remains to be seen whether this inconsistency is due to different research methods, or the fact that the noradrenergic pathway has not been as well investigated in single-gene studies (Morley and Hall, 2003).

✔/✗ **Animal research:** there have been many studies using non-human animals in order to study aggression through the generations. There are fewer ethical concerns with using animals in this way and the quicker breeding cycles of such animals allow for inter-generational effects to be seen relatively quickly. Much of the research involves mice. Mice have proved to be a useful model for human behaviour since they have genes and proteins that serve some similar functions in humans (Southwick, 1970). However, it is self-evident that there are also many qualitative and quantitative differences between mice and men!

Conclusion

So what does all this research tell us about aggression and genetics? It shows that, while genetics have an influence on aggression, it is not 'aggressive genes' that are inherited whose presence will cause criminal tendencies and whose absence will result in a perfect child, but rather that genes can trigger a genetic sensitivity to the environment, causing the combination of aggressive genes and an 'aggressive' upbringing to have negative and aggressive results.

The truth is that we cannot be certain whether or not testosterone causes aggression. The evidence suggests that testosterone is more closely linked to aggression in non-human animals but the link seems less strong in humans. We are left with the age-old problem of cause and effect, and studies contradict one another as to the precise role testosterone plays in human aggression. One benefit of this contrasting research is that there is plenty of material for an essay arguing the precise role of testosterone and aggression! Genetics also appear to play a vital part in aggressive behaviour. Psychologists need to be aware of the reductionist approach whereby we hope to find a single gene (or hormone or neurotransmitter or part of the brain) responsible for everything. However, as Sapolsky (1998) puts it so well, 'even if you completely understood how genes regulate all the important physical factors involved in aggression – testosterone synthesis and secretion, the brain's testosterone receptors, the amygdala neurons and their levels of transmitters, the favourite colour of the hypothalamus – you still wouldn't be able to predict levels of aggression accurately in a group of normal individuals'.

AGGRESSION AS AN ADAPTIVE RESPONSE

Evolutionary explanations of human aggression

A (very) brief theory of evolution

Although Darwin published his groundbreaking book, *On the Origin of Species*, in 1859, it was not until the 1970s that psychology took an evolutionary approach to human behaviour. It's helpful to understand the essential features of this theory, as listed below (adapted from Cartwright, 2001).

- Animals are grouped into species – for example, humans belong to the species *Homo sapiens*.

- Within each species, some variation exists. People are not identical to one another in either looks or behaviour.

- Many looks and behaviours are determined by the genome of the individual. The genome consists of DNA strands inherited from their parents (50 per cent from each parent).

- Individuals pass on their DNA to their offspring. Offspring are not identical to their parents since genes can suffer from mutations or not be 'switched on'. Some genes are expressed only if they occur in certain combinations. Thus, certain characteristics may 'skip' a generation.

- The majority of mutations are harmful and tend to be selected against. However, sometimes a mutation may confer some benefit to the animal.

163

- All animals require resources and often these are limited. Hence there is competition among organisms.

- Some organisms will be more successful in the competition than others. Indeed, some of the mutated variations will have an advantage over other organisms (the 'survival of the fittest').

- Since they are more successfully adapted to their environment, successful variants will breed more and produce more offspring.

- If the variant is sufficiently different, then a new species may occur and natural selection will have led to evolutionary change.

- As a consequence of natural selection through this process of adaptation, organisms will become expertly designed, not only in their structure, but also in their behaviours.

- Since we've been around in some form or another for about 5 million years, by now we (humans) should be fairly well adapted to our environment and reproductive survival – if not for Britain in the early twenty-first century, at least as a hunter-gatherer on the African savannah.

Sociobiology (sometimes called evolutionary psychology) is the term used to explain human behaviour through the theory of evolution by natural selection, with the additional consideration of the influence of social factors on behaviour.

The evolutionary explanation of aggression

The evolutionary explanation of aggression suggests that aggression serves an important function in terms of both individual survival as well as procreation potential. In essence, competition arises when resources are limited and therefore animals/species must actively compete in order to increase their own 'fitness'. Therefore aggression is advantageous at both the individual and genetic levels. Newman *et al.* (2005) discovered that forms of a gene linked to aggressive behaviour in macaque monkeys have been around in primates for at least 25 million years. For the

aggression gene to survive so long, it must have provided some advantage to its hosts.

A simple explanation for aggression is that human beings are somehow 'programmed' for violence by their basic nature and that humans have an inbuilt tendency for violence. Sigmund Freud suggested that we all possess a powerful 'death wish' (thanatos). This death wish is directed outwards towards others as aggression. A related view suggests that aggression springs mainly from an inherited fighting instinct that human beings share with other species (Lorenz, 1966). In the past, males seeking desirable mates found it necessary to compete with other males. One way of eliminating competition was through successful aggression, which drove rivals away or even eliminated them through fatal conflict. Aggression can thus be seen to serve an adaptive purpose, one that has evolved as a natural element in the behavioural repertoire of some species because it facilitates survival and adaptation to the environment. Because males who were adept at such behaviour were more successful in securing mates and in transmitting their genes to offspring, this may have led to the development of a genetically influenced tendency for males to 'aggress' against other males. Males would not be expected to aggress against females, because females view males who engage in such behaviour as too dangerous to themselves and potential future children, resulting in rejection of them as potential mates. For this reason, males have weaker tendencies to aggress against females than against other males (Denisiuk, 2004).

Spriggs (1999) argued that, as hunter-gatherers, our ancestors formed groups 25,000 years ago on the African savannah. The social structure of these groupings provided better opportunities for food, mating, safety and companionship. These ancestral hunter-gatherer social groups were dominated by the physical strength, stamina and stature of the males. Before plant domestication some 10,000 years ago, fruits, berries and nuts were not always easily available. This problem-solving ability of learning to capture small animals, and then larger ones, ensured our survival as a species. Our ancestors survived on their hunting abilities, assisted by an adaptive 'aggressive' tendency necessary to accomplish the task. Once the cultural habits of male dominance were established, they were reinforced by further continued successes – in most, but not all, cases, success in using force over females to dominate gene distribution. The adaptive response of the female to this aggressive tendency was to adapt to the trait, thus gaining resources for her children. Another possibility is that the male became aggressive to gain the favour of the female and thus pass on his genes. Finding great advantage in this arrangement to their gender, males dominated by the use of strength and stamina in a harsh and unforgiving world. Since evolutionary success was built on the foundation of the aggressive male and responsive female, evolution continued to favour those social groups dominated by 'naturally selecting' cultures in which this aggression and response dominated. However, because of child-rearing and the investment required (typically by the females), males took the most and gave little back. It is argued by some that things haven't changed a great deal. In the past, males controlled most of the resources and used those resources in a variety of manipulative methods. The species survived, and the survival behaviour became embedded into genetic instructions to ensure that survival.

But what led us down this genetic path? In any group, conditions vary, leading to various cumulative results. Some male hunters were more successful then others. Some clans had numerically more sons, sons that were better at accumulating resources. This may also partly explain why, in various cultures, it is sometimes seen as more desirable to have males in childbirth. Those men who combined the traits of strength, stamina and cunning began to outperform and bring back more resources than others. As a result, their stature grew, while that of others withered. This male dominance in hunting led to battles for dominance in territory and the selection of females, who are essential elements in gene transference. It is hypothesised that, in some groups, this may have led to the creation of a single dominant male who controlled access to the females; if other males wanted access, they found it necessary to form an alliance with the dominant male. Alternatively, this sexual dominance was eventually cracked by the cunning resourcefulness of the females. To do this, the females had to most likely 'cheat' on their dominant male by stealing away from the group for a dalliance with a non-dominant male (Spriggs, 1999).

Sometimes we can try to hypothesise about our evolutionary past by studying non-human animals. Smuts (1995) describes how aggression in male primates is used to sexually coerce females. She cites Jane Goodall (1986), who recounts the so-called 'chimpanzee dating'

game. Among the many scenarios, males gather around attractive oestrous females and try to lure them away from other males for a one-on-one sexual dalliance. The females try to resist the demands of less desirable males. The males use aggression to counter this female resistance. Chimpanzee males appear to use force in order to try to increase the chances that a female will mate with them, or to decrease the chances that she will mate with someone else. However, this form of sexual coercion is not widespread in all primate species. For example, vervet monkeys and bonobos (pygmy chimpanzees), rarely if ever try to coerce females sexually. Smuts (1995) notes that female primates often form female (and less frequently male) friendship groups to counteract this aggression from unwelcome males. She suggests that such alliances can even be seen in human behaviour throughout the world. She cites the South American Yanomamo people, whose men frequently abduct and rape women from neighbouring villages and severely beat their wives for suspected adultery. However, among the Aka people of the Central African Republic, male aggression against women has never been observed. She notes that most human societies, including our own, fall between these two extremes.

Females tend to be much more choosy in selecting a mate since they have a greater investment in their offspring (Buss and Malamuth, 1996). Women tend to select men who are able to provide for potential offspring through the resources they can bring to any relationship. Men are therefore more competitive with each other (intrasexual competition) for access to women. This has created a strong demand for men who are able to provide valuable resources, resulting in the characteristics of assertiveness, aggressiveness and sensitivity to hierarchy found in men. In primitive hunting cultures, such men literally brought home the bacon!

Sadalla, Kenrick and Vershure (1987) also report that dominant behaviour in males increases their attractiveness to females. Although male dominance enhanced their sexual attractiveness, it didn't improve their likeability. However, this dominant trait may have arisen as a result of social coercion. For example, a woman who chose a dominant aggressor for a sexual partner may have chosen him in order to stay alive, rather than expressed a personal preference for dominant men.

Evaluation of evolutionary explanations of aggression

✗ **Unfalsifiability of evolutionary explanations:** given that evolutionary psychology hypothesises on human behaviour from thousands of years ago, it is difficult to test empirically. Some scientists argue that evolutionary hypotheses are scientifically indefensible. This follows from the Popperian view of science involving hypothesis testing using empirical methods. The counter-argument is that evolutionary psychology progresses because of its ability to 'digest apparent anomalies and generate novel predictions and explanations' based on the Lakatosian Philosophy of Science (Ketelaar and Ellis, 2000). (If you wish to investigate the Lakatosian Philosophy of Science further, I suggest you go into a dark room, lie down and reconsider.)

✗ **Different types of aggression:** Krahe (2001) notes that there are many different types of sexual assault. For example, assaults on children, on post-menopausal women and on individuals genetically related to the aggressor are widespread, and yet do not seem to serve any obvious reproductive fitness for the aggressor. How can these forms of aggression be explained by the evolutionary perspective?

✗ **Reductionist argument:** as we have seen in this chapter, there are other explanations for aggression, from the biological to the social environment. Trying to explain a behaviour as complex as aggression by using one explanation is reductionist. Indeed, it cannot conclusively be shown that aggressive tendencies are adaptive in humans. Opponents suggest that aggression is the product of environment and learning. Evolutionary theorists don't deny learning, but insist there's also an innate mechanism or drive.

✗ **Cross-cultural differences in aggression:** a common criticism of the evolutionary explanation of aggression is that individual differences in aggression levels, both within and between cultures, weaken the argument. Bloom and Dess (2003) provide an illuminating example of why this may not be so. They give the example of the callus-producing mechanism, which causes blisters, that is universal in all humans. However, there are large differences within and between cultures in the thickness and distribution of calluses or blisters. For example, academics get very few, tennis players get them on their hands, carpet layers on their knees and Yanomamo people get them on their feet. Thus there are huge variations within and between cultures, but the mechanism remains universal. The mechanism is universal subject to contextual variations – perhaps the same is true with regard to aggression.

STRETCH AND CHALLENGE: The Selfish Gene

Richard Dawkins's 1976 book, *The Selfish Gene*, has sold over a million copies, and is concerned with a gene-centred view of evolution. Although not an easy read, it would give you an interesting perspective on the evolutionary perspective. However, the account by Dawkins is not without criticism and this should be borne in mind by readers.

Infidelity and jealousy

Jealousy can be a potent cause of aggression. Daly and Wilson (1988) report that an unexpectedly high proportion of homicides are committed by men who have just been left (or are about to be left) by their partners. Jealousy is defined as an emotional state that is aroused by a perceived threat to a relationship or position. It motivates behaviour (including aggression) that counters the threat (Buss *et al.*, 1992). Jealousy is a reaction related to fear and rage, and makes one want to protect, maintain and prolong the association of love. Infidelity involves a sexual partner (particularly a spouse) being unfaithful. Infidelity can be sexual, emotional, or both. *Sexual infidelity* is any behaviour that involves sexual contact, such as kissing, intimate touching, oral sex or sexual intercourse. *Emotional infidelity* involves the formation of a emotional attachment to or affection for another person, and can involve such behaviours as flirting, dating, intimate conversations or falling in love. Although 99 per cent of married people expect their spouse to be faithful (Treas and Giesen, 2000), marital infidelity figures are much higher. Greeley (1994) reports that 11 per cent of females and 21 per cent of males admit to extra-marital sex. Of course, infidelity does not just relate to marriage, and people in long-lasting relationships usually expect their sexual partners to be faithful too.

Much of the anger and blame in situations where a partner has been unfaithful focuses on the partner rather than the rival. De Weerth and Kalma (1993) concluded that women experience stronger feelings of anger at both their partner and rivals than do men. They asked students at a Dutch university to indicate how

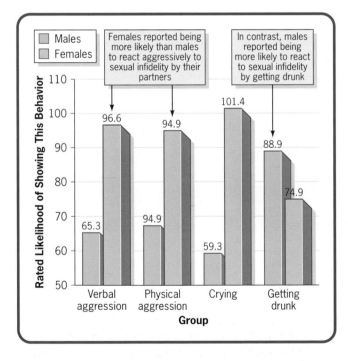

Figure 4.16 *Gender differences in sexual jealousy: as shown here, females indicated that they would be more likely than males to respond aggressively to sexual infidelity by their lover*
Source: *based on data from de Weerth and Kalma (1993)*

they would react if they learned their lover was having an affair with another person. The results are shown in Figure 4.17. Females reported that they would be more likely to respond with verbal and physical abuse of their lover, whereas males more often responded that they would get drunk! Of course, this relates specifically to sexual jealousy, not emotional jealousy (see below) and may merely be indicative of the way Dutch students behave.

The evolutionary explanation for infidelity and jealousy is related to the evolutionary approach to mating behaviour. There appear to be marked gender differences in what men and women look for in a potential partner (intersexual selection). Men and women appear to use different criteria when it comes to sexual selection. In a comprehensive study of 37 cultures on six continents and five islands, Buss (1989) found that women value prospective male suitors on a cluster of characteristics related to resource potential. These included good financial prospects, ambition, industriousness, older age and emotional maturity. However, men value potential female partners in terms of fecundity, defined as the ability to produce and care for children. Fecundity is assessed in terms of a preference for youthful looks and physical attractiveness. More specifically men prefer 'baby face', or infantile, features (i.e. large eyes and a small nose) since these are assessed as correlated with attractiveness, fertility and perceptions of few medical problems (Cunningham, 1986).

The evolutionary perspective specifies that men and women are similar in all domains except the ones in which they have faced different adaptive problems throughout human evolutionary history. Buss (1995) and other evolutionary psychologists argue that men and women differ in their responses to infidelity in ways that have resulted from different adaptations to different reproductive problems. The evolutionary perspective does not dispute that both forms of infidelity – emotional and sexual – are disturbing to both sexes. Instead, evolutionary psychologists believe that the cues that trigger sexual jealousy are weighted differently in men and women (Buss *et al.*, 1999).

Men should be more distressed over acts of sexual infidelity, because men have faced the adaptive problem of uncertain paternity. While a woman is always certain a child is hers, men are not since they never know for certain the moment of fertilisation. Therefore men run the risk of investing resources in a child that is not their own. It follows that if a man senses that his partner is being sexually unfaithful, this triggers an 'alarm' and evokes sexual jealousy and possible aggression. Some male aggression can be viewed as sexual jealousy and possessiveness, which arise from paternal uncertainty (Archer, 1996). When a male is not sure if 'his' child is indeed his, he will become jealous, which will bring out aggressiveness in him as he tries to find out the child's paternity.

Women, on the other hand, are certain of maternity, making their concern of a different nature. A woman's adaptive problem is finding a father who is willing and able to invest his resources in a child for the long term. According to evolutionary theory, this is why emotional infidelity is more upsetting to a woman than sexual infidelity. If she finds that the father of her child is emotionally involved with another woman, it is a potential threat that he will begin to invest his resources in the new relationship. Specifically, if her mate becomes interested in another woman, this will result in a loss of his time, attention, energy, resources, protection and commitment to her children. This loss is essential to her child's survival and is a cue for sexual jealousy (Buunk et al., 1996). This signals an 'alarm' of a different nature in the woman: emotional jealousy (Ahrndt, 2005).

There is a great deal of evidence to back up these sex differences supporting this perspective (Buss et al., 1999; Buunk et al., 1996). Much of the experimental support comes from studies that use forced-choice, hypothetical scenarios created by Buss et al. (1992).

Participants are instructed to think of a serious, committed romantic relationship that they have had in the past, that they currently have or that they would like to

How Science Works

Practical Learning Activity 4.6: Scientific justification for male behaviour?

The evolutionary argument seems to suggest that men are programmed by their genes to be sexually unfaithful. Discuss whether this might be used by some men to explain infidelity.

have. They are then asked to indicate which would cause them more distress: imagining their partner forming a deep emotional attachment to another person, or imagining their partner enjoying passionate sexual intercourse with another person. In selecting the choice that is the most distressing, results generally show that women are more distressed than men at the thought of their partner becoming emotionally involved with another, while men are more distressed than women at the prospect of their partner becoming sexually involved (Ahrndt, 2005).

In another study, Buss et al. (1999) set up the scenarios so that each form of infidelity was mutually exclusive (partner engaged in sexual or emotional infidelity but not both). The results showed that a larger percentage of men than women reported greater distress in response to sexual infidelity (when there was no emotional involvement) relative to distress in response to imagining their partner engaging in emotional infidelity (with no sexual involvement).

Box 4.1: An example of some of the possible infidelity scenarios used (Nannini and Meyers, 2000)

An example of one scenario representing the condition of sexual infidelity follows.

Your boyfriend/girlfriend arrives home from a week-long business trip only to inform you that he/she met someone that he/she found very physically attractive. Although they had few common interests they engaged in sexual intercourse throughout the week. You are sure that your partner loves you very much and highly values your relationship together. Your partner has reassured you that even if he/she did have sex with someone else his/her attraction to the person was purely physical.

For the remaining two conditions of infidelity for this particular scenario version, the narrative remained the same, with the exception of those parts that detailed the nature of the imagined partner's involvement with the individual outside of the romantic relationship.

The condition of emotional infidelity for this scenario version read as follows.

Your boyfriend/girlfriend arrives home from a week-long business trip only to inform you that he/she met someone that he/she found very intriguing. They spent the entire week together exploring their common interests. You are sure that your partner loves you very much and highly values your relationship together. Your partner has reassured you that even if he/she enjoyed the company of someone else while he/she was away they did not engage in sexual intercourse.

The last condition of infidelity – both sexual and emotional involvement – for this scenario version read as follows.

Your boyfriend/girlfriend arrives home from a week-long business trip only to inform you that he/she met someone that he/she found very intriguing. They spent the entire week together exploring their common interests. Before your partner returned home they had engaged in sexual intercourse. You are sure that your partner loves you very much and highly values your relationship together.

What methodological criticisms might be made of these scenarios?

Buss *et al.* found further support for the evolutionary perspective, with 61 per cent of the men, but only 13 per cent of the women, reporting greater distress with the sexual aspect of the infidelity, while 39 per cent of men and 87 per cent of women were more distressed with the emotional aspect of the infidelity. Buss *et al.* contend that 'Based on the cumulative weight of the evidence … the evolutionary account of jealousy appears to be in good scientific standing' (1999: 149).

Harris (2003) conducted a meta-analysis on sex differences in emotional responses to infidelity. The meta-analysis included 32 studies and generally it was found that men were more likely to report that sexual infidelity would distress them more than emotional infidelity, while women were more likely to report that emotional infidelity would distress them more than sexual infidelity.

Evaluation of the evolutionary explanation of infidelity and jealousy

✗ **Double-shot hypothesis:** the double-shot hypothesis states that participants are most distressed by the infidelity, sexual or emotional, that most clearly implies that the other infidelity, sexual or emotional, is also occurring. Thus, an individual may be more distressed by emotional infidelity than sexual infidelity because she/he assumes that if there has been emotional infidelity there has also been sexual infidelity, but does not assume that there has been emotional infidelity if there has been sexual infidelity (Ahrndt, 2005). Men are thought to be capable of sex without emotional involvement, while women typically are not. Because of this assumption, when given the choice between their partner's commission of sexual or emotional infidelity, men will choose sexual infidelity as more distressing than emotional infidelity because they assume that it is likely that if a woman is having sex, she must also be emotionally involved. In this case, men will choose sexual infidelity as more distressing because it implies that both sexual and emotional infidelity are occurring. Conversely, women assume that because men are able to have 'meaningless sex' without emotional attachment, a man's emotional infidelity is more distressing because it implies that he is sexually *and* emotionally involved. This would prompt a woman to be more distressed by emotional than sexual infidelity (Harris and Christenfeld, 1996). There is certainly some research to support this hypothesis (Cramer *et al.*, 2000).

✗ **Operationalisation of infidelity:** Dreznick (2004) suggests that there may be an alternative explanation to evolutionary theory, such as a difference in beliefs of what constitutes infidelity. If men do not perceive emotional infidelity to be infidelity, then they would not be particularly jealous in response to a partner's emotional infidelity.

✗ **Methodology:** researchers have questioned whether the hypothetical forced-choice method is a valid measure of sex differences in responses to infidelity. Some researchers have suggested that the results may simply be a product of the methodology employed (Harris, 2002, 2003). The first problem involves the use of hypothetical questions. Many participants may have experienced infidelity at first hand and there seems no reason to not ask about these real instances rather than use hypothetical examples. Indeed, Harris (2002, 2003) did ask about real instances of infidelity and found no male/female difference in the degree to which they were distressed by emotional vs sexual infidelity. Furthermore, both males and females reported focusing slightly more on emotional than sexual aspects of their partner's infidelity. A related problem involves the forced-choice nature of the method. Participants have to state which type of infidelity would distress them more: sexual or emotional. This does not allow the participant to specify their level of or the quantity of their agreement. When continuous measures of emotional distress are used it should be the case that men should be much more distressed by sexual than emotional infidelity and women should be much more distressed by emotional than sexual infidelity. However, this does not appear to be the case (Ahrndt, 2005). Even in Buss *et al.*'s original study (1992), 49 per cent of men said they would be more distressed by sexual infidelity and 51 per cent of men by emotional infidelity, while 19 per cent of women reported that they would be more distressed by their partner's sexual infidelity and 81 per cent of the women reported they would be more distressed over emotional involvement. These results are not explained by evolutionary theory. As Hupka and Bank (1996) argue, *most* men should become upset over the sexual infidelity and *most* women over emotional infidelity in order for the evolutionary perspective to be supported.

Conclusion

Even if we accept that the evolutionary explanation is adequate to explain human (male) aggression it does mean that there is an inevitability to the continued dominance of this male 'aggression'. Just because this direction of evolution allowed us to arrive at this place in time successfully, does not mean it has to continue (Spriggs, 1999). Indeed, in modern societies, extreme levels of aggression are likely to be damaging to the 'fitness' of the individual since violent individuals are likely to be caught and punished, perhaps with imprisonment. Furthermore, a fairly high proportion of murderers commit suicide, which is hardly fitness-maximising (Cartwright, 2001).

Explanations of group display in humans (for example, sports events and lynch mobs)

There are numerous explanations for group displays in humans. The best known are described below.

Deindividuation

Although we all carry a sense of our own identity,

sometimes we lose it by becoming part of a large group or crowd, such as a mob or army. Deindividuation into a group results in a loss of individual identity and a gaining of the social identity of the group. The three most important factors for deindividuation in a group of people are:

1. anonymity – knowing you won't be accountable for your actions

2. diffusion of responsibility – feeling less responsibility for your actions because they are shared in the group (see below)

3. group size – a larger group increases the above two factors.

✔ Specification Hint

There are very many explanations for group display in humans. The specification requires you to know 'explanations', so this means that you must learn a minimum of TWO. Deindividuation has already been discussed on pages 140–142, and can also be used as an explanation for group display in humans.

Bystander apathy

This refers to the phenomenon where an individual is less likely to intervene in an emergency situation when a group of other people are present than when they are alone. There are two main explanations for this apathy. These are as follows.

1. **Pluralistic ignorance:** in ambiguous situations, people look to others for help as to what to do (social reality). In an emergency situation, if all the other bystanders are also uncertain and looking for guidance, then looking to others can produce the wrong guidance, sometimes resulting in no action at all.

2. **Diffusion of responsibility:** the presence of other people can influence the decision-making process. If there are lots of people present, then a diffusion of responsibility occurs whereby each person feels less responsible for dealing with the emergency. Rather surprisingly, the more bystanders there are present, the less likelihood there is that one of them will accept responsibility. In essence, 'someone else can help'.

STRETCH AND CHALLENGE: The case study of Kitty Genovese

Kitty Genovese was a New Yorker who was murdered in 1964 in the Queens area of New York. Her murder was apparently witnessed by up to 38 people who did little to help her despite the attack lasting approximately half an hour. The outcry that followed the crime led psychologists to investigate 'bystander apathy'. Indeed, bystander apathy is sometimes referred to as the 'Genovese Syndrome'. The Genovese case is a fascinating one, and highlights many areas of psychological interest. Her attacker (Winston Moseley) was caught and still resides in a US prison.

Further details of the case and its importance to psychology can be found on the web or in the book *Classic Case Studies in Psychology* (Rolls, 2005).

Contagion theory

This suggests that groups exert a hypnotic effect on their members. This effect, combined with the anonymity aspect of groups, results in irrational, emotional or 'mob' behaviour (Le Bon, 1995, originally published in 1896). The theory also suggests that the behaviour of the group is formed by its members coming together as a group, not as a result of any pre-existing individual tendencies they may have. The main problem with the theory is that much group behaviour is not irrational or 'mob-like'.

Convergence theory

This theory argues that the behaviour of a group is a result of like-minded individuals coming together. In other words, if a group becomes violent (a mob or riot), convergence theory would argue that this is not because the crowd encouraged violence but rather because people who wanted to become violent came together in the crowd. The main problem with this theory is that although some groups are the meeting of like-minded people, some crowds actually spur individuals into behaviour in which they would otherwise not engage.

Emergent-norm theory (Turner and Killian, 1987)

Another theory to explain group behaviour is the snappily titled 'emergent-norm theory of crowd dynamics', proposed by Turner and Killian (1972). They argue that crowd behaviour is neither irrational nor entirely predictable. They argue that groups of similar people often gather together for some collective purpose (say, to cheer on their respective team), but this may change during the course of the match day and specific factors (such as the result, a referee's decision or policing of the crowd) may alter the norms within the crowd. Individuals within the crowd may begin the day with the idea of having a joyous celebration of victory, but events may emerge during the day that have an adverse and negative violent effect on their behaviour.

Emergent-norm theory takes a different approach to older theories that concentrate on instinctual or irrational behaviour. It suggests that group behaviour involves norm-governed behaviour. No longer is the group seen as governed by a 'weak collective mind' but by rational group processes. These group processes are governed by normative influence – that is, people act in a compliant way, motivated by seeking approval and avoiding punishment of the group. Turner and Killian (1987) argue that one problem with many groups of people that come together to form groups is that they have few established norms to regulate their behaviour and so the main problem is trying to explain how a norm emerges within the group (hence the title 'emergent-norm theory') (Manstead and Hewstone, 1995)

People who gather in a group may be very different and they may not share clear norms as to what kind of behaviour is expected. In addition, they may have little history of coming together as a group.

As Hogg and Abrams (1988) state, 'because the group lacks formal organization (it may have no specific goal, no obvious leaders and no well defined boundary to membership) the norm must be specific to the situation to some degree'. People in the group tend to focus their attention on group members who are particularly distinctive in terms of their behaviour (in other words, they stand out from the crowd). It is these individuals' behaviour that implies the group norms. Thus in any group there is a pressure to conform to the nonconformist norms of these distinctive individuals. People are conforming to the new norms that have emerged in the crowd. Inaction by the group majority against these distinctive individuals is further interpreted as a tacit acceptance of these new emergent norms.

Emergent-norm theory acknowledges that members of a group communicate with each other as to the appropriate norms of action. However, the group is over-influenced by the behaviour of these distinctive individuals, whose behaviour is probably rare in most people's daily lives – for example, violence. These emergent norms are a product of the group and do not continue beyond the membership of the group.

Evaluation of emergent-norm theory

✔ **Useful model:** emergent-norm theory appears to be a useful theory and can act as a combination of both convergence theory and contagion theory. It suggests that group behaviour is a combination of like-minded individuals (e.g. sports fans or racists), anonymity (lost in the crowd, or wearing a hood in the case of the Ku Klux Klan), and shared emotion that leads to group behaviour. People may gather with expectations and norms for appropriate behaviour but the interactions in the group influence the way new expectations and norms emerge, allowing for behaviour that would not normally be expected. Emergent-norm theory thus takes into account the fact that crowds communicate and that behaviour in a crowd can be unpredictable.

✘ **A normless environment?** The idea that groups form together in a normless environment has been criticised. Surely very few groups gather in a social vacuum and many norms of behaviour are present before the group collects rather than emerging after the group has already gathered. In most occasions

Evaluation of emergent-norm theory continued...

when groups form there is a common sense of purpose, and norms are already established. For example, sports fans know many of the norms that are expected at a sports event, although it is true that others may emerge during the event. Nevertheless, Turner and Killian (1987) insisted that there is a lack of tradition of established norms in groups. Some academics have criticised Turner and Killian's idea that certain distinctive individuals shape the group's norms, arguing that this is an 'elitist version of Allportian individualism; instead of crowd behaviour being explained in terms of the personalities of all participants it is tied to the personality of a dominant few' (Reicher, 2001). A further criticism involves the use of normative influence in the explanation. Although the behaviour of some people in a group may be due to compliance it does not explain why others resist and do not follow the emergent norms.

✗ **Self-awareness?** Individuals in a group of people would have to be very self-aware in order to identify what norms were emerging during a group display. After all, there is even less need for people to follow and comply with norms if they feel deindividuated (which people often feel in a group). Much of the research into group behaviour suggests that individuals in groups are not self-aware, they are deindividuated and not necessarily governed by norms. One problem for emergent-norm theory is to explain exactly how these individuals in groups who appear uninhibited and not self-aware manage to work out the emerging group norms and, further, why do they follow these group norms?

Social identity theory (Reicher, 1987)

Reicher (1987) believed that there is more to group behaviour than is explained by emergent-norm theory. He argued that group behaviour involves inter-group (between different groups of people) behaviour, such as opposing sports fans, confrontations with the police, and so on. Reicher argued that this element of group behaviour has been under-emphasised and that even in the absence of direct confrontation there is often a symbolic confrontation between the group and some other group or agency (such as the government).

Another key feature of the theory is that people do not lose their identity in a group (as proposed by deindividuation theory), but they assume the shared identity of the group – people change their personal identity to fit in with the shared social identity of the group. According to this explanation, individuals become members of specific groups for a specific purpose (e.g. to support a team) because of shared interests and attitudes. Prior to joining the group, individuals shared a sense of social identity that promotes belonging to the group. These general shared group norms provide a basis for the type of behaviour that is expected in the group. Social identity theory explains crowd behaviour in terms of informational influence. That is, an individual first categorises him- or herself as part of some social identity; second, creates or discovers the norms of that group; and, third, assigns those stereotypes to him- or herself (called 'self-stereotypes'). These norms and self-stereotypes help provide a framework for future behaviour.

However, these norms and self-stereotypes do not indicate how to behave across all the situations and contexts that the group might face. Confronted with this, group members look to the behaviour of other consistent or key group members for help and guidance as to how to act. Thus groups have shared norms that they bring to the group, but they also develop context-specific norms for conduct (much like emergent-norm theory) (Manstead and Hewstone, 1995).

Social identity theory proposes two ways in which norms form in a group. The first involves the relationship to an outgroup (people who are not members of the group, such as opposing fans, the police). It is suggested that the group have existing norms (such as football rivalries between nearby towns) for outgroup members and inductive inference from the behaviour of other ingroup members (key members may start throwing bottles, which may be taken as normative behaviour in that instance). This latter idea is similar to the distinctive behaviour of key group members in emergent-norm theory. The resulting explanation is a generally cohesive and parsimonious theory that can well explain group dynamics in a wide variety of situations.

This theory seems to be able to explain how people change their behaviour according to group membership and the situation they find themselves confronted with. It can also explain how the same groups can behave differently in different situations. For example, it can explain how a solicitor can be a peaceful rugby supporter one Saturday, an opera-goer the next Saturday and an aggressive football hooligan the following Saturday.

Reicher conducted several experiments that have supported social identity theory. In one of these he managed to increase the feeling of social identity in a group (by repeatedly calling the participants 'social science students'), or decrease the feelings of group membership (by referring to the participants by code numbers). When social identity was pronounced, their answers on a question of punishing sexual offenders followed the answers of other 'social science students' (the group were told previously that social science students favoured punishments). When the group's social identity was not emphasised, they did not produce similar group answers. In other words, Reicher showed that interpersonal influence was high from similar others when social identity was emphasised.

Aguirre, Wenger and Vigo (1998) used the time it took for the evacuation of occupants of the World Trade Center at the time of the explosion of 26 February 1993, to test predictions from emergent-norm theory. They examined data from a survey carried out in the first week of May 1993, of 415 people who worked at the World Trade Center. Many of the theory's predictions were supported. They found that enduring social relationships in each group were particularly important facets for levels of cooperation within each group, suggesting that group dynamics are important determinants of behaviour.

Evaluation of social identity theory (Reicher, 1987)

✔ **Research support:** social identity theory provides a more detailed and comprehensive explanation for group behaviour, and explains why different groups behave in different ways according to the situation or context they find themselves in. Milgram and Toch (1969) analysed the US race riots in the 1960s and showed that violence was not irrational or directionless; in fact, many rioters reported feeling a real sense of positive social identity with other group members. In Britain, Reicher (1987) examined the riots that occurred in the St Pauls district of Bristol in 1980. Much like Milgram and Toch, he found that the rioting was not uncontrolled – on the contrary, aggression was primarily directed at symbols of government such as the police and banks. Indeed, rioters even stopped to direct the traffic and private property tended not to be damaged. During and after the riot, people from St Pauls felt a stronger sense of shared social identity (Manstead and Hewstone, 1995).

✔ **Dynamic behaviour of crowds:** social identity theory involves a new transformation of identity that group members have chosen to adopt. This theory emphasises the dynamic nature of group behaviour. People are not acting like sheep and losing their identity in a group; rather they are individuals who actively decide to join specific groups, identify with the group's shared identity and norms, and then incorporate these in their sense of self-belonging to the group. It explains the dynamics of group behaviour at both an individual and collective level.

✔ **Sports events and football hooliganism:** emergent-norm theory doesn't readily explain why football is more prone to hooliganism than other sports events. However, Stott and Adang (2003) suggest that the

Evaluation of social identity theory (Reicher, 1987) continued...

dynamics of the crowd are a mixture of internal and external crowd influences. Social identity theory suggests that collective crowd behaviour is influenced by the shared identity of the members of the crowd. In terms of many football supporters, this will involve their loyalty to a particular team, their feelings for the opposition, and any other factors that they believe they share (for example, shared history or experiences) or have in common (for example – and excuse the stereotype – white, macho, working class). This also occurs with national teams – for example, Scottish football fans often unite around their hatred of the English, even when they're not playing England. Although crowd behaviour is affected by this sense of social identity, research suggests that the behaviour of a crowd is also determined by how the two sets of fans interact during the match and how each group believes it has been treated during the event. Stott and Adang place particular emphasis on the way authorities control football crowds, suggesting that the police in particular can play a vital part in influencing crowd behaviour to minimise the likelihood of violence. Light levels of good-humoured policing can often mitigate against the 'them versus us' norm, and prevent it emerging and provoking aggression.

Evaluation of explanations of group displays in humans

✗ **Operationalisation of group display:** there is no agreed definition for what constitutes a group display. Does it incorporate a crowd, a social movement, a psychology class, a church congregation, a protest march, a riot, people fleeing from a disaster, a Women's Institute meeting? Does it include a group of strangers who have just met and a group of friends who have been meeting for 20 years? The answer is that it probably includes all these groups of people. It is self-evident that these groups are very diverse and that the dynamics of each group may have little in common. It seems unlikely that one explanation can adequately explain all the different types of behaviour that these groups would display. Another problem was highlighted by Levy (1989), who studied an episode of non-violent group behaviour at a US professional football game. Although she found support for a number of different group explanations, she had difficulty distinguishing between the different explanations. She argued that many of the explanations overlapped and it was difficult to disentangle the value of each.

✗ **Retrospective explanations:** one major problem with the explanations of group displays in humans is that they typically involve looking back at past events and explaining them using a particular explanation or theory. For example, Zimbardo *et al.* (1973) explained the Prison Simulation Experiment in terms of deindividuation when many nowadays explain it in terms of adhering to the norms and expectations the prisoners and guards brought to their roles. It seems relatively easy to look back at an event, as Reicher (1987) did with the St Pauls riots, and then explain the behaviour displayed in terms of a particular theory. Psychodynamic theory is perhaps the best example of this, with some academics arguing that it can explain everything but predict nothing. Many of the explanations we have looked at for group behaviour are equally poor at predicting group behaviour. In other words, it is difficult to predict when a group will be aggressive and when it will remain peaceful. The mark of a good established theory or explanation is that it should be able to predict behaviour.

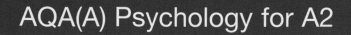
How Science Works

Practical Learning Activity 4.7: When is a crowd not a crowd? When is a punch not a punch?

- With a friend, try to agree a definition of what constitutes a 'group' or a 'crowd'. Try to think of instances where people gather together but that wouldn't fit your definition. Remember, it is always important to try to disprove a hypothesis or theory rather than merely try to find support for it.
- Try to define the term 'aggression'.
- Try to think of instances of behaviour that might **not** fit your definition.

SUMMARY

CHAPTER

Social psychological approaches to aggression

- **Aggression** is behaviour directed towards the goal of harming another living being, that is intended to harm or injure. It can include psychological as well as physical injury.

- **Social Learning Theory (SLT)** is often called modelling or observational learning (**Bandura, 1973**). SLT suggests that aggression and other forms of behaviour are primarily learned through observation or imitation. Humans aren't born aggressive, but learn through direct experience or by observing the actions of others.

- There are four component processes to the theory: **attention, retention, production and motivation**.

- Research that supports SLT includes **Bandura et al.'s (1961) Transmission of Aggression through Imitation** and **(1962) Imitation of Film-mediated Aggressive Models**. SLT has many useful applications and makes cognitive sense. However, it ignores the biological factors and the differences in individuals due to genetic, brain and learning differences.

- **Deindividuation Theory** is a social psychological account of how the individual acts in a group or crowd. It explains how rational individuals become aggressive hooligans when they lose a sense of individual identity.

- Research that supports this theory includes **Zimbardo et al.'s Prison Experiment (1973)**, where a simulated prison was constructed in Stanford University and 24 emotionally stable male participants were recruited.

- Other studies into deindividuation include the **Trick or Treater Study (Diener et al., 1976)** and the **Darkened Room Arousal Study (Gergen et al., 1973)**.

- There are also other theories, such as biological or instinct theories, that explain aspects of human aggression.

- Aggression in institutions such as hospitals and prisons is a significant problem throughout the world. Deindividuation Theory is one explanation for some of this aggression. **The Importation Model (Irwin and Cressey, 1962)** suggests that prisoners bring their aggressive tendencies from outside the prison. The violence of prisoners is a product of their experiences outside prison. Various factors, such as age and educational attainment, are also correlated with aggression in prisons. Three categories of prisoners have been identified: the criminal or thief subculture; the convict subculture; the conventional or straight subculture.

- **Situational models** propose that aggression in institutions occurs because there are factors present in the institution that make violence more likely to occur. Such factors include organisational, physical and staffing factors.

- **The Deprivational Model** is an example of a situational model and suggests that it is what goes on within the institution that leads to aggression. Various deprivations experienced by prisoners (deprivation of liberty, autonomy, goods and services, heterosexual sex and security) all lead to an increased likelihood of aggression.

- More recently, an Interaction Model, which unites the importation and situational (deprivation) models, has been proposed.

Biological explanations of aggression

- **Neural and hormonal mechanisms** do play an important part in many human behaviours. Many behavioural differences between men and women are linked to hormonal differences. **Testosterone** levels have been shown to affect aggression levels in many non-human studies using the **'subtraction and replacement'** paradigm. The relationship between aggression and testosterone levels in humans is far from clear-cut. Evidence suggests that aggression increases testosterone levels (Klinesmith *et al.*, 2006; Sapolsky, 1997).

- Genetic factors are implicated in aggression levels, as shown by heritability studies. There is some evidence that the **MAOA gene** influences aggression in humans and animals, but further research is needed to determine the exact nature of this relationship.

- **Twin and adoption studies** have been used to try to determine the genetic influence on aggression. Although figures vary from study to study there is good evidence of a genetic factor in aggression. Genes may trigger a heightened sensitivity to environmental factors that lead to aggression.

- An over-emphasis on genetic factors of aggression can lead to a **reductionist view** of human aggression.

Aggression as an adaptive response

- **The evolutionary explanation of aggression** suggests that aggression serves an important function in terms of individual survival and procreation potential. In our evolutionary past, males found it necessary to compete with rival males for desirable mates. An aggressive male who could wipe out the competition would pass on his aggressive genes to the next generation. Thus aggression can be seen as serving an **adaptive purpose**. A major problem with the evolutionary explanation of aggression is that it is impossible to test scientifically.

- **Jealousy** is a major cause of aggression. **Sexual infidelity** and **emotional infidelity** also play a part in many aggressive incidents between partners. The evolutionary explanation suggests that men will be more upset by sexual infidelity since they then face the problem of paternal uncertainty, whereas women will be more upset by emotional infidelity. Using hypothetical scenarios, Buss *et al.* (1992) found support for this idea.

- There are many explanations for group display (or crowd behaviour) in humans. **Deindividuation, bystander apathy, contagion theory and convergence theory** are all explanations that are relevant.

- **Emergent-norm theory (Turner and Killian, 1987)** argues that similar types of people gather for some collective purpose, but that different norms may emerge during the event, which can lead to aggression. This theory suggests that group behaviour is governed by the norms in the group, and how these norms emerge is the goal of much of the research.

- **Social identity theory (Reicher, 1987)** suggests that people in a group assume the shared identity of the group. Crowd behaviour is explained in terms of informational influence. Social identity theory emphasises the dynamic nature of crowds and explains behaviour at an individual and collective level.

- A problem with many of the explanations of group displays is that they can retrospectively explain crowd behaviour that has become aggressive but are less successful in predicting which crowds will act aggressively.

Essay Questions

Social psychological approaches to aggression

1. Critically consider ONE social psychological theory of aggression. (25 marks)
2. Outline and evaluate explanations of institutional aggression. (25 marks)

Biological explanations of aggression

3. Discuss the role of neural and hormonal mechanisms in aggression. (25 marks)
4. Critically consider the role of genetic factors in aggressive behaviour. (25 marks)

Aggression as an adaptive response

5. Describe and evaluate evolutionary explanations of human aggression. (25 marks)
6a. Outline explanations of group display in humans. (15 marks)
6b. Critically evaluate one or more of your explanations (in part 6a) of group display in humans. (10 marks)

It should take you 30 minutes to answer each question.

Gender

What's covered in this chapter?

You need to know about:

Psychological explanations of gender development
- Cognitive Developmental Theory, including Kohlberg and Gender Schema Theory
- Explanations for psychological androgyny and gender dysphoria, including relevant research

Biological influences on gender
- The role of hormones and genes in gender development
- The biosocial approach to gender development
- Evolutionary explanations of gender roles

Social contexts of gender role
- Social influences on gender role – for example, the influence of parents, peers and schools, media
- Cross-cultural studies of gender role

INTRODUCTION

How Science Works

Practical Learning Activity 5.1

1. Try to find definitions of the following terms:

- sex
- gender
- sexual identity
- gender identity
- gender dysphoria
- transsexual
- gender (or sex) role
- gender (or sex) stereotypes
- sex typing
- intersex
- hermaphrodite
- gender (or sex) differences (or 'psychological sex differences')
- psychological androgyny.

2. Ask people if they believe there's a difference between 'sex' and 'gender'; if so, what do they understand the difference to be?

3. Also, excluding the act of sex (or sexual behaviour), can 'sex' mean different things?

✔ Specification Hint

The specification refers to 'gender', 'gender development', gender role', 'psychological androgyny' and 'gender dysphoria'.

Before we start discussing theories and research studies relating to these, it's important to define them – and other related terms – so we know how they're used in this area of investigation. We won't then need to define them each time they appear in different theories or research studies.

The 'vocabulary' of sex and gender

Feminist psychologists (such as Unger, 1979) distinguish between sex and gender. *Sex* refers to the biological facts about us, which are summarised as 'male' and 'female'. However, sex is a *multidimensional* variable, as shown in Box 5.1. *Gender*, by contrast, is what culture makes out of the 'raw material' of biological sex. It's the *social equivalent* or *social interpretation* of sex. As Maracek *et al.* (2004) put it, 'sex is to gender as nature is to nurture; that is, sex pertains to what is biological or natural, whereas gender pertains to what is learned or cultural ...'.

Sexual identity is an alternative way of referring to our biological status as male or female. Corresponding to gender is *gender identity,* our classification of ourselves (and others) as male or female, boy or girl, etc.

For most people, their sexual and gender identities correspond. However, some individuals experience *gender dysphoria* (or dysmorphia) – that is, anxiety, uncertainty or persistently uncomfortable feelings about their assigned gender (based on their anatomical sex). Gender dysphoria is the major symptom of *gender identity disorder,* in which individuals believe their gender identity is different from their sexual identity (their anatomical sex). These individuals usually become *transsexuals* – that is, they choose to undergo hormonal and surgical procedures that will 'correct' their sexual identity and bring it into line with their gender identity.

Figure 5.1 A transsexual: gender is more flexible than we might sometimes think

Gender (or *sex*) *role* refers to the behaviours, attitudes, values, beliefs and so on that a particular society either expects from, or considers appropriate to, males and females on the basis of their biological sex. To be *masculine* or *feminine*, then, requires males or females to conform to their respective gender roles. All societies have carefully defined gender roles, although their precise details differ between societies. *Gender* (or *sex*) *stereotypes* are widely held beliefs about psychological differences between males and females, which often reflect gender roles.

Sex typing is the process by which children acquire a sex or gender identity and learn gender-appropriate behaviours (adopt an appropriate gender role). Sex typing begins early in western culture, with parents often (still) dressing their newborn baby boy or girl in blue or pink respectively. Even in the earliest days of infancy, our gender influences how people react to us (Condry and Ross, 1985). Indeed, usually the first question asked by friends and relatives of new parents is 'Boy or girl?'

The categories of biological sex described in Box 5.1 are usually highly correlated, so a person tends to be female (or male) in all respects. The categories also tend to be correlated with non-biological aspects of sex, including the sex the baby's assigned to at birth, how it's brought up, its gender identity gender role identity and so on. These facts help to explain why, whether we choose to focus on sex or gender, we

Box 5.1: Five categories of biological sex

1. **Chromosomal sex:** normal females inherit two X chromosomes, one from each parent (XX); normal males inherit one X chromosome from the mother and one Y chromosome from the father (XY). Two chromosomes are needed for the complete development of both internal and external female structures, and the Y chromosome must be present for the complete development of male internal and external structures (Page *et al.*, 1987). For many years it was believed that if the Y chromosome were absent, female external genitals would develop. However, a *female-determining gene* has been located on the X chromosome (Unger and Crawford, 1996). Female embryos begin synthesising large quantities of oestrogen (see below), which is thought to play a key role in the development of the female reproductive system. A gene on the Y chromosome called TDF (*testis-determining factor*) appears to be responsible for testis formation and male development (Hodgkin, 1988).
2. **Gonadal sex:** this refers to the sexual or reproductive organs (ovaries in females, testes in males). *H-Y antigen*, controlled by genes on the Y chromosome, causes embryonic gonads to be transformed into testes. If H-Y antigen isn't present, gonadal tissue develops into ovaries (Amice *et al.*, 1989).

3. **Hormonal sex:** when the gonads are transformed into testes or ovaries, genetic influences cease and *sex hormones* take over biological sex determination. The male sex hormones are called *androgens*, the most important being *testosterone* (secreted by the testes). The ovaries secrete two distinct types of female hormone: *oestrogen* and *progesterone*. Although males usually produce more androgens, and females more oestrogens, *both* males and females produce androgens and oestrogens. So, strictly, there are no exclusively 'male' or 'female' hormones (Muldoon and Reilly, 1998).

4. **Sex of the internal reproductive structures:** the Wolffian ducts in males and the Mullerian ducts in females are the embryonic forerunners of the internal reproductive structures. In males, these are the prostate gland, sperm ducts, seminal vesicles and testes; in females, the Fallopian tubes, womb and ovaries.

5. **Sex of the external genitals:** in males, the external genitals are the penis and scrotum; in females, the outer lips of the vagina (*labia majora*). In the absence of testosterone (which influences both the internal and external structures of chromosomal males), female structures develop.

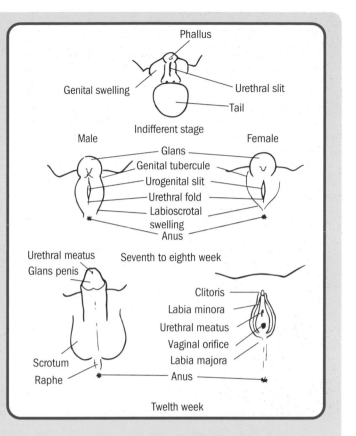

Figure 5.2 Prenatal differentiation of male and female genitalia. From a relatively undifferentiated state, development proceeds by means of the relative enlargement of structures that have analogues in members of the other sex (from Unger, 1979)

assume that 'male' and 'female' are *dichotomous* categories; in other words, each of us can only be one *or* the other.

However, things aren't always as straightforward in reality as this assumption implies. Although estimates vary, it's been suggested that around 1 in 4,500 live births involves an infant whose genitals are sufficiently ambiguous to make the immediate classification of male or female very difficult (Warne, 1998, in Liao and Boyle, 2004). The general term for such sexually undifferentiated infants is 'intersex'. Either pre- or post-natally, disorders can occur leading to an *inconsistency* or low correlation between the categories. These disorders can tell us a great deal about the development of gender identity, gender role and gender role identity. People with such disorders are collectively referred to as *hermaphrodites* (from the mythical Greek god/goddess Hermaphrodite, who had attributes of both sexes). *True hermaphrodites* – either simultaneously or sequentially – have functioning organs of both sexes; they are very rare, and their external organs are often a mixture of male and female structures.

Case Study 5.1: Mr Blackwell: hermaphrodite (Goldwyn, 1979)

- In an article called 'The fight to be male', Goldwyn cites the case of Mr Blackwell, only the 303rd true hermaphrodite in medical history.
- He's described as a handsome and rather shy 18-year-old Bantu. Although he had a small vaginal opening as well as a penis, he was taken to be male and was raised as a boy. But when he was 14 he developed breasts and was sent to hospital to discover why this had happened. It was found that he had an active ovary on one side of his body and an active testicle on the other. He expressed his wish to remain male, and so his female parts were removed.
- Goldwyn points out that if his internal ducts had been differently connected, Mr Blackwell could have actually fertilised himself without being able to control this.

Pseudohermaphrodites ('intersex' individuals) are more common. Although they, too, possess ambiguous internal and external reproductive structures, they're born with gonads that match their chromosomal sex (unlike true hermaphrodites).

- In *complete androgen insensitivity syndrome* (CAIS) (or *testicular feminising syndrome*), pre-natal development in a chromosomally normal (XY) male is feminised. The internal reproductive structures of either sex fail to develop, and the external genitals fail to differentiate into a penis and a scrotum. Normal-looking female external genitals and a shallow ('blind') vagina are present at birth. At puberty, breast development occurs, but the individual fails to menstruate. Very little or no surgery is needed for the adoption of a female appearance.

- *Congenital adrenal hyperplasia* (CAH) (or *adrenogenital syndrome*/AGS) is the most common and most studied intersex condition (Hines, 2004b), in which a chromosomally normal female (XX) is exposed to an excessive level of androgens during the critical period of prenatal sexual differentiation.

While the internal reproductive structures are unaffected, girls with CAH are born with masculinised or ambiguous genitals: the androgens have caused phallic enlargement (the clitoris is larger than normal) and some degree of labial fusion (the outer lips of the vagina are joined together). These individuals are usually raised as females.

- In *DHT-deficient males* (or *5-alpha-reductase deficiency*), a genetic disorder prevents the normal prenatal conversion of testosterone into dihydrotestosterone (DHT). This hormone is necessary for the normal development of male external genitals. These males are usually incorrectly identified as females and raised as girls (but see Case Study 5.2).

Case Study 5.2: The Batista family: an overnight sex change? (Imperato-McGinley *et al.*, 1974)

- Imperato-McGinley *et al.* studied a remarkable family who live in Santo Domingo in the Dominican Republic (in the Caribbean). Of the ten children in the Batista family, four of the sons have changed from being born and raised as girls into muscular men: they were born with normal female genitalia and body shape, but when they were 12, their vaginas healed over, two testicles descended and they grew a full-size penis.
- The Batistas are just one of 23 affected families in their village in which 37 children have undergone this change. All these families have a common ancestor, Attagracia Carrasco, who lived in the mid-eighteenth century. She passed on a mutant gene that shows only when carried by both parents.

- In *chromosome abnormalities* there's a discrepancy between chromosomal sex and external appearance, including the genitals. The most common examples are Turner's syndrome (where a female has a single sex chromosome: XO) and Klinefelter's syndrome (where a male has an extra X chromosome: XXY).

Gender stereotypes and psychological gender differences

How Science Works

Practical Learning Activity 5.2

- Conduct a survey in which you ask people to list examples of 'typical' feminine and masculine characteristics. Are the responses significantly different – or are the similarities greater than the differences?
- Do males and females give different responses – either for the same or opposite gender? Either way, do your findings surprise you? Explain your answer.
- If the responses are significantly different, do they represent *mere* stereotypes, or do you think there are real, actual differences between males and females?
- If the differences are real, how might they arise?

Assuming that these stereotypes do correspond to real male–female differences, there's a strong tendency (both among the general public and psychologists up to the mid-1970s) to regard them as *mutually exclusive*; in other words, men tend to be masculine and women tend to be feminine (the more masculine you are, the less feminine you are, and vice versa). This is equivalent to the view that biological sex is dichotomous (see above).

However, as we saw above, intersex is a very real phenomenon. The psychological equivalent to intersex is *androgyny*: androgynous people display *both* masculine *and* feminine characteristics ('andro' = 'male', 'gyne' = 'female').

There appears to be a high degree of agreement across 30 countries regarding the characteristics associated with each gender group (Williams and Best, 1994). For example, male-associated terms included 'aggressive', 'determined' and 'sharp-witted', while female-associated terms included 'cautious', 'emotional' and 'warm'. However, as far as actual differences are concerned, many stereotypes about males and females have little empirical foundation (see Box 5.2).

Box 5.2: Some findings relating to gender differences

- **Aggression:** according to Maccoby and Jacklin (1974) and Weisfeld (1994), boys are more aggressive verbally and physically than girls, a difference that appears as soon as social play begins (at around two-and-a-half years). While both genders become less aggressive with age, boys and men remain more aggressive throughout development. However, some studies have shown that women score high for certain kinds of indirect, non-physical aggression (Durkin, 1995), while others have found no gender differences at all (e.g. Campbell and Muncer, 1994). According to Schaffer (2004), when both physical and non-physical aggression are taken into account, the gender difference almost disappears.
- **Verbal ability:** from preschool to adolescence, the genders are very similar with respect to verbal ability. But at age 11 females become superior, and this increases during adolescence and possibly beyond (Maccoby and Jacklin, 1974). But again, evidence suggests that any such differences are so small as to be negligible (Hyde and Linn, 1988).
- **Spatial ability:** males' ability to perceive figures or objects in space and their relationship to each other is consistently better than females' in adolescence and adulthood (Maccoby and Jacklin, 1974). But while there's male superiority on some spatial tasks, *within-sex* variability is large. Moreover, when between-sex differences are found, they're usually small (Durkin, 1995).
- **Mathematical ability:** mathematical skills increase faster in boys, beginning at around age 12–13 (Maccoby and Jacklin, 1974). But while there are significant sex differences, these are in the *reverse* direction to the stereotype (Hyde *et al.,* 1990).

(See the 'Stretch and Challenge' text, below.)

Maccoby and Jacklin's (1974) review concluded that hardly any of the many psychological attributes they examined clearly differentiated the sexes. This was later confirmed by Ruble and Martin (1998). According to Schaffer (2004), 'personality and cognitive differences are far fewer in number than is commonly believed, and, where they do exist, moderate in extent and are quite probably becoming less evident as society redefines the role of the sexes'.

STRETCH AND CHALLENGE

According to Baron-Cohen (2003a, 2003b), the *female* brain is predominantly hardwired for *empathy*, while the *male* brain is predominantly hardwired for *understanding and building systems*. He calls this the *Empathising-Systemising* (E-S) *Theory*.

According to the theory, a person (whether male or female) has a particular 'brain type', of which there are three common types:

1. for some individuals, empathising is stronger than systemising (the female brain/E-type)
2. for others, systemising is stronger than empathising (the male brain/S-type)
3. yet others are equally strong in their empathising and systemising ('balanced brain'/B-type).

Anecdotal evidence shows that girls display more empathy and sensitivity towards others. For example, baby girls as young as 12 months old respond more empathically to others' distress, showing greater concern through more sad looks, sympathetic vocalisations and comforting. This echoes what's found in adulthood: more women report sharing their friends' emotional distress, and they also spend more time comforting people. Women are also more sensitive to facial expressions, better at decoding non-verbal communication, picking up subtle nuances from tone of voice or facial expression, or judging a person's character.

Boys, from toddlerhood onwards, are more interested in cars, trucks, planes, guns and swords, building blocks, constructional and mechanical toys (i.e. *systems*). They seem to love putting things together and 'building' things. Boys also enjoy playing with toys that have clear functions, buttons to press, things that will light up or devices that will cause another object to move. Girls prefer dolls, soft toys and domestic articles (Golombok and Fivush, 1994).

Males are also generally better at map-reading and mental rotation (both tests of systemising), and all these differences are reflected in 'typical' male and female *occupations*. Baron-Cohen believes that *hormonal factors* are the most likely cause of these male–female differences (see below, pages 200–202). He also proposes that E-S Theory can help explain *autism*, claiming that autistic children, and adults, whether male or female, have a predominantly male (S-type) brain (see Chapter 6).

Synoptic Material

The meaning of sex differences

Durkin (1995) suggests that 'The overwhelming conclusion to be drawn from the literature on sex differences is that it is highly controversial'. A statistically significant difference *doesn't* imply a larger behavioural difference. Rather, what determines a significant result is the *consistency* of the differences between groups. So, for example, if all the girls in a school scored 0.5 per cent higher than all the boys on the same test, a small but highly significant result would be produced (Edley and Wetherell, 1995).

Eagly (1983), however, has argued that in at least some cases a significant difference *does* reflect a substantial sex difference. By combining the results of different but comparable studies (*meta-analysis*), substantial sex differences emerge on some measures. According to Eagly, research has actually tended to conceal rather than reveal sex differences. However, the differences within each gender are at least as great as the differences between them (Maccoby, 1980; see Box 5.2).

The politics of sex difference research

According to Edley and Wetherell (1995), debates in the nineteenth century about which sex is more intelligent were clearly more than just academic. Early attempts to prove that men's brains are larger and more powerful were just as much about justifying men's dominant social position as about trying to discover the 'natural' order of things.

Similarly, the argument over inherent or natural sex differences is often part and parcel of a more general political debate about how society should be organised. For example, the claim that women are naturally more subjective, empathic and emotional (see 'Stretch and Challenge', above) leads very neatly to the decision that they're best suited to childcare and other domestic tasks that are devalued by men precisely because they're typically performed by women.

More specifically, within psychology as a whole, but perhaps in the study of gender in particular, there's a strong bias towards publishing studies that have produced 'positive' results (where statistically significant sex differences have been found). When sex differences *aren't* found, the findings tend to remain unreported; the far more convincing evidence for 'sex similarity', therefore, is ignored, creating the very powerful impression that differences between men and women are real, widespread and 'the rule'. Indeed, the very term 'sex similarities' sounds very odd (Unger, 1979; Jackson, 1992; Tavris, 1993).

PSYCHOLOGICAL EXPLANATIONS OF GENDER DEVELOPMENT

According to Bussey and Bandura (2004):

Gender development is a fundamental issue, because some of the most important aspects of people's lives, such as the talents they cultivate, the conceptions they hold of themselves, and others, the social opportunities and constraints they encounter, and the social life and occupational paths they pursue, are heavily prescribed by societal gender typing. It is the primary basis on which people get differentiated, with pervasive effects on their daily lives.

Cognitive Developmental Theory

Kohlberg's Cognitive Developmental Theory

Other theories of gender role development (such as Social Learning Theory / SLT; see below, pages 209–213) implicitly assume that the child already knows which gender s/he is, and proceeds accordingly to learn the appropriate role (Durkin, 1995). But where does that knowledge come from in the first place? According to *cognitive developmental theory* (CDT; Kohlberg, 1966; Kohlberg and Ullian, 1974), it arises in the same way as all knowledge, namely from the child's active construction of an understanding of the world through interaction with it. This view of the child as 'discovering' the world through its exploration of it is a basic principle of Piaget's (e.g. 1950) theory of cognitive development, on which Kohlberg's account was based (see Chapter 6).

Children's discovery that they're male or female *causes* them to identify with members of their own gender (*not* the other way round, as SLT and psychoanalytic (Freudian) theories suggest). While rewards and punishments influence children's choices of toys and activities, these don't mechanically strengthen stimulus–response connections, but provide children with *information* about when they're behaving in ways that other people deem appropriate (Bandura, 1977a; see final main section of this chapter, pages 209–213).

According to Kohlberg, young children acquire an understanding of the concepts 'male' and 'female' in three stages (see Box 5.3).

Once children acquire gender constancy, they come to value the behaviours and attitudes associated with their gender. Only at this point do they identify with the adult figures who possess the qualities they see as being most relevant to their concept of themselves as male or female (Perry and Bussey, 1979). This usually means imitating same-sex models and following sex-appropriate activities; Maccoby and Jacklin (1974) called this 'self-socialisation', because it doesn't depend directly on external reinforcement.

Box 5.3: Stages in the development of gender identity

- **Stage 1 (Gender labelling or basic gender identity):** this occurs somewhere between one and a half and three years, and refers to the child's recognition that it is male or female. According to Kohlberg, knowing one's gender is an achievement that allows us to understand and categorise the world. But this knowledge is fragile, with 'man', 'woman', 'boy' and 'girl' being used as little more than labels, equivalent to a personal name. Children sometimes choose the incorrect label and don't yet realise that boys invariably become men and girls always become women (Slaby and Frey, 1975).

- **Stage 2 (Gender stability):** by age three to five, most children recognise that people retain their gender for a lifetime. For example, if asked 'When you were a baby, were you a little boy or a little girl?' or 'Will you be a mummy or a daddy when you grow up?', children from four onwards (but not before) can answer correctly (Slaby and Frey, 1975). But they still rely on superficial, physical signs to determine their gender (Marcus and Overton, 1978). So, if someone is superficially transformed (for example, a woman has her long hair cut very short, or a man puts on women's clothes), children of this age are likely to infer that the person has changed gender (Emmerlich *et al.*, 1977, in Durkin, 1995). McConaghy (1979, in Durkin, 1995) found that if a doll was dressed in transparent clothing, so that its male or female genitals were visible, children of this age would judge its gender by its clothes (*not* its genitals).

- **Stage 3 (Gender constancy or consistency):** at around age six to seven, children realise that gender is *immutable* (i.e. permanent) – even if a woman has her head shaved, her gender remains female. Gender constancy represents a kind of *conservation* (Piaget's term to describe understanding that things remain the same despite changes in their appearance) and, significantly, appears shortly after the child has mastered the conservation of quantity (Marcus and Overton, 1978; see Chapter 6). So we can only conclude that gender understanding is complete when the child appreciates that gender is constant over time *and* situations.

Gender Schema Theory (or Gender Schematic Processing Theory)

Gender schema theory (GST), or *Gender schematic processing theory* (GSPT), addresses the possibility that gender identity *alone* can provide children with sufficient motivation to assume sex-typed behaviour patterns (e.g. Martin and Halverson, 1981, 1983; Bem, 1985; Martin, 1991). The key difference between this approach and Kohlberg's is that for the initial understanding of gender (gender schema) to develop, the child needn't understand that gender is permanent. Like SLT, this approach suggests that children learn 'appropriate' patterns of behaviour by observation. But, consistent with CDT, children's active cognitive processing of information also contributes to their sex typing.

It has its roots in information-processing theories of cognitive development (see Gross, 2005) and Kohlberg's theory. Just as the self-concept can be thought of as a 'schema' or 'self-theory', so the child's gender schema begins to develop as soon as s/he notices the differences between males and females, knows his/her own gender, and can label the two groups fairly reliably – all of which happens by age two or three (Bee, 2000). Once children have a gender identity, they look increasingly to the environment for information with which to build and enrich the appropriate gender schema: 'an organized body of knowledge about the attributes and behaviours associated with a specific gender' (Durkin, 1995). This schema provides a basis for interpreting the environment and selecting appropriate forms of behaviour; in this way, the child's self-perception becomes sex-typed. For example, children learn that strength is linked to the male role stereotype and weakness to the female stereotype, and that some dimensions (including strength–weakness) are more relevant to one gender (males) than the other (Rathus, 1990). So a boy learns that the strength he displays in, say, wrestling

Evaluation of Kohlberg's CDT

✔ **Experimental evidence supporting Kohlberg:** evidence suggests that the concepts of gender identity, stability and constancy occur in that order across many cultures (Munroe *et al.,* 1984). It's somewhat more advanced in children's understanding of their own as opposed to other people's gender (Leonard and Archer, 1989), presumably because parents and others draw a child's attention more to its own gender-specific characteristics than to others' (Schaffer, 1996).

Slaby and Frey (1975) divided a group of two- to five-year-olds into 'high' and 'low' gender constancy. The children were then shown a silent film of adults simultaneously performing a series of simple activities. The screen was 'split', with males appearing on one side and females on the other. Children rated as high on gender constancy showed a marked same-sex bias, as measured by the amount of visual attention they gave to each side of the screen. (While this reached statistical significance in the case of boys, it didn't with the girls.) This supports Kohlberg's claim that gender constancy is a *cause* of the imitation of same-sex models, rather than an effect.

Similarly, Ruble *et al.* (1981) found that high gender constancy preschoolers showed greater responsiveness to the implicit messages of television toy commercials compared with low constancy children. This affected both their tendency to play with the toys and their judgements as to which sex they were appropriate for.

Several studies have found evidence for self-socialisation (see above) (Slaby and Frey, 1975; Ruble, 1987; Stangor and Ruble, 1987). Children actively construct their gender-role knowledge through purposeful monitoring of the social environment (Whyte, 1998).

✘ **Inability to explain early gender-appropriate behaviour:** a major problem for CDT is that it predicts there should be little or no gender-specific behaviour before the child has acquired gender constancy. But even in infancy, both boys and girls show a marked preference for stereotypical male and female toys (Huston, 1983; see 'Stretch and Challenge', above). As far as CDT is concerned, infants might have developed a sense of gender identity, but they're some years away from achieving gender stability and constancy (Fagot, 1985).

---

influences how others perceive him. Unless competing in some sporting activity, most girls don't see this dimension as being important. But while boys are expected to compete in sports, girls aren't, and so a girl is likely to find that her gentleness and neatness are more important in others' eyes than her strength (Rathus, 1990).

🔍 How Science Works

Practical Learning Activity 5.3

- Why should children notice gender so early?
- Why is it such an important category?

One suggestion (Maccoby, 1998) is that because gender is clearly an either/or category, children seem to understand very early that this is a key distinction; it therefore serves as a kind of magnet for new information. Alternatively, adults and other children emphasise gender differences in countless small ways (we saw examples above of asking about a newborn baby's sex and dressing baby boys and girls in different colours).

Whatever the origin of this early schema, once established, a great many experiences are assimilated to it, and children may begin to show preference for same-sex playmates or for gender-stereotyped activities (Martin and Little, 1990). However, the gender schema undergoes change as the child's general cognitive abilities develop, as described in Box 5.4.

Box 5.4: Developmental changes in children's gender schema (based on Bee, 2000)

- Preschoolers first learn some broad distinctions about what kinds of activities or behaviour go with each gender, both by observing other children and through the reinforcements they receive from parents. Examples include 'men have short hair' and 'girls play with dolls'. They also learn a few gender 'scripts' – whole sequences of events that normally go with a particular gender, such as 'cooking dinner' (female) and 'building with tools' (male).
- One study (Bauer, 1993) even suggests that boys (but not girls) may be aware of, and more willing to imitate, gender-matched scripts as early as the age of two.
- Between ages four and six, the child learns a more subtle and complex set of associations for his/her *own* gender – what children of the same gender like and don't like, how they play, how they talk, what kinds of people they spend time with. Not until about age eight to ten does the child develop a schema of the opposite gender that matches the complexity of the same-gender schema (Martin *et al.*, 1990).
- When gender constancy develops at about five or six, children's understanding of 'what people who are like me do' becomes more elaborated. This 'rule' is treated as *absolute* (as with other rules; see Chapter 6).
- By late childhood and early adolescence, it's understood that these 'rules' are just social conventions, and gender-role schemas become more flexible (Katz and Ksansnak, 1994). Teenagers have largely abandoned the automatic assumption that what their own gender does is better or preferable; in fact, a significant minority of teenagers begin to define themselves as *androgynous* (see below, pages 193–196).

Evaluation of GST/GSPT

✔ **Supporting evidence:** Fagot (1985) found that two-year-olds who can correctly label the genders spend 80 per cent of their time in same-gender groups, whereas those who cannot spend only 50 per cent of theirs in same-gender groups. Also, early labellers are subsequently more sex-typed in their choice of toys and have greater knowledge of gender stereotypes (Fagot and Leinbach, 1989).

Martin and Little (1990) tested three- to five-year-olds on gender identity, stability and constancy, as well as on clothing and toy stereotypes, toy preferences and peer preferences. They found that children require only gender identity for their preferences and knowledge to be influenced. This is exactly what GST/GSPT would predict.

Also consistent with the theory is the finding, from several experiments (e.g. Martin and Halverson, 1983), that when children view pictures or watch films of individuals in cross-gender activities (such as a male acting as a nurse, or a female as a doctor), they either miss the point, distort the information or quickly forget it (and insist that the man was the doctor and the woman the nurse). This demonstrates the *resilience* of children's gender-role beliefs and attitudes. When they process gender-related information in terms of their schemas, they admit data that are consistent with their schemas, and disregard or reject data that are inconsistent with them.

The theory also accounts for the finding that children appear to be more influenced by the gender-appropriateness of an activity performed by a model than by the model's gender. The schema 'this is for

Evaluation of GST/GSPT continued...

boys/girls' is more influential than unqualified imitation ('do everything that grown-ups do') (Durkin, 1995).

✗ Evidence that appears to contradict the theory: in other respects, the link between understanding and behaviour isn't so clear – on the contrary, some studies suggest that children can act without knowing. For example, Perry *et al*. (1984) found that two- to five-year-olds demonstrated sex-typed activities well before knowledge of gender-role stereotypes. Boys' knowledge lagged about a year behind their preferences, while among girls the trends were more obscure (Schaffer, 1996).

Eisenberg *et al*. (1982) observed three- to four-year-olds at play, then questioned them about the reasoning for their choice of particular toys. There were few references to gender-role stereotypes; the children justified their choices in terms of what the toy could do and how this fitted in with their preferred activities – not in terms of conscious attempts to act in accordance with learned stereotypes.

Bussey and Bandura (1992) found that both three- and four-year-olds reacted in a gender-stereotypical way to peers' behaviour that didn't conform to their gender. They disapproved of boys feeding, changing nappies and comforting dolls, and girls driving dumper trucks. They also expected the peer's friends to react in the same disapproving way. However, many of these same children hadn't even attained gender identity, let alone gender constancy. Even the youngest behaved towards peers in a gender-stereotypical way, despite their limited gender-linked knowledge. As Bussey and Bandura (2004) conclude, 'Neither children's gender identity stability and constancy nor gender classificatory knowledge predicted gender-linked conduct.'

✗ Alternative theoretical interpretations: Bussey and Bandura (1992) present their findings in the context of *Social Cognitive Theory* (Bandura, 1986), according to which gender development begins as a result of 'predominantly external sanctions' (such as parental controls) but shifts gradually to a self-regulated process governed by perceptions of anticipated outcomes; these perceptions are mediated by the social environment. According to this approach, the major mechanism involved is *self-evaluation*.

✔/✗ Are schemas causes or effects and do they really affect behaviour? So, among preschoolers there's no evidence to suggest that gender schemas, at least in any conscious and verbalised form, are a necessary precondition for sex-typed behaviour. Schaffer (1996) wonders if the influence might be in the *opposite* direction: children's monitoring of their own and others' behaviour might lead to the development of gender schemas.

However, once they're acquired, gender schemas almost certainly affect our attention to and processing of information relevant to males and females, and thereby guide our actions. Like all schemas, we tend to encode and remember information consistent with our gender schemas; gender stereotypes are a form of schema – once learned they'll guide action so that a child will conform with learned standards and social expectations (Schaffer, 1996).

Although cognitive developmental approaches are currently the most influential accounts of gender-role development, they've been criticised on a number of counts.

- Like social learning theorists, cognitive developmental theorists say little about *why* the genders are differentially valued (Bem, 1993). Instead, the social environment is taken as 'given', and the focus is on universal cognitive processes (such as schemas) that act on data that arise from the environment.
- Most cognitive developmental accounts centre around the (isolated) *individual* looking out at society and trying to make sense of it An alternative view is that cognitive development itself proceeds in an *interactive* context, and the construction of social role (including gender role) knowledge is a *collective* activity. This doesn't mean the cognitive processes are irrelevant, only that they occur within a *social* context. According to Bem (1989, 1993) the bases for gender differentiation *don't* lie within the child's mind, but in the child's socially organised experiences. Bem (1989) found that only about 50 per cent of a sample of American three- to five-year-olds could correctly identify the sex of toddlers photographed nude. Those who could, performed better on a gender constancy test. This suggests the possibility that, rather than originating in the child's 'concept of physical things – the bodies of himself and of others' (Kohlberg, 1966), gender role knowledge depends at least partly on social experiences, and the ways the culture organises gender differentiation (Durkin, 1995).
- As we saw at the beginning of the chapter, the sex/gender distinction corresponds to that between nature and nurture. This dichotomy is now commonplace in mainstream psychology; indeed, it has been the basis for much psychological research intended to determine what's learned and what's inherent, what's malleable and what's not (Maracek *et al.*, 2004). According to Money's *biosocial theory* (see pages 202–206), gender identity is learned through socialisation, while sex is a biological given. *Feminist psychologists* (e.g. Unger, 1979), basing their work on Money's research, maintain that while gender is socially constructed, sex is a (non-constructed) biological category. However, *social constructionist approaches* (commonly misunderstood as nothing more than the 'nurture' end of the nature–nurture debate) attempt to challenge (by deconstructing) the very notion of dichotomous biological sex (Kitzinger, 2004). This is an approach that some feminist psychologists have been developing for some time. Kitzinger quotes Kessler and McKenna (1978), who argue that:

> To take the sexes for granted, to treat the existence of two sexes as an irreducible fact, obscures each individual's responsibility for creating the world in which she/he lives ... gender is a social construction, a world of two sexes is a result of the socially shared, taken-for-granted methods that members use to construct reality.

The existence of *intersex* individuals shows that our western male/female dichotomy *isn't* a biological 'given'. Anthropologists have described 'third sex' categories in other cultures (see pages 216–217), and European and North American feminists have been criticised for assuming that all cultures organise their social world through a perception of human bodies as male or female (Kitzinger, 2004). Kitzinger argues that, instead of asking how successfully intersex people can be surgically and socially modified in order to become male or female, psychologists could be exploring how the myth of two biological sexes is reproduced, regulated – and sometimes resisted.

- According to Maracek *et al.* (2004), social constructionists challenge the idea that sex is the biological bedrock and gender is a mere cultural overlay. More specifically, they question the following aspects of the conventional sex-gender distinction: (i) the idea of gender as a property of individuals; (ii) the idea of gender as static and enduring aspects of individuals; (iii) the formulation of sex and gender as a dichotomy; and (iv) the claim that biological sex is a bedrock that stands apart from and untouched by language and culture. They take a dynamic approach to gender: rather than regarding it as individual personality or trait differences, they construe gender as a *social process* – the shared labour through which we're continually producing one another as male or female people. This is called 'doing gender'. Maracek *et al*. (2004) quote West and Zimmerman (1987), who put it like this:

> *Rather than as a property of individuals, we conceive of gender as an emergent feature of social situations: both as an outcome of and a rationale for various social arrangements and as a means of legitimating one of the most fundamental divisions of society.*

To social constructionists, sex, biology and bodies *aren't* ahistorical 'givens': what any cultural group takes to be natural doesn't reside outside the realm of interpretation and language. As Maracek *et al*. (2004) say:

> *What are taken as biological facts are actually situated understandings lodged within webs of assumptions that shift from one cultural setting to another, from one epoch to another, and ... perhaps from one subgroup to another within the same culture ...*

In a very fundamental way, there are no 'facts' – not even those regarding biological entities and processes – that aren't culturally determined.

Psychological androgyny

Prior to the 1970s, the prevalent view (within both psychology and society at large) was that an individual could be *either* masculine *or* feminine. It was assumed that people who achieved a good fit with their gender role (a masculine male and a feminine female) were better adjusted and psychologically healthier than those who didn't (Moghaddam, 1998).

According to Brown (1986), many widely used psychological tests (developed between the 1930s and 1960s) had this assumption built into them. Because of the way the tests were designed and scored, it was impossible for an individual to register as both highly masculine *and* highly feminine: these were mutually exclusive, either/or categories. This made it impossible for any *androgynous* people – that is, individuals who display both masculine and feminine characteristics.

The Bem Sex Role Inventory (BSRI) (1974)

By the early 1970s, several researchers had challenged this traditional view: the same individual *could* be high on both, low on both, or medium on both, since masculinity and femininity were *independent* dimensions. This shift in perspective owed a great deal to the feminist movement, including feminist psychologists such as Bem. To 'discover' androgyny, it was necessary to incorporate this new conception into a new sort of test that would produce two logically independent scores; the Bem Sex Role Inventory (BSRI) (1974) was the first and most influential of these tests (Moghaddam, 1998) (see Gross, 2008).

The BSRI made it possible to measure androgyny by logically and empirically separating scores on masculinity and femininity: it comprises two *independent* scales.

Evaluation of the BSRI

✔ **Popular and widely used test:** the BSRI is the most widely used measure of sex-role stereotyping in adults (Hargreaves, 1986) and probably the most popular modern social psychological method for measuring gender identity (Wetherell, 1997).

✘ **Methodological problems:** quite independently of Bem, Spence *et al.* (1975) devised an alternative test of androgyny – the Personal Attributes Questionnaire (PAQ). Like the BSRI, this produces two independent scores (one for masculinity, one for femininity). However, the two tests assessed androgyny quite differently, which underlined a major problem with the BSRI relating to the very concept of androgyny itself. The BSRI defined androgyny as the difference between an individual's masculinity and femininity scores, such that the smaller the difference, the higher the androgyny score. This (unwittingly) allowed for the *same* androgyny score to be obtained in two very *different* ways: either by an individual scoring *high* on both scales or *low* on both. But surely two such individuals are likely to be very different types of people, in which case what do their androgyny scores mean? By contrast, PAQ allowed for four categories of persons:

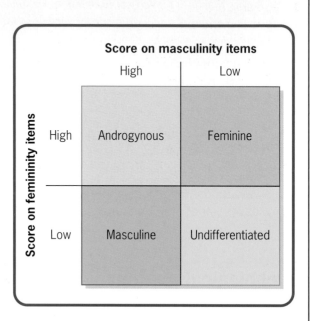

Figure 5.3 *Four sex-role types are created when we think of masculinity and femininity as separate dimensions rather than two ends of the same dimension*

1. the highly sex-typed male – *high* masculinity, low femininity
2. the highly sex-typed female – *low* masculinity, *high* femininity
3. the androgynous person – *high* masculinity, *high* femininity
4. the 'undifferentiated' person – *low* masculinity, *low* femininity.

The crucial difference is that Bem didn't distinguish between 3 and 4: she confounded them. Consequently, she compared her original (1974) results with those of Spence *et al.* and concluded that the four-categories approach was superior: androgyny was now defined as only high in both masculinity and femininity (not low in both too). Her revised BSRI (1977) is considered to be equivalent to PAQ.

The BSRI and Gender Schema Theory

During the 1980s, Bem (e.g. 1984) reformulated her ideas as *gender schema theory*. In our everyday lives, we perceive the world *through* our schemas, such that the world as we know it is composed of the categories represented by our schemas (Edley and Wetherell, 1995).

The male/female distinction is one of the most important classification systems in human social life (Bem, 1987). The social world that children grow up in is thoroughly gendered, and gender differentiation is everywhere imposed from 'outside' (toys, clothes, hairstyles, socialisation practices, the media and so on). Consequently, children soon learn to interpret their

How Science Works

Practical Learning Activity 5.4

- Do the findings regarding the greater number of 'cross-gender' girls than 'cross-gender' boys surprise you?
- Similarly, are you surprised by the finding regarding the association between higher self-esteem and an androgynous or masculine self-concept?
- How might you account for these findings?
- Is being androgynous or having masculine characteristics desirable in and of itself, or is it possible that in some societies high self-esteem may be associated with feminine characteristics? In other words, can the kind of culture one lives in determine which gender role is most closely associated with self-esteem?

experiences through this same set of categories, including, importantly, their sense of self. However, while some children see themselves as entirely defined by a particular gender category (so that self and gender are almost synonymous), others can imagine at least some degree of difference between self and gender. Clearly, the former are strongly sex-typed compared with the latter (as measured by the BSRI).

Perhaps because young children's ideas about sex roles are still quite rigid, there's little sign of androgyny among children below the age of nine or ten. But from about 11 years onwards, variations in androgyny, masculinity and femininity clearly do exist (Bee, 2000). In the USA, 25–35 per cent of high-school students define themselves as androgynous (e.g. Rose and Montemayor, 1994). More girls than boys seem to show this pattern, and more girls fall into the masculine category than boys into the feminine category (see 'Evaluation of the BSRI', above.)

More striking is the finding that either an androgynous or a masculine gender-role self-concept is associated with higher self-esteem among *both* boys and girls (e.g. Rose and Montemayor, 1994).

Bee (2000) suggests that these findings make sense if we assume the existence of a 'masculine bias' in western societies: traditionally, masculine qualities, such as independence and competitiveness, are more highly valued by both men and women than are many traditionally feminine qualities. If such a bias exists, then the teenage boy's task is simpler than the girl's. He can achieve high self-esteem and success with his peers by adopting a traditional masculine gender role, while a girl who adopts a traditional feminine gender role is adopting a less valued role; she has to make a greater effort to behave in ways not expected of her in order to be seen as competent and achieve a level of self-esteem comparable to the boy's.

Spender (1980) calls this general tendency for 'masculine' attributes and occupations to be valued while 'feminine' ones are derogated or downgraded, the 'plus male, minus female' phenomenon. According to Hefner *et al.* (1975, in Taylor, 1986), 'both men and women are trapped in the prisons of gender ... but the situation is far from symmetrical; men are the oppressors and women the oppressed'.

A major hypothesis derived from the BSRI is that androgyny is a good indicator of psychological well-being / mental health. Some supporting evidence exists, such as Bem's (1975) finding that androgynous individuals show gender-role adaptability across situations: they'll behave as the situation requires even though this means behaving in a gender-inappropriate way. Lubinski *et al.* (1981) found that androgynous people report feeling greater emotional well-being, and Spence *et al.* (1975) reported that they have higher self-esteem. However, other evidence is more in line with the findings for adolescents described above. A review by Taylor and Hall (1982) suggested that masculinity – both in males and females – may be a better predictor than certain measures of androgyny. Psychological well-being (measured by, for example, self-esteem, adjustment, absence of anxiety, depression and psychosomatic symptoms) is generally more strongly related to masculinity than femininity on the BSRI and seems not to distinguish reliably between sex-typed and androgynous individuals (Taylor, 1986).

Synoptic Material

The concept of androgyny and feminist psychology

The concept of androgyny implied that women were no longer expected or encouraged to restrict their behaviour to traditional gender-role-specific traits. Bem (1977), together with other feminist psychologists (e.g. Maracek, 1978), prescribed androgyny as a liberating force, leading women to fuller lives. However, while clearly an improvement over the traditional view that masculinity and femininity are opposites and mutually exclusive, the androgynous perspective still maintains that personality comprises feminine and masculine elements. Further, it implies that these elements are *equivalent*, when, in fact, masculine traits are more highly valued (Doyle and Paludi, 1991; see above). As Hare-Mustin and Maracek (1988) argue:

> when the idea of counterparts implies symmetry and equivalence, it obscures differences in power and social value … Arguing for no differences between women and men, however, draws attention away from women's special needs and from differences in power and resources between women and men.

So, while the concept of androgyny is in some ways very radical, it retains aspects of the traditional view: masculinity and femininity are still implicitly seen as inherent characteristics of individuals, rather than socially determined ('constructed') categories (see the 'Synoptic Material' section, pages 192–193). This focus on individuals (who may be androgynous regardless of biological sex or gender) detracts from considering social and political inequalities between gender groups (Paludi, 1992).

Bem herself seems to have taken some of these criticisms on board in her later work. For example, in 1981 she wrote:

> the concept of androgyny is insufficiently radical from a feminist perspective because it continues to presuppose that there is a masculine and a feminine within us all – that is, that the concepts of masculine and feminine have an independent and palpable reality rather than being themselves cognitive constructs derived from gender-based schematic processing. A focus on the concept of androgyny thus fails to prompt serious examination of the extent to which gender organises both our perceptions and our social world.

Eichler (1980, in Wetherell, 1997) sees androgyny as a meaningless ideal. If our society was actually androgynous, the concept itself wouldn't exist: 'sex' (apart from its strictly biological sense) would be considered an irrelevant variable and defunct as a term of reference for social organisation. It's illogical to aim towards achieving androgyny while simultaneously regarding it as the *combination* of highly desirable feminine and masculine qualities.

Gender dysphoria

✔ Specification Hint

The specification uses the term 'gender dysphoria', which is actually used very rarely by psychologists or psychiatrists discussing abnormal behaviour. At the beginning of the chapter, gender dysphoria was defined as anxiety, uncertainty or persistently uncomfortable feelings about one's assigned gender (based on one's anatomical sex). Dysphoria is the major symptom of *gender identity disorder* (GID), which is the term used by official psychiatric classifications of mental disorders. For the rest of this section, therefore, the focus will be on GID (rather than gender dysphoria as such).

Gender identity disorder (GID)

What is it?

According to the Diagnostic and Statistical Manual of Mental Disorders (DSM-IV-TR, 2000 – the official classificatory system of the American Psychiatric Association), gender identity disorder (GID) belongs to the category of 'Sexual and Gender Identity Disorders' (the others being paraphilias, such as fetishism, sexual masochism and sexual sadism, and sexual dysfunctions, including sexual arousal disorders and orgasmic disorders). The criteria for GID are listed in Box 5.5.

Box 5.5: DSM-IV-TR criteria for gender identity disorder

- Strong and persistent identification with the opposite sex.
- In children, presence of four or more of the following:
  (a) repeatedly stated desire to be or insistence that she or he is the other sex
  (b) preference for wearing opposite-sex clothes
  (c) preference for cross-sex roles in play or persistent fantasies of being of the opposite sex
  (d) preference for stereotypical play of the opposite sex
  (e) preference for playmates of the opposite sex.
- In adolescents and adults, such symptoms as desire to be the opposite sex, passing as member of the opposite sex, desire to be treated as member of the opposite sex, conviction that his or her emotions are typical of the opposite sex.
- Persistent discomfort with one's biological sex or a sense of alienation from the gender roles of that sex.
  (a) In children, manifested by any of the following. In boys, finding penis disgusting and convinced that it will disappear with time; dislike of stereotyped boys' play activities. In girls, rejection of urinating while sitting; belief that they will grow a penis; aversion to developing breasts and menstruating; aversion to conventional female clothing.
  (b) In adolescents and adults, manifested by any of the following. Strong desire to get rid of secondary sex characteristics via hormones and/or surgery; belief that he or she was born the wrong sex.
- Not concurrent with a physical intersex condition.
- Causes marked distress or impairment in social or occupational functioning.

How Science Works

Practical Learning Activity 5.5

- Which of the criteria listed in Box 5.5 correspond to 'gender dysphoria'?
- What are secondary sex characteristics? Give some examples.
- What's meant by 'Not concurrent with a physical intersex condition'?
- What's the difference between people with GID cross-dressing and transvestites?

What causes GID?

Genetic factors

Bennett (2006) cites one of the few studies of the genetic processes involved in GID (Coolidge et al., 2002), which found that 2 per cent of their sample of over 300 monozygotic (MZ) (identical) and dizygotic (DZ) (non-identical/fraternal) twins showed some evidence of GID based on self-report measures.

Applying statistical modelling techniques to their data, Coolidge et al. revealed that 62 per cent of the variance in reported symptoms could be attributed to biological factors, and 38 per cent to environmental factors. They concluded that the causes of GID are primarily biological – not psychological.

Biological factors
Hormones
Identifying the biological processes through which these genetic effects may be mediated remains unclear (Bennett, 2006). Although one obvious candidate is *hormones*, studies of sex hormonal disturbance in adulthood are surprisingly difficult to carry out: as we noted earlier, many people with GID take opposite-sex hormones as part of a treatment programme or by buying them on the black market. Even though it may be possible to study only transsexuals who've not taken such exogenous hormones for a few months, relatively little is known at present about the long-term effects of earlier hormone treatment (Davison *et al.*, 2004).

Given these difficulties of interpretation, what evidence there is doesn't support a hormonal explanation. Gladue (1985) reported few, if any, hormonal differences between men with GID, male heterosexuals and gay men. Similar results have been reported for women.

But what about studies of children? The case of the Batista family (Imperato-McGinley *et al.*, 1974; see Case Study 5.2) strongly suggests that hormones determine gender identity, although the abnormal sample involved makes generalising to the general population problematical.

Other research shows that human – and other primate – offspring whose mothers take sex hormones during pregnancy often behave like members of the opposite sex and have anatomical abnormalities. A much-cited example is Ehrhardt and Money's (1967, in Money and Ehrhardt, 1972) study of girls whose mothers had taken synthetic progestins (which are precursors to male sex hormones) to prevent uterine bleeding during pregnancy. The girls became quite tomboyish (e.g. climbing trees, playing with guns) as preschoolers. Young boys whose mothers have taken female hormones during pregnancy tend to be less boyish than their peers and to engage in less rough-and-tumble play (Yalom *et al.*, 1973).

However, there's no evidence that either group of children dislike their gender (Bennett, 2006). Also, some of the girls studied by Ehrhardt and Money were *intersex*: they had ambiguous genitals, which often led them to be raised as boys. Such cases formed the basis for Money and Ehrhardt's (1972) *biosocial approach* (see next section, pages 201–206), which maintains that it's the gender of rearing that's crucial in determining gender identity, and not genetic/chromosomal sex. Not only did Money and Ehrhardt seriously play down the influence of hormones on behaviour – including their own data – in formulating their theory, but the theory has been seriously challenged by the case of the penectomised twin (see pages 204–205). Perhaps of most relevance here is the fact that the DSM criteria for GID explicitly remove intersex conditions from the criteria. In other words, we cannot accept evidence for the role of hormones if these are associated with intersex conditions.

Social and psychological factors
Psychoanalytic explanations
The earliest psychological theory of GID was proposed by Stoller (1968), a psychoanalyst. He claimed that extreme stress in adult life profoundly disturbs all aspects of the person's identity, and in some cases may disturb gender identity. While Stoller's theory remained highly influential for many years, it's since been widely criticised, and empirical studies have generally failed to confirm predictions from the theory (Frude, 1998).

Other psychoanalytic explanations suggest that male transsexuals have an ambiguous core gender identity. According to Ovesey and Person (1973, in Bennett, 2006), male transsexualism stems from extreme separation anxiety early in life before the individual has fully established his own sexual identity. To alleviate this anxiety, the individual resorts to fantasies of *symbiotic fusion* with the mother – that is, mother and child become one and the danger of separation is removed. In the transsexual's mind, he literally becomes the mother, and to sustain this fantasy attempts to switch his core identity from male to female.

Ovesey and Person explain the desire for the removal of the penis by noting that the transsexual *doesn't* experience castration anxiety. In Freud's theory of the Oedipus complex, all boys, somewhere between three and five years, fear having their penis cut off as punishment by a jealous father for desiring their mother. What makes the male transsexual different is that his anxiety *ends* only when he is castrated. The penis is clear evidence that he has failed to psychically fuse with the mother. For the same reason, transsexuals reject homosexuality – this too would underline their maleness. Instead, they prefer to reject any sexual experience, and generally have little or no sexual experience – even masturbation. The motivation for security takes precedence over their sex drive, reflecting their fear of early maternal deprivation (Bennett, 2006).

Conditioning approaches

Perhaps the most widely accepted theory of GID is that it arises from conditioning early in life. Parents of people with GID often report that they encouraged and gave attention to their child when s/he cross-dressed. This appears to be particularly relevant in boys, where they may be taught how to put on make-up, and other feminine behaviours. Many mothers and other female relatives find it cute when the feminine boy dresses in the mother's old dresses and high-heeled shoes. Family albums typically contain photographs of young boys dressed in women's clothing. Such family reactions to an atypical child probably contribute in a major way to the conflict between his/her anatomical sex and the acquired gender identity. More subtly, girls who display high levels of tomboyish behaviour tend to have parents who do the same, and are 'daddy's girls' (Green, 1974, 1987).

A factor that may contribute to this pattern of adult behaviour is the child's physical attractiveness. Boys with GID have been rated as *more* attractive than control children, while girls with GID have been rated as *less* attractive (Zucker *et al.*, 1993). Also, male patients report having had a distant relationship with their father, while females report a history of physical or sexual abuse (Bradley and Zucker, 1997).

Conditioning experiences may also explain why more children than adults are identified as having GID: early life experiences are dominated by the family. But, as the individual grows up, peers, schoolteachers and others outside the family exert an influence; this makes it more likely that the person will be punished for behaving in 'inappropriate' ways. However, as Bennett points out, while this approach can explain the development of non-gender-typical behaviours, it cannot so easily explain the strength of their beliefs about their gender, and their resistance to any form of psychological therapy. According to Hines (2004a), 'The strong, persistent desire to change sex, and the willingness to undergo surgery and hormone treatment despite formidable obstacles, including, in some cases, social stigmatization and job loss, may suggest a biological imperative.' However, as we noted above, efforts to identify genetic or hormonal abnormalities in adults

STRETCH AND CHALLENGE

Freud's account of gender development is related to his account of moral development, which, in turn, is part of his theory of psychosexual development (see Gross, 2005; Gross and Rolls, 2008). Up until the resolution of the Oedipus complex at about age five, gender identity is assumed to be flexible; when the child identifies with the same-sex parent, it acquires both a superego and gender identity.

There are at least three reasons for doubting a Freudian interpretation of the development of gender identity.

1. Children of a particular age don't appear to acquire gender identity in 'one fell swoop' (Krebs and Blackman, 1988).
2. Children who grow up in 'atypical' families (e.g. single-parent or lesbian couples) aren't necessarily adversely affected in terms of their gender identity (Golombok *et al.*, 1983). Indeed, children reared in fatherless families (whether lesbian or heterosexual) appear to have *more secure attachments* (Golombok *et al.*, 1997). When children raised in gay or lesbian households are followed up into adulthood, there are no indications that gender identity or sexual orientation is affected by having two same-sex parents. Studies of the parenting abilities of gays and lesbians indicate they're just as capable, warm and child-orientated as heterosexual parents – sometimes more so (presumably because of their greater motivation in the face of a sceptical and hostile world). The claim that children need a parent of each sex for healthy development isn't supported by the existing evidence (Golombok, 2000).
3. While identification might promote gender identity, children are aware of gender roles well before the age at which Freud believed their Oedipus complex is resolved. For example, boys prefer stereotypically masculine toys and girls stereotypically feminine toys in infancy (O'Brien *et al.*, 1983).

Figure 5.4 Harmless fun – or a contributory cause of gender identity disorder?

with GID have been largely unsuccessful. The prenatal hormone environment may influence gender identity (Hines, 2004a).

Socio-cultural influences

Researchers in this field are very much aware of the culture-relative nature of masculinity-femininity, and of the difference between enjoying activities more typical of the opposite sex and actually believing that one is of the opposite sex (Davison *et al.*, 2004). Most small children engage in varying amounts of traditional opposite-sex play, with no gender identity conflicts whatsoever (Green, 1976).

However, our society is very intolerant of boys who 'cross over', whereas girls can play games and dress in a manner more typical of boys and still be accepted. Indeed, the male bias within western cultures makes pursuit of certain masculine behaviours and characteristics highly desirable and an important influence on

females' self-esteem (see the discussion of androgyny, above).

BIOLOGICAL INFLUENCES ON GENDER

The role of hormones and genes in gender development

✔ Specification Hint

Much has already been said – at the beginning of the chapter – about the role of hormones and genes in *sexual differentiation* – that is, development as a male or female. We considered both normal development – that is, where all the categories of biological sex (see Box 5.1) are consistent with one another, and abnormal development – that is, cases of *intersex,* where there are discrepancies between genetic (chromosomal) sex and both internal reproductive organs and external genitalia.

Cases of intersex are crucial in relation to the *biosocial approach* to gender development; this will be discussed before consideration of the *evolutionary explanations* of gender roles.

Gonadal hormones and sexual differentiation

Although sexual differentiation begins with the sex chromosomes (XX or XY), they don't exert most of their influence directly. Instead, their main job is to direct the gonads to develop as either testes (in males) or ovaries (in females). After that, hormones from the gonads, particularly androgens from the testes, provide the major biological influences on sexual differentiation.

The influence of hormones on sexual differentiation begins early in gestation (pregnancy) and involves the internal and external genitalia, as well as the brain and behaviour. It has been studied extensively in non-human mammals, ranging from rodents to primates, and appears to apply, at least to some extent, to human development as well. According to Hines (2004a),

'Infants enter the world with some predispositions to "masculinity" and "femininity", and these predispositions appears to result largely from hormones to which they were exposed before birth.'

The gonads are originally identical in both XY and XX embryos. However, in XY individuals, genetic information on the Y chromosome causes the gonads to become testes, and by week eight of gestation they're producing hormones (particularly the primary androgen, testosterone). If the gonads don't become testes, they become ovaries, which don't appear to produce significant amounts of hormones prenatally. Consequently, XY foetuses have higher levels of testosterone than XX foetuses, particularly between 8 and 24 weeks of gestation. Between then and birth, gonadal hormone levels are low in both sexes, but a surge of testicular hormones after birth makes testosterone once again higher in boys than in girls (for about the first six months).

Gonadal hormones, intersex conditions and human behavioural development

Hormones clearly influence the human genitalia, but hormonal influences on behaviour are harder to establish; this is partly because behaviour is subject to social (and other) influences after birth. In addition, it's unethical to manipulate hormones experimentally in humans during early life in the way it's done with non-humans (but even here, ethical issues arise). For this reason, the natural experiments represented by cases of intersex individuals are of particular importance.

According to Hines (2004a, 2004b), girls with CAH (compared with unaffected sisters / first cousins and girls matched for demographic background) are usually treated post-natally to normalise hormones, sex-assigned and raised as girls, and surgically feminised.

Play behaviour

These girls show increased preferences for male-typed toys (such as cars, trucks and guns) and reduced preferences for female-typed toys (such as dolls, cosmetics and kitchen equipment). These findings have been reported by researchers in several different countries (including the USA, Canada, the Netherlands, Germany, Sweden and the UK), using interviews and questionnaires, as well as direct observation of children's toy choices. Girls with CAH also choose boys and other girls equally as favourite playmates, whereas their unaffected relatives choose other girls 80–90 per cent of the time (Hines and Kaufman, 1994).

This male-typical behaviour occurs despite the girls having been surgically feminised and raised as girls, and despite their parents being encouraged to promote feminine behaviour in their daughters – which they do.

What does this imply for normal development? Normal variability in prenatal androgen appears to influence sex-typical play, without causing genital ambiguity. Testosterone levels during pregnancy have been found to be higher in mothers of healthy girls with extremely male-typical toy, playmate and activity preferences (such as for rough-and-tumble play) than in mothers of girls with extremely female-typical behaviour (Hines et al., 2002). The girls were three and a half at the time of the study. Other evidence shows that levels of available testosterone in the maternal circulation during pregnancy, along with the daughters' own testosterone levels in adulthood, predict male-typical gender-role behaviour in daughters at the age of 27–30 years. Individual variability in testosterone during pregnancy could be genetic.

Core gender identity

Despite Money and Ehrhardt's claim that sex of rearing is more important than chromosomal or hormonal sex (see below), there's considerable evidence that points to the greater influence of biology.

Although for the vast majority of CAH individuals (or those with other intersex conditions), core gender identity *is* consistent with sex of rearing, some do experience gender dysphoria – and some express a desire to change sex. Although dysphoria is rare among intersex individuals, it's more frequent than in the general population (e.g. Zucker et al., 1996).

Sexual orientation

Females with CAH are more likely than their sisters, or demographically matched controls, to report bisexual or homosexual erotic interests. These findings have been reported in the USA, the UK, Germany and Canada (Hines, 2004a, 2004b). Nevertheless, the majority of CAH women describe themselves as heterosexual. Women with CAH also report reduced erotic interest in general (i.e. in either males or females; Zucker et al., 1996).

These outcomes for adult sexuality could be influenced by problems related to ambiguous genitalia and surgery. Feminising surgery doesn't usually produce genitalia that are identical to those of normal females, and surgery can make intercourse problematic. Individuals with CAIS almost always report a heterosexual orientation (i.e. towards men) and are just as likely as other women to form long-term heterosexual relationships or to marry (Hines *et al.*, 2003); this suggests that their inability to respond to androgens, or their feminine appearance and socialisation, is more important than the Y chromosome in determining sexual orientation (Hines, 2004b). For example, their knowledge of exposure to masculinising hormones and of physical virilisation at birth might influence their sexual behaviour.

The biosocial approach

How Science Works

Practical Learning Activity 5.6

- What conclusions can you draw about the role of hormones and genes in gender development from the research described above?
- What are the advantages and disadvantages of studying gender development in intersex individuals?

According to Edley and Wetherell (1995), to ask 'What is the biological basis of masculinity (or femininity)' is to pose a false question. In their view:

It requires us to separate what cannot be separated: men [and women] are the product of a complex system of factors and forces which combine in a variety of ways to produce a whole range of different masculinities [and femininities].

Biosocial theory takes social factors into account in relation to biological ones. It sees the *interaction* between biological and social factors as important, rather than biology's direct influence. From birth, the way adults respond to a child is influenced by the child's sex; as far as other people are concerned, the baby's sex is just as important as its temperament. Clearly, adults bring sexual stereotypes to their interactions with children, but are these expectations responsible for creating differences in the children or do adults react to differences that are already present? What is the direction of influence? (Schaffer, 2004). The 'Baby X' experiments tried to answer this question (see Key Study 5.1).

Key Study 5.1: The 'Baby X' experiments (based on Schaffer, 2004)

Aim/hypothesis (AO1)

A series of studies, starting in the 1970s and collectively known as the 'Baby X' experiments, set out to answer the question regarding the direction of the influence between children's sex and the way they're typically treated by parents and other adults. One example is the study conducted by Condry and Condry (1976).

Method/design (AO1)

A sample of over 200 adults, both men and women, were shown a videotape of a nine-month-old baby who was introduced to some as a boy ('David') and to others as a girl ('Dana'). Both in appearance and dress the baby was neither markedly masculine nor feminine.

The baby was shown responding to various toys, such as a teddy and a doll, and to such stimuli as a jack-in-the-box and a sudden loud buzzer; for each of these the adults were asked to describe the emotion the baby displayed.

Results/findings (AO1)

The results clearly showed the influence of the baby's presumed gender. For example, when 'David' reacted to the jack-in-the-box by crying, most of the adults labelled this as *anger*; when 'Dana' showed exactly the same behaviour, it was identified as *fear*.

Conclusions (AO1)

The same baby reacting in the same way was judged to respond differently, depending on the gender label supplied. As Condry and Condry concluded, differences between male and female infants appear to be in the eye of the beholder.

Evaluation (AO1/AO2)

There have been many other studies investigating reactions to Baby X. While using the same basic approach, there are variations among these studies in procedural details and in samples, such as whether the baby is presented live or on videotape, whether the adults are asked to interact with the baby or not, the amount of experience that adults have of children, the kind of judgements they're expected to make, and so on.

For example, Smith and Lloyd (1978) dressed babies in unisex snowsuits and gave them names that were sometimes in line with their true gender and sometimes not. When adults played with them, they treated the babies according to the gender they *believed* them to be. For example, they were more likely to offer the babies same-sex toys, and 'boys' were more likely to be encouraged to play vigorously and explore the toys actively, while 'girls' were treated more gently and as more dependent on adult help. This indicates that a person's (perceived) biological make-up becomes part of his/her social environment through others' reactions to them.

However, not all such studies have obtained such clear-cut results. So when adults were asked to rate the baby's personality characteristics (how friendly, cooperative etc.), few differences emerged according to gender labelling: the baby's real characteristics proved more important in determining how the child was perceived. Also, children asked to interact with a Baby X are more strongly influenced by beliefs about its gender than adults are (Stern and Karraker, 1989, in Schaffer, 2004).

Schaffer concludes like this:

> the gender-labelling effect is not as strong as originally thought. Whether a child is considered to be male or female is only one of several influences on the way others react. It is strongest when little other information is available about the child such as his or her real characteristics or when that information is ambiguous. However, when gender-label effects are found, they are almost invariably in keeping with cultural stereotypes of the sexes and may well therefore play a part in children's gender development.

According to Money and Ehrhardt (1972), 'anatomy is destiny': how an infant is labelled sexually determines how it's raised or socialised. In turn, this determines the child's gender identity, and from this follow its gender-role identity and sexual orientation. Psychologically, sexuality (i.e. gender identity) is *undifferentiated* at birth; it becomes differentiated as masculine or feminine in the course of the various experiences of growing up.

As we saw above, much of the evidence for biosocial theory comes from studies of *intersex* individuals. What such individuals are is a 'natural experiment': their gender of rearing is 'out of synch' with their chromosomal/hormonal/anatomical status, which makes it possible to assess the relative influence of environmental and biological factors on gender identity.

Money and Ehrhardt (1972) report their findings from CAH individuals, who were initially raised as boys.

When the mistake was discovered, their genitals were surgically corrected, and they were reassigned and raised as girls. Money and Ehrhardt claim that it's possible to change the gender of rearing without any undue psychological harm being done, provided this occurs within a 'critical' or 'sensitive' period of about two and a half to three years. After this, reassignment to the opposite gender can cause extreme psychological disturbance.

Money and Ehrhardt also studied ten people with CAIS. They showed a strong preference for the female role, which also supports the view than gender of rearing is more important than biological sex. The case of Daphne Went also tends to support this view (see Case Study 5.3).

Case Study 5.3: Daphne Went: a case of CAIS (Goldwyn, 1979)

Daphne Went, a motherly-looking woman, possessed two testes where most women have ovaries. She is one of 500 or so 'women' in the UK with CAIS.

Her development began along the male route, but it was never finished. The egg was fertilised by a Y sperm and two normal testes developed. They secreted their first hormone, which absorbed the female parts, but when they produced testosterone her body didn't respond to it. So, apart from the womb, everything developed along female lines.

When at puberty she developed no pubic hair and didn't menstruate (despite breast development and female contours, as a result of the action of oestrogen), there was clearly something wrong! Hormones didn't bring on her periods, because she had no womb. Chromosomally, Mrs Went is male; as far as the gonads are concerned, she's also male (she has testes). But her external appearance is female. She's married, has adopted two children, and leads an active life as a woman.

Evaluation of biosocial theory

✗ **Controversial additional evidence:** in addition to the study of intersex individuals, there are a few cases of XY infants with normally functioning testes who've been assigned and raised as girls, again with surgical feminisation. This can occur, for example, when the infant is born with a severely underdeveloped penis – or no penis at all (Hines, 2004b).

There are also a few cases where male infants have suffered accidental penile destruction (usually during surgery/circumcision) and have been reassigned as females. The most famous and well-documented case involves the twin boy whose penis was destroyed during circumcision. This has caused great controversy, partly because of Money's insistence that, despite blatant – and ultimately tragic – evidence to the contrary, the findings support the view that gender identity (and gender role) is *learned*. This is described in Case Study 5.4.

Diamond and Sigmundson (1997) re-examined the medical notes and impressions of therapists who'd been originally involved with the Reimer twins. New data also came from interviews with John (David) himself, his mother and his wife in 1994/95 (when John was 29/30). In the light of these new data, Diamond and Sigmundson challenged two basic assumptions ('postulates') of Money and Ehrhardt's biosocial theory, namely:

1. individuals are psychosexually neutral at birth
2. healthy psychosexual development is intimately related to the appearance of the genitals.

They concluded that John was a mature and forward-looking man with a keen sense of

humour and balance. Although still bitter over
his experience, he accepted what had
happened and was trying to make the most of
his life with support from his wife, parents and
family. He had job satisfaction and was
generally self-assured. However, tragically, he
committed suicide in 2004.

Diamond and Sigmundson's conclusions
completely reverse those drawn by Money and
Ehrhardt. They argue that cases of infant sex
reassignment need to be reviewed after
puberty: five- and ten-year post-sex
reassignment follow-ups just aren't sufficient.
No support exists for the postulate that
individuals are psychosexually neutral at birth or
that healthy psychosexual development is
dependent on the appearance of the genitals.
(See Synoptic Material, page 206.)

Figure 5.5 David Reimer in 2000

✔ **Some supporting evidence:** in another case of a boy whose penis was destroyed when he
was just two months old, he was reassigned as a girl at seven months, and now identifies as a
bisexual woman; she shows no signs of gender dysphoria (Bradley *et al.,* 1998). It's difficult to
account for the difference between the outcomes of this case and David Reimer's, but this
second case is clearly consistent with biosocial theory.

✘ **Intersex individuals are atypical:** just because some people appear to be flexible in their
psychosexual development, doesn't in itself disprove that 'built-in' biases still have to be
overcome (Diamond, 1978). Intersex individuals are, by definition, an *atypical* sample; this is
the opposite side of the coin to the advantage that they allow the influence of environmental
and biological factors to be separated. There's no evidence that people *in general* are as
flexible in their psychosexual development. The first postulate was based on studies of
intersex individuals (Diamond and Sigmundson, 1997).

Case Study 5.4: The case of the penectomised twin (Money and Ehrhardt, 1972)

- In 1966, at the age of eight months, while undergoing a routine circumcision, Bruce Reimer's penis
  was accidentally burnt off (*penectomised*). After consulting with Money, his parents decided it was
  in Bruce's best interests to raise him as a girl (Brenda).
- At 22 months, Brenda was surgically castrated (*orchiectomy*), he was given oestrogen injections,
  and a vaginal canal was constructed. He was subsequently raised as Joan.
- At age four, Joan preferred dresses to trousers, took pride in her long hair and was cleaner than

Case Study 5.4: The case of the penectomised twin (Money and Ehrhardt, 1972) continued...

her twin brother, Kevin. At age nine, although Joan had been the dominant twin since birth, she expressed this by being a 'fussy little mother' to Kevin.

- In *Man and Woman, Girl and Boy* (1972), Money and Ehrhardt referred to Joan's 'tomboyish traits' in passing, focusing on the ways she conformed to the stereotypes of female gender role. No mention was made of the rejection and teasing she'd encountered in school. Significantly, when she reached her teens she was an unhappy adolescent, with few friends, uncertain about her gender identity, and maintaining that boys 'had a better life'.
- When Joan was 12, she (reluctantly) began taking oestrogen, and soon breast development and fat around her hips and waist began to appear. But she resisted any further (vaginal) surgery. By 14, the female hormones were now competing with her male hormonal system. She decided to stop living as a girl, changed her name (back) to John, and underwent sex reassignment surgery just before her sixteenth birthday. A rudimentary penis was constructed, but this neither resembled nor performed like the real thing. His popularity with girls caused him terrible distress and unhappiness, and at 18 he tried to commit suicide – on two separate occasions.
- At 21, he had a second operation on his penis, which produced a significant improvement. Two years later, he met and fell in love with a single mother of three children – they married in 1990 (Colapinto, 2000). Colapinto met him in 1997 (he was then 31 and renamed David Reimer).

Synoptic Material

According to Ceci and Williams (1999), Diamond and Sigmundson's (1997) review helps to redress the existing imbalance in the nature–nurture debate regarding the influences on the development of gender identity. As developmental psychologists, they believe that most textbooks stress the importance of how children are raised, to the detriment of biological explanations.

The 'supremacy of socialisation' is, of course, what Money and Ehrhardt's biosocial theory advocates. Ceci and Williams say that perhaps the single most striking aspect of the John/Joan case given by Diamond and Sigmundson is how quickly John, who spent 10–20 years being raised as a female, was able to adopt a male gender identity and role. This strongly suggests that biological influences aren't as irrelevant as many psychologists seem to believe.

The second postulate *reduces* a person's total sexuality to just those behaviours and experiences that relate to the genitals. However, an individual's sexual profile comprises at least five levels: gender patterns, reproduction, sexual identity, arousal and physiological mechanisms, and sexual orientation (PRIMO). According to Diamond and Sigmundson, John's reassignment to Joan addressed only the gender patterns; it was just *assumed* that sexual identity and the other levels would follow. Joan did indeed become aware of what was expected of her as a girl, but John didn't feel comfortable with this. Standing while urinating is a dramatic illustration of this. Sex reassignment also failed at the other four levels.

John/Joan (later David Reimer) appeared on the *Oprah Winfrey Show*, declaring that Money had consigned him to a childhood of humiliation, confusion and misery (Usborne, 2004). Biology ultimately proved irrepressible; gender identity is 'hardwired' into the brain virtually from conception (Diamond, 1982; Diamond and Sigmundson, 1997). As Diamond (in Usborne, 2004) says, 'David didn't give permission for what was done to him. Even though he didn't have a penis, he still knew he was male.' Agreeing with Diamond, Reimer (in Fletcher, 1997) argues that, 'The organ that appears to be critical to psychosexual development and adaptation is not the genitalia but the brain.'

Evolutionary explanations of gender roles

✔ Specification Hint

Much of what's usually discussed under this heading is covered in Chapter 2 on Relationships, specifically, the middle section on *Human Reproductive Behaviour* (pages 61–75): (i) the relationship between *sexual selection* and *human reproductive behaviour*; (ii) evolutionary explanations of *parental investment* – for example, sex differences, parent–offspring conflict. That section also describes some of the basic principles of Darwin's *evolutionary theory* and *evolutionary psychology* (*neo-* or *modern Darwinism*).

Some additional material is presented here, which can be regarded largely as an *evaluation* (AO2) of evolutionary psychological explanations of gender roles in relation to sexual selection, mate preferences and parental investment. (Alternatively, this additional material can be thought of as 'Stretch and Challenge'.)

Only the third and last section of this part of the specification points to *human* behaviour (by reference to 'the influence of parents, peers and schools, media. Cross-cultural studies of gender role'). However, as in Chapter 2, it's perfectly acceptable to give examples from non-human animals, provided these are relevant to, and throw light upon, the research involving humans.

According to Kenrick *et al*. (2004):

> *Human behaviour represents an amalgam of influences. Since its inception, the evolutionary approach to understanding these influences has often aroused controversy ... Today's evolutionary models have been expanded and modified in the face of logical argument and new data. Those models now emphasize issues such as female choice, male parental investment, gender similarities as well as differences, and environmental variability in human behaviour ... The view of behavioural predispositions as adaptations to recurrent problems of survival and reproduction is complementary to other perspectives ...*

They go on to say that we don't need to choose between evolutionary explanations and those that emphasise culture, learning or cognition:

> *The human brain was designed by the same natural forces that shaped other natural phenomena, but it is a brain designed to think, learn, and to construct cultures. To isolate or ignore any of these facets limits our understanding of human behaviour ...*

The psychology of gender is perhaps the best area of research for integrating these different approaches and perspectives.

How Science Works

Practical Learning Activity 5.7

- Read (or re-read) pages 64–73, which discuss *parental investment* and *sexual selection*.
- Identify just how these two 'general principles' explain the relationships between (a) sex differences in morphology and behaviour and (b) sex differences in mating strategies.
- While non-human examples are relevant, the emphasis should be on human parental investment and sexual selection.

Differential parental investment and sexual selection

Differential parental investment refers to the fact that males and females differ in the amount of resources they invest in offspring (Trivers, 1972). Eggs are generally more costly to produce than sperm and, in mammals, this is compounded by a lengthy period of gestation, requiring a large amniotic sac that takes priority over the female's own nutritional intake for several months. After birth, the female nurses the newborn, again sacrificing her own nutritional intake to feed her offspring. Human young need to be fed and cared for even after they're weaned. So the minimum parental investment for female mammals is considerable.

Males can father young with much less investment: all it takes is one act of sexual intercourse. Kenrick *et al.* (2004) cite the example of the Xavante hunter-gatherer people, where the average number of offspring for males and females was 3.6. However, the variance was 3.9 for women and 12.1 for men. In other words, some Xavante men had many offspring and others had few. Only one of 195 women was childless at age 20, but 6 per cent of men were still childless at age 40. One man fathered 23 children, whereas for a woman the highest number of children was 8. This pattern holds for most species; females, compared to males, tend to have fewer offspring and a greater investment in them.

Some of the physical differences between males and females are due simply to natural selection based on differential parental investment. The female body needs to produce eggs and, in mammals, to nurture the foetus and the newborn baby. So why are males usually larger than females, when a relatively larger body would seem to be of more use to females that must directly contribute bodily resources to the young? And why are males more likely to have decorative features such as antlers or brilliant plumage, and to use some of those features to compete with other males?

Darwin's answer was *sexual selection* (*intra-* and *inter-*; see pages 69–71). Because females invest more in any given offspring, a bad choice of mate would prove more costly for a female than for a male. Thus, females, compared to males, tend to be more selective. However, human males, compared with other mammalian species, invest quite heavily in their offspring and exercise greater discrimination in mating.

Male parental investment

Without paternal investment, human offspring have lower survival rates, and sex differences tend to be smaller when males invest more in their offspring (Geary, 1998). Accordingly, men and women are relatively similar in size and decoration, in contrast to peacocks and peahens. In some species, the typical 'sex roles' are completely reversed (as in some species of birds): where this happens, larger and more colourful females compete for sexual access to males. Consistent with parental investment theory, males in these species invest relatively more in offspring than do females (Kenrick *et al.*, 2004).

However, because men and women still contribute fundamentally different resources to produce offspring, the characteristics they desire in mates are also different. Women directly invest their bodily resources; their reproductive potential peaks in the mid-twenties and ends with the menopause (Dunson *et al.*, 2002). Consistent with this, men's judgements of female attractiveness have been linked to indicators of youth and physical health (see pages 64–67). Men invest indirect resources (such as food, money and protection) that don't necessarily diminish as they get older. So women would be expected to value men's ability to provide those resources more than their youth.

Environmental influences on behaviour

According to Kenrick *et al.* (2004), 'an evolutionary perspective doesn't assume that human behaviour is based in rigid reflexes and closed instincts, but it does assume domain-specific biases relative to what is learned and how information is connected …'. Research on humans and other animals has revealed different learning biases adapted to recurrent problems faced by the animals' ancestors.

For example, mothering is particularly sensitive to environmental constraints. Contrary to the belief that females are infinitely warm and nurturing, Hrdy (1999) argues that mothers are strategic actors that respond to environmental conditions in ways that enhance the chances of their own survival, as well as that of their offspring. This behaviour can appear ruthless at times. We all know that mothers will kill attackers to protect their offspring, but, in rare circumstances, they might desert offspring to protect limited resources. Hrdy describes the South American Ache foragers, in which one mother's newborn was left behind because its father had died during the pregnancy and the mother's new husband wouldn't provide for the child. Also, when a close birth interval between two children threatened the older child's milk supply, the newborn was killed.

Infanticide has been documented on all continents. For example, in Denmark, all cases of female–female murder between 1933 and 1961 were infanticide (Daly and Wilson, 1988). These examples illustrate very real trade-offs that mothers must make between different offspring under particular environmental conditions. In primates (including humans), these strategic choices can lead to acts that seem contrary to widely held images of mothering, including favouring one child over another, abandonment and even infanticide (Hrdy, 1999).

Cross-cultural studies of gender-linked behaviour

Kenrick et al. (2004) maintain that one advantage of adopting an evolutionary perspective on gender is that it leads to questions concerning universal issues.

- Are there cross-cultural regularities in the behaviours of human males and females?

- Do those regularities reflect different problems faced by the two sexes across different species, or are they unique to humans?

- How do those regularities fit with general evolutionary models (such as parental investment theory)?

In many ways, men and women within any culture are more alike than they are different. On most behavioural dimensions, there are probably more differences *within* a sex than between the sexes. This holds true for spatial abilities, verbal intelligence, friendliness and many other characteristics (see above, pages 185–187).

At first glance, such overlap makes it difficult to imagine universal sex differences in behaviour that compare to the universal sex differences in morphology (such as having testicles or ovaries); and even some of these show overlap (within any culture, there are women who are taller than most men).

The evolutionary perspective assumes that sex-linked behaviours arose as adaptations to the problems of survival and reproduction faced by our ancestors. When ancestral men and women faced similar demands in a given domain, we'd expect small or non-existent sex differences; but when they faced different demands, we'd expect larger differences. Given a similar diet and family background, the average man is slightly taller, heavier, and more muscular than the average woman: 'Behavioural differences are more like these differences in height and weight than the morphological differences in male and female sex organs' (Kenrick et al., 2004).

Because reproductive competition is central to evolutionary theory, evolutionary theorists have been particularly interested in the relationships between sex and behaviours related to social dominance and aggression (see Chapter 3), and mating (see Chapter 2).

SOCIAL CONTEXTS OF GENDER ROLE

Social influences on gender role

✔ Specification Hint

The specification states 'Social influences on gender role, for example the role of parents, peers and schools, media'. This means that the examiner cannot ask you specifically about any one or more of these, but these are the kinds of influence you need to know about. More emphasis will be given here to the role of parents and the media.

Practical Learning Activity 5.8

- How does Social Learning Theory (SLT) differ from Classical Learning Theory (in particular, operant conditioning)? (See Gross, 2005; Gross and Rolls, 2008.)

Social Learning Theory

According to Durkin (1995), early formulations of *social learning theory* (SLT) claimed that socialising agents, such as parents, teachers, peers and the media, convey repetitive messages about the importance of gender-role-appropriate behaviour.

The child is *positively reinforced* (rewarded) for behaving in gender-appropriate ways and *punished* for behaving in gender-inappropriate ways (based on the principles of *operant conditioning*). This is one means by which children *learn* their gender roles. But these socialising agents also *model* examples of appropriate and inappropriate behaviour and the consequences of conforming or not conforming with gender norms. Through *observational learning*, the child acquires knowledge regarding gender roles without actually 'doing' anything: the child sees *others* (the models) being reinforced or punished. Indeed, according to Perry and Bussey (1984), gender-role stereotypes are acquired mainly through observational learning.

The influence of parents

In one of the earliest versions of SLT, Bandura and Walters (1963) drew on examples of gender role learning to illustrate that their theory could account for social learning in general. They pointed out that parents in many different cultures present their off-spring with direct example (modelling) and instruction in appropriate gender role behaviours; they also provide their children with toys and play materials that are stereotypically male or female.

So one reason girls and boys learn to behave differently is that they're *treated differently* by their parents and others. As the 'Baby X' experiments show (see Key Study 5.1), when informed of a child's biological sex, parents and other adults often react to it according to their gender-role expectations. Thus, girls and boys are given different toys, have their rooms decorated differently and are even spoken to in different ways (Rubin *et al.*, 1974). Boys tend to be positively reinforced more for behaviours reflecting independence, self-reliance and emotional control, while girls are more likely to be reinforced for dependence, nurturance, empathy and emotional expression (Block, 1979).

Fathers have been found to reinforce these sex-typed behaviours more than mothers do (Kerig *et al.*, 1993), especially in their sons (Siegal, 1987); in other words, fathers treat their children in a more *gendered* way (Maccoby, 1990). Typically, fathers interact in a more instrumental and achievement-orientated way, and give more attention to their sons; mothers attend equally to their sons and daughters (Quiery, 1998).

However, Karraker *et al.* (1995) found that this strong sex typing of infants at birth has declined, and that there were no differences between mothers and fathers in this respect.

Evaluation of SLT in relation to parental influence

✔ **Findings supporting SLT:** Sears *et al.* (1957) found that parents allowed sons to be more aggressive in their relationships with other children, and towards themselves, than daughters. For some mothers, 'being a boy' meant being aggressive, and boys were often encouraged to fight back. Although parents believe they respond in the same way to aggressive acts committed by sons and daughters, they actually intervene much more frequently and quickly when girls behave aggressively (Huston, 1983).

Boys were more likely to imitate aggressive male models than were girls (Bandura *et al.*, 1961, 1963). Children are also more likely to imitate a same-sex model than an opposite-sex model, even if the behaviour is 'gender-inappropriate' (see Chapter 3).

Parents tend to encourage their same-gender children to join them in traditionally gender-appropriate activities, such as cooking and shopping for mothers and daughters, and car washing and fishing for fathers and sons (Bandura and Walters, 1963; Huston, 1983; Lytton and Romney, 1991). Fathers begin to make themselves more available to their sons during the second year by talking to them more than to daughters (Lamb, 1977); by middle childhood, they tend to interact more with their sons than their daughters (Sears, 1965).

Alongside this greater availability of different parental models, the child begins to attend selectively to models, taking into account both their gender and the gender-appropriateness of the model's behaviour (Bandura, 1977a, 1986). There's research evidence to support *both* claims (e.g. Bussey and Bandura, 1984).

Some supporting evidence comes from studies of media portrayals of males and females (see below).

Figure 5.6 *Do children spontaneously imitate gender-appropriate behaviour, or do parents actively encourage this?*

✗ **Findings not supporting SLT:** according to Maccoby and Jacklin (1974), there are no consistent differences in the extent to which boys and girls are reinforced for aggressiveness or autonomy. In fact, there appears to be remarkable uniformity in how the genders are socialised. This view is supported by Lytton and Romney (1991), who found very few gender differences in terms of parental warmth, overall amount of interaction, encouragement of achievement or dependency, restrictiveness and discipline, or clarity of communication.

These findings are surprising, because most psychologists would agree on the importance of parents as the major agents of socialisation. But perhaps the focus on reinforcement is misleading, since the main social learning mechanism might be modelling (Durkin, 1995). Although Bandura *et al*.'s research is often cited, the evidence concerning imitation and modelling is actually inconclusive, and some studies have failed to find that children are more likely to imitate same-gender than opposite-gender models. Barkley *et al*. (1977) reviewed 81 studies testing the prediction that children will imitate same-gender models; only 18 supported the prediction. Indeed, children have been shown to prefer imitating *behaviour* that's appropriate to their own gender *regardless* of the model's gender (Maccoby and Jacklin, 1974; Masters *et al*., 1979).

While modelling plays an important part in children's socialisation, there's no consistent preference for the same-gender parent's behaviour (Hetherington, 1967). Instead, children prefer to imitate the behaviour of those with whom they have most contact (usually the mother). Also, there's no significant correlation between the extent to which parents engage in sex-typed behaviours and the strength of sex typing in their children (Smith and Daglish, 1977). However, whether fathers adopt either traditional (sex-typed) or egalitarian attitudes has been found to correlate with four-year-olds' perceptions of gender roles (Quiery, 1998).

The influence of the media

Evaluation of SLT in relation to media influence

✔ **Findings supporting SLT:** a large body of evidence suggests that gender-role stereotypes are portrayed by the media, as well as by parents and teachers (Wober *et al.,* 1987). In US TV programmes, males outnumber females by two or three to one on almost every kind of programme; in made-for-children programmes, it's more like five to one (Huston and Wright, 1998). Males are shown in more dominant roles, with higher occupational status, while women are often presented in a narrow range of traditional feminine occupations, such as housewife, secretary and nurse, or in a more subordinate role (Durkin, 1985, 1986).

In commercials, the frequency of males and females is more equal, but women are more likely to be shown using products – especially domestic products – while men are shown receiving their services; the voiceover (the 'expert' pronouncing on the merits of the product) is nearly always male (e.g. Manstead and McCulloch, 1981). In both commercials and regular programmes, women are more often shown at home or in romantic situations, while men more often appear in work settings, with cars or playing sport. Men are also shown solving problems and being more active, aggressive, powerful and independent, whereas women are usually portrayed as submissive, passive, attractive, sensual, nurturing, emotional and less able to deal with difficult situations (Golombok and Fivush, 1994; Huston and Wright, 1998). Bee (2000) cites research showing that commercials for boys' and girls' toys are produced differently: those for boys are fast, sharp and loud ('action-packed'), while girls' are gradual, soft and fuzzy. Even six-year-olds notice these differences in style.

Figure 5.7 Rachel from Friends *– a heavily sex-typed character*

Children categorised as 'heavy' viewers of television hold stronger stereotyped beliefs than 'lighter' viewers (Gunter, 1986). This isn't too surprising perhaps, given that before starting school (at age six), the average American child has already been exposed to thousands of hours of TV; by 18, the average child has spent more time in front of the TV than in a classroom (Huston *et al.,* 1990).

Books, too, including picture books and early reading books, are quite stereotyped. As in TV commercials, the leading characters are more likely to be male (Bee, 2000).

✘ **Findings not supporting SLT:** the fact that 'heavy' TV watchers hold stronger stereotyped beliefs doesn't, of course, mean that TV is responsible. These data are *correlational*; all we can conclude is that the greater the exposure to TV, the stronger the stereotypes. It's possible that highly sex-typed children like to watch lots of TV because it confirms their own limited worldview.

What's more, the correlations are generally weak at best, but they're often minimal or non-existent; one study actually found that 'heavy' viewers scored *lower* on a test of gender stereotype acceptance (Durkin, 1995). Durkin also cites studies showing that children sometimes change their stereotypes as a result of exposure to counter-stereotyped TV content.

The view that TV can impact upon a passively receptive child audience with messages about gender-role stereotyping, and mould young children's conceptions of gender, is over-simplistic (Gunter and McAleer, 1997). Gunter and McAleer maintain that children respond selectively to particular characters and events, and their perceptions, memories and understanding of what they've seen may often be mediated by the dispositions they bring with them to the viewing situation. While 'heavy' TV viewers might hold stronger stereotyped beliefs than 'lighter' viewers, no precise measures have been taken of the programmes they actually watch.

How Science Works

Practical Learning Activity 5.9

- Conduct a *content analysis* of children's television programmes and/or the commercials that are screened during these programmes.
- You could limit yourself to a single channel (terrestrial or cable etc.), recording, say, one hour per day for five days; alternatively, you could sample one or more terrestrial channels and compare with one or more cable channels.
- You would need to design a grid comprising a number of predetermined categories, so that all you need to do while watching is tick the appropriate box. These categories could be based on the research described above (e.g. 'male is the main character' / 'female is the main character' / 'male character is boss or some other dominant role' / 'female is housewife, secretary or nurse, or in subordinate role'.

The influence of peers

As we saw when evaluating Kohlberg's cognitive theory of gender identity development, children's play is sex-typed from an early age (usually two years). According to Huston (1985) and others, children seek like-minded peers with similar resources; the peers themselves are likely to possess strong gender role stereotypes.

Figure 5.8 Same-sex peers represent a crucial influence on the child's gender development

According to Maccoby (1990), gender differences emerge primarily in social situations such as peer settings, rather than in individual tests. Children soon begin to show preferences for same-gender playmates and segregate into predominantly same-gender groups, where they resist adult interventions aimed at encouraging them to be nice to the opposite gender.

Peers are also likely to be intolerant of others' cross-gender behaviour. For example, Langlois and Downs (1980) compared peer and maternal reactions to preschoolers' play with opposite-gender toys. When boys played with girls' toys, mothers accepted this, but their (male) peers ridiculed and even hit them. As Durkin (1995) says, 'From early childhood, gender is not just another thing to learn about, but a vital social category that determines whom one mixes with and how one behaves ...'. We noted earlier that a young child's gender identity and gender role stereotypes are rigid and inflexible compared with those of older children, adolescents and adults. Once these have developed, the critical variable may not be *vertical reinforcement* (i.e. from parents and other adults) but *horizontal social engagement* (play with peers) (Durkin, 1995).

213

The influence of schools

Schools also highlight the importance of gender and provide a lot of information about gender roles (Meece, 1987, in Durkin, 1995). Not only does going to school represent a more formal structuring of the child's daily life, but it also raises prospects of the future – of what you're going to be when you grow up. Meece reviews extensive evidence showing that schools maintain widely gender-biased practices in terms of the opportunities and advice (including career counselling) they offer.

Cross-cultural studies of gender role

Cross-cultural psychology

As Best and Thomas (2004) point out, despite ample research and theory concerning gender and gender differences, the vast majority of the data come from studies of western, primarily US, samples. Such studies represent only a small portion of the world's population (what Moghaddam and Studer, 1997, call psychology's *First World*; see Chapter 2) and fail to consider the entire range of variation in human behaviour.

Cross-cultural research helps to correct this imbalance by examining gender-related behaviours within the context of numerous cultural variations. According to Smith and Bond (1998), *cross-cultural psychology* (CCP):

> examines the degree to which psychological processes and behaviours are relatively invariant across cultures, universal, or tend to vary systematically with cultural influences ... Cross-cultural psychology becomes critical when investigating the robustness or generalizability of a psychological theory or empirical finding in cultural settings that differ from the one in which it was originally derived.

So CCP studies both (a) *variability* in behaviour among the various societies and cultural groups around the world (Smith and Bond, 1998) *and* (b) what's *similar* across different cultures, and thus likely to be our common human heritage (the *universals* of human behaviour) (Jahoda, 1978).

It helps to correct *ethnocentrism*, the strong human tendency to use our own ethnic or cultural group's norms and values to define what's 'natural' and

'correct' ('reality'; Triandis, 1990). 'First World' research findings, and the theories based upon them, have been applied to *people in general*, as if culture makes no difference. An implicit equation is made between 'human being' and 'human being from western culture' (the *Anglocentric* or *Eurocentric bias*).

Cross-cultural psychologists *don't* make this equation, because, for them, cultural background is the crucial *independent variable*. But, as we've seen, they also consider the search for universal principles of human behaviour as perfectly valid (and consistent with the 'classical' view of science; see Chapter 10).

The emic–etic distinction

This distinction, first made by Pike (1954), refers to two distinct approaches to the study of behaviour:

1. the *etic* looks at behaviour from *outside* a particular cultural system

2. the *emic* looks at behaviour from the *inside*.

'Etics' refers to culturally general concepts, which are easier to understand (because they're common to all cultures), while 'emics' refers to culturally-specific concepts, which include all the ways that particular cultures deal with etics. It's the emics of another culture that are often so difficult to understand (Brislin, 1993).

The research tools that the 'visiting' psychologist brings from 'home' are an emic for the home culture, but when they're assumed to be valid in the 'alien' culture and are used to compare them, they're said to be an *imposed etic* (Berry, 1969).

Logically, emic concerns (those relating to *intracultural validity*) should always *precede* etic concerns (those relating to *intercultural validity*) (Best and Thomas, 2004) – that is, researchers should first ensure that their procedures are appropriate *within* each of the cultures being studied, and only then can they ask whether the methods will allow valid comparisons *between* cultural groups.

An etic method that's sensitive to emic concerns is called a *derived etic*; this is considered appropriate for making comparisons between groups (Best and Thomas, 2004). However, research has to start somewhere and, inevitably, this usually involves an instrument or observational technique rooted in the researcher's own culture (Berry, 1969). Many attempts to replicate American studies in other parts of the world involve an imposed etic: they all assume that the situation being studied has the same meaning for members of the alien culture as it does for members of the researcher's own culture (Smith and Bond, 1998).

How Science Works
Practical Learning Activity 5.10

- Can you think of some possible examples of imposed etics in the context of gender? You might like to look back at the section on androgyny (pages 193–196).
- What are some of the advantages of cross-cultural research? (See Gross, 2005.)
- Describe the difference between cross-cultural psychology (CCP) and *cultural psychology*. (Again, see Gross, 2005.)

The emic–etic issue in relation to gender roles

The emic–etic issue is illustrated by researchers who have translated masculinity–femininity scales developed in the USA into other languages, and administered and scored them using American scoring systems.

Although there's some evidence of cross-cultural generality, Best and Thomas (2004) cite several studies showing the lack of 'translatability'. For examples, Kaschak and Sharratt (1983) reported a dramatic failure of the translated items in their attempt to develop a sex role inventory with Costa Rican university students. Using Spanish translations of 200 items, including the PAQ (Spence and Helmreich, 1978) and the BSRI (Bem, 1974) (see above), they found that only two of the 55 PAQ items and half the 60 BSRI items discriminated between men and women. This means that many items representing masculinity–femininity in the USA *don't* do so in Costa Rica. Similar failures have occurred with BSRI items used in South India, Malaysia, and Mexico. As Best and Thomas say, 'Clearly, evaluating masculinity–femininity across cultures requires careful attention to culture-specific (emic) definitions of the concepts.'

Cultural relativism

This really represents the most direct challenge to the biological approach. If gender differences reflect biological differences, then we'd expect to find the same differences occurring in different cultures. Any differences that exist between cultures with regard to gender roles (*cultural relativism*) support the view that gender role is *culturally determined*.

Margaret Mead (1935) claimed that the traits we call masculine and feminine are completely unrelated to biological sex. Just as the clothing, manner and head-dress considered to be appropriate in a particular society, at a particular time, aren't determined by sex, so temperament and gender role aren't biologically but *culturally* determined. She studied three New Guinea tribes living quite separately from each other within a 100-mile radius.

1. The *Arapesh* were gentle, loving and cooperative. Boys and girls were reared in order to develop these qualities, which in western society are stereotypically feminine. Both parents were said to 'bear a child', and men took to bed while the child was born.

2. The *Mundugumor* were ex-cannibals. Both males and females were self-assertive, arrogant, fierce and continually quarrelling, and they both hated the whole business of pregnancy and child-rearing. Sleeping babies were hung in rough-textured baskets in a dark place against the wall, and when they cried, someone would scratch gratingly on the outside of the basket.

3. The *Tchambuli* represented the reversal of traditional western gender roles. Girls were encouraged to take an interest in the tribe's economic affairs, and the women took care of trading and food gathering. Men were considered sentimental, emotional and incapable of making serious decisions, spending much of the day sitting around in groups, gossiping and 'preening' themselves.

However, by 1949, after she'd studied four other cultures (Samoa, Manus, Iatmul and Bali), Mead had rather dramatically changed her views about gender roles. From a rather extreme cultural determinism, she now concluded that women were 'naturally' more nurturing than men, expressing their creativity through childbearing and childbirth, and superior in intellectual abilities requiring intuition.

While motherhood is a 'biological inclination', fatherhood is a 'social invention'; by implication, societies that encourage a gender role division other than that in which dominant, sexually energetic men live with passive, nurturant women, are 'going against nature'. Significantly, by this time Mead has given birth to a child of her own (Booth, 1975).

Are there cultural universals?

A finding that may seem to support Mead in her search for 'natural' differences is that there's no known society in which the female does the fighting in warfare (including the Tchambuli and Arapesh; Fortune, 1939).

However, there's more to aggression than warfare. Malinowski (1929), studying the Trobriand Islanders, reported that, in order to foster their tribe's reputation for virility, groups of women would catch a man from another tribe, arouse him to erection and rape him! This 'gang rape' was carried out in a brutal manner, and the women often boasted about their achievement.

But even if men were, universally, the hunters and warmakers, does this necessarily mean that males are naturally more aggressive than females? According to Wade and Tavris (1994), early researchers *assumed* that men are naturally aggressive (and women are naturally nurturant). Consequently, they often defined nurturing in a way that *excluded* the altruistic, caring

activities of men. For example, men can nurture the family by providing food for mother and child, and sometimes by going off to fight in faraway places, sacrificing their own lives if necessary in order to provide a safe haven for their people.

While most cultures distinguish between 'men's' and 'women's' work, and while biological factors undoubtedly play some part in the sexual division of labour, the content of this work varies enormously between cultures. As Hargreaves (1986) observes, in some cultures, 'men weave and women make pots, whereas in others these roles are reversed; in some parts of the world women are the major agricultural producers, and in others they are prohibited from agricultural activity'.

Figure 5.9 Is there any work that a man or woman couldn't do by virtue of his or her gender?

Stretch and Challenge: Are there more than two genders?

The production of sexual bodies

According to Maracek *et al*. (2004), social constructionists don't deny that genes, hormones and brain physiology may have effects on behaviour and morphology. But their interest is in the accounts people give about sexual bodies, the cultural meanings given to the body, and the social implications of those meanings.

In the USA, it's standard medical practice to surgically alter an infant's genitals if they're considered to be ambiguous. Primarily, it's the size of the phallic structure that will determine if the child will undergo surgical procedures that are difficult, painful, and may produce infertility or permanent loss of capacity for sexual pleasure; the size difference between a medically acceptable penis and a medically acceptable clitoris is a mere 1.5 cm – a difference that may not be obvious to a lay person. According to Maracek *et al*.:

The purpose of 'corrective' surgery is to create male and female genitals as unmistakably different structures. Surely, this is a radical example of social construction: The physical body is reconstructed to match what is considered to be the proper appearance of male or female anatomy.

Sex categories

The sex categorisation itself represents a more fundamental cultural construction. In contemporary western societies, biological sex and sex category are confused with each other – that is, the agreed-upon criterion for classification as a member of one or the other sex is male or female genitalia. What's more, the idea of two, and only two, sex categories has achieved the status of biological, psychological and moral certainty (Maracek *et al.*, 2004). But our genitals aren't usually available for public inspection. In fact:

> the demonstrable existence of one or another kind of genitalia is actually irrelevant to the ascertainment of sex category in everyday life. People rely instead on insignias of sex (apparel, names, hair length) as proxies for the genitals that cannot be seen. (Maracek et al., 2004)

In other words, we make inferences about people's ('private') genitals (as male *or* female) based on very public aspects of their appearance, based on the assumption that the latter are reliable indicators of the former. However, social constructionists have challenged the common-sense idea that there can be only two sexes, as determined by sexual dimorphism. Maracek *et al.* give examples that include the internet, where people can experiment with sex categories (e.g. in some chat rooms, individuals manipulate names, biographies, verbal style so as to assume a sexual identity other than their offline one).

While this is a very recent and western example, many older cultures have recognised a third – or fourth – sex for much longer. Some examples are given in Box 5.6.

Box 5.6: Some examples of a third (and a fourth) sex

- Among the Sakalavas in Madagascar, boys who are thought to be pretty are raised as girls and readily adopt the female gender role. Similarly, the Alentian Islanders in Alaska raise handsome boys as girls; their beards are plucked and they're later married to rich men. They, too, seem to adapt quite readily to their assigned gender role.
- Studies of certain Native American peoples reveal the possibility of more than two basic gender roles. For example, the *berdache*, a biological male of the Crow tribe, simply chooses not to follow the ideal role of warrior. Instead, he might become the 'wife' of a warrior, but he's never scorned or ridiculed by his fellow Crows. (Little Horse in the film *Little Big Man*, starring Dustin Hoffman, was a berdache.)
- Some *hijras* in India are physical hermaphrodites, others have male genitalia, and still others were born with male genitalia but opted to undergo castration. *Hijras* adopt female names and wear women's clothing – but they don't try to pass as women. Their heavy make-up, long, unbound hair and sexualised gestures set them apart from women in general (Nanda, 1990, in Maracek *et al.*, 2004).
- In Thailand, *kathoeys* have male genitalia but dress in women's clothing. But a *kathoey* isn't a man who wishes to be (or become) a woman, nor do they believe they have a 'woman's mind' trapped inside the 'wrong body' (in the way that many transsexuals in western countries describe themselves). Rather, they take some pride in their male genitals and they don't wish to pass as women; they act in dramatic, loud, brash ways that violate the norms of femininity in Thai culture.
- The Mohave Indians recognised *four* distinct gender roles: (i) traditional male; (ii) traditional female; (iii) *alyha*; and (iv) *hwame*. The *alyha* was the male who chose to live as a woman (mimicking menstruation by cutting his upper thigh and undergoing a ritualistic pregnancy); the *hwame* was a female who chose to become a man.

SUMMARY

Psychological explanations of gender development

- An important distinction is made between **sex** (the biological facts about us, summarised as 'male' or 'female') and **gender** (the social interpretation of sex). Corresponding to these are **sexual identity** and **gender identity** respectively.

- Biological sex is a **multi-dimensional** variable, comprising **chromosomal, gonadal** and **hormonal sex**, as well as **sex of the internal reproductive structures** and **external genitals**.

- **Gender dysphoria** is the major symptom of **gender identity disorder** (**GID**). Individuals with GID usually become **transsexuals**.

- To be **masculine** or **feminine** requires males or females to conform to their respective **gender** (or **sex**) **roles**; these are often reflected in **gender** (or **sex**) **stereotypes**.

- Acquiring an appropriate gender role is achieved through the process of **sex typing**.

- While the various categories of sex are usually correlated, both with each other and with gender categories, there are inconsistencies and ambiguities, as in **hermaphroditism**.

- **True hermaphrodites** (such as Mr Blackwell) are very rare, but **pseudo-hermaphrodites** (**intersex** individuals) are more common, as in **complete androgen insensitivity syndrome** (**CAIS**) (or **testicular feminising syndrome**), **congenital adrenal hyperplasia** (**CAH**) (or **adrenogenital syndrome / AGS**), **DHT-deficient males** (or **5-alpha-reductase deficiency**) and **chromosome abnormalities**.

- The psychological equivalent to intersex is **androgyny**.

- While there appears to be considerable agreement cross-culturally regarding typical male and female characteristics, there's very little empirical evidence for (between-) **gender differences**. Within-gender differences are at least as common as those between the genders.

- According to Baron-Cohen's **empathising-systemising** (**E-S**) **theory**, female brains are predominantly hardwired for **empathy** (E-type) and male brains for **understanding** and **building systems** (S-type). These differences are reflected in typical male/female **occupations**, and **autistic** individuals have a predominantly male brain.

- Within psychology in general, and in the study of gender in particular, there's a strong **bias** towards publishing studies that find **significant sex differences** and overlooking those that don't.

Psychological explanations of gender development

- According to Kohlberg's **cognitive developmental theory (CDT)**, the child's gender knowledge arises, as with all knowledge, from active construction of an understanding of the world through interaction with it.

- This development of **gender identity** proceeds through three stages: **gender labelling / basic gender identity** (one to three years); **gender stability** (three to five); and **gender constancy / consistency** (six to seven).

- Children's discovery that they're male or female **causes** them to identify with same-gender individuals: imitating them and following sex-appropriate activities ('self-socialisation').

- A major problem for CDT is its inability to account for gender-specific behaviour that occurs *before* the child has acquired gender constancy.

- **Gender Schema / Schematic Processing Theory** proposes that gender identity **alone** is sufficient for children to assume sex-typed behaviour patterns; the child's self-perception becomes sex-typed.

- Once established, the gender schema assimilates many different experiences. But it undergoes change as the child's general cognitive abilities develop.

- The evidence for gender schema theory is mixed, and much of the supporting evidence is correlational (are gender schemas causes or effects of gender-appropriate behaviour?).

- Also, cognitive developmental approaches say little about why the genders are differentially valued and the construction of gender-role knowledge is a **collective activity** that takes place within a **social context**.

- **GST** seems to assume that gender is an either/or, socially constructed category, while sex is a (non-constructed) biological category. But some **feminist psychologists**, adopting a **social constructionist approach**, argue that the existence of intersex individuals shows that our western male/female dichotomy isn't a biological 'given' and question many aspects of the sex-gender distinction.

- The **Bem Sex Role Inventory (BSRI)** made it possible to measure psychological androgyny by taking masculinity and femininity as two **independent** dimensions.

- A major hypothesis derived from the BSRI is that androgyny is a good indicator of psychological well-being / mental health. While some supporting evidence exists, other evidence suggests that masculinity – both in males and females – may be a better predictor. This is consistent with the 'plus male, minus female' phenomenon.

- While the concept of androgyny may be very radical, feminist psychologists have criticised its implicit view of masculinity/femininity as inherent characteristics of individuals, rather than socially constructed categories.

- **Genetic** and **hormonal factors** have been implicated in the causation of **gender identity disorder (GID)**, but evidence for the role of hormones is excluded if these are associated with intersex conditions. Strong evidence comes from the case of the Batista family (McGinley *et al.*).

- **Psychoanalytic** accounts of GID include the concept of **symbiotic fusion** as a way (in males) of alleviating extreme separation anxiety from the mother. Freud's account is related to his more general theory of psychosexual development.

- Perhaps the most widely accepted theory of GID is that it arises through **conditioning** early in life. The **culture-relative** nature of masculinity/femininity also needs to be taken into account, including the male bias of most western societies.

Biological influences on gender

- Although **sexual differentiation** begins with the sex chromosomes (XX or XY), their main function is to direct the gonads to develop as either ovaries (female) or testes (male). After that, gonadal hormones – especially **androgens** from the testes – provide the major biological influences.

- Human behaviour is subject to both prenatal biological and post-natal (social and other) influences; this makes the natural experiments represented by cases of intersex individuals especially important.

- Girls with CAH are usually hormonally and surgically normalised, and raised as girls. Despite this, they tend to show greater male-typical behaviour (compared with unaffected sisters / first cousins and other controls), some display gender dysphoria, and are more likely to report bisexual or homosexual interests.

- According to Money and Ehrhardt's **biosocial theory**, based on the study of intersex individuals, it's the **interaction** between biological and social factors that determines a child's gender development.

- Social factors include adults' responses to the child, which are influenced by their sexual stereotypes (as illustrated by the 'Baby X' experiments).

- Psychologically, gender identity is **undifferentiated** at birth; it becomes differentiated as masculine or feminine according to how the child is socialised during its first two and a half to three years. Gender reassignment after this **critical/sensitive period** can cause extreme psychological disturbance.

- The case of Daphne Went also supports Money and Ehrhardt's claim that gender of rearing is more important than biological sex. However, cases of penectomised XY infants reassigned as females (notably David Reimer) challenge this conclusion.

- According to Kenrick *et al.*, we don't need to choose between **evolutionary** explanations and those that emphasise culture, environmental influences, learning or cognition. The psychology of gender is perhaps the best research area for integrating these different approaches and perspectives.

- **Differential parental investment** and **sexual selection** are two general principles used to explain the correlation between (a) sex differences in morphology and behaviour, and (b) sex differences in mating strategies.

- Males and females differ in both the **amount** and **nature** of the resources they invest in offspring; this explains the different characteristics they desire in mates.

Social contexts of gender role

- **Social learning theory** (**SLT**) incorporates the principles of **operant conditioning** with **observational learning** (**modelling**). As major socialising agents, parents treat boys and girls differently according to their gender-role expectations (**sex typing**).

- Evidence for SLT is inconclusive. Some studies have failed to find that children are more likely to imitate same-gender models (as SLT predicts) than opposite-gender models; others have found a preference for imitating gender-appropriate **behaviour** regardless of the model's gender.

- SLT also provides a framework for investigating the influence of the **media**.

- A large body of evidence suggests that gender-role stereotypes are portrayed by the media (especially in commercials) – as well as by parents and teachers.

- Much of this evidence is only **correlational**, and children aren't passive recipients of media content but respond selectively to what they see.

- Once a young child's gender identity and gender role stereotypes have developed, **horizontal social engagement** (play with peers) may be the critical variable (rather than **vertical reinforcement** from parents/other adults).

- **Schools** maintain widely gender-biased practices regarding the opportunities and advice they offer, as well as providing a great deal of information about gender roles.

- Most of the data regarding gender and gender differences come from psychology's **First World**. **Cross-cultural psychology** (**CCP**) helps to correct this imbalance by examining gender-related behaviours within various cultural contexts.

- CCP studies both **variability** in, and the **universals** of, human behaviour, helping to correct **ethnocentrism** and the **Anglocentric/Eurocentric bias**.

- The research tools used by 'visiting' psychologists are an **emic** for the home culture; when they're assumed to be valid in the 'alien' culture, they're said to be an **imposed etic**. An etic method that's sensitive to emic concerns is called a **derived etic**.

- The emic–etic issue is illustrated by researchers who have translated masculinity–femininity scales developed in the USA into other languages. Despite some evidence of cross-cultural generality, several studies show the lack of 'translatability'.

- **Cultural relativism** represents the most direct challenge to the biological approach; any differences between cultures with regard to gender roles support **cultural determinism**. This is illustrated by Mead's study of three New Guinea tribes: the **Arapesh**, **Mundugumor** and **Tchambuli**.

- **Social constructionists** have challenged the common-sense idea that there are / can only be two sexes, as determined by sexual dimorphism. Many older cultures have recognised a third/fourth sex for a long time.

Essay Questions

Psychological explanations of gender development
1. Describe and evaluate Kohlberg's explanation of gender development. (25 marks)
2. Discuss explanations of psychological androgyny and/or gender dysphoria. (25 marks)

Biological influences on gender
3a. Describe the role of hormones in gender development. (9 marks)
3b. Discuss evolutionary explanations of gender roles. (16 marks)
4. Describe and evaluate the biosocial approach to gender development. (25 marks)

Social contexts of gender role
5. Discuss social influences on gender role (for example, the influence of parents, peers and school, and the media). (25 marks)
6. 'The distinction between male and female is a culturally determined construct, not a biological fact.' Critically consider cross-cultural studies of gender roles. (25 marks)

It should take you 30 minutes to answer each question.

A2 Unit 3

Cognition and development

6 Chapter

What's covered in this chapter?

You need to know about:

Development of thinking
- Theories of cognitive development, including Piaget, Vygotsky and Bruner
- Applications of these theories to education

Development of moral understanding
- Theories of moral understanding (Kohlberg) and/or pro-social reasoning (Eisenberg)

Development of social cognition
- Development of the child's sense of self, including Theory of Mind (Baron-Cohen)
- Development of children's understanding of others, including perspective taking (Selman)
- Biological explanations of social cognition, including the role of the mirror neuron system

✓ Specification Hint

In the specification, the three major theories of cognitive development that you *must* know about (Piaget, Vygotsky and Bruner) appear together in one bullet point, and their applications to education ('Application of these theories …') appear in a separate bullet point. It makes better sense to consider the application to education of each theory as the theory is discussed. Also, in the examination you might be asked about both the theory and its applications in the same question.

Theories of cognitive development

Different theories of cognitive development (that is, how the child's thinking develops) rest on very different images of what the child is like.

- Piaget sees the child as (a) an organism *adapting to its environment*; and (b) a *scientist* constructing its own understanding of the world.

- For Vygotsky, by contrast, the child is a participant in an *interactive process*. Through this process, socially and culturally determined knowledge and understanding gradually become *individualised*.

- Bruner, like Vygotsky, emphasises the *social* aspects of the child's cognitive development.

Piaget's theory

Much of Piaget's research was conducted in the 1930s and 1940s with Swiss children, and was published in French. His work wasn't translated into English until the 1950s. Piaget (e.g. 1950) was interested in how *intelligence* changes as the child grows (what he called *genetic epistemology*). He *wasn't* interested in why some children are more intelligent than others.

He maintains that cognitive development occurs through the interaction of innate capacities and environmental events, proceeding through a series of *stages* which are:

- *hierarchical* – they build on each other, such that earlier stages are necessary for later stages to develop

- *invariant* – every child passes through the stages in the same order or sequence, and there's no regressing (going backwards) to earlier stages (except as the result of brain damage)

- *universal* – every child passes through the same stages, regardless of culture

- *qualitatively different* – each stage involves a *different kind of intelligence*; we don't become more intelligent as we get older – rather, the *nature* of our intelligence changes.

What underlie the stage changes are a number of *functional invariants*. These are fundamental aspects of development, which remain the same, and work in the same way, through each of the stages. The crucial functional invariants are: *assimilation, accommodation* and *equilibration*. The major cognitive structure that changes in the course of development is the *schema* (plural = *schemas* or *schemata*).

Schemas (or schemata)

A schema is the basic building block, or unit, of intelligent behaviour (see Box 6.1).

Assimilation, accommodation and equilibration

Assimilation is the process by which we incorporate

Box 6.1: Schemas

- Piaget saw schemas as mental structures that organise past experience. They provide a way of understanding and predicting future experience. According to Bee (2000), schemas are more the action of categorising than actual categories.

- Life begins with simple schemas, largely confined to inborn reflexes (such as sucking and grasping). These operate independently of each other, and are triggered only by particular stimuli. As the baby develops, schemas become integrated with each other. They also become less reflex and more deliberate, and under the baby's voluntary control.

new information into existing schemas. For example, babies will reflexively suck a nipple and other objects (such as a finger). But if the baby is to learn to suck from a bottle or drink from a cup, the innate sucking reflex must be modified through *accommodation*.

When a child can deal with most, if not all, new experiences by assimilating them, it's in a state of *equilibrium* (the process of seeking 'mental balance'). This is brought about by the process of *equilibration*. But if existing schemas are inadequate to cope with new situations, *cognitive disequilibrium* occurs. To restore balance, the existing schema must be 'stretched' in order to take in ('accommodate') new information or meet the demands of new situations. So, for example, the baby needs to change how it sucks (including what it does with its tongue) when drinking from a cup – as well as the position of its head. Later on, it will drink while actually holding the cup, so different schemas will be used together in a voluntary way (see above).

Assimilation and accommodation are necessary and complementary processes, which, together, constitute the fundamental process of *adaptation* (see Figure 6.1).

How Science Works
Practical Learning Activity 6.1

1. Observe a baby of, say, up to 12 months, trying to identify as many schemas as you can. These might be simple, innate (inborn) single reflexes (such as sucking or grasping), or they might be more complex, involving an integration of two or more simple reflexes (such as drinking from a cup).
2. The idea is that most behaviour *isn't* reflex (biologically 'ready-made'), but is built up from more simple abilities to form more complex, voluntary actions.

Stages of cognitive development

Each of Piaget's stages represents a stage in the development of intelligence (hence, 'sensorimotor intelligence', 'pre-operational intelligence', and so on). Each stage is also a way of summarising the various schemas a child possesses at any one time (see Table 6.1). The ages shown in Table 6.1 are only approximate: children move through the stages at different rates (due to both biological and environmental differ-

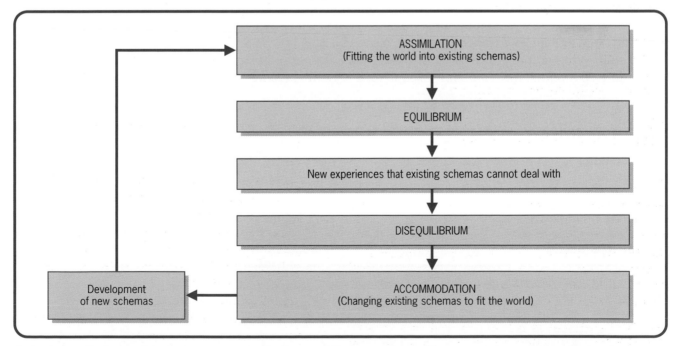

Figure 6.1 Relationship between assimilation, equilibrium, disequilibrium and accommodation in the development of schemas

ences). There are also transitional periods, in which children's thinking is a mixture of two stages. For Piaget, development is a gradual and continuous process of change; the child moves from one stage to the next through cognitive disequilibrium.

The sensorimotor stage

This lasts for approximately the first two years of life. Babies learn about the world, and interact with it, mainly through their senses ('sensori-') and by doing ('motor'). Based on observations of his own children, Piaget divided the sensorimotor stage into six sub-stages. A crucial development that takes place during the course of these sub-stages is *object permanence*, as described in Box 6.2.

Box 6.2: The development of object permanence (OP)

- In the second sub-stage (*primary circular reactions*: one to four months), a baby will look where an object disappears for a few moments, but won't search for it. If the object doesn't reappear, the baby appears to lose interest ('out of sight' is 'out of mind').
- In *secondary circular reactions* (four to ten months), the baby will reach for an object that's partially hidden. This suggests the baby realises that the rest of the object is attached to the visible part. But if the object is completely hidden, the baby makes no attempt to retrieve it.
- In the *coordination of secondary circular reactions* (ten to twelve months), a baby will search for a hidden object ('out of sight' is no longer 'out of mind'). But it will keep looking for it where it was last hidden – even when it's hidden somewhere else.
- Between 12 and 18 months (*tertiary circular reactions*), the child will look for the object where it last saw it hidden. But object permanence isn't yet fully developed.
- The final stage (*invention of new means through mental combinations*: 18–24 months) involves the ability to *infer invisible displacements*. The child can now look for an object that's been hidden – without having actually seen this happen. For example, the child watches you place a small toy in a matchbox, which is then put under a pillow. When it's not looking, you slip the toy out of the matchbox and leave it under the pillow. When you give the child the matchbox, it will open it, expecting to find the toy. When it discovers the toy's not there, it will look for it under the pillow. Before 18 months, it would have failed to look under the pillow.

Stage	Approximate age
Sensorimotor	0–2 years
Pre-operational	2–7 years
Concrete operational	7–11 years
Formal operational	11 years onwards

Table 6.1: Piaget's four stages of cognitive development

Evaluation of Piaget's account of object permanence

✗ **Methodological limitations:** according to Bower and Wishart (1972), how an object is made to disappear can influence the baby's response. If a four-month-old is looking at and reaching for an object suspended in front of it, and the lights are then turned off, it continues to search for it for up to one and a half minutes (detectable through the use of infrared cameras). This suggests that the baby *does* remember the object is still there – so 'out of sight ' *isn't* 'out of mind'. This finding was replicated by Hood and Willatts, 1986, in Bremner, 2003).

✗ **It develops earlier than Piaget claimed:** Bower and Wishart's study shows that Piaget's claims concerning when OP develops *underestimates* babies' abilities. In other words, OP develops earlier than Piaget claimed. For example, Baillargeon (1987) showed that babies as young as three and a half months can display OP, nor is it necessary for babies below six months to see the whole object in order to respond to it.

The sensorimotor stage is also important for the development of the *general symbolic function* (GSF), which refers to (a) self-recognition (see pages 260–262); (b) symbolic thought (such as language); (c) deferred imitation (the ability to reproduce something that's no longer present) (Meltzoff and Moore, 1983); and (d) representational (or make-believe) play – that is, using one object as though it were another. Like deferred imitation, this depends on the infant's growing use of mental or internal (interiorised) images of things and people in their absence.

With development of the GSF, the child begins to think in something like an 'adult' sense.

How Science Works

Practical Learning Activity 6.2

- Try to find definitions – and give examples – of the following terms:
  - seriation
  - artificialism
  - syncretic thought
  - transductive reasoning
  - animism.
- Without reading any further, say what you understand by the term 'egocentrism'? (See, for example, Gross, 2005.)
- How do these examples illustrate the pre-logical thought of the pre-operational child?

The pre-operational stage

The GSF continues to develop, but the child continues to be influenced by *how things look* rather than by logical principles or *operations* (hence, 'pre-operational'). Piaget subdivided the stage into (i) the *pre-conceptual* (two to four years) and *intuitive sub-stages* (four to seven years).

The *absolute* nature of the pre-conceptual child's thinking makes relative terms such as 'bigger' and 'stronger' difficult to understand (things tend to be just 'biggest' or just 'big'). The intuitive child *can* use relative terms, but its ability to think logically is still limited. The intuitive sub-stage has probably been investigated and discussed more than any other; in particular, *egocentrism* and *conservation*.

Egocentrism

In order to understand egocentrism (and *conservation*; see below), we need to be familiar with the process of *centration*. This involves focusing on just a single perceptual quality at a time. A pre-conceptual child asked to divided apples into 'big and red' ones and 'small and green' ones will either put all the red (or green) apples together irrespective of size, or all the big (or small) apples together irrespective of colour. Until the child can *decentre*, it will be unable to classify things logically or systematically.

According to Piaget, pre-operational children are *egocentric* – that is, they see the world from their own standpoint and cannot appreciate that other people might see things differently. They cannot put themselves 'in other people's shoes' to realise that others don't know or perceive everything they themselves know or perceive.

Consider the following example (Phillips, 1969) of a conversation between an experimenter and a four-year-old boy:

Experimenter:	*'Do you have a brother?'*
Child:	*'Yes.'*
Experimenter:	*'What's his name?'*
Child:	*'Jim.'*
Experimenter:	*'Does Jim have a brother?'*
Child:	*'No.'*

If the child could see things from Jim's point of view, he'd know that Jim *does* have a brother – the child himself!

The 'classic' Piagetian demonstration of egocentrism is the Swiss mountain scene experiment, described in Key Study 6.1.

Key Study 6.1: The Swiss mountain scene (SMS) experiment (Piaget and Inhelder, 1956)

Aim/hypothesis (AO1)

This was an experimental demonstration of egocentrism. It was predicted that children below the age of seven would be unable to see the mountain scene model from any perspective other than their own.

Method/design (AO1)

Three papier mâché model mountains of different colours, one with snow on top, one with a house and one with a red cross, were used (as shown in Figure 6.2).

The child walked round the model, exploring it, then sat on one side while a doll was placed at another. The child was then shown ten pictures of different views of the model, including the doll's and its own. The child was asked to select the picture representing the doll's view (the dependent variable).

Results/findings (AO1)

Four-year-olds were completely unaware that there were perspectives other than their own: they always chose the picture that matched *their own* view of the model. Six-year-olds showed *some* awareness of other perspectives, but they often selected the wrong picture. Only seven- and eight-year-olds *consistently* chose the picture that represented the doll's view.

Conclusions (AO1)

Piaget concluded that children under seven are subject to the *egocentric illusion:* they fail to understand that what they see is *relative to their own position*. Instead, they believe that their own view represents 'the world as it really is'.

Evaluation (AO1/AO2)

For Piaget, the child's *age* is the crucial independent variable. But critics see the task itself as an unusually difficult way of presenting a problem to a young child. Borke (1975) and Hughes (in Donaldson, 1978) have shown that when the task is presented in meaningful context (making what Donaldson calls 'human sense'), even three and a half-year-olds can appreciate the world as another person sees it.

Similarly, Gelman (1979) showed that four-year-olds (a) adjust their explanations of things to make them clearer to a blindfolded listener, and (b) use simpler forms of speech when talking to two-year-olds. We wouldn't expect either finding if four-year-olds were truly egocentric, as Piaget claims.

These are all examples of *perspective taking*, and according to Siegal (2003), 'A reasonable conclusion is that young children are not egocentric all of the time, but their perspective-taking skills clearly improve during childhood ...'. Perspective taking is discussed further towards the end of the chapter (see pages 268–271).

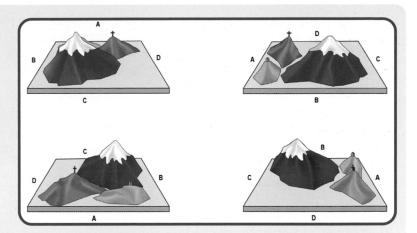

Figure 6.2 Piaget and Inhelder's three-mountain scene, seen from four different sides (from Smith, P.K.. Cowie, H. and Blader, M. (1998), Understanding Children's Development (3rd edn). Oxford: Blackwell.

Conservation

Conservation is the understanding that any quantity (such as number, liquid quantity, length or substance) remains the same despite physical changes in how objects are arranged. Piaget believed that pre-operational children cannot conserve, because their thinking is dominated by the *perceptual* nature of objects ('how things look'). The inability to conserve is another example of centration. Some typical conservation experiments are described in Key Study 6.2.

Key Study 6.2: Conservation experiments

Aim/hypothesis (AO1)

Whatever the material used (coloured liquid, counters, plasticine etc.), the aim is the same – namely, to demonstrate that children younger than seven cannot conserve, as shown by their answering the *post-transformation question* by saying that the quantity has actually changed.

Method/design (AO1)

Again, this is the same regardless of the particular material used. The materials are presented and the child is asked, 'Is there the same amount/number ...?' (the *pre-transformation question*). Then, in full view of the child, the materials are rearranged/changed in some way and the question is repeated (the *post-transformation question*).

1. In the case of *liquid quantity*, the child is shown two beakers of coloured liquid (A and B) and asked 'Is there the same amount of liquid in A and B?' Then the liquid from B is poured into the taller and thinner beaker C. The question is repeated.

2. To test conservation of *number*, two rows of counters are put in a one-to-one correspondence and the child is asked 'Is there the same number of counters in A and B?' One row is then pushed together (to form row C) and the question is repeated.

3. *Substance or quantity* conservation is tested using plasticine. Two equal-sized balls of plasticine are presented and the child is asked 'Is there the same amount of plasticine in A and B?' One ball is then rolled into a sausage shape, and the question is repeated.

Findings (AO1)

In all cases, pre-operational children answer the pre-transformation question correctly (namely, 'Yes – there's the same ... in A and B'). This is referred to as *identity*). But in case 1, they typically answer the post-transformation question by saying there's more liquid in C, because 'it looks more' or 'it's taller'. Children of seven and over answer 'yes' to the second question.

In case 2, pre-operational children usually think there are more counters in A than in C – because 'it's longer' (despite being able to count). Older children answer 'yes' to the second question.

In case 3, the pre-operational child typically thinks that there's more plasticine in C (the sausage) than in A. Older children, again, answer 'yes' to the post-transformation question.

Conclusions (AO1)

According to Piaget, although the pre-operational child understands identity, it *centres* on just one dimension of the stimulus material (for instance, the height of the liquid in the beaker). It fails to take width into account, unlike the older child, who understands that 'getting taller' and 'getting narrower' tend to cancel each other out (*compensation*).

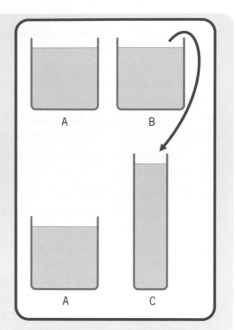

Figure 6.3 The conservation of liquid quantity: although the child agrees that there's the same amount of liquid in A and B, when the contents of B are poured into C, the appearance of C sways the child's judgement so that C is now judged to contain more liquid than A ('it looks more' or 'it's taller'); although the child has seen the liquid poured from B into C and agrees that none has been spilled or added in the process (what Piaget calls 'identity'), the appearance of the higher level of liquid in the taller, thinner beaker C is compelling

Figure 6.4 Number conservation using counters: two rows of counters are put in a one-to-one correspondence and then one row is pushed together; the pre-operational child usually thinks there are more counters in A than in C because A is 'longer', despite being able to count correctly and agreeing that A and B have equal numbers

If the liquid from C is poured back into B, the younger child will again say that A and B contain the same amount of liquid. But they cannot perform this operation *mentally* – that is, they lack *reversibility* (understanding that what can be done can be undone *without any gain or loss*). These same limitations apply to the other forms of conservation.

Evaluation (AO1/AO2)

Rose and Blank (1974) showed that when the pre-transformation question was dropped, six-year-olds often succeeded on the number conservation task. They also made fewer errors on the standard (two-question) form of the task when tested a week later. Samuel and Bryant (1984) replicated these findings, using conservation of number, liquid quantity and substance.

According to Donaldson (1978), the standard form of the task unwittingly 'forces' the child to give the wrong answer against its better judgement. Because children are asked the same question twice, they infer that they're expected to give a *different* answer the second time ('Why else would the experimenter ask me the same question twice?'). Donaldson argues that *contextual cues* may override purely linguistic ones. Children may think their first answer has been rejected – so they give a different answer in order to please the experimenter. This is the problem of a *clash of conversational worlds* between child and adult (Siegal, 2003).

According to Piaget, it shouldn't matter *who* rearranges the counters in number conservation experiments, or *how* this happens. However, when 'Naughty Teddy' (a glove puppet operated by the experimenter) is brought out of its box and 'accidentally' rearranges one row of counters, pre-operational children show conservation of number (and length) (McGarrigle and Donaldson, 1974; Light *et al.*, 1979). This also applies when the transformation is made by a person other than the experimenter (Hargreaves *et al.*, 1982; Light, 1986).

Class inclusion tasks

Another way in which Piaget studied centration (and classification) was through *class inclusion tasks*. If a pre-operational child is presented with several wooden beads, mostly brown but a few white, and asked 'Are they all wooden?', the child will respond correctly. If asked 'Are there more brown or more white beads?', the child will again respond correctly. But if asked, 'Are there more brown beads or more beads?' the child will say there are more brown beads.

The brown beads are more numerous than the white, and they can be perceived in a more immediate and direct way than the wooden beads as a whole (despite the first question being answered correctly). The 'bead-ness' of the beads is less obvious and more 'abstract' than either their colour or their number. For Piaget, the child fails to understand the relationship between the whole (the *superordinate class* of wooden beads) and the parts (the *subordinate classes* of brown and white beads).

However, Donaldson (1978) asks if the difficulty the child experiences is to do with what's expected of it and

How Science Works

Practical Learning Activity 6.3

- Why do you think pre-operational children say there are more brown beads?
- Do you consider this to be an unnecessarily difficult task for the child? (See Key Study 6.2.)
- Can you think of a different way of presenting the task that would be easier for the child?
- Present the two forms of the task to two groups of, say, five- to six-year-olds and compare the success rates.
- What conclusions can you draw from your findings about (a) Piaget's method of testing class inclusion; and (b) pre-operational children's ability to classify objects and to decentre?

Piaget's standard procedure might convey the implicit message: 'Take note of the transformation because it's relevant.' But, in fact, the task involves an *irrelevant* perceptual change (nothing is added or taken away). By contrast, studies like 'Naughty Teddy' might imply the message: 'Ignore the transformation, it makes no difference.' If children do better in this form of the task, it may be because they've failed to notice that any transformation has occurred – *not* that they can conserve!

So if something is actually changed (a *relevant* change), children should do *worse* in the accidental/incidental transformation condition than those tested in the standard way. This prediction has been supported in several studies (e.g. Light and Gilmour, 1983; Moore and Frye, 1986). This lends indirect support to Piaget.

Chapman and McBride (1992) conducted a similar study with four- to ten-year-olds, involving sleeping horses. Although they replicated the results reported by Donaldson, most children couldn't effectively justify their answers. When this was taken into account, the difference in correct answers produced by the standard form of the task and the 'sleeping' form disappeared.

In both studies, a majority of children still failed even under conditions where task demands are reduced. This suggests a deep *conceptual* difficulty, as well as a linguistic one (Siegal, 2003).

According to Gelman (1978), the word 'more' has a different meaning for children and adults. Adults use 'more' to mean 'containing a greater number'. But for children, 'more' refers to the general concept of larger, longer, occupying more space, and so on.

how the task is presented. She describes a study with six year olds using four toy cows: three black and one white. They were laid on their sides and the children were told they were 'sleeping'.

Of those asked 'Are there more black cows or more cows?' (equivalent to Piaget's method), 25 per cent answered correctly. But of those asked 'Are there more black cows or more sleeping cows?', 48 per cent answered correctly.

The concrete operational stage

The child can now perform logical operations – but *only in the presence of actual objects* (hence, 'concrete' operations). Conservation is an example of such an operation, which requires the ability to *decentre* (see above).

Further examples of the child's ability to decentre include its understanding that objects can belong to more than one class or category: for example, Andrew is Bob's brother *and* Charlie's best friend. Children also become significantly *less* egocentric. Their viewpoint becomes increasingly *relative*, enabling them to see things from different perspectives.

Seriation – that is, children's ability to put things in order of size (or any other dimension) – increases, but they still have difficulty with *transitivity tasks*.

How Science Works

Practical Learning Activity 6.4

- Alan is taller than Bob, and Bob is taller than Charlie. Who's taller, Alan or Charlie?
- Depending on your answer, how do you think a seven- to eleven-year-old would answer?
- Try it out on children of this – and other – age groups.
- Try it out on some fellow A-level students who aren't studying psychology.

Concrete operational children cannot solve transitivity problems like the one above entirely in their heads. They can usually only solve them using real (concrete) objects (such as dolls).

Box 6.3: Horizontal and vertical décalage

- Some types of conservation are mastered before others, and their order is invariant.
- *Liquid quantity* develops by age six to seven, *substance/quantity* and *length* by seven to eight, *weight* by eight to ten, and *volume* by eleven to twelve.
- This step-by-step acquisition of new operations is called *décalage* (displacement or 'slips in the level of performance').
- In conservation, décalage is *horizontal*: there are inconsistencies *within* the same kind of ability or operation (for example, a seven-year-old can conserve number but not weight).
- *Vertical décalage* refers to inconsistencies *between* different abilities or operations (for example, a child may have mastered all kinds of classification, but not all kinds of conservation).

The formal operational stage

The concrete operational child is basically concerned with manipulating *things* (even if this is done mentally). These are called *first-order* operations. By contrast, the formal operational thinker can manipulate *ideas* or *propositions*; s/he can reason solely on the basis of verbal statements (*second-order* operations).

'Formal' here refers to the ability to follow the *form* of an argument without reference to its particular content. For example, in transitivity problems (see above), 'If A is larger than B, and B is larger than C, then A is larger than C' is a form of argument whose conclusion is logically true, *regardless* of what A, B and C refer to.

Formal operational thinkers can also think *hypothetically* – that is, they can consider what *might* be as well as what actually *is*. For example, if they're asked what it would be like if people had tails, they might say 'Dogs would know when you were happy,' or 'Lovers could hold tails in secret under the table.' Concrete operational thinkers might tell you 'not to be so silly' or say where on the body the tail might be. This would reveal their dependence on what they've actually experienced (Dworetzky, 1981).

This ability to imagine and discuss things that have never actually been encountered demonstrates the formal operational thinker's continuing *decentration*. The more *systematic thinking* of this stage is demonstrated in a study by Inhelder and Piaget (1958). Participants were given five containers filled with clear liquid; four were 'test chemicals', the other an 'indicator'. When the correct combination of one or more test chemicals was added to the indicator, it turned yellow; participants had to find the right combination. Pre-operational children simply mixed the chemical randomly, and concrete operational children, although more systematic than this, generally failed to test all possible combinations. Only formal operational thinkers considered all the alternatives, systematically varying one factor at a time. Also, they often wrote down all the results and tried to draw general conclusions about each chemical. This approach illustrates *hypothetico-deductive reasoning*.

Evaluation of Piaget's theory

✔ **A major influence within developmental psychology:** some years ago, Piaget's theory was regarded as the major framework, or paradigm, within child development. According to Schaffer (2004), it remains the most comprehensive account of how children come to understand the world. Siegal (2003) argues that 'he [Piaget] set the agenda for a vast body of productive research in the twentieth and twenty-first centuries'.

✗ **Declining influence:** despite Piaget's work remaining a vital source of influence and inspiration, both on psychology and education (see below), today there are hardly any 'orthodox' Piagetians left (Dasen, 1994). As Flavell (1982), and others (e.g. Siegal, 2003), have remarked:

Like all theories of great reach and significance ... it has problems that gradually come to light as years and years of thinking and research get done on it. Thus, some of us now think that the theory may in varying degrees be unclear, incorrect and incomplete.

Evaluation of Piaget's theory continued...

✔ **Cross-cultural support:** the few cross-cultural studies of the sensorimotor stage have shown the sub-stages to be universal. Overall, it seems that ecological or cultural factors *don't* influence the sequence of stages, although they *do* affect the rate at which they're attained (Segall *et al.,* 1999).

Dasen (1994) cites studies he conducted in remote parts of the central Australian desert with eight- to fourteen-year-old Aborigines. He gave them conservation of liquid, weight and volume tasks (basically the same as used by Piaget), plus two tests of *spatial relationships:*

1. two landscape models, one of which could be turned through 180 degrees – participants had to locate an object (doll or sheep) on one model, then find the same location on the second model
2. a bottle was half-filled with water, then tilted into various positions; a screen hid the water level – participants were shown outline drawings of the bottle and had to draw in the water level.

On conservation tasks, Dasen found the same shift from pre-operational to concrete operational thought as Piaget had with Swiss children. But this took place between the ages of ten to thirteen (rather than five to seven). A fairly high proportion of adolescents and adults also gave non-conservation answers.

On the spatial tasks, there was again the same shift from pre- to concrete operational thought as for Swiss children. But they found these tasks easier than the conservation tasks. In other words, operational thinking develops *earlier* in the spatial domain; this is the *reverse* of what's found for Swiss (and other European) children.

STRETCH AND CHALLENGE

According to Dasen, these findings make perfect sense in terms of Aboriginal culture, where things *aren't quantified*. Water is vital for survival, but the exact quantity is unimportant. Counting things is unusual, and number words only go up to five (after which everything is 'many'). By contrast, finding one's way around is crucial: waterholes must be found at the end of each journey and family members meet up at the end of the day after having split up in order to search for water. The acquisition of a vast array of spatial knowledge is helped by the mythology, such as the 'Dreamtime' stories that attribute a meaning to each feature of the landscape and to routes travelled by ancestral spirits.

Conservation experiments have also been conducted with Eskimo, African (Senegal and Rwanda), Hong Kong and Papua New Guinea samples. Consistent with Dasen's findings, children from non-western cultures often show a considerable lag in acquiring operational thought. But this applies mainly to those having minimal contact with white culture. Where Aborigines, for example, live in white communities and attend school there, they perform at a similar level to whites. Even where there's a lag in development compared with whites, the stages still appear in the same order. So (as with the sensorimotor sub-stages), 'Cultural factors ... can affect rate of attainment; they do not alter developmental sequence' (Schaffer, 2004). As Dasen (1994) puts it:

The deep structure, the basic cognitive processes, are indeed universal, while at the surface level, the way these basic processes are brought to bear on specific contents, in specific contexts, is influenced by culture. Universality and cultural diversity are not opposites, but are complementary aspects of all human behaviour and development.

234

✗ **Lack of cross-cultural support:** the aspect of Piaget's theory that has received the least support from cross-cultural studies is the formal operational stage. Dasen has argued that only one-third of adolescents and adults actually attain formal operations, and that in some cultures this capability doesn't 'exist' at all. But formal operational thought can take many forms. According to Segall *et al.* (1999), it's more accurate to argue that formal operational thinking 'in effect, scientific reasoning ... is not what is valued in all cultures'.

✗ **Neglect of social factors:** Meadows (1995) maintains that Piaget implicitly saw children as largely independent and isolated in their construction of knowledge and understanding of the physical world ('the child as scientist'). This excludes the contribution of other people to children's cognitive development. As we shall see below, the social nature of knowledge and thought is a basic feature of Vygotsky's (and, to a lesser degree, Bruner's) theory. According to Vygotsky (1987):

The child [in Piaget's theory] is not seen as part of the social whole, as a subject of social relationships. He is not seen as a being who participates in the societal life of the social whole to which he belongs from the outset. The social is viewed as something standing outside the child.

Applying Piaget's theory to education

Piaget actually wrote very little about the educational implications of his developmental theory (Davis, 2003). However, it has three main implications for education (Brainerd, 1983), namely the concept of *readiness*, the *curriculum* (what should be taught) and *teaching methods* (how the curriculum should be taught).

1. *Readiness* relates to limits set on learning by a child's current stage of development (see Box 6.4). According to Schaffer (2004), Piaget's most relevant contribution to education (especially the teaching of maths and science; see below) is the recognition that careful thought must be given to the individual child's capacity for handling particular experiences. What's needed is a *child-centred approach,* whereby the tasks set by the teacher are adapted as precisely as possible to the child's cognitive level.

2. Regarding the *curriculum,* the greatest impact of Piaget's theory has been on science and maths: teaching materials should consist of concrete objects that children can easily manipulate. But rather than trying to base a curriculum on Piagetian stages, it would be more useful to modify the curriculum in line with what's known about them, and not allow them to limit teaching

Figure 6.5 In the traditional classroom (left), the teacher is at the centre of the learning process imparting ready-made ('academic'/'school') knowledge; by contrast, in the Piagetian classroom (right), the child actively discovers knowledge for him/herself, often through interaction with other children in small groups

methods (Ginsburg, 1981). However, even today, an understanding of number conservation remains a criterion for an *attainment target* in the UK National Curriculum for maths (Davis, 2003; see below).

3. Central to a Piagetian perspective is the view that children learn from actions rather than from passive observation (*active self-discovery / discovery learning*). As far as *teaching methods* are concerned, teachers must recognise that each child needs to construct knowledge for him/herself, and that deeper understanding is the product of active learning (Smith *et al.*, 1998). Piaget's account of development could be used by those involved in early education as a *formalisation* of many of the assumptions underlying child-centred education.

Some evaluative points

- Piaget's theory seems to suggest that there are definite sequences in which concepts should be taught. For example, different types of conservation appear at different times (see Box 6.3). But many traditional schools don't base their teaching on this – or any other – developmental sequence (Elkind, 1976).

- Both Vygotsky and Bruner were unhappy with Piaget's concept of 'readiness' and proposed a much more active policy of intervention. Instead of waiting until the child is 'ready', Bruner (1966) argued that

'any subject can be taught effectively in some intellectually honest form to any child at any stage of development'. This is related to his theory of the '*spiral curriculum*' (see below). The equivalent active form of intervention advocated by Vygotsky is represented by the related concepts of *scaffolding* and the *zone of proximal development* (again, see below).

Vygotsky's theory

Vygotsky didn't produce a fully formed theory or coherent body of research, and many of his ideas weren't spelled out in detail. His works were originally published in the former Soviet Union in the 1920s and 1930s, but weren't translated into English until the early 1960s (Vygotsky, 1962).

Vygotsky and Piaget agree that development doesn't take place in a vacuum: knowledge is constructed as a result of the child's active interaction with the environment. But, as we've seen, for Piaget, that environment is essentially *asocial* (so his account is described as *constructivist*). But, for Vygotsky

> *Human nature cannot be described in the abstract; whatever course children's mental growth takes is to a large extent a function of the cultural tools that are handed down to them by other people (Schaffer, 2004).*

So, for Vygotsky, cognitive development is a thor-

Box 6.4: The role of the teacher in the Piagetian classroom

- It's essential for teachers to assess very carefully each individual child's current stage of cognitive development (this relates to the concept of readiness). The child can then be set tasks tailored to its needs which become *intrinsically motivating* (desirable in themselves).

- Teachers provide children with learning opportunities that enable them to advance to the next developmental step. This is achieved by creating *disequilibrium* (see above). Rather than providing the appropriate materials and allowing children to 'get on with it', teachers should create a proper balance between actively guiding and directing children's thinking patterns, and providing opportunities for them to explore by themselves (Thomas, 1985).

- Teachers should be concerned with the *learning process* rather than its end product. This involves encouraging children to ask questions, experiment and explore. Teachers should look for the reasoning behind children's answers, particularly when they make mistakes.

- Teachers should encourage children to *learn from each other.* Hearing other (often conflicting) views can help break down egocentrism, and working in pairs can promote long-lasting perspective-taking (e.g. Doise and Mugny, 1984). This has powerful implications for the British educational system (and any others), which from infant school through to university assesses understanding and knowledge at an individual level (Davis, 2003).

oughly *social* process (hence, he's a *social constructivist*). His aim was to spell out and explain how the higher mental functions (reasoning, understanding, planning, remembering and so on) arise out of children's social experiences. He did this by considering human development in terms of three levels: the *cultural, interpersonal* and *individual*. He had much more to say about the first two than the third, so we'll concentrate on those here.

The cultural level

Children don't need to 'reinvent the world anew' (as Piaget seemed to believe). They can benefit from the accumulated wisdom of previous generations; indeed, they cannot avoid doing so through interactions with caregivers. So each generation stands on the shoulders of the previous one, taking over the particular culture – including its intellectual, material, scientific and artistic achievements – in order to develop it further before handing it on, in turn, to the next generation (Schaffer, 2004). Each child 'inherits a number of *cultural tools*.

How Science Works

Practical Learning Activity 6.5

- Give some examples of what you think Vygotsky means by 'cultural tools'.
- Try to include examples of tools that are inherited by *every* generation (and which, arguably, are part of how we define being human), as well as those that are very recent but also very powerful and influential.

Cultural tools can be:

- *technological* (clocks, bicycles and other physical devices)

- *psychological* (concepts and symbols, such as language, literacy, maths and scientific theories)

- *values* (such as speed, efficiency and power).

It's through such tools that children learn to conduct their lives in socially effective and acceptable ways, as well as understanding how the world works. Schaffer (2004) gives the example of *computers* as a major – and relatively recent – cultural tool:

There are few instances in history where a new technical

Figure 6.6 The computer: a powerful and pervasive cultural tool

invention has assumed such a dominant role in virtually all spheres of human activity as the computer ... in the space of just a few decades computing expertise is regarded as an essential skill for even quite young children to acquire ...

For Vygotsky, the most essential cultural tool is *language*.

Box 6.5: The importance of language as a cultural tool

- It's the pre-eminent means of passing on society's accumulated knowledge: how others speak and what they speak about is the main channel of communicating culture from adult to child.
- It enables children to regulate their own activities. At about age seven, speech becomes internalised to form internal thought; an essential *social* function thus becomes the major tool for *cognitive* functioning.

The interpersonal level

It's here that culture and the individual meet, and it's the level at which Vygotsky made his major contribution.

Internalisation and the social nature of thinking

The ability to think and reason by and for ourselves (*inner speech* or *verbal thought*) is the result of a fundamentally *social* process. At birth, we're social beings capable of interacting with others, but we're able to do little – either practically or intellectually – by or for ourselves. But we gradually become more self-sufficient and independent, and by participating in social activities our abilities become transformed.

For Vygotsky, cognitive development involves an active *internalisation* of problem-solving processes that takes place as a result of mutual interaction between the child and those with whom s/he has regular social contact (initially the parents, but later on with friends, classmates and teachers). This is the reverse of Piaget's view (or, at least, his original view). Piaget's image of 'the child as scientist' is replaced by *the child as apprentice*, who acquires the culture's knowledge and skills through graded collaboration with those who already possess them (Rogoff, 1990). According to Vygotsky (1981), 'Any function in the child's cultural development appears twice, or on two planes. First it appears on the social plane, and then on the psychological plane.' So cognitive development progresses from the *intermental* to the *intramental* (from joint regulation to self-regulation). But intermental (social) regulation has to work with the 'raw material' of the baby's innate abilities or capacities; an example is given in Box 6.6.

Box 6.6: Pointing as an example of cultural development from the physical to the social

- Initially, a baby's pointing is simply an unsuccessful attempt to grasp something beyond its reach.
- When the mother sees her baby pointing, she takes it as an 'indicatory gesture' that the baby wants something. So she helps it, probably by making the gesture herself.
- Gradually, the baby comes to use the gesture deliberately. The 'reaching' becomes reduced to movements that couldn't themselves achieve the desired object – even if were within the baby's reach. The baby cries, looks at the mother, and will eventually speak while pointing. The gesture is now directed towards the *mother*, rather than the object; it's become a 'gesture for others', rather than a gesture 'in itself' (Meadows, 1995).

Scaffolding and the zone of proximal development (ZPD)

Vygotsky (1978) defined the *zone of proximal development* (ZPD) as

> the distance between actual developmental level as determined by independent problem solving and the level of potential development through problem solving under adult guidance or in collaboration with more capable peers.

'Joint collaboration' is best viewed as active, shared participation for the purpose of solving a problem. The adult or peer, with greater understanding of the problem, actively facilitates or encourages the child in his/her own definition and redefinition of the problem to promote the achievement of a solution. In this way, the adult's or peer's role in regulating or managing the child's performance is gradually reduced, with the child being given more opportunity to perform the task independently ('transfer of responsibility') (Rogoff, 1986; Slee and Shute, 2003).

How Science Works
Practical Learning Activity 6.6

- Give some examples of skills/knowledge that children acquire through joint collaboration.
- Try to observe a parent and/or more experienced peer engaging in joint collaboration. It might be interesting to compare (a) the way that a mother and a father go about it, including whether their behaviour is influenced by the child's gender (see Chapter 5); (b) the way an adult and a more experienced peer go about it.

The concept of sensitive guidance for development was taken up and elaborated by several researchers, who used the term *scaffolding* (Wood *et al.*, 1976; Wood *et al.*, 1978; Bruner and Haste, 1987; Wood, 1988; Wood and Wood, 1996).

Scaffolding refers to the kind of guidance and support adults provide children in the ZPD. Through joint collaboration and transfer of responsibility, the developing thinker doesn't have to create cognition 'from scratch': there are others available who've already 'served' their own apprenticeship. An example of scaffolding is given in Key Study 6.3.

Key Study 6.3: A demonstration of scaffolding (Wood *et al.*, 1976)

Aim/hypothesis (AO1)

Wood *et al.* (1976) were interested in how mothers of four- and five-year-olds 'tutored' them on a construction task that they were unable to perform alone.

Method/design (AO1)

The task comprised fitting wooden blocks together with pegs to make a pyramid. The mothers were observed as they attempted to assist their child to complete the pyramid.

Results/findings (AO1)

Mothers provided different levels of support for the children's performance, ranging from full demonstration of the task, through verbal instruction on how to do it, to simply encouraging the child to perform the task. Not all such tutoring was equally effective; for example, children became frustrated with full demonstration (an example of adult imposition of a solution) or were given verbal instructions that were too difficult.

Conclusions (AO1)

Children's learning was best promoted by providing assistance as soon as the child got stuck, and refraining from intrusive assistance when the child was making progress. Wood called such an instructional style 'contingent teaching': 'These mothers ensured that the child wasn't left alone when he was overwhelmed by the task, and also guaranteed him greater scope for initiative when he showed signs of success' (Wood, 1988). Similarly, Bruner (1987) argues that the most useful help is that which adapts itself to the learner's successes and failures. For example, the helper uses a general instruction initially until the child runs into difficulties; at this point, a more specific instruction or demonstration is given. This style allows the child considerable autonomy, but also provides carefully planned guidance in its ZPD.

Evaluation (AO1/AO2)

This demonstration of scaffolding illustrates very well what Vygotsky called sensitive guidance, as well as what the ZPD means in practice: children will benefit from their mothers' guidance (that is, learn) only if it's adapted to the child's performance.

While Wood *et al.*'s sample may have been small, their basic findings have been replicated in several other studies. Also, the concepts of sensitive guidance, scaffolding and ZPD are relatively 'culture fair' – that is, they can quite easily be applied to different cultures, where the particular skills and problems involved will differ.

The individual level

STRETCH AND CHALLENGE

The claim that Vygotsky's theory, unlike Piaget's, isn't truly developmental, isn't strictly accurate. While emphasising the cultural and interpersonal levels, at the individual level he identified a number of stages, derived from experimental work on the sorting of blocks of various colours and shapes (Vygotsky, 1962).

- Initially, objects are sorted into unorganised 'heaps'.
- Later, they're grouped in terms of functional, concrete uses, such as knife with fork and spoon (a kind of categorisation that adults also use).
- Then come 'chain complexes', in which groups of objects are sorted consecutively according to certain criteria (such as shape or colour), but the crucial criterion changes over time. (Compare this with Piaget's 'syncretic thought'; see page 227.)
- Then come 'diffuse complexes', in which the criteria for selection are fluid, and based on unreal attributes that would surprise an adult.
- 'Pseudo-concepts' predominate the thinking of the preschooler. Superficially, the child appears to be using true concepts, at least enough to allow them to communicate with adults. But what the child understands is very different from an adult's understanding of the 'same' concept name.
- True, abstract thought appears in adolescence, but earlier, more concrete, forms of thinking continue to operate. (Compare this with the finding that many adults fail to achieve Piaget's formal operations – even in western cultures; see above.) Piaget's stage theory has very much overshadowed the stage aspects of Vygotsky's theory, which is acknowledged most for its emphasis on the social, language-driven nature of children's cognitive development (Slee and Shute, 2003).

Evaluation of Vygotsky's theory

✔**Theoretical strengths:** Vygotsky's theory clearly 'compensates' for one of the main limitations of Piaget's theory. As Segall *et al*. (1999) put it, 'Piaget produced a theory of the development of an "epistemic subject", an idealised, non-existent individual completely divorced from the social environment.' For Vygotsky, culture (and especially language) plays a key role in cognitive development. The development of the individual cannot be understood – and cannot actually *happen* – outside the context of social interaction.

✔**Relevance to cross-cultural psychology:** although Vygotsky's theory hasn't been tested cross-culturally as Piaget's has, it has influenced cross-cultural psychology through the development of *cultural psychology* (e.g. Cole, 1990; see Chapter 5) and related approaches, such as 'socially shared cognition' (Resnick *et al*., 1991) and 'distributed cognition' (Salomon, 1993). According to these approaches, 'cognitive processes are not seen as exclusively individual central processors, but ... are situation specific ... therefore cognition is not necessarily situated "within the head" but is shared among people and settings' (Segall *et al.*, 1999).

Evaluation of Vygotsky's theory continued...

✔ **Stimulus for other researchers:** although Vygotsky didn't carry out much empirical research himself, the specific nature of many of his ideas has made it possible for others to follow them up. This has resulted, for example, in a substantial body of research into scaffolding, peer tutoring and other aspects of the educational process (see above and below).

We saw above how Rogoff has pointed out the limitations of his concept of scaffolding, but it's 'versatile' enough for her to have incorporated it into the broader concept of guided participation. The two concepts refer to many of the same basic principles and processes. Bruner (e.g. 1966) is one of the leading figures to have been influenced by, and helped extend, Vygotsky's ideas – and to apply them to education (see below).

✗ **The 'coldness' of his theory:** Schaffer (2004) believes that Vygotsky's neglect of *emotional factors* is a serious omission; he makes no reference to struggles, the frustrations of failure, the joys of success, or generally what *motivates* the child to achieve particular goals: 'While cognition was given a social appearance, Vygotsky's treatment of the child is as "cold" as Piaget's' (Schaffer, 2004).

Applying Vygotsky's theory to education

As we've seen above, much of Vygotsky's theory is directly or indirectly concerned with formal schooling; Rogoff's criticism of the concept of scaffolding is a good illustration of this. And, according to Davis (2003):

By emphasising the social nature of development, Vygotsky's theory is not only a theory of learning, it also offers a theory of teaching, since language is the prime medium for sharing knowledge in formal contexts such as schools and informally in the home ...

The zone of proximal development (ZPD)

The ZPD defines those functions that haven't yet matured but are in the process of maturing (Vygotsky, 1978). These could be called the 'buds' or 'flowers' rather than the 'fruits' of development. The actual developmental level characterises mental development *retrospectively* (what the child has been able to do in the past), while the ZPD characterises it *prospectively* (what the child *could* do – with help).

Box 6.7: Applying the concept of ZPD to education

Suppose a child is currently functioning at level 'x' in terms of attainment. Through innate/environmental means, the child has the potential to reach level 'x + 1'.
The area between 'x' and 'x + 1' is the child's ZPD. The ZPD may be different for different children, and those with a large ZPD will have a greater capacity to be helped than those whose ZPD is small. Irrespective of the size, Vygotsky saw the teacher as responsible for giving children the cues they need or taking them through a series of steps towards the solution of a problem.

Source: based on Sutherland (1992)

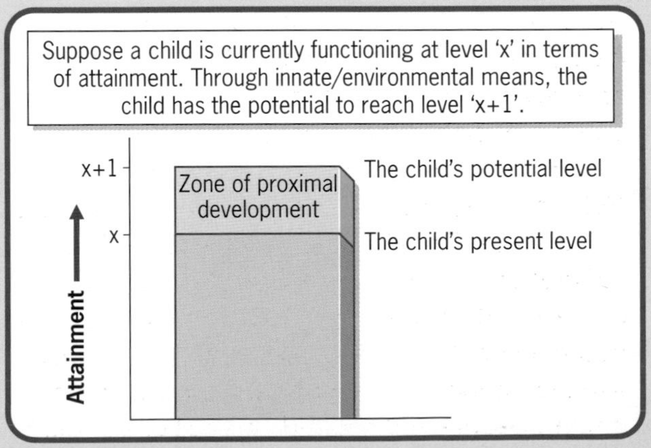

Suppose a child is currently functioning at level 'x' in terms of attainment. Through innate/environmental means, the child has the potential to reach level 'x+1'.

x+1 — Zone of proximal development — The child's potential level

x — The child's present level

Attainment

Figure 6.7 Vygotsky's zone of proximal development

Collaborative learning

In *collaborative learning,* children at similar levels of competence work together, either in pairs or groups. Slavin's (1990) *Student Teams Achievement Divisions* (STAD) involves small groups of varying ability, gender and ethnic background, working on a topic. These groups show greater achievement than controls taught by more conventional methods.

Educators now believe that *both* collaborative learning and *peer tutoring* can offer an effective environment for guiding a child through its ZPD. This may be because these settings encourage children to use language, provide explanations and work cooperatively or competitively, all of which help produce cognitive change (Pine, 1999).

The role of the teacher

Vygotsky defines intelligence as the capacity to learn from instruction. Rather than teachers playing an *enabling* role, Vygotsky believes they should guide pupils in paying attention, concentrating and learning effectively (a *didactic* role; Sutherland, 1992). By doing this, teachers scaffold children to competence.

Bruner's theory

As we noted earlier, Bruner's emphasis on how cognitive development is influenced by social factors makes his theory more like Vygotsky's than like Piaget's. However, Bruner was also much influenced by Piaget's ideas. For example, they both believe that:

- children's underlying cognitive structures mature over time, so that they can think about and organise their world in increasingly complex ways

- children are actively curious and explorative, capable of adapting to their environment through interacting with it; abstract thinking grows out of action – competence in any area of knowledge is rooted in active experience and concrete mental operations.

Bruner places much greater emphasis than Piaget on the notion that humans actively construct *meaning* from the world. In *Actual Minds, Possible Worlds* (1986), Bruner states that:

> *Contrary to common sense there is no unique 'real world' that pre-exists and is independent of human mental activity and human symbolic language; that which we call the world is a product of some mind whose symbolic procedures construct the world.*

Box 6.8: Vygotsky and the National Curriculum

- In the UK, the past 20 years have seen an almost complete U-turn in educational policy and practice. The emphasis has shifted from *child-centred* to *curriculum-centred* education (Davis, 2003).

- The Plowden Report (1967) ('Children and their primary schools') stated that 'at the heart of the educational process lies the child'. In the mid-1980s, the then Secretary of State for Education declared that 'at the heart of the educational process lies the curriculum'. These two views can be seen as reflecting the theories of Piaget and Vygotsky, respectively.

- The Education Reform Act (1988) introduced a compulsory National Curriculum (NC) for all five- to sixteen-year-olds in England and Wales. English, maths and science were identified as 'core' subjects, and *attainment targets* were specified (descriptions of the knowledge children should have acquired as they work through the system). These targets at *key stages* provide the benchmark for assessment at ages 7, 11, 14 and 16.

- Assessment involves *criterion referencing* (as opposed to *norm referencing*) – that is, measuring a child's performance relative to a specified criterion (a given attainment target). The assessment tests are 'standard assessment tasks' (SATs).

- Sutherland (1992) argues that Vygotsky didn't 'advocate mechanical formal teaching where children go through the motions of sitting at desks and passing exams that are meaningless to them ... On the contrary, Vygotsky stressed intellectual development rather than procedural learning'.

- Vygotsky rejected any approach advocating that teachers have rigid control over children's learning. Rather, as with Piaget, teachers' control over children's activities is what counts. Teachers extend and challenge children to go beyond where they otherwise could have.

As such, the world we live in is 'created' by the mind. Bruner argues that the idea that we construct the world should be quite acceptable to developmental or clinical psychologists, who find that people can attach quite different meanings to the 'same' event (see Chapter 7) (Slee and Shute, 2003).

There are also some basic areas of disagreement between Bruner and Piaget, reflecting the influence of Vygotsky. In particular, Bruner (e.g. 1966) stresses the role of language and interpersonal communication, and the need for active involvement by expert adults (or more knowledgeable peers) in helping the child to develop as a thinker and problem solver. Not only does language play a crucial role in the scaffolding process, but for Bruner language is intimately related to the child's cognitive growth. Indeed, thinking would be impossible without language.

Bruner (1987) also argued that children's competences are greater than Piaget's theory leads us to believe. Like Vygotsky, he places great emphasis on the child as a social being whose competences 'are interwoven with the competences of others'.

Bruner (1966) identified three major themes in understanding cognitive growth and the conditions that shape it. These relate to (i) *modes of representation*; (ii) the impact of *culture* on cognitive growth; Bruner notes that cognitive growth is shaped as much 'from the outside in as the inside out'; and (iii) the *evolutionary* history of human beings; Bruner believes that humans are particularly suited to adapting to their environment by social means rather than by morphological (bodily/physical) means (see Chapter 2). We shall say most about the first of these.

Modes of representation

Unlike Piaget, Bruner (1966) doesn't identify stages of development as such. Instead, he describes three *modes of representing the world*, different forms that our knowledge and understanding can take. So he's as much concerned with knowledge in general as he is with cognitive growth. The three modes are the *enactive, iconic* and *symbolic*, and they develop in that order (and he does refer to them as 'stages').

The enactive mode

At first, babies represent the world through *actions*; any knowledge they have is based upon what they've experienced through their own behaviour. So the enactive mode corresponds to Piaget's sensorimotor stage. Past events are represented through appropriate motor responses. Many of our motor schemas, such as bicycle riding, tying knots, aspects of driving, get represented in our muscles, so to speak, and even when we have the use of language, it's often extremely difficult to describe in words alone how we do certain things.

How Science Works

Practical Learning Activity 6.7

- Ask one or more adults to describe/explain one or more of the above motor schemas. (You may prefer to choose your own examples, or ask the participant to choose.)
- Does it make any difference if the skill (e.g. driving a car or swimming) has been acquired recently (or is in the process of being acquired)?

Through recurrent events and environmental conditions, we build up almost automatic patterns of motor activity, which we 'run off' as units in the appropriate situation. But although infants can perform actions, they don't know how they perform them. To this extent, Bruner agrees with Piaget that the infant's intelligence is one in which things are 'lived rather than thought' (Piaget, 1954, in Slee and Shute, 2003). Also like Piaget, Bruner sees the onset of *object permanence* as a major *qualitative* change in the young child's cognitive development.

The iconic mode

An icon is an *image*, so this form of representation involves building up mental images of things we've experienced. As Bruner says,

> *A second stage in representation emerges when a child is finally able to represent the world to himself by an image or spatial schema that is relatively independent of action.*

A mental image is a genuine cognitive representation: it represents a body of information but takes a different form from what it represents. Images are normally *composite* – that is, made up of a number of past encounters with similar objects or situations. Iconic knowledge is inflexible, focuses upon small details, is self-centred (it focuses on the child as an observer), and is subject to distortion because of the child's needs and feelings. Perception is also closely tied to action or doing, and is unsteady due to the child's unreliable concentration.

This mode corresponds to the last six months of the sensorimotor stage (where schemas become interiorised) and the whole of the pre-operational stage (where the child is at the mercy of what it perceives in drawing intuitive conclusions about the nature of reality: things are as they *look*).

The symbolic mode

Bruner's main interest was in the *transition* from the iconic to the symbolic mode. He and Piaget agree that a very important cognitive change occurs at around six to seven years. For Piaget, this is the start of logical operations (albeit tied to concrete reality), while Bruner sees it as the appearance of the symbolic mode. An experiment demonstrating the transition from iconic to symbolic modes is described in Key Study 6.4.

Key Study 6.4: The transition from iconic to symbolic modes (Bruner and Kenney, 1966)

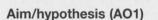

Aim/hypothesis (AO1)

The aim of the experiment was to demonstrate the transition from the iconic to the symbolic mode of representation. It was predicted that children under seven would succeed on a reproduction task (which requires only the iconic mode), while only those seven and over would succeed on a transposition task (which requires the symbolic mode).

Method/design (AO1)

Bruner and Kenney arranged nine plastic glasses in a 3 × 3 matrix. Three- to seven-year-olds were made familiar with the matrix. The glasses were then scrambled, and the children were asked to put them back as they were before (the *reproduction task*). In the *transposition task*, the glasses were removed from the matrix, and the glass that had been in the bottom right-hand square was placed in the bottom *left*-hand square; the child had to rebuild the matrix in this transposed manner.

Results/findings (AO1)

Children generally could reproduce at a younger age than they could transpose. The reproduction task involves the iconic mode (60 per cent of the five-year-olds could do this, 72 per cent of the six year olds and 80 per cent of the seven-year-olds). But the transposition task involves the symbolic mode (the results were 0 per cent, 27 per cent and 79 per cent, respectively).

Conclusions (AO1)

Clearly, the five year olds were dominated by the visual image of the *original* matrix, while the six- to seven-year-olds translated their visual information into the symbolic mode. They relied upon verbal rules to guide them, such as 'It gets fatter going one way and taller going the other.' So a child using images but not symbols can reproduce but not restructure.

Evaluation (AO1/AO2)

This is a cleverly designed study, in which the prediction, derived directly from Bruner's theory, is tested in a very direct and clear-cut way. Although there was no *independent* evidence that the younger children were dominated by the iconic mode, the fact that the older children's performance on the transposition task was guided by verbal rules *is* independent evidence of their use of the symbolic mode. In other words, if the only evidence for the older children's use of the symbolic mode is the fact that they were successful on the transposition task, this could be seen as *circular*: they succeed on the task because they use the symbolic mode, and we know they use the symbolic mode because they succeed on the task! The verbal rules show that they use the symbolic mode *over and above* their success on the task.

Language comes into its own as an influence on thought. The child is now freed from the immediate context and is beginning to be able to 'go beyond the information given' (Bruner, 1957). According to Bruner (1966), 'The idea that there is a name that goes with things and that the name is arbitrary is generally taken as the essence of symbolism.' Thus, a written sentence describing a beautiful landscape doesn't look like a landscape, whereas a picture of a landscape does. The landscape is symbolised in the language that describes it.

Without the ability to symbolise, and in particular, to use language, the child would grow into adulthood dependent upon the enactive and iconic modes of representing and organising knowledge of the world.

The impact of culture

According to Bruner, development is culturally – and historically – embedded (Bruner, 1986; Bruner and Haste, 1987). In Bruner's words, 'It can never be the case that there is a "self" independent of one's cultural-historical context.' In this way, Bruner's view is closely allied with Vygotsky's. Culture is the means by which 'instructions' about how humans should grow are carried from generation to generation (Bruner, 1987) – that is, culture helps transmit knowledge and understanding.

Bruner also assumes that the child is a *social* being (again, in agreement with Vygotsky). Bruner and Haste (1987) are critical of the legacy left by Piaget, suggesting that while the child is active in the construction of the world, the picture that emerges from Piaget's theory is one of a rather isolated child working alone at problem-solving tasks. They emphasise that the child is in fact a social operator, who through social life, 'acquires a framework for interpreting experience, and learns how to negotiate meaning in a manner congruent with the requirements of a culture' (Bruner and Haste, 1987).

Applying Bruner's theory to education

Bruner's modes of representation lie at the heart of the '*spiral curriculum*', according to which the principles of a subject come to be understood at increasingly more complex levels of difficulty. Like Vygotsky, Bruner was unhappy with Piaget's concept of 'readiness', and proposed a much more active policy of intervention, based on the belief that 'any subject can be taught effectively in some intellectually honest form to any child at any stage of development' (Bruner, 1966).

This has contributed to the idea of the 'competent infant' – that is, the belief that infants and young children, regardless of background, have much more capacity to learn academic skills than they actually display (Elkind, 1987). Elkind argues that Bruner, as well as other educators, may not have appreciated how sincerely parents and educators would take up this statement as a rallying call. A new optimism was generated regarding the infant's abilities and competences, that overstepped the mark (Slee and Shute, 2003).

Educators need to provide learners with the means of grasping the structure of a discipline – that is, the underlying principles and concepts (rather than just mastering factual information). This enables learners to go beyond the information given and develop ideas

Evaluation of Bruner's theory

✔ **Theoretical strengths:** as we've seen, Bruner has helped to build on some of Vygotsky's ideas and make them more widely known; scaffolding and the view of individual development as mediated through social and cultural influences are two important examples. His theory also represents an important alternative to Piaget's, although, as we've also seen, there's considerable overlap between them; arguably, they're more complementary than opposed theories.

Slee and Shute (2003) believe that Bruner's work may not have received the attention it deserves in mainstream developmental and educational psychology. Nonetheless, his research and writing have important implications for psychologists' understanding of the developing child: 'By emphasizing the constructive nature of cognitive development and the influence of cultural factors, Bruner has added a richer dimension to our contemporary understanding of the nature of the child's thinking' (Slee and Shute, 2003).

of their own. Teachers also need to encourage learners to make links, and to understand the relationships within and between subjects (Smith *et al.,* 1998).

DEVELOPMENT OF MORAL UNDERSTANDING

> ### ✔ Specification Hint
>
> The specification states 'Theories of moral understanding (Kohlberg) and/or pro-social reasoning (Eisenberg)'. 'Theories' is plural, so what you need to know *could* be: (a) two theories of moral understanding (one of which must be Kohlberg's); (b) two theories of pro-social reasoning (one of which must be Eisenberg's); or (c) one theory of each (Kohlberg and Eisenberg).
>
> As far as (a) is concerned, the 'obvious' other theory is Piaget's; this had a great influence on Kohlberg and is a sort of application of Piaget's general theory of cognitive development.
>
> For these reasons, we've decided to cover Piaget's and Kohlberg's theories in detail, and Eisenberg's more briefly.

According to Haste *et al.* (1998), historically four main questions have been asked about moral development.

1. How do conscience and guilt develop, acting as sanctions on our misdeeds? This relates to Freud's *psychoanalytic theory* (see Gross, 2005; Gross and Rolls, 2008).

2. How do we come to understand the basis of rules and moral principles, so that we can make judgements about our own and others' behaviour? This relates to the *cognitive-developmental theories* of Piaget, Kohlberg and Eisenberg.

3. How do we learn the appropriate patterns of behaviour required by our culture? This relates to *learning theories*, including Bandura's *social learning theory* (SLT) (or *social cognitive theory*; see Gross, 2005, and Chapter 5).

4. How do we develop the moral emotions that motivate our concern for others? Eisenberg's theory is also relevant here.

The second question has dominated research into moral development for 30 years, through work within the cognitive-developmental theoretical framework (Haste *et al.,* 1998). Kohlberg's theory has been the focus of research during this time, but Piaget (1932) pioneered this approach. What all theories have in common is the belief that it's the reasons *underlying* behaviour, rather than the behaviour itself, that make it right or wrong.

Piaget's theory

Piaget argued that morality develops gradually during childhood and adolescence. While these changes are usually referred to as qualitatively different stages of moral development, Piaget explicitly *didn't* use the concept of developmental stages in relation to moral development. Rather, he identified two *types of moral orientation*, namely *heteronomous* and *autonomous* (see Table 6.2, page 248). Instead of seeing morality as a form of cognition, Piaget discussed morality in the context of affects and feelings (Eckensberger, 1999).

Understanding rules

To discover how moral knowledge and understanding change with age, Piaget began by looking at children's ideas about the rules of the game of marbles. He believed that the essence of morality lies in rules, and that marbles is a game in which children create and enforce their own rules free from adult influence. Piaget felt that in this way he could discover how children's moral knowledge *in general* develops. As he noted:

> *Children's games constitute the most admirable social institutions. The game of marbles, for instance, as played by boys, contains an extremely complex system of rules . . . that is to say, a code of laws, a jurisprudence of its own . . . All morality consists of a system of rules.*

Pretending that he didn't know the rules, Piaget asked children to explain them to him, and during the course of a game, to tell him who made the rules, where they came from and whether they could be changed.

He found that children aged from five to nine or ten tended to believe that the rules had always existed in their present form, and that they'd been created by older children, adults or even God. The rules are sacred and cannot be changed in any way (an *external law*). Nevertheless, children unashamedly broke the rules to suit themselves, and saw nothing contradictory in the idea of both players winning the game.

As for children of ten and over, they understood that the rules were invented by children themselves and could be changed – but only if all players agreed. The function of rules is to prevent quarrelling and ensure fair play. They adhered rigidly to the rules, and discussed the finer points and implications of any changes. Piaget called this moral orientation towards cooperation with peers *mutual respect*, in contrast with the *unilateral respect* shown by younger children towards adult authority.

Moral judgement and punishment

Piaget also told children pairs of stories about children who'd told lies, stolen or broken something (see Box 6.9).

Box 6.9: Examples of pairs of stories used by Piaget

- *Example 1a:* A little boy called John was in his room. He was called in to dinner and went into the dining room. Behind the door there was a chair and on the chair there was a tray with 15 cups on it. John couldn't have known that the chair was behind the door, and as he entered the dining room, the door knocked against the tray and the tray fell on the floor, breaking all the cups.

- *Example 1b:* One day, a little boy called Henry tried to get some jam out of a cupboard when his mother was out. He climbed on to a chair and stretched out his arm. The jam was too high up, and he couldn't reach it. But while he was trying to get it, he knocked over a cup. The cup fell down and broke.

- *Example 2a:* A little girl called Marie wanted to give her mother a nice surprise and so she cut out a piece of sewing for her. But she didn't know how to use the scissors properly and she cut a big hole in her dress.

- *Example 2b:* A little girl called Margaret went and took her mother's scissors one day when her mother was out. She played with them for a bit and then, as she didn't know how to use them properly, she made a hole in her dress.

How Science Works

Practical Learning Activity 6.8

- Piaget asked children who they believed was the naughtier and should therefore be punished more.
- Who do you think (a) five- to nine- or ten-year-olds and (b) children over ten judged to be the naughtier?
- Why?
- In view of the fact that Piaget's research was conducted in the early 1930s with middle-class Swiss children, what might you change about the stories if you were repeating the study today? Try rewriting them according to your suggestions.
- Test this out with a sample of younger and older children.

Moral judgement

Piaget was more interested in the *reasons* children gave for their answers than the answers themselves. While five- to nine- or ten-year-olds could distinguish an intentional act from an unintentional one, they tended to base their judgements on the severity of the outcome or the sheer amount of damage done. So John and Marie were typically judged as naughtier (*objective* or *external responsibility*).

By contrast, children aged ten or above judged Henry and Margaret to be naughtier, because they were both doing something they shouldn't have. Although the damage they caused was accidental, older children saw the motive or intention behind the act as being important in determining naughtiness (*internal responsibility*).

Punishment

Younger children believed that naughty people should pay for their crimes. In general, the greater the suffering the better, even though the form of punishment might be quite arbitrary. Such *expiatory* punishment ('paying the penalty for') is seen as decreed by authority and accepted as just because of its source (*moral realism*). Thus, when a child in a class doesn't admit to a misdeed and the rest of the class doesn't identify the offender, younger children see *collective punishment* (the whole class is punished) as fair.

If someone has been naughty (such as telling a lie) and isn't found out, then suffers some misfortune (e.g. falls over and cuts his/her leg), younger children often construed this as a punishment for the misdeed (*immanent justice*). God (or an equivalent force) is in league with those in authority to ensure that the 'guilty will always be caught in the end'.

In the case of older children, punishment was seen as bringing home to the offender the nature of the offence, and as a deterrent to behaving badly in the future. They also believed that collective punishment was wrong, and that 'the punishment should fit the crime'. So if one child steals another child's sweets, the offender should give his/her own sweets to the victim (based on the *principle of reciprocity*) or be punished in some other appropriate way. Older children no longer saw justice as being tied to authority (*moral relativism*), and there was less belief in immanent justice.

Box 6.10: Heteronomous and autonomous morality

- Piaget called the morality of young children *heteronomous* ('subject to another's laws or rules'). Older children display *autonomous* morality ('subject to one's own laws or rules') and see rules as the product of social agreements rather than sacred and unchangeable laws (the *morality of cooperation*).
- Piaget believed that the change from heteronomous to autonomous morality occurs because of the shift at about seven from egocentric to operational thought (see above). This suggests that cognitive development is *necessary* for moral development, but since the latter lags at least two years behind the former, it cannot be *sufficient*.
- Another important factor is the change from *unilateral respect* (the child's unconditional obedience to parents and other adults) to *mutual respect* within the peer group (where disagreements between equals have to be negotiated and resolved).

	Understanding rules	Moral judgement and punishment
5–9/10-year-olds: **Heteronomous moral orientation** ('subject to another's laws or rules')	• *Rules represent an external law* • *Unilateral respect*	• *Objective/external Responsibility* Belief in: • *expiatory punishment* • *moral realism* • *collective punishment* • *immanent justice*
10-year-olds and above: **Autonomous moral Orientation** ('subject to one's own laws or rules')	*Mutual respect*	• *Internal responsibility* Belief in: • *principle of reciprocity* • *moral relativism* No longer believe in: • *collective punishment* • *immanent justice*

Table 6.2: Summary of Piaget's theory of moral development

Evaluation of Piaget's theory

✔ **Stimulus for research into perspective taking:** Piaget argued that *egocentrism* could be overcome via *social interaction with peers*. Intellectually, and in terms of status, adults are too far removed from children, but peers provide the ideal potential source of *sociological conflict* necessary for developmental change to take place (through resolution of conflict). Although there's no *logical* reason why conflict resolution should result in developmental advance (Bryant, 1990), Piaget's claims have inspired some important research into the potential impact of peer interaction on *perspective-taking* (Davis, 2003; see below, pages 268–271).

✘ **Gender bias:** Piaget believed that popular girls' games (such as hopscotch) were too simple compared with boys' most popular game (marbles) to merit investigation. While girls eventually achieve similar moral levels to boys, they're less concerned with legal elaborations. This apparent *gender bias* is even more evident in Kohlberg's theory (see below).

✘ **Piaget oversimplified children's understanding of intention:** this is much more complex than he believed, and children are capable of applying their understanding of intention to moral decision making. The preschool child *isn't* amoral, as Piaget claimed (Durkin, 1995).

Piaget's stories (see Box 6.9) make the *consequences* of behaviour explicit rather than the intentions behind it (Nelson, 1980). When three-year-olds see people causing negative consequences, they assume that their intentions are also negative. But when information about intention is made explicit, even three-year-olds can make judgements about them, *regardless* of the consequences. This suggests that the main difference between three-year-olds and older children concerns (a) the ability to separate intentions from consequences; and (b) the use of these separate pieces of information to make moral judgements.

Armsby (1971) found that 60 per cent of six-year-olds (compared with 90 per cent of ten-year-olds) judged that a child who deliberately breaks a cup is more 'guilty' (and so more deserving of punishment) than one who accidentally breaks a TV set. This suggests that at least some six-year-olds are capable of understanding intention in the sense of 'deliberate naughtiness'.

✔/✘ **Cross-cultural support:** the evidence here is mixed. Many of the age trends described by Piaget have been supported by later studies, including cross-cultural data, mainly from Africa (Eckensberger and Zimba, 1997). But based on his idea of a balance between the individual and society, Piaget *didn't* assume that the developmental changes he observed in his Swiss sample would necessarily be found in other cultures. On the contrary, he claimed that the essential issue was whether the cultural context would allow certain changes to occur. This relates to *contextualisation*, which is evident in current cross-cultural research (Eckensberger, 1999). An interesting example is given in Key Study 6.5.

Key Study 6.5: Lying and truth telling in China and Canada (Lee *et al.*, 1997)

Aim/hypothesis (AO1)

Lee *et al.* tested the claim that the understanding of lying is greatly influenced by the social norms and values in which individuals are socialised.

Method/design (AO1)

A total of 120 children from the People's Republic of China and 108 Canadian children (aged seven, nine and eleven) were presented with four brief stories. Two of the stories involved a child who intentionally performed a good deed (valued by adults in both cultures) and two involved a child who performed a bad deed (disapproved of by adults in both cultures). When the story characters were questioned by a teacher about who committed the act, they either lied or told the truth. The participants were asked to evaluate the story characters' deeds and their verbal statements as either 'naughty' or 'good'.

Results/findings (AO1)

Overall, the Chinese children rated truth telling less positively and lie telling more positively in *pro-social settings* compared with Canadian children. Both groups rated truth telling positively and lie telling negatively in *antisocial situations.*

Conclusions (AO1)

The first finding indicates that the emphasis on self-effacement and modesty in Chinese culture overrides children's evaluations of lying in certain situations. The second finding reflects the emphasis in *both* cultures on distinguishing between misdeed and truth/lietelling.

Evaluation (AO1/AO2)

Lee *et al.*'s results suggest a close link between socio-cultural practices and moral judgement in relation to lying and truth telling. China is a Communist-collectivist society, which values the community over the individual, promoting personal sacrifice for the social good (see Chapter 2). Taking the credit for a good deed is viewed as a violation of both traditional Chinese cultural norms and Communist-collectivist doctrine.

In western culture, 'white lies' and deceptions to avoid embarrassment are tolerated, and concealing positive behaviour isn't explicitly encouraged (especially in the early years). Taking credit for good deeds is an accepted part of individualistic self-promotion in the west – but in China this is seen as a character flaw.

The study demonstrates that cultural and social factors are key determinants in children's moral development – over and above cognitive development (Lee *et al.*, 1997).

Kohlberg's theory

Kohlberg's theory has dominated research in the field of moral reasoning for 30 years. Kohlberg was greatly influenced by Piaget and, like him, believed that morality develops gradually during childhood and adolescence. Also like Piaget, he was more interested in people's *reasons* for their moral judgements than in the judgements themselves. For example, our reasons for upholding the law, as well as our views about whether there are circumstances in which breaking the law can be justified, might change as we develop.

Kohlberg assessed people's moral reasoning through

the use of *moral dilemmas*. Typically, these involved a choice between two alternatives, both of which would be considered socially unacceptable. One of the most famous of these dilemmas concerns 'Heinz'.

Box 6.11: The Heinz dilemma

In Europe, a woman was near death from a special kind of cancer. There was one drug that the doctors thought might save her. It was a form of radium that a druggist in the same town had recently discovered. The drug was expensive to make, but the druggist was charging ten times what the drug cost him to make. He paid $400 for the radium and charged $4,000 for a small dose of the drug. The sick woman's husband, Heinz, went to everyone he knew to borrow the money, but he could only get together about $2,000, which was half of what the drug cost. He told the druggists that his wife was dying and asked him to sell it cheaper or let him pay later. But the druggist said, 'No, I discovered the drug and I'm going to make money from it.' So Heinz got desperate and considered breaking into the man's store to steal the drug for his wife.

1. Should Heinz steal the drug? (Why or why not?)
2. If Heinz doesn't love his wife, should he steal the drug for her? (Why or why not?)
3. Suppose the person dying isn't his wife but a stranger. Should Heinz steal the drug for the stranger? (Why or why not?)
4. (If you favour stealing the drug for a stranger.) Suppose it's a pet animal he loves. Should Heinz steal to save the pet animal? (Why or why not?)
5. Is it important for people to do everything they can to save another's life? (Why or why not?)
6. Is it against the law for Heinz to steal? Does that make it morally wrong? (Why or why not?)
7. Should people try to do everything they can to obey the law? (Why or why not?)
8. How does this apply to what Heinz should do?

Source: Kohlberg. L. (1984)

- In July, 2004, a 100-year-old man, Bernard Heginbotham, who killed his 87-year-old wife by slitting her throat, avoided a prison sentence because the judge said he acted out of love. Her health was failing and she'd been moved from one care home to another. He became very distressed and decided to end her suffering.

How Science Works

Practical Learning Activity 6.9

- Read Box 6.11 and try answering the questions about Heinz.
- You might like to repeat the exercise with a sample of children of nine and under, and adolescents and adults.
- Should he have killed his wife?
- Can slitting someone's throat ever be justified as an act of love?
- Should his age have been taken into account when passing sentence?
- Should he have been sent to prison?
- You might like to discuss these questions in the form of a class debate.

Kohlberg first started using the Heinz (and other) dilemmas in 1956, with 72 Chicago boys (10–16 years), 58 of whom were followed up at three-yearly intervals for 20 years (Colby *et al.*, 1983; Kohlberg, 1984; Colby and Kohlberg, 1987). Based on the answers given by this sample to the Heinz and other dilemmas, Kohlberg identified six qualitatively different stages of moral development, differing in complexity, with more complex types being used by older individuals. The six stages span *three levels* of moral reasoning:

1. at the *pre-conventional level*, we don't have a personal code of morality; instead, it's shaped by the standards of adults and the consequences of following or breaking their rules

2. at the *conventional level,* we begin to internalise the moral standards of valued adult role models

3. at the *post-conventional level*, society's values (such as individual rights), the need for democratically determined rules and *reciprocity* (or *mutual action*) are affirmed (stage 5); in stage 6, individuals are guided by *universal ethical principles*, in which they do what their conscience dictates – even if this conflicts with society's rules.

Box 6.12: Kohlberg's three levels and six stages of moral development, and their application to the Heinz dilemma

Level 1: Pre-conventional morality

Stage 1 (punishment and obedience orientation): what's right and wrong are determined by what is and isn't punishable. If stealing is wrong, it's because authority figures say so and will punish such behaviour. Moral behaviour is essentially the avoidance of punishment.

- Heinz *should* steal the drug. If he lets his wife die, he'd get into trouble.
- Heinz *shouldn't* steal the drug. He'd get caught and sent to prison.

Stage 2 (instrumental relativist orientation): what's right and wrong are determined by what brings rewards and what people want. Other people's needs and wants are important, but only in a reciprocal sense ('If you scratch my back, I'll scratch yours').

- Heinz *should* steal the drug. His wife needs to live and he needs her companionship.
- Heinz *shouldn't* steal the drug. He might get caught and his wife would probably die before he got out of prison, so it wouldn't do much good.

Level 2: Conventional morality

Stage 3 (interpersonal concordance or 'good boy–nice girl' orientation): moral behaviour is whatever pleases and helps others, and doing what they approve of. Being moral is 'being a good person in your own eyes and the eyes of others'. What the majority thinks is right by definition.

- Heinz *should* steal the drug. Society expects a loving husband to help his wife regardless of the consequences.
- Heinz *shouldn't* steal the drug. He'd bring dishonour on his family and they'd be ashamed of him.

Stage 4 (maintaining the social order orientation): being good means doing one's duty – showing respect for authority and maintaining the social order for its own sake. Concern for the common good goes beyond the stage 3 concern for the family: society protects the rights of individuals, so society must be protected by the individual. Laws are accepted and obeyed unquestioningly.

- Heinz *should* steal the drug. If people like the druggist are allowed to get away with being greedy and selfish, society would eventually break down.
- Heinz *shouldn't* steal the drug. If people are allowed to take the law into their own hands, regardless of how justified an act might be, the social order would soon break down.

Level 3: Post-conventional morality

Stage 5 (social contract-legalistic orientation): since laws are established by mutual agreement, they can be changed by the same democratic process. Although laws should be respected, since they protect individual rights as well as those of society as a whole, individual rights can sometimes supersede these laws if they become destructive or restrictive. Life is more 'sacred' than any legal principle, and so the law shouldn't be obeyed at all costs.

- Heinz *should* steal the drug. The law isn't set up to deal with circumstances in which obeying it would cost a human life.
- Heinz *shouldn't* steal the drug. Although we could understand why he'd want to steal it, even such extreme circumstances don't justify a person taking the law into his own hands. The ends don't always justify the means.

Stage 6 (universal ethical principles orientation): the ultimate judge of what's moral is a person's own conscience operating in accordance with certain universal principles. Society's rules are arbitrary and may be broken when they conflict with universal moral principles.

- Heinz *should* steal the drug. When a choice must be made between disobeying a law and saving a life, one must act in accordance with the higher principle of preserving and respecting life.
- Heinz *shouldn't* steal the drug. He must consider other people who need it just as much as his wife. By stealing the drug, he'd be acting in accordance with his own particular feelings, with utter disregard for the values of all the lives involved.

Source: based on Crooks and Stein (1991), Rest (1983)

Both Kohlberg and Piaget see cognitive development as necessary for, and setting a limit on, the maturity of moral reasoning, with the latter lagging behind. For example, formal operational thought is needed to achieve stages 5 and 6, but cannot guarantee it. Because formal operations are achieved by only a relatively small proportion of people, it's not surprising that only about 15 per cent of people reach stages 5 and 6 (Colby *et al.*, 1983; see Table 6.3).

Kohlberg's levels of moral development	Age group included within Kohlberg's developmental levels	Corresponding type of morality (Piaget)	Corresponding stage of cognitive development (Piaget)
Pre-conventional (stages 1 and 2)	Most 9-year-olds and below; some over-9s	Heteronomous	Pre-operational (2–7)
Conventional (stages 3 and 4)	Most adolescents and adults	Heteronomous (e.g. respect for the law / authority figures) *plus* autonomous (e.g. taking intentions into account)	Concrete operational (7–11)
Post-conventional (stages 5 and 6)	10–15% of adults, not before mid-30s	Autonomous (10 and above)	Formal operational (11 and above)

Table 6.3: The relationship between Kohlberg's stages and Piaget's moral orientations / stages of cognitive development

Evaluation of Kohlberg's theory

✔ **Is there empirical support?** Kohlberg's *longitudinal* (follow-up) study showed that those who were initially at lower stages had progressed to higher stages. This suggests 'moral progression' (Colby *et al.*, 1983), consistent with the theory. (A major advantage of longitudinal studies is that the participants act as their own controls – the same individuals are compared with *themselves* over time.) Based on these findings, Kohlberg argued that stages 1–5 are *universal*, occurring in an *invariant* (fixed) sequence. Rest's (1983) 20-year longitudinal study of men from adolescence to their mid-thirties also showed that the stages seem to occur in the order Kohlberg described.

Evaluation of Kohlberg's theory continued...

✔/✘ **Are the stages universal?** Snarey's (1987) review of 45 studies conducted in 27 countries provides 'striking support for the universality of Kohlberg's first four stages'. But the results of Kohlberg and Nisan's (1987) study of Turkish youngsters, from both a rural village and a city, over a 12-year period, contradict this conclusion. Their overall scores were lower than Americans', and rural youngsters scored lower than the urban residents.

These (and other) findings suggest that cultural factors play a significant part in moral reasoning. According to the socio-cultural approach, what 'develops' is the individual's skill in managing the moral expectations of his/her culture expressed through linguistic and symbolic practices. This contrasts with Kohlberg's cognitive-developmental approach, which focuses on individual processes 'inside the head' (Haste *et al.*, 1998).

✘ **Is it gender-biased?** According to Gilligan (1982, 1993), because Kohlberg's theory was based on an all-male sample, the stages reflect a male definition of morality; in other words, the theory is *androcentric* (literally, 'male centred').

Men's morality is based on abstract principles of law and justice, whereas women's is based on principles of compassion and care. In turn, the different 'moral orientations' of men and women rest on a deeper issue, namely how we think about *selfhood*. An ethic of justice (male) is a natural outcome of thinking of people as separate beings who, in continual conflict with each other, make rules and contracts as a way of handling that conflict. A 'female' ethic of caring/responsibility follows from regarding selves as *connected* with one another.

✔/✘ **So do females and males 'think differently'?** According to Johnston (1988), each gender is competent in each mode (justice vs care/compassion), but there are gender-linked preferences. While boys tended to use a justice orientation, they'd also use the care orientation if pressed. Likewise, girls preferred a care orientation, but they too switched easily. Haste *et al.* (1998) believe that Johnston's findings support Gilligan's argument that there's more than one moral 'voice', but not her claim that the 'caring' voice is more apparent among women. Several studies show that gender differences in moral orientation are less important than the kind of dilemmas being studied. One of these is described in Key Study 6.6 (see page 255).

How Science Works

Practical Learning Activity 6.10

- What do you think Gilligan might mean by a 'male definition of morality'?
- How might this differ from a female definition of morality?

Eisenberg's theory of pro-social moral reasoning

Kohlberg's concept of moral reasoning is *prohibition-orientated*. In the case of Heinz, for example, one prohibition (stealing) is pitted against another (allowing his wife to die). But not all 'moral conflicts' are like this. Eisenberg (1982, 1986; Eisenberg *et al.*, 1991) argues that if we want to understand developmental changes in helping or altruism (see Chapter 2), we need to examine children's reasoning when faced with a conflict between (a) their own needs, and (b) others' needs, in a context where the role of laws, rules and the dictates of authority are minimal. This refers to *pro-social moral reasoning*.

Key Study 6.6: Studies of hypothetical and real-life dilemmas (SoHARD) (Walker, 1989)

Aim/hypothesis (AO1)

Walker wanted to test the claim that gender differences in moral orientation (based on Gilligan's research) are less important than the kind of dilemmas being considered.

Method/design (AO1)

Walker studied a large sample of males and females (aged 5–63). Participants were scored for both moral stage and orientation, on both *hypothetical dilemmas* (such as Heinz) and *personally generated, real-life dilemmas*.

Results/findings (AO1)

The only evidence of gender differences was for adults on real-life dilemmas.

● When asked to produce real-life dilemmas, females reported more *relational/personal* ones; these involved someone with whom the participant had a significant and continuing relationship (for example, whether or not to tell a friend that her husband was having an affair).

● Males reported more *non-relational/impersonal* ones. These involved acquaintances or strangers (for example, whether or not to correct a shop assistant's error in giving too much change).

Regardless of gender, relational/personal dilemmas produced a *higher* level of response than non-relational/impersonal ones.

Conclusions (AO1)

This last finding is the crucial one: it's the *opposite* of Gilligan's claim that Kohlberg's stages are biased against an ethic of care. Both females and males tended to use the ethic of care mostly in relational/personal dilemmas, and most people used *both* orientations to a significant degree. The nature of the dilemma is a better predictor of moral orientation than is gender (Walker, 1996).

Evaluation (AO1/AO2)

Walker (1984, 1995) also refuted Gilligan's claim that Kohlberg's scoring system is biased against females, making them more likely to be rated at the conventional level and males at the post-conventional level. He reviewed all the available research evidence relating to gender differences (80 studies, 152 separate samples, and over 10,000 participants), and found that overall the differences were non-significant for all age groups. After controlling for educational or occupational differences favouring men, Walker concluded that there was no evidence of a systematic gender difference in moral-stage scores.

In a series of studies during the 1980s, Eisenberg presented children of different ages (sometimes followed up until early adulthood) with illustrated hypothetical stories. The story character can help another person – but always at some personal cost.

Based on children's responses to this and other similar dilemmas, Eisenberg identified six stages of pro-social moral reasoning. These are described in Table 6.4.

Box 6.13: A hypothetical story used by Eisenberg to assess pro-social reasoning

A girl named Mary is going to a friend's birthday party. On her way, she sees a girl who has fallen down and hurt her leg. The girl asks Mary to go to her home and get her parents so the parents can take her to the doctor. But if Mary does run and get the child's parents, she will be late for the birthday party and miss the ice cream, cake and all the games.
   What should Mary do? Why?

Level 1 (hedonistic, self-focused orientation): the individual is concerned with selfish, pragmatic consequences, rather than moral considerations. For example, 'She wouldn't help, because she might miss the party.' What's 'right' is whatever is instrumental in achieving the actor's own ends/desires. Reasons for helping / not helping include direct gain for the self, expectations of future reciprocity, and concern for others whom the individual needs and/or likes.

(This is the predominant mode for preschoolers and younger primary schoolers.)

Level 2 (needs-of-others orientation): the individual expresses concern for the physical, material and psychological needs of others, even though these conflict with his/her own needs. For example, 'She should help, because the girl's leg is bleeding and she needs to go to the doctor.' This concern is expressed in the simplest terms, without clear evidence of self-reflective role-taking, verbal expressions of sympathy or reference to internalised affect, such as guilt.

(This is the predominant mode for many preschoolers and primary schoolers.)

Level 3 (approval and interpersonal orientation and/or stereotyped orientation): stereotyped images of good and bad persons and behaviours and/or considerations of others' approval/acceptance are used in justifying pro-social or non-helping behaviours. For example, 'It's nice to help' or 'Her family would think she did the right thing.'

(This is the predominant mode for some primary schoolers and secondary-school students.)

Level 4a (self-reflective empathic orientation): the individual's judgements include evidence of self-reflective sympathetic responding, role taking, concern with others' humanness, and/or guilt or positive affect related to the consequences of one's actions. For example, 'She cares about people,' and 'She'd feel bad if she didn't help because she'd be in pain.'

(This is the predominant mode for a few older primary schoolers and many secondary-school students.)

Level 4b (transitional level): the individual's justifications for helping / not helping involve internalised values, norms, duties or responsibilities, or refer to the need to protect the rights and dignity of others. But these aren't clearly or strongly stated. For example, 'It's just something she learnt and feels.'

(This is the predominant mode for a minority of people of secondary-school age and older.)

Level 5 (strongly internalised stage): as for 4b, above, but internalised values, norms etc. are much more strongly stated. Additional justifications for helping include the desire to honour the individual and societal contractual obligations, improve the conditions of society, and belief in the dignity, rights and equality of human beings. It's also characterised by the wish to maintain self-respect for living up to one's own values and accepted norms. For example, 'She'd feel bad if she didn't help because she'd know she didn't live up to her values.'

(This is the predominant mode for a very small minority of secondary-school students and no primary schoolers.)

Table 6.4: Stages of pro-social moral reasoning (based on Eisenberg, 1982, 1986)

✔ **Theoretical importance and contrast with Kohlberg's theory**

- In a review of her research, Eisenberg (1996) points out that, as predicted, children almost never said they'd help in order to avoid punishment or out of blind obedience to adult authority figures. This would be expected, given that children are rarely punished for *not* acting in a pro-social way (but *are* for wrongdoing). This contrasts sharply with what's been found for prohibition-orientated moral reasoning (the focus of Kohlberg's theory).

- For Kohlberg, other-orientated reasoning emerges relatively late, but Eisenberg expected to find it by the preschool years. Even four- to five-year-olds often appeared to orientate to others' needs, showing what seemed to be primitive empathy. References to empathy-related processes (such as taking the other's perspective and sympathising) are particularly common in pro-social reasoning.

- Contrary to Kohlberg's claims, even individuals who typically used higher-level reasoning occasionally reverted to lower-level reasoning (such as egotistic, hedonistic reasoning). This was especially likely when they chose not to help, suggesting the role of *situational variables*; these are also implicated in some cross-cultural studies. For example, children raised on Israeli kibbutzim are particularly likely to emphasise reciprocity between people, whereas city children (both Israeli and from the USA) are more likely to be concerned with personal costs for helping others.

- If individuals' moral reasoning can vary across situations, then the relationship between their typical level of moral reasoning and their actual pro-social behaviour is likely to be weak. This prediction is supported by Eisenberg's research.

- One additional factor that Eisenberg's research has revealed is *emotion* – in particular, *empathy*. Whether or not children help others depends on the *type* of emotional response that others' distress induces in them (rather than *whether or not* they respond emotionally). Children (as well as adults) who respond *sympathetically/empathically* (associated with lowered heart rate) are more likely to help than those who experience *personal distress* (associated with accelerated heart rate). (See the discussion of pro-social behaviour in adults in Gross, 2005.)

- According to Eckensberger (1999), emotions (especially positive ones) are increasingly being seen as the basis for moral development. This represents a move away from Kohlberg's theory and a return to Piaget's. Piaget's and Kohlberg's theories are commonly referred to as cognitive-developmental, and, as we saw earlier, Kohlberg was very much influenced by Piaget. But instead of seeing morality as a form of cognition, Piaget in fact discussed morality in the context of affects (emotions) and feelings; mutual respect and empathy were central (Eckensberger, 1999). In this respect, Eisenberg and Piaget have more in common with each other than either has with Kohlberg.

DEVELOPMENT OF SOCIAL COGNITION

How Science Works
Practical Learning Activity 6.11

- Try to define the 'self' (or self-concept). Try not to use the word 'self' in your definition (but it's very difficult not to).
- What different components make up the self/self-concept?
- What factors do you think might influence the development of the self/self-concept?
- What do you think the following terms refer to: self-recognition, self-definition, the psychological self, the categorical self?
- In what order do you think these develop in the child?

Development of the child's sense of self

What is the self?

'*Self*' and '*self-concept*' are used interchangeably to refer to an individual's overall self-awareness. According to Murphy (1947), 'the self is the individual as known to the individual', and Burns (1980) defines it as 'the set of attitudes a person holds towards himself'.

According to Leary (2004), the self is a *cognitive structure* that permits self-reflection and organises information about oneself. It also has *motivational features*, in particular:

- *self-consistency* (to maintain, if not verify, one's existing view of oneself)

- *self-evaluation* (self-assessment – to see oneself accurately)

- *self-enhancement* (to maintain a positive image of oneself).

Our existing view of ourselves is our *self-image* (how we describe ourselves, what we think we're like). This includes social roles, personality traits and physical characteristics (our *body image / bodily self*). Our self-evaluation determines our *self-esteem* (or *self-regard*), which refers to how much we like the kind of person we think we are. Coopersmith (1967) defined self-esteem as 'a personal judgement of worthiness, that is expressed in the attitudes the individual holds towards himself'.

The second major component of the self-concept is *self-esteem*. According to Greenwald (1980), the *self-esteem motive* acts like a totalitarian political regime which suppresses information and rewrites history to preserve a particular image of the government. The 'totalitarian ego' distorts facts about the self and rewrites one's memory of personal history in order to maintain one's own positive evaluation. This corresponds to *private* self-enhancement (Leary, 2004).

Self-esteem is partly determined by how much the self-image differs from the *ideal self* (*ego-ideal* or *idealised self-image*), the third major component of the self-concept. This refers to the kind of person we'd *like to be*.

Factors influencing the development of the self-concept

Argyle (1983) identifies four major influences, namely (i) the reaction of others; (ii) comparison with others; (iii) social roles; and (iv) identification (see Gross and Rolls, 2008). The importance of these factors extends beyond childhood, since our self-concept is constantly being revised. But the most significant 'change' is probably the time when it's first being formed.

The reaction of others

Both Cooley's (1902) *theory of the looking-glass self* and Mead's (1934) *symbolic interactionist* theory see the reaction of others as central to the formation of the self-concept (see Gross, 2005). Any attempt to explain how we come to be what we are, and how we change, involves us asking what kind of evidence we use. Kelly (1955), like Cooley and Mead, believes that we derive our pictures of ourselves through what we learn of others' pictures of us. So the crucial evidence is the reaction of others to us, both what they say about us and the implications of their behaviour towards us. We filter others' views of us through our views of them, building up continuous and changing pictures of ourselves out of our interaction with others.

Preschool children are extremely concerned with how adults view them, and few things are more relevant than the reactions to them of *significant others* (parents, older siblings and other people whose opinions the child values). Strictly speaking, it's the child's *perception* of others' reactions that makes such an important contribution to how the child comes to perceive itself. After all, the child has no frame of reference for evaluating parental reactions: parents are all-powerful figures and what they say is 'fact'. If a child is consistently told how beautiful she is, she'll come to believe it (it will become part of her body image). Equally, if a child is repeatedly told how stupid or clumsy he is, this too will become accepted as the 'truth', and the child will tend to act accordingly.

The first child is likely to develop high self-esteem and the second low self-esteem. Argyle (1983) explains this in terms of *introjection* (a process very similar to identification), whereby we come to incorporate into our own personality the perceptions, attitudes and reactions to ourselves of our parents. It's through others' reactions that the child learns its *conditions of worth* – that is, which behaviours will produce *positive regard* (approval, encouragement, praise etc.) and which will not (Rogers, 1959).

When the child starts school, the number and variety of significant others increase to include teachers and peers. At the same time, the child's self-image is becoming more differentiated, and significant others then become important in relation to different parts of the self-image. For example, teachers matter as far as the child's academic ability and progress are concerned, parents are important as far as how loveable the child is, and so on.

Coopersmith's (1967) study of nine- and ten-year-old white, middle-class boys, found that the optimum conditions for the development of high self-esteem involve a combination of firm enforcement of limits on the child's behaviour, plus a good deal of acceptance of the child's autonomy and freedom within those limits. Firm management helps the child to develop firm inner controls; a predictable and structured social environment helps the child to deal effectively with the environment and, hence, to feel 'in control' of the world (rather than controlled by it). Coopersmith followed these boys through into adulthood, and found that the high-self-esteem boys consistently outperformed the low-self-esteem boys, both educationally and occupationally.

STRETCH AND CHALLENGE: The schizophrenic self

In contrast with the parents of high-self-esteem boys in Coopersmith's study is the study of interaction between parents and their schizophrenic children. These parents tend to deny *communicative support* to the child, and often fail to respond to the child's statements and demands for recognition of its opinions. When the parents do communicate with the child, it's often in the form of an interruption or an intrusion, rather than a response to the child. In fact, they respond selectively to those of the child's utterances that they themselves have initiated – rather than those initiated by the child.

Laing (1970) suggests that these kinds of communication patterns within the family make the development of *ego boundaries* in the child very difficult – that is, there's a confusion between *self* and *not-self* (me and not-me). This impaired autonomy of the self and appreciation of external reality represent fundamental characteristics of schizophrenic adolescents and adults (see Chapter 7).

Comparison with others

According to Bannister and Agnew (1976), the personal construct of 'self' is intrinsically *bipolar* – that is, having a concept of self implies a concept of not-self. (This is similar to Cooley and Mead's view that self and society are really two sides of a coin.) So one way in which we come to form pictures of what we're like is to see how we compare with others. Indeed, certain components of self-image are only meaningful through comparison with others. For example, 'tall' and 'fat' aren't absolute characteristics (like, say, 'blue-eyed'): we're tall or fat only relative to others who are shorter or thinner.

How Science Works

Practical Learning Activity 6.12

- What *level of measurement* does this example correspond to? (See Chapter 11.)
- Can you think of a psychological characteristic, much researched by psychologists, that is also meaningful only by comparing people, but is often taken to be 'absolute'? It's measured in a way that suggests every individual has 'so much' of it, but, in reality, an individual's score is (implicitly) a comparison with other people's scores.

Parents and other adults often react to children by comparing them with other children (such as siblings). If a child is told repeatedly that she's less clever than her big sister, she'll come to incorporate this into her self-image, and will probably have lower self-esteem as a result. (If pre-conceptual children fail to understand relative terms, she might just incorporate this as 'I'm not clever' or 'I'm stupid'; see the discussion of Piaget's theory, above.) In turn, this could adversely affect her future academic performance, so that she doesn't achieve in line with her true ability. A child of above average intelligence who's grown up in the shadow of a brilliant sibling may be less successful academically than an average or even below-average child who's not had to face such unfavourable comparisons.

According to Tesser (2004), recent research has shown the *converse* to be true – that is, one's view of self can affect how we compare ourselves with others. For example, the poorer our performance in, say, athletics, the more charitable we are in evaluating others' athletic performance. If I do poorly, then others who do poorly are 'OK'; if I do well, the people who do poorly are rated down. Under some conditions, when we're outperformed by others, we *don't* downgrade our view of self, but upgrade their performance instead (Alicke *et al.*, 1997). It's less threatening to be outperformed by a 'genius' (who's 'out of our league') than by someone of normal/average ability.

Social roles

As we noted earlier, social roles are part of what people commonly regard as part of 'who they are'. Kuhn and McPartland (1954) asked seven-year-olds and under-graduate students to give 20 different answers to the question, 'Who am I?' The children gave an average of five answers, while the students gave an average of ten. As we get older, we incorporate more and more roles into our self-image, reflecting the increasing number and variety of roles we actually take on. The pre-schooler is a son or daughter, perhaps a brother or sister, has other familial roles, and may also be a friend to another child. But the number and range of roles are limited compared with those of the older child or adult.

Developmental changes in the self-concept

Achieving identity, in the sense of acquiring a set of beliefs about the self (a *self-schema*), is one of the central developmental tasks of a social being (Lewis, 1990). It progresses through several levels of complexity, and continues to develop through the lifespan (see Gross, 2005).

During the first few months, the baby gradually distinguishes itself from its environment and from other people, and develops a sense of *continuity through time* (the *existential self*). But at this stage, the infant's self-knowledge is comparable to that of other species (such as monkeys). What makes human self-knowledge distinctive is becoming aware that we have it – we're conscious of our existence and uniqueness.

According to Maccoby (1980), babies are able to distinguish between themselves and others on two counts:

1. their own fingers hurt when bitten (but they don't have any such sensations when they bite their rattle or their mother's fingers)

2. probably quite early in life, they begin to associate feelings from their own body movements with the sight of their own limbs and the sounds of their own cries. These sense impressions are bound together into a cluster that defines the *bodily self*, so this is probably the first aspect of the self-concept to develop.

Other aspects of the self-concept develop by degrees, but there seem to be quite clearly defined stages of development. Young children may know their own names, and understand the limits of their own bodies, and yet be unable to think about themselves as coherent entities. So self-awareness/self-consciousness develops very gradually.

According to Piaget, an awareness of self comes through the gradual process of *adaptation to the* environment (see above). As the child explores objects and accommodates to them (thus developing new *sensorimotor schemas*), it simultaneously discovers aspects of its self. For example, trying to put a large block into its mouth and finding that it won't fit is a lesson in selfhood, as well as a lesson about the world of objects.

Self-recognition

One way in which the development of bodily self has been studied is through *self-recognition*, which involves more than just a simple discrimination of bodily features. To determine that the person in a photograph or a film, or reflected in a mirror, is oneself, certain knowledge seems to be necessary:

- at least a rudimentary knowledge of oneself as continuous through time (necessary for recognising

ourselves in photographs or movies) and space (necessary for recognising ourselves in mirrors)

- knowledge of particular features (what we look like).

Although other kinds of self-recognition are possible (such as one's voice or feelings), only *visual* self-recognition has been studied extensively, both in humans and non-humans. Many non-human species (such as birds, fish, chickens and elephants) react to their self-images as if they were other animals: they don't seem to recognise them as their own reflections at all. But self-recognition has been observed in the higher primates – chimpanzees and other great apes. Gallup's study with chimpanzees is described in Key Study 6.7.

Key Study 6.7: Mirror, mirror ... (Gallup, 1977)

Aim/hypothesis (AO1)

Gallup was interested in observing whether any non-human species, in this case wild-born chimpanzees, are capable of self-recognition. Traditionally, it has been thought that this ability is unique to human beings.

Method/design (AO1)

Gallup placed a full-length mirror on the wall of each chimp's cage. At first, they reacted as if another chimp had appeared: they threatened, vocalised or made conciliatory gestures. But this quickly faded out, and after three days had almost disappeared. They then used their image to explore themselves (such as picking up food and placing it on their face), which couldn't be seen without the mirrors.

After ten days' exposure, each chimp was anaesthetised and a bright red spot was painted on the uppermost part of one eyebrow ridge, and a second spot on the top of the opposite ear, using an odourless, non-irritating dye.

Results/findings (AO1)

After recovering from the anaesthetic, the chimp was returned to its cage, from which the mirror had been removed; it was observed to see how often it touched the marked parts of its body. The mirror was then replaced, and each chimp began to explore the marked spots about 25 times more often than it had done before.

The procedure was repeated with chimps that had never seen themselves in the mirror, and they reacted to the mirror image as if it were another chimp (they didn't touch the spots).

Conclusions

The first group had, apparently, learned to recognise themselves through exposure to their mirror image. It's generally agreed that passing the 'mirror test' is strong evidence that a chimp has a self-

Key Study 6.7: Mirror, mirror ... (Gallup, 1977) continued...

concept, and that only chimps, orang-utans and humans consistently pass it; lower primates (monkeys, gibbons and baboons) are unable to learn to recognise their mirror image.

However, Gallup infers much more than this. He claims that:

not only are some animals aware of themselves but ... such self-awareness enables these animals to infer the mental states of others. In other words, species that pass the mirror test are also able to sympathise, empathise and attribute intent and emotions in others ... abilities that some might consider the exclusive domain of humans.

In other words, Gallup is claiming that chimps have a *theory of mind.* We shall discuss this claim, and evidence of theory of mind in children, below.

Self-definition

Piaget, Mead and many others have pointed to the importance of language in consolidating the early development of self-awareness, by providing labels that permit distinctions between self and not-self ('I', 'you', 'me', 'it'). The toddler can then use these labels to communicate notions of selfhood to others. One important kind of label is the child's *name.*

Names aren't usually chosen at random; either the parents particularly like the name they choose, or they want to name the child after a relative or famous person. Names aren't neutral labels in terms of how people react to them and what they associate with them. Indeed, they can be used as the basis for *stereotyping.*

Jahoda (1954) described the naming practices of the Ashanti tribe of West Africa; children born on different days of the week are given names accordingly, because of the belief that they have different personalities. Police records show that among juvenile delinquents there was a very low percentage of boys born on Mondays (believed to have quiet, calm personalities), but a very high rate of Wednesday-born boys (thought to be naturally aggressive).

How Science Works

Practical Learning Activity 6.13

- Try to account for these findings?
- Are they merely a coincidence, or might there be an expectation–behaviour link that accounts for them?

The findings can be explained in terms of the *self-fulfilling prophecy.* It's reasonable to believe that Ashanti boys were treated in a way that was consistent with their name, and that, as a result, they 'became' what their name indicated they were 'really' like. In English-speaking countries, days of the week (e.g. Tuesday) and months of the year (e.g. April, May and June) are used as names, which have associations that may influence others' reactions towards them (for example, 'Monday's child is fair of face, Tuesday's child is full of grace ...').

Christenfeld and Larsen (2008) identify a number of ways in which our names could influence us. For example, if our family name comes near the beginning of the alphabet we're likely to enjoy certain advantages compared with those whose names come towards the end. Rare names and rare spellings, and those that are stereotypically black rather than white, tend to judged as less favourable by others. Although it's very difficult to disentangle the effects of nature and nurture:

it seems that ... names do shape, in some ways, the fate of their bearers. Perhaps the thousands of baby-naming books should add a new section reporting not only on the past of a name, but also on the future ... (Christenfeld and Larsen, 2008)

When children refer to themselves as 'I' (or 'me') and others as 'you', they're having to reverse the labels that are normally used to refer to them by others ('you', 'he', 'she'). Also, of course, they hear others refer to themselves as 'I' and not as 'you', 'he' or 'she'. This is a problem of *shifting reference.* Despite this, most children don't invert 'I' and 'you'. However, two interesting exceptions are autistic and blind children, who often use 'I' for others and 'you' for self (see below). This may be associated with the abnormal interactions and relationships these children experience, which, in turn, further support the theories of Cooley and Mead.

The categorical self

Age and *gender* are both parts of the central core of the self-image. They represent two of the categories regarding the self that are also used to perceive and interpret the behaviour of others.

Age is probably the first social category to be acquired by the child (and is so even before a concept of number develops). Lewis and Brooks-Gunn (1979) found that six- to twelve-month-olds can distinguish between photographs, slides and papier mâché heads of adults and babies. By 12 months, they prefer interacting with

unfamiliar babies to unfamiliar adults. Also, as soon as they've acquired labels like 'mummy', 'daddy' and 'baby', they almost never make age-related mistakes.

Before age seven, children tend to define the self in *physical* terms: hair colour, height, favourite activities and possessions. Inner, psychological experiences and characteristics aren't described as being distinct from overt behaviour and external, physical characteristics. During middle childhood through to adolescence, self-descriptions now include many more references to internal, psychological characteristics, such as competencies, knowledge, emotions, values and personality traits (Damon and Hart, 1988). However, Damon and Hart also report important cultural differences in how the self-concept develops.

Synoptic Material

The self-concept as a cultural phenomenon

In Maori culture, the person is invested with a particular kind of power (*mana*), given by the gods in accordance with the person's family status and birth circumstances. This is what enables the person to be effective, whether in battle or everyday dealings with others. But this power isn't a stable resource and can be increased or decreased by the person's day-to-day conduct. For example, it could be reduced by forgetting a ritual observance or committing some misdemeanour. People's social standing, successes and failures are seen as dependent on external forces, not internal states (such as personality or level of motivation). In fact, mana is only one of these eternal forces which inhabit the individual.

People living in such a culture would necessarily experience themselves quite differently from what people in western culture are used to. Instead of representing themselves as the centre and origin of their actions, which is crucial to the western concept of the self, 'The individual Maori does not own experiences such as the emotions of fear, anger, love, grief; rather they are visitations governed by the unseen world of powers and forces' (Potter and Wetherell, 1987).

According to Mosovici (1985), 'the individual' is the greatest invention of modern times. Only recently has the idea of the autonomous, self-regulating, free-standing individual become dominant, and this has fundamental implications for the debate about free will and determinism (see Gross, 2005).

Smith and Bond (1998) argue that we need to distinguish between *independent* and *interdependent* selves: the former is what's stressed in western, *individualist* cultures, and the latter in non-western, *collectivist* cultures (see Chapter 2).

School highlights others' expectations about how the self should develop. It also provides a social context in which new goals are set and comparisons with others (peers) are prompted. This makes evaluation of the self all the more important (Durkin, 1995). This comparison becomes more important still in adolescence (see Gross, 2005).

The psychological self

Maccoby (1980) asks what children mean when they refer to themselves as 'I' or 'me'. Are they referring to anything more than a physical entity enclosed by an envelope of skin?

How Science Works

Practical Learning Activity 6.14

- What do you think children (say, three- to five-year-olds) mean when they refer to themselves as 'I' or 'me'?
- How might you go about testing this age group? (What method/materials would you use?)
- Ask a sample of adults the same question(s) you'd ask the children.
- How different (if at all) are their respective answers?
- What surprises (if any) were there in your findings?
- What conclusions can you draw from your findings?

Flavell *et al.* (1978) investigated development of the psychological self in two and a half- to five-year-olds. In one study, a doll was placed on the table in front of the child, and it was explained that dolls are like people in some ways – they have arms, legs, hands and so on (which were pointed to). Then the child was asked how dolls are different from people, whether they know their names and think about things and so on. Most children said a doll *doesn't* know its name and *cannot* think about things – but people can.

They were then asked, 'What is the part of you that knows your name and thinks about things?' and 'Where do you do your thinking and knowing?' A total of 14 out of 22 children gave fairly clear localisation for the thinking self, namely, 'in their heads', while others found it very difficult. The experimenter then looked directly into their eyes and asked, 'Can I see you thinking in there?' Most children thought not.

These answers suggest that by three and a half to four years, a child has a rudimentary concept of a private, thinking self that's not visible even to someone looking directly into its eyes. The child can distinguish this from the bodily self, which it knows is visible to others. In other words, by about age four, children begin to develop a *theory of mind*, the awareness that they – and other people – have mental processes (e.g. Wellman, 1990; Leekam, 1993; Shatz, 1994). This is discussed further below.

Theory of mind

As we've just seen, one aspect of the child's psychological self is the development of a *theory of mind* (ToM). Also, when discussing self-recognition in chimpanzees, we noted Gallup's claim that they possess a ToM. In fact, the term 'theory of mind' was originally coined by Premack and Woodruff (1978) based on their efforts to understand the cognitive and language abilities of chimpanzees. They defined ToM as the ability to attribute mental states (knowledge, wishes, feelings and beliefs) to oneself and others. As we spend time with others, we take into account their feelings, thoughts and behaviour in order to try to understand why they behave as they do.

Indications of the existence of ToM awareness are found in everyday use of language, such as 'I think she was upset' and' I'm sure you'll like this.' To understand that children have a developing sense of another, researchers must first rule out the possibility that the child is: (a) not behaving egocentrically (e.g. indicating that another child wants something based *not* on their knowledge of the other's desire but on their *own* desire);

✔ Specification Hint

The specification states 'Development of the child's sense of self, including Theory of Mind (Baron-Cohen) ...'. The reference to Baron-Cohen means that you could be asked specifically about his research into theory of mind. But much of his research in this area has been focused on people (children and adults) with *autism*, who, it is claimed, *lack* a theory of mind. So, although autism isn't mentioned in the specification, it's virtually impossible to discuss Baron-Cohen's research without discussing autism. In the section that follows, we've included plenty of material on the 'normal' development of theory of mind, but Baron-Cohen's research will be discussed in the context of autism.

STRETCH AND CHALLENGE

Gallup (1998) believes that self-awareness (or self-consciousness) is the expression of some underlying process that allows organisms to use their experience as a means of modelling the experience of others. The best support for this *mind-reading hypothesis* (MRH) comes from mirror studies involving human infants and young children.

A number of researchers (e.g. Lewis and Brooks-Gunn, 1979) have used modified forms of Gallup's technique with 6–24-month-old children. The mother applies a dot of rouge to the child's nose (while pretending to wipe its face), and the child is observed to see how often it touches its nose. It's then placed in front of a mirror, and again the number of times it touches its nose is recorded. At about 18 months, there's a significant change: while touching the dot was never seen before 15 months, between 15 and 18 months, 5–25 per cent of infants touched it compared with 75 per cent of the 18–24 month olds.

In order to use the mirror image to touch the dot on its nose, the baby must also have built up a schema of how its face should look in the mirror before (otherwise it wouldn't notice the discrepancy created by the dot). This doesn't develop until about 18 months. This is also about the time when, according to Piaget, *object permanence* is completed; object permanence, therefore, would seem to be a necessary condition for the development of self-recognition.

Gallup's research also points to the *right prefrontal cortex* as the brain area that mediates self-awareness and mental states (such as deception and gratitude), and this is the brain region that grows most rapidly between 18 and 34 months.

As additional support for his MRH, Gallup cites studies by Povinelli and his colleagues, involving chimps. These studies are often taken to show that chimps have a ToM. But ironically, Povinelli (1998) himself disagrees with Gallup's MRH. While agreeing that passing the mirror test indicates that chimps possess a self-concept, he disagrees that this means they also possess the deep psychological understanding of behaviour that seems so characteristic of humans.

If chimps *don't* genuinely reason about mental states, what can we say about their understanding of self based on the mirror test? Povinelli has tried to answer this by shifting his attention from chimps to two-, three- and four-year-old children. In a series of experiments, children were videotaped while they played a game. The experimenter secretly placed a large, brightly coloured sticker on top of the child's head. Three minutes later, they were shown either (a) a live video image of themselves, or (b) a recording made several minutes earlier, which clearly depicted the experimenter placing the sticker on the child's head.

With the live image (equivalent to seeing themselves in the mirror), most two- and three-year-olds reached up and removed the sticker from their head. But with the recording, only about a third did so. This wasn't because they failed to notice the stickers (most could identify the sticker when they were specifically asked about it) or because they failed to 'recognise' themselves in the recording (they confidently responded with 'Me' and stated their name when asked, 'Who is that?'). However, they seemed to be recognising just facial and bodily features: when asked, 'Where is that sticker?' they often referred to the 'other' child (e.g. 'It's on his/her head'), as if they were trying to say, 'Yes, that looks like me, but that's not *me* – she's not doing what I'm doing right now.' By about age four, a significant majority of the children passed the delayed self-recognition test.

For Povinelli, these findings suggest that self-recognition in chimps – and human toddlers – is based on recognition of the self's *behaviour*, not the self's psychological states (necessary for a ToM). Chimps and toddlers possess explicit mental representations of the positions and movements of their own bodies (the *kinaesthetic self-concept*).

265

or (b) not simply using past experience to infer something about another child (Slee and Shute, 2003).

In a major review of the field, Flavell (1999) has identified three main waves of research into the development of ToM.

1. The first wave largely involved Piaget's account of *egocentrism*, which restricts pre-operational children's ability to appreciate other perspectives apart from their own (see above). Research studies confirm a gradual increase in children's perspective-taking abilities (see below).

2. A second wave related to development of the child's *metacognitive abilities* – that is, awareness of its own mental processes (see Gross, 2005).

3. The third, and now dominant, wave relates to the development of ToM. A vast amount of research began in the early 1980s and currently almost dominates the field of cognitive development. As noted above in the 'Specification Hint', much of this research has been related, directly or indirectly, to autism, where Baron-Cohen is a major figure (see below).

The normal development of ToM

Research into understanding false beliefs

One of the most important aspects of understanding the mind is the realisation that just as I have a mind (feelings, desires, beliefs and so on), so do other people. Equally important is the realisation that other people's beliefs etc. may sometimes *differ* from our own – that is, different people may *represent* the world in different ways. If I believe, for example, that there's a cabbage in the fridge, and you believe that it's a cauliflower, we cannot both be right. Although we could both be mistaken (it's actually broccoli), assuming that it is in fact a cabbage,

then your belief is incorrect; in other words, you have a *false belief* about the world.

A major way of investigating ToM is to present children with *false-belief tasks*. Wimmer and Perner (1983) carried out the first study of children's understanding of false belief. With four-, six- and eight-year-olds, they used models to act out a story about a little boy called Maxi who put some chocolate in a *blue* cupboard. Then Maxi left the room, and while he was out of the room the children saw Maxi's mother transfer the chocolate to a *green* cupboard. The children were asked to predict where Maxi would look for the chocolate when he came back into the room. While most of the six- and eight-year-olds gave the correct (*blue* cupboard) answer, most four-year-olds said that he'd look in the *green* cupboard.

Of course, this is the *wrong* answer: Maxi couldn't possibly know that the chocolate had been moved. But four-year-olds assume that Maxi sees things as they themselves do and that he'll know that the chocolate is in the green cupboard (where it actually is). They fail to understand that Maxi's beliefs about the world are different from how the world really is, and that he'll act on the basis of his *false belief*.

This was a very important result, because it indicated that young children's reasoning about other people's behaviour may be quite different from the assumptions that adults make about other people's behaviour. The discovery of such a major developmental difference stimulated a huge amount of research into how children think about the mind, and the relationship between mind and behaviour (Smith *et al.*, 1998).

A much-cited study by Baron-Cohen *et al.* (1985) is described in Key Study 6.8.

Key Study 6.8: The Sally Anne experiment (Baron-Cohen *et al.*, 1985)

Aim/hypothesis (AO1)

This was essentially a replication of the Wimmer and Perner 'Maxi' study, retaining the vital elements but adapted to make it shorter and simpler, and more appropriate in content for older children (Mitchell, 1997). The title of the study is 'Does the autistic child have a 'theory of mind?' So it wasn't simply a replication of the earlier study, but an attempt to directly test the *ToM hypothesis* – that is, the claim that a *lack* of ToM is at the core of autism.

According to the current edition of the Diagnostic and Statistical Manual of Mental Disorders (DSM-

IV-TR, 2000), published by the American Psychiatric Association (see Chapter 7), autism involves three fundamental impairments: (i) qualitative impairments in social interaction; (ii) qualitative impairments in communication; and (iii) repetitive and stereotyped patterns of behaviour and lack of normal imagination. The Sally Anne experiment was an attempt to test the ToM hypothesis as an explanation for all three impairments (see Gross, 2008).

Method/design (AO1)

A crucial difference between this and the 'Maxi' study is that the latter involved only normal children, while Baron-Cohen *et al.* tested 20 autistic children (mean chronological age / CA just under 12; mean verbal mental age / vMA 5.5); 14 Down's syndrome children (mean CA just under 11; mean vMA just under 3); and 27 normal children (mean CA 4.5; mean vMA assumed to be equivalent to their CA). The normal and Down's syndrome children served as control groups, with the autistic children as the experimental group.

After first checking that the child knew which doll was which (Sally or Anne: the *naming question*), Sally placed a marble in her basket; then she left the scene, and Anne transferred the marble and hid it in her box. Then, when Sally returned, children were given the Sally Anne test: success or failure depended specifically on their response to the third of three questions:

1. 'Where is the marble really?' (*reality question*)

2. 'Where was the marble in the beginning?' (*memory question*)

3. 'Where will Sally look for her marble?' (*belief question*)

The *correct answer* required the child to attribute a *false belief* to Sally (she'll look in the *wrong place*). The first two questions acted as *control* questions, used to ensure that (a) the child has attended to and knows the current location of the marble, and (b) s/he remembers where it was before.

Results/findings (AO1)

All the children passed the naming question, as well as the reality and memory questions. As predicted, the autistic children were significantly less likely to pass the false-belief question (20 per cent) compared with both the normal children (85 per cent) and those with Down's syndrome (86 per cent). Those who failed pointed to where the marble *really* was, rather than to any of the other possible locations.

Conclusions (AO1)

These findings strongly support the ToM hypothesis: autistic children are unable to attribute beliefs to others, which puts them at a serious disadvantage when having to predict other people's behaviour. Baron-Cohen *et al.* regard this failure as representing a specific deficit; it cannot be explained in terms of the general effects of mental retardation, since the more severely retarded Down's syndrome children performed slightly *better* than even the normal children.

Evaluation (AO1/AO2)

Despite the ToM hypothesis being both convincing and powerful, a substantial amount of evidence has accumulated which is undermining it (Mitchell, 1997). Even in successful replications of the Sally Anne study (and in the Baron-Cohen *et al.* study itself), a minority of autistic children reliably succeed in answering the belief question correctly (or acknowledging false belief in some other way).

The Sally false-belief task involves a *first-order belief* ('I think Sally thinks the marble is in the basket'). A *second-order belief* involves understanding that someone else can have beliefs about a third person ('I think that Anne thinks that Sally thinks that the marble is in the basket'). Baron-Cohen (1989) found that *all* the autistic children failed this second-order belief task. However, many adults with Asperger's syndrome (an *autistic spectrum disorder* not associated with retarded language development) *pass* such second-order ToM tests (Ozonoff *et al.,* 1991; Bowler, 1992). Both studies contradict Baron-Cohen's (1989) claim that lack of ToM is the core cognitive deficit in autism.

However, these studies cannot be taken as conclusive evidence for an *intact* ToM in these individuals: such second-order tests can easily produce *ceiling effects* (see Chapter 11) if used with participants whose mental age (MA) is above six years (Baron-Cohen *et al.,* 1997). This is because children with normal intelligence pass second-order tests at about six years (Perner and Wimmer, 1985). Unfortunately, second-order tests have often been regarded as 'complex' or high-level tests of ToM. While they *are* more complex than first-order tests, normal four-year-olds pass them. Both types of test are simply *probes* for four- or six-year-old-level skills; we cannot just assume they're suitable as tests of whether an *adult* (with autism, Asperger's syndrome or any other condition) has a fully functional ToM.

How Science Works

Practical Learning Activity 6.15

- In what ways did the normal children and those with Down's syndrome function as control groups?
- Can you suggest *other* groups that might have been used?
- In what sense were the reality and memory questions *control questions*? What would have been the effect of not including them?
- While (lack of) ToM is very similar to Piaget's concept of *egocentrism*, what are some of the important *differences* between them? (See Gross, 2008.)

Perspective taking

Are there different types of perspective taking?

Baron-Cohen *et al.* (1985) make a distinction between *conceptual* and *perceptual* perspective taking (PT). The former is what's being tested by their false-belief task, while the latter is tested by the 'three mountains' task (Piaget and Inhelder, 1956; see above, Key Study 6.1 pages 228–229). In terms of this distinction, Piaget and Inhelder's task involves only visuo-spatial skills (seeing things from another's perspective), whereas ToM involves attributing beliefs to other people (including false beliefs). Evidence that autistic children are successful on perceptual perspective-taking tasks, but unsuccessful on the false-belief tasks, indicates very clearly that the two types of task are testing quite different abilities/skills.

Specification Hint

There's considerable overlap between (certain parts of) Piaget's theory of cognitive development (we've already looked at the differences between egocentrism and ToM), ToM, and perspective taking (PT). These, in different ways, all constitute aspects of 'development of the children's understanding of others'. Perspective taking is specified in this part of the specification, and the work of Selman is also specified. So you could be asked a question about perspective taking (in general) and/or Selman's research.

In a complementary way, Flavell *et al.* (1990) distinguish between two levels of PT ability:

1. *level 1* (two- to three-year-olds) – the child knows that some other person experiences something differently (*perceptual* PT)

2. *level 2* (four- to five-year-olds) – the child develops a whole series of complex rules for figuring out precisely what the other person sees or experiences (*affective* and *cognitive* PT).

In a study of children's ability to distinguish between appearance and reality, Flavell (1986) showed children a sponge painted to look like a rock. They were asked what it looked like and what it 'really' was. Three-year-olds said either that it looked like a sponge and was a sponge, or that it looked like a rock and was a rock. However, four- to five-year-olds could say that it looked like a rock but was in fact a sponge.

Gopnik and Astington (1988) allowed children to *feel* the sponge before asking them the questions used in Flavell's study. The children were then told, 'Your friend John hasn't touched this, he hasn't squeezed it. If John just sees it over here like this, what will he think it is? Will he think it's a rock or a sponge?' Typically, three-year-olds said that John would think it was a sponge (which it is), while four- to five-year-olds said he'd think it was a rock (because he hadn't had the opportunity of touching/squeezing it). In other words, the older children were attributing John with a false belief, which they could only do by taking John's perspective. Evidence like this has led several theorists (e.g. Gopnik and Wellman, 1994) to propose that four- to five-year-olds have developed quite a sophisticated ToM.

Social role-taking perspectives in childhood

According to Selman (1976, 1980), how people 'see' the world involves much more than their visual perceptions. The ability to take account of others'

Box 6.14: Selman's (1976) stages of social role taking

Stage 0: Egocentric viewpoint (three to six years)
The child has a sense of differentiation of self and others but fails to distinguish between the social perspective (thoughts, feelings) of others and self. The child can label others' overt feelings, but doesn't see the cause-and-effect relationship between reasons and social actions.

Stage 1: Social informational role taking (six to eight years)
The child is aware that others have a social perspective based on their own reasoning, which may or may not be similar to the child's. However, the child tends to focus on one perspective rather than integrating different viewpoints.

Stage 2: Self-reflective role taking (eight to ten years)
The child is conscious that each individual is aware of the other's perspective and that this awareness influences self and the other's views of each other. Putting the self in the other's place is a way of judging his/her intentions, purposes and actions. The child can form a coordinated chain of perspectives, but cannot yet abstract from this process to the level of simultaneous mutuality.

Stage 3: Mutual role taking (10–12 years)
The child realises that both self and other can view each other mutually and simultaneously as subjects; the child can step outside the two-person dyad and view the interaction from a third-person perspective.

Stage 4: Social and conventional system role taking (12–15 years and over)
The person realises that mutual perspective taking doesn't always lead to complete understanding. Social conventions are seen as necessary because they're understood by all members of the group (the *generalised other*), regardless of their position, role or experience.

expectations and desires, predicting how they might react, and understanding what they're trying to communicate, is integral to a wide range of human social behaviours; these include joint problem solving, communication and persuasion, sympathising and empathising, and understanding of fairness and justice.

Using techniques adapted from Piaget's, Kohlberg's and Eisenberg's study of moral development, Selman (1976) tapped children's reasoning about a set of social dilemmas in which conflicting feelings might be involved. For example, participants are asked to consider a story about a child, Holly, who's confronted with an urgent choice between (a) climbing up a tree to save a friend's distressed kitten, and (b) honouring an earlier promise to her father that she'd never again engage in reckless tree climbing. The child is asked a series of questions: 'Does Holly know how her friend feels about his kitten?' 'How will Holly's father feel if he finds out she climbed a tree?' 'What would you do?' and so on.

Taking a cognitive developmental approach, Selman identifies five stages of social role taking. These stages involve gradual, qualitative progress from egocentric reasoning to an eventual understanding of the complexities of mutual PT within a social system organised around conventions and normative expectations (Durkin, 1995). The stages are described in Box 6.14.

How Science Works

Practical Learning Activity 6.16

Durkin (1995) gives an example (taken from Selman, 1976) of a response to the task:

Q: What do you think Holly will do, save the kitten or keep her promise?
A: She will save the kitten because she doesn't want the kitten to die.
Q: How will her father feel when he finds out?
A: Happy, he likes kittens.
Q: What if her father punishes her if she gets the kitten down?
A: Then she will leave it up there.
Q: Why?
A: Because she doesn't want to get into trouble.

- At what stage would you classify this person's response?
- Give your reasons.

Selman classifies this response at Stage 0 (four to six years, but the age isn't specified). He comments that the child seems to focus on the act of saving the kitten, and assumes that everyone else sees things in this way. When pressed about breaking a promise to the father, the child lurches to a quite different viewpoint, and seems to be quite unaware of the inconsistency.

Subsequent research has supported the broad developmental claims of Selman's model: individuals progress gradually to higher stages over time, with little evidence of regression to lower stages (e.g. Selman, 1980, in Durkin, 1995). This establishes that the model deals with a meaningful conceptual development. But it raises further questions, such as the relationship between PT ability and the development of social behaviour (which mirrors the question of the relationship between level of moral reasoning and moral behaviour in relation to Kohlberg's theory; see above).

PT and social behaviour

Some studies have found that children with more advanced role-taking skills are more likely to volunteer appropriate pro-social assistance to peers when needed, and to be more popular. But others have failed to find a consistent relationship between popularity and PT. Training in PT skills aimed at improving social competence has produced mixed results.

These findings indicate that social PT is unlikely to be the only attribute or social cognitive ability involved in harmonious peer relationships (Durkin, 1995). Selman himself doesn't predict a straightforward relationship, arguing that the critical factor in social performance may not simply be the individual's stage of reasoning, but how s/he *uses* PT skills in everyday interactions (Selman *et al.*, 1982). *Knowing what to do* to resolve a problem may be just as important as the ability to take someone else's perspective for successful social interaction (Shure, 1982, in Durkin, 1995).

Damon (1983) suggests that rather than thinking of PT as a general *ability* that children acquire, it's more useful to regard it as a common *activity* in which children consider perspectives other than their own. These perspectives could involve others' thoughts, feelings, vision, interpersonal relationships, goals and expectations – a whole range of issues that arise in different situations where people interact. The extent to which children engage in PT may well be correlated with success in resolving social problems and gaining from interactions with others. Viewing it as a multifaceted process helps us think of PT not as a 'driving force' of social cognition and social behaviour, but as a set of skills that themselves grow out of what the child knows about social interactions (Durkin, 1995).

Biological explanations of social cognition

Up until the mid-1990s, neuroscientists and psychologists would have attributed an individual's understanding of someone else's actions – and, especially, their intentions – to a rapid reasoning process similar to that used in solving a logical problem: some sophisticated cognitive mechanism in the brain processes the information presented to the senses and compares it with similar previously-stored experiences, allowing the individual to reach a conclusion about what the other person is up to and why. Although such complex deductive operations probably do occur in some situations (especially when someone's behaviour is difficult to interpret), the ease and speed with which we typically understand simple actions suggests a much more straightforward – biological – explanation.

Mirror neurons

In the early 1990s, Rizzolatti and his colleagues stumbled upon such a biological explanation. They identified a class of neurons in the monkey brain that fire when an individual performs simple, goal-directed motor actions (such as grasping a piece of fruit). The surprising discovery was that these same neurons also fire when the individual sees *someone else* perform the same act. Because this newly discovered subset of brain cells seemed to directly reflect acts performed by another, they were named *mirror neurons* (Rizzolatti *et al.*, 2006).

When human volunteers observed an experimenter grasping objects or performing meaningless arm gestures, there was increased neural activation in their hands and arm muscles that would be involved in the same movements; this suggested a mirror neuron response in the motor areas of their brains. In order to locate the exact brain areas involved, Rizzolatti and his team used *positron-emission tomography* (PET), a major *brain-imaging technique*; this involves a moving X-ray beam taking pictures from different positions around the head, which are then converted by the computer into 'brain slices' (apparent cross sections of the brain). A radioactive tracer is added to a substance used by the body (such as oxygen or glucose), and as the marked substance is metabolised, PET shows the

pattern of how it's being used (for example, changes occur when the eyes are opened or closed).

Based on scans of volunteers' brains while they observed grasping actions performed with different hand grips (then, as a control, looking at stationary objects), three main areas were activated:

1. the superior temporal sulcus (STS), known to contain neurons that respond to observations of moving body parts

2. the inferior parietal lobule (IPL) (which corresponds to the monkey IPL), and

3. the inferior frontal gyrus (IFG) (which corresponds to the monkey ventral premotor cortex, including F5).

While these encouraging results suggested the existence of a mirror mechanism in the human brain, they didn't reveal its full scope.

Understanding intention

When we perform an act such as picking a flower and smelling it before passing it to someone else, in reality we're carrying out a series of linked motor acts whose sequence is determined by our *intent*: one series of movements picks the flower and brings it to one's nose to smell, but a partly different set of movements grasps the flower and hands it to the other person (Rizzolatti *et al.*, 2006).

Initially using monkeys again, Rizzolatti and his team set out to explore whether mirror neurons provide an understanding of intention by distinguishing between similar actions with different goals. If the monkey's task was to grasp a piece of food and bring it to its mouth, there was very different neuronal activity during the grasping part of the action compared with when the task was to grasp the same item and put it in a container. While the grasping was overtly the same, the brain responds differently according to the action's final goal. When the monkey then watched an experimenter perform the same two tasks, most of the mirror neurons were activated differently. The patterns of firing exactly matched those observed when the monkey performed the acts itself.

Human participants were then tested using *functional magnetic resonance imaging* (fMRI). While MRI can identify the slightest reduction in blood flow in a vein or artery, it provides only still images of brain slices. By contrast, fMRI monitors blood flow in the brain over time as people perform different kinds of task.

Rizzolatti's participants were presented with video clips showing (a) a hand grasping a cup against an empty background, using two different grips; (b) two scenes containing objects such as plates and cutlery, arranged either as though they were ready for someone to have afternoon tea, or as though left over from a previous meal ready to be cleaned up; (c) a hand grasping a cup in either of these two contexts ('grasping a cup to drink' / 'grabbing the cup to take it away').

The results showed not only that human mirror neurons distinguish between 'grasping' and 'grabbing', but that they respond strongly to the intention component of an act (that is, depending on whether the action was performed in the 'drinking' or 'clearing away' contexts). In both cases, mirror neuron activity was stronger compared with (a).

Understanding emotion

According to Rizzolatti *et al.* (2006):

> *Given that humans and monkeys are social species, it is not difficult to see the potential survival advantage of a mechanism, based on mirror neurons, that locks basic motor acts onto a larger motor semantic network, per-mitting the direct and immediate comprehension of others' behaviour without complex cognitive machinery. In social life, however, understanding others' emotions is equally important. Indeed, emotion is often a key contextual element that signals the intent of the action ...*

As with actions, humans undoubtedly understand emotions in more than one way When we observe another person experiencing emotion, that sensory information can trigger a cognitive elaboration, ultimately resulting in a logical conclusion about what s/he is feeling. Alternatively, it may produce a direct mapping of the sensory information onto the motor structures that would produce experience of that emotion in us. The first way of recognising emotions involves no feeling, whereas in the second case the mirror mechanism elicits the same emotional state in the observer ('I feel your pain'). In other words, mirror neurons provide a direct *internal* experience, and therefore understanding, of another person's emotion (and this also applies to their acts and intentions). This provides a biological basis for empathy, and for the well-known contagiousness of yawns, laughter, and good and bad moods (Dobbs, 2006).

Box 6.15: A disgusting example of mirror neurons in action

A paradigmatic example of how mirror neurons provide the biological basis of empathy is the emotion of *disgust,* whose expression has important survival value for fellow members of the species. In its most primitive form, it signals that something is bad and, most probably, dangerous. Wicker (2003, in Dobbs, 2006) published a research report called 'Both of us disgusted in *my* insula: the common neural basis of seeing and feeling disgust'.

Using fMRI, Wicker (in collaboration with Rizzolatti *et al.*) found that experiencing disgust oneself and seeing an expression of revulsion on someone else's face caused the *same* set of mirror neurons to fire in the *anterior insula* (a part of the cortex active in synthesising convergent information). In other words, the observer and the observed share a neural mechanism that enables a form of direct experiential understanding (Rizzolatti *et al.,* 2006).

Similar findings for *pain* were reported by Singer and her colleagues (Rizzolatti *et al.,* 2006).

Synoptic Material

To claim that identifying the mirror neuron system provides us with a complete understanding of our ability to perceive other people's intentions and emotions is *reductionist*. In other words, the claim maintains that once we've located the mirror neurons and collected sufficient evidence regarding when and how they function, then we'll know all there is to know about social cognition (social cognition is *reduced to* / explained in terms of the mirror neuron system). But this is surely an overstatement.

However, although such a mirror mechanism for understanding emotions cannot fully explain all social cognition, it does provide for the first time a functional neural basis for some of the interpersonal relations on which more complex social behaviours are built. For example, it may be a *substrate* (the underlying structure) that allows us to empathise with others (Rizzolatti *et al.,* 2006); this leaves room for social and environmental (cultural) factors to play their part. Paradoxically, some researchers claim that mirror neurons may actually be responsible for – or, at least, have contributed to – the development of culture.

For example, according to Ramachandran (in Dobbs, 2006),

> mirror neurons will do for psychology what DNA did for biology: they will provide a unifying framework and help explain a host of mental abilities that have hitherto remained mysterious and inaccessible to experiments.

They may clarify not only how we come to learn and to understand others, but also how humans took a 'great leap forward' about 50,000 years ago, acquiring new skills in social organisation, tool use and language that made human culture possible. However, there was no growth spurt in human brains at that time; indeed, they've remained at basically their present size for about 200,000 years (Dobbs, 2006). So, what changed? Ramachandran and others speculate that the change was a *genetic* adaptation that gave key neurons the mirroring capacity they now have, paving the way for accelerating advances in understanding, communication and learning. For the first time, information could be spread, built on and modified to create the intellectual and social dynamic of culture.

STRETCH AND CHALLENGE: Mirror neurons and autism

According to Ramachandran and Oberman (2006), saying that people with autism cannot interact socially and empathise because they lack a ToM (see above) doesn't go very far beyond restating the symptoms. What Ramachandran and his colleagues (and other researchers) have been doing since the late 1990s is trying to identify the brain mechanism whose known functions may match those that are disrupted in autism. The key mechanism may already have been found, in the form of *mirror neurons.*

Mirror neurons seem to be performing the precise functions that people with autism fail to perform. So it seems logical to hypothesise that the mirror neuron system in such people is deficient in some way. Oberman *et al.* (2005) took *electroencephalogram* (EEG) measurements (recordings of the electrical activity of the cortex) of the brains of ten high-functioning autistic children and compared them with ten age- and gender-matched controls. Their findings supported the hypothesis that there's a lack of mirror neuron activity in the brains of autistic children.

It follows from Oberman *et al.*'s findings that, if treatments could be developed to restore mirror neuron activity, then at least some of the symptoms of autism could be alleviated (Ramachandran and Oberman, 2006) (see Gross, 2008).

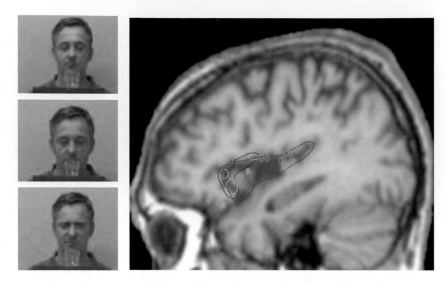

Figure 6.8 Feeling disgust activated similar parts of the brain when human volunteers experienced the emotion while smelling a disgusting odour or when the same subjects watched a film clip (left) of someone else disgusted. In this brain cross section, neuron populations activated by the experience of disgust are outlined in red, and those activated by seeing disgust are circled in yellow. (Blue outlines the region of investigation, and green indicates areas examined in a previous study.) These overlapping neuron groups may represent a physical neural mechanism for human empathy that permits understanding the emotions of others

SUMMARY

Development of thinking

- Piaget sees the child as (a) an organism **adapting to its environment**, and (b) a **scientist** constructing its own understanding of the world. He was interested in how **intelligence** changes as the child grows (**genetic epistemology**).

- Cognitive development occurs through the interaction of innate capacities and environmental events, proceeding through a series of **hierarchical, invariant, universal** and **qualitatively different stages**.

- Underlying the stage changes are **functional invariants** – in particular **assimilation, accommodation** (together constituting **adaptation**) and **equilibration**.

- The major cognitive structure that changes in the course of development is the **schema**, the basic building block of intelligent behaviour.

- Each of Piaget's stages represents a stage in the development of intelligence and summarises the schemas a child possesses at any particular time; movement through the stages takes place through **cognitive disequilibrium**.

CHAPTER

- The **sensorimotor stage** (birth to two years) is divided into six sub-stages, a crucial development being **object permanence**. In the final sub-stage (**invention of new means through mental combinations**: 18–24 months), object permanence is complete with the ability to **infer invisible displacements**.

- Also important is the development of the **general symbolic function** (**GSF**), including self-perception, symbolic thought (such as language), deferred imitation and representational/make-believe play.

- The **pre-operational stage** (two to seven years) is subdivided into the **pre-conceptual** (two to four) and **intuitive sub-stages** (four to seven).

- The pre-operational child cannot **decentre**. One form this takes is **egocentrism**, as demonstrated by the famous Swiss mountain scene experiment.

- Piaget believed that pre-operational children cannot **conserve** because their thinking is dominated by how things **look**. This inability to conserve is another example of centration.

- Typical conservation experiments (number, liquid quantity, length and substance) involve a pre-transformation question, then some perceptual change is made to the material (counters, coloured liquid in beakers etc.), and finally a post-transformation question.

- The child may, unwittingly, be forced into giving the wrong answer on the post-transformation question; when the pre-transformation question is dropped (e.g. Rose and Blank), or when 'Naughty Teddy' rearranges the counters, many more children show conservation.

- Centration (and classification) is also studied through **class inclusion tasks**. Pre-operational children fail to grasp the relationship between **superordinate** and **subordinate classes**.

- In the **concrete operational stage**, the child can now perform logical operations (such as conservation), but **only in the presence of actual objects**. Even then, there are inconsistencies **within** conservation (**horizontal décalage**) and inconsistencies **between** different abilities (**vertical décalage**).

- The concrete operational child is no longer egocentric, but cannot yet perform **transitivity tasks** entirely in its head.

- While the concrete operational child's logical thinking consists of **first-order** operations (manipulating **things**), the **formal operational** thinker can manipulate **ideas** or **propositions** (**second-order** operations). Examples include the ability to follow the **form** of an argument (regardless of the content), and the ability to think **hypothetically** and **systematically**.

- While there may be few 'orthodox' Piagetians left, Piaget continues to be a huge influence on both psychology and education. Considerable **cross-cultural** support exists, especially for conservation, although cultural factors can affect the **rate** of attainment; much less support exists for formal operations.

- Critics have emphasised Piaget's failure to recognise the role of **social** influences on the child's thinking; his **domain-general approach** is giving way to a more **domain-specific approach**.

- The three main implications of Piaget's theory for **education** are (i) the concept of **readiness** (a **child-centred approach**); (ii) the **curriculum**; and (iii) **teaching methods** (**active self-discovery / discovery learning**).

- Teachers must set the child tasks that become **intrinsically motivating**. They should also provide learning opportunities that enable the child to advance to the next developmental step (by creating **disequilibrium**), as well as encouraging children to **learn from each other**.

- Vygotsky agrees with Piaget that knowledge is constructed as a result of the child's active interaction with the environment. But while Piaget's account is **constructivist**, Vygotsky's is **social constructivist**: human development proceeds at three levels, the cultural, interpersonal and individual.

- At the **cultural level**, each child inherits a number of **cultural tools** (**technological**, **psychological** and **values**). A major – and relatively recent – cultural tool is the **computer**.

- For Vygotsky, the crucial cultural tool is **language**. This is the pre-eminent means of passing on society's accumulated knowledge and enables children to regulate their own activities.

- Culture and the individual meet at the **interpersonal level**. Cognitive development involves an active **internalisation** of problem-solving processes, which occurs through mutual interaction between the child and parents, friends and teachers. Vygotsky's **the child as apprentice** replaces Piaget's **the child as scientist**.

- Cognitive development progresses from the **intermental** to the **intramental** (from joint regulation to self-regulation). But intermental (social) regulation has to work with the 'raw material' of the baby's innate abilities, such as **pointing**.

- **Joint collaboration** refers to active, shared participation for the purpose of solving a problem; through **scaffolding**, responsibility is gradually transferred from the adult / more advanced peer so that the child can perform the task independently. This all happens within the child's **zone of proximal development** (**ZPD**).

- At the **individual level**, Vygotsky identified a number of stages, derived from experimental work on the sorting of different coloured and shaped blocks: 'heaps', functional categories, 'chain complexes', 'diffuse complexes', 'pseudo-concepts' and true abstract thought.

- Although Vygotsky's theory hasn't been tested cross-culturally, it has influenced cross-cultural psychology through the development of **cultural psychology** (and related approaches).

- Much of Vygotsky's theory is concerned, directly or indirectly, with **formal schooling**. While the child's actual developmental level characterises mental development **retrospectively**, the **ZPD** characterises it **prospectively**.

- While Bruner was influenced by Piaget's ideas, he placed much greater emphasis on the notion that humans actively construct **meaning** from the world: the world we live in is 'created' by the mind.

- Like Vygotsky, Bruner stresses the role of culture and language as influences on cognitive growth; indeed, thinking would be impossible without language.

- Bruner identified three **modes of representation**: the **enactive**, **iconic** and **symbolic**. While not stages in the Piagetian sense, they develop in this order.

- He was mainly interested in the **transition** from the iconic to the symbolic mode (as demonstrated by Bruner and Kenney). Language comes into its own, freeing the child from the immediate context and enabling it to 'go beyond the information given'.

- Bruner's modes of representation lie at the heart of the **spiral curriculum**. This involves a rejection of Piaget's concept of readiness and has contributed to the idea of the 'competent infant'.

- Educators need to help learners grasp the underlying concepts and principles – rather than just mastering factual information.

Development of moral understanding

- The question as to how we come to understand the basis of rules and moral principles, enabling us to make judgements about our own and others' behaviour, has dominated research into moral development for 30 years. This is reflected in the **cognitive-developmental theories** of Piaget, Kohlberg and Eisenberg.

- Piaget's pioneering research identified two **types of moral orientation**: **heteronomous** ('subject to another's laws': five to nine or ten years) and **autonomous** ('subject to one's own laws': ten years and over).

- Regarding **understanding rules**, heteronomous individuals display a belief that **rules represent an external law**, and **unilateral respect**. Autonomous individuals don't believe that rules represent an external law, and display **mutual respect**.

- Regarding **moral judgement and punishment**, heteronomous individuals display **objective/external responsibility** and belief in **expiatory punishment**, **moral realism**, **collective punishment** and **immanent justice**. Autonomous individuals display **internal responsibility** and believe in **moral relativism** and the **principle of reciprocity**.

- A major weakness of Piaget's theory is that he oversimplified – and underestimated – children's understanding of **intention**.

- Far from assuming that his two moral orientations are universal, Piaget argued for **contextualisation**. This is illustrated by Lee *et al.*'s study of lying and truth telling among Chinese and Canadian children.

- Like Piaget, Kohlberg believes that people's **reasons** for their moral judgements are more important than the judgements themselves. He used hypothetical **moral dilemmas**, the most famous of which involves Heinz and his dying wife.

- Based on people's answers to several questions about each of these dilemmas, Kohlberg identified **three levels of moral reasoning**, each comprising two stages. **Level 1: Pre-conventional morality** comprises **stage 1 (punishment and obedience orientation)** and **stage 2 (instrumental relativist orientation)**; **Level 2: Conventional morality** comprises **stage 3 (interpersonal concordance / 'good boy–nice girl' orientation)** and **stage 4 (maintaining the social order orientation)**; **Level 3: Post-conventional morality** comprises **stage 5 (social contract-legalistic orientation)** and **stage 6 (universal ethical principles orientation)**.

- The ethical principles that are taken as universal (especially **justice**, which is central to Kohlberg's theory) appear **not** to be so, and stages 5 and 6 seem to be related to the degree of industrialisation (rather than westernisation).

- Even more controversial is Gilligan's claim that the theory is **gender-biased (androcentric)**. While men's morality is based on abstract principles of law and justice, women's is based on principles of compassion and care. In turn, these 'moral orientations' reflect how men and women think differently about **selfhood**.

- The evidence doesn't support Gilligan's claim that the 'caring' voice is more apparent among women. Several studies show that gender differences in moral orientation are less important than the **kind** of dilemmas being studied (**hypothetical** or **personally generated, real-life**).

- While Kohlberg's concept of moral reasoning is **prohibition-orientated**, Eisenberg is concerned with **pro-social moral reasoning**: the reasoning that's involved when we're faced with a conflict between our own and others' needs in a context where the role of laws and demands of authority are minimal.

- Based on children's responses to illustrated hypothetical stories, in which the story character can help another in need – but always at some personal cost – Eisenberg identified six stages of pro-social moral reasoning (or **orientations**): **Level 1 (hedonistic, self-focused)**; **Level 2 (needs of others)**; **Level 3 (approval and interpersonal and/or stereotyped)**; **Level 4a (self-reflective, empathic)**; **Level 4b (transitional level)**; **Level 5 (strongly internalised stage)**.

- One distinctive feature of Eisenberg's theory (compared with Kohlberg's) is the role of **emotion**. In particular, if we respond **empathically**, we're more likely to help another person than if we experience **personal distress**. This is true of both adults and children.

- Emotions (especially positive ones) are increasingly being seen as the basis for moral development.

Development of social cognition

- The **self** (or **self-concept**) is a **cognitive structure** that also has **motivational features**, in particular **self-consistency**, **self-evaluation** and **self-enhancement**.

- Major components of the self-concept are **self-image** (including **body image / bodily self**), **self-esteem** (or **self-regard**) and **ideal self** (**ego-ideal** or **idealised self-image**).

- Factors influencing the **development** of the self-concept include the **reaction of others**, which is central to both Cooley's **theory of the looking-glass self** and Mead's **symbolic interactionist** theory

- Others' reactions are incorporated into the child's personality through **introjection**; this is how the child learns its **conditions of worth** (behaviours that will produce **positive regard**).

- Parents of **schizophrenic** children deny them **communicative support**, making the development of **ego boundaries** (self/not-self) very difficult.

- Other factors influencing the development of the self-concept are **comparison with others** and **social roles**.

- The first developmental change in the self-concept involves the baby's sense of **continuity through time** (the **existential self**).

- Development of the bodily self has been studied through **self-recognition**, based on Gallup's study involving chimpanzees.

- Other aspects of the self-concept to develop are **self-definition** (including the effect of **names** on the child's behaviour), the **categorical self** (characteristics such as **age** and **gender**), and the **psychological self** (what's referred to by 'I'/'me').

- Western, **individualist** cultures tend to stress **independent** selves, whereas non-western, **collectivist** cultures stress **interdependent** selves.

- Part of the psychological self is development of a **theory of mind (ToM)**. Research into the development of ToM in children is now dominated by research into the link between ToM and **autism**.

- While Gallup takes the results from his studies of chimpanzees as support for his **mind-reading hypothesis (MRH)**, Povinelli argues that self-recognition in chimpanzees (and toddlers) involves recognition of the self's **behaviour** as well as a **kinaesthetic self-concept**: what they lack is recognition of the self's psychological states necessary for a ToM.

- A major way of investigating ToM is to present children with **false-belief tasks**. Baron-Cohen *et al.*'s 'Sally Anne' experiment found that autistic children failed on the false-belief task, indicating a specific deficit (the **theory of mind mechanism / ToMM**).

- However, not only did some of the autistic children pass the **first-order** (false-) **belief** task, but later studies have shown that many adults with Asperger's syndrome (an **autistic spectrum disorder**) pass **second-order** tasks.

- Baron-Cohen *et al.* distinguish between **conceptual** and **perceptual perspective taking (PT)**.

These are being tested in the Sally Anne false belief task, and Piaget and Inhelder's Swiss mountain scene experiment, respectively. Flavell *et al.* distinguish between **perceptual** PT and **affective** and **cognitive** PT.

- Taking a cognitive-developmental approach, Selman identifies five stages of **social role taking**. Stage 0: **Egocentric viewpoint** (three to six years); stage 1: **Social informational role taking** (six to eight); stage 2: **Self-reflective role taking** (eight to ten); stage 3: **Mutual role taking** (10–12); and stage 4: **Social and conventional system role taking** (12–15-plus).

- Social PT is unlikely to be the only social cognitive ability involved in harmonious peer relationships. **Knowing what to do** to resolve a problem may be just as important for successful social interaction as the ability to take another's perspective.

- Rizzolatti first discovered **mirror neurons** in the macaque monkey brain; the fact that the same distinct sets of neurons fired when the monkey ate some food and when it watched a person eat the food suggested that the neurons were a true representation of the act.

- **Brain-imaging techniques** (such as **positron emission tomography**/PET) were then used with human volunteers. Using **functional magnetic resonance imaging** (fMRI), it was found that not only do human mirror neurons distinguish between 'grasping' and 'grabbing', but they respond strongly to the **intention** component of an act.

- One way in which humans understand **emotion** involves a direct **internal** experience of another's emotions, providing a biological basis for empathy. The appearance of mirror neurons may represent a huge step forward in human evolution.

Essay Questions

Development of thinking

1a. Outline and evaluate any ONE theory of cognitive development. (13 marks)
1b. Assess the application of this theory to education. (12 marks)
2. Critically consider Vygotsky's theory of cognitive development. (25 marks)

Development of moral understanding

3a. Outline Kohlberg's theory of moral understanding. (9 marks)
3b. Discuss Kohlberg's theory in terms of the influence of gender and/or cultural factors. (16 marks)
4. Discuss Eisenberg's theory of pro-social reasoning. (25 marks)

Development of social cognition

5. Describe and evaluate research into the development of perspective taking in children. (25 marks)
6. Critically consider psychological research into the development of the child's sense of self, including theory of mind (Baron-Cohen). (25 marks)

It should take you 30 minutes to answer each question.

Psychopathology

What's covered in this chapter?

You need to know about:

Schizophrenia
- Clinical characteristics of schizophrenia
- Issues surrounding the classification and diagnosis of schizophrenia, including reliability and validity
- Biological explanations (for example, genetics, biochemistry) and psychological explanations (for example, behavioural, cognitive, psychodynamic and socio-cultural) of schizophrenia
- Biological therapies and psychological therapies for schizophrenia (for example, behavioural, psychodynamic and cognitive-behavioural), including their evaluation in terms of appropriateness and effectiveness

Depression
- Clinical characteristics of depression
- Issues surrounding the classification and diagnosis of depression, including reliability and validity
- Biological explanations (for example, genetics, biochemistry) and psychological explanations (for example, behavioural, cognitive, psychodynamic and socio-cultural) of depression
- Biological therapies and psychological therapies for depression (for example, behavioural, psychodynamic and cognitive-behavioural), including their evaluation in terms of appropriateness and effectiveness

Specification Hint

The specification only requires you to know about ONE type of psychopathology (or mental disorder). To give you more choice (and because you may be interested in learning about one or both of the others), we've included discussion of *two* (schizophrenia and depression) in this chapter. There may be times when reference to/comparison with another mental disorder could count as AO2 material.

While you need to know about both biological and psychological explanations, you're not required to know about any specific ones. Examples are given (which are the most likely ones that you'd know about), but examination questions cannot ask you specifically about one or more of these. In keeping with the general rule (and depending on the particular wording of the question), the more explanations you discuss, the less detailed each one needs to be (the 'breadth versus depth trade-off').

This chapter begins with a discussion of classification and diagnosis of mental disorder *in general*.

THE CLASSIFICATION AND DIAGNOSIS OF PSYCHOLOGICAL ABNORMALITY

How Science Works

Practical Learning Activity 7.1

● Remind yourself of the various definitions of psychological abnormality (see Gross and Rolls, 2008).
● Remind yourself of the main features of (a) the biological; (b) psychodynamic; (c) behavioural; and (d) cognitive approaches to abnormality (again, see Gross and Rolls, 2008).
● Explain the relationship between the biological approach, the medical model, and the classification and diagnosis of psychological abnormality.

Classification

All systems of classification of psychological abnormality stem from the work of Kraepelin, who published the first recognised textbook of psychiatry in 1883. Kraepelin claimed that certain groups of symptoms (a *syndrome*) occur together regularly enough to be regarded as having an underlying physical cause (in much the same way as a particular medical disease and its syndrome can be attributed to a biological abnormality). He regarded each 'mental illness' as distinct from all others, with its own origins (causes or *aetiology*), symptoms, course and outcome.

Kraepelin (1896) proposed two major groups of serious mental diseases:

1. *dementia praecox* (his term for what we now call schizophrenia), caused by a chemical imbalance, and

2. *manic-depressive psychosis* (now known as bipolar disorder), caused by a faulty metabolism.

This classification helped to establish the *organic* or *somatic* (bodily) nature of mental disorders. It also provided the basis for the Diagnostic and Statistical Manual of Mental Disorders (DSM) and the International Classification of Diseases (ICD). DSM is the official classification system of the American Psychiatric Association. It's the 'bible' of American psychiatrists, but it's also used widely throughout the world. DSM was first published in 1952 (DSM-I), and the latest version is DSM-IV-TR (2000). ICD is published by the World Health Organization (WHO). Mental disorders were included for the first time in 1948 (ICD-6), and the latest version is ICD-10 (1992).

Both DSM and ICD use the term 'mental disorder', but both have dropped the traditional distinction between 'neurosis' (e.g. phobic disorders, obsessive-compulsive disorder) and 'psychosis' (e.g. schizophrenia and depression). However, ICD-10 retains the term 'neurotic' and DSM-IV-TR still uses 'psychotic'. *Psychosis* is the technical term for what the lay person calls madness (Frith and Cahill, 1995). Psychotic symptoms include delusions, hallucinations, passivity experiences and thought disorder. These account for why 'crazy' people are seen as 'out of their head' or 'in another world'. Unlike *neurotic symptoms* (such as anxiety, including panic attacks and phobias), psychotic symptoms are outside the normal realm of experience. This means that they're also outside our common-sense powers of understanding and empathy. Schizophrenia is by far the commonest of the psychoses, and is considered to be one of the most serious of all mental disorders.

Reliability of psychiatric diagnosis

The classic study examining the reliability (or otherwise) of psychiatric diagnosis is Rosenhan's (1973) 'Being sane in insane places' (see Gross and Rolls, 2008). Although Rosenhan's conclusions have been questioned (notably by Spitzer, 1976), the study highlights the issue of reliability, as well as the related issue of validity. If psychiatrists cannot agree among themselves about a particular patient's diagnosis, then it's impossible to know whether any diagnosis that's made is correct (i.e. valid) – that is, that this is the disorder the patient 'actually' has. Diagnosis is the process of identifying a disease and allocating it to a category on the basis of symptoms and signs. Clearly, any system of classification will be of little value unless psychiatrists can agree with one another when trying to reach a diagnosis (*inter-rater/inter-judge reliability*), and represents a fundamental requirement of any classification system (Gelder *et al.*, 1989, 1999).

According to Davison *et al.* (2004), despite some categories still having greater reliability than others, reliability has improved significantly since the publication of DSM-III in 1980 and is now acceptable for most of the major categories. However, problems remain, as outlined below.

- Specifying a particular number of symptoms from a longer list that must be evident before a particular diagnosis can be made seems very arbitrary. For example, DSM-IV-TR insists on depressed mood plus *four* other symptoms to be present to diagnose major depression (see Table 7.6, page 311). But why four? (Pilgrim, 2000; Davison *et al.*, 2004).

- There's still room for subjective interpretation on the part of the psychiatrist. For example, in relation to mania, the elevated mood must be 'abnormally and persistently elevated' for a diagnosis of mania to be made. Likewise, one of the five axes of DSM requires comparison between the patient and an 'average person'. These examples beg all sort of questions. As Davison *et al.* (2004) say, 'Such judgements set the stage for the insertion of cultural biases as well as the clinician's own personal ideas of what the average person should be doing at a given stage of life.'

- However, in defence of diagnosis, Clare (1980) argues that the nature of physical illness isn't as clear-cut as critics of the medical model claim; reliability between doctors regarding angina, emphysema and tonsillitis is no better than that for schizophrenia (Falek and Moser, 1975). Clare believes that psychiatrists are at fault – *not* the process of diagnosis itself.

Validity of psychiatric diagnosis

As we noted above, reliability is a necessary prerequisite for validity. Validity implies a degree of 'objectivity', but is actually more difficult to assess; this is because for most disorders there's no absolute standard against which diagnosis can be compared. However much we improve reliability, this is no guarantee that the patient has received the 'correct' diagnosis (Holmes, 1994).

Predictive validity

The primary purpose of making a diagnosis is to enable a suitable treatment programme to be selected. Treatment cannot be chosen randomly, but is aimed at eliminating the underlying cause of the disorder (where it's known). But in psychiatry there's only a 50 per cent chance of predicting correctly what treatment a patient will receive on the basis of diagnosis (Heather, 1976). One reason for this seems to be that factors other than diagnosis may be equally important in determining a particular treatment. This is related to the issue of *bias* within psychiatry (see below and Box 7.4, pages 313–314).

Construct validity

This is the most relevant form of validity in relation to diagnosis. According to Davison *et al.* (2004), the categories are *constructs* because they're *inferred* – not proven – entities. For example, a diagnosis of schizophrenia doesn't have the same status as a diagnosis of, say, diabetes. With physical disease, there's a real sense in which patients 'have' it, and it's feasible to distinguish them from their disease. But even in the more extreme psychotic states, it's impossible to divorce the condition from the person (Marzillier, 2004).

Construct validity is determined by evaluating the extent to which accurate statements and predictions can be made about a category. For example, to what extent does the construct form part of a network of lawful relationships? These relationships could concern:

- possible causes (such as genetic predisposition or biochemical imbalance; see below)

- characteristics of the disorder that aren't symptoms as such but are associated with it (such as poor social skills in schizophrenia; see below)

- predictions about the course of the disorder and probable response to particular treatments (see above).

Davison *et al.* believe that the DSM diagnostic categories do indeed possess some construct validity – some more than others. However, according to Mackay (1975):

> The notion of illness implies a relatively discrete disease entity with associated signs and symptoms, which has a specific cause, a certain probability of recovery and its own treatments. The various states of unhappiness, anxiety and confusion which we term 'mental illness' fall far short of these criteria in most cases.

Pilgrim (2000) argues that calling madness 'schizophrenia' or misery 'depression' merely *technicalises* ordinary judgements. What do we add by calling someone who communicates unintelligibly 'schizophrenic'? Similarly, Winter (1999) argues that 'diagnostic systems are only aids to understanding, not necessarily descriptions of real disease entities'.

How Science Works

Practical Learning Activity 7.2

- If, as we noted above, factors other than diagnosis contribute to determining a particular treatment, what might these other factors be?
- Another way of asking this question is 'What kinds of *bias* might be involved in psychiatry that influence the way that different patients are diagnosed and treated?'

Culture and gender bias in assessment and treatment

According to Davison *et al.* (2004), studies of the influences of culture on psychopathology and its assessment have proliferated in recent years. The reliability and validity of various forms of psychological assessment have been questioned on the grounds that their content and scoring procedures reflect the culture of white Europeans and so may not accurately assess people from other cultures.

One way in which cultural biases may work is by causing psychiatrists (and clinical psychologists) to over- or underestimate psychological problems in members of other cultures (Lopez, 1989, 1996). For example, not only are African-Caribbean people in the UK more likely to be diagnosed as schizophrenic or compulsorily committed to psychiatric hospital, they're also more likely to be given major tranquillising drugs or electroconvulsive therapy (ECT) than white people (Fernando, 1988). This is mirrored in a study by Blake (1973, in Davison *et al.*, 2004), which showed that clinicians were more likely to diagnose a patient as having schizophrenia if the case summary referred to the person as African-American than if s/he was described as white. A hospital-based study found that African-American patients were over-diagnosed with schizophrenia and under-diagnosed as having a mood disorder (Simon *et al.*, in Davison *et al.*, 2004).

All ethnic minorities are less likely to be referred for psychotherapy than indigenous whites, and similar differences have been reported between working-class and middle-class groups. Women are also more likely than men to be diagnosed as psychiatrically ill (Winter, 1999; see below). Winter believes that one viable explanation for these differences is that

> general practitioners and psychiatrists, who are predominantly white, middle class and male, may be biased against, or insufficiently sensitive to the cultural and social situations of, black, working-class or female clients.

Should a very emotionally withdrawn Asian-American be perceived as displaying a characteristic that's judged more positively in Asian cultures than in Euro-American culture, or be seen as having a psychological disorder? A clinician who attributes this behaviour to a cultural difference rather than to a psychological disorder risks overlooking an emotional problem that s/he would be likely to diagnose if the patient were a white male. The effect of cultural bias in clinical assessment works both ways (Lopez, 1989).

Clinicians who encounter clients claiming to be surrounded by spirits might view this belief as a sign of schizophrenia. But in Puerto Rican cultures such a belief is common. Native Americans taught by their culture to cooperate with others are less likely to warm to the task of taking an aptitude test, which, by its

Box 7.1: Culture-bound syndromes (CBSs)

A large number of studies have found that, in a wide range of non-western cultures, there are apparently unique ways of 'being mad' (Berry *et al.,* 1992) – that is, there are forms of abnormality that aren't easily accommodated by the categories of ICD or DSM. These *culture-bound syndromes* (CBSs), or 'exotic' disorders, are first described in, and then closely or exclusively associated with, a particular population or cultural area, with the local, indigenous name being used. DSM-IV-TR defines them as 'locally specific patterns of aberrant behaviour and troubling experience that may or may not be linked to a persistent DSM-IV diagnostic category' (APA, 2000).

For example, *Koro, jinjin bemar, suk yeong, suo-yang* (usually called just 'Koro') refers to an acute panic/anxiety reaction to the belief, in a man, that his penis will suddenly withdraw into his abdomen, or in a woman that her breasts, labia or vulva will retract into her body. This is reported in Southeast Asia, south China and India. Other examples include *amok, brain fag, dhat* and *ghost sickness.*

These disorders are 'outside' the mainstream of abnormality as defined by, and 'enshrined' within, the classification systems of western psychiatry, which determines the 'standard'. The underlying assumption is that mental disorders in the West are *culturally neutral,* that they can be defined and diagnosed *objectively,* while only CBSs show the influence of culture (Fernando, 1991).

At the same time, cross-cultural studies suggest that the concept of mental disorder isn't merely an expression of western values, but represents a basic human way of perceiving certain behaviour as evidence of abnormal psychological processes. According to Price and Crapo (1999), 'mental disorders occur in all cultures … all cultures appear to label some specific behaviours in a way that is similar to the categories and definitions used by Western psychiatry …'.

nature, is highly individualistic and competitive (Davison *et al.,* 2004).

Much more attention is now paid to how symptoms of a given disorder may differ depending on the culture in which it appears (see the discussion of whether or not schizophrenia is culture-free in 'Synoptic Material', page 303). In DSM-IV-TR, cultural differences are dealt with (a) in descriptions of each disorder in the main body of the manual; (b) in an appendix that provides a general framework for evaluating the role of culture and ethnicity; and (c) by describing *culture-bound syndromes* (CBSs) in the appendix (see Box 7.1).

SCHIZOPHRENIA

Clinical characteristics of schizophrenia

As we noted above, what we now call schizophrenia Kraepelin originally called *dementia praecox* ('senility of youth'). He believed that the typical symptoms (delusions, hallucinations, attention deficits and

✔ Specification Hint

When describing the clinical characteristics of schizophrenia (as with depression), it's sometimes necessary to consider issues relating to classification and diagnosis. For example, people who are diagnosed as schizophrenic may display a wide range of different symptoms, and different types/sub-types are recognised. But, conversely, there's some debate as to whether these sub-types really are different. There's also overlap between schizophrenia and, say, mania.

So, it's not as straightforward as it may seem simply to describe the clinical characteristics of any particular category of psychopathology. This point could have value as AO2 material.

bizarre motor activity) were due to a form of mental deterioration that began in adolescence. But Bleuler (1911) observed that many patients displaying these symptoms *didn't* go on deteriorating, and that illness often begins much later than adolescence. Consequently, he introduced the term schizophrenia instead (literally 'split mind' or 'divided self') to describe an illness in which 'the personality loses its unity'.

The lifetime risk of developing schizophrenia is about 1 per cent, affecting males and females in equal numbers. It usually appears in late adolescence / early adulthood (so Kraepelin got that right), and somewhat earlier for men than for women.

According to Clare (1976), the diagnosis of schizophrenia in the UK relies greatly on Schneider's (1959) *first rank symptoms* (see Table 7.1).

Schneider's first rank symptoms (FRSs) are *subjective experiences*, which can only be inferred on the basis of the patient's verbal report. Slater and Roth (1969) regarded hallucinations as the *least* important of all the major symptoms. This is because they aren't exclusive to schizophrenia, but are found in patients with mania and delusional depression (this is also true of delusions; see below). Slater and Roth identified four additional symptoms, which are *directly observable* from the patient's behaviour (see Table 7.2, page 287).

So who's right: Schneider or Slater and Roth?

According to Claridge and Davis (2003), 'first rank symptoms' imply that

certain experiences of people clinically labelled 'schizophrenic' are so bizarre, incomprehensible, and distant from the normal that we are surely convinced that these must be central to the disorder.

Passivity experiences and thought disturbances

- *thought insertion* (thoughts are inserted into one's mind from outside and are under external influence)
- *thought withdrawal* (thoughts are removed from one's mind and are externally controlled)
- *thought broadcasting* (thoughts are broadcast to / otherwise made known to others)
- external forces may include the Martians, the Communists and the 'government'

Auditory hallucinations (in the third person)

- *hallucinatory voices* are heard discussing one's thoughts or behaviour as they occur (a kind of running commentary), or arguing about oneself (or using one's name), or repeating one's thoughts out loud / anticipating one's thoughts
- they're often accusatory, obscene and derogatory, and may order the patient to commit extreme acts of violence
- they're experienced as alien or under the influence of some external source, and also in the light of concurrent delusions (e.g. the voice of God or the devil; see text, below)
- the hallucinations of patients with *organic* psychoses (where there's known brain pathology) are predominantly *visual*

Primary delusions

- *false beliefs* (incompatible with reality, usually of *persecution* or *grandeur*) held with extraordinary conviction, impervious to other experiences or compelling counter-argument / contradictory evidence
- the patient may be so convinced of their truth that they act on the strength of their belief, even if this involves murder and rape (as in the case of Peter Sutcliffe, the 'Yorkshire Ripper')

Table 7.1: Schneider's (1959) first rank symptoms of schizophrenia

Thought process disorder

- the inability to keep to the point, being easily distracted/side-tracked (*derailment*)
- in *clang associations* (e.g. 'big', 'pig', 'twig'), words are 'thrown together' based on their sound rather than their meaning; this produces an apparently incoherent jumble of words ('*word salad*')
- also, the inability to finish a sentence, sometimes stopping in the middle of a word (*thought blocking*), inventing new words (*neologisms*), and interpreting language (e.g. proverbs) literally

Disturbance of affect

- events/situations don't elicit their usual emotional response (*blunting*)
- there's a more pervasive, generalised absence of emotional expression (as in minimal inflection in speech, and lack of normal variation in facial/bodily movements used to convey feelings: *flattening of affect*)
- loss of appropriate emotional responses (e.g. laughing / getting angry for no apparent reason, changing mood very suddenly, giggling when given some bad news: *incongruity of affect*)

Psychomotor disorders

- muscles in a state of semi-rigidity (*catalepsy*)
- grimacing of facial muscles, limb twitching, stereotyped behaviours (such as constant pacing up and down), or assuming a fixed position for long periods of time, even several years in extreme cases (*catatonic stupor*)

Lack of volition

- *avolition* (apathy): lack of energy, apparent lack of interest / inability to carry out routine activities (such as grooming, personal hygiene)
- *anhedonia* (inability to experience pleasure): lack of interest in recreational activities, lack of interest in sex
- *asociality* (severe impairment in social relationships): few friends, poor social skills, little interest in being with others

Table 7.2: Major symptoms of schizophrenia (based on Slater and Roth, 1969)

In other words, FRSs seem to describe the 'fundamental', core, features of schizophrenia. But like Slater and Roth, Bleuler regarded hallucinations and delusions as *accessory* (secondary) symptoms – that is, they are psychological consequences of a more primary, physical process that constitutes the real core. Claridge and Davis believe that the DSM and ICD criteria for diagnosing schizophrenia are a confused mix of these views – although there's a bias towards FRSs. They consider this bias to be understandable, since 'Reporting that aliens in outer space are responsible for the thoughts in your head certainly seems more crazy than bemusing your neighbours with your stream of consciousness style of conversation!' But, unlike most diagnostic categories, there's *no essential* symptom that must be present for a diagnosis of schizophrenia to be made (Davison and Neale, 2001).

Positive and negative symptoms

Most of Schneider's FRSs are what are known as *positive symptoms* (or Type I) – that is, excesses or distortions, the *presence of active symptomatology*. They're what define, for the most part, an *acute* episode, and are occurrences beyond normal experience (Javitt and Coyle, 2004). Typically, patients have several acute episodes, between which are less severe, but still very debilitating, symptoms.

Most of Slater and Roth's symptoms are *negative* (Type II) symptoms. They consist of behavioural deficits, *lack of* or *poverty* of behaviour. These symptoms tend to endure beyond the acute episodes, and have a profound effect on patients' lives. The presence of several negative symptoms is a strong predictor of a poor quality of life two years after leaving hospital (Davison *et al.*, 2004).

Evaluation of the positive/negative distinction

✔ **Important for research:** as we shall see below, the distinction between positive and negative symptoms is very important in relation to research into the *causes* of schizophrenia. According to Claridge and Davis (2003), currently the most widely quoted research classification is based on this distinction. But despite its popularity, they believe there are several problems with the distinction.

✘ **Are they 'types' or states?** Subjective accounts of psychotic experience suggest that it's doubtful whether negative symptoms define a *type* of schizophrenia. It's more likely that positive and negative symptoms represent alternating *states* occurring at different times within the same individual.

✘ **'Type' or end-state?** If it *does* define a 'type' of schizophrenia, the negative form probably refers to the chronic end-state. Some patients progress into this after years of adaptation to their more acute ('florid') episodes.

✘ **Are negative symptoms unique to schizophrenia?** If a diagnosis of schizophrenia is based on an initial episode that consists solely of negative symptoms, it won't be very convincing. For example, how do negative symptoms differ from those of depression (see below)?

✘ **Ambiguity:** 'negative symptom' is ambiguous. It could be a way of coping with positive symptoms (say, in the form of social withdrawal). Alternatively, it could be an effect of antipsychotic medication. Or it could be a manifestation of depression.

✔ **Provides template for understanding variety of schizophrenic symptoms:** despite these criticisms, the positive/negative distinction (or some elaboration of it) is probably along the right lines as a rough template of how schizophrenic symptoms can vary. It's easily recognisable to psychiatrists and psychologists.

Varieties of schizophrenia

DSM-IV-TR distinguishes three types of schizophrenia (as initially proposed by Kraepelin). These are *disorganised, catatonic* and *paranoid*. These are described in Table 7.3, page 290.

Other types that have been identified include *simple* and *undifferentiated*.

Simple schizophrenia

This often appears during late adolescence, and has a slow, gradual onset. The main symptoms are gradual social withdrawal and difficulty in making friends, aimlessness and idleness, blunting of affect, loss of volition and drive, and a decline in academic or occupational performance. Such people may become drifters or tramps, and are often regarded by others as idle and 'layabouts'. But there are no major psychotic symptoms as in the other types. Only ICD actually distinguishes this type, which is still used in some countries.

Undifferentiated (atypical)

This category is meant to accommodate patients who can't easily be placed elsewhere – that is, psychotic conditions that meet the general diagnostic criteria for schizophrenia, but don't conform to any of the subtypes (due to either insufficient or overlapping symptoms). 'Residual' is used when the patient no longer meets the full criteria but still shows some signs of illness. This is a 'supplementary' type used in DSM.

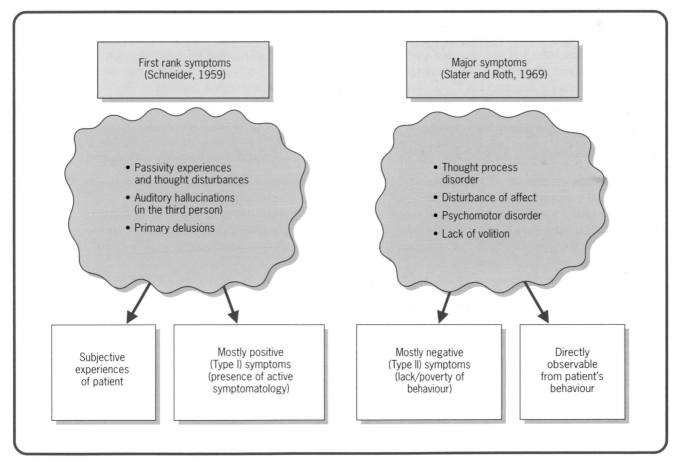

Figure 7.1 Summary of different attempts to define the major characteristics of schizophrenia

Disorganised schizophrenia

- This is probably the nearest thing to many people's idea about what a 'mad' or 'crazy' person is like (see text, above). It's what Kraepelin called hebephrenic.
- It's normally diagnosed only in adolescents and young adults.
- Mood is shallow and inappropriate; thought is disorganised, and speech is incoherent; this makes it difficult for the listener to follow.
- Delusions and hallucinations are fleeting and fragmentary, and behaviour is irresponsible, unpredictable, silly or mischievous, childish or bizarre; the person may sometimes become violent (if, for example, s/he's is approached while hallucinating).
- The person may become incontinent, and tends to ignore personal appearance and hygiene.

Catatonic schizophrenia

- The patient may alternate between extremes such as (a) hyperkinesis (hyperactivity) and stupor (a marked reduction of spontaneous movements and activity), or (b) automatic obedience ('command automatism') and negativism (apparently motiveless resistance to all instructions/attempts to be moved or doing the opposite of what's asked).
- There may be episodes of apparently purposeless motor activity combined with a dreamlike (oneroid) state with vivid scenic hallucinations.
- Other characteristics are mutism, posturing (the voluntary assumption of inappropriate and bizarre postures) and waxy flexibility (maintenance of the limbs and body in externally imposed positions).
- Onset may be more sudden than other types of schizophrenia. But the patient is likely to have shown previous apathy and withdrawal from reality.

Paranoid schizophrenia

- This is dominated by relatively stable, often paranoid delusions (although delusions of grandeur are also quite common); these may be accompanied by vivid auditory hallucinations.
- Also common are ideas of reference; the patient incorporates unimportant events within a delusional framework, and reads personal significance into other people's trivial actions – for example, they might think that overheard fragments of a conversation, or something on TV or in a magazine, are about them.
- Paranoid schizophrenics also tend to be agitated, argumentative, angry and sometimes violent.
- But in other respects, the patient is less disturbed (the personality is better preserved) than in the other kinds; the person remains emotionally responsive, and s/he is more alert and verbal than other types; although their language is filled with references to delusions, it isn't disorganised.
- It's the most homogeneous type – that is, paranoid schizophrenics are more alike than those in other categories.

Source: based on Gelder *et al*. (1999), Davison and Neale (2001)

Table 7.3: The three types of schizophrenia as identified by DSM-IV-TR

Evaluation of the sub-types

✗ **Are they really different?** With the possible exception of paranoid, psychiatrists find it very difficult to tell these 'subtypes' apart. Some patients present symptoms of one subgroup at one time, then those of another subgroup later (Gelder *et al.,* 1999). This dramatically reduces the *reliability* of diagnosis (Davison and Neale, 2001).

✗ **Are sub-types 'real' or are they subject to 'external forces?** Catatonic symptoms are much less common now than 50 years ago. This could be because drug therapy works effectively on bizarre motor processes. Alternatively, the apparently high prevalence of catatonic schizophrenia during the early twentieth century may have been due to misdiagnosis (Boyle, 1991). There are similarities between it and encephalitis lethargica (sleeping sickness). Many cases of the latter may have been diagnosed as catatonic schizophrenia. This was portrayed in the film *Awakenings* (based on the book by Oliver Sacks).

✗ **Poor predictive validity:** assigning someone to a particular sub-type provides very little information that helps either in treatment or predicting the outcome of the illness (Davison and Neale, 2001).

Explanations of schizophrenia

Biological explanations

Is schizophrenia a neurological disorder?

When Kraepelin first identified dementia praecox, he was convinced that it was a physical disease like any other. The neuropathological changes associated with *general paralysis of the insane* (caused by syphilis) and *Alzheimer's disease* had just been discovered. He expected that similar 'markers' would be found for schizophrenia (and manic-depressive illness).

However, schizophrenia was classified as a *functional psychosis* until 1978, when the then new CT scan was used for the first time to study the brains of chronic schizophrenics (by Johnstone *et al.* at the Clinical Research Centre in Middlesex, England; Gershon and Rieder, 1992). It revealed that chronic schizophrenics show an increase in the size of the lateral cerebral ventricles (the fluid-filled spaces in the middle of the brain). Other X-ray evidence confirmed that there was less brain tissue (especially in the medial temporal lobe). This was subsequently confirmed by MRI scans. MRI scans, together with post-mortem examinations, also revealed that schizophrenics have a smaller hippocampus. Part of the limbic system is also smaller.

> ✓ **Specification Hint**
>
> The specification says 'Biological (for example, genetics, biochemistry) and psychological (for example, behavioural, cognitive, psychodynamic and socio-cultural) explanations ...'. This requires you to know *at least one* of each type of explanation, *but one of each type will do.* Some explanations are overlapping, and it's also useful for analysis and evaluation (AO2) to be familiar with other (biological or psychological) explanations. So we've decided to include three biological accounts. These are also helpful for considering explanations of other mental disorders.

Gershon and Rieder also cite research that has shown reduced blood flow in the frontal cortex of schizophrenics. This implies decreased neuronal activity. Post-mortems also show that certain groups of neurons are organised in an abnormal way, or are connected differently, compared with those of non-schizophrenics.

STRETCH AND CHALLENGE: Some general considerations regarding research problems and strategies (AO2) (based on Claridge and Davis, 2003)

- Schizophrenia is *heterogeneous* (there are many different symptoms that can be involved, and different sub-types are officially recognised – but see text above). This makes it almost certain that attempts to give a *single* explanation will fail.
- Patients don't just differ from each other (*between*-subject differences). The same patient can show considerable variation on different occasions (*within*-subject differences). For example, individual schizophrenics show enormous day-to-day fluctuations in simple physical responses (such as galvanic skin response (GSR)). But most studies take only a single measure. This may be a general problem in any psychological research. But it may be a particular problem in the case of schizophrenia, because what causes this individual instability of function may itself be an important clue to the nature of the disorder.
- People with acute symptoms may be distracted by delusional thoughts about the experimenter. Or they may just not be looking at the computer screen that test stimuli are presented on. A partial solution to this problem is to test people who are taking antipsychotic medication. But then we cannot be sure whether their performance reflects a genuine feature of the illness or an effect of the drugs!
- This makes the study of schizoid and schizotypal personality disorder (SPD, or *schizotypy*) very important. The symptoms of schizophrenia can sometimes appear in a rather muted (toned-down) form. This gave rise to the idea of the *schizophrenic spectrum* (a range of schizophrenia-like disorders). SPD has received the most attention as a possible mild variant of schizophrenia. Diagnostic criteria for SPD include ideas of reference, odd beliefs or magical thinking, unusual perceptual experiences, odd thinking and speech, suspiciousness, inappropriate affect, odd eccentric behaviour or appearance, a lack of close friends, and excessive social anxiety.
- If people high on schizotypy share important characteristics with schizophrenics, then by studying the former it becomes possible to study 'schizophrenia' without the confounding effects of acute mental disturbance or medication. This 'schizotypy strategy' is used to examine possible *mechanisms* involved in psychotic disorder. This includes the *genetics* of schizophrenia (see text below).

Evaluation of the neurological disorder explanation (NDE)

✔ **Evidence for cause rather than effect:** all these differences are found when patients first develop symptoms (and may even precede the onset of symptoms). This suggests that they're *not* the result of being ill for a long time or of medication (Harrison, 1995). Also, these differences don't progress over time, nor is there any evidence of neural scar tissue (*gliosis*) that's normally found in degenerative disorders (such as Alzheimer's and Huntington's). This suggests a *neurodevelopmental disorder* – that is, a failure of brain tissue to develop normally (such as failure of neuronal growth or neuronal connections) or a disturbance in the 'pruning' of neurons that normally takes place between three and fifteen years of age (Gershon and Rieder, 1992)

✗ **Correlational data:** the cognitive and affective abnormalities involved in psychosis are so severe that

Evaluation of the neurological disorder explanation (NDE) continued...

it's reasonable to expect brain abnormalities to be involved (Frith and Cahill, 1995), but the data are largely *correlational*.

✗ The differences between normal and schizophrenic brains are relative: these differences are apparent only if a group of schizophrenics is compared with a group of non-schizophrenics. That is, no one can yet diagnose schizophrenia in an individual based *solely* on a brain scan or looking down a microscope (Harrison, 1995).

✗ How do such differences arise? Even if we could diagnose schizophrenia just from a brain scan, this wouldn't answer the more fundamental question as to why some people develop these disorders and others don't.

✗ No consistent differences between normal and schizophrenic brains: individual studies have regularly shown differences between schizophrenics and control samples. But replicable effects *across* studies have remained elusive (Claridge and Davis, 2003). For example, a review by Chua and McKenna (1995) concluded that there was no reliable evidence for gross structural or functional cerebral abnormality that could be said to characterise schizophrenia as a diagnostic category. The only exception was lateral ventricular enlargement. But the degree of enlargement is modest, many patients don't show any enlargement at all, and enlarged ventricles are found in other disorders (such as mania) (Davison and Neale, 2001). Also, enlarged ventricles are more of a vulnerability factor than an immediate cause of the disorder.

✔/✗ No single brain abnormality can explain all symptoms: it's more likely that different brain circuits underlie different clusters of symptoms. For example, people with known abnormalities in their temporal lobe often show schizophrenia-like symptoms. Neuroimaging studies involving schizophrenic patients support this link, and suggest that it's specifically *positive* symptoms that are associated with this dysfunction (Bogerts, 1997). *Negative* symptoms may be related to the *frontal* lobe. Schizophrenics show 'hypofrontality'. This is seen as either (a) reduced activity relative to other brain regions, or (b) failure of the prefrontal cortex (PFC) and associated structures to be appropriately activated by cognitive tasks (Velakoulis and Pantelis, 1996). Performance deficits on neuropsychological tests of frontal lobe function are much greater in those rated high on negative symptoms (Mattson *et al.,* 1997). This suggests that their core cognitive failure is *indirect,* due to *motivational* effects (see Table 7. 2 above).

Biochemical explanations of schizophrenia

Genetics may have its effect through body chemistry and related biological processes. So biochemical explanations are *complementary* to genetic theory, not alternatives to it. According to the *dopamine hypothesis,* what directly causes schizophrenic symptoms is an *excess* of the neurotransmitter dopamine. In order to appreciate the dopamine hypothesis (and explanations of other disorders involving neurotransmitters), we need to consider the process of neurotransmission. This is described in Box 7.2.

The evidence for this hypothesis comes from three main sources.

1. Post-mortems on schizophrenics show unusually high levels of dopamine, especially in the limbic system (Iversen, 1979).

2. Anti-schizophrenic drugs (such as chlorpromazine) are thought to work by binding to dopamine receptor sites – that is, they inhibit the ability of the dopamine (D2) receptors to respond to dopamine, thus reducing dopamine activity. They produce side effects that are

Box 7.2: The process of neurotransmission

- Information is transmitted in the brain via a combination of electrical impulses and neurotransmitters.
- *Within* a nerve cell (or *neuron*), information is conveyed by electrical impulses. But, for transmission *between* neurons, transmitters are needed.
- When an electrical impulse arrives at the end of the neuron, a neurotransmitter is released into a tiny gap (the *synaptic gap* or *cleft*) between it and the beginning of the next neuron. The first neuron is referred to as the *pre-synaptic* neuron, and the second ('receiving') neuron as the *post-synaptic* neuron.
- The released neurotransmitter attaches to *post-synaptic receptors*. This action triggers another electrical impulse.
- Once it's done its job, the neurotransmitter is then recycled, in one of two ways: (i) it may be taken back by the neuron that released it (*reuptake*); or (ii) it may be broken down chemically in the synaptic gap into simpler compounds by *monoamine oxidase* (MAO). Serotonin (5-HT), norepinephrine (noradrenaline) and dopamine are major neurotransmitters, collectively known as MAO transmitters.

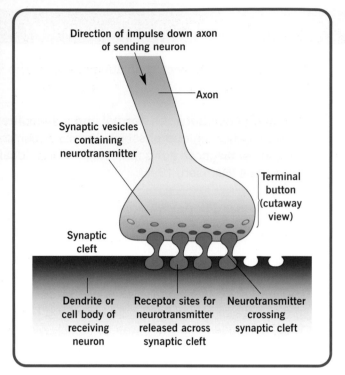

Figure 7.2 The synapse

similar to the symptoms of Parkinson's disease, which is known to be caused partly by low levels of dopamine in particular nerve tracts.

3. High doses of L-dopa (used in the treatment of Parkinson's disease) can sometimes produce symptoms very similar to the psychomotor disorders seen in certain types of schizophrenia. High doses of amphetamines can induce *amphetamine psychosis* (AP), which closely resembles paranoid schizophrenia and can exacerbate the symptoms of a patient with schizophrenia. Both these drugs are believed to increase the activity of dopamine. Dopamine-containing neurons are concentrated in the basal ganglia and frontal cortex. These areas are concerned with the initiation and control of movement. Degeneration of the dopamine system produces Parkinson's disease (see above). Antipsychotics are given to counteract AP.

Evaluation of biochemical explanations

✗ **Inconclusive evidence:** overall, the evidence is inconclusive (Lavender, 2000). For example, there's no consistent difference in dopamine levels between drug-free schizophrenics and normals, nor is there any evidence of higher levels of other metabolites indicating greater dopamine activity (Jackson, 1986).

✗ **Cause or effect?** Even if there were evidence of higher dopamine levels, this could just as easily be a *result* of schizophrenia as its cause. If dopamine *were* found to be a causative factor, this might only be

Evaluation of biochemical explanations continued...

indirect. For example, abnormal family circumstances give rise to high levels of dopamine, which, in turn, trigger the symptoms (Lloyd *et al.*, 1984).

✗ **Dopamine hypothesis couldn't explain all cases:** it's unlikely that any problems with dopamine production/receptivity will prove to be the basic biochemical abnormality underlying all forms of schizophrenia – although it may play a crucial role in some forms (Jackson, 1990). According to Lavender (2000):

> *if schizophrenia is not a clearly identifiable syndrome but an umbrella term covering a range of symptoms with unclear onset, course, and outcome, then it is obvious that much of the work investigating a specific biological basis will inevitably be inconclusive. So far, this appears to be the case ...*

As Bentall (1990) argues, perhaps the time has come to concentrate on specific symptoms, before trying to find the biochemical cause(s).

✗ **Incomplete explanation:** the dopamine hypothesis cannot be a complete explanation. For example, it takes several weeks for antipsychotics to gradually reduce positive symptoms, even though they begin blocking D2 receptors very quickly (Davis, 1978). Their eventual therapeutic effect may be due to the effect this blockade has on *other* brain areas and neurotransmitter systems (Cohen *et al.*, 1997).

✗ **Other neurotransmitters implicated:** newer anti-schizophrenic drugs implicate *serotonin*. Serotoninergic neurons are known to regulate dopaminergic neurons in the mesolimbic pathway (MLP; see below and Figure 7.3). So, dopamine may be just one piece in a much more complex jigsaw (Davison and Neale, 2001). *Glutamate*, another transmitter found in many parts of the human brain, may also be involved.

✔ **Refining the hypothesis:** improved technologies for studying neurochemical factors in humans, plus inconsistent data, have led to the claim that what schizophrenics have is an excess of dopamine *receptors*, or that their D2 receptors are *oversensitive*. This refined dopamine hypothesis is based on several post-mortem and PET scan studies. Having too many – or oversensitive – receptors is functionally equivalent to having too much dopamine itself, and seems to be associated mainly with *positive* symptoms (Davison and Neale, 2001).

✔ **Further refinements:** an excess of dopamine located in the *mesolimbic pathway* (MLP) seems to be most relevant to understanding schizophrenia. The therapeutic effects of antipsychotic drugs on the positive symptoms occur by blocking D2 receptors there. The

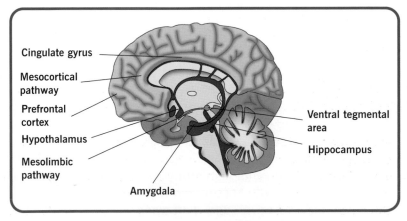

Figure 7.3 The brain and schizophrenia

mesocortical pathway (MCP) begins in the same brain region as the MLP, but projects to the prefrontal cortex (PFC) (see Figure 7.3).

The PFC also projects to limbic areas which consist of neurons that are activated by dopamine. These *dopaminergic* neurons in the PFC may be underactive and so fail to exert inhibitory control over dopaminergic neurons in the limbic area. This produces overactivity in the MLP. The PFC is thought to be especially relevant to negative symptoms. Consequently, underactivity of the dopaminergic neurons in this part of the brain may also be the cause of negative symptoms. This proposal has the advantage of explaining how positive and negative symptoms can be present at the same time in the same patient. Also, because antipsychotics don't have major effects on dopaminergic neurons in the PFC, we'd expect them to be relatively ineffective in treating negative symptoms – and they are (Davison and Neale, 2001).

The genetic theory of schizophrenia

As Table 7.4 shows, relatives of patients with schizophrenia (proband or index case) have a greater risk of being diagnosed themselves as the genetic relationship becomes closer. This was confirmed by Kendler *et al.* (1996).

How Science Works

Practical Learning Activity 7.3

Table 7.4 includes data from both *family resemblance studies* (including dizygotic/DZ and monozygotic / MZ twins) and *twin studies* (monozygotic twins reared apart / MZRA).

● What's the difference between MZs and DZs?
● From a purely genetic perspective, what degree of similarity regarding schizophrenia would you expect for the two types of twin: (a) reared together (in the same birth family; and (b) apart (in two separate families, one of which may be the birth family)?
● From the data in Table 7.4, why can't we draw the simple conclusion that the correlation between the risk of developing schizophrenia and degree of family resemblance / blood tie is due to the greater genetic similarity?
● What's the main advantage of studying MZRAs compared with MZs reared together?
● Identify a major disadvantage of studying twins (whether raised together or separately).

(See Gross, 2005.)

Family resemblance studies confound genetic and environmental influences. In other words, there's no way of telling whether the correlation between the risk of developing schizophrenia and degree of family resemblance / blood tie is due to the greater genetic similarity or the greater similarity of environments. This is because, as the blood tie increases, so does the similarity of the environment.

The two major alternative designs, *twin* and *adoption studies*, both face problems of their own. For example, they presuppose that schizophrenia is a distinct syndrome that can be reliably diagnosed by different psychiatrists.

Twin studies

As Table 7.5 shows, there's a wide variation in the concordance rate for schizophrenia in different studies, for both MZs and DZs. This suggests that different countries use different criteria for diagnosing schizophrenia.

By the same token, if the highest concordance rate for MZs is 69 per cent (using a 'broad' criterion), this still leaves plenty of scope for the role of environmental factors. If schizophrenia were totally genetically determined, then we'd expect to find a 100 per cent concordance rate for MZs. In other words, if one member of an MZ pair has schizophrenia, the other twin should also have it in every single case. In fact, most diagnosed cases *don't* report a family history (Frith and Cahill, 1995). Nevertheless, the average concordance rate for MZs is five times higher than that for DZs (50 per cent and 10 per cent respectively; Shields, 1976, 1978).

Relationship to proband	Percentage with schizophrenia
Spouse	1.00
First cousin	2.00
Grandchild	2.84
Niece/nephew	2.00–2.65
Child	9.35
– with one schizophrenic parent	6.00
– with two schizophrenic parents	46.00
Sibling	7.30–10.00
Dizygotic (DZ) twin	12.00–12.08
Monozygotic (MZ) twin	44.30
Monozygotic twin reared apart (MZRA)	58.00

Table 7.4: Summary of major European family and twin studies of the genetics of schizophrenia (based on Gottesman et al., 1987; Gottesman, 1991)

Study	'Narrow' concordance*		'Broad' concordance*	
	% MZs	% DZs	% MZs	% DZs
Rosanoff et al. (1934); USA (41 MZs, 53 DZs)	44	9	61	13
Kallmann (1946); USA (174 MZs, 296 DZs)	59	11	69	11–14
Slater (1953); England (37 MZs, 58 DZs)	65	14	65	14
Gottesman and Shields (1966); England (24 MZs, 33 DZs)	42	15	54	18
Kringlen (1968); Norway (55 MZs, 90 DZs)	25	7	38	10
Allen et al. (1972); USA (95 MZs, 125 DZs)	14	4	27	5
Fischer (1973); Denmark (21 MZs, 41 DZs)	24	10	48	20

* 'Narrow' based on attempt to apply a relatively strict set of criteria when diagnosing schizophrenia. 'Broad' includes 'borderline schizophrenia', 'schizoaffective psychosis', 'paranoid with schizophrenia-like features'.

Table 7.5: Concordance rates for schizophrenia for identical (MZ) and non-identical (DZ) twins (based on Rose et al., 1984)

A more precise estimate for the relative importance of genetic and environmental factors comes from studies where MZs reared apart (MZRAs) are compared with MZs reared together (MZRTs). According to Shields (1976, 1978), the concordance rates are quite similar for the two groups, suggesting a major genetic contribution.

Adoption studies

Adoption studies arguably provide the most unequivocal test of genetic influence, because they allow the clearest separation of genetic and environmental factors. For example, Heston (1966) studied 47 adults born to schizophrenic mothers and separated from them within three days of birth. As children, they'd been reared in a variety of circumstances, though not by the mother's family. They were compared (average age 36) with controls matched for circumstances of upbringing, but where mothers hadn't been schizophrenic. Five of the experimental group, but none of the controls, were diagnosed as schizophrenic.

Rosenthal et al. (1971) began a series of studies in 1965 in Denmark, which has national registers of psychiatric cases and adoptions. They confirmed Heston's findings, using children separated from schizophrenic mothers, on average at six months.

In what's considered to be one of the major schizophrenia adoption studies, Kety et al. (1975) used a different design from earlier studies. Two groups of adoptees were identified: (i) 33 who had schizophrenia, and (ii) a matched group who didn't. Rates of disorder were compared in the biological and adoptive families of the two groups of adoptees – the rate was greater among the biological relatives of the schizophrenic adoptees than among those of the controls, a finding that supports the genetic hypothesis. Further, the rate of schizophrenia wasn't increased among couples who adopted the schizophrenic adoptees, suggesting that environmental factors weren't of crucial importance (Gelder et al., 1989).

The reverse situation was studied by Wender et al. (1974), who found no increase among adoptees with normal biological parents but with a schizophrenic adoptive parent. Gottesman and Shields (1976, 1982), reviewing adoption studies, conclude that they show a major role for heredity.

Box 7.3: The equal environments assumption

- Twin studies are based on the *equal environments assumption*: (a) MZs aren't treated more similarly than same-sex DZs; or (b) if they are, this doesn't increase MZs' similarity for the characteristic in question relative to same-sex DZs.
- According to Lilienfeld (1995), this assumption has stood up surprisingly well to careful empirical scrutiny. For example, researchers have identified MZs and DZs whose *zygosity* has been misclassified (MZs mistaken for DZs, and vice versa). If similarity of rearing were the key factor underlying the greater concordance for MZs, then *perceived* zygosity (as opposed to actual zygosity) should be the best predictor of concordance. However, twin similarity in personality and cognitive ability is related much more closely to *actual* than perceived zygosity (Scarr and Carter-Saltzman, 1979).
- Also, the greater similarity in parental rearing for MZs seems to be due largely or entirely to the fact that MZs elicit more similar reactions from their parents (Lytton, 1977). It seems, therefore, that the greater similarity of MZs is a *cause*, rather than an effect, of their more similar parental treatment.

Evaluation of the genetic theory

✗/✔ **The random placement assumption:** this refers to the assumption that adoptees are placed with parents who are no more similar to their biological parents than by chance. This is crucial when evaluating the results of adoption studies. Rose *et al*. (1984) consider selective placement to be the rule (rather than random placement) and so a major, if not fatal, stumbling block for adoption studies. But Lilienfeld (1995) believes the random placement assumption is largely or entirely warranted.

✔ **Supporting evidence:** perhaps the most reasonable conclusion is that there's converging evidence, from multiple sources, implicating genetic factors in the aetiology of schizophrenia. Its heritability seems to be comparable to that of any medical condition known to have a major genetic component, such as diabetes, hypertension, coronary artery disease and breast cancer (Lilienfeld, 1995).

✗/✔ **But how is it inherited and what exactly is inherited?** The precise mode of inheritance remains controversial (Frith and Cahill, 1995; Lilienfeld, 1995). The most popular current view is the 'multifactorial' (*polygenic*) model: a number of genes are involved that determine a predisposition, which then requires environmental factors to trigger the symptoms of the illness. This is referred to as a *diathesis-* (i.e. predisposition) *stress model.* Zubin and Spring (1977), for example, claim that what we probably inherit is a degree of *vulnerability* to exhibit schizophrenic symptoms. Whether or not we do will depend on environmental stresses, which may include viral infections during pregnancy (especially influenza A), severe malnourishment during pregnancy, birth injury or difficult birth, being born in winter, as well as 'critical life events' (see below).

✗/✔ **The influence of environmental factors:** according to Claridge and Davis (2003), 'the contribution of genetic influences is one of the few factual certainties about schizophrenia. Even in the absence of the discovery of specific genes, this is clear from kinship data . . .'. But, as the *diathesis-stress model* maintains, any inherited factors can only account for a greater *vulnerability* or likelihood of developing schizophrenia. They don't *guarantee* that the vulnerable individual will actually become schizophrenic. So, just as Claridge and Davis are certain that genetic factors are involved, they're equally certain that the genetic data tell us that environmental factors must also be important. But these can be interpreted as *biological* factors (viral infections, birth complications etc.; see above) or as *social.* For example, Tienari (1991) examined the rate of schizophrenia in Finnish people who'd been adopted and whose biological mothers were schizophrenic. As predicted, having a biological mother with schizophrenia increased the rate of schizophrenia in the adoptees, even if they were adopted by non-schizophrenic families. But the schizophrenic genetics revealed itself only if the adoptive family was psychologically disturbed in some way. So, even vulnerable individuals could be protected from schizophrenia if their family of rearing were healthy.

Psychological explanations

✔ Specification Hint

As we've seen above, the diathesis-stress model incorporates both 'vulnerability' factors (usually taken to mean prenatal, including genetic influences) and 'triggering' factors (usually taken to mean post-natal, environmental influences). The latter are also what's normally understood by 'psychological'. So, 'psychological explanations' include those that focus on the non-genetic, environmental half of the diathesis-stress model. The specification gives several examples; here we shall focus on two or three different accounts, which all come under the heading 'socio-cultural'.

The 'schizophrenogenic mother' and family communication

Early theorists regarded family relationships as crucial, especially that between mother and son. This view was so popular at the time that the term 'schizophrenogenic mother' was coined. This described the cold, dominant, conflict-inducing parent (Fromm-Reichmann, 1952). She was rejecting, overprotective, self-sacrificing, insensitive to others' feelings, rigid and moralistic about sex, and afraid of intimacy.

There was little supporting evidence. But the families of schizophrenics differ in some ways from those of non-schizophrenics. For example, they show vague patterns of communication and high levels of conflict (Davison and Neale, 2001). But which is cause and which is effect? Could it be that the abnormal communication and high conflict levels are *caused by* having a schizophrenic in the family?

Some evidence exists that these may play some part in causing schizophrenia. Goldstein and Rodnick (1975) studied adolescents with behaviour problems and their families over a five-year period. Several developed schizophrenia and related disorders during this period, and abnormal communication did seem to predict the later onset of schizophrenia. However, the parents of manic patients (those with bipolar disorder; see below) also display such deviant communication. So, it cannot be a *specific* causal factor in schizophrenia.

Further evidence comes from the Finnish adoption study by Tienari (1991) referred to above. The adoptive families were classified according to the level of maladjustment they displayed (based on clinical interviews and psychological tests). Adoptees with a biological schizophrenic mother were more severely schizophrenic themselves if reared in a disturbed family. So should we conclude that both a genetic predisposition and a harmful family environment are necessary for schizophrenia (as the diathesis-stress model would maintain)? Again, the disturbed family environment could be a *response* to having a disturbed child (Davison and Neale, 2001).

The family interaction model

During the 1950s and 1960s, several British psychiatrists, notably R.D. Laing, Cooper and Esterson, united in their rejection of the medical model of mental disorder. They denied the existence of schizophrenia as a disease entity. Instead, they saw it as a metaphor for dealing with people whose behaviour and experience fail to conform to the dominant model of social reality. They thus spearheaded the *antipsychiatry movement* (Graham, 1986).

In *Self and Others* (1961), Laing proposed the *family interaction model*. Schizophrenia can only be understood as something that takes place *between* people (*not* inside them). To understand individuals we must study not individuals but interactions between individuals (this is the subject matter of *social phenomenology*).

Labelling theory

Laing (1967) proposed another model of schizophrenia. The *conspiratorial model* maintains that

Figure 7.4 R.D. Laing (1927–1989)

Evaluation of the family interaction model

✔ **Supporting evidence:** the family interaction model was consistent with American research, especially that of Bateson *et al*. (1956). This showed that schizophrenia arises within families that use 'pathological' forms of communication, in particular contradictory messages (*double-binds*). For example, a mother induces her son to give her a hug, but when he does she tells him 'not to be such a baby'. This research is, of course, consistent with the studies by Goldstein and Rodnick (1975) and Tienari (1991) described above. Laing and Esterson (1964) presented 11 family case histories, in all of which one member becomes a diagnosed schizophrenic. Their aim was to make schizophrenia intelligible in the context of what happens within the patient's family and, in so doing, to further undermine the disease model of schizophrenia.

✗/✔ **Cause or effect?** As with other correlational evidence, both Bateson *et al*.'s and Laing and Esterson's studies are open to two interpretations. According to Laing and Esterson, it's the family that is 'schizophrenic', and one particularly vulnerable member becomes a scapegoat for the whole family's pathology. Alternatively, the patient is already ill and part of the family's way of dealing with this is to develop abnormal ('schizophrenic') forms of communication. Supporters of biochemical or genetic explanations would argue that there's sufficient data to account for how people become schizophrenic without having to bring family environmental factors into it. But supporters of the diathesis-stress model would claim that only environmental factors (such as disturbed families) can explain how vulnerability is turned into actual schizophrenic illness.

schizophrenia is a label, a form of violence perpetrated by some people on others. The family, GP and psychiatrists conspire against the schizophrenic in order to preserve their definition of reality (the status quo). They treat schizophrenics as if they were sick and imprison them in mental hospitals, where they're degraded and invalidated as human beings.

The influence of labelling is demonstrated in Rosenhan's famous 1973 study. As we noted earlier, Rosenhan's aim was to show that psychiatrists are unable to tell the difference between the 'sane' and the 'insane', and that, therefore, psychiatric classification and diagnosis are totally unreliable. But he also discussed the effects of *diagnostic labelling* at great length.

Rosenhan claims that his results demonstrate dramatically what several authors (such as Scheff, 1966) have claimed, namely that psychiatric (diagnostic) labels tend to become *self-fulfilling prophecies*. Psychiatric labels stick in a way that (other) medical labels don't. More seriously, *everything* the patient says and does is interpreted in accordance with the diagnostic label once it's been applied. For example, after admission the pseudo-patients kept a written record of how the ward was run. This was documented by the nursing staff as 'Patient engages in writing behaviour'. In other words, the writing was seen as a symptom of their pathological behaviour. Rosenhan argues that mental disorder is a purely *social* phenomenon, the consequences of a labelling process.

According to Scheff (1966), the crucial factor in schizophrenia is the act of assigning a diagnostic label to the individual. This label influences (a) how the person will continue to behave (based on stereotyped ideas of mental illness), and (b) how others will react to them. The labelling process creates a *social role*, which *is* the disorder. Without it, deviant behaviour (or the breaking of *residual rules*) wouldn't become stabilised. Residual rules are what's 'left over' after all the formal and obvious ones (about violence, stealing etc.) have been recognised. Examples would be 'Don't report hearing voices' or 'Don't talk to yourself out loud while walking down a busy street.' Scheff believes it's quite common for people to commit 'one-time violations'. If a 'normal' person is unlucky enough to be caught violating a residual rule, they might be diagnosed as suffering from, say, schizophrenia. Rosenhan's experiment shows how easy it is to 'slip into' the role of psychiatric patient.

Evaluation of labelling theory

✔**Theoretical significance:** according to Lilienfeld (1995), Rosenhan's experiment 'provides a sorely needed reminder of the human mind's propensity to rearrange or reframe facts to achieve consistency with preexisting beliefs'. This refers to the staff's interpretation of the pseudo-patients' behaviour in terms of the diagnostic label they were given on admission.

✔**Intuitive appeal:** most people who've worked for any length of time in a psychiatric setting have witnessed abuses of the diagnostic process. Patients are sometimes given labels that are unjustified (Davison and Neale, 2001).

✗ **More than just a label:** Miller and Morley (1986) argue that the label 'schizophrenic' isn't just a label, but there's a reality of some kind behind it. They also believe that it's a mistake to argue for *either* 'labelling' *or* 'mental illness' (it's a false dichotomy).

✗ **Why is the label applied in the first place?** Labelling theory and Rosenhan's study have usefully highlighted how people labelled as mentally ill are treated. But they cannot account for why someone begins to show deviant behaviour in the first place (MacLeod, 1998). Also, if diagnostic labels really are so powerful, why were the genuine patients in Rosenhan's study not deceived by them? The pseudo-patients' actual behaviour seemed to have been more powerful than whatever adverse effects the labels may have exerted on these observers' perceptions (Lilienfeld, 1995).

✗/✔ **Just how sticky are psychiatric labels?** Neisser (1973) supports Rosenhan's claim that psychiatric labels are 'irreversible'. Instead of the pseudo-patients being discharged with a diagnosis of 'normal' or 'normal: initial diagnosis in error', they were given the discharge diagnosis of 'schizophrenia in remission'. It's almost as if the psychiatrist can never be wrong ('heads I win, tails you lose'). But Lilienfeld argues that 'schizophrenia in remission' conveys useful information. Schizophrenia tends to be a chronic disorder, which often recurs after periods of remission. 'In remission' indicates the increased risk of subsequent episodes.

✗ **Historical relativity:** according to MacLeod (1998), labelling theory is an example of a theory that fitted the practices of a particular place and time. For example, it seems to be especially applicable to *involuntary* hospital admissions. When Scheff conducted his research in the 1960s, 90 per cent of all psychiatric admissions were involuntary. When Bean (1979) replicated Scheff's study in the UK, the figure was only 18 per cent. Not only will there be national and cultural differences in admission rates, but the US figure is likely to have fallen in that time.

✗ **Cultural relativity:** labelling theory implies that definitions of abnormality will vary across cultures, reflecting different social norms and values – for example, the visions of a shaman vs the hallucinations of a diagnosed schizophrenic; the only difference is that shamans are perceived by their culture as wise. Murphy (1976) studied the Eskimo and Yoruba peoples. Contrary to labelling theory, both cultures have a concept of being crazy that's quite similar to our definition of schizophrenia. The Eskimo's *nuthkavihak* includes talking to oneself, refusing to talk, delusional beliefs and bizarre behaviour. The Yoruba's *were* encompasses similar symptoms. Both cultures also have shamans, but they draw a clear line between their behaviour and that of crazy people.

Synoptic Material: Is schizophrenia culture-free?

During the 1970s and 1980s, psychiatrists and clinical psychologists became increasingly interested in 'cultural psychiatry'. According to Berry *et al*. (1992), the central issue in the cross-cultural study of mental disorder is whether phenomena such as schizophrenia are:

● *absolute* (found in all cultures in precisely the same form)
● *universal* (present in some form in all cultures, but subject to cultural influence)
● *culturally relative* (unique to particular cultures and understandable only in terms of those cultures).

Of these three possibilities, only the first corresponds to a 'culture-free' view of abnormality. Berry *et al*. reject this view of abnormality, on the grounds that 'cultural factors appear to affect at least some aspects of mental disorders, even those that are so closely linked to human biology'. Universality is a more likely candidate for capturing the objective (biological) nature of mental disorder. Schizophrenia is the most commonly diagnosed mental disorder in the world, and of the major disorders, the largest number of culture-general symptoms has been reported for schizophrenia (WHO, 1973, 1979; Draguns, 1980, 1990).

However, according to Brislin (1993), there are at least three possible ways in which culture-specific factors can influence schizophrenia: (i) the form that symptoms will take; (ii) the precipitatory factor involved in the onset of the illness; and (iii) the prognosis.

1. When schizophrenics complain that their minds are being invaded by unseen forces, in North America and Europe these forces keep up to date with technological developments. So in the 1920s, these were often voices from the radio; in the 1950s, they came from television; in the 1960s it was satellites in space; and in the 1970s and 1980s spirits were transmitted through microwave ovens. In cultures where witchcraft is considered common, the voices or spirits would be directed by unseen forces under the control of demons.
2. Day et al. (1987) studied schizophrenia in nine different locations in the USA, Asia, Europe and South America. Acute schizophrenic attacks were associated with stressful events 'external' to the patient (such as losing one's job or the unexpected death of a spouse), which tended to cluster within a two- to three-week period prior to the onset of obvious symptoms. Some events could only be understood as stressful if the researchers had detailed information about the person's cultural background.
3. Lin and Kleinman (1988) found that the prognosis for successful treatment of schizophrenia was better in non-industrialised than industrialised countries. The former provide more structured, stable, predictable and socially supportive environments that allow schizophrenic patients to recover at their own pace and to be reintegrated into society.

Therapies for schizophrenia
Biological therapies

✓ Specification Hint

As with explanations, you only need to know about ONE of each type of therapy (i.e. biological and psychological). Once again, the specification gives only examples, so that exam questions cannot require you to discuss any particular therapy. Here we've decided to present two or more of each type, both to give you choice and to enable you to compare and contrast different therapies within the same category in order to gain AO2 marks.

How Science Works

Practical Learning Activity 7.4

- Remind yourself of (a) biological therapies (including drugs and electroconvulsive therapy / ECT), and (b) psychological therapies (including psychoanalysis, systematic desensitisation and cognitive behavioural therapy) (see Gross and Rolls, 2008).
- Try to identify some of the recurring problems/issues associated with the use of different therapies – especially biological ones. (Again, see Gross and Rolls, 2008.)

STRETCH AND CHALLENGE: Some general considerations regarding the use of therapies for psychopathology

Before considering the appropriateness/effectiveness of particular treatments in relation to schizophrenia, it's useful to be aware of these issues as they apply to the treatment of psychopathology in general.

- Especially in the case of biological therapies, *side effects* represent a continuing source of controversy and debate.
- There are also *ethical* issues raised by any kind of therapy/treatment situation; these are perhaps most evident again in the case of biological therapies, where side effects may be permanent and irreversible (as in psychosurgery).
- There are issues regarding *social power* and the use of particular treatments (such as major tranquillisers / anti-psychotic drugs, and ECT) as *agents of social control.*
- When we ask 'Is therapy effective?' (which usually denotes *psychological* therapies), we're asking a deceptively simple question that really comprises two interrelated questions: (i) 'Does it work?' (this is related to *outcome research*); and (ii) 'How does it work?' (this related to *process research*). Each question, in turn, comprises several other, overlapping, questions. *Outcome questions* include the following.
  - Is psychotherapy (in general) effective?
  - Is any one kind of psychotherapy more effective than another?
  - What constitutes a satisfactory outcome?
  - How should psychological change be measured (and for how long after the end of treatment)?
  - How much and what kind of change is necessary for a judgement of improvement to be made?
- *Process questions* include the following.
  - What are the necessary components of effective therapy?
  - What are the mechanisms by which change is brought about (what are the 'active ingredients')?
  - Are different therapies effective because of the particular techniques and tools they use, or are there *common factors* that apply to *all* therapies?

Although the specification doesn't require you to know about these issues specifically, they're clearly relevant to any discussion of particular treatments for specific mental disorders. A useful discussion can be found in Gross (2005).

Drug therapies (chemotherapy)

Without question, the most important development in the treatment of schizophrenia was the introduction, in the 1950s, of *antipsychotic drugs* (or *neuroleptics*), so named because they produce side effects similar to the symptoms of a neurological disorder, such as Parkinson's disease (see above).

Traditionally one of the most commonly prescribed antipsychotic drugs, *phenothiazine*, is related to the group of antihistamine drugs (used to treat the common cold and asthma). A French surgeon extended the use of antihistamines to reduce surgical shock: his patients became sleepy and less anxious about the impending surgery. A new phenothiazine derivative, *chlorpromazine*, was then found to be very effective in calming patients with schizophrenia. As we saw above, phenothiazine works by blocking dopamine (D2) receptors in the brain, thus reducing the influence of dopamine on thought, emotion and behaviour.

Chlorpromazine (trade name Thorazine or Largactil) was first used in the USA in 1954 and quickly became the treatment of choice for schizophrenia. By 1970, more than 85 per cent of all patients in state mental hospitals were receiving chlorpromazine or another phenothiazine. Other antipsychotics that have been used for years to treat schizophrenia include the *butyrophenones* (e.g. haloperidol, Haldol) and the *thioxanthenes* (e.g. thiothixene, Navane). Both types seem generally to be as effective as the phenothiazines, and work in similar ways (Davison *et al.*, 2004).

Advantages/benefits of the traditional antipsychotic drugs

- Fifty years ago, straitjackets were commonly used and many psychiatric wards had one or more padded cells. Before the 1950s, over half of those admitted to a mental hospital and diagnosed with schizophrenia remained in hospital for the rest of their days. For most patients, 'treatment' consisted of little more than long-term care and custody ('patient warehousing') (Frude, 1998). The introduction of powerful neuroleptic drugs brought enormous changes.

- The management of such patients was revolutionised by these drugs; they rapidly reduced many of the most disturbing symptoms and sharply decreased the average length of stay in hospital. Schizophrenia changed from a 'long stay' to a 'short stay' condition,

although many patients needed to be readmitted from time to time when experiencing further acute episodes. Of the 300,000 people in the UK who've suffered at least one acute episode, fewer than 3 per cent are now cared for permanently in mental hospitals. Many are now treated mostly on an outpatient basis; of those admitted to hospital, the vast majority stay only a few weeks or months (Frude, 1998).

- These classes of drugs can reduce the *positive* symptoms (see Table 7.1), enabling many patients to be released from hospital; however, they're not a cure.

- Patients who respond positively are kept on *maintenance doses* – that is, just enough to continue the therapeutic effect. They take their medication and return to the hospital or clinic occasionally for the dose to be adjusted.

Limitations / side effects of the traditional antipsychotic drugs

- They have little effect on the *negative* symptoms (see Table 7.2).

- About 30 per cent of patients with schizophrenia don't respond favourably to these antipsychotics (although some may respond to newer antipsychotics, such as clozapine; see below).

- Even those on maintenance doses (see above) may make only marginal adjustment to the community. For example, they may be unable to live unsupervised or to hold down the kind of job for which they might be qualified. Their social relationships are likely to be sparse, and readmission to hospital is common. While the antipsychotics have significantly reduced long-term institutionalisation, they've also initiated the *revolving-door* pattern of admission, discharge and readmission (Davison *et al.*, 2004). However, Davison *et al.* cite a study by Herz *et al.* (2000) that tested the effectiveness of a new treatment, which involved:
  - educating patients about relapse and recognising early signs of relapse
  - monitoring early signs of relapse by staff
  - weekly supportive group or individual therapy
  - family educational sessions
  - quick intervention, involving both increased doses of medication and crisis-orientated problem-solving therapy, when early signs of relapse were detected.

Staff were able to accurately recognise early signs of relapse and implement procedures to deal with it. Over an 18-month period, the new treatment cut relapse rates in half and reduced rehospitalisation rates by 44 per cent.

- Although antipsychotic drugs may be an important protective factor against relapse, relapse rates of 40 per cent in the first year following the start of treatment, and 15 per cent in successive years, are typical; overall, they appear to *delay* relapse rather than prevent it (Bennett, 2006).

- Commonly reported side effects (*anticholinergic*) include dry mouth, dizziness (due to low blood pressure), blurred vision, restlessness, constipation, glaucoma and sexual dysfunction. In addition, there's a group of particularly disturbing side effects (*extrapyramidal side effects*), which stem from dysfunctions of the nerve tracts that descend from the brain to the spinal motor neurons. Extrapyramidal side effects resemble the symptoms of Parkinson's disease, including *acute dystonia* (involuntary muscle contraction / muscular rigidity), *tardive dyskinesia* (an abnormal motion of voluntary and involuntary muscles), producing chewing movements and other movements of the lips, fingers and legs; together these cause arching of the back and a twisted neck and body posture, affecting about 20 per cent of those taking phenothizines over an extended period (APA, 2000), and *akathisia* (an inability to remain still; people pace and fidget constantly). These symptoms can be treated by drugs used with patients who have Parkinson's disease. In *neuroleptic malignant syndrome*, which can be fatal, severe muscular rigidity is accompanied by fever; the heart races, blood pressure increases, and the patient may lapse into a coma. This affects about 1 per cent of cases.

- Because of these side effects, about half the patients taking the whole range of antipsychotics stop taking them after a year, and up to 75 per cent after two years. For this reason, patients are often treated with long-lasting antipsychotics (such as fluphenazine decanoate, Proloxin); these are injected every two to six weeks (Davison *et al.*, 2004). The longer an individual has been taking phenothiazines, the less likely any side effects are to disappear – even after the drug is discontinued (Bennett, 2006).

- Because of all these side effects, psychiatrists face a dilemma: if medication is kept to a minimum (in order to reduce the side effects), the chances of relapse are increased. But the higher the dose, the greater the chances of serious, untreatable side effects developing.

Newer drug therapies

Clozapine (Clozaril), an *atypical neuroleptic*, can produce therapeutic gains in schizophrenic patients who don't respond well to traditional antipsychotics (Kane *et al.*, 1988, in Davison *et al.*, 2004), and it has proven more effective in reducing positive symptoms than traditional antipsychotics. It also has the advantage of reducing negative symptoms (Bennett, 2006; Frude, 1998). Patients on clozapine are also less likely to drop out of treatment (Kane *et al.*, 2001, in Davison *et al.*, 2004) and maintenance of discharged patients reduces relapse rates. Although the precise biochemical mechanisms of clozapine's therapeutic effects are unknown, we do know that it has a major impact on serotonin receptors (Davison *et al.*, 2004).

Although clozapine also produces fewer motor side-effects, those it does produce are serious. *Agranulocytosis* involves an impairment to the functioning of the immune system in 1–2 per cent of patients by lowering the number of white blood cells, making patients more susceptible to infection and even death (Bennett, 2006). Other side effects include seizures, dizziness, fatigue, drooling and weight gain. Patients must be carefully monitored through regular blood tests.

On the back of the success of clozapine, research has produced *olanzapine* (Zyprexa) and *risperidone* (Risperdal). Both produce fewer motor side effects than traditional antipsychotics, they appear to be as effective in reducing positive symptoms (perhaps even better), and are superior in reducing rehospitalisation rates. Risperidone also reduces negative symptoms (Wilson *et al.*, 1996). It appears to improve short-term memory, which is correlated with improvements in learning social skills in psychosocial rehabilitation programmes (Davison *et al.*, 2004). This is a good illustration of how biological and psychological therapies can *complement* each other – in this case, through the effects of drugs on the patient's cognitive abilities.

Electroconvulsive therapy (ECT) and psychosurgery

According to Davison *et al.* (2004), the general warehousing of patients in mental hospitals in the early

ECT was also used with schizophrenic patients after its development by Cerletti and Bini in 1938. A meta-analysis ('study of studies') by Tharyan (2002, in Bennett, 2006) concluded that about half those treated with ECT showed short-term improvements in overall level of functioning compared with those given a 'dummy' shock. But this effect didn't last, and ECT is less effective than antipsychotic medication; even combining the two treatments is only beneficial in the short term and only one in every five to six people appears to benefit. For these reasons,

> ECT in the treatment of schizophrenia has largely been curtailed, with an increased emphasis on medication and psychosocial treatments. However, some have still advocated its use when other treatments have proven unsuccessful (Tharyan and Adams, 2005) (Bennett, 2006).

In 1935, Moniz, a Portuguese psychiatrist, introduced the *prefrontal lobotomy*, a surgical procedure that destroys the nerve tracts connecting the frontal lobes to lower brain centres. His initial reports claimed high success rates (Moniz, 1936), and until the mid-1950s thousands of psychiatric patients – not just those diagnosed with schizophrenia – underwent one or other kind of psychosurgery. One of the main reasons for its demise was the introduction of antipsychotic drugs.

Psychological therapies
Psychodynamic approaches

Like Kraepelin, Freud saw schizophrenia as an organic problem, rather than as primarily a psychological one; he renounced the idea of using psychoanalysis with psychotics in general. He considered schizophrenics incapable of establishing the close interpersonal relationship necessary for psychoanalysis to proceed,

---

Synoptic Material

Davison *et al.* (2004) quote Kopelowicz and Liberman (1998), who claim that:

> *For veteran practitioners who have long considered only biological treatments as effective ... evidence that supports the protective value of psychosocial treatments ... may serve as an antidote to the insidious biological reductionism that often characterises the field of schizophrenia research and treatment ...*

How Science Works
Practical Learning Activity 7.5

- What do you understand by the term 'biological reductionism'?
- Put into your own words what Kopelowicz and Liberman are saying.
- What other kinds of reductionism are there?
- Give some other examples of reductionism from within psychology.

(See Gross, 2005.)

1900s, combined with the shortage of trained staff, created a climate that allowed experimentation with radical biological interventions. In the early 1930s, Sakel introduced the practice of inducing a coma with large doses of insulin. This presented serious risks to health, including irreversible coma and death, and the treatment was gradually abandoned.

Evaluation of drug therapies

According to Davison *et al.* (2004):

> *Antipsychotic drugs are an indispensable part of treatment for schizophrenia and will undoubtedly continue to be an important component. They are surely preferable to the straitjackets formerly used to restrain patients. Furthermore, the recent success of clozapine, olanzapine, and risperidone has stimulated a continued effort to find new and more effective drug therapies ...*

However, some critics have described antipsychotics as 'pharmacological straitjackets'. Also, Davison *et al.* argue that the continuing improvement in antipsychotic medications shouldn't lead us to neglect the importance of psychosocial factors in the efforts to control schizophrenia.

and he did little, either in his clinical practice or through his writing, to adapt his therapy to the treatment of people with schizophrenia.

However, Harry Stack Sullivan, an American psychiatrist, pioneered the use of psychoanalysis with hospitalised schizophrenic patients. In 1923, he established a ward dedicated to psychoanalytic treatment of young, recent-onset patients. In Sullivan's view, schizophrenia reflects a return to early childhood forms of communication. The individual with schizophrenia has a fragile ego, and, unable to handle the extreme stress of interpersonal challenges, s/he *regresses*. So their current difficulties in living and 'personality warps' are the lasting remains of earlier unsatisfactory personal experiences and social relationships. The schizophrenic person uses language in a defensive way, rather than as a positive means of communication; their speech (or lack of it) serves to keep people at a distance, thereby protecting their low self-esteem.

The chief barrier to communicating with such people is their anxiety; one of the therapist's main tasks, therefore, is to avoid inducing unnecessary anxiety in the patient. Therapy requires the patient to learn adult forms of communication and to achieve insight into the role the past has played in current problems. Sullivan's treatment approach involved examining the individual's life history, and the historical roots and current consequences of his/her maladaptive interpersonal patterns (as displayed in the relationship with the therapist and in everyday life). Based on his belief that these individuals had a basic mistrust of others – longing for close relationships but at the same time being terrified of them – Sullivan recommended the very gradual nonthreatening development of a trusting relationship. For example, the therapist should sit to one side of the patient, in order not to force eye contact (which he considered too threatening in the early stages of treatment). After many sessions, as the patient gains greater trust of the therapist, s/he is encouraged to examine his/her interpersonal relationships.

A similar approach was adopted by Frieda Fromm-Reichmann (1952), who worked for a time with Sullivan after emigrating from Germany.

How effective are psychodynamic approaches?

Sullivan's approach was important because it encouraged the psychological treatment of people with schizophrenia. Although great claims were made for the success of the analyses carried out by Sullivan and

Fromm-Reichmann, it seems that many of their patients were only mildly disturbed and might not even have been diagnosed as schizophrenic by DSM-IV-TR criteria (Davison *et al.*, 2004).

According to Roth and Fonagy (2005), there are few well-controlled studies of individual psychodynamic psychotherapy with schizophrenic patients. They cite one comparison which showed that psychodynamic therapy confers no additional benefit when combined with medication, and is less effective than medication when those receiving therapy alone are compared with those receiving medication alone.

Roth and Fonagy conclude that, on the whole, research into the effectiveness of expressive, insight-orientated psychotherapy tends to be largely negative; indeed, the emotional intensity of psychodynamic treatments may be harmful for at least some patients (at least during the more acute phase of a psychotic episode). Such treatment may, by its nature, simply be too intensive and intrusive for some of these patients to handle. Supportive therapy, in which the patient receives help in coping with problems of everyday life, has been shown to be significantly more helpful, particularly on measures such as relapse rate and the number of days spent in work. However,

> Although formal psychotherapy may not be judged appropriate, there is some suggestion that the development of a good therapeutic alliance between clinician and patient promotes better compliance with medication … and may be a helpful adjunct to treatment (Roth and Fonagy, 2005).

More recent *psychosocial* interventions take a more active, present-focused and reality-orientated approach; therapists try to help patients and their families deal more directly with the everyday problems they face in coping with this disruptive and debilitating illness. This approach is based on the assumption that much of the stress experienced by people with schizophrenia is due to their difficulties in negotiating everyday social challenges, including the pressures that arise in the family after they leave hospital (Davison *et al.*, 2004). These newer and more effective approaches include (a) *social skills training* (SST).

Social skills training (SST)

SST is designed to teach people with schizophrenia how to succeed in a wide variety of interpersonal situations, including discussing medication with their psychiatrist, ordering meals in a restaurant, filling out job application forms and interview skills ('vocational rehabilitation'), saying no to offers of drugs for the stress, learning about safer sex, and reading bus timetables. People with schizophrenia are seriously challenged by all of these and must work hard to (re-acquire them); doing so enhances the quality of their lives outside institutional settings (Davison et al., 2004).

How effective is SST?

Evidence suggests that severely disturbed patients can be taught new social behaviour that helps them function better – fewer relapses, better social functioning and better quality of life (Kopelowicz et al., 2002, in Davison et al., 2004). Some studies demonstrate benefits lasting for up to two years following treatment. But others indicate that even if training leads to improvements within the context in which training takes place, these fail to generalise over a longer time span and to community ('real life') settings (e.g. Emmelkamp, 1994, in Roth and Fonagy, 2005).

Even when deliberate attempts are made to help patients generalise their skills to community settings, SST has a very modest impact. Offered on its own, SST doesn't appear to have significant benefits (Roth and Fonagy, 2005). But today it's usually a component of treatments that go beyond the use of medications alone, including *family therapies* for lowering expressed emotion (Davison et al., 2004).

Cognitive-behavioural therapy (CBT)

It was once believed that it was futile to try to change the cognitive distortions of patients with schizophrenia. However, early attempts to change the *behaviour* of these patients, using behaviour modification techniques (such as the token economy: see Gross, 2005), exposure and distraction, gradually gave way to cognitive-behavioural approaches. Although these vary in their emphasis and, to some degree, rationale, all interventions have the primary aim of modifying hallucinations and delusional beliefs (Roth and Fonagy, 2005). In fact, two major CBT approaches involving schizophrenic patients can be identified: one is broadly referred to as *stress management* (Bennett, 2006) and is related to 'personal therapy'; the other, *belief modification* or *reattribution therapy*, is directly aimed at changing the patient's thinking.

Stress management (SM) and 'personal therapy'

How Science Works

Practical Learning Activity 7.6

- Remind yourself of what's involved in *stress management* (see Gross and Rolls, 2008).
- How do you think stress management might be of benefit to patients with schizophrenia? (That is, what specific techniques/coping mechanisms might be of most value and how might they work?)
- Remind yourself of what's involved in *rational-emotive behaviour therapy* (REBT; Ellis, 1973). (Again, see Gross and Rolls, 2008.)

SM approaches involve a detailed evaluation of the problems and experiences an individual is having, their triggers and consequences, and any strategies s/he may use to cope with them. Once the problems have been identified, the therapist and patient (client) work together to develop specific strategies to help the client cope more effectively with them. Potential strategies include cognitive techniques such as (a) distraction from intrusive thoughts or challenging their meaning; (b) increasing or decreasing social activity as a means of distraction from intrusive thoughts or low mood; and (c) using breathing or other relaxation techniques to help the client to relax (Bennett, 2006).

'Personal therapy' is a broad-based cognitive-behavioural approach to the multiplicity of problems faced by discharged schizophrenic patients. This individualistic therapy takes place both one-to-one and in small groups. A key element (derived from family therapy studies) is teaching patients how to recognise inappropriate affect; if ignored, this can build up and produce cognitive distortions and inappropriate social behaviour. Patients are also taught to notice small signs of relapse, such as social withdrawal or inappropriate threats against others. If left unchecked, such behaviours are likely to interfere with the patient's efforts to live by conventional social rules, including keeping a job and making and maintaining relationships.

Personal therapy also includes some *rational-emotive behaviour therapy* (Ellis, 1973), designed to help patients avoid turning life's inevitable frustrations and challenges into catastrophes; this, in turn, helps them to reduce their stress levels (see Gross and Rolls, 2008). Muscle-relaxation techniques help the patient to detect the gradual build-up of anxiety or anger, and then to apply the relaxation skills to help control these emotions. They're taught that emotional volatility (or dysregulation) is part of the biological diathesis (or predisposition) in schizophrenia, which they must learn to live with. Patients are also encouraged to continue taking their medication in a maintenance mode (see above).

So the goal of personal therapy is teaching the patient internal coping skills, new ways of thinking about and controlling his/her own emotional reactions to whatever challenges the environment presents.

How effective is SM?

SM has been used both with people who are at particularly high risk of a first episode of schizophrenia and with those who've already experienced an acute schizophrenic episode (chronic patients). In an attempt to prevent high-risk people from having their first episode, McGorry *et al.* (2002, in Bennett, 2006) randomly allocated such individuals to either (a) a needs-based intervention (supportive psychotherapy focusing on social, work or family issues), or (b) low-dose risperidone therapy combined with CBT (called a specific preventive intervention). Each intervention lasted for six months. By the end of treatment, 36 per cent of people in (a) had a first-episode psychosis compared with just 10 per cent of those in (b).

Other studies have evaluated interventions designed to promote recovery *following* an acute schizophrenic episode. For example, Tarrier *et al.* (2000, in Bennett, 2006) assigned individuals to either drug therapy alone, or in combination with SM or supportive counselling. The SM intervention involved twenty sessions in ten weeks, followed by four booster sessions over the following year. By the end of the first phase of treatment, those receiving SM showed a greater improvement than those in the counselling group; those receiving drugs showed only a slight deterioration. One-third of those receiving SM achieved a 50 per cent reduction in psychotic experiences (compared with 15 per cent of those in the counselling group); the percentages free of all positive symptoms were 15 and 7 respectively. None of those in the drugs-only group achieved this. One year later, there remained signifi-

cant differences between the three groups, favouring those in the SM group. Similar results came from a study by Startup *et al.* (2005, in Bennett). However, by the two-year follow-up, the SM group's advantage in Tarrier *et al.*'s study had vanished (although both this and the counselling group were still better off than the drugs-only group).

How effective is CBT as a whole?

In chronic patients, CBT doesn't reduce the likelihood of relapse or readmission, but it does produce significant improvement in mental state, more so on delusions than hallucinations. In more acute patients, the evidence is mixed regarding CBT's capacity to shorten initial episodes or improve specific symptoms; there's no indication that it reduces relapse rates. According to Roth and Fonagy (2005):

> *Overall, it seems reasonable to conclude that though expectations of improvement should be modest, CBT can make an important contribution to patients' quality of life and mental state. Its long-term effects are unclear . . . though some individual studies suggest an incubation effect . . .*

In other words, it may take a good while for the beneficial effects to appear. Roth and Fonagy also note that some forms of CBT can have adverse effects, especially for more vulnerable individuals.

DEPRESSION

Mood (affective) disorders

Depression is one of the *mood* (or *affective*) *disorders*. These involve a prolonged and fundamental disturbance of mood and emotions. When depression (major depressive disorder) occurs on its own, it's referred to as *unipolar disorder*. Mania (manic disorder) usually occurs in conjunction with depression (when it's called *bipolar disorder*), but in the rare cases in which mania occurs alone, 'bipolar' is also used. Most patients with mania eventually develop a depressive disorder (Gelder *et al.*, 1999). Strictly, mania on its own, and mixed episodes of both mania and depression, are called 'Bipolar 1'. 'Bipolar 2' refers to major depression combined with *hypomania* (less extreme than full-blown mania).

Mania is a sense of intense euphoria or elation. A characteristic symptom is a 'flight of ideas': ideas come rushing into the person's mind with little apparent logical connection, and there's a tendency to pun and play with words. Manics have a great deal of energy and rush around, usually achieving little and not putting their energies to good use. They need very little sleep, may appear excessively conceited ('grandiose ideas' or delusions), and display *disinhibition*, which may take the form of a vastly increased sexual appetite (usually out of keeping with their 'normal' personality), or going on spending sprees and building up large debts.

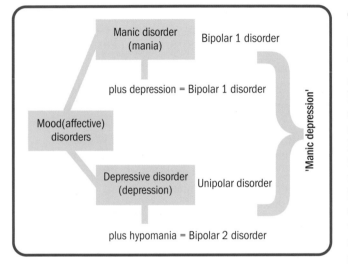

Figure 7.5 The relationship between manic and depressive disorders

'*Manic-depressive*' refers to both the unipolar and bipolar forms of affective disorder. Bipolar disorder is much less common than unipolar, occurring in fewer than 10 per 1,000, usually before age 50. Each episode lasts about three months (Gelder *et al.*, 1999). Bipolar 1 (mixed episodes of mania and depression) is more common than either Bipolar 1 (mania alone) or Bipolar 2 (depression and hypomania). It affects about 1 per cent of the population, usually first appears in the twenties, and occurs equally often in men and women.

The clinical characteristics of depression

The depressed person experiences a general slowing down and loss of energy and enthusiasm for life. It may begin at any time from adolescence onwards, with the average age of onset being the late twenties. The age of onset has decreased over the past 50 years as the prevalence has increased. With treatment, each episode lasts two to three months, but six months or longer if untreated. It affects 20 to 30 men per 1,000, but 40 to 90 women per 1,000 (see Box 7.4, page 313). One exception to this general rule is that Jewish men and women are about equally likely to be diagnosed with depression. Jewish men are also more likely to be diagnosed with depression than other male groups (Levav *et al.*, 1997). About 10 per cent of patients eventually commit suicide (Gelder *et al.*, 1999).

- Sad, depressed mood, most of the day, nearly every day for two weeks, or loss of interest and pleasure in usual activities

plus
At least four of the following:

- Difficulties in sleeping (insomnia); not falling asleep initially; not returning to sleep after awakening in the middle of the night, and early morning awakenings; or, in some patients, a desire to sleep a great deal of the time
- Shift in activity level, becoming either lethargic (psychomotor retardation) or agitated
- Poor appetite and weight loss, or increased appetite and weight gain
- Loss of energy, great fatigue
- Negative self-concept, self-reproach and self-blame; feelings of worthlessness and guilt
- Complaints or evidence of difficulty in concentrating, such as slowed thinking and indecisiveness
- Recurrent thoughts of death or suicide

Table 7.6: DSM-IV-TR Criteria for depression (major depressive disorder)

According to Davison and Neale (2001), there's no question that these are the major symptoms of depression. What's controversial is whether a patient with five symptoms for a two-week duration is distinctly different from one who, say, has only three for ten days. If one twin has been diagnosed with depression, a co-twin with fewer than five symptoms for less than two weeks is also likely to be diagnosed with depression. Also, such patients are likely to have recurrences (Kendler and Gardner, 1998). Davison and Neale argue that these findings show that 'depression seems to exist on a continuum of severity, and the DSM diagnostic criteria identify patients at a relatively severe end of the continuum'.

Are there different kinds of depression?

An important distinction is made between *major depressive disorder* (or 'clinical depression') and *dysthymic disorder* (or 'chronic depression'). The difference is in the duration, type and number of symptoms. Patients who meet the DSM-IV-TR criteria for dysthymic disorder have three or more symptoms (instead of five required for a diagnosis of major depressive disorder), including depressed mood but *not* suicidal thoughts, and cannot be without these symptoms for more than two months (see Table 7.6).

According to Claridge and Davis (2003), mood disorders and anxiety disorders have much in common.

- They occur much more frequently than other (types of) disorder.

- Their symptoms are much more continuous with normal personality.

- There's considerable symptom overlap between them (such as a focus on negative and threatening events and stimuli). It's even been proposed that there should be a new DSM category, namely 'Mixed Anxiety-Depression' (MAD). Many patients with severe psychological impairment don't necessarily meet the full diagnostic criteria for either anxiety or depressive disorder.

- According to DSM, 80–90 per cent of depressed patients have symptoms associated with anxiety disorders (such as poor concentration, sleep disturbance, loss of energy, irritability, health worries and panic attacks). Conversely, 'depressed mood' is an associated feature of all anxiety disorders.

- Stress is an important causal factor in both, as well as a consequence of both.

The idea that 'depression' may actually comprise a cluster of loosely connected, distinct disorders has been around since the early 1900s. Claridge and Davis claim there are at least two quite distinct forms of depression.

1. *Melancholic type*, characterised by profound anhedonia (the inability to find pleasure in life), associated with apathy, inactivity, excessive sleeping and severely depressed mood. They can't feel better even temporarily when something good happens.

2. *Agitated type*, characterised by difficulty in recovering from emotionally stressful events, and obvious signs of anxiety and restlessness.

Endogenous versus exogenous depression

A distinction deeply embedded within psychiatric thinking is that between *endogenous* ('from the inside') and *reactive* (or 'exogenous', from the outside) depression.

- Endogenous referred to depression arising from biochemical disturbances in the brain. Reactive was seen as being caused by stressful life experiences. These were also classified as psychotic and neurotic depression respectively, implying that the former is much more serious.

- But the distinction is controversial. According to Gelder *et al*. (1999), both types of cause are present in every case, and there appears to be a continuum of severity (as opposed to distinct patterns; see above). Champion (2000) believes that endogenous depression can no longer be defined in terms of the absence of external causes, but by the *presence* of more severe symptoms.

The heterogeneity of mood disorders

As with schizophrenia, people with the same unipolar (or bipolar) diagnosis can vary greatly from one another. For example, some bipolar patients experience the full range of symptoms of both mania and depression almost every day (a *mixed episode*). Others have symptoms of only one or the other during any one episode (Davison and Neale, 2001).

Some depressed patients may be diagnosed as having psychotic features if they're prone to delusions and

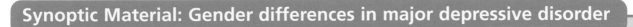
Synoptic Material: Gender differences in major depressive disorder

In England, a woman is about 40 per cent more likely to be admitted to a psychiatric hospital than a man. However, as in other countries, rates of hospitalisation rise rapidly among the elderly, and women outnumber men by two to one in the elderly population (75 and over). When admission rates for other categories of disorder are taken into account (such as the very similar rates between males and females for schizophrenia), it's depression that contributes most to the high overall rate of treated mental illness among women (Cochrane, 1995). There are no sex differences in the rate of bipolar disorder (Strickland, 1992). But (as we saw above) women are two to three times more likely to be diagnosed with unipolar disorder than men (Williams and Hargreaves, 1995).

Box 7.4: Are women naturally disposed towards depression?

- A popular and widely held view is that women are naturally more emotional than men, and so are more vulnerable to emotional upsets. Hormonal fluctuations associated with the menstrual cycle, childbirth, the menopause and oral contraceptives have all been proposed as the mechanism that might account for the sex difference (Cochrane, 1995). Cochrane believes that there's no evidence that biochemical or physiological changes involved in the menopause, for example, have any direct effect on psychological functioning. The hormonal changes of the menstrual cycle may not be sufficient on their own to cause clinical depression. But they may tend to reactivate memories and feelings from a previous period of major depression (caused by other factors) (Williams and Hargreaves, 1995).

- According to Callaghan and O'Carroll (1993), some studies suggest that one in ten women who've just given birth is sufficiently depressed to need medical or psychological help (*mood disorder with post-partum onset / post-natal depression*). But no specific causal hormonal abnormality has been identified. Social factors may be just as important as physical ones, such as her adjustment to a new role and the attention being diverted from her to the baby.

- Hormonal changes cannot explain why the discrepancy in the female/male rates of depression is so large or why only *some* women are affected. One study found that when women who've recently given birth were compared with a sample of non-pregnant women of the same age, depression rates were very similar (8.7 and 9.9 per cent, respectively) (Cooper *et al.*, 1988, in Cochrane, 1995). Not only does the risk of depression *not* increase following childbirth, it seems to be good for you!

- Cochrane identifies a number of *non-biological explanations* of women's greater susceptibility to depression:

  (a) Girls are very much more likely to be abused, particularly sexually, than boys, and victims of abuse are at least twice as likely to suffer clinical depression in adulthood as non-victims. Abuse alone could account for the female/male difference in depression.

  (b) A woman's acceptance of the traditional female gender role involves accepting that she'll have relatively little control over her life. This may contribute to *learned helplessness,* which has been used to account for the development of depression (see text below and final bullet).

  (c) The female/male difference in the rate of depression is at its greatest between the ages of 20 and 50. Most women will experience marriage, childbearing, motherhood and the 'empty-nest' syndrome during these years. Being a full-time mother (especially of young children) and wife, and not having paid employment outside the home, are increasingly being seen as risk factors

313

for depression. This is especially true if they lack an intimate, confiding relationship (Brown and Harris, 1978).

(d) Cochrane (1983) argues that depression may be seen as a coping strategy that's available to women. This contrasts with those of men (such as alcohol, drugs and their work). It's more acceptable for women to admit to psychological symptoms, which may represent a means of changing an intolerable situation. But Callaghan and O'Carroll (1993) warn that 'Unhappiness about their domestic, social, and political circumstances lies at the root of many women's concerns. This unhappiness must not be medicalized and regarded as a "female malady".'

● Ussher (2000) cites the observation that women are more likely to attribute problems to internal, stable and global factors. In other words, they tend to blame their own shortcomings, which they see as permanent and general, for the things that go wrong in their lives (see the discussion of attribution theory in text below).

hallucinations. The presence of delusions seems to be a useful distinction among people with unipolar depression (and this was seen as a characteristic of endogenous depression; see above). Such patients don't respond well to the usual antidepressants. But they do respond favourably to a combination of antidepressants and antipsychotics. This is more severe than depression without delusions, and involves more social impairment and less time between episodes (Coryell *et al.*, 1994).

According to DSM, both bipolar and unipolar can be sub-diagnosed as *seasonal* if there's a regular relationship between an episode and a particular time of the year.

Explanations of depression

Specification Hint

The specification states: 'Biological (for example, genetics, biochemistry) and psychological (for example, behavioural, cognitive, psychodynamic, and socio-cultural) explanations'. As with schizophrenia, you only need to know about ONE explanation of each type. Again, as with schizophrenia, different biological and psychological explanations are overlapping, and it's useful for analysis and evaluation (AO2) to be familiar with more than one. Box 7.4 indicates some of the major (kinds of) explanation; although this was looking specifically at gender differences in depression, the points raised can be used for AO2 analysis and evaluation.

Biological explanations

The role of genetic factors

First degree relatives (parents, siblings and children) of severely depressed patients have a higher risk of affective disorders (10–15 per cent) than the general population (1–2 per cent). This increased risk is even higher among relatives of patients with early onset. But curiously, among first degree relatives of patients with bipolar disorder there are more cases of major (unipolar) depressive disorder than bipolar disorder (Davison and Neale, 2001).

Concordance for bipolar disorder (about 70 per cent) is the same among MZs reared together or apart. This compares with 23 per cent for DZs. Adoption studies confirm the importance of genetic factors. The natural parents of adoptees with a bipolar disorder have a higher rate of affective disorder than do natural parents of adoptees without bipolar disorder (Gelder *et al.*, 1999). Genetic factors in unipolar (depressive) disorder seem to be less decisive than in bipolar disorder. Also, there's some evidence that genetic factors are more important in women than in men (Davison and Neale, 2001; but see Box 7.4, above).

Neurochemical explanations

The monoamine hypothesis

Serotonin (5-HT), norepinephrine (noradrenaline) and dopamine are collectively known as *monoamine oxidase* (MAO) *transmitters*. By far the most studied of these is 5-HT (Claridge and Davis, 2003). According to the *monoamine hypothesis* (MAOH), a depletion of serotonin, noradrenaline and/or dopamine underlies the melancholic symptoms of depression. High levels induce mania.

The supporting evidence is based largely on working backwards from what's known about the mechanisms of drugs that either induce or reduce depressive symptoms. It was discovered in the mid-1950s that depression was a common side effect of one of the first effective drugs for treating high blood pressure (reserpine). It was known that reserpine reduced the levels of brain 5-HIAA (a chemical produced when 5-HT is broken down). Also in the 1950s, tricyclics and monoamine oxidase inhibitors (MAOIs) were found to be effective in relieving depression. *Tricyclics* prevent some of the reuptake of both noradrenaline and serotonin (see Box 7.2). This leaves more of the transmitter in the synaptic gap, making transmission of the next nerve impulse easier.

The newest antidepressants are called *serotonin reup-take inhibitors* (SRIs), because they act more selectively on serotonin. (This is why they're sometimes called SSRIs – *specific serotonin reuptake inhibitors*.) They raise levels of serotonin (5-HT) and have a well-established antidepressant effect. Examples include fluoxetine (most familiarly marketed as Prozac). Because SRIs are effective in treating unipolar depressive disorder, a stronger link has been established between low levels of 5-HT and depression (Gelder *et al.,* 1999; Davison and Neale, 2001).

MAOIs prevent the enzyme monoamine oxidase (MAO) from breaking down the neurotransmitters (see Box 7.2). This increases the levels of both 5-HT and noradrenaline in the brain. Like the tricyclics, this compensates for the abnormally low levels of these in depressed people.

Evaluation of the MAOH

✔ **Theoretical importance:** the MAOH is the longest-standing and most persistent biological theory of depression (Claridge and Davis, 2003).

✗ **The delayed benefits of antidepressants:** it's known that all the main antidepressants have an immediate effect on the levels of 5-HT and noradrenaline in the brain. But it sometimes takes up to seven to fourteen days for them to have any noticeable effect on patients' symptoms. It seems that, by the time the drugs begin to 'work', the neurotransmitter levels have returned to their previous state. So, a simple increase in neurotransmitter levels isn't a sufficient explanation for why the drugs alleviate depression (Davison and Neale, 2001).

✔/✗ **Indirect support:** an indirect way of testing the role of 5-HT is to measure concentrations of a particular *metabolite.* This is a by-product of the breakdown of the neurotransmitters found in urine, blood serum and cerebro-spinal fluid (CSF). These are found to be lower in patients with depression, especially in those who commit violent suicide (Claridge and Davis, 2003). But this could be the result of many different kinds of biochemical abnormality. Also, the lower concentrations probably aren't a direct indication of levels of either 5-HT or noradrenaline *in the brain*. Metabolites measured this way could reflect neurotransmitters anywhere in the body (Davison and Neale, 2001).

✗ **Lack of support from more direct measures:** a more direct test comes from experimental depletion studies involving normal participants. When they're given drugs that reduce levels of 5-HT and noradrenaline in the brain, these people *don't* usually experience depressive symptoms (Claridge and Davis, 2003). Nor do the symptoms of unmedicated depressed patients become worse (Delgado, 2000).

Psychological explanations

Cognitive explanations

Beck's theory of depression

Beck's (1967, 1987) central idea is that depressed individuals feel as they do because their thinking is dominated by *negative schemas*. This is a tendency to see the world negatively, which is triggered whenever the person encounters new conditions that resemble in some way the conditions in which the schemas were originally learned (usually in childhood and adolescence).

These negative schemas fuel and are fuelled by certain cognitive biases, which cause the person to misperceive reality. So (a) an *ineptness schema* can make depressed people expect to fail most of the time; (b) a *self-blame schema* makes them feel responsible for all misfortunes; and (c) a *negative self-evaluation schema* constantly reminds them of their worthlessness. The main specific cognitive biases are described in Box 7.5.

Negative schemas, together with cognitive biases or distortions, maintain the *negative triad*. This refers to negative thoughts about the self, the world and the future.

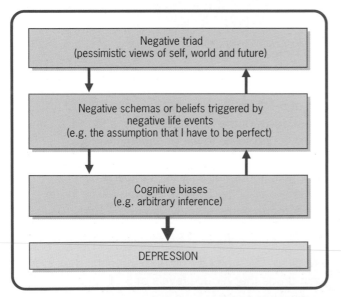

Figure 7.6 *The interrelationship among different kinds of cognitions in Beck's theory of depression*

Box 7.5: The main cognitive biases in Beck's theory of depression

- *Arbitrary inference:* a conclusion drawn in the absence of sufficient evidence – or any evidence at all. For example, a man concludes that he's worthless because it's raining the day he's hosting an outdoor party.
- *Selective abstraction:* a conclusion drawn on the basis of just one of many elements in a situation. For example, a worker feels worthless when a product doesn't work, even though she's only one of several people who contributed to making it.
- *Overgeneralisation:* an overall sweeping conclusion drawn on the basis of a single, perhaps trivial, event. For example, a student regards his poor performance in a single class on one particular day as final proof of his worthlessness and stupidity.
- *Magnification and minimisation:* exaggerations in evaluation performance. For example, a man believes that he's completely ruined his car (*magnification*) when he sees a small scratch on the rear bumper. A woman believes herself to be worthless (*minimisation*) despite a succession of praiseworthy achievements.

Source: based on Davison and Neale (2001)

Evaluation of Beck's theory

✔**Major cognitive theory:** it's widely agreed that Beck's theory has been the most influential of the cognitive models of depression (that is, the view that depression is caused by how people *think*) (Champion, 2000).

✔**More general theoretical influence:** Freud saw people as victims of their passions. The id is the dominant part of the personality, and the ego is able to exert little control over our feelings (see Gross and Rolls, 2008). But, in Beck's theory, the cause–effect relationship is *reversed*. Our emotional reactions are essentially a function of how we *construe* the world (interpret and predict it). Depressed people see themselves as victims, and Beck sees them as victims of their own illogical self-judgements.

✔**Do depressed people really think as Beck maintains?** The evidence initially came from Beck's clinical observations (Beck, 1967). Further support comes from various sources, including self-report questionnaires, and laboratory studies of memory and other cognitive processes (Davison and Neale, 2001).

✔/✘ **What's cause and what's effect?** Perhaps the greatest challenge facing any cognitive theory of depression is to show that depressed people's thoughts are the *cause* of their depression rather than the effect. Many experimental studies have shown that a person's mood can be influenced by how s/he construes events. But manipulating people's affect (mood or feeling) has also been shown to change their thinking. Beck (and others) have found that depression and certain kinds of thinking are *correlated.* But a specific causal relationship cannot be determined from such data (as with all correlations; see Gross and Rolls, 2008). Probably the relationship works *both* ways. In recent years, Beck himself has come to this more *bidirectional* position. There's certainly no unequivocal support for the claim that negative thinking causes depression (Davison and Neale, 2001).

✔/✘ **How to measure cognition?** Recently, researchers have recognised that the measure of cognition most widely used in Beck's theory (the Dysfunctional Attitudes Scale) is *multidimensional*. That is, it comprises subscales that assess different aspects of dysfunctional attitudes (such as a strong need to impress others and a desire to be perfect). These more specific components of dysfunctional thinking may have more success in predicting the subsequent occurrence of depression when they interact with a stressor that's specific to them – for example, a personal failure in someone with a strong need to be perfect (Davison and Neale, 2001).

✔**Important influence on therapy:** Beck's theory has stimulated considerable research into the treatment of depression. The form of therapy based on cognitive theories in general is called *cognitive behaviour therapy* (CBT; see above). Evidence concerning the effectiveness of Beck's form of CBT can be taken as (indirect) support for the theory it's based on. Beck (1993) reviewed its effectiveness in treating unipolar depressive disorder (for which it was originally designed), as well as generalised anxiety disorder, panic disorder and eating disorders. These *outcome studies* show very clearly that CBT is very highly effective. CBT is also being used to treat bipolar disorder, obsessive-compulsive disorder, as well as patients with HIV and cancer. (See the section on therapies, below.)

Learned helplessness theory (LHT)

Strictly, learned helplessness theory (LHT) is the original of three related cognitive theories of depression. (Only two will be discussed here.) The basic premise of LHT is that depression in humans is a form of *learned* helplessness (LH) (Seligman, 1974). This is based on Seligman's experiments with dogs.

Dogs were given inescapable electric shocks. Soon after receiving the first shocks, the dogs seemed to give up and passively accept the painful stimulation. Later, even though the shocks could now be avoided, the dogs stopped trying. Most of them lay down in a corner and whined. A control group, which hadn't received the inescapable shocks, learned the avoidance response relatively easily.

On the basis of these observations, Seligman proposed that animals acquire a sense of helplessness when confronted with uncontrollable aversive stimulation. Later, this sense of helplessness impairs their performance in stressful situations that *can* be controlled. They seem to lose the ability and motivation to respond effectively to painful stimulation. By extension, LH could provide an explanation for at least certain forms of depression in humans. Seligman believed that, like his dogs, many depressed people appear passive when faced with stress. They fail to initiate actions that might allow them to cope. Also like depressed people, Seligman's dogs lost their appetite and lost weight. They also showed reduced levels of noradrenaline.

How Science Works

Practical Learning Activity 7.7

- In general terms, how valid is it to apply findings from experiments with non-humans to human behaviour?
- If your answer to the previous question includes 'It depends on the non-human species involved', how valid is it in the case of dogs?
- In this particular case, is it reasonable to generalise from the observation of LH in dogs to depression in humans?

Evaluation of the attributional theory

✔ **Theoretical value:** this clearly is an improvement on LHT, because it adds in cognitive factors that are missing from the latter. There's a vast amount of research into attribution within social psychology, so Abramson *et al.* are drawing on a well-established research area to supplement the idea of helplessness. The concept of attributional style represents a *diathesis,* a predisposition to develop a particular mental disorder under stressful conditions (see the discussion of schizophrenia above, page 300).

✔ **Empirical support:** Seligman *et al.* (1979) gave their ASQ to college students. As predicted by the theory, mildly depressed students more often attributed their failures to personal (internal), global and stable inadequacies than did non-depressed students.

✗ **Where does the depressive attributional style come from?** This is a problem faced by most cognitive explanations of psychopathology. In general terms, it's thought to stem from childhood experiences, but there's little empirical support for this claim. However, Rose *et al.* (1994) found that depressive attributional style is related to sexual abuse in childhood, as well as to parental overprotectiveness, harsh discipline and perfectionistic standards.

Evaluation of LHT

✗ **Contradictory findings:** by 1978, research with humans began to reveal several inadequacies of LHT. For example, some studies indicated that helplessness sometimes actually *improves* performance. Also, many depressed people blame themselves for their failures, but this is incompatible with the claim that they see themselves as helpless. Finally, the experience of being unable to control the outcome of one particular situation (helplessness) doesn't necessarily lead to clinical depression in most people.

✗ **There's more to depression than helplessness:** the above findings suggest very strongly that LH cannot tell the whole story. LHT was revised by Abramson, Seligman and Teasdale in 1978. The major change they proposed was in terms of *attribution theory principles.* When we experience failure, for example, we try to explain it (just as we try to account for our successes) – this is perfectly 'normal'. What's associated with depression is a particular *pattern* of attributions (or *attributional style*) – that is, a tendency to make particular kinds of *causal inferences* rather than others.

   The 'depressed attributional style' is based on three key dimensions, namely *locus* (whether the cause is internal or external, to do with the actor him/herself or some aspect of the situation), *stability* (whether the cause is stable or unstable, a permanent feature of the actor or something transient), and *global* or *specific* (whether the cause relates to the 'whole' person or just some particular feature or characteristic).

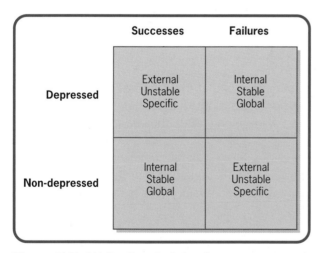

Figure 7.7 Attributional styles for success and failure in depressed people (based on Abramson et al.*, 1978; Abramson and Martin, 1981)*

The depressed person believes that his/her failure: (a) is caused by *internal* factors ('I'm stupid'); (b) reflects *stable,* long-term, relatively permanent factors ('I never do well on tests or exams'); (c) reflects a *global,* pervasive deficiency – that is, failure applies to all or most aspects of his/her life ('I get everything wrong').

   People diagnosed as clinically depressed are more likely to show this pattern when given, for example, the *Attributional Style Questionnaire* (ASQ) (Seligman *et al.,* 1979). But equally important, the person who's *prone* to becoming depressed may also display this attributional style. It's believed to play a mediating role between negative life events and adverse physical and mental health outcomes. When such depression-prone people experience stressors, they're more likely to develop the symptoms of depression, and their self-esteem is shattered (Peterson and Seligman, 1984).

Overall evaluation of helplessness theories

Davison and Neale (2001) point out some general problems with all three helplessness-related theories, as follows.

✗ **Which type of depression is being explained?** Seligman (1974) was originally trying to explain the similarity between LH and what used to be called reactive depression (see above, page 312).

✗ **Biased samples and inappropriate measures of depression:** some research has been conducted with clinical populations (people actually diagnosed as having a depressive disorder) (e.g. Abramson *et al.*, 1978). But many studies have involved college students selected on the basis of the Beck Depression Inventory (BDI) or have simply tried to predict increases in BDI scores. But the BDI wasn't designed to diagnose depression, only to assess its severity among those already diagnosed. Selecting people based on raised BDI scores doesn't produce a group of people that's comparable to those with clinical depression. For example, high scorers have been found to score much lower when re-tested two to three weeks later. Also, the finding that the ASQ can predict BDI scores doesn't necessarily mean that it can predict the onset of actual clinical depression.

✗ **Are the findings specifically about depression?** We've already noted the comorbidity of depression and anxiety. We need to be sure that the theories are truly about depression, rather than about negative affect in general. Depressive attributional style seems to be related to anxiety and general distress, as well as depression.

✗ **Is the depressive attributional style stable?** A key assumption is that the depressive attributional style is a persistent part of the make-up of the depressed person. As a diathesis, it must be 'in place' before the person experiences some stressor. But Hamilton and Abramson (1983) showed that it disappears following a depressive episode.

✔ **Stimulus for research:** despite these problems, Davison and Neale conclude that these theories have clearly stimulated a great deal of research and theorising about depression. This is likely to continue for many years to come.

Synoptic Material: The influence of culture

There are an estimated 340 million people worldwide affected by depressive disorders. This makes it the most common of all mental disorders (Lyddy, 2000). According to Price and Crapo (1999), various researchers have denied the presence of native concepts of depression among groups as diverse as the Nigerians, Chinese, Canadian Inuit (Eskimos), Japanese, Malaysians and the Hopi Native Americans. Price and Crapo ask:

> *If depression, as currently defined in Western culture and psychiatric diagnosis, is not found in non-Western cultures, how do we know that 'depression' is not merely a Western folk-concept, analogous to other culture-specific conditions, such as koro, kayak-angst, amok, or susto?*

These are all examples of *culture-bound syndromes* (CBSs). These were discussed above (see Box 7.1).

According to Kaiser *et al.* (1998), DSM-IV-TR recognises the vital role of culture in the expression and diagnosis of disorders. It encourages clinicians to keep cultural considerations in mind when assessing patients. In the section dealing with depression, conditions that appear most often in specific cultures are outlined, as well as cultural variations in the manifestation of symptoms. For example, in some cultures people tend to present with *somatic* complaints (such as aches and pains), while in others *affective* symptoms are more common (such as sadness). The task of the clinician is to take the norms of the individual patient's cultural reference group into account, while at the same time avoiding cultural stereotypes (Kaiser *et al.*, 1998).

Figure 7.8 *Amok – a culture-bound syndrome. But aren't western mental disorders also influenced by culture?*

Therapies for depression

Biological therapies

Drug therapy (chemotherapy)

We've already described the three major types of drug used to treat depression when considering the monoamine hypothesis (MAOH) above. According to Gelder *et al.* (1999), the main difference between MAOIs, tricyclics and SSRIs is in their side effects, rather than their effectiveness or speed of action. They all increase 5-HT (serotonin) function, and many also increase noradrenaline function. Most can be given just once per day, but they usually 'kick in' only after 10–14 days. They should be withdrawn slowly: sudden cessation can cause restlessness, insomnia, anxiety and nausea.

Monoamine oxidase inhibitors (MAOIs)

Iproniazid was originally used in 1952 as a treatment for tuberculosis – it elevated patients' mood (without, incidentally, affecting the disease). Iproniazid and related drugs (e.g. *phenelzine* or Nardil) inhibit the activity of an enzyme known as monoamine oxidase (MAO), and gradually increase the activity levels of neurons that utilise noradrenaline (a monoamine) and 5-HT.

How effective are MAOIs ?

These are generally less effective than tricyclics when used to treat severe depression, and no more effective for mild depression. Success rate is about 50 per cent (Bennett, 2006). They're seldom the first choice of treatment, because of their side effects (including raised blood pressure and cerebral haemorrhage); these can be caused by eating certain foods (such as cheese, bananas, pate, yeast extract (e.g. Marmite), fish that contain tyramine, and red wine) or taking other drugs (such as decongestants and tricyclic antidepressants). More recent *reversible selective* MAOIs have been developed to avoid these problems.

Tricyclics

These are so named because their basic chemical structure includes three carbon rings. *Imipramine* (Tofranil) and *amitryptyline* were the first to be introduced and are still used as a standard for comparing other antidepressants. They seem to act by blocking the reuptake of dopamine and noradrenaline, but some also block the reuptake of serotonin; others block serotonin alone, and some have no known effect on any of these systems (Hamilton and Timmons, 1995).

How effective are tricyclics?

They're effective in the treatment of both mild and severe depression, and traditionally have been the first choice of treatment in the latter; 60–65 per cent of those who take tricyclics experience some improvement in symptoms (Hirschfeld, 1999, in Bennett, 2006). However, they have many side effects, including toxic effects on the cardiovascular system. They're lethal in overdose, and so present grave dangers to suicidal patients. In addition, beneficial effects aren't usually felt for two to three weeks after the patient starts taking the drug; this delay in effectiveness can make it difficult to persuade a patient to keep taking it (Frude, 1998). It's also important to keep taking the drugs after improvements in mood have been achieved; about 50 per cent of users will relapse within a year if they're stopped prematurely (Montgomery *et al.*, 1993, in Bennett, 2006). These tricyclics are gradually being replaced by modified tricyclics (such as *lofepramine* and *trazedone*), which cause fewer side effects (Gelder *et al.*, 1999).

Specific serotonin reuptake inhibitors (SSRIs)

The 'second generation' drugs selectively inhibit the reuptake of serotonin into presynaptic neurons – that is, they make more serotonin available. Examples include *paroxetine* and *fluoxetine* (Prozac). Prozac has rapidly become the most commonly prescribed antidepressant medication (Costello *et al.*, 1995), having been taken by more than 38 million people (Boseley, 1999) since its introduction in 1988.

How effective are SSRIs?

Prozac (dubbed 'vitamin P') was marketed as a wonder drug (Munro, 2000). It produces fewer side effects than tricyclics (such as dry mouth and constipation), but its biggest selling point has been that it's almost impossible to kill yourself with an overdose. However, since its launch in 1988 in the USA (and in the UK shortly afterwards), there's been a spate of disturbing accounts of violence and suicide committed by people prescribed the drug. Victims and families of killers have sued the manufacturer (Eli Lilly) in 200 court cases (Boseley, 1999).

About 250,000 people worldwide taking Prozac have attempted suicide (because of the drug), and about 25,000 will have succeeded. Eli Lilly knew as long ago as 1979 that Prozac can produce in some people a strange, agitated state of mind that can trigger an unstoppable urge to commit murder or suicide. This is a recognised mental disorder called *akathisia*, which has long been associated with antipsychotic drugs (such as chlorpromazine; see above). But whereas antipsychotics remove the will to act on the suicidal/violent feelings, Prozac doesn't (Boseley, 1999). However, Bennett (2006) cites two studies presenting a rather different picture. A meta-analysis by Fergusson *et al.* (2005) found no evidence of any greater risk of

---

STRETCH AND CHALLENGE: The Prozac phenomenon

In January 2000, Eli Lilly's patent expired, meaning that cheap generic versions of Prozac are set to flood the international market; this will make it available to those previously unable to afford it. This is especially significant given that the World Health Organization (WHO) predicts that depression will be the leading form of ill health across the globe by 2010, with an estimated one person in three being affected (Munro, 2000). According to Munro:

Drugs like Prozac are firmly entrenched in both professional and public minds as the treatment of choice for depression. There is a growing concern that the widespread use of antidepressants is blocking the development of other forms of treatment, such as cognitive therapy. Such a trend could be exacerbated by the increased affordability of fluoxetine …

Some feel that an overemphasis on medication has grown from aggressive marketing by the drug companies. With Prozac, people for the first time were going to their doctors *asking for* antidepressants *by name.* In 1995, 13.2 million prescriptions were written for *all* types of antidepressant in the UK. In 2002, 26 million prescriptions were written for SSRIs *alone* (Dilner, 2004).

A recent survey of GPs in the UK found that 80 per cent admit they're overprescribing drugs such as Prozac (and Seroxat), when patients may simply need someone to talk to. One in three GP appointments now involves patients who are reporting depression (Frith, 2004).

suicide associated with SSRIs compared with tricyclics; similarly, Yerevanian *et al.* (2004) found that suicide rates didn't differ between SSRIs and tricyclics, and that suicide rates were higher following discontinuation of both classes of drugs than during active treatment.

Another SSRI, Seroxat, is proving at least as controversial. Seroxat is among the biggest-selling drugs in the world, taken by 600,000–800,000 people in the UK, many of them under 30 (Laurance, 2004). In 2003, Seroxat was banned in the UK for under-18s because of an increased suicide risk. The ban applied to all other SSRIs – except Prozac. According to the Seroxat

Users' Group, it's *still* being prescribed to children and under-18s despite the ban (Townsend, 2004).

Depressed people selected for clinical trials are usually only moderately depressed, not actively suicidal, as well as free from other physical and psychiatric illness (Fisher and Greenberg, 1995; Lyddy, 2000). Nevertheless, assigning a depressed person to a placebo condition when there's an effective treatment *is* ethically problematic.

Khan *et al.*'s finding that placebo-group participants reported symptom reduction isn't surprising according to Fisher and Greenberg. A response to a placebo is just

How Science Works

Practical Learning Activity 7.8

One aspect of the controversy surrounding Prozac is its use as a 'designer drug'. Kramer (1993) advocates that everyone could benefit from taking it, since it makes people more assertive and playful, and improves relationships. Kramer believes that in the near future, we'll be able to change our 'self' as easily as we change our clothes ('cosmetic psychopharmacology').

● Even if this were possible, do you think it's right?

STRETCH AND CHALLENGE: The effectiveness of antidepressants and the placebo effect

When we ask 'How effective are antidepressants?', what this usually means is: how much more effective are antidepressants than placebos ('dummy drugs', usually inert sugar pills). Fisher and Greenberg (1995) looked at 15 separate reviews of the literature relating to antidepressants, plus two large-scale meta-analyses. Overall, the effectiveness of antidepressants appears to be modest, with a high relapse rate (over 60 per cent) among those who respond positively to the drugs but are then taken off them. Their benefits also tend to wane after a few months, even while they're still being taken.

Fisher and Greenberg also discuss the *methodology* of drug trials. In a classic *double-blind design*, neither the patient nor the researchers know whether the patient is receiving a drug or a placebo. But when the (*inactive*) placebo doesn't produce as many bodily sensations as the (*active*) drug, participants soon learn to discriminate between them. For example, imipramine causes dry mouth, tremor, sweating and constipation. These side effects could be used by those administering the drug/placebo to identify the 'ons' and the 'offs', and they might convey their resulting expectations regarding the effects of the pill to the participants.

For these reasons, *active* placebos (such as atropine), which *do* produce side effects, are sometimes used. In one of the reviews cited by Fisher and Greenberg, 68 studies conducted (between 1958 and 1972) which had used an inert placebo were compared to seven using atropine. The antidepressant was found to be superior to the placebo in 59 per cent of the former, but in only 14 per cent (one study) of the latter.

How effective is ECT?

Many psychiatrists believe that for severe depression, bilateral ECT is preferable, as it acts more quickly and fewer treatments are needed. (This was the standard practice up until the 1950s.) But, as we saw above, applying an electrode to just one side of the head (the *non-dominant* – right – side for most people) doesn't prevent memory and other cognitive dysfunction altogether.

Sackeim (1989) reviewed controlled comparisons of real and *sham* (simulated or 'dummy', where the doctors 'go through the motions' but no actual electric current is passed through the patient's brain) ECT. He concluded that real ECT is significantly more effective than sham ECT. Also, bilateral is slightly more effective than unilateral. ECT is also more effective than antidepressant medication, and probably the most effective available treatment for severe depression. However, the use of medication following treatment can help prevent relapse.

Current psychiatric opinion in the UK is represented by the RCP *ECT Handbook* (1995), according to which 'ECT ... is an effective treatment in severe depressive illness'. Reviews of the research (e.g. Breggin, 1997) have generally failed to find any controlled studies showing the benefits of ECT lasting longer than four weeks. Also, the relapse rate is high.

✔ Specification Hint

The specification gives 'cognitive-behavioural therapy' as an example of a psychological therapy that you may choose to discuss in relation to your selected mental disorder. Because Beck's treatment of 'automatic thoughts' was designed specifically to help people with depression, this is the form of CBT that we've chosen to discuss here.

How Science Works
Practical Learning Activity 7.10

- Remind yourself of what's involved in *cognitive behavioural therapy* (CBT); this was discussed in relation to stress management in Gross and Rolls (2008).
- The specific form of CBT that was discussed there was self-instructional training (Meichenbaum, 1977).
- Two other major forms of CBT also discussed in Gross and Rolls are rational emotive behaviour therapy (REBT) (Ellis, 1973, 1990) and treatment of 'automatic thoughts' (Beck, 1963, 1967, 1987, 1997). These were both discussed in relation to individual differences: psychopathology (abnormality).

Psychological therapies
Cognitive-behavioural therapy
Treatment of 'automatic thoughts' (Beck, 1963, 1967, 1987)

According to Mahoney (1974) and Meichenbaum (1977), many (if not most) clinical problems are best described as disorders of thought and feeling. Since behaviour is to a large extent controlled by the way we think, the most logical and effective way of trying to change maladaptive behaviour is to change the maladaptive thinking that underlies it. Beck (1993) defines CBT as

> the application of the cognitive model of a particular disorder with the use of a variety of techniques designed to modify the dysfunctional beliefs and faulty information processing characteristic of each disorder.

CBT is derived from various sources, including behaviour therapy and psychoanalysis, which define and operationalise cognition in different ways. However, the attempt to change a person's thinking (*cognitive restructuring*) is always a means to an end, namely 'lasting changes in target emotions and behaviour' (Wessler, 1986).

Beck sees the client as a colleague of the therapist who researches verifiable reality (Wessler, 1986). For example, if a client expresses the negative thought, 'I'm a poor father because my children aren't better disciplined,' Beck would take the second part of the statement and seek factual evidence about its truth. He'd also focus on the evaluative conclusion that one is a poor father because one's children sometimes misbehave.

In these and other ways, clients are trained to distance themselves from things, to be more objective, to distinguish fact from fiction, and fact from evaluation, to see things in proportion, and not to see things in such extreme terms. By the end of treatment, typically 20 sessions, clients have learned specific techniques for changing their faulty beliefs, thereby relieving their depressed mood (Wilson *et al.*, 1996).

As well as trying to alter maladaptive thought patterns, Beck's treatment approach has a strong behavioural element (Bennett, 2006). After an initial *education phase,* in which the individual learns the relationships between cognitions, emotions and behaviour, *behavioural activation* and *pleasant event scheduling* is introduced, aimed at increasing physiological activity and engagement in social or other rewarding activities. For profoundly depressed people, this may simply involve encouraging them to get out of bed in the morning or go for walk. Cognitive factors are usually addressed only after the client has experienced some improvement in mood or energy. Once this has been achieved, they're taught to identify the faulty thinking responsible for low mood and to challenge these thoughts.

Clients are, typically, given 'homework' to do in between sessions; these assignments are aimed at providing them with goals that they can achieve, which, in turn, will help them to think good of themselves. These assignments usually involve some form of *behavioural hypothesis testing* or practice in using new coping skills. Hypothesis testing involves direct, behavioural challenges of negative thoughts. For example, someone who believes they're incapable of 'chatting up' a member of the opposite sex whom they find attractive will be asked to do just that (in a bar or at a party). But the therapist, at least, should be confident the client is capable of coping with the situation: failure will reinforce the ineptness schema, for example – the very thing the task was designed to disprove.

Because there's a significant risk of relapse in the year following the end of treatment, one or two 'booster' sessions during this period can be a useful means of preventing relapse (Bennett, 2006).

How effective is Beck's treatment of 'automatic thoughts'?

A widely cited study by Rush *et al.* (1977, in Davison *et al.*, 2004) indicates that Beck's cognitive therapy was more successful than imipramine in alleviating unipolar depression. But the unusually low rate of improvement for those taking the drug suggested that these patients may have been poorly suited for this form of treatment. However, the effectiveness of Beck's therapy in this study and in a 12-month follow-up (Kovacs *et al.*, 1981, in Davison *et al.*, 2004) encouraged many other researchers to conduct further evaluations; these confirmed its effectiveness. There's also evidence that Beck's therapy has *prophylactic* (i.e. preventative) effects.

Another widely cited study is the Treatment of Depression Collaborative Research Program (TDCRP) (Elkin *et al.*, 1989) (discussed in Key Study 7.1). This was a large, complex and expensive study, which compared the effects of Beck's cognitive therapy (CT), antidepressant medication and *interpersonal psychotherapy* (IPT). We need to say a little about IPT before we can appreciate the findings of the TDCRP.

Box 7.6: Brief psychodynamic therapy and interpersonal dynamic therapy (IPT)

According to Hoyt (2003), beginning with Freud, numerous theoreticians and clinicians have applied the psychoanalytic concepts of the unconscious, resistance and transference to brief forms of treatment. Indeed, many of Freud's cases were 'brief', just a few sessions lasting weeks or months. By contrast, in the UK, classical psychoanalysis requires the client to attend three to five sessions per week for several years (Fonagy, 2000); for many, this is far too expensive, as well as too time-consuming. Early pioneers include Alexander and French (1946) and Ferenczi (1952).

Various short-term dynamic methods have been developed to 'bring the patient to a greater awareness of his or her maladaptive defences, warded-off feelings, and counterproductive relationship patterns' (Hoyt, 2003). What they all emphasise is increased therapist activity within a limited, central focus. There may be a 'contract' for a specified number of weeks as opposed to the open-ended arrangement of classical analysis. For example, Malan's (1976) *brief focal therapy* lasts for one session per week for about 30 weeks, targeting fairly specific psychological problems (such as a single area of conflict or relationship in the client's current life). Although all the basic techniques of psychoanalysis may be used (see Gross and Rolls, 2008), there's considerably less emphasis on the client's past, and client and therapist usually sit in armchairs facing each other.

This form of therapy is practised by many clinical psychologists (as well as psychiatrists and social workers), who haven't received a full-blown psychoanalytic training (Fonagy and Higgitt, 1984; Fonagy, 1995). Fonagy (2000) cites evidence for the effectiveness of brief dynamic psychotherapy.

Interpersonal psychodynamic therapy (IPT) is a variant of brief psychodynamic therapy that stresses the interactions between a client and his/her social environment. One of the pioneers was American psychiatrist Harry Stack Sullivan, who argued that patients' basic difficulty is misperceiving reality stemming from disorganised interpersonal relationships in childhood, in particular the relationship with the parents. In contrast with Freud, for whom the analyst was a blank screen for transference, Sullivan advocated that the therapist was a 'participant observer' in the therapy process (See pages 307–308)

IPT (Klerman *et al.*, 1984) concentrates on the client's current interpersonal difficulties and on discussing – even directly teaching – better ways of relating to others. The therapist combines empathic listening with suggestions for behavioural changes and how to implement them. The core of this approach is to help the depressed person examine the ways in which his/her interpersonal behaviour might interfere with obtaining pleasure from relationships. Clients are helped to improve their communication (verbal and non-verbal) and social skills, reality testing and ability to meet their current social role obligations. The focus is on the person's current life, rather than exploring past – often repressed – causes of present-day problems.

In a review of depression treatment outcome studies (Leichsenring, 2001, in Davison *et al.*, 2004), the success rate of short-term psychodynamic treatment is comparable to that of CBT. One of the outcome studies included in this review is the Treatment of Depression Collaborative Research Program (Elkin *et al.*, 1989), which suggested that IPT is particularly effective for removing the symptoms of unipolar depression as well as for maintaining treatment gains (Frank *et al.*, 1990). (See Key Study 7.1.)

Key Study 7.1: The Treatment of Depression Collaborative Research Program (TDCRP) (Elkin *et al.*, 1989)

Aim/hypothesis (AO1)

In 1977, the US National Institute of Mental Health (NIMH) initiated the first comparison of two psychological treatments – Beck's cognitive therapy (CT) and interpersonal psychotherapy (IPT). These were compared with each other and with pharmacotherapy (the use of psychoactive drugs, in this case the antidepressant imipramine) and placebo drug intervention. This was a large, complex study, both widely cited and controversial.

Method/design (AO1)

Since Beck's CT had been designed specifically for use with depressed patients, the comparison psychological treatment also had to meet this criterion. It also had to be explicit and standardised enough to allow other therapists to be trained to use it (preferably using a manual), and it had to have been shown to be effective with depressed patients. It also needed to be quite distinct from CT. IPT met all these criteria. Imipramine was a well-tested tricyclic, widely regarded at the time as a standard treatment for depression; it was used as a reference against which to evaluate the two psychological treatments.

The placebo condition was used as a control condition against which to compare the effectiveness of imipramine, but also as a partial control for CT and IPT because of the presence of clinical management (strong support and advice). Using a *double-blind design* similar to that used in the imipramine condition, participants received a placebo that they believed might be an effective antidepressant. But they were also given much more psychological support – and even direct advice when considered necessary – than in most placebo conditions.

All treatments lasted 16 weeks (with slight differences in the number of sessions for different conditions). A total of 60 patients were randomly allocated to each of the four conditions; all were closely monitored throughout. A large number and wide range of assessments were made both before and at the end of treatment, as well as three times during treatment and again at 6-, 12- and 18-month follow-ups. Measures included some that tapped *processes* of change. For example, do IPT patients learn to relate better to others during therapy and, if so, is this improvement correlated with clinical outcome? Do CT patients display less cognitive distortion towards the end of treatment compared with the early sessions? The perspectives of the therapist, patient, an independent clinical evaluator blind to the treatment condition and, whenever possible, a significant other from the patient's life (such as a spouse), were also tapped.

Three domains of change were assessed: (i) depressive symptomatology; (ii) overall symptomatology and life functioning; and (iii) functioning related to particular treatment approaches.

Results/findings (AO1)

The results have been published in a series of reports, including Elkin *et al.* (1996).

- By the end of the 16-week treatment phases, all the interventions appeared to be equally effective. Of those in the IPT condition, 55 per cent were clinically 'improved', compared with 57 per cent in the imipramine condition, 51 per cent in the CT condition and 29 per cent in the placebo condition. (Even those in the placebo condition showed substantial improvement.)

- Imipramine worked fastest during treatment in reducing depressive symptoms. But, by 16 weeks, the two psychological therapies had caught up.

- On some measures, the less severely depressed placebo patients were doing as well after 16 weeks as similar patients in the active treatment conditions. But severely depressed patients in the placebo condition were doing less well. There was some evidence that IPT was more effective than CT with the more severely depressed patients, and CT proved significantly less effective than imipramine.

- As predicted by the rationale of the different treatments, IPT patients showed greater improvements in social functioning than CT or imipramine patients, while CT reduced certain types of dysfunctional attitudes more than the other treatments.

- At the 18-month follow-up, the active treatment conditions didn't differ significantly, and of those patients across the four conditions who'd improved markedly right at the end of treatment, only 20–30 per cent remained completely depression-free. However, IPT patients reported greater satisfaction with their treatment, and those in both IPT and CT reported significantly greater effects of treatment on their capacity to establish and maintain interpersonal relationships and to recognise and understand sources of their depression.

Conclusions and evaluation (AO1/AO2)

The findings regarding the effectiveness of CT with the most severely depressed patients caused much debate, not least because this led the American Psychiatric Association to recommend against its use with this group of patients. However, the results have been questioned from a number of perspectives (Bennett, 2006). For example, psychiatrists were puzzled by the much greater effectiveness of the placebo than is usually found, and psychologists were surprised that CT proved less effective than in earlier studies.

Jacobson and Hollon (1996) point out that the differences between the imipramine and the two psychological treatments weren't consistent across the three sites at which the study was conducted; they also claim that some of the therapists weren't sufficiently skilled. They also note that 33 per cent of the imipramine patients dropped out before the end of treatment; of the remaining 67 per cent, half hadn't recovered when treatment ended, and of those who did recover, half had relapsed within months of medication being withdrawn – far more than those in the CT condition. The use of imipramine itself is problematical, given its side effects (see text above).

It's the *long-term* results that suggest the superiority of the psychological therapies. Relapse rates following the end of treatment are often far higher for drug treatments than for CT, even when the initial treatment is successful. For example, Hollon *et al.* (2005, in Bennett, 2006) found that in the year following the end of treatment, the relapse rate for those successfully treated with CT was 31 per cent, compared with 47 per cent for those initially treated with drugs which were then replaced with a placebo, and 76 per cent for those who received neither medication nor placebo.

Given the complexity of the research, and the many claims and counter-claims (as well as different interpretations of the 'same' data), Davison *et al.* (2004) conclude that 'there is little in the many findings from this milestone study of comparative outcome [the TDCRP] that can gladden the hearts of proponents of any of the interventions'. According to Roth and Fonagy (2005), the TDCRP set a standard against which other studies can be judged.

As an overall conclusion to their review of treatments for depression, Roth and Fonagy (2005) maintain that:

while treatments for depression are effective in the short term for at least a proportion of patients, longer term impacts are limited. Given the nature of the disorder, this is a creditable achievement, but it is clear that there needs to be a focus on the most pernicious aspect of life with this disorder – the tendency to relapse. Hand in hand with this, there may be need to adopt a more complex framework for classifying depression . . . greater consideration of developmental pathways, as well as personality variables, may be relevant factors for future research to consider.*

CHAPTER

SUMMARY

The classification and diagnosis of psychological abnormality

- All systems of classification of psychological abnormality stem from the work of Kraepelin, who distinguished between **dementia praecox** (what's now called schizophrenia), caused by a chemical imbalance, and **manic-depressive psychosis** (now known as bipolar disorder), caused by a faulty metabolism.

- This classification helped to establish the **organic/somatic** nature of mental disorders. It also provided the basis of the **Diagnostic and Statistical Manual of Mental Disorders (DSM)** and the **International Classification of Diseases (ICD)**.

- Although the traditional distinction between 'psychosis' and 'neurosis' has been dropped by DSM and ICD, the term **psychosis** is still used to refer to serious mental disorders, with schizophrenia being by far the commonest of the psychoses, and one of the most serious.

- Rosenhan's classic study challenges the **reliability** of psychiatric diagnosis. A fundamental requirement of any classification system is that different psychiatrists agree with each other (**inter-rater/inter-judge** reliability).

- Despite improvements in overall reliability, some categories are less reliable than others and there's still room for subjective interpretation by the psychiatrist.

- In relation to psychiatric diagnosis, **construct validity** (as opposed to **predictive** validity) is the most relevant but is very difficult to establish.

- For psychiatry to be considered an objective discipline, it needs to be seen as **value-free**. While there's evidence that psychiatry is **culture-** and **gender-biased**, in DSM cultural differences are now dealt with (a) in descriptions of each disorder within the main manual; (b) in an appendix that deals with evaluating the role of culture and ethnicity; and (c) by describing **culture-bound syndromes (CBSs)**.

Schizophrenia: clinical characteristics

- Bleuler first introduced the term schizophrenia ('split mind' / 'divided self') to describe an illness in which 'the personality loses its unity'.

- Schneider's **first rank symptoms** (FRSs) refer to **passivity experiences and thought disturbances** (thought insertion, withdrawal and broadcasting), **auditory hallucinations (in the third person)** (hallucinatory voices) and **primary delusions** (false beliefs, usually of persecution or grandeur).

- FRSs are **subjective experiences**, which can only be inferred from the patient's verbal report. Also, hallucinations and delusions aren't peculiar to schizophrenia.

- Slater and Roth identified four additional symptoms: **thought process disorder** (derailment, 'word salad', thought blocking); **disturbance of affect** (blunting, flattening of affect, incongruity of affect); **psychomotor disorders** (catalepsy, catatonic stupor); and **lack of volition** (avolition, anhedonia, asociality). These are all **directly observable** from the patient's behaviour.

- While the DSM and ICD criteria are a confused mix of these two groups of symptoms, there seems to be a bias towards FRSs. But unlike most diagnostic categories, there's no **essential symptom** required for a diagnosis of schizophrenia.

- Most FRSs are **positive symptoms** (Type I) – the **presence of active symptomatology** – while most of Slater and Roth's are **negative symptoms** (Type II) – **lack** or **poverty** of behaviour.

- The distinction between positive and negative symptoms is crucial for research into the **causes** of schizophrenia, as well as providing a template for understanding the variety of schizophrenic symptoms. It's also easily recognised by psychologists and psychiatrists.

- DSM identifies three **types** of schizophrenia: **disorganised** (or **hebephrenic**), **catatonic** and **paranoid**. Paranoid is the most **homogeneous** category. Other types include **simple** and **undifferentiated** (**atypical**).

Schizophrenia: explanations

- Because of the confounding effects of acute mental disturbance and medication, people with **schizotypy** (schizoytpal personality disorder / SPD) are studied in an attempt to examine possible **mechanisms** involved in schizophrenia.

- Scanning techniques and post-mortems have revealed differences in the brains of schizophrenics (including increased lateral cerebral ventricles and reduced tissue in the medial temporal lobe) compared with non-schizophrenics.

- However, the data are **correlational** and the differences are only **relative**, nor can any single brain abnormality explain **all** schizophrenic symptoms.

- A major **biochemical** explanation is the **dopamine hypothesis**. Crucially, the claimed higher dopamine levels could as easily be **caused by** the disorder as be its cause. Other **neurotransmitters**, such as **serotonin** and **glutamate**, have also been implicated.

- Refinements of the dopamine hypothesis include the claim that crucial brain areas involved are the **mesolimbic pathway** (MLP) (positive symptoms), and the **mesocortical pathway** (MCP) which projects to the **prefrontal cortex** (PFC) (negative symptoms).

- The finding that relatives of schizophrenic patients have a greater risk of being diagnosed themselves as the blood relationship becomes closer (**family resemblance studies**) is consistent with the **genetic theory**.

- However, family resemblance studies **confound** genetic and environmental influences. While the two major alternative designs – **twin studies** and **adoption studies** – allow for the separation of these two sets of factors, they both face problems of their own.

- One shared problem is the assumption that schizophrenia is a distinct syndrome that can be reliably diagnosed. A twin study problem relates to the **equal environments assumption** (EEA). An adoption study problem is the **random placement assumption**.

- The wide variation in **concordance rate** in different twin studies suggests that different countries use different criteria for diagnosing schizophrenia, and even the highest for monozygotic (identical) twins (MZs) leaves plenty of scope for environmental factors.

- The finding that the concordance rates for MZs reared apart (MZRA) and together (MZRT) are quite similar suggests a major genetic contribution.

- The most popular current view of how schizophrenia is inherited is the **polygenic model**. This, in turn, is related to the **diathesis-** (i.e. predisposition) **stress model**. Any inherited factors can only account for a greater **vulnerability** or likelihood of developing schizophrenia. Environmental stressors can either be **biological** (e.g. viral infections) or **social** (e.g. being raised in a psychologically disturbed adoptive family).

- One early **psychological** explanation is the **schizophrenogenic mother** (Fromm-Reichmann). Related to this was the view that schizophrenia is caused by **abnormal family communication** patterns.

- Laing proposed his **family interaction model** within the context of **social phenomenology**. Some support comes from Bateson *et al.*'s study of **double-binds**.

- Laing's **conspiratorial model** is based on **labelling theory**. Scheff argues that the crucial factor in schizophrenia is **diagnostic labelling**, which tends to produce **self-fulfilling prophecies**. Without the label, deviant behaviour (the breaking of **residual roles**) wouldn't become stabilised.

- Critics of labelling theory argue that labelling cannot account for why the label is applied in the first place – there must be some reality behind it. They also claim that 'schizophrenia' isn't as 'sticky' (irreversible) as Rosenhan maintained, and that labelling theory is **historically relative**.

- While Eskimo and Yoruba cultures both have a concept of 'crazy' that's quite similar to 'schizophrenia', **cultural psychiatry** suggests at least three possible ways in which culture-specific factors can influence schizophrenia: the **form** the symptoms will take, the **precipitatory** factor involved, and the **prognosis**.

Schizophrenia: therapies

- All therapies involve **side effects**, raise **ethical issues** and issues regarding **social power/control**. There's also an important distinction between **outcome research** ('Does therapy work?') and **process research** ('How does it work?').

- Of all the **biological** treatments for schizophrenia, by far the most important development was the introduction of **antipsychotic drugs** (**neuroleptics**).

- **Chlorpromazine** (a derivative of **phenothiazine**) became the standard form of **chemotherapy** in US state mental hospitals. Other drug groups include the **butyrophenones** and the **thioxanthenes**.

- While antipsychotics can reduce positive symptoms, enabling many patients to live in the community, they have little effect on negative symptoms and about a third don't respond favourably to them. Long-term institutionalisation has been replaced by the **revolving-door** pattern of admission, discharge and readmission. They tend to **delay** relapse, rather than prevent it.

- Particularly disturbing side effects (**extrapyramidal**) include **acute dystonia**, **tardive dyskinesia**, **akathisia** and **neuroleptic malignant syndrome**.

- Newer drug therapies include **clozapine** (an **atypical neuroleptic**), which can help patients who don't respond well to traditional antipsychotics, and which is more effective in reducing positive symptoms. It also reduces negative symptoms.

- Although producing fewer motor side effects, clozapine can cause **agranulocytosis**. Both **olanzapine** and **risperidone** produce fewer such side effects and are at least as effective in reducing positive symptoms, compared with traditional antipsychotics.

- Despite their undoubted advantages, antipsychotics have been described as 'pharmacological straitjackets'.

- **Electroconvulsive therapy** (**ECT**) is less effective than antipsychotic medication and is rarely used today.

- Like ECT, the use of **psychosurgery** (specifically, the **prefrontal lobotomy**, pioneered by Moniz) has largely disappeared following the introduction of antipsychotic drugs.

- Freud considered schizophrenics incapable of benefiting from **psychoanalysis**. Harry Stack Sullivan pioneered the use of psychoanalysis with hospitalised schizophrenic patients; through building up their trust, the therapist could help the patient learn adult forms of communication and gain insight into the past's influence on current problems.

- There are few well-controlled studies of **individual psychodynamic psychotherapy** with schizophrenic patients. But the emotional intensity of such treatments may be harmful for at least some patients, especially in the acute phases of a psychotic episode.

- More recent **psychosocial** interventions try to help patients and their families deal more directly with the everyday social challenges. These newer, more effective approaches include **social skills training (SST)**.

- Different forms of **cognitive-behavioural therapy (CBT)** all share the primary aim of modifying hallucinations and delusions. One major approach involving schizophrenic patients is **stress management (SM)** (related to 'personal therapy', which includes some **rational-emotive behaviour therapy / REBT)** .

- The long-term effects of CBT as a whole are unclear, but for less vulnerable individuals there may be an incubation effect.

Depression

- **Depression** (or major depressive disorder) is one of the **mood** (or **affective) disorders**. When it occurs alone, it's referred to as **unipolar disorder**. When it occurs with **mania** (manic disorder) it's called **bipolar disorder** ('Bipolar 1'). In rare cases where mania appears on its own, 'bipolar' is also used ('Bipolar 1').

- 'Bipolar 2' refers to major depression combined with **hypomania**.

- **'Manic-depressive'** refers to both the unipolar and bipolar forms of affective disorder.

Depression: clinical characteristics

- The DSM criteria are controversial with regard to the number of symptoms (in addition to depressed mood) that are required – and how long they must have lasted – before a diagnosis can be made.

- Depression seems to exist on a continuum of severity, but DSM emphasises symptoms only at the severe end ('clinical depression'). However, DSM distinguishes between this and **dysthymic disorder** ('chronic depression'), which requires only three or more symptoms (instead of five required for clinical depression), including depressed mood but **not** suicidal thoughts.

- Mood disorders and **anxiety** disorders have much in common. This is especially true in the case of **agitated type** depression (as distinct from **melancholic type**).

- Another distinction, deeply embedded within psychiatry, is that between **endogenous** ('from the inside') and **reactive** (or 'exogenous', 'from the outside'). The former is closer to the severe end of the continuum and the distinction is no longer made in terms of causes.

- Depression, like schizophrenia, is **heterogeneous**. Some depressed patients may report delusions and hallucinations; delusions tend to be associated with unipolar disorder.

- Women are two to three times more likely than men to be diagnosed with unipolar disorder. Explanations for this gender difference have ranged from women's greater **hormonal** predispositions to **non-biological** explanations (such as learned helplessness, sexual abuse, female

Essay Questions

Schizophrenia

1a. Outline clinical characteristics of schizophrenia. (5 marks)

1b. Explain issues associated with the classification and diagnosis of schizophrenia. (5 marks)

1c. Outline and evaluate ONE OR MORE psychological explanations of schizophrenia. (15 marks)

2. Outline and evaluate ONE OR MORE biological explanations of schizophrenia. (25 marks)

3a. Explain the use of ONE biological therapy as applied to the treatment of schizophrenia. (10 marks)

3b. Outline and evaluate psychological therapies as treatments for schizophrenia. (15 marks)

Depression

4a. Outline clinical characteristics of depression. (5 marks)

4b. Explain issues associated with the classification and diagnosis of depression. (5 marks)

4c. Outline and evaluate ONE OR MORE biological explanations of depression. (15 marks)

5. Discuss ONE OR MORE psychological explanations of depression. (25 marks)

6a. Explain the use of cognitive behavioural therapy as applied to the treatment of depression. (10 marks)

6b. Outline and evaluate biological therapies as treatment for depression. (15 marks)

It should take you 40 minutes to answer each question.

Media psychology

What's covered in this chapter?

You need to know about:

Media influences on social behaviour
- Explanations of media influences on antisocial and pro-social behaviour
- The effects of video games and computers on young people

Persuasion, attitude and change
- Persuasion and attitude change, including the Hovland-Yale and Elaboration Likelihood Models
- The influence of attitudes on decision making, including roles of cognitive consistency/dissonance and self-perception
- Explanations for the effectiveness of television in persuasion

The psychology of 'celebrity'
- The attraction of 'celebrity', including social psychological and evolutionary explanations
- Research into intense fandom – for example, celebrity worship, stalking

EXPLANATIONS OF MEDIA INFLUENCES ON ANTISOCIAL BEHAVIOUR

There are a number of explanations put forward to explain the effect that media influences have on anti-social behaviour. They can be classified into two broad types:

1. explanations of situational (or short-term) effects

2. explanations of socialisation (or long-term) effects.

✔ Specification Hint

If the question asks for two explanations, you could use two named explanations such as Social Learning Theory (SLT) and Desensitisation. However, in order to broaden the scope of your answer, you could divide the two explanations into situational (short-term) effects and socialisation (long-term) effects. This would allow you to include more information (possibly too much) and yet still meet the requirements of the question.

Explanations of situational (or short-term) effects

Cognitive priming

This explanation is that aggressive ideas shown in the media (particularly films) can 'spark off' other aggressive thoughts in shared memory pathways (Berkowitz, 1984). After viewing a violent film, the viewer is 'primed' to respond aggressively because the memory network involving aggression is activated. Huesmann (1982) also proposed that children may learn problem-solving scripts through observation and that aggressive scripts may be learnt through observation of violent scenes. If the children find themselves in a similar situation in real life they may recall aspects of the violent script as a solution. In some ways, this echoes the 'context dependant' theory of remembering (PSYA 1).

Arousal

Bandura (1973) suggested that arousal increases the dominant behaviour in any situation. If the feeling of arousal is attributed to anger, then aggression is likely to result. Research has shown that the arousal produced by (violent) pornography facilitates aggressive behaviour (Zillmann, 1989).

Sponsor effects

Wood *et al.* (1991) suggest that demand characteristics are a type of 'sponsor effect'. This means that (aggressive) behaviour shown in the media is somehow portrayed as acceptable behaviour. Viewers are more likely to accept a message in the media if they think it's 'sponsored' or condoned by someone they respect and admire (see the section on Bandura, pages 134–139). Watching a very violent film may suggest to young people that this sort of violence is acceptable behaviour within society, especially if it involves movie stars who are thought of as role models. Hearold (1986) showed that watching violent films was associated with both violent behaviour and general antisocial behaviour.

All the above explanations suggest that participants 'assume a more permissive atmosphere when they are shown a violent film, and that their inhibitions about misbehaviour generally are reduced' (Felson, 2000). An important evaluation is that these explanations appear to have only short-term effects on aggressive behaviour.

Routine activity explanation

This suggests that watching television is likely to decrease violence in society. This is because people are so busy watching television that they have less time to interact with others and actually be violent! Also, watching television is often a solitary occupation, which therefore decreases the time for family interaction and hence levels of domestic violence. Messner (1986) did, indeed, find lower levels of violent and non-violent crime in cities with high levels of television viewing.

Explanations of socialisation (or long-term) effects

Social Learning Theory (SLT) (Bandura, 1983)

This is easily the best-known explanation and has already been described in detail in Chapter 4 (see pages 134–139). It's argued that television can shape behaviour through imitative learning. Watching role models perform violently may increase violent behaviour in those viewers already motivated to aggress. Television may also teach viewers the negative or positive consequences of their violence. Paik and Comstock (1994) found the effect on antisocial behaviour was greater if the actor was rewarded for her/his actions.

The cultivation effect (Gerbner and Gross, 1976)

This suggests that television creates (or cultivates) a distrust or unrealistic fear in viewers. This causes viewers to misperceive (or exaggerate) threats in real life and react in a more violent way. This is also referred to as the 'mean world' effect. It is true that content analysis of television has shown that there is far more violence on television than in real life, but correlations between the amount of television viewing and fear of crime tend to be very low (Wober, 1978). Indeed, where other contributory factors are accounted for, the correlations disappear altogether. The main problem with this explanation is that people who are particularly fearful are likely to avoid any threatening situations in the first place. Thus, increasing the level of fear might actually help to reduce the level of violence. In addition, any correlations (if indeed they do exist in the first place) between television and heavy viewing can be explained by a third intervening variable. Viewers who watch relatively light amounts of television tend to be middle class and live in areas where crime rates are much lower than those heavy viewers who live in relatively high crime rate areas. Thus the greater fear of crime is due to the neighbourhood in which they live, not due to their viewing habits. Even Gerbner et al. (1986) have accepted some of this argument, but they insist that television viewing causes a resonance effect that reinforces the fears of their neighbourhood. Gunter (1987) has simply argued that viewers are sophisticated watchers of television and there is no evidence that they confuse television representations of crime with real life.

Desensitisation

This suggests that repeated exposure to violence in the media reduces the impact of the violence. People become 'desensitised' to the violence and it has less impact on them (habituation). They become less anxious about violence per se and may, therefore, engage in more violent behaviour. Belson (1978) conducted a study of over 1500 teenage boys and found no evidence that high exposure to television violence would desensitise them into becoming more violent. Indeed, he found no evidence that watching violence on television even reduced boys' consideration for other people or respect for authority. Hagell and Newburn (1994), in a study of juvenile offenders, found that they watched less television if anything, and no more screen violence than their non-offending counterparts (Gauntlett, 1995). However, it could also be argued that desensitised individuals might be *less* aroused by violence and therefore not be so easily provoked by real-life violence. Similarly, desensitised individuals may become indifferent to the violent message. Both of these latter possibilities would result in the desensitised individual being *less* violent, not *more*.

These explanations refer to longer-term effects on aggressive behaviour and thus may be more important processes than the situational explanations outlined above.

Other factors affecting subsequent aggression

There are a number of other factors that have been shown to influence subsequent aggression in a viewing audience. These include those described below.

Meaning and context of the communication

It's been shown that the interpretation by the viewer of the film plays a part in subsequent feelings of aggression. Berkowitz and Alioto (1973) found that viewing American football produced an aggressive reaction in viewers only if they thought players were trying to hurt each other, rather than just being professionals trying to win a game. Aggression is in the eye of the beholder and viewers impart different meanings to behaviour. The context of the behaviour can also affect meaning. Many cartoons are very violent (e.g. Tom and Jerry) but may not be interpreted as aggressive. The reality of the incident appears important in these interpretations.

Identification

Several studies have shown the importance of viewers' identification with the observed aggressor. Viewers who show a high degree of identification with violent television characters tend to be more highly aggressive themselves (Berkowitz, 1985).

Evaluation of explanations of antisocial behaviour

✗ **Research difficulties:** a number of researchers suggest that media influences on antisocial behaviour have been unduly influenced by political desires to blame television for all kinds of social problems (Gauntlett, 1995). It is far easier to blame 'video nasties' and call for them to be banned as an explanation and cause of violence among young people than it is to attribute the blame to other possible factors, such as education or poverty. As long ago as 1960, Joseph Klapper wrote that media research is too simplistic, involving as it often does the mere counting up of incidents of aggression to assess what type of programme is under consideration. These criticisms appear equally valid today and sophisticated methodologies remain difficult to design and elusive in practice. Further criticisms of much of the research into antisocial behaviour include the fact that it often seems based on the assumption that the audience members all consume the media in the same way and are equally influenced by it. This assumption is not supported by the facts (Dorr and Kovaric, 1981). Second, there is an assumption that the amount of television watched influences the amount of behaviour change. Again, this is not supported by the facts. The measure of the number of hours of television watched is a questionable one. It has been found that for 50 per cent of the time when children have the television on they are doing something else and paying little attention to the content on the screen. Finally, Cumberbatch (1989) questions why people think viewers (particularly children) will copy or imitate violent acts on the screen. They may acquire the knowledge of violent acts from television but this isn't likely to increase their desire to replicate them. Indeed, motivation is a more powerful determinant than knowledge and, in any case, most programmes show that violence or aggression does not gain any rewards.

Synoptic Material: If it's significant it must be of interest ...

Cumberbatch (1989) argues that media effects are filtered and selected before the public gets a chance to read them. He argues that many academic journals are more interested in publishing 'significant' research findings that demonstrate that violent media cause violent effects in people. Thus there is a research bias in favour of 'positive' findings. Cumberbatch questions how much research that has not found any link between violence in the media and real-life violence has been excluded from publication in academic journals. In addition, armed with the knowledge that research that shows 'no effect' is less likely to be published, academics will inevitably not choose to research such areas.

- Investigate how material is chosen for publication in academic journals.
- Is it possible that journals are biased in the material they select for publication?
- If this is the case, what worries might psychologists have about this?

Research relating to antisocial behaviour

Laboratory studies

These occur in carefully controlled environments in the hope that a causal link can be found between watching violence and behaving aggressively.

Imitation of Film-mediated Aggressive Models (IF-MAM) (Bandura, Ross and Ross, 1963)

This is the best-known experimental study of observational learning and aggression. It is covered in detail in Chapter 4 (pages 136–137).

Violent Programme Study (VPS) (Liebert and Baron, 1972)

Two groups of children were randomly assigned to either a:

- violent condition – watched a violent episode of a detective show

- non-violent condition – watched an equally arousing sports event.

Afterwards, during periods of play, those in the violent group were assessed as behaving more aggressively than those in the non-violent group.

However, not all the violent condition children acted aggressively and aggression levels were measured quantitatively (amount), not qualitatively (type).

Karate Kid Study (KKS) (Bushman, 1995)

Randomly assigned students viewed 15 minutes of aggression from the film *Karate Kid III* (experimental group) or an equally arousing non-violent clip from *Gorillas in the Mist* (control group). After this, each participant completed a 25 trial reaction time task against an (imaginary) opponent. If they 'won' the reaction time trial, they could 'punish' their opponent by subjecting them to white noise. They could select the 'punishment' level (65–105 decibels) each time they 'won' a trial. Trials were actually fixed so that they won 50 per cent of the time. Participants who had watched the violent *Karate Kid III* video clip delivered more punishment (longer duration and higher intensity) than those in the non-violent control group. It's worth noting that *Karate Kid III* is rated PG by the British Board of Film Classification, suggesting that it's not particularly violent.

Evaluation of laboratory experiments

✗ **Ecological validity**: the lab situation is different from real life and violence within the lab is different from violence outside the confines of the lab. The removal of all possible extraneous variables may enhance the methodological aspects of the experiment, but at the expense of creating a 'real-life' situation for the participants.

✗ **Legitimised aggression**: in the lab, the aggressive behaviour is legitimised by the experimental situation. Participants are told that the use of electric shocks and/or white noise is part of the experimental process.

✗ **No punishment as a consequence of actions**: performing aggressive behaviours in the lab never results in punishment (unlike real life).

✗ **Intention to harm**: many lab studies don't involve any intention to harm.

✔ **Applies to some aggressive individuals**: however, it may be the case that some aggressive people neither fear punishment nor worry about the possible consequences of their violence. Therefore lab results may be applicable to such individuals.

✗ **Demand characteristics and compliance**: the lab situation may provide clues as to how participants are expected to behave. Compliance is also likely since:

- behavioural standards expected in the situation are unclear
- the experimenter is likely to appear an influential figure
- participants wish to present themselves in a psychologically healthy light (Rosenberg, 1969).

Synoptic Material: What about ethics?

Howitt (1989) makes an interesting point about the beliefs of many of the researchers who conduct laboratory experiments into media violence and then measure any 'real-life' effects. If the experimenters really believe that their own findings show a real effect on the participants and that this effect may be long term, then how can they justify showing participants violent or aggressive stimulus material? Surely from an ethical viewpoint such research should not be conducted. Howitt (1989) suggests that the researchers don't actually believe in any long-term effects and their argument that a thorough 'debrief' was conducted would not be an acceptable defence except for the fact that the effects are minimal.

Consider other ethical issues that are of relevance in terms of violent media effects research.

Field experiments

These involve the manipulation of the independent variable in a real-life setting.

Hockey Game Study (HGS) (Josephson, 1987)

Josephson showed groups of boys either a violent or non-violent film. Later, both groups took part in a game of hockey. The boys in the 'violent film' condition were rated as most aggressive during the game. It was suggested that their behaviour was due to the effects of 'cognitive priming' since there were 'cues' in the violent film that mirrored aspects of the game.

Natural experiments

These involve a fortuitous and naturally occurring event. The independent variable is not manipulated by the experimenter.

Notel Study (NS) (Joy *et al.*, 1986)

Joy *et al.* (1986) examined the change in children's aggression after the introduction of television in a remote Canadian town (called 'Notel'). Results were compared with two other towns that already had television. Physical and verbal aggression levels increased in all three towns but were most marked in Notel.

Evaluation of field experiments

✔ **Few demand characteristics**: since participants are often unaware of taking part in a field study, there can be no demand characteristics.

✔/✗ **Mixed findings:** meta-analyses have failed to find clear-cut results. Wood *et al.* (1991) found that in:

- 16 studies participants acted more aggressively after watching a violent film
- 7 studies participants in the control groups acted more aggressively
- 5 studies there was no difference between control and experimental groups.

Evaluation of the Notel Study

✗ **Sample**: the sample size was small (N=45) and selective (only children aged 6–11 years).

✗ **Uncontrolled variables**: prior to the introduction of television, the children of Notel were just as aggressive as those in the other communities, suggesting that media effects don't explain aggressive behaviour. After all, you'd have expected the Notel children to be *less* aggressive if television was such a powerful influence. This suggests there were other differences between the three communities.

St Helena Study (SHS) (Charlton, 2000)

This study examined the effects of the introduction of television to the island of St Helena in the Atlantic. A total of 859 children were examined and behavioural measures recorded. There was no increase in anti-social behaviour five years after the introduction of television, but pro-social behaviour had actually increased.

Evaluation of natural experiments

✔ **Design considerations:** natural experiments take advantage of a naturally occurring event and as such involve no manipulation of the independent variable.

✗ **Methodological limitations:** there are many uncontrolled (confounding) variables in these natural experiments. It's therefore difficult to draw any firm conclusions about media influence on violent behaviour.

✗ **Cause and effect:** any relationship between introduction of television and increased levels of violence may not be causal.

Longitudinal studies

These generally use correlational analysis whereby measures of viewing behaviour are measured against levels of aggressive behaviour. In addition, participants are followed over a long period of time.

High School Study (HSS) (Milarvsky *et al.*, 1982)

A total of 3,200 students identified the television programmes they watched over a four-week period and then measures of aggression were obtained. This procedure was repeated over a number of years. There was little evidence of a correlation between exposure to television violence and aggressive behaviour. All the correlations were positive, but not to a statistically significant level. Support for these non-significant findings was also provided by Wiegman *et al.* (1992) in the Netherlands.

Cross-National Study (C-NS) (Huesmann and Eron, 1986)

This was based on earlier work where Eron *et al.* (1972) reported that the amount of television violence viewed at age eight was positively correlated to aggressive behaviour ten years later. However, this relationship was only found for boys using peer aggressive rating scale measures. This peer rating measure included antisocial measures, not merely aggression.

Using a similar methodology, a three-year longitudinal study of primary school children in five countries purported to show some positive correlations between aggression and the viewing of violence (Huesmann and Eron, 1986). However, Cumberbatch (1997) questions much of the research, suggesting that some of the correlations were not significant, or actually negative – that is, the more television violence watched the less aggressive the students were!

Evaluation of longitudinal studies

✗ **No consistent findings:** longitudinal studies have not shown a consistent pattern of results. There are as many negative findings as positive ones. The conclusion remains that these studies 'have not demonstrated a relationship between the amount of violence viewed on television and subsequent aggressive behaviour' (Felson, 2000). However, after Johnson *et al.* (2002) published substantive evidence (700 participants tracked over 17 years) of a correlation between viewing violence and subsequent aggressive behaviour, the American Psychiatric Association concluded that 'the debate is over … television violence has been shown to be a risk factor to the health and well-being of the developing child'.

✗ **No cause and effect:** even if the findings were consistent, we're still left with the major problem that correlational studies cannot prove cause and effect. There may be other variables that can explain any correlational relationship found.

345

How Science Works

Practical Learning Activity 8.1: Content analysis of TV programmes

Identify a number of popular television programmes – it might be best to concentrate on soap operas.

Devise a 'tick box' questionnaire where you could analyse the themes and behaviours seen on the programmes in a one-week period. Try to assess the number of antisocial and pro-social acts that you see.

It might be worth asking a friend to use the same rating-scale questionnaire but to watch the programmes separately.

● What problems did you encounter?
● What was the point in asking a friend to collect data separately?
● Did you come to the same conclusions?

Effects of specific media on violence

There is less research into this area, but the following studies have been carried out.

● **Music:** Barongan, Hall and Gordon (1995) found that music and music with violent themes increased aggression.

● **Violent stories:** some increase in aggression has been found after the reading of violent books or comics (Bushman and Anderson, 2001). However, Japan has many violent cartoon magazines and this finding contrasts markedly with the low levels of aggression in Japanese society and the high levels of violence depicted in its comic books.

● **Violent news:** this appears to increase aggression, but the effect is smaller than for other programmes (Paik and Comstock, 1994)

● **Aggressive sports:** viewing aggressive sports shows a small increase in aggression (Sachs and Chu, 2000).

● **Violent video games:** in a recent meta-analysis of 32 previous studies, Sherry (2001) concluded that the video game effect was 'less significant than the effect of television violence on aggression'. Anderson and Bushman (2001), in a similar review, could explain 4 per cent of violent behaviour measured as due to the playing of violent video games. Effects were most noticeable in the 6–12 age range.

Conclusion

Given the evidence, it would be surprising if media effects had absolutely no influence on viewers. It's likely that there's a small effect, but it's very weak and affects only a small number of predisposed individuals. Nevertheless, given the large population influenced by the media, this small effect may have important consequences (Felson, 2000). Paik and Comstock (1994) suggest that violent media account for about 10 per cent of the variance in societal violence, which is about the same effect as that of cigarettes on lung cancer rates (Wynder and Graham, 1950).

MEDIA INFLUENCES ON PRO-SOCIAL BEHAVIOUR

If violence on television causes people to be more aggressive, than shouldn't the good-hearted qualities in television cause its audience to be kinder to others? – Cooke (1993)

Many of the psychological processes outlined above with respect to antisocial behaviour can apply equally to pro-social behaviour. Pro-social behaviour here refers to altruism, helpfulness, generosity and other positive social skills. A number of studies have shown how observation of helping behaviour encourages helping behaviour in the bystander (Bryan and Test, 1967).

Explanations relating to media influences on pro-social behaviour

The following explanations have previously been addressed to antisocial behaviour, pages 340–342, but can also be applied to pro-social behaviour.

Cognitive priming

Pro-social behaviours shown in the media may 'spark off' other pro-social thoughts in memory pathways. After watching pro-social acts, the viewer might be more likely to behave in helpful ways.

Arousal

Watching people help others or share resources might result in heightened arousal towards pro-social behaviour. An example of this might occur when watching, say, *Comic Relief*.

Sponsor effects

Seeing others perform pro-social behaviour might suggest that this sort of behaviour is desirable. An example might include watching celebrities run the London Marathon for charity.

Social Learning Theory

You will need to refer to pages 134–140 for a more detailed account of SLT. It seems reasonable to assume that if antisocial behaviours are learnt through observational learning, then pro-social behaviours are also learnt in this way. A number of pro-social teaching packages have been developed based on the principles of SLT (Goldstein *et al.*, 1998). Some of these are still in use today. Bandura is currently researching 'pro-social' modelling, and examining whether positive modelling can result in cooperation, empathy, sharing and so forth.

Research relating to pro-social behaviour

Australia Naturally (Noble, 1983)

Grant Noble demonstrated that television can be a source of education for young viewers. He questioned 240 children aged 7–11 years who had watched a nature programme called *Australia Naturally*. The children were asked factual knowledge questions and questions that investigated moral, environmental views. Compared to a control group who had not seen the programmes, the moral lessons had been learned by the children to an even greater extent than the factual information, suggesting that complex messages ('be aware of the balance of nature') had a greater impact than simpler ones ('don't throw rubbish'). Noble concluded that television can contribute to social learning in children.

Good News Studies (GNS) (Holloway *et al.*, 1977)

Holloway *et al.* (1977) produced support for the cognitive priming effect of the impact of good news. They invited participants into the lab for an experiment and, while they sat in the waiting room, played them a news programme over the radio. They were then asked to participate in a study involving bargaining with a fellow participant (actually a confederate). Those who had heard the pro-social news story were more likely to be cooperative in their bargaining, particularly if the news story involved an account of someone who had intentionally given help.

Good News Study follow-up (Blackman and Hornstein, 1977)

This replicated the Holloway *et al.* (1977) study but also asked participants to rate their beliefs about human nature at the end of the study. Participants who had listened to the pro-social news report anticipated other people would be more cooperative, and generally reported a higher proportion of decent and honest people in the world.

Although these findings only report short-term effects in male participants, they do illustrate how participants responded to other pro-social acts not mentioned in the news report (e.g. helpfulness, cooperation). The participants' pro-social actions were different from those on the news report. It's suggested that these related pro-social concepts were activated, or 'primed', in their minds by the original pro-social news report (Berkowitz, 1985).

'Lost Your Marbles Game' (Silverman and Sprafkin, 1980)

This involved groups of three-, five- and seven-year-olds watching clips of *Sesame Street*. The experimental clips were designed to teach cooperation, compared to control clips which weren't. In pairs, children played a game of marbles after watching the programme clips. In order to win, the children had to cooperate with one

347

another by taking turns. There were no differences in the levels of cooperation shown by those in the control or experimental groups. It was suggested that these findings may have been the result of the very brief presentation of the programme clips and/or due to the artificial nature of the cooperation.

Evaluation of media influences on pro-social behaviour

✔ **Experimental support:** Hearold (1986) conducted a review of previous pro-social research studies (a meta-analysis) and concluded that:

Although fewer studies exist on pro-social effects, the effect size is so much larger, holds up better under more stringent experimental conditions and is consistently higher for both boys and girls, that the potential for pro-social overrides the small but persistent negative effects of antisocial programs. (Hearold, 1986: 135)

Note: There are as many as five evaluative points contained in this quotation!

✔ **Evidence for pro-social modelling:** Lovelace and Huston (1983) concluded that pro-social studies do *generally* produce pro-social behaviour in viewers. There has been far less research into the pro-social effects of television, perhaps because people believe that television is saturated with antisocial behaviour. Cumberbatch (1989) argues that antisocial acts are more obvious and easier to count, whereas pro-social acts are more subtle and therefore this has led to the under-counting of pro-social acts. Cumberbatch (1998) counted 20 altruistic acts per hour over a three-year period on US television (1975–1978) compared to the average six/seven antisocial acts per hour. Much of the research into pro-social effects examines the positive effects of television programmes that were made explicitly for 'pro-social' purposes. Pro-social acts also occur on more mainstream television programmes; however, very few researchers have ever investigated the positive effects of programmes where the primary aim was entertainment rather than the promotion of a pro-social message.

✔ **Methodological issues:** many of the studies described above have the advantage of strict experimental control and allow the presentation of the pro-social behaviour clearly and unambiguously. However, many of the studies use brief clips from programmes some of which are specifically produced for use in the lab. In addition, measures of pro-social behaviour are conducted in an artificial situation. Generalising such findings may be difficult. A further problem with pro-social behaviour measurements is that the measures are based on value judgements – admittedly ones that most people would agree on. However, Lee (1988) notes that the 'pro-social' term originated as a contrast to antisocial aggressive behaviours. However, this dichotomy is not always seen in television. For example, many heroes and heroines on television (e.g. Batman and Superman) perform many pro-social acts (e.g. saving the world from nasty criminals) but are usually assessed by media researchers as representing violence and aggression. Much media research into antisocial and pro-social behaviours fails to recognise the complexities of many such characters. Surely a TV hero who kills a villain who was about to destroy the world should be feted as someone who has performed a pro-social act rather than someone who is antisocial? Gauntlett (1995) claims that 'the content analysis approach and method is severely flawed by its inability to recognise the content or meaning of acts'.

The effects of video games and computers on young people

Since the 1970s, video games have had a major impact on how people, particularly young people, spend their leisure time. Nintendo is one of the largest manufacturers of video games, and from 1983 to 1995 sold three games every second worldwide. Indeed, this was one game for every teenager on Earth. The explosion of the video game industry has led to concern about the effects these games have on young people. In terms of video games, there has been an increase in the violence and brutality of the games and increasingly realistic graphics and sound that yield blood-gushing, bone-crunching special effects. Newer games are often played from a 'first person shooter' perspective: players kill video characters directly rather than via another character. With the advent of newer technologies, 'reality vests' allow the player to feel the victim's death struggle. So-called 'skinning' allows players to place pictures of their friends, enemies or even teachers on to the characters that they subsequently hunt down. During game play these reality devices vibrate and twitch when, for example, the player's character chokes or shoots an opponent or is shot by an opponent. This tactile stimulation enhances the sensory experience of video game play, further differentiating it from more passive audio-visual media, such as TV (Ballard, 1999).

The main concern relates to violence within the games, although concerns have also been raised with regard to addiction and criminal activities. However, there are claims that games can have a positive benefit in that there are creative and pro-social games with educational value, and also games that help to release stress and aggression in a non-destructive way (Bowman and Rotter, 1983). Virtual reality and video games have also been shown to have beneficial effects as learning aids within the healthcare sector (Gold et al., 2006). Such media have also been used for the rehabilitation of stroke patients, to teach children about diabetes and asthma management, and as therapy in moderating certain phobias (Lieberman, 2001; Aoki et al., 2004).

Synoptic Material: Safer children in a digital world – the Byron Review

On 6 September 2007, the prime minister, Gordon Brown, asked Dr Tanya Byron to conduct an independent review looking at the risks to children from exposure to potentially harmful or inappropriate material on the internet and in video games. She published her findings on 27 March 2008. The full report is extremely long, but an executive summary (only 12 pages) is available at: http://www.dfes.gov.uk/byronreview/pdfs/Executive%20summary.pdf.

- Read the summary of the Byron Review and make brief notes on the key points.
- While reading the summary consider what you think the prime minister hoped to come out of the report.
- If you were a well-known media psychologist, what concerns might you have about being asked to conduct such a review?
- What do you feel about so-called 'media'-friendly psychologists? What about psychologists who prefer to conduct their research quietly in their university laboratories and never venture into the 'media' arena? Are there any concerns with either approach?

Positive effects of playing video games on computers

Some scientists argue that video games can have a positive influence on children, and that they have great potential for getting people to learn and think about things. Gee (2003) sees some benefits from specific video games. He believes some games can empower learners, develop problem solving and help understanding. For example, certain games have an interactive component whereby players actively create and customise the game that they play, and their decisions impact on all aspects of the game. Some games allow for creativity and individualism from the players. Games offer a sense of control and mastery, and often reward non-linear thinking and the resetting of goals as the game progresses. Many games encourage the players to reflect on their choices, to review earlier decisions and then learn from their mistakes. They encourage independent thinking, perseverance and commitment.

Kestenbaum and Weinstein (1985) conducted a study into the relationship between heavy computer game use in adolescent male participants and personality and psychopathological factors. They argue that playing computer games has a calming effect in that they can help manage conflict and can discharge aggression by allowing the open expression of competition. Furthermore, they argue that most of the concern about computer game use is the domain of anxious parents.

How Science Works

Practical Learning Activity 8.2: The effects of video games on young people

Try to devise a questionnaire that some of your friends could complete that measures the extent to which they play video games and what types of video games they play.

Try to devise some questions that ask about their feelings towards the different games and their views on whether these games have any effect on them or on other people.

● What difficulties do you anticipate with this methodological approach?
● How else might you investigate this area?

Negative effects of playing video games on computers

Most of the research into the effects of video games on young people has focused on the negative effects. These can be categorised in the ways outlined below.

Physical effects

A number of studies have show that gaming provokes epileptic seizures (Funatsuka *et al.*, 2001). Indeed, prior to its release in the United States, Nintendo's *Pokémon* had to be reformatted due to its association with epileptic seizures in more than 700 Japanese viewers (AMA, 2006).

A research report from 2006 suggested that video games can have a short-term effect on the functioning of different areas of the brain (Matthews *et al.*, 2006). The study randomly assigned 44 adolescents to play either a violent video game (*Medal of Honor: Frontline*) or a non-violent but equally fun and exciting video game (*The Need for Speed*) for 30 minutes. Then brain scans (functional magnetic resonance imaging) were used to measure brain function immediately following the play time. Adolescents who played the violent game showed increased activity in the amygdala, which stimulates emotions, and decreased activity in the prefrontal lobe, which regulates inhibition, self-control and concentration. These so-called 'fight or flight responses' did not show up on the brain scans of the adolescents playing the non-violent *Need for Speed* computer game. The key difference between this study and many other earlier correlational studies is that it involved a carefully controlled laboratory study where the measurements (i.e. brain scans) were objective and unbiased.

Behavioural effects

Results from many studies suggest a correlation between exposure to or playing violent games and negative actions such as aggressive thoughts and aggressive behaviours. Anderson and Bushman (2001) conducted a meta-analysis of previous studies and measured the effects of exposure to violent video games on five variables (aggressive behaviour, aggressive thoughts, pro-social behaviour (i.e. cooperation), aggressive mood and physiological arousal). They found that short-term exposure to video game violence was significantly associated with temporary increases in aggression among all participants. Lin and Lepper (1987) found evidence that impulsiveness and aggression were related to the frequency of computer game use. This study involved male and female youngsters in Florida, where participants were asked about their computer game use and perceptions of their own aggressiveness ratings. These were compared to various teacher aggression rating scales. The aggressive effect from the use of computer video games was evident only in boys.

Some studies have investigated the effect on children's play after they had played either an aggressive or non-aggressive video game. Silvern and Williamson (1987) arranged for children to play either a violent video game (*Space Invaders*) or to watch a violent cartoon (*Roadrunner*). They then monitored the children's behaviour in a free-play situation and found increased physical and verbal aggression in those children who had played the violent video game. Obvious criticisms of this study involve the observational measures of the children's behaviour and whether findings can generalise beyond the experimental situation since it

Key Study 8.1: The effects on rewards and punishment after playing the video game *Mortal Kombat* (Ballard, 1999)

Aim/hypothesis (A01)

This study examined the effects of video game violence by gender of the competitor and/or confederate.

Method/design (A01)

A total of 119 middle-class or upper-middle-class male college students took part (96 participants were white, with the remainder (N=23) African-American).

Participants played one of four increasingly violent video games against either a male or female competitor and then engaged in a memory task in which rewards (jelly beans) and punishment (hand immersed in cold presser device, i.e. iced water) were administered.

Different versions of the video game *Mortal Kombat* were chosen as the violent video game, as it allowed the researchers to vary the level of violence within the game context. At the time of the study, *Mortal Kombat* was the top-selling and most violent video game in the USA. *NBA Jam* was chosen as the non-violent video game since it was considered to be equally exciting and as engaging as *Mortal Kombat*, but with no violence.

After playing different versions of the video games, the participants tested their 'competitor' (actually a confederate) on his or her recall of 20 word pairs that they had supposedly memorised ahead of the experiment. It was pre-arranged with the confederate that they would get 5 of the 20 word pairs incorrect. If the confederate correctly recalled a word pair they were rewarded with jelly beans; when they got it wrong the participant could plunge the confederate's hand into the iced water. Thus the participant's reward and punishment behaviour could be accurately measured. Reward behaviour was quantified by counting the total number of jelly beans the participant gave to reward the confederate for the 15 correct responses. Punishment behaviour was quantified as the amount of time that the participant held the confederate's hand in the iced water after each incorrect response.

After playing the different video games, the participant and competitor drew slips of paper to assign roles. It was arranged for the participant to always draw the 'teacher' role (just like in the Milgram (1963) procedure). The participant was instructed to reward the 'learner' (their competitor) with jelly beans for a correct answer and to punish him/her, using the cold presser device (i.e. iced water), for an incorrect answer. Participants were told to use their discretion in rewarding and punishing the 'learner'. Confederates were instructed to display high levels of concentration during this 'task', to be stoic during the ice water immersion, and not to respond verbally or physically to rewards. Each participant's hand was placed in the iced water as a short demonstration and for them to understand how painful it can be.

Results (A01)

Reward levels (measured by the number of jelly beans awarded) of male confederates were affected by level of game violence. In other words, participants rewarded male confederates with significantly more jelly beans under the *NBA Jam* game condition than any of the *Mortal Kombat* conditions. However, female confederates were rewarded similarly regardless of the game played. In terms of punishment behaviour, confederates were punished significantly more aggressively under the *Mortal Kombat* game condition than the *NBA Jam* condition. However, closer analyses indicated that *level* of game violence in the *Mortal Kombat* conditions did not significantly affect punishment of male confederates but punishment of female confederates was influenced by the level of game violence in the *Mortal Kombat* conditions. Indeed, for female participants, punishment increased in a linear fashion as level of game violence increased; for males the key factor was whether the game was violent or not. The amount of violence in the violent game did not increase punishment level.

Discussion

The researchers did find generally that the type of game (violent versus non-violent) affected both reward and punishment behaviour. However, a key finding was that the gender of the confederate was important. The male participants rewarded other males significantly less under the violent game conditions, while females were rewarded similarly across conditions. Although few studies have examined the impact of video game violence on reward behaviour, Silvern and Williamson (1987) found that pro-social behaviour decreased after children played a violent video game. The results of this study seem to support these findings.

In terms of punishment behaviour, the level of violence in game playing did not affect punishment levels towards males but did have a negative (increased) effect on the punishment of females. These results are consistent with other research examining the effects of gender of victim and media violence (Donnerstein, 1983; Huesmann and Malamuth, 1986). In other words, women and men were treated differently by the participants after exposure to increasingly violent media. Further, there was not just a difference in punishment behaviour between the non-violent and violent games, but punishment became more stringent for women as the level of violence in the games escalated.

Conclusions (A01)

Ballard concluded that 'the results suggest that video game violence may decrease reward behaviour toward others, particularly males, and increase punitive behaviour toward others, especially females'. The effect of game violence appears to be moderated by the gender of the victim.

Ballard concluded that violent video game play may have an immediate negative effect on interpersonal interactions. However, she notes that these are likely to be relatively minor although females may be the more likely victims of such hostility. Ballard doubts that violent video games play a direct part in serious violence. Rather, violent video games may, over time, have a desensitising effect, which is one factor, along with biological and environmental risk factors, that contributes to violent behaviour.

Source: Ballard (1999)

- Can you think of any methodological criticisms of this study?

involved only 28 children and only one specific (fairly non-violent) video game (Harris, 2001).

Many studies have found evidence for the short-term negative effects of violent video games. However, Gentile and Stone (2005), although they confirm an association between violent video games and aggressive behaviours, note that it is difficult to definitively conclude a causal effect on long-term aggressive behaviours. Perhaps not surprisingly, research conducted by the video game industry has concluded that there is no causal relationship between video game violence and aggression (Harris, 2001).

Psychosocial effects

With the increasing availability of computer games, there has been corresponding concern about the amount of time young people spend playing them. Figures vary as to the number of young people addicted to video games. Grüsser *et al.* (2007) surveyed 7,000 gamers and found that approximately 12 per cent of these could be classified as addicted using the World Health Organization criteria. Shotton (1989) conducted a study in the UK on computer game addiction and surveyed 127 people (50 per cent were children) who reported being addicted to home computer games for at least five years. He found that, compared to a control group, those in the addicted group were highly intelligent, motivated and high-achieving people. Furthermore, a five-year longitudinal study of the younger participants found that a proportionately high number had done well

educationally, gone on to university and secured high-ranking jobs. Shotton concluded that addiction to computer games was usually a harmless addiction. However, this study has been criticised for only including participants who were self-aware of their addiction and it is possible that the largest detrimental effects are experienced by those who do not acknowledge their addiction (Harris, 2001).

As with findings on long-term aggression, it is probably true to say that there is currently insufficient research to definitively conclude that video game overuse is an addiction.

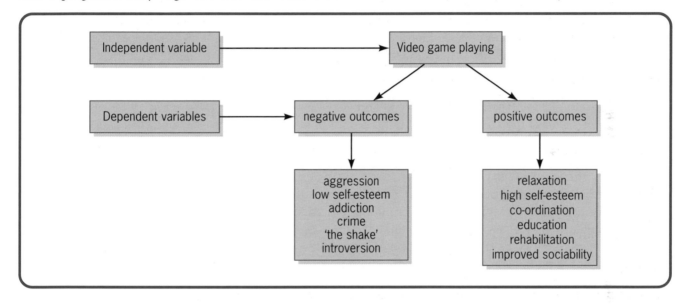

Figure 8.1 The positive and negative effects of computer games on young children (from Harris, 2001, page 13)

Evaluation of the effects of video games and computers on young people

✗ **Effects of long-term exposure:** although there does appear to be a fair body of research evidence that suggests there are some potential short-term negative effects of computer game use on subsequent behaviour, there is less research into the effects of long-term exposure. Therefore the long-term negative effects appear to be somewhat speculative. Given that there is also research which suggests that there are potential benefits associated with computer (game) use, the widespread concern surrounding computer game use may be a little misplaced. Further laboratory or longitudinal research is required to investigate further. Such research should also involve larger, more randomly selected samples involving children from different socio-economic backgrounds.

✗ **Causation problem:** the key question that surrounds much of the research into computer game use

Evaluation of the effects of video games and computers on young people continued...

concerns causation. Do young people who exhibit more negative behaviour do so as a result of playing these violent games or do aggressive individuals play these sorts of games because they appeal to their inherent nature? There appear to be three possible models or explanations.

1. Causal effects model: the use of violent computer games increases aggressiveness in young people.
2. Self-selection model: aggressive young people prefer playing violent computer games compared to their less aggressive peers.
3. Third variable model: both computer game use and aggressiveness are affected by a third variable such as the degree of parental control or discipline (Harris, 2001).

✗ **Methodology:** there are always criticisms that can be made of all different research methods. Laboratory experiments are criticised for creating an unnatural environment involving meaningless behavioural measures that are prone to demand characteristics. Field experiments are criticised for not being able to distinguish between violence created by a computer game and normal rough-and-tumble play behaviour. Finally, correlational studies are dismissed as irrelevant because 'cause and effect' cannot be established (see below). Anderson and Bushman (2001) accept that some of these criticisms are valid for some of the studies. However, the weight of evidence from all these studies suggests that violent video games do have a significant negative effect on young people. They argue that variables known to influence real-life aggression and violence have been shown to have the same effects in laboratory studies. Field experiments have found examples of aggressive behaviours that are directly modelled on the violence observed in the video game. Furthermore, the increased incidence of aggressive acts such as hitting, biting, hair pulling and so forth just because they may be occasionally seen in a natural play environment does not make them part of 'normal' play behaviour. Although specific incidents such as these may not be seen directly in the game just played, an increased incidence of them in children who have just played a violent video game can be attributed to the effects of the violent game.

✗ **Limited research on video games:** the vast majority of this research has focused on media other than video games (i.e. television, music, movies and arcade games). With the increasing focus on the amounts of time spent on video games by youth, and recognition of the tendency towards high levels of violence depicted in the games marketed to youth, researchers need to spend more time and effort concentrating on this area of the media in order to better determine the precise relationship of video game violence and aggressive behaviours. Due to the active and repetitive learning aspects of violent video games there is a real worry that violent video game effects may be larger than violent film and television effects.

Conclusion

Despite research that shows some link between video game playing and negative behaviour, there is little evidence of a *substantial* link between exposure to violent interactive video games and serious violence (Olson, 2004). In the meantime, the controversy continues, with both sides arguing the merits of their research findings. On two points the contrasting groups appear to agree. First, that if there are any effects, then violent video games and computer use are 'just one of many factors that contributes to societal violence and is certainly not the most important one' (Anderson, 2003). Second, that further longitudinal studies that test the link between violent video exposure and later aggression are essential.

Persuasion is the process of changing attitudes. There are many different definitions of an attitude but one adequate definition was provided by Petty and Cacioppo (1981), who wrote 'the term attitude should be used to refer to a general enduring positive or negative feeling about some person, object or issue'. This research is fraught with complications because an attitude cannot be observed or measured directly. Hence, much research involves the use of questionnaires and surveys that attempt to gauge a person's beliefs or opinions about the object under consideration.

The traditional communication (Hovland–Yale) approach

Much of the early research into persuasion and attitude change took place at Yale University in the 1950s and 1960s, examining factors that influence wartime propaganda. The Second World War had recently ended and the US government was particularly interested in this research area. One of the principal researchers at Yale was Carl Hovland, hence the research is often known under the heading of the Hovland–Yale approach. This approach concentrated on four factors that affected the communication process that influenced persuasion and attitude change.

1. The communicator: who is it that is seeking to persuade us?

2. The message: what is the content of the message?

3. The channel: how is the message conveyed?

4. The audience: to whom is the message directed?

The communicator

Experts appear to be more persuasive than non-experts. The same arguments are more convincing if the audience believes that the person delivering the message knows what they are talking about. Hovland and Weiss (1951) examined the role of the communicator's credibility in attitude change. They arranged for participants to read an article about the possibility of designing a nuclear-powered submarine. At this point in time, nuclear subs did not exist and they told half the participants that the article had been written by Robert Oppenheimer (who helped invent the first nuclear bomb) and the other half that it was from the Soviet newspaper *Pravda*. It was suggested that Americans would view Oppenheimer as a high-credibility source and *Pravda* as a low-credibility source. As expected, the message supported by the high-credibility source produced more attitude change than the low-credibility source (Lippa, 1994). Baron and Byrne (1997) suggest that this is why television adverts often put their experts in white coats, to emphasise the scientific status of the message. Nowadays the white-coated expert is seen less on television, but virtually every shampoo and anti-wrinkle cream has some pseudo-scientific name attached to it.

The credibility, status and attractiveness of the communicator appear to play an important part in persuasion. This is why personalities such as Tiger Woods are paid so much money to promote particular products. People who are attractive are usually well liked and we usually agree with people we like. There is some research that suggests that people who speak rapidly are more persuasive than those that speak slowly. It is believed that this is because people think that the person conveying the message must know what they are talking about (Baron and Byrne, 1997). Sorokin and Baldyreff (1932) played listeners two records of a classical music piece; unbeknownst to them they heard exactly the same performance. However, listeners were told beforehand that one of the performances had been judged as significantly better by music critics; 96 per cent of participants considered the performances were different and 59 per cent agreed with the alleged opinion of the experts.

students in the 'good weather', group were more likely to support the arguments for the exams. The arguments were judged as more persuasive because they were in a good mood caused by the sunny weather. However, when asked about the weather respondents did not acknowledge this as a factor in their judgements. Perhaps these factors have an unconscious effect and are all the more powerful because of it (Smith and Mackie, 2000).

Repeated messages are also found to be particularly effective persuasion techniques. The idea that repeated exposure to a stimulus produces a more positive attitude was first introduced by William James, one of the founding fathers of psychology, as long ago as 1890. He suggested that, 'the more often a stimulus was presented, the more likely the individual would (consciously) recognise it, and the more chances the person would have to intentionally consider and form an attitude about it' (Bargh, 2001). In the late 1960s Robert Zajonc proposed a slightly modified version of this, arguing that cognitive (thought) or motivational processes are not required for the liking effect to occur. It requires only repeated exposure. In the light of this, Zajonc coined the term 'the mere exposure effect', which states that 'mere repeated exposure of the individual to a stimulus is a sufficient condition for the enhancement of his [*sic*] attitude toward it'. The stimulus can refer to people, objects, consumer products, places and so on. Given time and repeated exposure we can grow to like most things.

To support his idea, Zajonc (1968) conducted various experiments where participants were shown different unfamiliar stimuli (Turkish words, Chinese-like characters and photos of strangers). Some of the words and photos were shown more frequently than others and the participants were asked to rate either how 'good' they thought the meaning of each word was or how much they liked the men in the photos. More positive ratings were given for the more frequently shown words or photos, providing support for the 'mere exposure' effect. Similar findings have been shown with a variety of non-human animals. For example, Harrison and Fiscaro (1974) even found that crickets show a marked preference for familiar surroundings by varying light levels in their environment.

Kunst-Wilson and Zajonc (1980) showed that people grow to like songs the more they hear them, even when they are unaware of having heard them previously. This finding may explain why some songs that we initially dislike become less irksome with repeated playing. Advertisers ruthlessly exploit their awareness of the 'mere exposure' effect and this explains why some adverts seem to be repeated endlessly. By repeated exposure, viewers start to like the product without ever having tried it! The repeated effect is particularly crucial for newly launched brands, which compete against other brands. Although performance of the product is obviously an important factor, familiarity is also a key ingredient to product success. Indeed, Baker (1999) has found that the familiarity of the product has a significant impact against superior-performing brands. Greater familiarity with VHS format video recorders led to them becoming the industry standard in the early 1980s despite the superior performance of the Betamax format. Of course, there is a point where an advert is repeated so often that you become sick to death of it!

The 'message repetition' idea is also shown in research on sales promotions beyond advertising. Bennett (1999) finds that the mere exposure effect works with sports sponsorship or product placements, most notably in the UK at major soccer matches. Bennett even argues that the effect may be more powerful here since this type of sponsorship is less overt than conventional advertising.

There are a few limitations to the 'message repetition' argument. First, some psychologists argue that it applies only to stimuli or messages that are inherently viewed as positive, or at least neutral. A greater familiarity with negative objects does not make us like them more. Second, message repetition does not work if people have *widely* conflicting interests, attitudes, personalities or opinions. In these circumstances, people may indeed dislike the message even more as a result of repetition (Freedman *et al.*, 1978). Third, repeated exposure can be overdone. After a certain number of exposures we will ignore the message. If the exposures continue, we will get irritated and 'take revenge' by assuming negative responses to the message. This explains why certain songs that are over-played on the radio can become increasingly annoying. Miller (1976) repeatedly showed people posters about stopping foreign aid. As predicted, they were persuaded most by moderate exposure to the message but after 200 exposures they reacted negatively to the message. Bornstein (1989) has found a similar effect with only 10 to 20 exposures, but acknowledges that the complexity of the message is also an important factor.

The channel

There are many different ways to get across a message – face to face, newspapers, television (see pages 370–374 below), email, internet, direct mail and so on. There is no one method that is better than others at persuading people – each is suited to different purposes. Face-to-face interaction seems a particularly good way of persuading people because the message can be tailored to fit the individual. However, mass media communication can persuade lots of people at the same time and thus reach thousands of people. With complicated messages, printed media are often more effective than visual messages, possibly because people pay more attention to and can recap written material (Lippa, 1994).

The audience

The Yale research found that different audience attributes (intelligence, personality and gender) affected the degree of persuasion of a message. The results were rather complex and difficult to decipher partly because some of the audience attributes varied in their effects. For example, intelligence may increase people's understanding of a message, but decrease their agreement with it since they might spot weak points in the message. Less intelligent members of the audience may not fully comprehend the message but still agree with it. Similarly, people with high self-esteem were found to be less distracted and withdrawn, and thus understand the message but are more sure of their own views and thus disagree with those trying to persuade them otherwise. Generally, studies suggest that people of moderate intelligence and moderate self-esteem are more readily persuaded by messages than those at either end of the continuum. Such people comprehend the message, but are not so convinced of their own opinions that they cannot be persuaded by carefully constructed arguments (Wood and Stagner, 1994).

Evaluation of the traditional communication (Hovland-Yale) approach

✔ **Positive contribution:** this traditional approach to persuasion and attitude change was one of the earliest systematic attempts to investigate the topic area. It provided a wealth of research into identifying factors that influence persuasion and when and how persuasion works. It also dealt with attitude change in practical ways and, indeed, much of the research is still relevant today and can be seen in advertising, speech writing and use by 'spin doctors' and lobbyists. This approach was less concerned with why people change their attitudes in response to these persuasive messages.

✗ **Criticisms of the approach:** contemporary critics would criticise the optimistic approach of Hovland, which implied that it is possible to discern general 'rules' for effective and persuasive communication. Although the approach suggests important factors in persuasion and attitude change it doesn't detail or determine the relative importance of each of these factors. Which are the most important factors? The message, the communicator, the audience, and so on? Although early research findings seem to discover governing laws of persuasion in laboratory settings, later research questioned many of these findings and these 'laws' did not hold up so well over time.

✗ **How does persuasion occur?** Perhaps the major weakness of the Hovland-Yale approach is that it is primarily an approach that concentrates on the steps in the persuasion process, and doesn't adequately deal with *how* persuasion actually occurs. It is based on the assumption that attitude change derives from an understanding or comprehension of a message. Obviously this is an important factor and can lead to persuasion and attitude change, but this does not guarantee that people are persuaded. As seen below, with the Elaboration Likelihood Model, persuasion can still occur even when a message is not fully understood or learned. The model has been superseded by more recent cognitively orientated models such as the Elaboration Likelihood Model (see below). Nevertheless, the work of the Yale group, competing messages) and thus people often don't have the time to process the messages sufficiently.

- Nature of argument: the message needs to be strong, and to be clearly argued and convincing. If the message reflects the pre-existing beliefs and attitudes of the listener then it is more likely to have a long-lasting effect. Occasionally the message has engaged the listener in all the steps described so far, but then the argument proposed is weak. In such circumstances, there is sometimes a 'boomerang' effect whereby the listener rejects the message completely.

If a message fails to make an impact through the central route then it may be processed via the peripheral route. If there are no peripheral cues present then the message will not have proved persuasive and attitude change will not result.

Peripheral route

A message using the peripheral route focuses on persuading people using devices that are not directly related to the actual subject matter. To use a previous example, this is why we see Tiger Woods advertising shaving foam. Tiger Woods becomes a peripheral cue because there is no obvious link between his ability as a golfer and shaving foam. Some key peripheral message cues have been identified by Cialdini (1993) (notice that none of these refers to the actual content of the message), as follows.

- Consistency refers to the process whereby people rely on thoughts that they have held in the past to evaluate the persuasiveness of a message.

- Likeability: some people who present messages are more likeable than others. This may explain why good-looking sports stars are in more demand for adverts then less attractive ones. Research has shown that physically attractive sources are persuasive (Berscheid and Walster, 1974), particularly when it comes to less involving topics.

- Expertise and authority: if a speaker has an air of authority about them, listeners are more likely to be persuaded by their message.

- Scarcity: if listeners believe that the message will be available for only a limited time, then they are more likely to be persuaded to take up the offer for fear of missing out.

Evaluation of the Elaboration Likelihood Model

✔ **Status of the theory:** the ELM is a relatively new model of persuasion and has gathered much support in the last few decades. Studies have shown that central processing leads to more lasting attitude change than does peripheral processing (Petty and Cacioppo, 1986). This may be because it involves more effort and time, whereas peripheral processing is more easily forgotten because it is more peripheral! Behaviour change as a result of attitude change from central route processing is also more long lasting. All in all, the ELM is probably the most influential cognitive theory of persuasion (Baron and Byrne, 1997). It is useful in that it recognises the way that similar messages can be processed differently by different people using different (central and peripheral) processes. Sometimes people have the ability and motivation to process messages using the central route; sometimes, people are more passive and process material via the peripheral route. Both these routes may still involve persuasion and attitude change.

✘ **The 'two route' metaphor:** one criticism of the ELM involves the use of the 'route' metaphor. This gives the impression that they don't occur concurrently. After all, you usually choose one route or the other, and can't go on to routes at the same time. This is not the case with ELM routes. Although the two routes may appear quite different, Petty and Cacioppo suggest that they operate on a continuum and illustrate the amount of mental processing that occurs when evaluating a persuasive message. However, the two routes *can* be processed at the same time and overlap with one another. When evaluating a

Evaluation of the Elaboration Likelihood Model continued...

message you may be thinking deeply about the content of the message and at the same time be thinking the speaker is a real expert in their field who appears very likeable (Benoit, 2008). Another problem is that the peripheral route seems to suggest a lack of thought about the message. Although there is arguably less thought allocated to the message, thoughtful processing still does occur, but on more peripheral issues such as 'How likeable is this person?'

✗ **Attitude change or attitude formation?** There have been negative criticisms of the theory, suggesting that many of the research studies concerned with the ELM investigate attitude only after they have perceived a message on a topic that they were not previously familiar with. Because they are not familiar with the message beforehand, pre-existing attitudes cannot be measured. Therefore, much ELM research does not measure attitude *change* as much as attitude *formation*. A further problem is that many of the attitude change measures concerned with the peripheral route involve transitory attitude change. Researchers have questioned whether it is possible to have transitory attitude change given that an attitude is usually defined as an enduring feeling towards an object or person. Again, the ELM research may not be measuring attitude change but attitude formation. Although Petty and Cacioppo (1981) have demonstrated that more permanent attitude change is possible through the peripheral route, some of these criticisms endure.

How Science Works

Practical Learning Activity 8.5: We get the message ...

● Choose a public safety campaign that is currently being promoted. This might be anti-smoking, healthy eating, drink-driving, anti-knife campaign and so on.
● Try to analyse the campaign in terms of your knowledge of the principles of persuasion. Give examples in the campaign that relate to the theory of persuasion. You could choose to do this with one advert rather than a number of adverts that contribute to an overall campaign.
● Devise your own campaign on an issue that is important to you. Use as many techniques as possible to persuade people to your view in order to change attitudes and behaviour.

THE INFLUENCE OF ATTITUDES ON DECISION MAKING INCLUDING ROLES OF COGNITIVE CONSISTENCY / DISSONANCE AND SELF-PERCEPTION

As seen above, an attitude can be used to refer to 'a general, enduring positive or negative feeling about some person, object or issue' (Petty and Cacioppo, 1981). Attitudes can influence in three ways (Rosenberg and Hovland, 1960).

1. Mood: what a person feels about something.

2. Cognitions: what a person believes about something.

3. Behaviour ('conative'): how a person responds to something.

Attitudes are a part of our cognitive equipment that helps us make sense of our world.

Rosenberg and Hovland (1960) suggested that attitudes affect mood, cognitions and behaviour, but research suggests that the link between these three elements is far from clear-cut. One early study was reported by LaPiere (1934). LaPiere travelled around the United States for two years with a Chinese couple.

He anticipated encountering a great many anti-oriental attitudes from the people who worked in the hotels and restaurants they visited. In fact, only on one occasion were they discriminated against. Six months later, LaPiere sent the 252 restaurants and cafés they had visited a questionnaire asking them if they would accept Chinese guests in their establishments. Just over 90 per cent of the 128 replies indicated that Chinese patrons would not be welcomed. LaPiere concluded that there is a large discrepancy between how one feels and how one acts.

In a similar study, Corey (1937) examined the attitudes of 67 university students towards cheating in classroom examinations. He then compared these attitudes with actual cheating in classroom tests. The students were allowed to 'self-mark' tests and submit their scores. Unbeknown to the students, their scripts had previously been marked and thus their true scores were known. There was no correlation between a student's reported attitude to cheating and actual cheating behaviour. Corey found that the best predictor of cheating was the difficulty of the test (i.e. the need to cheat in order to get good marks), not student attitude towards cheating. Incidentally, 76 per cent of the students cheated by reporting false scores.

A major problem with all attitude research is the obvious discrepancy between what people actually do and what they say they'll do. There is sometimes a marked difference between a person's reported attitude and their subsequent behaviour. It is suggested that this may be due to the inadequate methods that are used by psychologists to measure attitudes. LaPiere himself recognised this when he pointed out the danger of assuming that questionnaire-assessed 'attitudes' lead to actual behaviour in specific situations. In a quite damning paragraph, LaPiere (1932) concluded that:

The questionnaire is cheap, easy and mechanical. The study of human behaviour is time consuming, intellectually fatiguing and depends for its success upon the ability of the investigator . . . Yet it would seem far more worthwhile to make a shrewd guess regarding that which is essential than to accurately measure that which is likely to prove quite irrelevant.

A further explanation relates to the fact that attitude measures tend to concentrate on general attitudes and behaviour, whereas in real life they affect specific situations. Thus people may hold general anti-Chinese attitudes but behave politely when confronted with the specific situation of two Chinese people in their restaurant. However, even this stance has been questioned in later research. Ajzen and Fishbein (1977) argue the opposite – that inconsistency in attitudinal research findings was the result of studying single acts and not general behavioural trends. They argue that single acts are easier to study but general behavioural trends are a stronger and more accurate predictor of attitude. This is because a specific behaviour is often the product of many attitudes, not just one. Thus studying one specific act can present an inaccurate perception of how strong the attitude-to-behaviour relationship truly is. Somewhat confusingly, Ajzen and Fishbein state that you can't study specific attitudes by using general questions, and vice versa, because it will always show an inconsistency in attitude–behaviour relationships (Fazio and Powell, 1989).

It is generally concluded that attitudes form only one factor in the determinant of behaviour. They represent a predisposition to behave in particular ways, but how we actually behave depends on the specific situation. There are always situational factors that influence our behaviour in any circumstance, which may be in conflict with our general attitude. For example, in the LaPiere study, hoteliers and restaurant owners may have held general anti-Chinese attitudes, but the evident high status of the Chinese couple (good clothes, well spoken, accompanied by a white American) may have led them to alter their behaviour (Gross, 2005).

There are numerous theories or explanations that seek to explain attitude change. Many have concentrated on the idea of cognitive consistency – that is, with lots of different factors playing a part in determining our thoughts and behaviours we try to maintain some kind of coherence and consistency in them (Gross, 2005). Perhaps the two best-known explanations are the Cognitive Dissonance Theory (Festinger, 1957) and the Self-Perception Theory (Bem, 1965, 1967)

Cognitive Dissonance (Consistency) Theory

This theory is concerned with why people become motivated to change their attitudes. Festinger (1957) proposed the theory of cognitive dissonance, which is concerned with the way people change their attitudes when they realise that two thoughts or cognitions they hold are inconsistent. This conflict between two thoughts or cognitions creates a negative feeling of dissonance, or psychological discomfort. People deal with this dissonance either by changing one of the cognitions or adding a new cognition to explain the conflict. For example, a person who you consider a friend ignores you at a party. Your cognitions about your friend and their behaviour at the party conflict with one another. How could you deal with these conflicting thoughts that result in cognitive dissonance? You could change one of your thoughts. You might decide your friend is rude and actually has never been that nice and isn't really a good friend. You might decide his or her behaviour was not really that rude. Alternatively, you might add a new cognition and blame their new partner for turning them against you. Any of these new cognitions would help to reduce the feeling of cognitive dissonance and produce instead feelings of cognitive consistency. Festinger believed that the need to reduce dissonance is as basic as need for safety or to avoid hunger. It is a drive that compels us to be consistent, and the more important the issue and the greater the discrepancy between attitude and behaviour, the greater the feelings of dissonance experienced.

One key element of Cognitive Dissonance Theory is that it recognises that people do not always think rationally. However, people do try to rationalise their behaviour sometimes in an irrational way! People delude themselves by creating new cognitions that, if they thought about them rationally, must be wrong (Gross, 2005). The smoking example would be a case in point. People can make a case for continuing to smoke although, rationally, their arguments would not stand up.

Festinger argued that people selectively avoid information that will increase dissonance. Hence a smoker may not read a pamphlet detailing the dangers of smoking. We selectively choose television programmes and read books that confirm our attitudes and behaviour. We also choose our friends on the same basis, which is why many of our friends have similar views to ourselves. People who disagree with us or present differing views are likely to increase the discomfort felt by dissonance processes (Griffin, 1997). This selective exposure preference helps to reduce dissonance.

How Science Works

Practical Learning Activity 8.6: Cognitive dissonance and smoking

Surely everybody knows that smoking is bad for you. Yet many people continue to smoke. They must experience cognitive dissonance, knowing about the potential harm but continuing to smoke nonetheless. Outline some possible cognitions that smokers might produce in order to overcome their feelings of cognitive dissonance.

Festinger also stated that there are certain processes that increase the amount of dissonance experienced when there is a conflict between behaviour and attitude. The more important the issue, the greater the dissonance felt. The longer the delay between choosing the way to behave, the greater the dissonance felt; and the greater the difficulty in reversing the decision once made, the more the person will agonise over whether they made the right decision. These are sometimes called 'morning after' doubts, for obvious reasons (Griffin, 1997). Sometimes, once the decision is made, people will still continue to look for evidence afterwards to support their decision. The final process is called the 'minimal justification' hypothesis (see Key Study 8.2), which proposes counter-intuitively that the less the external incentive/reward (or justification) to change one's attitudes, the greater the change.

There have been a great many research studies that have investigated Cognitive Dissonance Theory. Many of these are forced compliance studies where participants are almost forced into holding conflicting opinions about something they don't really believe in. Perhaps the most famous is known as the $20 and $1 experiment (see Key Study 8.2).

Key Study 8.2: The $20 and $1 experiment (Festinger and Carlsmith, 1959)

Aim/hypothesis (A01)

Festinger and Carlsmith (1959) were testing two aspects of Festinger's (1957) theory.

1. If a person is induced to do or say something that is contrary to his [sic] private opinion, there will be a tendency for him to change his opinion so as to bring it into correspondence with what he has done or said.

2. The larger the pressure used to elicit the overt behaviour (beyond the minimum needed to elicit it) the weaker will be the above-mentioned tendency.

Method/design

A laboratory experiment was set up and 60 male students took part. They were asked to do some extremely boring repetitive tasks for 30 minutes. One task involved turning wooden pegs one at a time on a large board. Once they had completed these boring tasks they were asked to go to the waiting room and greet other participants who were waiting for their chance to participate. They were told that they must tell the waiting participant (who was actually a female confederate who was 'in' on the experiment) that the task they were about to do was extremely interesting. After this, the attitudes of the participants to the task was measured. It would appear to make sense that those paid the most would change their attitude the most. The greater the reward, the greater the attitude change. However, that was not what Festinger and Carlsmith had predicted and it was not what occurred.

Results (A01)

It was the participants who had been paid only $1 that changed their attitude the most. The $1 participants felt that the tasks had not been that boring, whereas the $20 participants had not changed their attitudes towards the tasks at all. So why had this occurred?

Conclusions (A01)

Festinger and Carlsmith argued that the $1 group had experienced more cognitive dissonance. There was a conflict between what they were saying to the next female participant and their attitude to the tasks. In order to reduce this dissonance they had changed or modified their view of the boring tasks (perhaps they weren't that boring after all!). The $20 group experienced much less dissonance. They knew the tasks were boring but could justify their lying (or 'counter-attitudinal advocacy') because they had been paid a decent sum of money to do so! The $1 group couldn't really reduce their cognitive dissonance by using this argument (since $1 was too little for this) so they changed their attitude to the task. They had to create another justification for their compliance (lying). This effect, whereby the smaller the reward or incentive, the greater the attitude change, is known as the 'less-leads-to-more effect' or the 'minimal justification' hypothesis (Gross, 2005).

How Science Works

Practical Learning Activity 8.7: *Aesop's Fables* – 'The Fox and The Grapes'

One hot summer's day a fox was strolling through an orchard till he came to a bunch of grapes just ripening on a vine which had been trained over a lofty branch. 'Just the things to quench my thirst,' quoth he. Drawing back a few paces, he took a run and a jump, and just missed the bunch. Turning round again with a One, Two, Three, he jumped up, but with no greater success. Again and again he tried after the tempting morsel, but at last had to give it up, and walked away with his nose in the air, saying: 'I am sure they are sour.'

- Explain how this story relates to cognitive dissonance.
- Give other examples of your everyday behaviour that relate to cognitive dissonance.

Evaluation of Cognitive Dissonance (Consistency) Theory

✗ **Nonsensical findings:** we have already mentioned that some of Festinger's conclusions may have been counter-intuitive. The idea that offering a large reward or incentive has less effect on attitude change than a smaller one created a great deal of hostility in social science circles (Griffin, 1997). Many psychologists were affronted that rewards might actually have a detrimental rather than helpful effect on behaviour. However, the $20/$1 study (outlined above) does seem to support this idea. However, further examination of the idea of cognitive dissonance led some to state that the theory was conceptually weak. Aronson (reported by Griffin, 1997) claimed that the theory failed to explain under what conditions dissonance occurs. Cognitive dissonance is criticised as a 'never fails' theory. When it is clear that dissonance has led to attitude or behavioural change, the case is supported, but when research fails to find attitude or behavioural change, it is claimed that the person did not experience sufficient dissonance to change their attitude or behaviour. Thus Cognitive Dissenance Theory can never be proved wrong. Aronson developed the theory, arguing that the amount of dissonance experienced is related to the effort invested in the behaviour. The more effort someone puts into something, the more they are going to buy into it. The greater the hardship associated with the choice, the greater the dissonance and therefore the greater the pressure towards attitude change (this is called the suffering-leads-to-liking effect) (Gross, 2005). An example of this may help. My son wanted to join a local football team. The two best teams invited him for trials. After the first trial, one offered him a place. The other told him it was difficult to say if he would get in but he should keep coming for training. After three weeks, they also offered him a place. Which did he accept? He signed for the team for which he had expended the most effort to get in.

✗ **Freedom of choice and negative consequences of action:** the Dissonance Theory was later expanded in a more complicated way. In the original $20 and $1 study the experimenter's request to persuade the next participant (actually the confederate) was not ostensibly a part of the experiment. Thus participants were free to choose to refuse this request – in other words, they were given freedom of choice over this request. Second, since the confederate had stated that she wasn't going to take part in the experiment until she was told that the experiment was interesting, the participant's lying led to negative consequences for the confederate (Hewstone and Stroebe, 1992). Other studies have confirmed that freedom of choice and negative consequences as a result of counter-attitudinal behaviour are important factors in the arousal of dissonance. Thus dissonance change is a complicated theory involving freedom of choice, incentive size and negative consequences as a result of any action.

Synoptic Material: Methodological issues

Demand characteristics problems with attitude studies (from Hayes, 2000)

Demand characteristics refer to the situation whereby participants form an expectation of the experiment and either consciously or unconsciously change their behaviour. This can occur in many ways.

Participants may seek the approval of the researcher and want to please the experimenter and get the 'right' result. They thus change their behaviour to try to fit in with what they think the researcher wants. However, in order to do this, they would need to try to 'second guess' what the study is about. Sometimes this is not obvious to the participants, although Orne (1962) argued that there are many clues during any experimental procedure that give participants an idea of what a study is about, what behaviour is being researched and what behaviours are expected of them. There are further problems associated with demand characteristics. For example, some participants wish to look good in the eyes of the researcher (social desirability effects), some become anxious about the study (evaluation apprehension) and this anxiety affects the results; and there is also 'enlightenment', whereby participants are becoming increasingly sophisticated about psychological research studies and this enhanced knowledge affects the results.

Rosnow (1968) examined students' views towards college fraternities (social groups within colleges and universities). Research participants were presented with one-sided arguments about either the merits or disadvantages of college fraternities. These groups changed their attitudes in line with the argument that they were presented with. One group received a balanced argument about the fraternity system. These students reported an anti-fraternity attitude. When questioned why, the participants stated that they were unsure how to react but were aware that the experimenter held anti-fraternity views and thus their attitude measures reflected this. The attitude measures reflected the experimenter's views and were not a product of the actual arguments presented.

Self-Perception Theory (Bem, 1965, 1972)

A challenge to Dissonance Theory soon came in the form of Self-Perception Theory (Bem, 1965, 1972). This theory suggests that we don't have privileged access to our own thoughts and feelings, and that any self-report of an attitude is an inference from observation of one's past behaviour (Gross, 2005). Indeed, it is argued that people are frequently in the same situation as outside observers when asked to indicate their own attitude. So in the $1/$20 experiment, participants remember that they told the next participant that the task was interesting and thus they will use this behaviour as a source of information unless there are good reasons to devalue this behaviour as a suitable source of information. Being paid $20 might be a good reason to devalue this behaviour; after all, they were bribed to say the task was interesting. If a participant was paid $1 there would be no reason to make this statement unless the task really was interesting and thus they also change their attitude because they infer that their behaviour reflected their true attitude. Self-perception theory can account for the $1/$20 experimental results without referring to clashing cognitions (Hewstone and Stroebe, 1992). To put it another way, the $20 group make a situational attribution ('I did it for the money'), whereas the $1 group make a dispositional attribution ('I did it because I really enjoyed it').

Evaluation of Self-Perception Theory

✔ **Research support:** many studies have supported Self-Perception Theory (Bem, 1965). However, studies can only show that participants may have inferred their own attitudes from their behaviour – they cannot prove that participants actually did go through such an inference process (Hewstone and Stroebe, 1992).

✘ **Placebo pill study:** Zanni and Cooper (1974) set out to test the two theories with a misattribution process study. Participants were asked to write an essay where they presented an argument that they disagreed with (a counter-attitudinal essay). They were given instructions which implied that they were free to choose whether or not to write the essay (high freedom of choice) or had no choice (low freedom of choice). As predicted by Dissonance Theory, participants under high choice who wrote the essay would experience dissonance (or tension) and thus change their attitude more than the low-choice group. This is indeed what the researchers found. Next, participants were told that they were being given a pill that would either make them feel relaxed or tense, or they were told nothing about the pill at all (the pill was a harmless sugar pill with no actual effects). According to Dissonance Theory, those participants who experienced dissonance (tension) would now be able to misattribute their tension to the pill and not to the behaviour (writing the essay they didn't agree with) and thus attitude change would not occur with those individuals. However, with Self-Perception Theory, the administration of the pill should have no effect on the attitude change. In actual fact, Cognitive Dissonance Theory was supported. Participants did misattribute the feeling of dissonance (tension) to the pill and attitude change did not occur in these circumstances (Hewstone and Stroebe, 1992). Thus feelings of dissonance are important for attitude change to occur.

✘ **Impression management:** this theory was proposed by Tedeschi and Rosenfeld (1981), and suggested that people have a social concern for appearing consistent to others. Thus dissonance effects in many experiments may not reflect genuine private attitude change but may merely be the result of participants feeling the need to appear to be consistent in their behaviour and attitudes. Thus attitude or behaviour change is motivated by social factors (such as the need to present a 'good' impression to others) and is not the result of cognitive factors.

Synoptic Material: Issues of cultural bias (Gross, 2005)

The $1/$20 experiment by Festinger and Carlsmith (1959) involved asking the participant to lie to another participant (actually a confederate). Lying is universally frowned upon by all cultures and thus this norm breaking would probably produce levels of dissonance across all cultures. However, it is argued that not all procedures that are designed to produce feelings of dissonance would produce the same amount of dissonance in all cultures. For example, Canadian and Japanese participants were asked to rate a number of music CDs. They were then asked to choose between two they had rated similarly. Canadians showed a dissonance effect, whereas the Japanese did not. It was suggested that the Japanese are less concerned when they lose the positive aspect of the unchosen item and are more willing to accept the negative aspects of the chosen item (Heine and Lehman, 1997).

The need to reduce conflict between an attitude and behaviour reflects an internal state. Many collectivist cultures do not demonstrate these tendencies. They value group cohesiveness more than individual desires or the need to express one's own attitudes. Dissonance appears to be strongest in individualistic societies such as the USA, with their emphasis on individual autonomy and perceived choice, but this effect is less clear in more interdependent (collectivistic) cultures (Gross, 2005). Cultural bias is not just restricted to attitude/behaviour conflict studies, it is also relevant to many other research areas in psychology.

Conclusion

Both theories mentioned (and indeed Impression Management Theory) have their supporters and detractors. Conflict between the competing theories has been reduced by the suggestion that Dissonance Theory best explains attitude change when people are faced with counter-attitude behaviour (cognitive dissonance) but Self-Perception Theory is best when faced with attitude-congruent behaviour (cognitive consistency). Tetlock and Manstead (1985) argued that no theory emerges as a clear winner and that researchers should examine the precise conditions under which particular theories find most favour. However Hogg and Vaughan (1995) state that:

> cognitive dissonance theory remains one of the most widely accepted explanations of attitude change and many other social behaviours. It has generated over one thousand research studies and will probably continue to be an integral part of social psychological research for many years … (cited in Gross, 2005: 421)

Explanations for the effectiveness of television in persuasion

Much of the research into television effects has concentrated on unintended effects associated with violence or aggression. However, television is also used as a form of media where broadcasters seek to persuade people to change their attitudes or behaviour as a result of watching television. These would include television advertising and public service broadcasting campaigns that seek to influence the consciousness of the public in a specific way. Public campaigns are usually related to health or safety concerns. One has only to think of Bob Geldof's Live Aid campaigns and concerts, which raised millions of pounds for various good causes in Africa, and the fact that many people seeking power see the control of television as a priority, to know that television can act as a powerful persuader.

A number of explanations have been proposed to explain television's effectiveness as an agent of persuasion.

Television's special role in everyday life

Some of the research into television and its effects have concentrated on the role that television plays in everyday life. Research has shown that television can mean many different things to different people

Figure 8.3 Rupert Murdoch of Sky TV: one of the most influential men in Britain?

(Gauntlett and Hill, 1999). Rogge and Jensen (1988) followed 420 West German families for a five-year period, examining their relationship with television. They reported on the idea of a meaningful relationship between individuals and their uses of television. They stated that, for some people, television can become part of the family structure, almost like a member of the family, which brings joy, distress, entertainment and shared meaning, as well as providing a sense of security in times of change.

One of the largest sets of data ever collected on people's experiences of television started in 1988 when 22,000 people in the UK kept a diary of their television viewing on 1 November 1988. Later, the British Film Institute invited 509 respondents to continue their research diaries for a further five years, from 1991 to 1996. By the close of the project, 427 respondents were still participating. Views of what television meant to people varied from 'nothing more than electronic wallpaper' to an essential 'window on the world'. People use television as a way to relax or escape from the pressures of everyday life. Some respondents viewed television as a good friend or good company when alone, while others reported considerable guilt about the amount of television they watched, the time they wasted and the passive nature of many of the programmes. It is obvious that television means different things to different people, but for some people television plays a very large part in their lives. Indeed, for some people particular programmes were reported to be the highlight of their week and it is clear that television gives many people a shared sensed of belonging. Indeed, talking about issues raised in television programmes remains an important part of many people's social lives.

The Hypodermic Effect explanation

This explanation supposes that television is such a powerful medium that it *injects* the message into the audience. It is also known as the 'silver bullet' or 'effects' model, in that much like a magic bullet the message can be precisely targeted at the audience with obvious subsequent effects on the audience. It suggests that the makers of television programmes can make us do whatever they want us to do. It is based on the assumption that audiences are passive recipients of the message and easily manipulated. It originated in the Frankfurt School, which examined the influence of Nazi propaganda techniques.

The Hypodermic Effect Model has never been taken that seriously by media researchers and there is little evidence of its validity, although there are a few studies that appear to provide support for it. Indeed, the Bandura *et al.* (1961) bobo doll studies have been cited as evidence of an uncritical audience passively copying an adult role model they had previously seen acting violently on film. Nowadays, it is viewed as outdated and not applicable to a modern audience that questions television material in a critical way and actively engages with much of the material presented. However, it might apply on the rare occasions where totalitarian regimes manipulate the media for their own good and a one-sided, biased portrayal may occur. Many of these regimes believe that control of the media, including television, will help to control the population at large. The Hypodermic Model may also apply in some forms of advertising where the viewer is less conscious of being manipulated. This could apply in sports sponsorships, for example, or in subliminal advertising. For these reasons, subliminal advertising is banned in the UK, perhaps in recognition that television has the potential to persuade with or without conscious awareness (McQueen, 1998). Although the model is largely discredited, it does have some continuing influence when people call for greater censorship in the media, mainly due to the latest moral panic over a particularly violent or aggressive television programme or criminal case (e.g. the James Bulger case). The direct effect of television does appear to be exaggerated, although it has to be recognised that there are ways that television has affected the general perceptions of the public. One simple example is the way that certain terms and catchphrases coined on television are now used in everyday language.

> ### ✔ Specification Hint: The effectiveness of television
>
> If the exam question asks about the effectiveness of television it should be possible to use the work of Hovland and the Yale University research team, which has been outlined above. Hovland established some general principles that relate to persuasive media messages. These general rules can also be applied to television persuasion.

Two Step Flow Theory (Katz and Lazarsfeld, 1960)

Paul Lazarsfeld and Elihu Katz adopted a different position to the Hypodermic Effect Theory, suggesting that mass media (and television) messages are filtered through what is known as opinion leaders. These opinion leaders receive messages through the medium of television and then pass on the information to other people in society (hence the 'two step flow' process). Thus the audience are active in the process of persuasion in that interpersonal communication occurs after perception of the message, and this is an important factor in determining which messages prove to be persuasive and which do not.

The process can be summarised as follows:

Source → message → mass media (television) → opinion leaders → general public

Lazarsfeld concluded that television has quite a limited direct effect on the audience. McQuail (1971) summarised the findings of 'limited effects' research as follows.

● Television merely reinforces existing opinions, it does not change opinion.

● People selectively tune in to hear the messages that they already favour.

● People respond to messages based on their existing predispositions.

Uses and Gratification Theory

This is another theory that explains how media (including television) work to get a message across. The basic idea is that people use the media to gratify or meet certain needs. People are active processors of the media and use the media to fulfil their needs. As Fiske (1987) stated, 'Television and its programmes do not have an "effect" on people. Viewers and television interact.' There are five areas of gratification.

1. Escape: these programmes allow viewers to escape from the reality of their lives.

2. Social interaction: people start to create personal relationships with the characters seen on television. This can be dangerous if it goes too far, but for many people it merely helps to create a common ground for everyday conversation.

3. Identification: people sometimes identify with a person on television. For example, this can be seen when people adopt the hairstyle of their favourite personality.

4. Inform and educate: people gain knowledge of the world around them and how it operates.

5. Entertain: people watch purely for the entertainment value.

How Science Works

Practical Learning Activity 8.8: Content analysis of programmes

● Think of a number of current television programmes and try to categorise them into the five areas of gratification outlined above.
● What difficulties are there with the categorisation of programmes in this way?

Public safety campaigns on television

Vast sums of money are spent each year on public safety campaigns designed to persuade people to change their behaviour in terms of health and safety issues. From AIDS in the 1980s to the use of mobile phones in cars and the annual drink-driving campaigns, advertisers have strived to develop effective campaigns. Some campaigns have been viewed as reasonably successful, while others have led to no observable change. Two campaigns will be mentioned here.

Pierce, Dwyer *et al.* (1986) report on a predominantly television-based large-scale anti-smoking campaign in Sydney, Australia. The 'Quit – For Life' campaign aired on prime-time television in 1983 and cost over half a million Australian dollars. A total of 87 per cent of smokers recalled seeing the ads and 50,000 telephone calls were made to the Quit Line in the three months following the campaign. Results showed a 2.8 per cent decrease in smoking in Sydney compared to a 1.6 per cent decrease in the rest of Australia where the ads were not seen. This difference was not significant and the researchers concluded that the effects were modest. Nevertheless, although such television campaigns have a modest effect on a minority of smokers, the campaigns are seen as cost-effective in terms of the medical costs saved by increasing the life expectancy of these reformed smokers.

One very thorough study examined the effect of a television campaign promoting the use of seat belts in the USA (Robertson *et al.*, 1974). Six different adverts were shown via cable television to 7,000 viewers and these were repeated 943 times over a nine-month period. Other cable viewers were not shown any of the adverts. To assess the effectiveness of the campaigns, daily observations of seat-belt use were made of car users in the city and the licence numbers of the vehicles were taken. This allowed the researchers to see which seat-belt users had seen the campaign. The results were disappointing in the extreme since the adverts had absolutely no effect whatsoever on seat-belt use (Gauntlett, 1995).

Dervin (1989) argues that public communication campaigns are effective only at great cost and within definite constraints. Furthermore, Gauntlett (1995) suggests that these campaigns only hope to influence the 2–3 per cent of the audience who are thought of as opinion leaders and agents of social change. Perhaps we expect too much of television as an agent of persuasion. Television appears to have only a marginal influence and the message is received best when it is reinforced by direct, face-to-face communications.

Advertising

Ninety per cent of my advertising budget is wasted, but I don't know which 90 per cent – Niall Fitzgerald, Unilever Chairman (1998)

Although huge budgets are spent on television advertising every year, there is conflicting evidence as to its effectiveness. It is difficult to find unequivocal data on the subject since companies are keen to keep advertising budgets and sales data to themselves. However, marketing research conducted by Stewart and Furse (1986) examined the impact of 1,000 television commercials and concluded that they caused trivial differences in viewers' recall and differentiation of the products concerned. Cashmore (1994) suggests that companies continue to spend on television advertising not because of its effectiveness but because they can find no other way of raising awareness of their brand against their competitors to a large audience simultaneously. It is estimated that television advertising fails from 90 to 99 per cent of the time (Gauntlett, 1995).

Two case studies are of interest. The Anchor Steam Brewing Company of San Francisco sold 103,000 barrels of beer in 1995 with no advertising campaign, while the California Raisin Advisory Board ran a television campaign promoting raisins, which cost $40 million annually. Its ads were incredibly popular, involving as they did clay animation dancing raisins backed by the Marvin Gaye song 'I heard it through the grapevine'. After four years, the campaign was stopped with sales lower than before the ads had started (Nolo, 2000).

Evaluation of the effectiveness of television in persuasion

✗ **Active audience:** it is now widely accepted that the Hypodermic Effect over-emphasised the passive nature of the audience. Nowadays researchers are interested not in what the media do to an audience but what the audience does with the media, and thus the Uses and Gratification Model finds more favour. Katz suggested that 'even the most potent of the mass media content cannot ordinarily influence an individual who has "no use" for it in the social and psychological context in which he [*sic*] lives. The 'uses' approach assumes that people's values, their interests, their associations, their social rôles, are pre-potent, and that people selectively "fashion" what they see and hear to these interests' (cited in McQuail, 1971). Television can act as a persuasive tool, but the audience does make a conscious choice as to the messages it hears and takes notice of. Television may be viewed simultaneously by people throughout the country and this is a common experience for all. However, it is also evident that television viewing is both personal and highly variable (Reardon, 1991). One problem with much of the research is that the idea of an 'active' audience means that television can be viewed or 'read' differently by different people. One person may 'see' a feminist perspective in their favourite soap opera or film, while others will not. One researcher may perceive 'violence', whereas the viewer may regard it as 'playful competition'. In addition, much of the laboratory experimental research concentrates on short-term effects and may be prone to demand characteristics.

✗ **Methodological difficulties:** it is rare for a public information campaign to be delivered only via television. Usually, information is also disseminated via radio, newspapers and other literature such as leaflets and posters. This makes it difficult to assess the effectiveness of television by itself. Similarly, research often involves the use of target groups and control groups. With national television campaigns it is difficult to determine who has watched what and how much attention they have given to the message.

✗ **Television advertising effectiveness?** It is extremely difficult to assess the effectiveness of television advertising. Apart from the fact that television campaigns seem poor at changing behaviour, advertising usually doesn't try to persuade people to do things they wouldn't normally do; it merely tries to persuade people to favour one product over another. Thus much advertising aims to change details of behaviour. Furthermore, most of the brands in the supermarket are the advertised brands, thus it is difficult to compare the sales of advertised and unadvertised products. More often than not, other factors play a part in the decision to purchase. The cost, packaging, image, promotional offer, the taste, appearance, and the prize draw or free gift offered with the product all have an effect on consumer purchasing decisions. Many people argue that advertising simply raises the consumer's awareness and recognition of the product. Once this is achieved, the product has to stand or fall on its own merits (Gauntlett, 1995).

General conclusions

Since attitude change is rarely studied for its own sake (except perhaps by psychologists) and more usually as a means of changing behaviour, one might consider it to be a worthless exercise since monetary incentives or legal sanctions seem to be far more effective agents of change. The seat belt example illustrates this. Despite a widespread campaign encouraging the use of seat belts, direct influence in the form of legislation (and penalties) brought about both behaviour and attitude change for the use of seat belts.

However, not all behaviours can be affected by so-called 'direct' strategies such as monetary incentives or legislation. Most people would not want all aspects of their behaviour to be controlled in this way. Certain behaviours, like smoking and drinking, cannot be completely controlled, although governments do introduce taxes and laws in an attempt to modify unhealthy behaviours. The use of legislation means that rules need to be constantly enforced, which can prove problematic in practice. Thus persuasion remains an essential way to influence behaviour, albeit in a more indirect way. In many instances, direct strategies complement indirect strategies, which is why many governments rely on mass-media campaigns (often television) to inform and persuade the population to change their attitude and/or subsequent behaviour (Hewstone and Stroebe, 1992).

How Science Works

Practical Learning Activity 8.9: Children and advertising

One area of where there is a great deal of concern over the effect of television advertising is the effect adverts have on children. Some researchers argue that children have a simpler relationship with television viewing, in that they find it harder to distinguish between programmes and adverts. However, others argue that this view ignores children's ability to process and evaluate adverts.

● Try to think up arguments for and against the use of television adverts directed at children.
● Are there particular adverts you think should not be directed at children? Which ones are they, and explain why not?

THE ATTRACTION OF CELEBRITY, INCLUDING SOCIAL PSYCHOLOGICAL AND EVOLUTIONARY EXPLANATIONS

I do have a tendency of being late, but I don't mean to. Anyway, just think. One day I'll lose. And I'll have to be on time when I lose – Boxer Chris Eubank apologising to a journalist for being late (in Giles, 2000)

The term 'fame' has a slightly different meaning to the word celebrity'. 'Fame' has an extremely long history of use relating to people who have become famous through their deeds, words or actions. The characteristic of celebrity is that it is a twentieth-century invention that is a product of the media and relates to the French word 'célébré' meaning 'well known, public'. Thus celebrities can be well known for nothing in particular, whereas famous people are deserving of individual recognition (Giles, 2000). Of course, sometimes these terms may overlap and people in the public eye may be both famous and a celebrity.

How Science Works

Practical Learning Activity 8.10: Famous or a celebrity?

Try to think of 30 people that most members of the public would recognise. See if there is agreement as to who would be classified as 'famous' and who might be classified as a 'celebrity'.

Figure 8.4 Truly famous or more celebrities?

There are a few 'celebrities' that profess to always wanting to be famous. Morrissey (former lead singer of The Smiths) wrote at the age of 18: 'I'm sick of being the undiscovered genius, I want fame NOW,' and Damon Albarn, of the bands Blur and Gorillaz, reckoned that from the age of 11 he knew he would become famous (Giles, 2000). It seems that many people envy and hope to become celebrities or famous, but what explanations are there for this desire?

Social psychological explanations

Popularity explanation

One explanation is very straightforward. Celebrities and famous people appear popular in the extreme. Crowds gather to get a glimpse of them. Some are idolised by their adoring fans. We see celebrities attending parties, eating the finest food, driving the most expensive cars and living in the best houses money can buy, accompanied by their good-looking partners. In short, we want some of their lifestyle. We aspire to live the life that they are living. We want their wealth, their lifestyle and their beauty. Celebrities act as role models for behaviour. Before the media played such an important part in all our lives, our role models were the hard-working husband or wife next door. Now we can look further afield and see celebrities we have never and will never meet, on our television screens every day. Why aspire to be like our neighbour when we can be like George Clooney or Madonna?

Media psychologists use the term 'parasocial' (Giles, 2002) to describe the relationship between celebrities and the audience because they exist beyond the person's social network. One aspect of the 'parasocial hypothesis' is that people misperceive celebrity gossip as evidence that these people are actually part of their own social network (De Backer *et al.*, 2007). Although we have never met these celebrities we may feel that we know a great deal about their lives – in fact, it may be true that we do know more about them than we do our neighbours. An incredible study by Aron *et al.* (1991) asked participants to generate visual images of particular individuals. They found that participants had more vivid images of the movie actress and singer Cher than they did of their own mothers!

Celebrities may occasionally behave appallingly (and be criticised for this), but generally they have led successful lives and have acquired many of the trappings of life that we would wish to obtain. The obvious reason why we pay so much attention to these celebri-

ties is through the process of Social Learning Theory, or imitative learning. We copy their behaviour because we want to be like them (see page 134, above): 'They have achieved success – I can too, by being like them.' The Learning Hypothesis explains interest in celebrities as a by-product of an evolved mechanism for acquiring fitness-relevant information on how to live our lives (De Backer *et al.*, 2007) (see also the evolutionary explanation, pages 376–379). This can even involve such minor behaviours as copying their current haircut, their fashion sense, or even buying the coffee we think they drink (or advertise). DeBacker *et al.* (2007) administered a survey to 838 participants and followed this up with 103 in-depth interviews. They found some support for both the Learning Theory argument in that the younger the (audience) person the more they 'learn' from the celebrity, and the greater the media exposure the more the celebrity is interpreted in terms of belonging to people's own social network (parasocial hypothesis). They suggest that the nature of celebrity changes across a person's lifespan, from that of a teacher to that of a friend.

Synoptic Material: Social Learning Theory

This theory suggests that we learn through watching the actions of others. We observe other people's behaviour and we copy what makes them successful and avoid actions that are seen to fail. Humans are more likely to copy the behaviours of higher-status individuals and such people would include the famous and/or celebrity figures. Celebrities act as role models for a wide range of behaviours. It is worth reviewing the Social Learning Theory in detail as outlined on pages 134–140. Although it is discussed primarily in relation to aggression, the theory can be applied to virtually all aspects of behaviour.

One explanation why people like celebrities so much may be the 'mere exposure effect'. In 1968, Robert Zajonc proposed 'the mere exposure effect', which states that 'repeated exposure of the individual to a stimulus is a sufficient condition for the enhancement of his [*sic*] attitude toward it'. The stimulus can refer to people, objects, consumer products, places and so on.

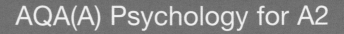
How Science Works

Practical Learning Activity 8.11: The most trusted celebrities?

In the USA, there is an index that measures the marketing power of celebrities – that is, it determines a celebrity's ability to influence consumers. The Davie Brown Index suggests that the top US celebrities include: Tom Hanks, Oprah Winfrey, Will Smith, Michael Jordan, Tiger Woods and Clint Eastwood.

● Try to develop a research project that might determine a UK equivalent Index.

Given time and repeated exposure, we can grow to like most things. Similar findings have been shown with a variety of non-human animals (Hill, 1978). For example, it's been found that crickets are more content in familiar surroundings, and that male wolf spiders are likely to be eaten if they try to mate with an unfamiliar female (Harrison and Fiscaro, 1974).

Why should familiarity be associated with such positive feelings? The answer may be that we (and other animals) have a biological predisposition for caution in encounters with novel, and thus potentially harmful, objects. The more we see someone, the more their image is familiar, and gives us a sense of comfort and trust when we see it. Thus the more we see, say, Jamie Oliver, the more we like him. It also appears that the 'mere exposure effect' works, even if we're not consciously aware of perceiving it. This might explain why certain celebrities seem to be on every possible form of the media. By repeated exposure to particular celebrities, viewers start to associate a positive attitude with them, without knowing much about them.

There are a few limitations to the 'mere exposure effect' argument. Some psychologists argue that it applies only to stimuli that are inherently viewed as positive or at least neutral. If people view a celebrity as having widely conflicting interests, personalities or opinions to their own, then they may dislike them even more as a result of repeated contact (Freedman *et al.*, 1978).

Personality Theory

It is argued that personality factors may contribute to the quest for fame. Simonton (1994) reports that some studies have measured personality factors through the use of a Thematic Apperception Test (where participants have to interpret 20 ambiguous pictures) and found that specific personalities had a greater need for recognition. Simonton (1994) concluded that Type A personalities were most likely to have the drive to succeed and the tendency to take risks.

However, most of these studies have involved retrospective analysis. That is, they find people who are famous and then try to determine their personality characteristics. Such studies lack real scientific credibility and tend to be mainly descriptive in nature.

STRETCH AND CHALLENGE: Personality tests

One of the best ways to find out about research is to participate in it. The BBC website has many experiments that you can do. One of these involves a personality test. You can access this at:
http://www.bbc.co.uk/science/humanbody/mind/surveys/whatamilike/index.shtml.

The test is 20 questions long and should take about 10 minutes. Give it a go and see what you make of the results. Can you think of any criticisms of personality tests such as these?

Outsider theory of celebrity

Another reason proposed for why people desire to be famous is that they feel isolated and rejected by the culture in which they live. Becoming famous helps them to feel wanted within the community. Cicero felt he was an outsider in Roman circles and his desire for greatness was fuelled by his feelings of rejection. Giles (2000) reports that the abnormally high number of Jewish Nobel Prize winners and the over-representation of African-Caribbeans and African-Americans in pop music and sport (two areas particularly associated with fame and celebrity) might suggest that an intermingling of cultural backgrounds helps create a fertile environment for achievement. Simonton (1994) provides some evidence to support this argument by listing the large number of homosexuals who have become famous in various fields, notably the arts and entertainment industries. Simonton (1994) suggests that 'unconventional lifestyles' lead people to become obsessively involved in their work and provide them with a desire for success in a culture in which they feel estranged (Giles, 2000).

Evolutionary explanations for celebrity

The evolutionary explanation for celebrity suggests that our brains today haven't adapted to the idea of the mass media; they are still adapted to living in small hunter-gatherer groups on the African savannah as we did 10,000 years ago. In this climate, it was important to survive by obtaining and gathering food, looking out for opportunities to reproduce, and competing with others for a higher place up the social pecking order. One way we did this was to gossip about the other people and keep an eye on the sexual goings-on in our group. Gossiping about our friends and family increased our knowledge of events in the group and helped to ensure our survival. If people kept up with the rivalries and affairs of others it ensured they were more likely to live a longer, healthier and easier life. In short, people who were good at gossiping were better at surviving.

Nowadays, though we live in a much larger social group and interact with larger numbers of people (65 million in the UK). We can't keep tabs on all of them, so we have to restrict our interest to smaller groups. Since we know comparatively little about our immediate friends and neighbours (although we'll still gossip about them as well) we use celebrities as a vehicle for our gossip and 'reproduction obsession'. This works well; it is also safer to gossip and take an interest in celebrities because, unlike our friends and neighbours, they won't find out about any false rumours we may have spread. Not only that, gossiping about celebrities to our friends and neighbours can help cement social relationships with our friends and neighbours. This is why people take such an interest in which celebrities are pregnant and who is dating whom. This obsession generalises into other areas of courtship such as weddings, what people look like, what they are wearing, what they are doing and who they are having an affair with. The celebrity magazines are fulfilling our Stone Age need for gossip. The obsession with the looks of celebrities also relates to reproductive strategies. Evolutionary psychologists can explain why a high proportion of female celebrities are blonde (blonde hair is associated with youth and youth with fertility), have firm breasts and small tummies (visual evidence that they are not pregnant).

Furthermore, because we see these celebrities every day our brains become confused and we start to think that we know them so well that we almost see them as friends. We confuse the information that we find out about celebrities as akin to having personal information on a friend. This can lead some people to neglect more meaningful personal relationships in favour of 'celebrity' relationships. Given this line of thinking it is easy to see why celebrity gossip features on so many media.

Such explanations might explain why we are attracted to celebrities, but why do people want to become celebrities? A sociobiological explanation might suggest that the most important aspect of our life is our attempt to reproduce our DNA (Dawkins, 1989) and thus the desire to become a celebrity can be viewed in the light of this. Fame makes us popular and brings us into contact with lots of people who are suitable candidates for us to reproduce with. Giles (2000) reports a story that a film star, when asked why he wanted to be famous, stated that it was because there were a lot of pretty women with whom he wanted to have sex! That may be the case for a lot of non-celebrity men, but being a famous film star probably helps in this respect. Another benefit of being a celebrity is that it allows them to overcome any shortcomings in their biological inheritance. However ugly or fat they may be, they have the advantage of being famous. Without naming names, we must all be able to think of celebrities who are thought of as 'sexy' but who in reality wouldn't turn heads if it wasn't for their fame.

Evaluation of celebrity explanations

✗ **Female preoccupation with celebrity?** Why are women more obsessed with celebrities than men? It is estimated that 67 per cent of readers of celebrity magazines are women. Could it be that on the African plain men gained no reproductive advantage from knowing about the gossip in the group? This seems unlikely – knowledge is power for males and females alike. Although it is hypothesised that women had to rely on more subtle Machiavellian techniques of survival (whereas men could rely more on brute

Evaluation of celebrity explanations continued...

strength), it surely would still have conferred some reproductive advantage for men to have been aware of alliances within their social group.

✗ **Fame as a means to reproductive fitness?** This argument sounds good until it is noted that many famous celebrities are also very attractive. Surely people don't strive to be famous simply to attract a potential mate? Ignoring the fact that celebrities' good looks may be manufactured by the surgeon's knife or the photographer's software package, it would appear to be true that the majority of celebrities are more physically attractive than the average member of the public. These attractive individuals would have a good chance of passing on their genes even without the added advantage associated with their celebrity status. Perhaps this 'gene pool' argument was true in the past, but with the emphasis on the visual media today, being beautiful is almost a prerequisite for being a celebrity. Fame as a sexual strategy cannot explain why some people place the importance of fame above any sexual strategies. Indeed, some celebrities appear to lead busy lives at the expense of having meaningful, stable relationships. Furthermore, how can such an explanation explain the high preponderance of homosexuals in the arts and entertainment worlds? Being a homosexual is one of the worst sexual strategies in order to pass on one's DNA (even recognising that some homosexuals do choose to have children). Here the evolutionary argument suggests that becoming a celebrity is a means of passing on something about our self to future generations without using children to achieve this goal. If we assume that most homosexuals do not want to pass on their DNA through having children, then they can leave their mark for the future though their fame. Homosexuals desire fame as a mark of posterity. Fame acts like a symbolic reproduction (Giles, 2000). In Roman times, the famous were preserved in pictures and statues; nowadays the famous are preserved on film, in newspapers and on YouTube. We can now replicate ourselves without the need to have children. Long-gone celebrities can still be seen on film and video as though they are still alive – their presence lives on long after their funeral. There is a clear evolutionary reason for the attraction of celebrity on a cultural rather than a purely biological level (Giles, 2000). This relates to Erikson's (1950) idea of 'generativity' – that is, a way of establishing and guiding the next generation. Celebrity and fame are a way of preserving one's identity for future generations. Being a celebrity means we leave our 'mark' long after we are dead. We defy death and can remain immortal in a symbolic sense (Giles, 2000).

✗ **Practical research difficulties:** investigating the psychology of celebrity is incredibly difficult. Psychology in its quest for scientific credibility has always avoided areas of research that are difficult to undertake in a quantitative way. If it can't be studied in the laboratory, the topic tends to be ignored. The psychology of celebrity is a case in point. The research area lends itself to a more qualitative analysis. Another problem with psychological research is the difficulty of obtaining participants. It is never easy to recruit 40 members of the 'normal' population who have the time to fill in a questionnaire on their behaviour and attitudes. Try gaining access to Madonna or Gwyneth Paltrow to find out about their experiences of fame! One further problem is that the area of celebrity is a relatively new one for psychological research. Usually, academics trawl through the previous literature to understand where the research is and how they can move it forward. There is little research in this area and thus it does not (as yet) form part of mainstream academic psychology (Giles, 2000). Researchers such as David Giles (currently at Winchester University) and John Maltby (Leicester University) are doing their best to address this.

Evaluation of celebrity explanations continued...

✗ **Unwanted celebrity status:** it is impossible to measure how many people desire to be 'celebrities'. It is likely to be only a small subset of the population at large. Of course, celebrity status is not always wanted. Gerry and Kate McCann might be regarded as 'celebrities', but their fame is certainly unwanted and the result of particularly distressing circumstances. Their desire to remain in the public eye is simply to promote public awareness of the Madeleine McCann case in the hope that members of the public may help in finding their missing daughter. Studying why people are attracted to 'celebrity' relies to a large extent on retrospective accounts by famous people of how and why they became famous. Such accounts can suffer from 'hindsight bias', where events in the past are reinterpreted in the present. Of course, people who are not currently celebrities can be asked about why they might wish to become so, but Giles (2000) reports that fame has acquired a vulgarity through the perceived low value of modern celebrity, and thus people may be less honest and open about such ambitions.

Research into intense fandom – for example, celebrity worship, stalking

Factors influencing celebrity worship

It is generally assumed that younger people (adolescents and teenagers) are most preoccupied with celebrities and that this interest wanes with age. Although some research has found little effect of age on celebrity worship, the majority of these studies have used a very restricted age range, often only looking at the age range 11–17 years (Levy, 1979; Hakanen, 1989). Most of the research has indeed found that age and measures of celebrity adulation demonstrate a statistically significant negative relationship (Ashe and McCutcheon, 2001; Maltby *et al.*, 2003). It seems that celebrity worship peaks between 11–17 years and then declines slowly thereafter.

Level of education also appears to be a factor associated with celebrity worship. Although this factor is compounded with age, generally it is found that the less education, the greater the amount of celebrity worship. Levy (1979) reported such findings, and McCutcheon, Lange and Houran (2002) found that the correlation was approximately -0.40. These findings appear to hold for both US and UK participants. As mentioned, one problem with these findings is that younger people have not had a chance to finish their education and thus the education measure is affected by the age variable. However, one study reported by McCutcheon *et al.* (2004) ignored any participant below the age of 25 years. It was hypothesised that

most people over the age of 25 have completed their education. The correlation coefficient measure remained at -0.32, suggesting that education remains an important factor in celebrity worship. McCutcheon *et al.* (2004) hypothesised that education is related to intelligence, and thus more intelligent people are better able to see through the cult of the celebrity. Alternatively, they suggest that people who have achieved in the education field may see a celebrity who is less educated than themselves and therefore find less to admire in their achievements. One measure of intelligence is 'cognitive flexibility', which involves the ability to adapt to different unexpected situations. Research suggests that celebrity worshippers do not possess 'cognitive flexibility' – indeed they are dogmatic and rigid to the point of being obsessive. Other measures, such as critical thinking and creativity, also seem to be less obvious in those people who score highest on celebrity attitude scales. It is hypothesised that celebrity worshippers may have comparatively poor social skills and that these hinder them in developing positive interpersonal relationships (McCutcheon *et al.*, 2004). In the absence of such relationships, celebrity worship seems to fill the void. Celebrities seem to provide another source of pseudo-friends for these individuals.

In terms of gender, it is not surprising to find that males are far more likely to cite sports stars as their favourite celebrities when compared to female choices. Females are more likely to choose their favourite celebrity from the entertainment and arts field (Smith, 1976; McCutcheon *et al.*, 2002). A study by Stever (1994) found that females were more likely to label their celebrity worship as 'intense' compared to male celebrity worship. However, this study examined celebrity worship with respect to Michael Jackson, who is more likely to attract a female fan base. Studies that have examined male and female fan reactions to their chosen favourite celebrities have generally very small differences between males and females. Females tend to report slightly more intense reactions, but this is not to a significantly different level from male reporting. Advertisers can be reassured that celebrity endorsements sell to male and female fans alike.

Auter and Palmgren (1992) did find that the amount of exposure to a TV sitcom did have a small effect on the positive perception of the celebrity involved. Ashe and McCutcheon (2001) found that those who watched films most frequently scored highest on a celebrity attitude scale. It is suggested that this provides some weak evidence for the 'mere exposure' effect mentioned above (Zajonc, 1968). Race and ethnicity factors have not proved to be particularly important in relation to the strength of celebrity worship. However, race and ethnicity are important factors determining the choice of celebrity to worship. One study in Florida found that black participants selected a black celebrity as their favourite 81 per cent of the time, with whites choosing a white celebrity 73 per cent of the time. Hispanics chose a white celebrity 60 per cent of the time and a black celebrity 25 per cent of the time. It appears that identification along racial lines is an important factor in celebrity worship. A possible reason that the effect was not marked for Hispanic participants was the lack of Hispanic celebrities.

Studies have examined the influence of personality on celebrity worship. It might be expected that there is a link between 'loneliness', 'shyness' and celebrity worship. Research suggests that a small minority of lonely and shy people do become celebrity worshippers because the celebrity fills a friendship void but that this is not the case for the vast majority of celebrity worshippers. Some of the individuals who are particularly lonely and shy may develop an unnatural obsession for their favourite celebrity and this can lead on to stalking behaviour (see below).

Some people believe that the world is a hostile and unfair place where people manipulate others for their own ends. Others adopt a more positive view that good will triumph in the end and people get what they deserve ('you reap what you sow'). The former attitude can be viewed as a Machiavellian approach and the latter as belief in a 'just world'. It is suggested that celebrity worshippers do not tend to see the world as Machiavellian in nature but instead believe in a 'just world'. Thus they may think that celebrities have got where they are because they deserve to. Celebrity worshippers appear to be very devoted and accepting of their favourite celebrity. Where the rest of us see deception and manipulation (do celebrities really use those products they advertise?), celebrity worshippers see truth and honesty. One study by Rubin and Peplau (1975) found a small significant correlation that supports this hypothesis, although others have found no such relationship.

Research measures into celebrity worship

Although celebrity worship is a relatively new research field, there have been a number of attempts to measure the variable. These involve a whole battery of self-report questions designed to capture the key elements associated with celebrity worship. Wann (1995) developed the Sport Fan Motivation Scale and identified eight factors that predicted sport fandom. These included self-esteem, escapism, entertainment, family and group membership approval, aesthetic appeal, excitement and financial reasons (e.g. betting). One of the recent established measures that used some of Wann's criteria is the Celebrity Attitude Scale (CAS) (Maltby et al., 2002). This involves 23 statements where the participant has to rate their scale of agreement (from strongly agree = 5 to strongly disagree = 1) (see Practical Learning Activity 8.12).

Maltby et al. (2003) administered the CAS to 1,732 British participants aged between 14 and 62 years. They reported three dimensions of celebrity worship.

1. Entertainment-social: fans become attracted to celebrities because of their ability to entertain them and become a social focus for many of their activities (e.g. discussions with friends, listening to music and so forth). Questions 4, 6, 9, 13, 14, 15, 18, 19, 21 and 22 relate to this dimension. Maltby et al. (2003) suggested that each of these three dimensions may relate to dimensions incorporated in Eysenck's Personality Theory.

2. Intense-personal: fans develop intensive and compulsive feelings about their favourite celebrity. Such feelings border on the obsessional. Questions 1, 2, 3, 5, 7, 8, 10, 11 and 12 relate to this dimension.

3. Borderline-pathological: fans develop uncontrollable behaviours and fantasies regarding their favourite

celebrity. Questions 16, 17, 20 and 23 relate to this dimension.

The entertainment-social dimension on the CAS relates to extraversion (sociable, sensation seeking, carefree and optimistic traits); the intense-personal dimension relates to Eysenck's neuroticism dimension (anxious, worrying and moody traits); finally, the borderline-pathological dimension relates to psychotism (solitary, troublesome, cruel, inhumane traits) (Giles and Maltby, 2006).

How Science Works

Practical Learning Activity 8.12: The Celebrity Attitude Scale (McCutcheon *et al.*, 2004)

Use the following scale in response to the items below:

5 = Strongly agree, 4 = Agree, 3 = Uncertain or neutral, 2 = Disagree, 1 = Strongly disagree

1. If I were to meet my favourite celebrity in person, he/she would already somehow know that I am his/her biggest fan
2. I share with my favourite celebrity a special bond that cannot be described in words
3. I am obsessed by the details of my favourite celebrity's life
4. My friends and I like to discuss what my favourite celebrity has done
5. When something good happens to my favourite celebrity I feel like it happened to me
6. One of the main reasons I maintain an interest in my favourite celebrity is that doing so gives me a temporary escape from life's problems
7. I have pictures and/or souvenirs of my favourite celebrity which I always keep in the same place
8. The successes of my favourite celebrity are my successes also
9. I enjoy watching, reading or listening to my favourite celebrity because it means a good time
10. I consider my favourite celebrity to be a soulmate
11. I have frequent thoughts about my favourite celebrity, even when I don't want to
12. When my favourite celebrity dies (or died) I will feel (or felt) like dying too
13. I love to talk to others who admire my favourite celebrity
14. When something bad happens to my favourite celebrity I feel like it happened to me
15. Learning the life story of my favourite celebrity is a lot of fun
16. I often feel compelled to learn about personal habits of my favourite celebrity
17. If I were lucky enough to meet my favourite celebrity, and he/she asked me to do something illegal as a favour, I would probably do it
18. It is enjoyable just to be with others who like my favourite celebrity
19. When my favourite celebrity fails or loses at something I feel like a failure myself
20. If someone gave me several thousand dollars (pounds) to do with as I please, I would consider spending it on a personal possession (like a napkin or paper plate) once used by my favourite celebrity
21. I like watching and hearing about my favourite celebrity when I am in a large group of people
22. Keeping up with the news about my favourite celebrity is an entertaining pastime
23. News about my favourite celebrity is a pleasant break from a harsh world

- Try to work out the extent to which you might be considered a 'celebrity worshipper'.
- Compare your results with those of your friends.
- What problems are there with such self-completion questionnaires?
- Can you think of some advantages and disadvantages associated with whether you completed the questionnaire anonymously or were required to identify yourself to the researchers?
- Are there any questions that you would omit from or add to the Celebrity Attitude Scale? Why?

Evaluation of research into intense fandom continued...

stalkers, who cause considerable distress to the people who are the objects of their affections and thus are likely to want to under-report their disturbing behaviour. In addition, many of the measures rely on rating scales and thus there is no agreed level of measurement for respondents to use. For example, is my 'Strongly agree' rating really any stronger than your 'Agree' rating? And, if it is, how much stronger is it? Do different people interpret the ratings in different ways? It seems likely that they do and thus there must be a degree of subjectivity in people's assessments of their own behaviour. Giles (2000) reports that such scales are also subject to culture-bound social desirability effects. Americans are more likely to agree with items that emphasise individuality or independence, whereas British respondents are more reluctant and/or modest in their ratings. Despite such criticisms, if a number of studies using different data collection techniques and different samples of people come to similar conclusions we can be more confident that the findings and conclusions are robust. It is arguable whether research into these new areas has reached that stage as yet.

X **Theory testing:** McCutcheon *et al.* (2004) attempted to test the Absorption Addiction Hypothesis. This hypothesis suggests that some individuals gradually become more absorbed and addicted to their favourite celebrities. It is evident that there should be far more individuals at the lower end of the continuum, who score high on the entertainment/social scale, and far fewer individuals who score high on the mild/pathology scale. They analysed the data from four research studies in the USA and UK and found this to be the case. Further support for the theory is that the dimensions that they identified with respect to celebrity worship do relate to earlier research findings related to personality types established by Eysenck (Eysenck and Eysenck, 1985). Since Eysenckian personality theory, is a relatively well-established theory it helps to support the explanations for celebrity worship proposed.

Conclusion

Television and the expansion of the mass media have brought more people into our homes and created more celebrities. Nowadays, individuals have to do less to be celebrities. Perhaps what Andy Warhol said in 1968 has been proved correct: 'In the future everyone will be famous for fifteen minutes.' For the most part, an interest in celebrities is not unhealthy; however, for some people it can have an adverse effect on their mental well-being and can result in stalking behaviour.

SUMMARY

CHAPTER

Media influences on social behaviour

- There are a number of explanations relating to media influences on **antisocial behaviour** including short-term effects involving **cognitive priming, arousal, sponsor effects** and **routine activity**.

- Long-term explanations include **SLT, the cultivation effect and desensitisation**.

- Laboratory research that supports the link between watching violence and aggressive behaviour includes the **Imitation of Film-mediated Aggressive Model (Bandura *et al.*, 1963), Violent**

Programme Study (Liebert and Baron, 1972) and **the *Karate Kid* Experiment (Bushman, 1995)**. Field, natural experiments and correlational studies also support these findings.

- There are a number of explanations relating to media influences on **pro-social behaviour**, including cognitive priming, arousal, sponsor effects and Social Learning Theory.

- Research that supports the link between watching and pro-social effects includes the **Good News Study (Holloway *et al.*, 1977)** and the **'Lost Your Marbles Game' (Silverman and Sprafkin, 1980)**.

- There are a number of pieces of research which suggest that video games can have a **positive effect** on young people's behaviour. Skills that are developed include **problem solving, creativity and individualism**.

- However, more studies seem to suggest that heavy exposure to **video games** has a **detrimental effect**. These effects can be **physical** (Matthews *et al.*, 2006) or **behavioural** (Anderson and Bushman, 2001). **Mary Ballard (1999)** conducted research into the effects of playing *Mortal Kombat* and found that such violent games can have an immediate negative effect on interpersonal interactions. Much of this research involves short-term effects and correlational data.

Persuasion and attitude change, including the Hovland-Yale and Elaboration Likelihood Models

- **Persuasion** is the process of changing attitudes. Early research by **Carl Hovland at Yale University** led to a concentration on four factors that influence the communication process: the **communicator, the message, the channel and the audience**. The **'mere exposure' effect** (Zajonc, 1968) supports the 'familiarity breeds likeability' aspect of message repetition. Strong emotions have been shown to affect the extent to which the message is perceived and attended to. Classical conditioning principles have been applied to the way emotions persuade an individual.

- The Yale research proposes a 'passive' audience reaction compared to the more 'active' audience approach suggested by the **Elaboration Likelihood Model (Petty and Cacioppo, 1981)**. This approach suggests that there are two cognitive processes that occur when a person listens to a persuasive message. **The central route** occurs when the person has the motivation and ability to think about the message. **The peripheral route** occurs when a person is uninterested in or distracted from the message. Persuasion can occur through either route, although the central route is more influential.

- **Attitudes** can influence mood, cognitions and behaviour. The major problem with attitude research is the discrepancy between what people actually do (behaviour) and what they say they'll do (their attitude). This was shown in an early study by LaPiere (1934), who travelled around the USA with a Chinese couple.

The psychology of addictive behaviour

What's covered in this chapter?

You need to know about:

Models of addictive behaviour
- Biological, cognitive and learning models of addiction, including explanations for initiation, maintenance and relapse
- Explanations for specific addictions, including smoking and gambling

Factors affecting addictive behaviour
- Vulnerability to addiction, including self-esteem, attributions for addiction and social context of addiction
- The role of media in addictive behaviour

Reducing addictive behaviour
- Models of prevention, including Theory of Reasoned Action and Theory of Planned Behaviour
- Types of intervention, including biological, psychological, public health interventions and legislation, and their effectiveness

MODELS OF ADDICTIVE BEHAVIOUR

✔ Specification Hint

The first bullet point suggests that the three types of model should be (or could be) *general* in nature; in other words, they apply more or less equally to any/all kinds of addiction. However, the second bullet point specifies smoking and gambling – that is, these two *must* be discussed, although others could be (such as alcoholism and drug addiction/abuse). Alcoholism and drug addiction have been researched more widely than any other type of addiction (probably because these have been around far longer than, say, television and fruit machines) and some of the early (biological) models of addiction were developed to account for alcoholism in particular, which means they're unlikely to apply straightforwardly to addictive behaviour that doesn't involve chemical substances (e.g. gambling). This should be borne in mind in relation to the first bullet point (and this observation could have AO2 value).

The diversity of drugs and 'ordinary' addictions

For thousands of years, people have taken substances to alter their perception of reality, and societies have restricted the substances their members are allowed to take. These substances, which we usually call 'drugs', are *psychoactive*, denoting a chemical substance that alters conscious awareness through its effect on the brain. Most drugs fit this description. Some (such as aspirin) are *indirectly* psychoactive: their primary purpose is to remove pain, but being headache-free lifts our mood. Others, however, are *designed* to change mood and behaviour, and are collectively referred to as *psychotherapeutic* drugs, such as those used to treat anxiety, depression and schizophrenia (see Chapter 7).

Some psychoactive drugs are used to produce a temporarily altered state of consciousness for the purposes of *pleasure*. These include *recreational drugs*, which have no legal restrictions (such as alcohol,

tobacco/nicotine and caffeine) and *drugs of abuse*, which are illegal (such as heroin and cocaine). However, just as recreational drugs can be abused (such as alcohol), so illegal drugs are taken recreationally (such as ecstasy). 'Drug addiction' and 'substance abuse', therefore, do not imply particular types of drug, only the extent to which the drug is used, and the effects – emotional, behavioural and medical – on the addict/abuser.

What counts as a recreational drug or a drug of abuse changes over time within a society, as well as between societies. For example, cocaine had been freely available over the counter in a huge variety of tonics and pick-me-ups before the 1930s, and was an ingredient of the original blend of Coca-Cola in the 1890s. At that time, it was seen as a harmless stimulant (Plant, 1999); now it's a Class A drug. Conversely, in the UK, cannabis was reclassified in 2004 from a Class B to a Class C drug (still illegal but seen as less dangerous and carrying a more lenient, if any, punishment).

According to Veitia and McGahee (1995):

> *Cigarette smoking and alcohol abuse permeate our culture and are widespread enough to be considered ordinary addictions ... The degree to which these drugs permeate our culture and the extent to which they are accepted by our society distinguish them from other addictive but illegal substances such as heroin and cocaine.*

The diversity of 'addiction': is there more to addiction than drugs?

How Science Works

Practical Learning Activity 9.1

- What do terms such as 'workaholic', 'shopaholic' and 'chocaholic' tell you about the nature of addictive behaviour?
- Can you define addiction in a way that can cover such non-drug behaviours?
- What might they all have in common?

The concept of addiction has been heavily criticised, leading some to reject it in favour of terms such as 'abuse' and 'dependence' (see below). However, some researchers argue that the concept should be *broadened*, in order to cover certain recent forms of 'addictive' behaviour that don't involve chemical substances at all. According to Shaffer *et al.* (1989):

> *Addictive behaviours typically serve the addict in the short run at the price of longer-term destructiveness. Physical dependence is not a requisite for addiction ... addictive behaviours organise the addict's life. All of life's other activities fit in the gaps that the addictive behaviour permits.*

The addiction can be to a substance or an experience: shopping, gambling or eating (or abstaining from eating; see Gross, 2005). Drawing on current definitions of substance dependence, pathological gambling and eating disorders, Walters (1999) suggests that addiction may be defined as 'the persistent and repetitive enactment of a behaviour pattern', which includes:

- *progression* (increase in severity)

- *preoccupation* with the activity

- *perceived loss of control*

- *persistence* despite negative long-term consequences.

Similarly, Griffiths (1999b) maintains that addiction isn't confined to drugs. Several other behaviours, including gambling, watching TV, playing amusement machines, overeating, sex, exercise, playing computer games and using the internet are all potentially addictive. Social pathologies are beginning to surface in cyberspace in the form of *technological addictions*, which are:

> *non-chemical (behavioural) addictions that involve human–machine interaction. They can be either passive (e.g. television) or active (e.g. computer games). The interaction usually contains inducing and reinforcing features (e.g. sound effects, colour effects ...) that may promote addictive tendencies. (Griffiths, 1995)*

Griffiths (1996, 2005) argues that these behaviours display the same *core components* of addiction (complementing Walters's 'four Ps' above), namely:

- *salience* – the activity becomes the most important one in the person's life; it dominates thinking (preoccupations), feelings (cravings) and behaviour (socialised behaviour deteriorates)

- *mood modification* – for example, the activity produces an arousing 'buzz' or 'high'

- *tolerance* – increasing amounts of the activity are needed to achieve the same effects

- *withdrawal symptoms* – discontinuation or sudden reduction of the activity produces unpleasant feelings and physical effects

- *conflict* – this may be between the addict and those around him/her, with other activities (such as work, social life and other interests) or within the individual him/herself

- *relapse* – reverting to earlier patterns of the activity soon after a period of abstinence or self-control.

How useful/valid is the concept of addiction?

Alcoholism and drug addiction as 'paradigm cases': addiction-as-disease

How Science Works

Practical Learning Activity 9.2

- Write a short description of an 'addict'.
- Conduct a survey in which you ask people (adults and children, if you so choose) to write a short description of an 'addict'.
- Are there are any common, recurring, features of these descriptions?

As we noted in the 'Specification Hint' above, early models of addiction were largely focused on addiction to alcohol and drugs. Until recently, the study and treatment of drug problems were organised around the concept of addiction: people with drug problems have problems because they're addicted to the drug (Hammersley, 1999). Addicts are compelled by a physiological need to continue taking the drug, experience horrible physical and psychological symptoms when they try to stop, and will continue taking it despite these symptoms because of their addictive need. Their addiction will also change them psychologically for the worse, they'll commit crimes to pay for the drug, neglect their social roles and responsibilities, and even harm the people around them. In addition, some drugs are considered more addictive than others, and substance users can be divided into addicts and non-addicts. As Bennett (2006) says, 'Ask someone to describe an addict and they will usually give a stereotypical description of someone addicted to "hard" drugs such as heroin or cocaine …'. This stereotype is based on the *addiction-as-disease* (AAD) model. In other words, alcoholism and drug addiction are 'paradigm cases', and the AAD model is the 'paradigmatic account of addiction in general. Even though the AAD model was developed as a way of trying to explain alco-

holism and (illegal) drug addiction, it has been criticised from several perspectives (see below). Given that we've considered several other addictions that are non-chemical/behavioural, the question arises as to how valid an addiction-as-disease model can be in trying to account for these.

Of the two that we're focusing on in this chapter, gambling would appear to be 'purely' behavioural (so that the AAD model doesn't seem appropriate), while smoking has both chemical and behavioural components (as do alcoholism and drug addiction), so that the AAD model would appear to be more appropriate.

Evaluation of the AAD model

✗ **Addiction is an oversimplified concept:** most professionals who deal with people with any kind of problem – medical, criminal, educational, social – will have seen many clients who aren't exactly addicts, but whose drug use seems to have contributed to, or worsened, their other problems (Hammersley, 1999).

✗ **Absolving addicts of their addictive behaviour:** while medical models such as this are generally persuasive, because they offer a diagnosis, definition and a pathology, they also appear to relieve the 'addict' of responsibility for his/her behaviour (Baker, 2000; see Chapter 7).

Sussman and Ames (2001) identify four major problems with this model (as it applies to drug abuse), as follows:

✗ **There's no independent means of verifying the existence of the disease:** in several conditions, the factors that produce certain symptoms can be assessed (for example, a viral infection can be measured through a throat culture, antibody production or high temperature). Also, the factors can be assessed independently of the resulting symptoms (for example, it can be established that high temperature is caused by a poison, virus or bacterium). But with behavioural disorders, it's often difficult to separate factors from symptoms (Davison and Neale, 1990). If the problem were merely one of *behaviour*, then no longer taking the drug would stop the problem. But relapse rates never fall to zero and are 65 per cent in the first year following treatment, halving each year after that. This is true regardless of the substance involved. High relapse rates imply underlying factors, but there are no independent measures of assessing the underlying factors.

✔ **Might the 'addicted brain' provide the independent assessment?** Even in the case of non-chemical addictions (such as those to exercise or gambling), the neurochemical reaction to the addictive behaviour is similar to that induced by drugs (Bennett, 2006). Recent research has thrown light on the 'addicted brain', which is described in Box 9.1 (See page 392).

✗ **Variation in disordered behavioural symptoms:** behavioural symptoms may be defined as more or less disordered depending on the social context. For example, someone who gets drunk and obnoxious

Evaluation of the AAD model continued...

once a month may be seen as an alcoholic in a church-going community, but not in a college dorm. Also, drug abuse can be seen as falling somewhere on a continuum, rather than a binary (yes/no) state, which is often used to define a disease ('you're either an addict or you're not'; see above). (This is related to the fundamental issue of how we define abnormality; see Gross and Rolls, 2008.) However, heart disease, for example, also falls along a continuum, which is why it can be 'missed' or misdiagnosed (even though there are objective tests that can detect it).

✗ **Variation in behavioural symptoms may not reflect the same underlying processes:** for example, it's unclear whether or not a person who drinks alcohol very occasionally, or one who drinks heavily periodically, or one whose drinking is always out of control, are subject to the same underlying influences. In other words, there are many patterns of drug abuse, but it's unclear whether they all reflect the same cause.

✗ **The aetiological factors for drug abuse as a behavioural disorder aren't known:** we don't know what makes people abuse drugs. If there's a common underlying cause, it's plausible that this has nothing to do with drug abuse behaviour. Indeed, drug abuse is associated with various problem behaviours, including crime, violence, sensation seeking and poor diet, which may precede the abuse as a disease.

Box 9.1: The 'addicted brain' (based on Claridge and Davis, 2003; Nestler and Malenka, 2004)

- Neurobiologists have long known that drugs have their effect because they ultimately boost the activity of the brain's reward system: a complex circuit of neurons that evolved to make us feel 'flush' after eating or sex. At least initially, stimulating this system makes us feel good, which encourages us to repeat whatever induced the pleasure.
- But new research indicates that chronic drug use can induce changes in the structure and function of the reward system's neurons that last for weeks, months or years following the fix.
- A key part of the circuit is the pathway extending from dopamine-producing neurons in the ventral tegmental area (VTA) to dopamine-sensitive neurons in the nucleus acumbens (NA), situated deep beneath the frontal cortex. These changes contribute significantly to the *tolerance*, *dependence* and *craving* that fuel repeated use, and that lead to relapses even after long periods of abstinence.
- The ventral tegmentum is an area in the midbrain, rich in dopamine neurons, which sends projections through the medial forebrain

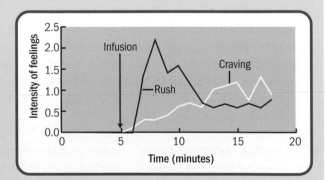

Figure 9.1 Graph of the addicted brain
Source: Nestler and Malenka (2004), reprinted with permission from Hans C. Breiter, Massachusetts General Hospital

bundle to a set of limbic brain regions, including the NA and amygdala, and to the prefrontal cortex. Together, these, and related structures, are known as the 'common reward pathway': their activation or stimulation is experienced as pleasurable and reinforcing. In fact, if rats are given unimpeded access to self-stimulation of the circuit (via an electrode implanted in the brain that delivers an electric current whenever they press a lever), they'll lever-press continuously to the point of self-starvation.

- There are also pathways linking the NA and VTA with other brain regions that can help make addicts highly sensitive to reminders of past highs (such as drug paraphernalia and places where they've scored), vulnerable to relapse when stressed, and unable to control the urge to seek drugs.

- The VTA–NA pathway acts as a 'rheostat of reward': it 'tells' other brain centres how rewarding an activity is. The more rewarding, the more likely the organism is to remember it well and repeat it.

- fMRI and PET scans show that the NA in cocaine addicts' brains 'lights up' when offered a snort, shown a video of someone using cocaine or even a photograph of white lines on a mirror.

- The amygdala and some areas of the cortex also respond. While being scanned, addicts rate their feelings of rush and craving on a scale of 0–3. Such studies show that (a) the VTA and sublenticular extended amygdala are important to the cocaine-induced rush, and (b) the amygdala and NA influence both the rush *and* the craving for more of the drug, which becomes stronger as the euphoria wears off (as shown in Figure 9.1).

- The NA has been called the 'Universal Addiction Site' (Leshner and Koob, 1999, in Claridge and Davis, 2003) because most, if not all, drugs (or activities) of abuse stimulate extracellular dopamine in this area. It has also been described as a *limbic-motor interface* because increased dopamine release in this area seems to play a pivotal role in providing certain stimuli with the incentive qualities needed to increase addictive behaviour. The same regions react in compulsive gamblers shown images of slot machines (see text below).

Synoptic Material

✔ **The need to distinguish between initiation, maintenance and relapse:** the last criticism of Sussman and Ames seems to imply a crucial distinction between initiation (aetiological factors – that is, how the behaviour gets started), maintenance (what keeps it going) and relapse (what makes the addictive behaviour recur after it's previously stopped). In other words, when we talk about addictive behaviour (as with *any* behaviour), we want to know about all three: the factors responsible for initiation may be different from those responsible for maintenance, which, in turn, may differ from those that account for relapse. Sussman and Ames seem to be saying that the fact that there may be more than one initiating factor (crime etc.) is a weakness of the AAD model. But there are often many causes of the 'same' illness or bodily state, and with behaviour this is exactly what we'd expect. No single explanation of any complex human behaviour is likely to be adequate.

Just as complex human behaviour comprises biological, cognitive and social, learned and unlearned factors, so different theoretical perspectives focus on and emphasise one of these types of factor. So while the AAD stresses the biological/bodily aspects of addictive behaviour, social psychologists and sociologists are likely to see 'addiction' as no more than a label for behaviour that deviates from social norms (for example, masturbation, fellatio, cunnilingus and homosexuality were viewed very differently 50 years ago from how they are today (Griffiths, 2001; see also Chapter 7; Gross, 2005; Gross and Rolls, 2008), while experimental psychologists / learning theorists will emphasise the process by which addictive behaviour is acquired, maintained and can be extinguished according to the same learning principles that apply to behaviour in general.

393

Box 9.2: Substance abuse, dependence and addiction

The Diagnostic and Statistical Manual of Mental Disorders, published by the American Psychiatric Association (DSM IV-TR. 2000; see Chapter 7) distinguishes between *substance abuse* and *substance dependence.* The DSM-IV-TR criteria for substance dependence are as follows.

- A maladaptive pattern of substance use leading to clinically significant impairment or distress, as manifested by three (or more) of the following, occurring at any time in the same 12-month period:

1. Tolerance, as defined by either of the following:
   (a) a need for markedly increased amounts of the substance to achieve intoxication or desired effect;
   (b) markedly diminished effect with continued use of the same amount of the substance.
2. Withdrawal, as manifested by either of the following:
   (a) the characteristic withdrawal syndrome for the substance (varies from substance to substance);
   (b) the same (or a closely related) substance is taken to relieve or avoid withdrawal symptoms.
3. The substance is often taken in larger amounts and over a longer period than was intended.
4. There is a persistent desire or unsuccessful efforts to cut down or control substance abuse.
5. A great deal of time is spent in activities necessary to obtain the substance (e.g. visiting multiple doctors or driving long distances), use the substance (e.g. chain-smoking), or recover from its effects.
6. Important social, occupational, or recreational activities are given up or reduced because of substance abuse.
7. The substance use is continued despite knowledge of having a persistent physical or psychological problem that is likely to have been caused or exacerbated by the substance (e.g. current cocaine use despite recognition of cocaine-induced depression, or continued drinking despite recognition that an ulcer was made worse by alcohol consumption).

Specify if:

- *With physiological dependence* – evidence of tolerance or withdrawal (i.e. either item 1 or 2 is present).
- *With psychological dependence* – no evidence of tolerance or withdrawal (i.e. neither item 1 nor item 2 is present.

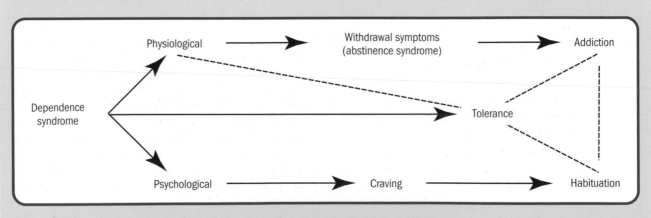

Figure 9.2 Summary of major components of dependence syndrome

So DSM distinguishes quite clearly between physiological and psychological dependence. The former is related to withdrawal and/or tolerance (which relates to the traditional concept of addiction), while the latter isn't. However, being deprived of something that's highly pleasurable can induce anxiety. Since the symptoms of anxiety (rapid pulse, profuse sweating, shaking and so on) overlap with withdrawal symptoms, people may mistakenly believe that they're physiologically dependent. Psychological dependence is, though, part of the overall *dependence syndrome* (see Figure 9.2).

According to Lowe (1995), 'psychological' dependence has little scientific meaning beyond the notion that drug taking (or whatever the addiction) becomes part of one's habitual behaviour; giving it up is very difficult because the person has become *habituated* to it. Physiologically addictive drugs may cause habituation *as well.*

Some dependent people can stay dependent for long periods *without* suffering any other problems. This applies particularly to people who otherwise fit well into society, and who haven't experienced financial, legal or health problems as result of their substance abuse – such as many smokers.

Most substance-dependent people have tried to give up several times, relapsing after weeks, months or even years. They often report strong craving or desire for the substance, and are at particular risk of resuming use when stressed, anxious, depressed, angry or happy. They also often feel they have difficulty controlling the amount they take once they start. When they relapse, they often return very quickly to their old, often destructive, habits (Hammersley, 1999).

Biological models of addictive behaviour

✔ Specification Hint

To reinforce a point made in the 'Specification Hint' above (page 389), you're only required to know about ONE model of each type: biological, cognitive and learning. Some times, it's easier to identify a distinct, specific model than at other times, and it's also useful to be familiar with a second model when evaluating the first. In relation to biological models, Box 9.1 describes some aspects of a more general *neurobiological* model; what follows expands and complements the description of the 'addicted brain'.

The neurobiology of addiction

Some have used the term 'hijacked' to describe the effect of addictive substances on normal brain functioning. What this denotes is:

the fact that cocaine and other drugs – indeed, all potentially addictive behaviours – activate and can subvert areas of our brain which evolved to regulate and sustain the most basic aspects of our existence. In other words, the same brain circuitry which subserves feeding, sex, and other essential survival behaviours, also underlies the development and maintenance of substance abuse .. . (Claridge and Davis, 2003)

Also, because these non-natural behaviours 'trick' the brain into thinking that a survival need has been met, it's not surprising that addicts typically have a diminished sexual libido (except sex addicts, of course) and appetite for food.

The *mesocorticolimbic dopamine pathway* (MDP) is involved in the pleasure and reinforcement associated with natural reward states (such as eating, drinking, mating and maternal behaviour), as well as with less basic needs (such as social interaction and novelty). Small *et al.* (2001, in Claridge and Davis, 2003) used brain imaging to show that when participants ate a piece of chocolate and rated the experience as 'pleasurable', there was increased regional blood flow in the striatum (part of the MDP). When they felt highly motivated to have some more chocolate, the same brain regions (the *caudomedial orbitofrontal cortex*) were active as those implicated in the experience of drug cravings.

Before the advent of brain imaging techniques, researchers relied mainly on research with non-human species; they had to make inferences about the rewarding properties of drugs from animals' behaviour. It's been demonstrated repeatedly that cocaine, heroin and several other addictive drugs are readily self-administered by several species of experimental animals (such as rats and monkeys). Because there's also a strong positive correlation between the human abuse potential of a particular drug and the degree to which animals will self-administer the substance, this experimental paradigm continues to serve as an excellent means of exploring the neurobiology of drug reinforcement.

The role of the prefrontal cortex

The prefrontal cortex (PFC) is thought to serve an 'executive' function in the brain by acting as a gating mechanism to moderate the suppression of limbic impulses. One way of studying its effects is to lesion (surgically remove) or block its function using antagonist drugs; another is to assess the behaviour of patients who've suffered frontal lobe damage.

In studies where the function of the PFC has been disrupted one way or another, people are unable to suppress inappropriate responses; in other words, they display a reduced ability to self-regulate their behaviour and loss of inhibitory control. In these cases, the individual's behaviour seems to be largely guided by previously conditioned responses that aren't suited to the current situation (Jentsch and Taylor, 1999, in Claridge and Davis, 2003; see below).

In recent years, the role of the PFC has gained increasing prominence in our understanding of the addiction process; especially important is our growing awareness of its role in *decision making* and in controlling behaviour that entails the risk of punishment (Bechara *et al.*, 2001, in Claridge and Davis, 2003). Currently the evidence suggests that specific regions of the PFC are responsible for regulating behaviour – specifically, for inhibiting the drive to respond to immediate reinforcement if the long-term consequences are likely to result in some negative outcome. One proposal is that impairments in the ability to make 'good' decisions lie at the heart of addictive behaviours. In other words, addicts tend to choose immediate rewards even if they result in long-term negative consequences. However, it's unclear whether this impairment is a *consequence* of drug taking (or other addictive behaviour) and over-activation of the reward circuitry, or whether there's a tendency or handicap in the adaptive functioning of the PFC that increases the risk of becoming addicted (Claridge and Davis, 2003).

Sensitisation and desensitisation

When the brain is activated excessively and chronically moved beyond its natural, balanced state, neurochemical changes begin to occur. According to Claridge and Davis (2003):

> What is insidious about the overuse of addictive activities or substances, however, is that they change the brain in ways that contribute to further seeking and further use – a process that, over time, creates a vicious downwardly spiralling cycle of behaviours that are difficult to resist and highly prone to relapse if abstinence is attempted …

Although the brain changes that occur are complex, and vary from one substance (or activity) to another, the two most significant (which operate in virtually opposite directions) are *desensitisation* and *sensitisation*.

Desensitisation is the neural mechanism underlying *tolerance* (see Box 9.2). When there are prolonged and repeated increases in extracellular dopamine (hyperdopaminergia), the brain attempts to compensate for the excessive stimulation by changing its function in some way. What seems to happen is that the dopamine receptors at the *post-synaptic* level (see Chapter 7) become less sensitive, which Claridge and Davis compare with closing some of the windows in a house when the outside temperature suddenly drops and becomes very cold. Unfortunately, one of the behavioural consequences of this neuroadaptation is an increased desire for more extensive addictive behaviour: the individual needs larger and/or more frequent doses to achieve the initial or desired effect of the behaviour. It appears that reduced activity in the PFC also takes place (hypofrontality); this underlies the difficulty addicts have in resisting impulses to use their drug. In other words, the executive function of the PFC is compromised (see above).

The problem with post-mortem studies is the question of *causality*. Did the drug addiction cause the brain changes, or were the addicts' brains like this *before* the addiction (implying that the brain changes caused the addiction)?

How Science Works

Practical Learning Activity 9.3

One way of studying desensitisation is to examine the brains of former drug addicts after their death. These post-mortems reveal a reduced density of dopamine receptors compared to normal brains.

- Can we necessarily infer from these findings that the addiction was responsible for the reduced receptor densities? Explain your answer.
- How might you get round this (potential) problem?
- In turn, what problems do such problem-solutions create?

Using PET-imaging with non-human primates, Ginovart *et al.* (1999, in Claridge and Davis, 2003) found reduced dopamine D2 receptor density after animals had been chronically exposed to amphetamines.

Sensitisation also plays a significant role in supporting addictive behaviours. Repeated but intermittent exposure to psychomotor stimulant drugs seems to produce increased behavioural and neurochemical responses to subsequent drug exposure. In animals, this can be seen in increases in their activity levels. Sensitisation also appears to function at the level of stimulus–reward or associative learning (see below).

How Science Works

Practical Learning Activity 9.4

- Based on what you know of the biological approach to abnormality (see Gross and Rolls, 2008), what other kinds of biological explanation of addictive behaviour can you identify? Briefly describe these alternatives.

Evaluation of the neurobiological approach

✔ **Substantial empirical support:** as we've seen, there's considerable research evidence to support the role of various brain structures and pathways in addictive behaviour.

✗ **Methodological problems:** as we've also seen, it's sometimes difficult to infer causality from post-mortem studies of human addicts. Animal experiments are subject to all the usual ethical issues associated with the use of animals in general, as well as the difficulties in interpreting the behaviour of organisms that cannot tell you what they're feeling (having to *infer* this from their overt behaviour).

✗ **A reductionist approach:** as with all attempts to explain human behaviour in biological terms, other, non-biological, factors tend to get overlooked or ignored. In other words, explaining addiction by reference to brain structure and function implies that once these have been identified, addiction has been fully explained. But, as discussed below, the same brain activity can be triggered when addicts aren't directly involved in their addictive behaviour as when they are; this suggests that *psychological* factors (such as conditioned responses and cognitive processes) are also involved. While these can be seen as *complementing* biological factors, neurobiological approaches tend to be *reductionist* (that is, they *exclude* non-biological factors).

Learning models of addictive behaviour

When discussing the neurobiology of addiction, Claridge and Davis (2003) note that burst-firing activity of the dopamine reward neurons occurs consistently not only during the *consummatory* phase of rewarding activities (i.e. when the activity is actually taking place, such as sniffing cocaine) but also well *before* the consumption begins. We saw in Box 9.1 that cocaine addicts' reward systems respond when merely offered a snort, watching a video of someone using cocaine, or even looking at a photograph of white lines on a mirror. The same brain regions react in compulsive gamblers when shown images of slot machines.

Classical (respondent or Pavlovian) conditioning

According to Claridge and Davis (2003), these examples strongly suggest that the common reward pathway is also involved in *associative learning* – that is, in establishing the conditioned reinforcement of environmental cues that signal the approach or onset of the natural reward state. Here they're referring to *classical conditioning*, a passive form of learning in which two stimuli become associated/linked with each other, one (the *unconditioned stimulus* / UCS) producing a particular response 'naturally' (the *unconditioned response* / UCR), the other (the *conditioned stimulus* / CS) producing the same response only through association with the first (the *conditioned response* / CR). (See Figure 9.3.)

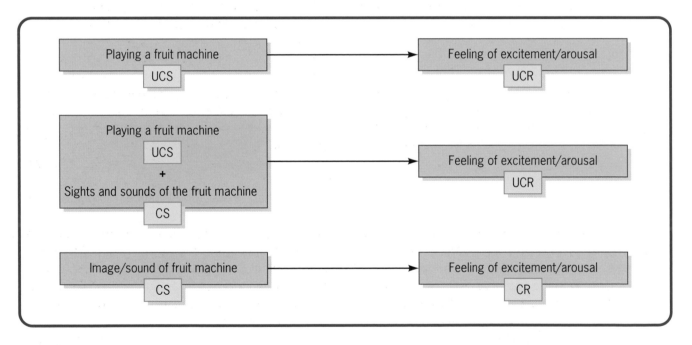

Figure 9.3 Diagrammatic representation of how classical conditioning can produce a response to a stimulus associated with the addictive behaviour

Evaluation of the classical conditioning explanation

✗ **The limited nature of respondent behaviour:** when Skinner (e.g. 1938) drew the distinction between respondent and operant behaviour, he was effectively distinguishing between involuntary and voluntary behaviour respectively. He claimed that most behaviour – human and non-human – is voluntary, in the sense that it's *not* triggered automatically by environmental stimuli (conditioned or unconditioned) as conveyed by 'respondent'; 'operant' denotes the organism *operating on its environment* in some way, with the reinforcement a consequence of that operant behaviour.

As applied to addiction, classical conditioning might be able to explain how a stimulus associated with a drug (e.g. drug paraphernalia) can come to produce a similar response to the one produced by the drug itself (as well as a similar reaction in the brain), but it cannot explain how or why the drug is taken in the first place. Unless the drug is forced upon the individual in some way, we need to account for how addiction is *initiated*, and classical conditioning (on its own) cannot do this because it can only account for involuntary behaviour.

✔/✗ **It can account for certain aspects of addiction – but not all addictions are the same:** because of the powerful nature of the response produced by most drugs, classical conditioning can better explain the *maintenance* of addictive behaviours (for example, through the process of *stimulus generalisation*). However, what about addictive activities that don't involve such powerful, biologically determined UCRs? For example, by definition, gamblers only win some of the time, so why doesn't gambling stop through extinction? The answer seems to rely on *operant* conditioning (see text below).

When experimental animals are presented with the CS *without* the UCS, the CR gradually weakens and eventually stops altogether (*experimental extinction*); this is equivalent to the addict being denied access to the substance or activity of their addiction and abstaining. However, when the UCS is later reintroduced, experimental animals will once again display the CS (through *spontaneous recovery*). This corresponds to the addict's *relapse*, and shows that in extinction the CS is merely *suppressed* (rather than 'destroyed').

✔ **There's more to classical conditioning than meets the eye:** although respondent behaviour accounts for only a small proportion of all behaviour, the nature of the CS has been reinterpreted since Pavlov's (1927) pioneering research (see Gross, 2005). Indeed, Pavlov himself described the CS as a 'signal' for the UCS, the relationship between the CS and the UCS as one of 'stimulus substitution', and the CR as an 'anticipatory response', suggesting that his dogs were *expecting* the food to follow the bell. These are essentially *cognitive* processes that underlie the overt behaviour (see text below).

How Science Works

Practical Learning Activity 9.5

- Draw a diagram similar to Figure 9.3 representing the classical conditioning of cocaine addiction.
- How is cocaine as a UCS different from playing a fruit machine as a UCS? (See Gross, 2005; Gross and Rolls, 2008.)

From an *evolutionary* perspective, the ability of environmental cues to signal the approach or onset of the natural reward state is clearly a very adaptive function: the organism will fare much better if it's able to discriminate between stimuli that predict when a rewarding event is likely to happen and those that don't (Claridge and Davis, 2003). A relatively large body of research supports the role of the *amygdala* in this process, because it maintains a representation of the affective (emotional) value of the CS (Jentsch and Taylor, 1999, in Claridge and Davis, 2003). This is a good example of how the function of brain structures complements, and is correlated with, psychological processes (here, acquiring conditioned responses through classical conditioning).

The strength of conditioned reinforcement is greatly enhanced when the CS is paired with certain kinds of UCS (in particular, *pharmacological* rewards, such as cocaine) rather than others (such as food). This demonstrates that classical conditioning is a more complex learning process than it might at first appear: its effects are mediated by which particular UCS is used (which suggests the role of biological factors). Other research has demonstrated the role of *cognitive* factors (see Gross, 2005).

Operant (instrumental or Skinnerian) conditioning

One of the best-known explanations of gambling behaviour is that it illustrates very well the process of operant conditioning, specifically a *variable ratio reinforcement schedule*. As in all cases of operant conditioning, the organism must perform some specified action in order to receive a particular positive reinforcement (reward) such as a rat pressing a lever that results in the delivery of a food pellet. The food reinforcement makes the rat more likely to repeat the behaviour (it's *strengthened* by the food).

In general terms, applying this framework to drug dependence is straightforward if we define dependence *operationally* as an excessive tendency to engage in drug-taking behaviour. According to Powell (2000):

> *This implies that the rewards to the addict are so salient, and sufficiently reliable, that he or she has become motivated to take the drug progressively more often in order to achieve these effects, eventually reaching a point where the desire overwhelms all else …*

One important aspect of Skinner's work was to examine the effects on behaviour of how regularly (or predictably) reinforcements are presented; one of the five major schedules of reinforcement identified by Ferster and Skinner (1957) is the *variable ratio* (VR) schedule. A VR10 means that a reinforcement is given – on average – every ten responses, but the number varies from trial to trial. So the number of responses required on any one occasion is unpredictable. Typically, in rats pressing levers for food, a VR schedule produces a very high – and steady – response rate (they press at a faster rate, over considerable periods of time); it also produces the highest resistance to extinction of any schedule. The classic example of human behaviour that's controlled by a VR schedule is gambling.

How Science Works

Practical Learning Activity 9.6

- How might gambling be explained in terms of a VR reinforcement schedule? (You might find it useful to use *cognitive terms* in your explanation.)

If a gambler is used to winning only on a certain proportion of occasions that s/he gambles, then not winning on any particular occasion will come as no surprise and won't cause the behaviour to extinguish (as might happen if s/he wins every time). Tied to this *irregularity* of success is the *unpredictability* (the gambler doesn't know when the next success will come); not winning won't 'throw' the gambler. However, wins and losses average themselves out over a large number of bets. (Of course, if s/he never won again, the behaviour would, eventually, cease).

Evaluation of the operant conditioning explanation

✔/✗ **Can explain some aspects of addictive behaviour, but not all addictions are the same:** the account above relates to *maintenance* of behaviour – the gambling will persist in the absence of reinforcement because the gambler is used to receiving only intermittent, irregular reinforcements. However, as with classical conditioning, its ability to explain initiation is very limited. Unlike classical conditioning as described above (where, basically, the UCS – the reinforcement – is either presented or it's not), a VR schedule describes a situation where the reinforcer is presented a specific *proportion* of times the response is made. As we've seen, the behaviour *persists* for much longer than it would if the reinforcement occurred every time (i.e. abstinence is more difficult to achieve); *relapse* (which only occurs after a period of abstinence) is, therefore, less likely to occur in the first place, but if it does, it can be also be explained in terms of spontaneous recovery.

But just because gambling is commonly given as the 'classic' example of human behaviour controlled by a VR schedule, this doesn't mean that other addictive behaviours can necessarily be explained in similar terms. The equivalent for the drug addict would be that only sometimes does snorting cocaine produce a high; while some highs may be higher than others, this is hardly equivalent to winning or not winning on, say, a fruit machine. Also, different classes of drug exert quite different pharmacological effects, so that the rewards that have contributed to the development of the addiction will vary from drug to drug (Powell, 2000).

✔ **A more versatile approach:** as well as accounting for maintenance/persistence of certain addictive behaviours, it also offers an explanation of how difficult it might be for someone to break their habit. For example, the decision to try to break a habit can be seen as reflecting the strength of its punishing outcomes: since most habits produce mixed effects, some pleasant and others aversive, addicts may find themselves in an *approach-avoidance conflict*, where motivation fluctuates between wanting to use and wanting to stop (Powell, 2000).

✗ **Limited explanatory power:** in the context of gambling, Sharpe (2002, in Bennett, 2006) claims that while VR schedules undoubtedly contribute to high levels of *social* gambling, they don't fully explain *pathological* gambling, where consistent and significant losses don't cause the individual to stop gambling (see text below). Sharpe suggests that large pay-outs, and in particular a 'big win' early in a gambling career, establish and sustain pathological gambling. These presumably distort expectations of the outcomes of gambling, and support losses in the expectation of future 'big wins'.

Social Learning Theory

Social Learning Theory (SLT) (e.g. Bandura, 1977a, 1977b) represents an attempt to reinterpret certain aspects of Freud's psychoanalytic theory in terms of classical and operant conditioning. As well as focusing on human social behaviour, Bandura and other SL theorists believe that there are important *cognitive mediating variables* between stimulus and response without which we cannot adequately explain human behaviour. Some of the most important cognitive variables include *self-concept, self-monitoring* (or self-regulation) and *self-efficacy* (our belief that we can act effectively and exercise control over events that influence our lives (Bandura, 1977a, 1986). Self-efficacy is crucially important for motivation: how we judge our own capabilities is likely to affect our expectations about future behaviour.

SL theorists also emphasise the role of *observational learning* (or *modelling*) – that is, learning through the behaviour of others – *models*. This occurs spontaneously, with no deliberate effort by the learner or any intention by the model to teach anything. Observational learning takes place without any reinforcement – mere exposure to the model is sufficient for learning to occur (Bandura, 1965).

✔ **Helps to explain the initiation of addiction:** as we saw above, both the classical and operant conditioning explanations find it difficult to explain how the addictive behaviour occurs in the first place. But SLT, through its emphasis on observational learning/modelling, together with its claim that mere exposure to the model is sufficient for learning to take place, can quite easily explain why someone would begin engaging in behaviour that leads to addiction. Although reinforcement of some kind might be necessary for the learned behaviour to actually show, this may only require the *model* to be rewarded (Bandura, 1965). So, for example, observing a model win at a fruit machine might be enough for a child to begin developing the habit.

✔ **Emphasis on cognitive factors:** the importance of cognitive factors is reflected in Bandura's (1986, 1989) renaming of SLT as *Social Cognitive Theory* (SCT). The application of SLT to the understanding (and treatment) of addictive behaviours has been formalised by Marlatt and Gordon (1985, in Powell, 2000) in their 'Relapse Prevention' (RP) model. This is discussed in the next section.

Cognitive models of addictive behaviour

'Relapse Prevention' (RP) model (Marlatt and Gordon, 1985)

Although the RP model concentrates especially on the factors that will influence the success or failure of an addict who attempts to become abstinent, there's considerable overlap with processes that may be involved in the initial development of an addiction (initiation).

For any addict, there will be a range of *discriminative stimuli* (DSs), a term borrowed from operant conditioning that refers to stimuli (or contexts) that indicate the appropriateness or 'rewardingness' of specific behaviours. For example, one addict may have learned that heroin use is more rewarding when he's feeling down rather than when he's happy, while another may have learned that heroin is particularly exciting when she's with other users but less so when she's on her own ('drug-using friends represent DSs for her heroin use'; Powell, 2000).

If, after becoming drug-free, an addict encounters one of these DSs, then s/he will be at high risk of relapse (for example, the female addict meets one of her drug-using friends). In terms of the RP model, the DSs arouse *positive outcome expectancies*, which trigger a motivation to use the drug. However, the addict's ability to survive the threat to his/her abstinence is influenced by various other factors, including the strength of his/her motivation not to use, knowledge of alternative strategies for coping with the situation, and self-efficacy. A shortfall in any of these factors will increase vulnerability to relapse. The model is summarised in Figure 9.4.

Powell (2000) gives the example of Mark, a heroin addict. He may know in principle that an alternative strategy for combating low mood is to listen to his favourite music. But if he temporarily loses sight of his reasons for wanting to stay drug-free (a common problem in treatment), he may be insufficiently motivated to try this alternative and go straight for the easier option of drug use. Similarly, if his self-efficacy is very low, and he feels he doesn't have the inner strength to apply the effort needed to let the music work, then he's likely to dismiss it as a possibility. As Powell says:

> *It is essential, then, that intervention focuses not only on equipping the addict with adequate strategies but also on the personal resources that allow him to use them effectively. Conversely, a high degree of self-efficacy combined with strong motivation to remain abstinent may be insufficient if the addict does not have the knowledge or skill to resolve the situation in some other way . . .*

The fewer alternatives an individual has accessible for dealing with a situation, the more salient his/her positive outcome expectancies for drug use become (and, by extension, for other addictive behaviours).

The outcome of high-risk situations, and how addicts

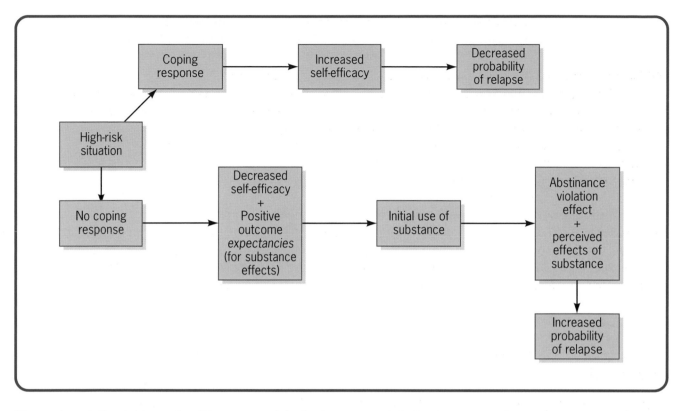

Figure 9.4 A Social Learning Theory model of relapse to addictive behaviour (from Powell, J., 2000 Drug and alcohol dependence. In L. Champion and M. Power (eds) Adult Psychological Problems: An Introduction (2nd edn). Hove: Psychology Press.

interpret it, has important consequences for their future progress. If they successfully resisted drug use, and they attribute this to their personal ability, then their level of overall self-efficacy will be raised and they'll feel more confident about their ability to successfully handle future threats. As we've seen, this, in turn, will make it more likely that they'll attempt alternative strategies in other high-risk situations, improving their chances of long-term abstinence.

One particularly destructive cognitive process is the *abstinence violation effect* (AVE), in which individuals see their drug use as incompatible with their previous determination to remain abstinent. These two cognitions ('I'm a drug addict' and 'I want to remain abstinent') are psychologically inconsistent, and this inconsistency creates a state of *cognitive dissonance* (Festinger, 1957). Dissonance is a negative drive state, a state of 'psychological discomfort or tension', which motivates the individual to reduce it by achieving consonance (consistency or balance). According to Festinger's cognitive dissonance theory, attitude change is a major way of reducing dissonance; this involves changing one or more cognitions ('the things a person knows about himself, about his behaviour and about his surroundings').

According to Powell (2000), the addict might reduce dissonance by assuming that some inherent personal quality makes abstinence impossible (a *personal/internal attribution*), such as 'Addiction is a disease I have, which I can't shake off – so there's no point in trying any more.' Such an interpretation will clearly undermine the addict's resistance to future temptations. A more constructive way of assessing a lapse would be to identify circumstantial factors that made it difficult to resist, permitting the development of contingency plans for the future. Viewed in this way, lapses can be used as learning experiences.

Perhaps the most efficient (and certainly the healthiest!) way a smoker could reduce dissonance is to quit smoking, but many people will work on the other cognition. For example:

- belittle the evidence about smoking and cancer (e.g. 'The human data are only correlational')

- associate with other smokers (e.g. 'If so-and-so smokes, then it can't be very dangerous')

- smoke low-tar cigarettes

- convince themselves that smoking is an important and highly pleasurable activity.

These examples illustrate how cognitive dissonance theory regards human beings not as rational but *rationalising* creatures: attempting to *appear* rational, both to others and themselves.

Evaluation of the RP model

✔**Theoretically rich:** as we've seen, the RP model has elements in common with major models of prevention (also referred to as 'models of health behaviour' within health psychology, such as the Theory of Reasoned Action and the Theory of Planned Behaviour), for which there is considerable empirical support. For example, in both theories, motivation (to comply with others' expectations) represents a major component, and in the Theory of Planned Behaviour, 'perceived behavioural control' has been measured as self-efficacy in some tests of the theory (see below, page 242).

The link with cognitive dissonance theory (CDT) also gives it a theoretical strength: CDT is a major theory of attitude change, which, as we've seen, can be applied to health matters, including drug taking and smoking.

✔**Substantial evidence in support of the general principles:** for example, Cummings *et al.* (1980, in Powell, 2000) found that alcoholics, smokers, opiate addicts, gamblers and overeaters were particularly likely to lapse when they experienced negative emotional states: 35 per cent of all lapses had been preceded by negative mood, with a further 16 per cent following some form of interpersonal conflict, and another 20 per cent being attributed to social pressure. These findings are consistent with the view that people often engage in addictive behaviour because of its effectiveness in escaping stress; they suggest, therefore, that stressful situations may be particularly risky to recent 'quitters'.

Miller *et al.* (1996, in Powell) followed the progress of alcoholics being treated as outpatients and found that one of the strongest predictors of relapse was lack of coping skills. Research in this area is flourishing; a whole issue of the journal *Addiction* (1996) was devoted to this topic.

✔**Implications for treatment:** the RP model implies that there's no single treatment or educational package that can be applied in exactly the same way to every client. Rather, the therapist must be aware of the many different factors that can influence attitudes to and expectations about use of a wide variety of drugs, and be willing to approach each individual's dependence free of any assumptions about underlying factors. However, within the broad theoretical framework of RP, there are principles for developing individual treatment that can be identified (Powell, 2000). These are discussed below (pages 434–435).

Explanations of gambling

✔ Specification Hint

Gambling has been given several times above as an example in relation to biological, learning and cognitive models of addictive behaviour in general. Here the specification requires 'Explanations for specific addictions, including smoking and gambling.' Depending on the wording of the question, one or more of the models discussed above could be drawn on in relation to gambling. What follows is additional material specifically dealing with gambling, but this should be seen as complementing what's already been covered. The same points apply to smoking.

Although identified as an impulse disorder in DSM-IV-TR (2000), pathological gambling is considered in the same behavioural terms as an addiction. The diagnostic criteria are summarised in Box 9.3.

Box 9.3: Diagnostic criteria for pathological gambling

Its diagnosis requires *five or more* of the following:

- a preoccupation with gambling
- a need to gamble with increasing amounts of money in order to achieve the desired excitement
- repeated, unsuccessful efforts to control, cut back or stop gambling
- its use as a way of escaping from problems or relieving dysphoric mood states
- a return to gambling following losses in the hope of 'getting even' ('chasing')
- lying to family members or others to conceal the extent of gambling
- committing illegal acts, such as forgery or fraud, to continue gambling
- jeopardising or losing significant relationships as a result of gambling.

Pathological gambling is usually the end point of a gradual shift through social, frequent, problem, and finally pathological, gambling. Each 'stage' involves a greater psychological and financial commitment to gambling, and an increase in associated problems. An estimated 60 per cent of pathological gamblers have committed criminal offences in order to continue gambling, and up to 30 per cent may have alcohol-related problems. This relationship with alcohol is important, as some have taken it to suggest that both alcohol and gambling problems reflect a more general 'addictive' personality. About 20 per cent of those in treatment for pathological gambling are reported to have attempted suicide (APA, 1994, in Bennett, 2006).

Bennett (2006) identifies several different explanations of the initiation (or *aetiology*) of pathological gambling.

Biological explanations

Some studies involving large numbers of twin pairs have found that shared environmental and genetic factors account for 35–54 per cent of the vulnerability to pathological gambling – with genetic factors being more important. One potential genetic process is through the dopamine D2 receptor gene. A variant of the D2 dopamine receptor, D2A1, has been found to be more prevalent in pathological gamblers compared with the general population.

The 'buzz' of winning or coming close to winning, which is the equivalent of the drug-taking 'high', appears to be mediated by a number of neurotransmitters. For example, dopamine levels have been found to rise after a winning streak, with activation of the reward system common to other addictions (see Box 9.1). Raised levels of norepinephrine (noradrenaline) have also been found following gambling episodes. These may impact on activity within both the brain and the sympathetic nervous system (see Gross and Rolls, 2008). In social gamblers (which most of us are from time to time), these neurochemical changes typically occur only while they're actually gambling. But in pathological gamblers, they occur while anticipating gambling or as a classically conditioned response to a gambling-related stimulus (Shinohara *et al.*, 1995, in Bennett, 2006).

405

These effects aren't trivial: withdrawal from gambling may produce symptoms similar to, or even more severe than, those experienced while coming off drugs (such as insomnia, headaches, loss of appetite, physical weakness, heart racing, muscle aches, breathing difficulty and chills).

Bennett (2006) describes a study by Meyer *et al.* (2004) that examined the effect of gambling on cardiovascular (heart rate) and neuroendocrine activity (cortisol – a stress hormone; see Gross and Rolls, 2008) among ten regular male blackjack players as they played in a casino. As shown in Figure 9.5, both heart rate and salivary cortisol were raised in the period of gambling compared with the control condition (sitting at a blackjack table, playing a game of cards without any money stakes involved).

The degree of increased heart rate during gambling was lower than that associated with the acute stress of parachute jumping, but was comparable to that evoked by the stress of public speaking and mental arithmetic – but lasted much longer. In addition, and unlike these other stressors, heart rate elevation continued after the gambling had finished.

Meyer *et al.*'s study provided the first demonstration that the arousal of gambling induces a secretion of salivary cortisol comparable to that observed in acute stress situations that last one to two hours. The sympathetic consequences of gambling (as well as dopamine – and endorphin – activity, neither of which was measured by Meyer *et al.*) may reinforce and encourage future gambling. However, the relevance of increased cortisol for the maintenance of gambling behaviour is unclear. Physiological responses to gambling enhance mood, and winning can produce a 'euphoric' state. Cortisol may contribute to such mood alterations (Bennett, 2006).

Socio-cultural factors

In general, greater access to gambling opportunities seems to increase both social and problem gambling. In the UK, despite some concerns, the introduction of the National Lottery in 1994 didn't result in wide-

Figure 9.6 An extremely accessible form of gambling

STRETCH AND CHALLENGE: The psychology of the National Lottery

The chances of winning the National Lottery are approximately 1 in 14 million. But despite these huge odds against, people persist with their dream of winning the elusive jackpot that will change their lives for ever. Why?

According to Griffiths (1997), part of the appeal of lotteries in general is that they offer a low-cost chance of winning a very large jackpot prize: without it, very few people would play. However, Griffiths identifies two other major reasons: (i) successful advertising and television coverage (this will be discussed in the next section of the chapter); and (ii) general ignorance of probability theory.

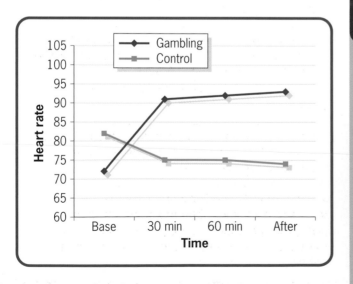

Figure 9.5 Heart rate during gambling and the control condition (Bennett, P., 2006)

Heuristic	Application to lottery participation
Availability heuristic (or bias): the belief that an event's probability is directly related to the frequency with which it's occurred in the past and that more frequent events are usually easier to remember than less frequent events (Kahneman and Tversky, 1973).	Winners are highly publicised, which gives the impression that wins are regular and commonplace, when in fact they're rare and occasional. Also, pleasant memories of an occasional small prize make winning more salient than losing.
Randomness bias: not expecting a random sequence to have any apparent biases and regularities (Teigen, 1994).	Despite the mechanical and random nature of the draw, many people seem to be trying to predict which numbers will be drawn (Haigh, 1995). So there's difficulty in choosing six random numbers from 49.
Representativeness bias: equating a 'random' sample with a 'representative' sample (Tversky and Kahneman, 1971).	A tendency to choose numbers that appear 'random' (irregular, no pattern), and avoid those that appear less random (adjacent numbers and repeating digits). This may explain the 'gambler's fallacy' (see below).
Gambler's fallacy: the belief that subsequent events will cancel out previous events to produce a representative sequence (Holtgraves and Skeel, 1992), and that the probability of winning will increase with the length of an ongoing run of losses (Wagenaar, 1988).	Choosing numbers that have been drawn the least (they're therefore 'due') and overestimating the chances of winning.
Illusory correlations: the use of superstitious behaviour in which it's believed variables correlate when they don't (Wagenaar, 1988).	Choosing 'lucky numbers' – birthdays, house numbers etc. – which causes players to discard statistical probabilities.
Flexible attribution: tendency to attribute success to personal skill and failures to some external influence (Wagenaar, 1988).	Preference for choosing one's own numbers, rather than buying 'lucky dips', so that any win is due to the player's own skill (game of luck), whereas losses are due to features of the game (game of chance).
Illusion of control: an expectancy of success that is greater than the objective probability warrants (Langer, 1975).	Being able to choose one's own numbers induces skill orientations, which cause players to feel inappropriately confident.
Sunk cost bias: continuing an endeavour once an investment has been made (Arkes and Blumer, 1985).	Continuing to buy lottery tickets while experiencing losses. The more money that's spent, the more likely people are to continue 'investing', and to inflate their estimations of winning.

Table 9.1: Heuristic strategies and biases that might be used by lottery players
Source: based on Griffiths (1997), Hill and Williamson (1998)

spread gambling problems. By the end of the first year, Lottery ticket sales had reached £3.3 billion (excluding a further £1.1 billion from scratchcards) (Griffiths, 1997). A 1998 survey by GamCare, for example, found that 65 per cent of the UK population had played the Lottery in 1997; this compared with 90 per cent of adults in Sweden and New Zealand over the same period (Bennett, 2006); 65 per cent also claim to play regularly (Hill and Williamson, 1998).

Probability

The chances of winning *something* are fairly high compared with other gambling activities, although, as we've seen, the chances of winning the jackpot are tiny. It's therefore likely that the ordinary 'social gambler' doesn't think about the actual probability of winning but relies on *heuristic strategies* for handling the available information. Heuristics are usually defined as 'rules of thumb' (i.e. simple 'if–then' rules or norms). There are many heuristics that may help explain the appeal of the National Lottery to the general public, and those that are probably most relevant are described in Table 9.1.

Evaluation of heuristics/ biases

✔ **They help us understand gamblers' irrational behaviour:** according to Griffiths (1997), these heuristics and biases give some insight into why gamblers don't learn from their past losses, and help to explain apparently 'irrational' behaviour.

✗ **They lack predictive value:** it's almost impossible to know which heuristic will be applied in a given situation, and it's quite possible for the same person to use a different heuristic in the same situation on different occasions (Griffiths, 1997).

Is the National Lottery addictive?

According to Gamblers Anonymous, within a year of the National Lottery starting, the number of calls it received had increased by 17 per cent (Griffiths, 1997). But how much of this was due to instant scratchcards? Griffiths argues that these are entirely different forms of gambling, particularly when comparing their respective *structural characteristics*.

While situational characteristics (including socio-cultural factors; see below) encourage people to begin gambling, structural characteristics are responsible for inducing people to carry on once they've started. They provide reinforcement, may satisfy gamblers' needs and may actually facilitate excessive gambling. In terms of the distinction between social ('soft') and pathological ('hard') gambling, the National Lottery is an example of the former (together with football pools and bingo), while scratchcards are an example of the latter (along with roulette, blackjack, horse/greyhound betting and fruit machines). The National Lottery has relatively low *event frequency* (despite the introduction of a second weekly draw in 1997).

Structural factors associated with gambling

Once in a gambling context, several factors may influence the extent of gambling – in particular, alcohol consumption among pathological gamblers (Ellery *et al.*, 2005, in Bennett, 2006). Bennett cites a study by Pols and Hawks (1991), which found that young game (fruit) machine players persisted for twice as long when losing after drinking moderate amounts of alcohol as they did when sober. The increasing location of game/fruit machines in pubs suggests that some of those who drink regularly may also come to gamble regularly. However, many regular casino gamblers drink *less* while gambling than they usually do (Bennett, 2006).

According to Griffiths and Parke (2003), psychology is used in the acquisition, development and maintenance of fruit-machine gambling through its application of conditioning (see above), and a number of structural characteristics, including familiarity, sound effects, and light and colour.

Conditioning

Fruit machines exploit the basic principle of positive reinforcement (see above) through the interdependence of a number of features, including:

- event frequency (the number of times a person can gamble within a given time period)

- the result of the gamble (a win or a loss)

- the pay-out interval (the actual time between gambling and when winnings are received).

This combination contributes to the 'addictiveness' of fruit-machine gambling. Because of the high event frequency, the loss period is also very brief. As a result, little time is given over to financial considerations and, more importantly, winnings can be re-gambled almost immediately.

Familiarity

Griffiths and Parke cite research by Griffiths and Dunbar (1997), which shows that the names of machines seem to be critically important, particularly in terms of gambling acquisition (i.e. initiation). Fruit machines are often named after a person, place, event, video game, cartoon character, television show or movie (such as *The Simpsons, Friends, Coronation Street, Blind Date, Indiana Jones, Cluedo, Tetris* and *Sonic the Hedgehog*). Not only is this something familiar to the player, but it may also be something that potential players like or identify with; these names are reflected in features, sound effects and lighting effects.

Griffiths and Parke suggest some possible reasons why a player would choose a machine with one of these such names.

- 'Celebrity endorsement': if *The Simpsons* creator (Matt Groening) or Homer Simpson (the central cartoon character) put their names on this machine, it must be a 'better' machine.

- Trust: players may believe they're unlikely to lose a lot of money with an international 'quality' brand such as *The Simpsons*, and that the jackpots are likely to be generous.

- Experience: regular viewers of the cartoon might believe their familiarity with the characters will help them when they play the machines.

- 'Fun': it might simply be that playing *The Simpsons* is more exciting, more humorous and so on.

The use of familiar, media-related machines in recent years may have a very persuasive effect on the money that players spend.

Synoptic Material: Evolutionary explanations

According to evolutionary psychologists, our motivational systems evolved during our hunter-gatherer past to support responses that aided survival and reproduction. This means that things we find pleasurable today may ultimately be rooted in behaviour that increased our *inclusive fitness* in the past. According to Workman and Reader (2004), most of us find some form of gambling pleasurable (whether 'social' or pathological – or somewhere in between). But given that the odds are stacked against us, why should such behaviour be so rewarding?

Long before the advent of evolutionary psychology (EP), France (1902, in Workman and Reader, 2004) suggested that among our hunter-gatherer ancestors, those who were prepared to take a risk and explore new areas for different food, shelter and mates were more likely to out-compete their more conservative, risk-aversive peers. The risk-takers were more likely, therefore, to survive in order to pass their genes on to future generations. Hence, we're left with the legacy of risk-taking genes; we still enjoy a gamble, but in (usually) non-life-threatening ways. France predicted that if gambling did indeed aid survival and – more importantly – reproduction, then we might expect to find it most strongly associated with males approaching sexual maturity: they'd become engaged in hunting and exploration (activities that might attract a mate). Females at this time are likely to take fewer risks as part of their preparation for child-bearing and child-rearing.

Evaluation of the evolutionary account of gambling

✗ **The problem of testing evolutionary hypotheses and circularity:** as with all aspects of EP, the problem is to test hypotheses from a theory that makes assumptions about what conditions were like for our ancestors. This is all they *can* do, in the absence of any direct evidence for what life was like so many thousands of years ago. However, if we have to accept the assumptions before we can test hypotheses based on them, we're in danger of making a *circular argument* – that is, accepting as 'true' something that the hypothesis is trying to *show* to be true!

✔ **Apparent empirical support:** France presented young male and female participants of various ages with a hypothetical gambling scenario. He asked them whether they'd be prepared to gamble on a two-day holiday: they could choose whether or not to draw a slip of paper that would determine the length of their holiday (drawing a long slip would add a day; drawing a short slip would remove a day). Among 11–15-year-olds, about 50 per cent of the girls and boys chose to gamble, while among 16–21-year-olds the percentage of males rose, whereas the percentage of females fell. This gender difference in attitudes to gambling at the point of reproductive maturity appears to support France's argument perfectly.

✗ **France's results beg as many questions as they answer:** as Workman and Reader point out, how do we know that this gender difference would be found if the study were replicated today? If it weren't found, then we could argue that it was related more to gender role socialisation at the end of the Victorian era than to evolutionary processes (see Chapter 5).

Although France's findings are consistent with EP, they're also consistent with other explanations, such as males being socialised into gambling at an age when they're just beginning to earn a living. As Workman and Reader (2004) say, the difficulty for evolutionary psychologists is to derive tests of hypotheses in which the outcome supports (or refutes) the evolutionary standpoint but doesn't also support (or supports less well) hypotheses derived from other psychological perspectives.

✔ **Some arguments in support of the evolutionary account:** Workman and Reader argue that France cleverly used a novel form of gambling (rather than a more traditional, gender-biased form such as the horses). This, to a large degree, removed the gender-socialisation element. Also, although the gender difference in gambling remains today, it's less marked than it was in France's day. Evolutionary psychologists don't reject socialisation accounts; rather, their argument concerns how easily males and females gravitate towards certain socialising factors. Even if there were no gender gap, the evolutionary argument about why, as a species, we find gambling so rewarding would still be worthy of consideration (Workman and Reader, 2004).

Explanations of smoking

The addictive nature of cigarette smoking has been described since 1920. It is classified as a Substance-Related Disorder in DSM-IV-TR (see above) and is referred to as a Nicotine-Related Disorder, since *nicotine* is the addicting agent of tobacco. It stimulates nicotine receptors in the brain; the neural pathways that become activated stimulate the dopamine neurons in the mesolimbic area that seem to be involved in producing the reinforcing effects of most drugs (Davison *et al.*, 2004; see Box 9.1).

Who smokes?

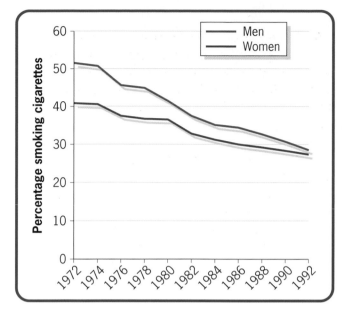

Figure 9.7 *Changes in smoking, 1972–1992 (after General Household Survey, 1994 Office for National Statistics © Crown copyright)*

How Science Works

Practical Learning Activity 9.7

- **What conclusions can you draw about smoking behaviour from the graph above?**

In general, data about smoking behaviour (General Household Survey, 1994, in Ogden, 2004) show that:

- smoking behaviour is on the decline, but this decrease is greater in men than in women (although more men smoke and more women have never smoked)

- smokers tend to be in the unskilled manual group

- there's been a dramatic reduction in the number of smokers smoking middle-tar cigarettes

- two-thirds of smokers report wanting to give up smoking

- 58 per cent of smokers say it would be fairly/very difficult to go without a cigarette for a whole day.

General approaches to explaining addiction

As we noted at the beginning of the chapter, the disease model of addiction (AAD) has been severely criticised, along with the concept of addiction itself. We also noted that both cigarette smoking and alcohol abuse can be thought of as 'ordinary addictions' because they're so widespread in our culture (Veitia and McGahee, 1995). However, in terms of the AAD model, alcoholism was much more the focus of theory and research than smoking.

Since the 1970s, behaviours such as smoking, drinking and drug taking have been increasingly described within the context of other behaviours. According to Ogden (2004):

> In the same way that theories of aggression shifted from a biological cause (aggression as an instinct) to social causes (aggression as a response to the environment/ upbringing), addictions were also seen as learned behaviours. Within this perspective, the term addictive behaviour replaced addictions and such behaviours were regarded as a consequence of learning processes . . .

Although this shift challenged the concepts of addiction, addict, illness and disease, there was still an emphasis on *treatment* (see below).

According to Ogden (2004), researchers often polarise a disease and a social learning (SL) perspective. For example, while some researchers argue that smoking is entirely due to the addictive properties of nicotine, others argue that it's a learned behaviour. However, implicit within each approach is the alternative explanation. For example, while AAD model may emphasise acquired tolerance following smoking behaviour, it implicitly uses an SL approach to explain why some people start smoking in the first place and why only some continue to the extent that they develop acquired tolerance; exposure and reinforcement must be part of the explanation.

So, although tolerance may be a disease model concept, it relies on some degree of SLT for it to operate. Similarly, people might smoke a greater number of cigarettes because they've learned that smoking relieves withdrawal symptoms. However, while this form of association is derived from an SL perspective, it implicitly uses a disease perspective in that it requires the existence of physical withdrawal symptoms. Therefore:

411

most researchers draw upon both disease and social learning perspectives. Sometimes, this interaction between the two forms of models is made explicit and the researchers acknowledge that they believe both sources of influence are important. However, at times this interaction is only implicit. (Ogden, 2004)

Smoking initiation and maintenance

In 1954, Doll and Hill suggested that smoking caused lung cancer. Fifty years later, about 30 per cent of the adult population still smoke even though most of them are aware of the related health risks. In fact, when people are asked about the risk of smoking compared with the risks of murder and traffic accidents, smokers are accurate in their perception of the risks of smoking (and their accuracy is similar to that of both ex-smokers and those who've never smoked) (Sutton, 1998, in Ogden, 2004).

Smoking in children

The early health promotion campaigns focused mainly on the determinants of smoking in adult men, but in recent years there's been an increasing interest in smoking in children. Because most children and adolescents try a puff of a cigarette, it's difficult to distinguish between actual initiation and maintenance of smoking behaviour. Ogden looks at these stages together.

Doll and Petro (1981, in Ogden, 2004) reported that people whose smoking is initiated in childhood have an increased chance of lung cancer compared with those who begin smoking later in life. This is particularly significant as most adult smokers start the habit in childhood and very few start smoking regularly after the age of 19/20. Although smoking in 11–15-year-olds fell, in both boys and girls, between 1982 and 1990, the decrease was smaller than that for adults (see above). In 1990, nearly 50 per cent of school children had at least tried one cigarette, and many try their first cigarette while still at primary school!

According to DiFranza (2008), new research (in the USA, Canada and New Zealand) has overturned the once taken-for-granted belief that cigarette addiction takes years to develop. Studies of adolescent smokers have shown that symptoms of addiction, such as withdrawal, craving and failed attempts at quitting, can appear within the first weeks of smoking. For example, of those who experience symptoms of addiction, 10 per cent do so within two days of their first cigarette, and 25–35 per cent do so within a month. In the New

Figure 9.8 The earlier smoking begins, the more dangerous the consequences

Zealand study, 25 per cent had symptoms after smoking one to four cigarettes; they were 200 times more likely to start smoking daily than those who didn't develop these symptoms so soon after starting to smoke.

Psychological and social predictors of smoking initiation

Models of health behaviour, such as the Theory of Reasoned Action (see below) have been used to examine the cognitive factors that contribute to smoking initiation. Additional cognitions that predict smoking behaviour include associating smoking with fun and pleasure, smoking as a means of calming nerves, and as being sociable and building confidence. Stress reduction is another likely candidate (see Gross and Rolls, 2008). In turn, how different people define, react to and deal with stress is related to *personality*, which is discussed – mainly in relation to *adults* – in Box 9.4 (again, see Gross and Rolls, 2008).

As Furnham and Heaven (1999) point out, personality needs to be considered alongside *social* factors; focusing on cognitive and personality factors places an emphasis on the individual and takes them out of their social context. As far as parents smoking is concerned, Lader and Matheson (1991, in Ogden, 2004) showed that children are twice as likely to smoke if their parents smoke. Conversely, if a child perceives the parents as being strongly *against* smoking, s/he is up to seven times less likely to be a smoker (Murray *et al.*, 1984, in Ogden, 2004). This appears to be the single most important influence.

Next most important is peer group pressure. Ogden

Box 9.4: Smoking and personality

- According to Cohen (1979, in Furnham and Heaven, 1999), personality may either represent a specific and direct causal factor in disease or it mediates/buffers the effects of causal factors. A third possibility is that personality factors influence certain types of health-related behaviours, which are either health-promoting or detrimental to health. Smoking is an example of the latter.
- Because smoking is (to some degree) a voluntary behaviour, its role in cancer and heart disease assumes an additional interest for personality psychologists: how do smokers and non-smokers differ (Furnham and Heaven, 1999)?
- Furnham and Heaven cite evidence that smokers have higher *extraversion* (E) scores than non-smokers, and, as E scores rise, so does cigarette consumption. One study found that smoking was associated with E, impulsiveness and sensation seeking. Another reported that both E and *neuroticism* (N) correlated with smoking, with deep inhalers forming the most neurotic group. Male smokers had higher average E scores than female smokers.
- One Canadian study (Patton *et al.*, 1993, in Furnham and Heaven, 1999) also found that current smokers (as opposed to those who'd never smoked and quitters) scored high on *psychoticism* (P). But female smokers were significantly higher on P than any of the other groups.
- However, personality variables such as E, N and P may be only three of a much longer list of factors that predict smoking (particularly among young people), such as peer pressure and conformity to group norms (see Gross and Rolls, 2008), having parents who smoke, school performance, self-esteem and the 'status' afforded by smoking (Furnham and Heaven, 1999).

(See Gross, 2005, for an account of E, N and P.)

cites studies in the USA that have examined the relationship between peer group identity and tobacco use. Individuals who identify themselves, and are identified by others, as being problem-prone, doing poorly at school, rarely involved in school sports, high in risk-taking behaviour (such as alcohol and drug use), and with low self-esteem, were more likely to have smoked. On the other hand, research has also found that high rates of smoking can be found in children seen as leaders of academic and social activities, who have high self-esteem and are regarded as popular by their peers.

Another influencing factor is the attitude of the school to smoking. Ogden cites a Cancer Research Campaign study (1991), which found that smoking prevalence was lower in schools with a 'no smoking' policy, especially where this applied to staff as well as students.

The cessation of smoking

In this chapter so far, we've identified three 'stages' of addiction: initiation, maintenance and relapse. But, crucially, relapse presupposes that the behaviour has stopped at some point; hence 'cessation' constitutes a fourth stage (in between maintenance and relapse). Here, it mainly denotes efforts made by the smoker to

quit (what's called self-help in Figure 9.9, together with some aspects of public health interventions), rather than clinical intervention.

Traditionally, smoking cessation was viewed as a dichotomy: an individual either smoked or didn't (they were categorised as smokers, ex-smokers or non-smokers). This view was consistent with the AAD model, but early attempts at promoting total abstinence (most notably in relation to alcoholism) were relatively unsuccessful; research now emphasises cessation as a *process*.

Prochaska and DiClemente (1984) adapted their *stages of change* (SoC) model to examine cessation of addictive behaviours, highlighting the processes involved in the transition from a smoker to a non-smoker (and drinker to non-drinker). They argued that cessation involves a shift across five basic stages (including relapse).

1. *Precontemplation:* the person is basically unaware of having a problem or fails to acknowledge it (denial).

2. *Contemplation:* the person begins to recognise that they have a problem and becomes prepared to do something about it.

3. *Preparation*: the person is now seriously considering taking some action to change their behaviour.

4. *Maintenance*: the behaviour change is sustained for a period of time.

5. *Relapse*: eventually, most of those who relapse will return to the action (preparation) stage.

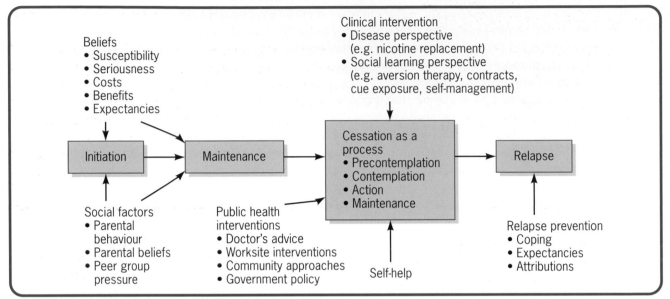

Figure 9.9 *The stages of substance use (from Ogden, J., 2004)*

Evaluation of the SoC model

✔ **Flexibility and realism of the model:** individuals don't progress through the stages in a straightforward, linear fashion, but may switch back and forth (the 'revolving door'); this illustrates the *dynamic* nature of cessation. Also, the model helps explain how a person can remain ambivalent about change over many years (Crouch, 2003).

✔ **Empirical support:** the model has been tested to provide evidence for the different stages for smokers (and outpatient alcoholics) (DiClemente and Prochaska, 1982, 1985; DiClemente and Hughes, 1990, all in Ogden, 2004) and for the relationship between stage of change for smoking cessation and self-efficacy (DiClemente, 1986, in Ogden, 2004).

In addition, DiClemente *et al*. (1991, in Ogden, 2004) examined the relationship between stage of change and attempts to quit smoking and actual cessation at one- and six-month follow-ups for almost 1,500 participants (mainly white, American females who'd started smoking at about 16 and smoked on average 29 cigarettes a day). The researchers categorised the contemplators into either (a) those who were smoking, seriously considering quitting within the next six months, but not within the next 30 days ('contemplators') or (b) those who were seriously considering quitting within the next 30 days (preparation stage). The latter were found to be more likely to have made an attempt to quit at both one and six months, had made more quit attempts, and were more likely to not be smoking at the follow-ups. Those in the preparation stage also smoked less, were less addicted, had higher self-efficacy, rated the benefits of smoking as less and the costs as more, compared with those at other stages. These results provide support for the SoC model and suggest that it's a useful tool for predicting the successful outcome of any smoking cessation intervention (Ogden, 2004).

> ### ✔ Specification Hint
>
> The specification states: 'Vulnerability to addiction including self-esteem, attributions for addiction, and social context of addiction ...'. These have been mentioned in the section above mostly in relation to gambling and/or smoking. Because in this section there's no reference to either of these specific addictive behaviours, feel free to draw on relevant examples from gambling and/or smoking. Equally, examples relating to other addictive behaviours are just as valid. Note that the specification refers to 'addiction' in the first section, and both 'addiction' and 'addictive behaviour' in the second, while the title of the *whole* section is 'The psychology of addictive behaviour'. As we've seen above, different terminology reflects different definitions and models – an important evaluative (A02) point in its own right.

How Science Works

Practical Learning Activity 9.8

- Look back over the first section and identify references to (a) self-esteem; (b) attributions for addiction; and (c) social context of addiction. (Remember that in this section, it doesn't matter whether the examples relate to specific addictive behaviours (such as gambling and smoking) or to addictive behaviour in general.)

Vulnerability to addiction

Extrapersonal versus intrapersonal factors

Sussman and Ames (2001) make a useful distinction between *extrapersonal* (or exogenous) and *intrapersonal* (or endogenous) *factors*.

- *Extrapersonal* factors are external to or outside the individual, and include environmental, cultural and social variables (such as interactions with others in different settings, and learning social behaviours from significant others – especially parents, close friends and role models). The role of the media (see below) would also count as an extrapersonal factor.

- *Intrapersonal* factors are internal characteristics of the individual, including genetics, personality (for example, as correlates of neurobiological processes), affective (emotional) states and cognitive factors (including attributions for addiction). Self-esteem, arguably, combines affective and cognitive elements.

These correspond to what Davison *et al.* (2004) call *socio-cultural* and *psychological* variables respectively.

It's sometimes difficult to differentiate extrapersonal from intrapersonal influences. For example, certain characteristics of role models (e.g. alcoholic parents) interact with individual reactivity to the role models (e.g. one individual might react to having alcoholic parents by using drugs to cope with emotional distress, while another might seek out positive support).

Extrapersonal factors

Sussman and Ames (2001) discuss four types of extrapersonal factors that are correlated with, or predict, drug use and abuse: *demographic* (gender, age and ethnicity), *environmental* (including variation in drug abuse worldwide), *cultural* and *social*. All of these could be thought of as part of the 'social context of addiction', but we'll concentrate on environmental, social and cultural factors.

Environmental influences

Environmental factors associated with, and perhaps motivating, experimentation with drugs, include neighbourhood disorganisation, economic deprivation and availability of drugs.

415

Neighbourhood disorganisation refers to a lack of centralised authority, or rapid changes in authority. This is associated with social disobedience, such as public drunkenness, drug dealing and gang-related activities. Building structures that provide many enclosed public areas, as well as abandoned buildings, lend themselves to a greater incidence of crime and drug use, and tend to be prevalent in dense, urban, disorganised neighbourhoods.

Economic deprivation may limit access to pro-social recreational opportunities and facilities (such as money for cinema tickets), and may also encourage drug-related crime (such as drug dealing) as an alternative means of generating income. Low socio-economic status (SES) tends to be associated with greater drug use among adults, such as use of crack cocaine among economically deprived groups and ethnic minorities in large metropolitan areas. But does drug use lead to lower SES ('downward drift') or does lower SES lead to drug use (alternative income or self-medication)?

Among adolescents, influences such as family dynamics and peer group association may affect the relative influence of socio-economic influences on drug use. Sussman and Ames (2001) suggest that familial and other social influences protect children from pro-drug influences, but for adolescents their protective function decreases. As adults, lower SES may become associated with several challenges to self-worth (self-esteem) and security; some young adults may choose self-medication under these disadvantaged circumstances. Conversely, young adults who are successful financially may be able to afford large quantities of expensive drugs, may become addicted, and then may suffer a rapid descent in SES. Probably, *both* downward drift and self-medication help explain the relationship between SES and drug use.

The *availability* of drugs in a person's neighbourhood includes (a) ease of distribution (the establishment of a 'business' structure, with relatively little resistance to transporting drugs in and out of a location); (b) access (an individual's knowledge of where to tap drug supplies along the distribution route); and (c) acquisition (an individual's ability to obtain the drug – for example, through establishment of trust, provision of services, or through money). Close proximity of drugs may result in frequent exposure, and may suggest ways of acquiring drugs.

Cultural influences

According to Sussman and Ames (2001), examples of cultural factors that might influence drug use include

life habits and rituals that are important and meaningful to the group, normative structures and expectations (cultural morality), and beliefs and attitudes about reasons for drug use and drug effects ....

Culture might determine which drugs are available, preferable and highly valued at any given time, whether experimentation is acceptable, and what one's expectations about the effects of a drug might be.

An example of a 'life habit' and 'normative structure' is the regular drinking of wine with meals in France (and increasingly in the UK – at least among people from middle-class backgrounds). Some French children learn that wine is a food; they learn to drink wine with meals and are able to buy wine in stores. But in the USA, it's illegal for anyone under 21 to buy alcohol, and children aren't supposed to drink it under any circumstances. Another example of a normative structure is the acceptance, availability and recreational use of marijuana in the Netherlands (as part of a harm-reduction approach), whereas in the USA, even the medical use of marijuana is highly controversial. The UK experience shows how attitudes towards particular drugs can change – and change again: cannabis was reclassified in 2004 from a Class B to a Class C drug (implying that it's less dangerous and addictive than Class B drugs). Despite the recommendations of a committee set up by the government to keep things as they are, the government announced in 2008 that it would *re-classify* cannabis as a Class B drug. In 2004, an estimated 3.3 million Britons (one in ten 16–59 year olds) would have used it; 25 per cent of 15–24 year olds used it in 2002 (Burke and Asthana, 2004).

As an example of a 'ritual' that involves 'beliefs pertaining to drug use', one unique cultural influence is the use of peyote, a hallucinogen, by certain groups of Native Americans in the Church for Spiritual Enlightenment in the USA (Sussman and Ames, 2001).

Another important cultural construct is *acculturation*, usually defined as the degree to which individuals adopt or prefer a culture to which they're more recently exposed (that is, immigrants to a new host culture) than their native culture (the one in which they were originally raised). It can be thought of as a social learning process, in which 'The degree to which a group or individual distance themselves from their native culture increases as more time is spent in the environment of a different culture …' (Sussman and Ames, 2001).

Level of acculturation in the new environment can affect drug use through exposure to cultural attitudes towards use or expectations of drug effects. Drug use or abuse might also occur when individuals are separated from traditional cultural groups that might discourage drug use. Alternatively, the stress resulting from failure to bond successfully with a new culture may increase the probability of drug use. Indeed, the very process of acculturation may involve risk factors that can reduce health status in general (*acculturative stress*). Examples of acculturative stress include lowered resistance to diseases such as hypertension and diabetes (Berry, 1998; see Gross and Rolls, 2008).

Social influences

These include the characteristics of the people in an individual's support system (the assistance people in social networks give each other), and the various effects the group has on the individual. The values and behaviours of parents, siblings, friends, peers and role models affect an individual's learning experiences. Observational learning (modelling) is very powerful. For example, if both parents smoke, a child is four times more likely to do so than if no other family member smokes; this also applies to exposure to alcohol (Davison *et al.*, 2004; see above).

Similarly, having friends who smoke predicts smoking, as well as increased drug use in general. Observing friends who seem to be enjoying using drugs may make us more curious about drug use (an 'informational' type of support). Also, we may wish to use drugs in order to have others to spend time with ('companionship' support). Alternatively, social support may directly influence our behaviour: this may include peer pressure to take drugs ('conformity' pressure) and access to drugs through friends or relatives who may purchase them ('instrumental' support). Research has

STRETCH AND CHALLENGE: Personality

Earlier in the chapter, we discussed personality in relation to smoking (see Box 9.4). A more general question that has been asked is 'Is there an addictive personality?' In other words, are there individual traits/characteristics that make it highly likely that an individual with those traits will develop some addictive behaviour or other?

From an historical perspective, the emphasis on personality and personality pathology in the development of addictive behaviours has fluctuated considerably (Claridge and Davis, 2003). Early theories (during the first half of the twentieth century) saw a disordered or maladjusted personality as the root cause of all addictions. By the 1970s, this view had been largely abandoned, because there was no evidence for one consistent *pre-addictive personality*. In recent years, personality pathology has regained its prominence. According to Claridge and Davis, 'Presently, the most prominent aetiological viewpoint is that of a *stress-diathesis* model whereby addictions develop from a reciprocal interaction between the psychological and biological vulnerability of the individual and their environmental circumstances …'.

Even the most extreme environmentalists have been forced to acknowledge that genes contribute to individual differences in behaviour. However, behavioural traits are very complex and therefore rarely affected by a single gene; indeed, they're *polygenic,* meaning that any given gene is likely to contribute only a small portion of the phenotypic (behavioural) variance (Crabbe, 2002, in Claridge and Davis, 2003).

Whatever the personality traits may be that cause the development of addictions, it's important to understand that those that predict who might *experiment* with substances (and other addictive behaviours) may be quite different from those that influence who will *abuse* these behaviours (Claridge and Davis, 2003). Some possible candidates for personality risk factors are: *sensitivity to reward*, *impulsivity*, and *proneness to anxiety and negative mood* (or *punishment sensitivity*).

417

consistently found that friend and peer use of drugs is one of the strongest predictors of drug use among teenagers. The deviant peer group tends to use drugs, will sometimes offer drugs, and role-model drug use (Sussman and Ames, 2001).

Although peer influence is very important in the decisions adolescents make about substance use, those with a high sense of self-efficacy are influenced *less* by their peers. Also, is it possible that, instead of social networks influencing an individual's substance use, individuals who are already abusers tend to select social networks that conform to their own drinking or drug use patterns (social selection as opposed to social influence)? Davison *et al.* (2004) cite a longitudinal study by Bullers *et al.* (2001) of over 1,200 adults, which found that an individual's social network predicted individual drinking, but individual drinking also predicted subsequent social network drinking. In fact, social selection seemed to be stronger. Similar results have been found in studies of adolescents.

Family conflict, poor supervision or drug-use tolerance by parents, family modelling of drug-using behaviour, and deviant peer group association are all examples of *differential socialisation* (the channelling of the development of beliefs, intentions, expectations, perceptions and modelling of social behaviour); these have all been found to influence the experimental use of drugs (Sussman and Ames, 2001).

Intrapersonal factors

According to Sussman and Ames (2001), intrapersonal factors, relative to extrapersonal factors, are likely to play a more active role following initiation to drug use, and help to explain why some individuals who use go on to abuse while others don't. These include personality, mood alteration/negative emotions, learning history and certain cognitive factors (such as attitudes, expectancies, and beliefs about risks and prevalence).

Sensitivity to reward

Meehl (1975, in Claridge and Davis, 2003) was one of the first to suggest that within the general population the capacity for pleasure or reward is a normally distributed, biologically based dimension. (This mirrors Eysenck's concepts of E and N; see Box 9.4.) Subsequent research has firmly rooted this personality construct in the neurobiology of the mesolimbic dopamine reward system (see Box 9.1).

Anhedonia describes the low end of the sensitivity to

reward dimension: it refers to the *reduced* ability to experience pleasure and reward from natural reinforcers (and is thought to reflect limited availability of dopamine). But there's accumulating evidence that susceptibility to addiction is linked to *both* ends of the scale. At the *low* end, there's good support for the notion that some anhedonic individuals engage in arousing behaviours as a form of compensation (such as skydiving) for their blunted affect and their inability to be aroused by weak levels of stimulation. Addictive behaviours (such as nicotine dependence) may serve the same mood-enhancing role. At the *high* end, people are also more likely to engage in addictive behaviours – but for very different reasons. Those high in sensitivity to reward tend to be more motivated to approach, and find pleasure from, natural rewards (the prime example being food).

Impulsive behaviour

This has been defined in different ways. Some see restlessness and the tendency to be easily distracted as essential elements, while others have defined it as low tolerance of frustration, which drives the individual to act spontaneously. Again, others have focused on the disinhibition of responding (poor self-regulation) when inhibition would be the appropriate response in a particular situation. Sussman and Ames (2001) define it as 'the tendency to act immediately in response to stimuli without consideration of consequences or various behavioural options'.

According to Bennett (2006), high levels of impulsivity in childhood (at its most extreme evident as childhood attention-deficit/hyperactivity disorder, ADHD) may be a risk factor for pathological gambling. He cites a retrospective study (Carlton and Manowicz, 1994), which found that adult pathological gamblers reported a higher rate of ADHD as children than is found in the general population. Prospective, longitudinal studies have replicated these findings. For example, Vitaro *et al.* (1999, in Bennett) measured impulsivity in four different ways in 13–14-year-olds, then measured gambling at age 17. The factors that predicted gambling included a tendency to respond excessively to positive outcomes, to require immediate reinforcement, and insensitivity to negative consequences – all characteristics of the pathological gambler.

In the case of drug addiction, it's more difficult to establish a *causal* relationship between impulsivity and addictive behaviour, since many of the studies are either correlational and/or have tested groups of drug-

Synoptic Material

From an evolutionary perspective, there's good reason why our genetic legacy has favoured high hedonic reward from eating. In times of famine and seasonal food shortages, an inherent love of eating was clearly adaptive. However, this same capacity has a very obvious *disadvantage* in environments like ours where highly palatable and calorie-dense food is too readily available:

> One result of this clash between our environment and our biology is the staggering percentage of overweight and obese individuals in most Western countries. Current estimates from the UK and North America indicate that more than 50 per cent of the adult population is overweight ... the emerging viewpoint ... is that eating can be just as addictive as snorting cocaine or drinking alcohol (Holden, 2001) (Claridge and Davis, 2003).

Those high on sensitivity to reward also tend to be more extraverted (see Box 9.4), more sociable and more attracted by novelty; all these other characteristics may contribute to their involvement in addictive behaviours. Many addictive behaviours occur in social settings, or are more likely to be initiated in the company of others (social drinking, the influence of peers on smoking – see text above – ecstasy and the club scene, 'coffee breaks'). Many addictive behaviours occur in the presence of some novelty or other, especially adolescents' experimentation with illicit drugs and sex. For the more sociable and extraverted individuals, the addictive behaviours themselves (the cigarettes, the alcohol, the casino) may not be the primary appeal; it might be the social contact and the novel experiences that are more rewarding. As Claridge and Davis say, 'for some individuals, addictions may be a secondary effect, developing as a consequence of their location within social events. However, over time, and after repeated exposure, the behaviours themselves take on primary appeal.'

dependent individuals. The major problem is that chronic drug taking can directly produce the same behavioural characteristics that are tapped by most measures of impulsivity. So it's impossible to know whether (a) it's impulsivity as a pre-existing personality trait that causes drug taking, or (b) whether drug taking causes impulsivity as a set of behavioural characteristics.

Proneness to anxiety and negative mood

There's a well-established link between substance abuse disorders and a variety of anxiety disorders. There's also good evidence that a personality profile whose main component is high N, and which Eysenck and Eysenck (1985) have called the 'addictive personality', is significantly higher in all addict groups (including substance abusers, compulsive gamblers and those with eating disorders).

However, because many of the studies supporting the association between anxiety and addiction have used addicts recruited from treatment and rehabilitation centres, the anxiety may be simply the distress of withdrawal that's being assessed (rather than a pre-existing, causal risk factor). (This is equivalent to the problem of establishing the direction of the causal link between impulsivity and drug taking discussed above). However, there's plenty of evidence – both retrospective and prospective – to support a causal link. For example, several studies have shown that anxiety disorders *precede* the substance abuse (Claridge and Davis, 2003).

The relief of a negative affective state (or the expectation of a desired affective state) may motivate an individual who's engaged in drug-taking behaviour to continue to use, and for those in recovery to lapse or relapse (Sussman and Ames, 2001). Several negative affective states have been found to influence relapse among adults, including anger, sadness, boredom, anxiety, depression, guilt, apprehension and anticipation of stressful events. Among at-risk young people, anger and depression have been found to be associated with substance abuse or dependence.

Once again, however, it's unclear whether these mood states or traits generally precede or are the result of drug use. Drug use could eventually make people feel more depressed or angry through their effect on neurotransmitter systems, withdrawal experiences or psychological dependence. If mood states precede drug use, the implication is that these people use drugs to 'self-medicate'. One factor motivating the use of addictive behaviours in general is simply their powerful ability to reduce the painful emotional consequences of stress; this *negative reinforcement* makes it more likely that the behaviour will be repeated when the individual is next faced with a stressful situation (see Box 9.5).

Box 9.5: The stress-reduction or self-medication pathway

The *stress-reduction* or *self-medication pathway* to addiction has received a great deal of research attention in recent years. Individuals high on traits such as anxiety and N are more reactive to stressful life events than more stable individuals and, in turn, this reactivity motivates them to seek quick and effective psychological relief from distress – in the form of drugs (Claridge and Davis, 2003). Consistent with this hypothesis is the argument that addicts don't select drugs randomly but as the result of an interaction between the psychopharmacological action of the drug and the form of the individual's distress (Khantizian, 1997, in Claridge and Davis, 2003).

For example, Khantizian argues that heroin addicts prefer opiates because their powerful muting action subdues the rage and aggression they experience, and cocaine has its appeal because it can relieve the distress of depression. It follows that the stress-reduction pathway is perhaps more relevant for addiction to alcohol, tranquillisers and the opiates, than for the popular stimulants such as crack/cocaine (Claridge and Davis, 2003).

A clearer understanding of the personality pathways has considerable practical importance and is crucial to the development of improved treatment methods (see text below). If we can understand the psychology of those at high risk for addiction, we can also improve our ability to target prevention efforts (Claridge and Davis, 2003).

Cognitive processes

Beliefs about risks and prevalence

These feature quite strongly in certain models of health behaviour (in particular the Health Belief Model), which are discussed in the next section. This, in turn, is related to unrealistic optimism and perceptions of invulnerability (see below).

Expectancies

The construct of *expectancy* is generally defined as the anticipated consequences of behaviour or beliefs held about alcohol and other drug effects (Sussman and Ames, 2001). For example, an expected consequence or outcome of alcohol use may include feeling more relaxed. Expectancies have both *cognitive* (that is, informational) and *motivational* (affective incentive) components.

Expectancies as a cognitive mediator of behaviour have been used to explain both volitional (voluntary) and non-volitional (involuntary) behaviours. Several researchers have produced evidence that outcome expectancies are correlated with alcohol use, contributing to both its initiation and maintenance. When individuals initially observe drug use or experiment with drugs, they're more likely to experience a positive outcome than a negative outcome.

Attitudes

Pro-gambling attitudes increase the likelihood of gambling and may be a consequence of early exposure to family influences. For example, Oei and Raylu (2004, in Bennett, 2006) found that parents' – and especially fathers' – attitudes towards gambling were predictive of their children's beliefs and attitudes. Although pro-gambling attitudes appear to lead to participation in gambling activities, they don't account for their maintenance (Sharpe, 2002, in Bennett, 2006). 'Self-talk' may be important at this time.

The role of media in addictive behaviour

As noted above, the media represent an extrapersonal (exogenous) factor. According to Sussman and Ames (2001), the increasing role of the media and worldwide access to information are influences on both drug use initiation and experimentation. The World Wide Web now provides incredible access to information about drugs of abuse and means of producing them. Different cultures may influence others' beliefs regarding drug use to the extent that they use a shared language on the web (for example, www.legalize.org/global/, in Sussman and Ames, 2001).

Television and movies may inadvertently promote drug use by conveying images of role models or idols, such as rock stars, romanticising heroin addiction, models who are tough chain smokers, movie stars happily addicted to alcohol, or rappers who like to sing about marijuana. Cinema images in particular are likely to be viewed internationally, influencing the host culture within which they're shown. Even if we don't consciously attend to such media images, through the *mere exposure effect* (e.g. Zajonc, 1980; see Chapter 2) they can affect preferences for objects. But do these preferences necessarily influence choice behaviour?

How Science Works
Practical Learning Activity 9.9

- Conduct a *content analysis* of television and/or newspapers and magazines, looking for images depicting use and/or abuse of drugs, alcohol, cigarettes, gambling and so on.
- Are these behaviours generally portrayed in a favourable or unfavourable light, or are they merely incidental to the action and/or the character concerned?
- Are these behaviours more likely to be displayed by men/women, young/old, white/non-white characters?
- While cigarette advertising is already banned in the UK, advertising alcohol isn't – although it must follow strict rules laid down by the Advertising Standards Authority (ASA). Do you think that all alcohol commercials should be banned, as has been done with cigarettes? You might want to hold a class debate on this issue.
- What rules do you think the ASA does – or should – stipulate for alcohol advertising?

Clearly, the media are important sources of information and, as such, influence behavioural options. For example, commercials that associate smoking with excitement-seeking cues and social popularity have been shown to be important influences on the initiation of smoking (Sussman and Ames, 2001). The media have the capacity for spreading information rapidly and affecting large groups; their potential international cultural impact cannot be overstated.

Gambling and the media

According to Griffiths (1993, 1995, in Griffiths, 1997), the gambling industry has consistently used techniques based both on appeals to expressive needs and the manipulation of situational factors to attract new custom. These marketing methods fall mainly into two categories, one of which is composed of situational characteristics that get people to gamble in the first place; these are primarily features of the environment, including location of the gambling outlet, the number of such outlets in a specified area, and the use of advertising in inducing people to gamble. These variables may be very important in the initial decision to gamble and may help to clarify why some forms of gambling are more attractive to particular socio-economic groups.

Griffiths (1997) believes that these characteristics have been crucial in the success of the National Lottery. Not only is it heavily advertised on billboards, television and in national newspapers, but the accessibility is so widespread that it's difficult to avoid in most shops. As Griffiths says, 'This means that the National Lottery is more salient than other forms of gambling, which do not have the same freedoms to advertise or have their own television show.'

Griffiths refers to studies of other lotteries around the world, which show that people from working-class backgrounds are over-represented and those from middle-class backgrounds are under-represented. Since television viewing is greater among the former, the impact of television-based marketing of lottery gambling may be increased for this social group.

The National Lottery is advertised in a very 'slick' way; it's designed either to make people think they've a good chance of winning the jackpot ('It could be YOU'), or to play on people's altruistic tendencies ('Everyone's a winner'). While it *could* be 'you', we know that the odds are 14 million to 1. Stewart (1996, in Griffiths, 1997) argues that there should be a government health warning that says 'It will almost certainly be SOMEONE ELSE'!

The National Lottery is very much sold on the premise that somebody has got to win the big jackpot, so why should it not be you. This is the major tactic – to makes the person believe that the almost impossible is within their grasp.

421

Viewers (including children and adolescents) are fast becoming persuaded that gambling is normal. The general public is being saturated with the principles of gambling and is growing up to believe that it's socially acceptable. As Griffiths says, the televised draw is itself a blatant form of advertising in which Camelot (which runs the Lottery) uses free air time each week (and is paid by the BBC for the privilege!). *The National Lottery Live* programme is watched by about 12 million viewers and again contributes to the Lottery's success. The televised draw highlights the simplicity of winning, while at the same time hiding the huge number of viewing losers (Walker, 1992, in Griffiths, 1997).

REDUCING ADDICTIVE BEHAVIOUR

Models of prevention

✔ Specification Hint

As we noted above, models of health behaviour are highly cognitive in flavour and some of the key constructs used in these models are as relevant to the previous section ('Factors affecting addictive behaviour') as they are to 'Reducing addictive behaviour'. So there's an important overlap between these two sections. The two models of health behaviour (what in the specification are called 'models of prevention') that you must know about are (i) Theory of Reasoned Action; and (ii) Theory of Planned Behaviour. In addition, we discuss the Health Belief Model and its link to research into unrealistic optimism and perceptions of invulnerability. Note that these models of health behaviour address 'health behaviour' in general (such as diet, exercise, sexual behaviour, as well as smoking and alcohol consumption), but use of illegal substances and gambling, for example, *aren't* specifically discussed. However, in this section, no particular addictive behaviours are mentioned, and tests of the models have sometimes involved addictive behaviours.

Understanding why people do or don't practise behaviours to protect their health can be assisted by the study of *models/theories of health behaviour*, such as:

- the Theory of Reasoned Action (TRA)

- the Theory of Planned Behaviour (TPB), and

- the Health Belief Model (HBM).

According to Ogden (2004), these various models/theories are often referred to, collectively, as *social cognition models*, because they regard cognitions as being shared by individuals within the same society. But Ogden prefers to distinguish between:

- social cognition models (such as TRA and TPB), which aim to account for social behaviour in general and are much broader than health models, and

- cognition models (such as HBM), which are specifically *health models*.

A fundamentally important question for health psychology is why people adopt – or don't adopt – particular health-related behaviours. Models of health behaviour try to answer this question, and those models discussed below belong to the family of *expectancy-value models* (Stroebe, 2000). These assume that decisions between different courses of action are based on two types of cognition:

1. *subjective probabilities* that a given action will produce a set of expected outcomes

2. *evaluation* of action outcomes.

Individuals will choose from among various alternative courses of action the one most likely to produce positive results and avoid negative ones. Different models differ in terms of the *types* of beliefs and attitudes that should be used in predicting a particular class of behaviour. They are rational reasoning models, which assume that individuals consciously deliberate about the likely consequences of behavioural alternatives available to them before engaging in action.

Theory of Reasoned Action (TRA)

This has been used extensively to examine predictions of behaviour and was central to the debate within social psychology regarding the relationship between attitudes and behaviour (see Gross, 2005). TRA assumes that behaviour is a function of the *intention* to perform that behaviour (Fishbein, 1967; Ajzen and Fishbein, 1970; Fishbein and Ajzen, 1975). A behavioural intention is determined by:

- a person's *attitude* to the behaviour, which is determined by (a) beliefs about the outcome of the behaviour, and (b) evaluation of the expected outcome

- *subjective norms* – a person's beliefs about the desirability of carrying out a particular health behaviour within the social group, society and culture to which s/he belongs.

Evaluation of TRA

✔/✗ **Supported by research evidence:** TRA has successfully predicted a wide range of behaviours, including blood donation, smoking marijuana, dental hygiene and family planning. However, attitudes and behaviour are only *weakly* related: people don't always do what they say they intend to.

✗ **Fails to take past behaviour into account:** the model doesn't consider people's past behaviour, despite evidence that this is a good predictor of future behaviour.

✗ **What about irrational and involuntary behaviour?** The model fails to account for people's irrational decisions (Penny, 1996). Similarly, Maes and van Elderen (1998) argue that, 'The assumption that behaviour is a function of intentions … limits the applicability … of the model to volitional behaviour – that is, to behaviours that are perceived to be under personal control …'.

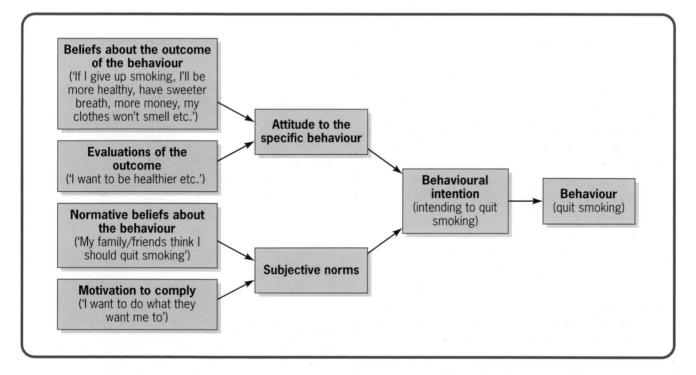

Figure 9.10 The main components of the Theory of Reasoned Action (adapted from Penny, 1996; Maes and van Elderen, 1998)

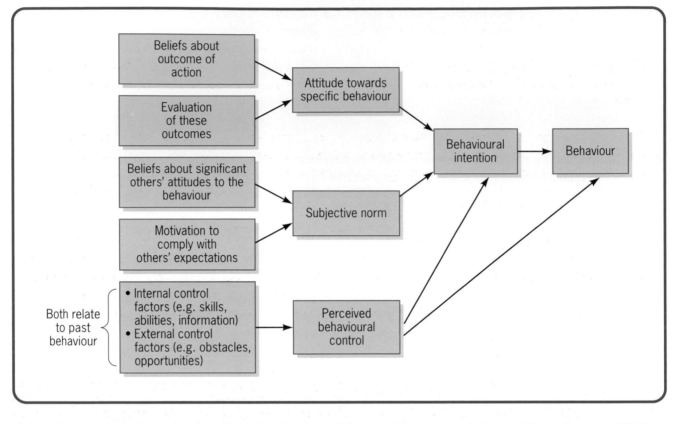

Figure 9.11 The main components of the Theory of Planned Behaviour (adapted from Ogden, 2004)

Theory of Planned Behaviour (TPB)

This represents a modification of TRA, in particular the addition of Bandura's (1977b, 1986) concept of *self-efficacy* (Ajzen, 1991). According to Ajzen, control beliefs are important determinants of *perceived behavioural control* (PBC) – that is, feeling confident that our current skills and resources will enable us to achieve the desired behaviour and overcome any external barriers. This is crucial to understanding motivation: if, for example, you think you're unable to quit smoking, you probably won't even try. PBC can have a *direct* effect on behaviour, bypassing behavioural intentions.

Evaluation of TPB

✔ **Much cited and influential model:** according to Walker *et al.* (2004), TPB is currently the most popular and widely used social cognition model in health psychology.

✔ **Substantial empirical support:** it's been used to assess a variety of health-related behaviours. For example, Brubaker and Wickersham (1990) examined its different components in relation to testicular self-examination: attitude, subjective norm and behavioural control (measured as self-efficacy) all correlated with the behavioural intention. Schifter and Ajzen (1985) found that weight loss was predicted by the model's components, especially PBC. TPB has been particularly successful in predicting behaviours such as smoking, alcohol consumption and exercise, with PCB and self-efficacy proving to

Evaluation of TPB continued...

be the key components (Dunn, 2007). Taking into account a large number of studies, TPB can account for about 60 per cent of the variability in people's intentions (Armitage and Conner, 2001, in Dunn, 2007).

✗ **The need for additional, non-cognitive components:** a number of commentators have suggested additional factors that may need to be taken into account. In particular, the model considers only cognitive determinants of attitudes and beliefs; one of the most promising 'extra' variables is 'anticipated regret' – that is, the strength of emotional disappointment that may occur if the intended behaviour isn't achieved (Richard *et al.*, 1995, in Dunn, 2007).

✔ **It takes a variety of variables into account:** like TRA, TPB has the advantage over the Health Belief Model (see text below) of including a degree of irrationality (in the form of evaluation), and it attempts to address the issue of social and environmental factors (normative beliefs). The extra 'ingredient' of PCB provides a role for past behaviour. For example, if you've tried several times before to quit smoking, then you're less likely to believe you'll be successful in the future and, therefore, you'll be less likely to intend to try (Ogden, 2000; Penny, 1996).

STRETCH AND CHALLENGE

✗ **Other theoretical limitations of the model:** according to Dunn (2007), the TPB (and the Health Belief Model) relates only to the *motivational* or *intention-formation stage*, and so doesn't address what can be called the *action stage* (the translation of intention into behaviour). Research has shown that even when intention is strong, people don't always follow through with the intended behaviour (Conner and Sparkes, 2005, in Dunn, 2007). Where intention has been deliberately manipulated, the impact on behaviour is still modest (Webb and Sheeran, 2006, in Dunn, 2007). As Dunn observes, 'It is said that "the road to hell is paved with good intentions", and good intentions, unfortunately, are not enough to ensure good behaviour.'

Much research has investigated the 'intention–behaviour' gap. One of the most promising research developments is *implementation intentions* (Gollwiotzer and Schaal, 1998, in Dunn, 2007). Asking someone to make an implementation intention requires them to make a specific plan as to when and where they'll carry out the behaviour. The reasoning behind this is that when they find themselves in that situation, they'll be cued to perform the behaviour. For example, Kellar and Abraham (2005, in Dunn, 2007) found that psychology undergraduates who'd been asked to plan vegetables for their lunch and evening meals, ate significantly more of those foods in the week following the plan-making compared with students who hadn't made specific plans. Similar effects have been found for a range of other health behaviours, including exercise, breast self-examination and consumption of vitamins (Sheeran *et al.*, 2005, in Dunn, 2007).

How Science Works

Practical Learning Activity 9.10

- Apply the example of deciding to quit smoking (or gambling) to TPB, as shown in Figure 9.11. Use Figure 9.10 to help you.
- You could do this individually or in pairs, and you could present your effort to the rest of the class.

Health Belief Model (HBM)

This was originally developed by social psychologists working in the US Public Health Service (Becker, 1974; Janz and Becker, 1984). They wanted to understand why people failed to make use of disease prevention and screening tests for early detection of diseases not associated with clear-cut symptoms (at least in the early stages), such as tuberculosis. It was later also applied to patients' responses to symptoms and compliance with / adherence to prescribed medication among acutely and chronically ill patients. More recently, it's been used to predict a wide range of health-related behaviours (Ogden, 2004).

The HBM assumes that the likelihood that people will engage in a particular health behaviour is a function of:

- the extent to which they believe they're *susceptible* to the associated disease

- their perception of the *severity of the consequences* of getting the disease.

Together, these determine the *perceived threat* of the disease. Given the threat, people then consider whether or not the action will bring benefits that outweigh the costs associated with the action. In addition, *cues to action* increase the likelihood that the action will be adopted; these might include advice from others, a health problem or mass-media campaigns. Other important concepts include *general health motivation* (the individual's readiness to be concerned about health matters), and *perceived control* (for example, 'I'm confident I can give up smoking' – Becker and Rosenstock, 1987; see Figure 9.12).

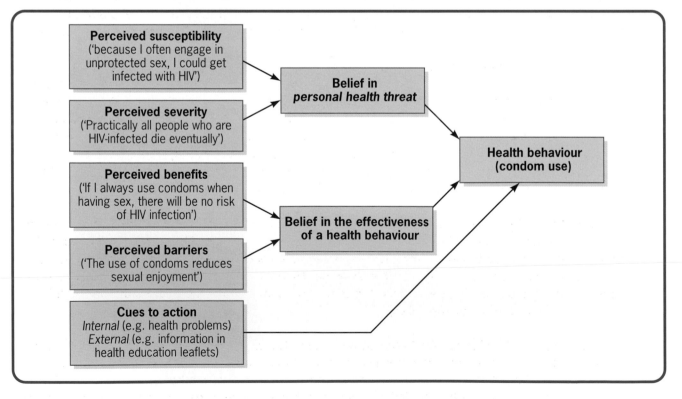

Figure 9.12 The main components of the Health Belief Model (adapted from Stroebe, 2000, reproduced with kind permission of the Open University Press/McGraw-Hill Publishing Company)

Evaluation of the HBM

✔ **Takes demographic variables and psychological characteristics into account:** it allows for demographic variables (such as age and gender) and psychological characteristics (such as ways of coping with stress and locus of control; see Gross and Rolls, 2008) that might affect health beliefs (Forshaw, 2002). For example, young women are likely to engage in dieting behaviour. So 'the HBM covers most, if not all, of the factors which, on the face of it, should be relevant in determining if a person engages in a particular behaviour' (Forshaw, 2002).

✔ **Supporting evidence:** there's considerable evidence supporting the HBM's predictions, in relation to a wide range of behaviours. Dietary compliance, safe sex, having vaccinations, regular dental check-ups and participating in regular exercise programmes are all related to people's perception of their susceptibility to the related health problem, their belief that the problem is severe and their perception that the benefits of preventative action outweigh the costs (e.g. Becker, 1974; Becker *et al.,* 1977; Becker and Rosenstock, 1984). According to Dunn (2007), these examples include behaviours that occur once or over a short period of time (such as immunisation and attending screenings) as well as those that are longer term (such as dieting, exercise and the use of condoms). The most important predictor of the likelihood of health behaviour seems to be perceived barriers, followed by susceptibility, benefits and severity. Relatively little research has been conducted on the effects of cues to action or health motivation (Dunn, 2007).

✗ **Conflicting evidence:** for example, Janz and Becker (1984) found that healthy behavioural intentions are related to *low* perceived seriousness (*not* high as the model predicts). Also, several studies have suggested an association between *low* susceptibility (*not* high) and healthy behaviour (Ogden, 2004).

✗ **It overestimates people's rationality:** the HBM has been criticised for assuming that people's behaviour is governed by rational decision-making processes (a criticism that applies to health models in general), ignoring emotional factors (such as fear and anxiety), and overemphasising the individual. A factor that might explain the persistence of unhealthy behaviours is people's inaccurate perceptions of risk and susceptibility. While fear might dissuade someone from experimenting with drugs in the first place (see PMT, below), once addictive behaviours have become habitual, they'll be carried out with little conscious deliberation. In addition, people under the influence of alcohol or other drugs may have impaired judgement and be unable to think logically (Dunn, 2007).

✗ **The importance of intention:** unlike TRA and TPB, there's no explicit reference to behavioural *intention* in the HBM. Instead, central beliefs and perceptions act directly on the likelihood of behaviour. But it's been shown that adding intention to the HBM increases its level of predictability, so it's now typically added when testing the model. However, this blurs the distinction between the HBM and other models. The trend is towards developing generic models of health behaviour that incorporate the best 'bits' of other models (Harris and Middleton, 1995).

✗ **The reinforcing effects of addictive behaviours:** a major factor that's not considered by HBM is the positive aspects of health-endangering behaviour patterns (such as the enjoyment of smoking; see above) (Stroebe, 2000). Although the HBM – and the other models of health behaviour – isn't explicitly aimed at explaining and predicting addictive behaviours, these are precisely the types of behaviour that cannot be adequately understood – or changed – without taking their reinforcing effects into account. It's *because* of their reinforcing properties that they become addictive and, hence, why they're so difficult to change (see below).

An evaluation of health belief models: what do we do about habitual behaviours?

As we noted above, addictive behaviours are reinforcing. Also, by definition, they're *habitual*. Not all habitual behaviours are addictive (and detrimental to health); indeed, they may be health-enhancing (such as routinely eating five pieces of fruit/vegetables per day); but all addictive behaviours are, by definition, habitual.

Behaviour becomes habitual if it's performed frequently and regularly and under environmental conditions that are stable. Once it's become habitual, it should no longer be guided by conscious deliberations (such as intentions and attitudes, subjective norms or PBC on which intentions are based) (Stroebe, 2000). Past behaviours that were performed regularly and in stable contexts were found to be much stronger predictors of future behaviour than were measures of intentions (Oulette and Wood, 1998, in Stroebe, 2000).

Does this mean that the health models we've discussed (which Stroebe calls 'rational reasoning models') shouldn't be applied to behaviours that have become habitual (including addictive behaviours)? In addressing this question, Stroebe distinguishes between two aspects of these models, namely *process* and *prediction*. The models outline how behavioural responses are guided by conscious intentions, which, in turn, reflect attitudes towards this behaviour, subjective norms and PBC. From this perspective, attitudes, subjective norms and control perceptions are linked to behaviour through their effects on behavioural intentions (Eagly and Chaiken, 1993; Oulette and Wood, 1998, in Stroebe, 2000). This description of the *action process* is invalid for habitual behaviours, which are cued *directly* by recurring features of the environment.

The automatic instigation and execution of habitual behaviour is similar in some respects to the spontaneous processing or MODE model (Fazio, 1990; Fazio and Towles-Schwen, 1999, in Stroebe, 2000). According to this model, the attitude-to-behaviour sequence is initiated when attitudes are accessed from memory by the presentation of relevant environmental cues: the more easily accessible (or easily recalled) the attitude, the greater the likelihood of such automatic activation of the attitude based on mere observation of the cues. In turn, the ease of recall will depend on how strong the association is in memory between the attitude object (e.g. cigarette smoking, playing fruit machines) and the individual's evaluation of it. If this association is weak, the automatic attitude-to-behaviour sequence

won't occur. Evidence exists that attitudes are highly accessible in cases of habitual behaviour.

For these reasons, rational reasoning models have become less valid as process models for habitual, and thus relatively automatic, behaviours. However, this *doesn't* mean that they're also invalid as *predictive* models: after all, habitual behaviours were once controlled consciously, so we must have once held attitudes, norms and control beliefs that were consistent with the behaviour. Where habits and intentions *conflict*, intentions (and attitudes) become poor predictors of behaviour; control beliefs will be the most valid predictors of behaviour, because they reflect the individual's assessment of the extent to which s/he has control over a given behaviour. Thus, in a study of alcoholics having psychotherapy to help them stop drinking, Jonas (1995, in Stroebe, 2000) found that PCB was the best predictor of therapy success.

Intervention

How Science Works

Practical Learning Activity 9.11

- For each of the three models discussed above, try to identify what they imply for intervention. (This requires you to first identify the key components of the model, then to consider how these might be manipulated in a way that would change behaviour in the desired direction.)
- Based on the discussion above of habitual behaviours (including addictive behaviours), how might such behaviours be changed (that is, how can habits be broken)?

Psychological interventions

Interventions based on cognition models (social cognition and health models)

TRA

According to the TRA, the effectiveness of strategies aimed at modifying health behaviour depends on the success in influencing the individual's intention to engage in the specific behaviour. Since intentions are taken to be the immediate determinant of behaviour, a change in behavioural intention should produce a change in the associated behaviour. The behavioural

Specification Hint

The specification states: 'Types of intervention, including biological, psychological, public health interventions, and legislation, and their effectiveness'. Interventions based on health models clearly represent psychological interventions. Strictly, you only need to know about one intervention of each type, but (as in other parts of the specification), it's always useful to be familiar with at least one other of each type (to provide A02 material through comparison and contrast, and, more generally, to provide a broader understanding of the topic). Note that there's a close link between health models and public health interventions (especially in the form of media campaigns). Note also – again – that no particular addictive behaviours are specified here, so you're free to 'mix and match' interventions and addictive behaviours.

and normative beliefs (which underlie the attitudes towards the behaviour and relevant subjective norms, respectively) should be the target of the intervention (Stroebe, 2000).

Whether one should focus more on behavioural or normative beliefs in designing a campaign to influence a specific behaviour will depend on the relative importance of attitudes and norms in determining the behaviour in question. Their relative importance will also vary between different populations, so it's important to conduct pilot studies when designing an intervention.

Taking smoking as an example, even though the negative health consequences represent salient outcomes, the belief that smoking is unhealthy no longer discriminates between smokers and non-smokers (Leventhal and Cleary, 1980, in Stroebe, 2000). In other words, since smokers generally acknowledge the harmful effects of smoking, information about these effects is unlikely to persuade smokers to quit. Similarly, the perceived threat of contracting HIV has been found to have only a small association with condom use among heterosexuals (Sheeran et al., 1999). Interventions that focus on the dangers of HIV and AIDS are, therefore, unlikely to be effective in

increasing condom use. As Stroebe (2000) says, 'To be effective, interventions have to focus on those beliefs which most strongly discriminate between people who do and do not intend to perform the behaviour in question.'

According to the model, it should also be possible to change attitudes towards some health-damaging behaviours by modifying the environment so as to increase the costs of the behaviour (for example, increases in the price of cigarettes and alcohol, restrictions on the sale of these). However, the person has to be aware of the changes, and the costs must be sufficiently high to outweigh the rewards.

TPB

Because the TPB is an extension of the TRA, the two models share many implications for intervention. However, one major difference is TPB's inclusion of PBC as a second predictor of behaviour. It follows that the first step in designing a successful intervention is to assess whether the behaviour is mainly determined by behavioural intentions or by PBC.

In the exceptional case where behaviour is mainly predicted by PBC, we need to examine further the lack of association between intention and behaviour. Stroebe gives the example of male homosexuals engaging in unprotected anal sex with casual partners. While most intend to use protection, those who fail to do so usually have low PBC; in this case, their control might be increased through some kind of skill training.

In the more usual situation where behaviour is mainly determined by the relevant behavioural intention, it's necessary first of all to establish the most important determinant of the intention (attitude, subjective

Figure 9.13 Princess Mabel of Amsterdam gives the starting signal of the new Stop Aids Now! *campaign*

How Science Works

Practical Learning Activity 9.12

● Based on what you know about how classical conditioning can help explain the development of addictive behaviour (see Figure 9.3), how do you think it might be used to *remove* addictive behaviour? A major application of classical conditioning is *aversion therapy*; think about the word 'aversive' and draw a diagram (following the pattern of Figure 9.3) to show how the process would work.

Patients would, typically, be given warm saline solution containing the emetic drug. Immediately before the vomiting begins, they're given a four-ounce glass of whisky, which they're required to smell, taste and swill around in the mouth before swallowing. (If vomiting hasn't occurred, another straight whisky is given and, to prolong nausea, a glass of beer containing emetic.) Subsequent treatments involve larger doses of injected emetic, or increases in the length of treatment time, or a widening range of hard liquors (Kleinmuntz, 1980). Between trials the patient may sip soft drinks to prevent generalisation to all drinking behaviour and to promote the use of alcohol substitutes.

Meyer and Chesser (1970) found that about half their alcoholic patients abstained for at least one year following treatment, and that aversion therapy is better than no treatment at all. Roth and Fonagy (2005) cite studies of aversion therapy using various emetics or electric shock in random control trials (RCTs – studies that explicitly compare two or more treatment conditions; see Chapter 7). Although results aren't consistent across trials, there appears to be only a short-term impact with both variants of this technique.

Smith *et al.* (1997, in Roth and Fonagy) matched 249 patients treated as inpatients in a multimodal treatment programme (including chemical or electrical aversion) with a similar number of controls from a separate outcome programme (an inpatient treatment that used mainly counselling). Although at six months, those who'd received the aversion therapy showed higher rates of abstinence, the benefit wasn't sustained at twelve months. According to Roth and Fonagy, 'Overall, there is little support for aversion techniques, and it is hard to recommend [their] use in standard service settings, given that (unsurprisingly) [there is] a high rate of attrition from such therapies.'

Covert sensitisation (Cautela, 1967) is a variant of aversion therapy. 'Covert' refers to the fact that both the behaviour to be removed and the aversive stimulus to be associated with it are *imagined*. The patient has to visualise the events leading up to the initiation of the undesirable behaviour: just as this happens, s/he has to imagine nausea or some other aversive sensation.

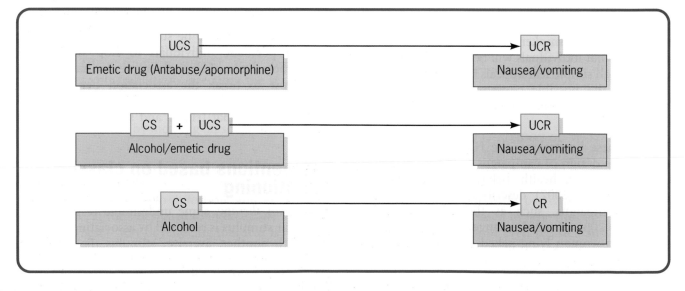

Figure 9.15 Diagrammatic representation of how aversion therapy can be used in the treatment of alcoholism

Figure 9.16 Malcolm McDowell in a scene from the film, A Clockwork Orange. *His eyes are clamped open, forcing him to watch a film portraying acts of violence and sadism, as part of aversion therapy. He's earlier been given an emetic drug, so that extreme nausea and violence will become associated*

'Sensitisation' is achieved by associating the undesirable behaviour with an exceedingly disagreeable consequence (Kleinmuntz, 1980). The patient may also be instructed to rehearse an alternative 'relief' scene in which, for example, the decision not to drink is accompanied by pleasurable sensations. Covert sensitisation is generally preferred on humanitarian grounds, but is no more effective than aversion therapy (Gelder *et al.,* 1989) or than aversion therapy and alternative interventions (Roth and Fonagy, 2005).

Aversion therapy had also been used to treat gambling behaviour. One of the earliest treatment studies (McConaghy *et al.,* 1983, in Bennett, 2006) compared the effectiveness of aversion therapy with *imagined sensitisation*. Aversion therapy involved participants reading aloud words on a series of cards, some of which were related to gambling activities and some of which described alternative actions (such as 'went straight home'). Each time they read out a gambling-related phrase they received a mild electric shock (described as 'unpleasant but not emotionally upsetting') for two seconds. Imagined sensitisation involved participants imagining a variety of gambling-related scenarios at the same time as using relaxation procedures to reduce arousal.

The latter approach proved the most effective on measures of gambling urge and behaviour over the year following treatment. Long-term follow-up, conducted between two and nine years after the end of therapy, found that 79 per cent of those who took part in the desensitisation programme reported control over or having stopped gambling. Just over 50 per cent of the aversion therapy group reported the same outcome.

Interventions based on operant conditioning

How Science Works

Practical Learning Activity 9.13

● Repeat the exercise as for Practical Learning Activity 9.12 – but substitute *operant* for classical conditioning.

Treatment for alcohol abuse using methods based on operant conditioning is often called *contingency management* (CM). This is based on the belief that environmental contingencies (of reinforcement and punishment) can play an important role in encouraging or discouraging drinking. It involves teaching patients and those close to them to reinforce behaviours that are *inconsistent* with drinking (such as taking Antabuse and avoiding situations that were associated with drinking in the past). The reinforcement usually takes the form of vouchers that can be exchanged for retail goods. CM also includes teaching job-finding and social skills, as well as assertiveness training for refusing drinks. Socially isolated individuals are assisted and encouraged to establish contacts with other people not associated with drinking. This approach also includes *couples therapy* (marital therapy). It's widely used with abusers of cocaine and opiates.

Other effective contingency-based treatments include providing reinforcers for staying sober, such as opportunities to win prizes, and abstinence-contingent partial support for housing, food, recreational activities and access to supportive therapy.

CM therapy (often referred to as the *community-reinforcement approach*) has generated very promising results (e.g. Azrin *et al.,* 1982; Sisson and Azrin, 1989; Smith and Meyers, 2000, all in Davison *et al.,* 2000). A review of the literature (Smith *et al.,* 2001, in Davison *et al.,* 2004) concludes that it's consistently found to be

433

- Attempts to identify the **addictive personality** currently favour a **stress-diathesis model**, according to which addictions develop from a reciprocal interaction between an individual's biological and psychological vulnerability and his/her environmental circumstances.

- Personality traits that predict who might **experiment** with drugs and so on may be quite different from those that influence who will **abuse** them. Possible candidates include **sensitivity to reward**, **impulsivity**, and **proneness to anxiety and negative mood** (**punishment sensitivity**).

- According to the **stress-reduction** or **self-medication pathway**, individuals high on N and anxiety are more likely to turn to drugs as a quick and effective relief from distress.

Reducing addictive behaviour

- The **Theory of Reasoned Action (TRA)** and **Theory of Planned Behaviour (TPB)** are **social cognition models**, which aim at accounting for social behaviour in general and are much broader than **cognition models** (such as the **Health Belief Model / HBM**), which are specifically **health models**.

- All three models are **expectancy-value models**, which assume that decisions between different courses of action are based on **subjective probabilities** (that a given action will produce certain expected outcomes) and **evaluation** of those outcomes.

- Individuals will choose among different courses of action the one most likely to produce positive results and avoid negative ones. Different models identify different **types** of beliefs and attitudes that predict a particular class of behaviour.

- TRA assumes that behaviour is a function of the **intention** to perform that behaviour; a behavioural intention is determined by a person's **attitude** (determined by beliefs about the outcome and evaluation of the expected outcome) and **subjective norms**.

- TPB is a modification of TRA, the main addition being Bandura's concept of **self-efficacy** in the form of **perceived behavioural control (PBC)**. This can have a **direct** influence on behaviour, bypassing behavioural intentions.

- A theoretical weakness of both the TRA and TPB is the **intention–behaviour gap**. One of the most promising research developments attempting to get round this problem is **implementation intentions**.

- HBM assumes that health behaviour is a function of (a) the extent to which people believe they're **susceptible** to the associated disease; and (b) their perception of the **severity of the consequences** of getting the disease. Together, these determine the **perceived threat**. Other important concepts are **cues to action**, **general health motivation** and **perceived control**.

- All three models emphasise people's **rational** decision making, including their assessment of personal susceptibility (for example, to HIV/AIDS). This makes them inappropriate for explaining and predicting addictive behaviours that are, by definition, **habitual** (cued **directly** by recurring features of the environment).

- **Protection motivation theory (PMT)** extends HBM to include **fear** as a motivating factor.

- Each of the major social cognition and health models implies **psychological interventions** for changing health behaviours (such as quitting smoking or having safe sex); these reflect the central concepts identified by the particular model.

- In relation to HIV/AIDS, most public health campaigns have emphasised vulnerability to, and severity of, infection – both designed to induce fear.

- Early experimental research suggested that you cannot frighten people into acting upon the message, and they may even be **inhibited** by it. What's necessary for change to occur is the **high availability factor**.

- According to McGuire, there's an **inverted U-shaped curve** in the relationship between fear and attitude change.

- Individuals must feel personally **vulnerable** to a threat before they're likely to form an intention to act on the recommendations of the message, especially if they're previously unfamiliar with a given health risk.

- To break the habits involved in smoking and other addictive behaviours, interventions need to teach people how to interrupt the association between their behaviour and internal stimulus conditions that trigger and maintain it.

- Interventions for alcoholism and gambling based on **classical conditioning** include **aversion therapy** and **covert** (or **imagined**) **sensitisation**.

- Interventions based on **operant conditioning** include **contingency management (CM)** (or the **community-reinforcement approach**), and **behavioural self-control training** (involving one/more of **stimulus control, modification of the topography of drinking** and **reinforcing abstinence**).

- **Cognitive** interventions include **cognitive-behavioural therapy (CBT)**, which can take different forms and involve specific techniques, such as **relapse prevention training** and **cognitive correction**. One or other of these has been used with substance and alcohol abuse, and pathological gambling.

- **Biological** interventions have included the use of **selective** (or **specific**) **serotonin reuptake inhibitors (SSRIs)** with pathological gamblers, **detoxification** (withdrawal) with alcoholics (involving **anxiolytic drugs**, such as **benzodiazepines**), **medication** (such as **disulfiram/Antabuse**) to maintain abstinence from alcohol.

- **Psychoactive drugs** (such as **fluoxetine/Prozac**) are also used to treat depression and other psychological disorders associated with drinking.

- Two widely used drug-therapy programmes for heroin addiction involve **heroin substitutes** (notably **methadone**) and **heroin antagonists**.

- Biological treatments for smoking include the use of nicotine gum, patches or inhalers.

- Drug addiction has also been treated recently through one or other type of brain stimulation: **deep brain stimulation (DBS)**, **cortical stimulation** and **transcranial magnetic stimulation (TMS)**.

- **Public health interventions** can take the form of **doctor's advice**, **worksite interventions**, **community-based programmes** and **government interventions** (such as restricting/banning advertising and increasing the costs).

Essay Questions

Models of addictive behaviour

1. Outline and evaluate **one or more** models of addiction, including explanations for initiation, maintenance and relapse. (25 marks)
2. Critically consider explanations for smoking and / or gambling. (25 marks)

Factors affecting addictive behaviour

3. Discuss research into individual differences in vulnerability to addiction. (25 marks)
4. (a) Outline research into the role of the media in addictive behaviour. (9 marks)
   (b) Discuss research into individual differences in vulnerability to addiction. (16 marks)

Reducing addictive behaviour

5. Outline and evaluate **two or more** models of the prevention of addiction. (25 marks)
6. Critically consider **two or more** types of intervention for addictive behaviour, including their effectiveness in dealing with initation and / or relapse. (25 marks)

Anomalistic psychology

What's covered in this chapter?

You need to know about:

Theoretical and methodological issues in the study of anomalistic experience
- Issues of pseudoscience and scientific fraud
- Controversies relating to Ganzfeld studies of ESP and studies of psychokinesis

Factors underlying anomalous experience
- Cognitive, personality and biological factors underlying anomalous experience
- Functions of paranormal and related beliefs, including their cultural significance
- The psychology of deception and self-deception, superstition and coincidence

Belief in exceptional experience
- Research into: psychic healing; out-of-body and near-death experience; psychic mediumship

This section of the specification is called 'Anomalistic psychology'. As explained in more detail below, this forms *part* of the subject-matter of *parapsychology*. Parapsychology has been defined in different ways, but is generally used to refer to the scientific study of *paranormal phenomena* ('paranormal' being another term for 'anomalous'). So the chapter might have been called 'Parapsychology', which, as well as anomalous experience (what the specification calls 'exceptional experience'), covers extrasensory perception (ESP), psychokinesis (PK) and apparitional phenomena (such as ghosts) (Henry, 2005a). But, of course, exam questions can only use the wording in the specification.

How Science Works

Practical Learning Activity 10.1

- Give some examples of anomalous/exceptional experience.
- What does 'extrasensory perception' mean? Give some examples.
- What does 'psychokinesis' mean? Give some examples.
- Give some (other) examples of 'apparitional phenomena'.
- Do you believe that any of these exist as real phenomena (regardless of how you might explain them)? In other words, as implied by the term 'extrasensory', do you believe that information can be exchanged between people that doesn't involve one or more of the sensory systems?

ANOMALISTIC PSYCHOLOGY AND PARAPSYCHOLOGY: DEFINING TERMS AND DEFINING THE FIELD

According to Henry (2005a), *parapsychology* (the term first introduced in the 1930s to refer to the scientific investigation of paranormal phenomena; Evans, 1987a) is the study of *psychic phenomena*, that is 'the exchange of information or some other interaction between an organism and its environment, without the mediation of the senses'.

For most psychologists, the sensory systems (vision/hearing, audition/hearing, gustation / taste, olfaction/smell, skin or cutaneous senses / touch, and proprioception / kinaesthetic and vestibular senses) are the only means by which we can acquire information about the environment (both physical objects and other people). However, there are some phenomena that seem to involve meaningful exchanges of information, and at the same time appear somehow to *exceed* the capacities of the sensory (and motor) systems as they're currently understood (Rao and Palmer, 1987) (e.g. '*extra*sensory perception'). For these reasons, such phenomena are considered to be *anomalous*, and are commonly referred to as *paranormal* (or 'psi', short for 'psychic ability').

As stated above, the subject matter of the field of parapsychology comprises extrasensory perception (ESP), psychokinesis (PK), anomalous (exceptional) experience and apparitional phenomena.

Extrasensory perception (ESP)

The term was first introduced in 1934 by J.B. Rhine. This was a general term used to cover three types of communication that supposedly occur without the use of the senses, namely *telepathy, clairvoyance* and *precognition*. This, and *retrocognition*, are defined in Box 10.1.

Psychokinesis (PK)

Psychokinesis (movement by the psyche) refers to ' the supposed power of the mind to manipulate matter at a distance without any known physical means' (Evans, 1987b), or the apparent ability to 'influence events simply by a direct volitional act of some sort, by wanting the event to happen in a certain way' (Morris, 1989). For PK, the direction of the influence is from person to environment (the reverse of ESP).

Box 10.1: The four types of extrasensory perception (ESP)

1. *Telepathy:* 'the transmission of information from one mind to another, without the use of language, body movements, or any of the known senses' (Evans, 1987b). It was previously called 'thought transference'.
2. *Clairvoyance:* 'the acquisition by a mind or brain of information which is not available to it by the known senses, and, most important, which is *not known at the time to any other mind or brain*' (Evans, 1987b).
3. *Precognition:* 'the apparent ability to access information about future events before they happen' (Morris, 1989).
4. *Retrocognition:* known information from the past is apparently picked up psychically (Henry, 2005a).

In all cases, the direction of influence is from environment to person.

Psychokinesis can be split into *macro-PK*, where solid objects are affected and the result can be seen by the naked eye (such as spoon bending), apports ('gifts' that 'materialise' from non-physical to physical reality) or moving an object purely via intention, and *micro-PK*, where ultra-sensitive instruments (such as strain gauges and random number generators / RNGs; see below) are apparently affected by intention and the significance of the results is assessed statistically.

Macro-PK is still highly controversial; it's an area where experimenters have to take particular care to guard against fraud (Wiseman, 2001; see below).

Naturally-occurring PK (*recurrent spontaneous PK / RSPK*) is associated with phenomena such as poltergeists. Direct mental interaction with a living system (DMILS) refers to PK on a live organism where physiology, such as electrodermal (skin conductance) activity or blood pressure, is altered purely by intention. Another example is distant and non-contact healing (Henry, 2005a).

Apparitional phenomena

Apparitions are experienced as *outside* the person and perceived as external to the self, the classic example

being a ghost. Sometimes the apparition appears to be fairly solid, at other times less obviously person-like. In previous centuries, reports of demon visitations were quite common. In the latter half of the twentieth century, reflecting technological developments, similar experiences have often been interpreted as visits by aliens. (This has parallels in the kind of 'thought-insertion' symptoms commonly reported by patients with schizophrenia; see Chapter 7.) In non-western cultures, experiences of spirits of some kind are often accepted as part of life, but in the west such reports are rare (though there are some well-known cases of visions of the Virgin Mary) (Henry, 2005a).

Anomalous or exceptional experience

In contrast to apparitions, anomalous experiences (such as out-of-body experiences / OBEs, near-death experiences / NDEs, past-life experiences / PLEs, and coincidence experiences / CEs) are felt as happening to the individual him/herself. There are other anomalous experiences (such as UFOs) and (other) exceptional experiences (such as altered states of consciousness and mystical experiences) that are traditionally studied by researchers other than parapsychologists. This is seen as a reason for categorising anomalous and exceptional experiences together.

For example, White (1993, in Henry, 2005a), offers a classification of exceptional experiences which brings together phenomena traditionally studied by parapsychologists and others interested in anomalous and exceptional experiences. These are:

- mystical experiences – including peak experiences, stigmata, transformational experience

- psychic experiences – including apports (see above), synchronicity, telepathy, PK (see above) and OBEs (see below)

- encounter-type experiences – including apparitions, angels, UFO encounters, sense of presence

- death-related experiences – such as NDEs (see below) and PLEs

- exceptional normal experiences – such as *déjà vu* and hypnagogia (sometimes spelled 'hynagogia').

How Science Works

Practical Learning Activity 10.2

● Try to find definitions of
  – peak experiences
  – stigmata
  – transformational experience
  – synchronicity
  – sense of presence
  – hypnogogia/hynagogia.

THEORETICAL AND METHODOLOGICAL ISSUES IN THE STUDY OF ANOMALISTIC EXPERIENCE

✔ Specification Hint

It seems sensible to consider 'Issues of pseudoscience and scientific fraud' as part of 'Controversies relating to Ganzfeld studies of ESP and studies of psychokinesis'. First, we need to describe those (and related) methods within a historical context; then we will consider the controversies surrounding them.

The historical roots of parapsychology (PP)

According to Evans (1987a), the history of PP can be conveniently divided into three overlapping phases or periods: *spiritualistic research / spiritualism, psychical research* and *modern PP.*

Spiritualistic research / spiritualism

Most Victorian scientists brought up as orthodox Christians were expected to believe in the reality of an immortal, non-physical soul. So a substantial number of them became involved in the minority religion of *spiritualism:* if souls or spirits survived the death of the physical body, they must exist *somewhere* in the universe and should, in principle, be contactable (for example, through mediums). Some of the outstanding brains of the time, including physicists, biologists and anthropologists, solemnly tried to induce spirit forms to materialise in their laboratories. The Society for Psychical Research was founded in London in 1882 and, soon after, the *Journal of the Society for Psychical Research.*

Other, more critical or sceptical, colleagues conducted their own experiments. Medium after medium was exposed as fraudulent, and the pioneers were shown to be gullible, incompetent or both. By 1900, scientific interest was moving away from seances and towards 'more plausible' aspects of the paranormal.

Figure 10.1 In the heyday of spiritualism, mediums were tied up inside a 'cabinet' in front of an audience; in a deep trance, they claimed to exude ectoplasm from various bodily orifices, and so create fully formed spirits that could move around the room, touching the astounded sitters (Blackmore, 2003)

Psychical research

This was the era of the 'ghost hunter'. Scientists and affluent amateurs turned to phenomena such as manifestations in haunted houses, poltergeist activity, demonic possession, apparitions and premonitions. There was also a growing number of casual studies of telepathy and precognitive dreams.

Modern PP

According to Blackmore (1995), a British parapsychologist, credit for the founding of PP (in the 1930s) was almost entirely due to J.B. Rhine and Louisa Rhine (although Louisa is often not mentioned, as in Evans's 1987a account; see 'Synoptic Material', page 262). They were biologists who wanted to find evidence *against* a purely materialistic view of human nature. Despite

STRETCH AND CHALLENGE: Sexism within the psychology profession

In 1974, Bernstein and Russo published an article in *American Psychologist* called 'The history of psychology revisited: Or, up with our foremothers'. It consisted largely of a quiz, which their psychology colleagues failed miserably! One of the questions was as follows:

The following are the last names of individuals who have contributed to the scientific study of human behaviour. What else do these names have in common?

Ausubel, Bellak, Brunswick, Buhler, Dennis, Gardner, Gibson, Glueck, Harlow, Hartley, Hoffman, Horowitz, Jones, Kendler, Koch, Lacey, Luchins, Lynd, Murphy, Premack, Rossi, Sears, Sherif, Spence, Staats, Stendler, Whiting, Yarrow.

(Answer: They are the surnames of female social scientists.)

While you may have recognised some of the names, this may only be because they had more famous and familiar husbands with whom they jointly published research (e.g. Gardner and Gardner, Harlow and Harlow (see Gross and Rolls, 2008), Kendler and Kendler, Luchins and Luchins, and Sherif and Sherif (again see Gross and Rolls, 2008); look at the 'References' section of any general psychology textbook). We automatically infer that the 'Harlow' in the list is Harry (of rhesus monkey fame) and that the 'Sherif' is Muztafer (of the autokinetic effect in conformity fame). We're *all* guilty!

Similarly, there's a strong tendency to assume that a psychologist whose name is unfamiliar to you is *male*. Even though *statistically* it's very likely that you'll be correct, this *isn't* the basis for making such assumptions. Rather, it reflects a *masculinist bias* – the belief that the contributions made by men to psychology are more important than those made by women. As Scarborough and Furumoto (1987, in Paludi, 1992) state, the history of psychology is the history of male psychology.

If the names in the answer to the question aren't what you'd call 'household names', that's precisely because the psychological literature's treatment of women psychologists has kept them invisible (Paludi, 1992). According to Stevens and Gardner (1982, in Paludi):

Figure 10.2 *Margaret Washburn and Mary Calkins: if these women are not household names, it is because psychological literature's treatment of women psychologists has kept them invisible*

The histories written by psychology's academicians are neither accurate nor complete, neglecting ... the most important contributions made by women ... they do not include Mary Calkins' theory of self nor her invention of the method of paired associates ... the monumentally important books of Margaret Washburn on abnormal behaviour ... and they totally ignore Magda Arnold's comprehensive theory of emotions and Margaret Harlow's contributions to an understanding of the importance of tactile stimulation in mothering.

sharing the same objectives, they wanted to dissociate themselves from spiritualism and bring their new science firmly into the laboratory. They renamed their research 'parapsychology', established a department of PP at Duke University in the USA, began to develop new experimental methods, and defined their terms operationally.

PP as science and its changing content
According to Roberts and Groome (2001):

We live in an age of science. However, there are many types of human experience which continue to defy any scientific explanation, as least in terms of the scientific knowledge that we have at the present time. In some cases we may have a partial explanation, but in other cases the underlying mechanism is completely unknown. These cases which completely defy any normal scientific explanation are referred to as 'paranormal' phenomena. In practice there is considerable overlap between what is regarded as 'paranormal' and what is ... merely 'unusual' ...

Because scientific knowledge changes so rapidly, and because most parapsychologists consider themselves to be scientists applying the accepted rules of scientific inquiry to difficult-to-explain phenomena, the field of PP is ever shrinking. For example, hypnosis, hallucinations and lucid dreams (where the dreamer seems to be controlling the dream content) used to be considered part of PP – until psychologists made progress in understanding them. This, in turn, suggests that 'paranormal' implies phenomena that *apparently* lie outside the range of normal scientific explanations and investigations. As Boring (1966) said, a scientific success is a failure for psychical research; in other words, PP is concerned with those phenomena that 'mainstream' or 'regular' psychology cannot explain with its currently available models and theories.

Parapsychologists who apply 'normal' scientific

methods are following a long tradition of scientists who investigated phenomena that *at the time* seemed mysterious (Utts and Josephson, 1996), or were given what we'd now consider bizarre, 'unscientific' explanations. Gregory (1987) gives the example of thunder and lightning: 'once considered to be the wrath of the Gods, but now understood as the same electricity that we generate and use for wonders of our technology'. In other words, once 'paranormal' phenomena have been accounted for scientifically, they'll no longer be called 'paranormal'. While they're still imperfectly understood (in terms of our current/conventional scientific knowledge and theories), it's convenient to call them paranormal: they're understandable *in principle*, but as yet we cannot explain them. This helps distinguish paranormal from 'supernatural' or 'beyond nature', which implies 'incompatible with scientific theorising and investigation' (Watt, 2001).

However, 'the phenomena of psi are so extraordinary and so similar to what are widely regarded as superstitions that some scientists declare psi to be an impossibility and reject the legitimacy of parapsychological inquiry' (Atkinson *et al.*, 1990).

Sometimes, 'extraordinary' can be construed as 'not real', and the history of PP is littered with accusations of fraud on the part of 'believers' by those who, for whatever reason, reject their claims. However, if psi 'really exists', what does this imply for many of our fundamental scientific beliefs about the world?

While strong opposition to PP is understandable, prejudgements about the impossibility of psi are inappropriate in science. Many psychologists who aren't yet convinced that psi has been demonstrated are nevertheless open to the *possibility* that new evidence may emerge that would be more compelling. Many parapsychologists believe that the case for psi has already been 'proven', or that experimental procedures exist that have the potential for doing so (Atkinson *et al.*, 1990).

Methods used to study PSI

According to Alcock (1981), definitions of ESP and PK are all negative, in the sense that they depend on ruling out 'normal' communication before the paranormal can be assumed. Progression in PP's experimental methods has necessarily been designed to exclude the 'normal' with even greater confidence. However, this inevitably leaves it open for critics to argue for even more devious ways in which sensory communication or outright fraud might occur (Blackmore, 1995).

ESP and Zener cards

The Rhines were convinced that the supposedly paranormal powers of the mind were essentially psychological phenomena, and so should be investigated with the tools of traditional psychological research. Throughout the 1930s, they conducted a lengthy series of *telepathy* experiments, in which the *receiver* had to guess the identity of a target being looked at by an *agent*. To make the task as easy as easy as possible, a set of simple symbols was developed and made into *Zener cards* (named after their designer), or 'ESP cards'. They come in a pack of 25 cards, comprising five circles, five squares, five crosses, five stars and five wavy lines (see Figure 10.4).

The rationale for these studies was that they allowed the experimenter to compare the results achieved with what would be expected by chance. So in a pack of 25 cards comprising five of each of five distinct symbols, we'd expect, on average, five to be *guessed* correctly (i.e. by chance alone). If receivers repeatedly scored above chance over long series of trials, this would suggest that they were 'receiving' some information about the cards. This would, in turn, imply that, if the experiments had been sufficiently tightly controlled as to exclude all normal or known sensory cues, then the information must be coming via ESP (Evans, 1987a).

Figure 10.3 Joseph and Louisa Rhine, founders of modern parapsychology

Figure 10.4 Zener card symbols

How Science Works

Practical Learning Activity 10.3

- Give a brief outline of how the Zener cards might have been used in (a) *clairvoyance* experiments and (b) *precognition* experiments.
- What different methods could have been used to determine that the order of the cards was random?
- Are some methods more reliable than others? Why?

In *clairvoyance* experiments, the cards were randomised out of sight of anyone before the receiver made his/her guesses; in *precognition* experiments, the card order was decided only *after* the receiver had made his/her guesses. However, devising procedures that rule out clairvoyance in favour of telepathy is difficult, and many researchers simply use the more general term, ESP, acknowledging this difficulty (Henry, 2005a).

Initially, the order of the cards in all the experiments was determined by shuffling, and later by the use of random number tables. It's extremely important for targets in ESP experiments to be properly randomised, so that results cannot be affected by any kind of systematic biases – shuffling *isn't* adequate (Blackmore, 1995).

What were the Rhines' findings?

The technique seemed to be successful, and the Rhines reported results that were way beyond what could be expected by chance (Blackmore, 1995). They claimed that they'd established the existence of ESP. However, these claims produced considerable opposition from the psychological establishment.

For example, were the Rhines' receivers physically completely isolated from the experimenter, so that information couldn't be passed unwittingly (for instance, by unconsciously whispering or other non-deliberate cues)? Were checks on the data records precise enough to ensure minor errors weren't made (unconsciously or deliberately) to bias the results in a pro-ESP direction?

The Rhines tightened up their procedures on both counts by (a) separating receiver and experimenter in different buildings, and (b) arranging independent verification and analysis of the results. As a consequence, the above-chance results became more rare, although they remained sufficiently common to constitute apparently indisputable evidence for ESP. However, then came another, more fundamental, criticism: when psychologists not committed to a belief in ESP tried to replicate the Rhines' findings in their own laboratories, they simply failed to produce any positive results.

In response to this potentially fatal blow, parapsychologists argued that a significant factor in ESP might be the *experimenter's attitude* to the phenomenon under investigation: sceptical or dismissive experimenters ('goats') might have a 'negative effect' on the results (the Rhines, and other believers, being 'sheep'). This argument seems to imply that only believers are fit to investigate ESP, which is contrary to the spirit of scientific research (Evans, 1987a; see Gross, 2005). The issue of *experimenter effects* is discussed later in the chapter (see pages 464–465).

Modern experiments of this type are better controlled than those of the Rhines. For example, the number of trials is pre-set, so that experimenters cannot stop when things are going well, the randomising procedures tend to be superior, and the target order is determined by machine, so that neither the person recording the participant's response, nor the experimenter, or anyone else in contact with the participant, knows the target order (thus preventing them from giving inadvertent clues) (Henry, 2005a).

The director of research at the Duke University Laboratory (the Rhines themselves had retired by this time) was later caught flagrantly modifying some experimental data in a pro-ESP direction. Fortunately, or unfortunately (depending on whether you're a goat or a sheep), this wasn't an isolated example.

How Science Works

Practical Learning Activity 10.4

- Are you a sheep or a goat? Why?
- Conduct a survey, asking people if they are 'sheep' or 'goats'. (You must, of course, first give them a brief account of ESP – and don't use the words 'sheep' or 'goats').
- Look for gender and age differences. Try to account for any differences that emerge.

Not only have experimental methods been tightened up since the early days of PP research, making the possibility of fraud much lower, but new statistical techniques for analysing and interpreting the data have been developed. According to Milton (2005), *meta-analysis* (MA) has become the leading means of combining the results of studies to provide an overall picture of an area of research, particularly in the social sciences and medicine. This includes PP research.

Free-response ESP

One drawback of the early Rhine research was that guessing long series of cards is extremely boring. By contrast, reports of psychic dreams, premonitions, and other cases of spontaneous psi were rife. The challenge was to capture these under laboratory conditions (Blackmore, 1995). Free-response ESP represents the most important attempts to meet this challenge.

Early experiments of this type used an entirely free choice of image, as in the telepathic drawings of Upton Sinclair and his wife in the 1930s (Henry, 2005a). Upton drew a sketch and his wife attempted to reproduce it; her attempts showed some failures but also many striking similarities. This type of experiment often produces dramatic results, with certain receivers drawing an image that seems very close to the original.

Box 10.2: The problem of fraud

According to Colman (1987), the history of PP is 'disfigured by numerous cases of fraud involving some of the most "highly respected scientists", their colleagues and participants'. For example, Soal (Soal and Bateman, 1954), a mathematician at Queen Mary College, London, tried to replicate some of the Rhines' telepathy experiments using Zener cards. Despite his rigid controls and the involvement of other scientists as observers throughout, accusations of fraud resulted in a series of re-analyses of the data. Marwick, a member of the Society for Psychical Research in London, finally proved (in 1978) that Soal *had* cheated (Blackmore, 1995).

Against this, it's misleading to suggest that experimenter fraud is rife in PP, or even that it's more common than in other disciplines. According to Roe (personal communication), books such as *Betrayers of the Truth* (Broad and Wade, 1982) show that fraud is more likely when the rewards are high and the chances of being caught (publicly exposed) are low. This characterises mainstream science (especially medicine), and is certainly *not* characteristic of PP.

As far as participant fraud is concerned, because certain psi effects (such as metal bending) can be replicated by magicians, and certain ESP effects by mentalists, it's sometimes argued that participants in psi experiments may have used similar tricks to achieve positive results. Some fakers and stage psychics use tricks, some mediums are fraudulent, and PP, like most other disciplines, has had a few cases of experimenter and participant fraud (see above). As Henry (2005a) points out:

This is one of the reasons that the modern parapsychological experiment is designed to control procedures so that fraud is effectively ruled out as an explanation. The controls include random automated target selection, automated result recording, predetermining the number of trials, screening and independent judging.

But there remains the question of the number of researchers achieving positive results. Many of the most significant results in PP seem to have been published by a relatively small number of experimenters (including Honorton; see text below). As in other disciplines, fraud seems a less plausible explanation if positive results are replicated under well-controlled conditions by many different investigators in different locations. Meta-analysis (MA) offers a tool to assess the significance of work by many different researchers involved in well-controlled studies (see Box 10.3).

Almost all experiments involve ordinary people, based on the assumption that if ESP and PK are genuine abilities or faculties, then, as with most other human abilities/faculties, a small proportion of people will be very bad at the task, most people somewhere near the middle, and a small proportion will be star performers (i.e. psi is *normally distributed*).

People who make special claims of having strong psychic abilities are relatively rarely tested, not only because few of them make credible claims that appear worth testing but also because ... the possibility that they might be fraudulent ... requires extensive, time-consuming and potentially expensive experimental controls to rule out the possibility of cheating. (Milton, 2005)

455

Box 10.3: Meta-analysis

Meta-analysis (MA) refers to the use of statistical methods to synthesise and describe experiments and their outcomes. Milton (2005) describes five major advantages that MA has over traditional 'research reviews', in which the reviewer describes individual studies and uses his/her (often subjective) judgement to draw an overall conclusion.

1. *Cumulative probability:* MA provides a precise estimate of how unlikely it is that the results of the entire group of studies being examined arose by chance alone. In order to make this calculation, the probability associated with each study's outcome is calculated and the probabilities are combined to reflect the overall outcome. In most PP meta-analyses, the results have been significantly above chance. In large groups of studies, the results go well beyond mere statistical significance and have astronomical odds against having arisen by chance (a 'fluke').

2. *File-drawer estimate:* a recurring issue within science in general, and PP in particular, is the concern that only successful studies tend to be published (i.e. those that produce significant results), while those that find no effect or an effect in the opposite direction from the one predicted are more often left in researchers' file drawers (and so *don't* get published; see Box 10.6, pages 463–464). This is because the editors of academic journals, or even the researchers themselves, believe that negative results aren't worth making public. If this is the case, then even a non-existent effect will appear to have been successfully demonstrated: with the usual cut-off point for statistical significance being set at 0.05, on average, one in 20 studies will be apparently successful by chance alone. This makes it necessary to know how many studies have been conducted in total (Milton, 2005). MA allows the calculation of the number of studies with an average zero effect that would have to be in the research 'file drawer' to bring the observed overall result in a MA down to the point at which it became statistically non-significant. In most MAs carried out in PP so far, the file-drawer estimates are so large that selective publication *doesn't* appear to be a reasonable counter-explanation for the observed results.

3. *Effect size:* MA focuses on studies not just in terms of their statistical significance levels (the traditional approach) but also allows diverse studies to be compared on a single measure, called an *averaged effect size.* When MA is used to assess the effectiveness of treatments for mental disorder, effect size refers to 'an index of the magnitude of the effects of a treatment ... averaged across all studies' (Lilienfeld, 1995; see Chapter 7). Most parapsychological research questions involve wanting to know about levels of performance in a certain task *under different conditions* – not just how unlikely the levels of performance were (Rosenthal and Rubin, 1992–3, in Milton, 2005).

4. *Study quality:* in an MA used in PP research, each study is typically assessed on a number of quality criteria, such as whether an adequately tested source of randomness was used in a PK experiment, whether there was adequate sensory shielding between receiver and target in an ESP study, and so on. Each study does or doesn't receive a full point for each criterion it passes and the points are added to reflect its overall quality (Milton, 2005). If psi experiment results were due to poor methodological controls rather than to genuine phenomena, we might expect each study's quality to be negatively related to its effect size; in other words, the better controlled the study, the smaller its outcome. However, in almost all PP MAs, *no* statistically significant relationships have been demonstrated between overall quality and effect size (Milton, 1995, in Milton, 2005).

5. *Replicability:* MA also allows the examination of whether only a few experimenters obtain statistically significant results. Where this has been done, a much higher proportion appear to do so than the 5 per cent expected by chance. For example, Honorton and Ferrari (1989) report that 30 per cent of studies and 37 per cent of experimenters obtained statistically significant results.

How Science Works

Practical Learning Activity 10.5

In the context of psychotherapy research, *effect size* is essentially an indicator of the extent to which people who receive psychotherapy improve relative to those who don't: the greater the difference between these two groups, the greater the effect size (Lilienfeld, 1995).

● What would effect size denote in the context of PP?

Another advantage of MA is that it allows researchers to examine whether certain variables are *correlated with* effect size. In the context of treatments for mental disorder again, Lilienfeld gives the examples of how experienced the therapist is and the age of the clients. In this way, they can determine not only the overall effectiveness of psychotherapy (*outcome research*), but also what factors, if any, influence its effectiveness (*process research*).

● Do you think this distinction between outcome and process research is likely to be relevant to PP research?
● If so, what variables might be correlated with ESP/PK that make it more or less likely to be demonstrated in experiments? (See pages 465–472.)

However, interpreting the results can be problematic. For example, the probability of drawing a house, face or tree is much higher than objects such as a garden swing or cooker. Also, it can be argued that people who know each other well may be able to use unconscious inference to anticipate what image the other party is likely to draw. Today, parapsychologists get round this problem by randomly selecting the images that people need to guess from a target pool (Henry, 2005a).

Remote viewing

Free-response methods include *remote viewing (RV) studies* (Targ and Puthoff, 1974, 1977). RV is a form of *clairvoyance*, in which an individual is able to 'see' a specific location some distance away, without receiving any information about it through the usual sensory channels. The experimenter selects a target site at random; the agent/sender travels to it and attempts to 'send' back images of the chosen site through mental intention. Targ and Puthoff reported a series of field studies involving Pat Price, a former California police commissioner, which sparked a debate between researchers as to whether Price's successes constituted genuine clairvoyance. While the target sites were usually within 30 minutes of the laboratory (for practical reasons), replications have taken place over thousands of miles (Henry, 2005a).

Despite the controversy, the research was sufficiently convincing for the US military to fund a substantial research programme. The CIA declassified this information and released details of more than 20 years of RV research (Blackmore, 1996). RV has been put to practical use in 'psychic archaeology' (finding lost sites), criminal investigations and, most controversially, predicting price fluctuations on the stock market.

The Ganzfeld

The most successful free-response method has been the *Ganzfeld* ('ganz' = 'whole'; 'feld' = 'field'), first used for psi research by Honorton in 1974. He argued that the reason ESP occurs in dreams, meditation and reverie is that these are all states of reduced sensory input and increased internal attention. He tried to find a way of producing such a 'psi-conducive' state without the expense of a 'dream laboratory'.

In practice, in this and other free-response experiments the image the receiver draws or describes is rarely identical to the target – but it often has many striking similarities; for example, the shape or colour may be right but the scale or function may be wrong (a cone rather than a pyramid, or the sun rather than an orange beach ball) (Henry, 2005a).

Typically, the receiver is asked to rank four images (selected randomly by computer) as to which s/he

Box 10.4: The Ganzfeld

- Halved ping-pong balls are taped over the *receiver's* eyes, and red light is shone into them, so all that can be seen is a pinkish glow. Soothing sea sounds or hissing 'white noise' (like a radio that's not properly tuned in) are played through headphones, while the receiver lies on a comfortable couch or reclining chair. While this doesn't constitute total sensory deprivation, the Ganzfeld deprives receivers of patterned input and encourages internal imagery. They typically report a pleasant sensation of being immersed in a 'sea of light'.

- The *sender* (an experimenter acting as an agent) is situated in a separate, acoustically isolated room. A visual stimulus (a picture, still photograph or brief video clip) is randomly selected from over 1,000 similar stimuli to serve as the *target*. While the sender concentrates on the target (for about 15 minutes), the receiver tries to describe it by providing a continuous verbal report of his/her ongoing imagery and free associations. This takes place after the receiver has listened to a 20-minute relaxation tape.

Figure 10.5 A receiver in the Ganzfeld

- The sender stays in the room for another ten minutes. From a separate room, the experimenter can both hear (via a microphone) and see (via a one-way mirror) the receiver, and is blind to the target (doesn't know what the target is).

- At the end of the experimental session, the receiver is presented with four stimuli (one of which is the target), and is asked to rate the degree to which each one matches the imagery and associations experienced during the session. A 'direct hit' is recorded if the receiver assigns the highest rating to the target.

- The sender is then called in and reveals the target. A typical experiment involves about 30 sessions.

thinks most resembles the target. Independently, a third party unconnected with the experiment is presented with a transcript of the receiver's continuous verbal report of his/her mentation about the target, plus a copy of the same four images; s/he is asked to rank the four images in terms of how closely each matches the transcript. Each of Honortons' 1,000+ targets differs from all the others in terms of the presence or absence of at least one of ten characteristics (such as colour, humans, animals, architecture, activity versus static). The receiver can be asked to answer ten questions about his/her image relating to each of these ten characteristics.

The 'Ganzfeld debate'

Honorton (1985) analysed 28 studies using the Ganzfeld procedure (totalling 835 sessions, conducted in ten different laboratories). He reported a 38 per cent correct selection of the target, which compares with a 25 per cent success rate by chance alone (i.e. by guessing). Statistically, this is highly significant: the chances of obtaining a 38 per cent success rate by chance alone is less than one in a billion (Honorton, 1985).

However, a critical review by Hyman (in the *Journal of Parapsychology*, 1985) pointed out discrepancies in the scoring systems used, and procedural flaws (such as the failure to use proper randomisation for selecting the targets). Hyman also claimed to have found correlations between the quality ratings for studies and outcome, with the 'sloppier' studies producing the 'better' results (see above). But, in the same journal, Honorton claimed to have found *no* evidence of such a correlation. Rosenthal provided a commentary on the debate, generally regarded as favouring Honorton's interpretation (Blackmore, 1995).

Hyman and Honorton issued a joint 'communiqué' (Hyman and Honorton, 1986), in which they agreed that the studies as a whole fell short of ideal, but that something beyond selective reporting, or inflated significance levels, seemed to be producing the non-chance outcomes. They also agreed that the significant outcomes had been produced by several different researchers. Further replication would decide which of their interpretations was correct.

This debate, which Morris (1989) describes as 'an outstanding example of productive interaction between critic and researcher', brought parapsychologists and sceptics together to try to agree what would constitute an acceptable experiment. As a consequence, Honorton designed a *fully automated* Ganzfeld, leaving little scope for human error or deliberate fraud. Several experiments produced significant results, which were published in the *Psychological Bulletin* in 1994. This is one of the world's most prestigious psychology journals, and meant that 'The Ganzfeld had achieved respectability' (Blackmore, 1997). However, despite many parapsychologists believing that the Ganzfeld is a genuinely repeatable experiment, most other scientists seem to reject the evidence: 'Unfair, say the parapsychologists. But we still do not know who is right' (Blackmore, 1997).

By 1997, over 2,500 Ganzfeld sessions had been conducted around the world, with an average success rate of 33 per cent. This appeared to provide impressive evidence for a psi effect. However, a MA of 30 subsequent Ganzfeld studies (Milton and Wiseman, 1999) found an effect near chance; Milton (1999) found a significant but lower effect size. Bem *et al.*'s (2001, in Henry, 2005a) re-analysis of 40 subsequent studies, including Milton and Wiseman's 30, suggested that those studies that followed the classic Ganzfeld procedure closely (such as using similar visual targets) did come very close to replicating the original effect size, whereas those trying something different (such as using musical targets) didn't (Henry, 2005a). The reasons for Milton and Wiseman's findings are unclear, either in normal or paranormal terms; this suggests that the next step in the search for strong evidence of psi will involve more systematic research to identify what, if any, variables affect performance in Ganzfeld ESP studies – if ESP is, indeed, a genuine phenomenon (Milton, 2005).

STRETCH AND CHALLENGE: Clairvoyance vs telepathy

Some Ganzfeld experiments don't use a sender, so that the target images could be acquired through *clairvoyance* (telepathy would require the involvement of another mind – the sender's). Honorton (1985) reported that where a sender was involved (*telepathy condition*), the results were generally more positive – but only when the experimenters were already experienced in using both sender and no-sender methods. Where experimenters consistently used one or other method, the *no-sender/clairvoyance condition* produced slightly more positive results.

Studies of psychokinesis (PK)

As with ESP studies, there are different types of PK study. But a way of characterising them as a whole is to describe them as being concerned with trying to demonstrate the effects of 'mind over matter' (see Box 10.5, page 461).

As we saw above, *macro-PK studies* involve the investigation of effects visible to the naked eye, such as metal bending (made famous by Uri Geller's spoon bending), while *micro-PK studies* investigate effects that require special instruments or statistical analysis to detect them, such as examining the effects of someone's intention on the rate of radioactive decay (Palmer and Rush, 1986).

Bio-PK or DMILS (distant influence upon living systems) studies examine the effects of people's inten-

Figure 10.6 Uri Geller (born 1946), British-Israeli psychic performer

tions upon other organisms' biological or physiological systems. For example, a DMILS study might explore whether someone's physiological activity decreases or increases in response to a distant person's intention that they become calm or excited (Braud and Schlitz, in Milton, 2005).

In a typical PK study, a computer might be connected to a micro-electronic random event generator (REG) (e.g. Schmidt, 1969) or random number generator (RNG) that by chance alone would produce two different outcomes equally often. The equipment is arranged so that each of the two outcomes is associated with a different event that the participant witnesses. For example, one outcome might lead to a light bulb getting brighter, the other to it becoming dimmer. The participant's task might be to try mentally to make the light bulb become brighter; his/her performance would be measured in terms of how often this happened above the 50 per cent chance baseline. To ensure that the REGs/RNGs used are unbiased (that their output is random), they're also run at times when no one is there to influence them. As in ESP studies, the results are assessed statistically.

In another form of the experiment, participants sit in front of a computer screen and are asked to increase the output (e.g. raise a simple horizontal line) shown on the display on one trial, decrease (lower) it on another, and leave it alone (keep it as horizontal as possible) in the control condition. Alternatively, the target might be a picture of snow with a varied rate of fall, or a sophisticated computer game. (*Psi Invaders* was modelled along the lines of *Space Invaders*, for example; Henry, 2005b). According to Henry (2005b):

> *These kinds of experiment offer an automated protocol, as the targets ... are random and determined automatically by machine and the results are recorded without human intervention ... Automating the experimental protocol in this way makes fraud very difficult indeed.*

Nelson and Radin's (1987, in Henry, 2005b) MA of the RNG-PK research comprised 832 experiments by 68 investigators including 258 control studies. The overall effect is small, at less than 51 per cent (where 50 per cent would be expected by chance), but it's highly significant – the odds against this happening by chance are in the order of over a *trillion* to one. From 1989 to 1996, Jahn *et al.* (in Henry, 2005b) conducted over 1,000 experiments with more than 100 participants, involving millions of trials. This series also produced a small – but highly significant – effect size in line with other MAs for this type of experiment (Nelson *et al.*, 1991, in Henry, 2005b). However, Steinkamp *et al.* (2002, in Henry, 2005b), in an MA of 300 RNG experiments with 100 controls, found *no* difference between the effect sizes of the two groups.

Unknown to the participant, experimenters sometimes switch between machines generating the random numbers that determine the display, or change the sampling rate, with no apparent effect on performance. In contrast, intention may be a critical factor. Also, RNG performance isn't affected by distance – whether the participants are next door to where the machine is situated or thousands of miles away makes no difference to their performance (Henry, 2005b).

Box 10.5: 'Mind over matter' meta-analyses

Dice

One group of studies involves people trying to influence the outcome of falling dice. For example, participants may try to make a rolled dice land so that a six is uppermost. This was first suggested to J.B. Rhine by gamblers, who claimed to be able to influence the outcome in dice-throwing situations in gaming casinos (see Chapter 9).

Radin and Ferrari (1991, in Delanoy, 2005) carried out an MA of 148 dice studies conducted between 1935 and 1987. The analysis found a highly significant overall effect for the combined experimental influence studies; the combined result for 31 control studies (where no conscious influence on outcome was attempted) didn't differ from chance. Based on 11 different study quality measures, there was a tendency for effect sizes to decrease as study quality increased – but the relationship wasn't significant.

Another methodological problem is that the probability of obtaining a specific outcome isn't equally distributed across all the die faces: the six typically has the least mass and is thus most likely to come up (the more pips cut into the die, the lighter the die face). Even after taking this 'non-random' factor into account, a significant overall effect was still found for a subset of 69 studies, where the targets were balanced equally across the six die faces.

A file-drawer analysis reveals that a 20:1 ratio of unreported, non-significant studies for each reported study was required to reduce the overall result to chance levels. Radin and Ferrari concluded that 'the aggregate evidence suggests the presence of a weak, genuine mental effect'.

RNG

A second group of studies involves influencing a random number generator (RNG) to behave in a non-random way. A participant attempts to mentally influence an RNG, which drives a visual display (such as a circle of sequentially flashing lights) based on prior instructions (such as to keep the lights flashing in a clockwise manner by visualising and wishing this to occur).

A meta-analysis by Radin and Nelson (1989, in Delanoy, 2005) involved the largest parapsychological database (832 studies, comprising 597 experimental studies and 235 control studies). The mean effect size for the experimental studies was very small, but still significantly higher than that for the control studies (which was close to chance). Using 16 study quality measures, effect size wasn't significantly related with study quality. The file-drawer estimate is enormous (requiring 54,000 unreported negative studies to reduce the observed effect to chance levels). Given these findings, Radin and Nelson concluded that 'it is difficult to avoid the conclusion that under certain circumstances, consciousness interacts with random physical systems'.

In contrast, a more recent MA (Steinkamp *et al.,* 2002, in Delanoy, 2005) found no differences between the effect sizes of 357 experimental RNG studies and 142 control studies. A significant correlation was found between effect size and study size, suggesting that any experimental effect stemmed mainly from the smaller studies. However, Delanoy points out that these results were presented at a conference, rather than published in a journal; she warns that the findings should, therefore, be treated with caution.

In our discussion of ESP and PK so far, we've seen just how divided opinion is between those who believe in the reality of psi ('sheep') and those who don't ('goats'). We've also seen that accusations of fraud – the deliberate invention or modification of procedures or results – have been a feature of the history of PP research. Arguably, this makes the study of psi unique as an area of psychological inquiry. At least as far as goats are concerned, parapsychologists are guilty unless proven innocent. In other words, if psi doesn't exist (as goats maintain), then any claims by sheep that it does must be based on fraudulent (or, at best, unreliable and/or invalid) data. So rather than simply trying to produce evidence that supports the existence of psi, parapsychologists are constantly having to show that they're *not cheating*! But how can you prove a negative?

The history of PP also seems to highlight a number of methodological issues that, while they recur throughout all areas of psychological research, assume a more exaggerated or extreme form in relation to psi. These include:

- the question of the 'conclusive' experiment
- the replication problem
- publication bias (or the 'file-drawer' problem)
- the inadequacy of controls
- experimenter effects.

The question of the 'conclusive' experiment

According to Abelson (1978), the editor of *Science*, 'extraordinary claims require extraordinary evidence' (quoted in Rao and Palmer, 1987). This implies that the strength of evidence needed to establish a new phenomenon is directly proportional to how incompatible the phenomenon is with our current beliefs about the world. If we reject the possibility of this new phenomenon (its *subjective probability* is zero), then no

amount of empirical evidence will be sufficient to establish the claim. However, as Rao and Palmer point out, 'In serious scientific discourse ... few would be expected to take a zero-probability stance because such a stance could be seen to be sheer dogmatism, and the very antithesis of the basic assumption of science's open-endedness.' Abelson's 'extraordinary evidence' sometimes means, in practice, demands for a 'fool-proof' experiment that would control for all conceivable kinds of error, including experimenter fraud. This assumes that, at any given time, one can identify all possible sources of error and how to control for them.

How Science Works

Practical Learning Activity 10.6

- Do you believe that this assumption is valid?
- Is there such a thing as 'perfect control'?
- Can anything be 'proved' in psychology (or any other science)?
- You might want to have a class debate on the issue.

(Try to answer these questions *before* reading on, including the text relating to 'The replication problem'.)

According to Rao and Palmer:

> The concept of a 'conclusive' experiment, totally free of any possible error or fraud and immune to all sceptical doubt, is a practical impossibility for empirical phenomena. In reality, evidence in science is a matter of degree ... a 'conclusive' experiment [should] be defined more modestly as one in which it is highly improbable that the result is artifactual ...

In other words, there are *no absolutes* in science (no certainty, no once-and-for-all 'proof'), only *probabilities*. In *this* sense, Rao and Palmer believe that a case can be made for 'conclusive' experiments in PP. The REG experiment seems to fit the bill (see above): it represents one of the major experimental paradigms in contemporary PP, it's regarded by most parapsychologists as providing good evidence for psi, and it's been closely scrutinised by critics. Despite this – and almost inevitably – they have been criticised.

For example, Hansel (1980) claimed that Schmidt's

highly significant results haven't been replicated by other researchers (see below), and these criticisms are routinely taken as valid by most sceptics (such as Alcock, 1981). Although Hyman (1981, in Rao and Palmer, 1987) is one of the few psi goats who has questioned Hansel's basic reasoning, he still agrees with Hansel's claim that the REG experiments don't provide an adequate case for the existence of psi. However,

> *There is no such thing as an experiment immune from trickery ... Even if one assembles all the world's magicians and scientists and puts them to the task of designing a fraud-proof experiment, it cannot be done (Rao and Palmer, 1987).*

The replication problem

This has been addressed above in relation to the use of MAs as a way of assessing the validity of PP research (see Box 10.3). Rao and Palmer argue that science is concerned with establishing general laws, not unique events. (This relates to the *idiographic-nomothetic* debate, see Gross, in press). The ability to repeat an experiment would seem to be a reasonable thing to demand of a field aiming to achieve scientific respectability (*New Scientist*, 2004).

However, many sceptics argue that only 'replication on demand' can produce conclusive proof of psi. According to Rao and Palmer, an experiment isn't either replicable or not replicable, but rather it's on a continuum:

> *In this sense of statistical replication, an experiment or an effect may be considered replicated if a series of replication attempts provides statistically significant evidence for the original effect when analyzed as a series (Rao and Palmer, 1987).*

In other words, does the evidence *overall / as a whole* support the existence of the effect being investigated? *On balance*, does the accumulated evidence, based on a large number of replication attempts point towards the existence of psi, or not?

However, while this is fine in principle, in practice it's proved impossible to reach any kind of consensus. As we've seen, different MAs can reach different conclusions, despite them (supposedly) following the same 'rules'. But there are times when different MAs are clearly following different rules. For example, four different MAs were conducted of the 30 Ganzfeld experiments reported between 1995 and 1999. Two of these MAs concluded that the findings were significant, while the other two concluded that they weren't. The biggest discrepancy between them was the inclusion (or not) of a hugely successful study by Dalton (1997) carried out at Edinburgh University. It was omitted from two of the MAs on the grounds that it was an 'outlier': because its results were so much better than any others, it should be discounted (an accepted practice in MA). But another accepted practice is that MAs must use *all* available data. So the other two included Dalton's study (*New Scientist*, 2004). So much for scientific objectivity!

Rao and Palmer argue that, once we give up the idea of *absolute* replication ('replication on demand'), parapsychological phenomena have been replicated in a statistically significant sense. Also, many parapsychologists argue that any failure to replicate should be taken as a *positive* result: it confirms what they knew all along, namely that paranormal phenomena are inherently elusive. You cannot expect to pin them down in the laboratory (*New Scientist*, 2004).

Publication bias (or the 'file-drawer' problem)

This too was discussed in Box 10.3 in relation to MA.

STRETCH AND CHALLENGE

Consistent with the discussion of individual MAs above, Rao and Palmer claim that the 'file-drawer' problem cannot explain away the significant number of replications in PP. But isn't it impossible ever to establish how many studies may have been 'binned'? Some answers are provided in Box 10.6.

Box 10.6: Solving the 'file-drawer' problem

- Parapsychologists are more sensitive to the possible impact of unreported negative results than most other scientists. In the USA, the Parapsychological Association (PA) has advocated publishing all methodologically sound experiments, regardless of the outcome. Since 1976, this policy has been reflected in publications of all affiliated journals (such as the *Journal of Parapsychology*) and in papers presented at annual PA conventions.

- There are relatively few parapsychologists, and most are aware of ongoing work in the various laboratories around the world. When conducting an MA, they actively seek out unpublished negative studies at conventions and through personal networks.

- There are also some areas where we can be reasonably certain we have access to *all* the experiments conducted; for example, research into the relationship between ESP performance and ratings obtained on the Defence Mechanism Test (DMT; Kragh and Smith, 1979, in Rao and Palmer, 1987). Because the administration and scoring of the test requires specialised training available only to a few individuals, it's relatively easy to keep track of the relevant experiments.

Source: based on Atkinson *et al.* (1990), Rao and Palmer (1987)

The inadequacy of controls

According to Alcock (1981), replication of an experimental result by other experimenters 'does not assure that experimental artifacts were not responsible for the results in the replication as well as in the original experiment'. This is perhaps like saying that 'two wrongs don't make a right'. While it's true that replicating an effect implies nothing directly about its cause, it's also a basic premise of experimental science that replication reduces the probability of *some* causal explanations, particularly those related to the honesty or competence of individual experimenters (Rao and Palmer). As Alcock (1981) himself says in another context:

It is not enough for a researcher to report his observations with respect to a phenomenon; he could be mistaken, or even dishonest. But if other people, using his methodology, can independently produce the same results, it is much more likely that error and dishonesty are not responsible for them.

Some more specific criticisms of ESP and PK research relating to inadequacy of controls have been discussed above.

Experimenter effects

Alcock (1981) and others have argued that replication must be conducted by investigators *unsympathetic to psi* (goats). This would exclude most – but not all – parapsychologists (Blackmore being a good example of one who would 'qualify'). Researchers' personal beliefs are rarely reported and may often be difficult to determine reliably. Rao and Palmer believe that if such a criterion were to be applied retrospectively to published research in psychology as a whole, there wouldn't be much left. So why should parapsychologists be singled out in this way?

According to Valentine (1992), *experimenter bias* has been demonstrated in a variety of psychological experiments, including reaction time, psychophysics, animal learning, verbal conditioning, personality assessment and person perception. According to Rosenthal (1966), what the experimenter is *like* is correlated with what s/he *does*, as well as influencing the participant's perception of, and response to, the experimenter. Experimenters can affect the outcome of experiments unwittingly through tone of voice and other forms of bodily communication; these can subtly (and unconsciously) convey expectations to participants (see Gross, 2005). These *experimenter effects* have long been explicitly recognised and discussed in PP.

One of the most reliable findings in parapsychological research is that some experimenters, using well-controlled methods, repeatedly produce significant results, while others, using exactly the same methods, consistently produce non-significant results.

The experimenter effect (EE) is one of PP's longest-standing controversies. This is largely due to the 'heads I win, tails you lose' interpretation that many 'sheep' place on the findings described in Box 10.7. In other words, the fact that positive results are obtained by experimenters with psi abilities – but not by those without – 'proves' that psi exists. Rather than being a confounding variable as sceptics would claim, believers argue that EEs in the context of parapsychological research actually demonstrate the phenomenon under investigation.

According to Palmer, of the Rhine Research Centre (in McCrone, 2004), 'the strongest predictor of ESP results generally is the identity of the experimenter'. The EE is

- Some experimenters seem capable of creating a climate in which participants' psi abilities are allowed to express themselves (*psi-permissive* experimenters), while others have the opposite effect and produce consistently negative results (*psi-inhibitory* experimenters). These differences seem to be related to:
  (a) the pleasantness/unpleasantness of the experimental setting for the participant – a relaxed participant is more likely to display psi abilities (Crandall, 1985)
  (b) the experimenter's expectations – participants are more likely to display psi abilities if the experimenter expects positive results (Taddonio, 1976).
- According to Schmiedler (1997), some experimenters have produced particularly high levels of positive results with participants who fail to repeat their performance later. This could be explained in terms of a highly motivated experimenter, who has strong psi abilities him/herself. S/he may somehow *transfer* these abilities to participants during the course of the experiments (but not beyond), distorting the findings in the process. These are referred to as *psi-conducive* experimenters.

now the object of intense research, with new explanations emerging. For example, some parapsychologists claim that it arises not through experimenters' influence over mind or matter, but because they use their extra-sensory powers to pick the right moments to sample a fluctuating process and catch any 'fluky', but natural, departures from randomness (McCrone, 2004).

FACTORS UNDERLYING ANOMALOUS EXPERIENCE

Cognitive, personality and biological factors

✔ Specification Hint

Research into the *biological factors* underlying anomalous experience has focused mainly on (a) NDEs, which we consider in the final section of this chapter (pages 481–486), and (b) perception without awareness (such as conscious awareness during anaesthesia, and blindsight; none of these examples has been given previously as an instance of anomalous experience). This illustrates the breadth of the term 'anomalous experience'. Note also that there's considerable overlap between cognitive, personality and biological factors. For example, (a) perception without awareness is discussed initially in relation to cognitive factors, but the examples of conscious awareness during anaesthesia, and blindsight, are discussed largely in physiological terms; and (b) important individual differences in perception without awareness and their overlap with individual differences in ESP abilities are discussed in relation to personality.

Cognitive factors

Wiseman (2001) reviews the research evidence relating to 'psychic fraud', an unusual form of deception which refers to people's claim to possess psychic abilities (such as faith healing and psychic surgeons – the ability to cure illness (see below) – psychic reading – the ability to divine the past and predict the future – mediumship – the ability to contact the dead (see below)). He identifies three major reasons why understanding psychic fraud is important.

1. Both the lay public and professionals sometimes turn to alleged psychics in times of need. People's vulnerability at such times gives the psychic power over them, as demonstrated by the mass suicide of almost all the several hundred followers of 'Reverend' Jim Jones's cult in the USA in the 1970s. He often

maintained their faith by faking biblical miracles, such as healing and 'walking on water'.

2. Scientists need to be able to distinguish genuine from fake psychic abilities.

3. An understanding of the techniques used to fake psychic ability may provide insight into the types of cognitive and social biases that disrupt perception, reasoning and memory. Cognitive psychologists investigate how observers attend to, perceive, understand and store information from the environment, as well as how this information is recalled and used during thinking and problem solving. Research into psychic fraud may reveal novel types of bias, and, like the study of visual illusions, it can provide important new insights into the limitations of human information processing.

Trying to identify the strategies used by fake psychics has involved collecting and collating information from sources such as magazines, books and videos outlining methods for faking psychic ability, investigations of fake psychics and the literature relating to the 'folk' psychology of magic and psychic fraud. In addition, experiments have tested the efficacy of some of these strategies.

Misframing

Sociologists use the term 'frame' to refer to abstract structures which observers use to define situations in a certain way (Goffman, 1974); many situations can be framed in different ways. For example, before observing an alleged medium, sceptics might expect to see some kind of trickery, whereas believers might expect a display of genuine mediumistic ability. Such expectations can play a major role in determining how the observer approaches a 'psychic' demonstration, and, in turn, how it's perceived and remembered. Jones and Russell (1980, in Wiseman, 2001) asked both 'sheep' and 'goats' to observe a staged demonstration of ESP. In one condition, the demonstration was successful (that is, ESP appeared to take place), while in the other it wasn't. Sheep who saw the unsuccessful demonstration distorted their memories of it and often stated that ESP *had* occurred. However, goats tended to recall the demonstrations accurately – even if it appeared to support the existence of ESP.

Wiseman and Morris (1995, in Wiseman, 2001) showed participants a film containing fake psychic demonstrations. They were then asked to rate the 'paranormal' content of the film and to answer a set of

recall questions. They were subsequently told that the film contained magic tricks and were asked to complete a second set of recall questions. The recall questions contained information that was both 'important' and 'unimportant' to the method of the tricks. Overall, the results suggested that sheep rated the demonstrations as more 'paranormal' than did goats, and goats recalled significantly more 'important' information than did sheep (even when told the film contained trickery).

Not surprisingly, fake psychics are eager to encourage observers to view their supposed abilities as genuine. A fake faith healer might assure an observer that he never accepts payment for his services, implying that he has no motive to deceive. However, Morris (1986, in Wiseman, 2001) has noted how fake psychics can be motivated by many other factors, including personal fame and power, raised self-esteem and a desire to be altruistic. Another motive may be sheer enjoyment, as in the case of the Cottingley fairies (Randi, 1982, in Wiseman, 2001).

The faker (or fakir) may also deliberately produce a credible psychic phenomenon, such as causing an object to move a small distance along a table top (as opposed to making it levitate above the table). This is based on the assumption that observers believe that PK can rarely be used to produce really large physical

Figure 10.7 In 1917, two young girls, Frances Griffiths and Elsie Wright, living in Cottingley, a small Yorkshire village, produced several photographs showing the girls with fairies. Finally, in 1983, Elise confessed that the pictures had been faked; the girls had drawn the fairies, cut them out and attached them to the ground with hatpins (Wiseman, 2001)

effects. The faker may also exploit an observer's physical and emotional needs – for example, claiming to possess healing powers to a seriously ill observer, or ability to communicate with the observer's deceased loved one.

Attention and distraction

It's often vital for fake psychics to ensure that observers don't attend to the parts of their performance that might 'give the game away'. They might do this by saying that they have little control over their ability and therefore cannot predict the phenomena that will occur. This strategy also helps the psychic if a performance doesn't go according to plan. Most observers only start to concentrate their attention fully when they believe that paranormal phenomena are about to happen. A fake psychic may take advantage of this by making secret preparations long before the demonstration begins; it's particularly effective if the performer is able to anticipate which phenomena observers might request.

Competent fakers can also manipulate the focal point of observers' attention. The carefully planned introduction of movement, colour, sound and body language (including the positioning of the feet and hands, and eye contact) can be used to attract observers' attention to a desired location. Also, confusion can be created to prevent attention being focused on any one location.

Switching methods

A fake psychic may develop several ways of fabricating a certain type of psychic ability, enabling him/her to switch methods during a performance. For example, Harris (1985, in Wiseman, 2001) describes a whole range of methods that may be used for PK metal bending. The faker may then switch methods to create the 'bundle-of-sticks' phenomenon:

An effect is produced several times under different circumstances with the use of a different technique each time ... the weak points of one performance are ruled out because they were clearly not present during other performances. The bundle of sticks is stronger than any single stick. (Diaconis, 1985, in Wiseman, 2001)

Controlling performing conditions

Psychics often state that their ability only manifests itself under certain conditions. A fake can exploit this by insisting on working under conditions that are favourable to fraud. For example, fake mediums insist that all of the sitters link hands during a seance, 'in order to bring forth spirit communication', for example. In reality, it's designed to prevent curious sitters from reaching out into the seance room and possibly discovering various forms of trickery (such as reaching rods and accomplices).

Many individuals have reported experiencing extraordinary phenomena during dark-room seances. Eyewitnesses claim that objects have mysteriously moved, strange sounds have been heard, or ghostly forms have appeared, and that these phenomena have occurred under conditions that make 'normal' explanations practically impossible. Sheep argue that conditions commonly associated with a seance (such as darkness, anticipation and fear) may act as a catalyst for these phenomena. Goats suggest that reports of seances are unreliable, and that eyewitnesses are either fooling themselves or being tricked by fraudulent mediums.

How Science Works

Practical Learning Activity 10.7

- Based on your knowledge of eyewitness testimony (EWT) and reconstructive memory (see Gross and Rolls, 2008), estimate:
  (a) the overall percentage of participants who reported movement of at least one of the objects
  (b) the percentage of goats who were certain the suspended ball *hadn't* moved
  (c) the percentage of sheep who were certain the suspended ball *hadn't* moved
  (d) the percentage of sheep who believed that at least one other object *had* moved
  (e) the percentage of goats who believed that at least one other object *had* moved
  (f) the percentage of sheep who answered 'yes' to the question, 'Do you believe that you have witnessed any genuine paranormal phenomena?'
  (g) the percentage of goats who answered 'yes' to the same question.
- Explain your reasons for making these estimates in terms of Loftus's EWT research.

Key Study 10.1: Eyewitness testimony in the seance room (Wiseman *et al.*, 1995)

Aim/hypothesis (AO1)

Wiseman *et al.* conducted an experiment to assess the reliability of testimony relating to seance phenomena.

Method/design (AO1)

Twenty-five participants attended three seances. They were first asked to complete a short questionnaire designed to assess whether they believed that genuine paranormal phenomena might sometimes occur during seances.

All the windows and doors in the seance room had been sealed and blacked out, and the chairs were arranged in a large circle. Various objects (a book, slate and bell) had been treated with luminous paint and placed on a small table in the middle of the circle. The medium (an actor) first pointed out the presence of a small luminous ball, suspended on a piece of rope from the ceiling. After turning out the lights, he asked everyone to join hands; he then asked the participants to concentrate on trying to move the ball, and then to try in the same way to move the objects on the table. During the seances, the slate, bell, book and table remained stationary.

After leaving the seance room, participants completed a short questionnaire asking them about their experience of the seance.

Results/findings (AO1)

The percentages for the items above were as follows: (a) 27; (b) 76; (c) 54; (d) 40; (e) 14; (f) 20; (g) 0.

Conclusions (AO1)

Despite the fact that neither the suspended ball nor any of the objects on the table – or the table itself – moved during the seance, almost a third of participants believed they'd witnessed movement of at least one of the objects. These results suggest that we're all vulnerable to trickery, but not surprisingly, a belief or expectation of paranormal phenomena during seances may add to that vulnerability.

Have 'outs' ready in case something goes wrong

Fakers have developed many kinds of 'outs' to enable them to escape or minimise the damage caused by something not going according to plan during their performance. By anticipating how a trick might go wrong, they develop various strategies to switch the method of that trick in order to 'rescue' the performance ('outs'). For example, if controls are imposed that prevent the type of trickery that was planned, the faker may explain away such failure by claiming that the conditions of the demonstration weren't psi-conducive.

Similarly, when some of the apparently 'bad tissue' ('tumour') removed from a patient by a psychic surgeon was discovered to be chicken intestine, the surgeon explained away this evidence by stating that it was a well-known fact that 'supernatural forces' convert the tumours into harmless substances once they've left the patient's body! The fact that the surgeon's claim cannot be disproved is, from a strictly scientific perspective, its greatest weakness.

Perception without awareness

The term 'perception without awareness' (PWA) or 'non-conscious processing' (Towell, 2001) (or 'preconscious processing') refers to people's perception of, and responses to, stimuli that are presented below the threshold of conscious awareness. Historically, the term 'subliminal perception' has been used to refer to the same phenomenon. 'PWA' is preferred because research has shown that there's no such thing as a fixed and easily measured sensory threshold. Also, modern cognitive psychologists may wish to distance themselves from the early subliminal perception studies, partly because many had methodological flaws, and also because of the extravagant claims based on them (such as that audiotapes containing subliminal suggestions can produce weight loss or influence consumers' buying preferences). There's scant evidence that gross human behaviour can be influenced by such complex subliminal messages, although there's good evidence that individuals can perceive and process simple information (such as single words or a simple line drawing) presented at levels that are too weak (e.g. too fast) for conscious awareness (Watt, 2001; see Gross, 2005, 2008).

While there's been a great deal of debate within cognitive psychology over whether or not there's evidence for PWA, many parapsychologists have noted similarities between PWA and ESP and hope to extend their understanding of the latter by studying the overlap between the two. According to Rhine (1977, in Watt, 2005), 'It is here, in the common unconscious functions of both sensorimotor and extrasensorimotor (or psi) character that parapsychology comes closest to psychology.'

Many parapsychologists have noted the often striking parallels between ESP and subliminal perception. For example, Schmiedler (1988, in Watt, 2005) described her 'shock of recognition [which] came from a list of personality variables associated with subliminal sensitivity; they looked just like the variables associated with ESP success'.

Some of these personality variables are discussed below in the section entitled 'Personality factors' (pages 470–472).

Biological factors

Conscious awareness during anaesthesia (CADA)

This (together with electrophysiological markers of non-conscious processing and blindsight) reveals the considerable impact that PWA can have on conscious experience – and our behaviour (Towell, 2001). It's

long been appreciated that we have more information at our disposal than we're capable of attending to, and the assumption is that outside the constraints of attention we're engaged in non-conscious passive processing.

Since the introduction of general anaesthesia about 160 years ago, there have been numerous reports of conscious awareness during it. Changes in people's electroencephalogram (EEG – a measure of electrical activity in the brain; see below) have been used in many studies in an attempt to monitor consciousness during surgery with anaesthesia. The introduction of paralysing muscle relaxants into routine major surgery, together with the trend towards lighter anaesthesia, has increased the risk of unplanned intra-operative 'wakefulness', in which patients may be unable to communicate this to staff because of paralysis. The overall incidence of CADA had been estimated at 0.2–0.9 per cent, but for women undergoing Caesarean section it's been put at 0.9–6.1 per cent (Towell, 2001); in the latter, subsequent recollections can range from 'dreams' to reporting exact operative details.

Electrophysiological markers of non-conscious processing

The EEG offers a millisecond-by-millisecond analysis of brain function. It measures the potential difference between two or more points on the scalp recorded via electrodes. When the EEG is time-locked to a stimulus onset and this is repeated several times, it's possible to record an *evoked potential* (EP); EPs have been used extensively as a tool to study early brain processing of stimuli that are thought to be non-conscious.

Libet and his colleagues have demonstrated that electrical stimuli applied directly to the somatosensory cortex of the brain (responsible for detecting bodily and sensory stimulation) don't produce an immediate sensation. We'd expect a verbal report of the sensation within 100 milliseconds/ms of the stimulus (based on the short conduction time – 20–30 ms – of the sensory pathways). However, stimuli were perceived about 500 ms later. This suggests that before conscious awareness of a stimulus can occur, it's necessary to achieve a state of 'neuronal adequacy', which takes up to 500 ms to develop (Libet *et al.*, 1979). More recently, Gomes (1998, in Towell, 2001) has suggested a minimum value of 230 ms.

Whatever the value of neuronal adequacy, it's clear that there are 'readiness potentials' of 1–2 seconds before the initiation of either planned or unplanned movements; these potentials, presumably, reflect the non-conscious preparation to move. A simple but fast reaction time of around 250 ms following the stimulus would be interpreted as a non-conscious, automatic response; longer, choice reaction times represent conscious processing of stimuli.

Prepulse inhibition of the startle response

The orbicularis oculi eye muscle blink reflex measures the startle response to sudden, unexpected sensory stimuli; it's thought to reflect neuronal excitability in the brainstem and doesn't involve higher brain functions. It's possible to modulate the blink reflex and startle response by presenting a weak stimulus (*prepulse*) prior to a stronger blink-inducing probe stimulus. It's assumed that the prepulse stimulus is preattentive and at very short latencies (the interval between stimulus presentation and onset of the response) may be non-conscious.

It's been widely reported that the timing of the prepulse stimulus can facilitate or inhibit the amplitude and latency of the blink reflex in normal adults. Inhibition of blink amplitude is called *prepulse inhibition* (PPI); it's best achieved using prepulse stimuli of around 120 ms. Absent or abnormal PPI has been demonstrated in patients with post-traumatic stress disorder, schizophrenia and schizotypal personality disorder; this is thought to reflect the impaired habituation and increased central nervous system arousal observed in people with these disorders (see Chapter 7).

Blindsight

This refers to the phenomenon whereby patients with damage to their primary visual cortex retain the ability to detect, localise and discriminate visual stimuli that are presented in areas of their visual field in which they report *subjective blindness* ('I cannot see'). Blindsight has been studied extensively by Weiskrantz (1986). There may be two forms of blindsight: (i) a form present in visually guided behaviour in both sighted and brain-damaged people; and (ii) another present only following brain damage. The evidence from blindsight research has been used to argue that we can see things and have perceptual belief without the distinctive visual awareness that accompanies normal sight. In other words, there's a sharp dissociation between visual *performance* and visual *awareness*.

Towell (2001) refers to a report that shows a blindsight individual could recognise facial expressions presented in the blind field. This is consistent with perception of emotional expressions in the absence of awareness in normal individuals (based on neuroimaging experiments). In both cases, it appears that the amygdala is activated via a colliculopulvinar pathway.

Towell also cites a report of a similar phenomenon to blindsight for hearing. A patient with total deafness caused by a bilateral lesion in the temporal lobes and central pontine area retained some ability to respond reflexively to sounds. When attempts were made to restore awareness of sound and voluntary responses to sounds by drawing attention to orienting head movements, performance improved and the patient began to respond successfully in a forced-choice situation. However, despite confidence in detection and localisation of sounds, she remained unaware of their meaning.

Several other aspects of blindsight include the proposal that it's very unlikely to result from dissociations within a single system, but rather from the interaction of distinct evolutionary systems. In addition, the intact motor abilities to respond to visual stimuli indicate that (a) patients' verbal responses result *not* from degraded vision, but from *proprioception* (that is, the provision of information about the position, location, and orientation of the body); and (b) above-chance correct verbal responses are forced guesses, rather than tentative beliefs. In other words, awareness doesn't imply the activation of belief systems.

Personality factors

Extraversion

According to Delanoy (2005), parapsychologists have long been interested in exploring why some people report having more psi experiences in their everyday life than do others. Also, while most experimental work is done with volunteer participants who haven't been selected for their supposed psi ability, findings indicate that some people appear to do better in experimental psi tests than others. One approach to examining possible reasons for these differences is to explore the relationship between psi ability and personality; one of the most frequently researched personality factors is *extraversion* (E). Briefly, extraverted individuals tend to be sociable and outgoing (see Gross, 2005).

Descriptive reviews of studies examining the relationship between psi and E (Eysenck, 1967; Palmer, 1977; Sargent, 1981) concluded that E was a psi-conducive trait. Honorton *et al.*'s (1998) MA of 60 studies initially found a significant overall effect, but the effect sizes were *heterogeneous* (not consistent with each other). Consequently, Honorton *et al.* (1998) divided the studies into smaller groups according to various procedural variables to see if they could discover the source of the heterogeneity.

Separating the 45 studies that used forced-choice procedures from the 15 that used free-response methods (see above) revealed significant effects in both groups of studies. But again, both groups had heterogeneous effect sizes. So the researchers next examined whether testing participants individually or in groups had any impact on the outcomes. Of the forced-choice studies, 21 had tested participants individually, and had heterogeneous effect sizes. But in the 24 forced-choice studies where participants were tested in groups, there was *homogeneity* (the effect sizes were consistent with each other) – but there was *no* significant E/psi effect. In other words, the only studies showing consistent results were those that didn't find a relationship between E and psi.

A further analysis of these surprising results revealed that in the forced-choice data, the significant – but inconsistent – effect was due to *flawed studies*, in which the E measure had been given *after* the ESP test. In other words, the participants knew how they'd performed on their psi task before completing the E questionnaire. This is a flaw because knowledge of their psi results may have influenced how they completed the questionnaire. This finding raises the possibility that the apparent psi/E relationship was due to psychological, as opposed to paranormal, factors (Delanoy, 2005). This led Honorton *et al.* to conclude that the E/psi relationship in forced-choice studies is *artefactual* (a consequence of the way the experiments were conducted, rather than a genuine relationship between the two variables).

What about the 14 free-response E studies? Honorton *et al.* again found a significant but heterogeneous E/psi relationship; dividing them according to individual or group testing procedures revealed that the two group-testing studies were responsible for the heterogeneity. The results for the 12 individual-testing studies were significant *and* homogeneous. In all but one of the 12, the E questionnaire was given prior to the ESP test, thereby avoiding the flaw contained in the forced-choice studies. For the 221 auto-Ganzfeld trials for which they had E data, Honorton *et al.* found a significant ESP/E relationship.

Why should there be a significant relationship between

E and psi at all? Watt (2005) identifies two explanations.

1. Extraverts are more sociable than introverts and hence more comfortable in an experimental settings that might be intimidating to introverts.

2. Extraverts tend to have lower levels of cortical arousal than introverts, and so would have the reduced physiological arousal thought to be psi-conducive. (Extraverts need greater levels of stimulation to produce the same level of cortical arousal as introverts: in the Ganzfeld, for example, introverts would be relatively more aroused since they need less stimulation in the first place.)

Variables common to PWA and ESP

According to Watt (2001), a state of dispersed attention or relaxation is known to facilitate sensitivity to subliminal stimulation. Similarly, ESP seems to be facilitated by an increased awareness of internal processes, feelings and imagery, by relaxation, and by a passive and non-analytical state of mind. These similarities have led to speculation that, once the extra-sensory information has reached an individual, it's processed in very similar ways to subliminal information; that is, both extra-sensory and weak-sensory information initially arrive at an unconscious or pre-conscious stage of processing. They both have the potential to emerge into consciousness, subject to various types of distortion and transformation of weak sensory material along the way, in particular *defensiveness*.

Defensiveness

How Science Works

Practical Learning Activity 10.8

● Try to define the term 'defensiveness'.
● Explain the concept of defensiveness in Freud's psychoanalytic theory. (See Gross and Rolls, 2008.)

'Defensiveness' can be defined in several ways. According to the cognitive approach, defence is seen as the cognitive reappraisal of threatening situations, leading to a reduction of subjective threat. A widely accepted definition is Dixon's (1981): defensiveness is unconscious resistance to unpleasant or threatening information.

Although pencil-and-paper measures of defensiveness do exist, the most commonly used is the Defence Mechanism Test (DMT). Simple pictures depicting a potentially threatening situation are shown for extremely short durations, and after each exposure the participant is asked to describe what they though they saw. The rationale behind the test is that, at such short durations, individuals can perceive little if anything of the stimulus picture; as a result, they'll project something of their own fears and attitudes into their descriptions, in the form of distortions and transformations. A trained scorer checks the individual's descriptions for signs of various types of defensiveness (Watt, 2001).

Johnson was the first parapsychologist to test the idea that individuals who are defensive to weak sensory information may also be resistant to extra-sensory information. As he put it: 'People who are prone to draw their preconscious blinds in matters of visual perception might act somehow similarly towards perceptions which are extra-sensory' (in Watt, 2001).

His expectations were confirmed: individuals who showed defensive reactions on the DMT tended to have lower ESP scores than individuals who weren't defensive. This led to a series of studies, conducted in Iceland, the USA and Holland, comparing DMT and ESP performance. A meta-analysis of these studies (Haraldsson and Houtkooper, 1992, in Watt, 2001) found a significant DMT–ESP correlation.

Watt considers this to be an important finding, as it suggests that ESP information is processed according to normal psychological principles. However, difficulties in administering the DMT have hindered

independent replication of the DMT–ESP studies. Consequently, Watt developed an alternative measure of defensiveness that enabled objective scoring of individuals' reactions to weak sensory stimuli. Watt and Morris (1995, in Watt, 2001) conducted two studies which found that defensive individuals tended to have lower ESP scores than individuals who weren't defensive. This finding provides converging evidence of the similarity between subliminal perception and ESP, underlining the claim that normal cognitive processes may be applied to information of extra-sensory origin.

Haraldsson *et al.* (2002, in Watt, 2005) identify an *experimenter effect* that casts some doubt on the validity of the earlier studies. However:

> *Taken as a whole, the evidence for a defensiveness–ESP relationship is consistent with the theory that psi information may initially be perceived at an unconscious level and that this information may be subject to distortions and transformations prior to its emergence in conscious awareness ... There are also preliminary indications of a similar defensiveness–PK relationship ... The defensiveness–ESP relationship is one example of how psychological factors may contribute to an understanding of parapsychological phenomena. (Watt, 2005)*

Functions of paranormal and related beliefs

Who believes?

Even if paranormal phenomena don't exist, paranormal *experiences,* and *belief* in paranormal phenomena, certainly do. Surveys have shown that a considerable number of people report experiences they interpret as paranormal in nature (Watt, 2001). While PK experiences are quite rare, ESP is relatively common. One random postal questionnaire survey found that 36 per cent believed in ESP, while 25 per cent had experienced it (Blackmore, 1984). A survey of over 1,200 adult Americans (Gallup and Newport, 1991) found that 75 per cent admitted to reading their horoscope in the newspapers, 25 per cent expressed a firm belief in astrology, claimed to have experienced telepathy and believed in ghosts, and almost 17 per cent claimed to have seen a UFO. Responding to an appeal in the *Daily Telegraph*, 59 per cent of respondents expressed some belief in paranormal phenomena (Blackmore, 1997).

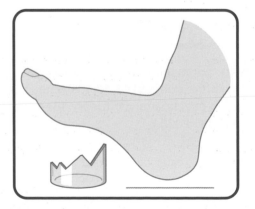

Figure 10.8 Example of threatening stimulus from Watt's studies comparing defensiveness and ESP (Source: Watt, 2005)

How Science Works

Practical Learning Activity 10.9

- Conduct a survey of adults, asking them:
  - (a) What do you understand by the term 'paranormal'?
  - (b) Can you give some examples of paranormal phenomena?
    (If they cannot answer either of these correctly, tell them what ESP means and give some examples.)
  - (c) Have you ever had any paranormal experiences (such as telepathy etc.)? If so, can you describe them?
  - (d) Whether or not you've had such an experience, do you believe in the paranormal? Why / why not?
- Are there any patterns in their answers? For example, are some paranormal experiences more common than others? Are there any gender-related trends? Are there recurring reasons given for belief in the paranormal?

According to Watt (2005), numerous polls and surveys have demonstrated that paranormal beliefs are widely held, across a variety of cultures (see below), ages, educational achievements and religious beliefs. A representative Gallup poll (Newport and Strausberg, 2001, in Watt, 2005) found that 54 per cent believed in psychic healing, 50 per cent believed in ESP and 42 per cent believed that houses can be haunted. In general, a higher proportion of females than males tend to report paranormal beliefs and experiences. While this may reflect females' greater psychic tendencies, Watt cites evidence which suggests that females are more willing than males to *report* having had such experiences.

Why do people believe?

For some, an interest in the paranormal represents no more than a bit of harmless fun (Roberts and Groome, 2001), but for many others it plays a major part in helping them to make important decisions, such as deciding to get married or change jobs on the advice of an astrologer, move house to escape a ghost or poltergeist, or take significant actions based on information they believe comes by telepathy or from a clairvoyant. Roberts and Groome maintain that belief in paranormal phenomena may cause fears and anxieties,

such as living in constant dread of alien abduction – or believing it's already happened – fear of ghosts, demons and the Devil.

Some accident or catastrophe may be blamed on the intervention of some unknown force: 'The disaster was fated, in the stars, or brought about by demons or the vengeful dead.' This type of attribution can create convenient excuses for those who are actually responsible, and in failing to face up to reality they may also fail to learn from their mistakes. According to Roberts and Groome:

> Telepathy, clairvoyance and astrology might all have the potential to enrich and improve our lives, provided that they are valid and genuine. However, if it turns out these paranormal phenomena are not genuine, then they represent a source of considerable confusion, misjudgement and bad decision-making . . .

For these reasons, paranormal phenomena need to be subjected to scientific investigation, in order to determine whether or not they are genuine.

In a more general sense, belief in the paranormal can be seen as one example of how we all try to interpret and make sense of our experience. By definition, unusual or anomalous events 'demand' an explanation in a way that 'ordinary' or 'expected' events don't. So, for some people, belief in paranormal phenomena represents a 'ready-made' explanation for (certain kinds of) unusual experiences. The basic cognitive process(es) involved in explaining the ordinary and the unusual may be identical (see above), but when someone arrives at a conclusion in terms of alien abduction, the actions of poltergeists or merely ESP, we might regard their reasoning as suspect!

According to French (2001):

> People need to make sense of anomalous experiences, and a paranormal explanation is probably seen as preferable to the notion that they are losing their sanity. Once a paranormal explanation has been accepted, it provides various secondary gains (such as a sense of being special) even though the sufferer may be genuinely afraid of further 'attacks'.

Of course, *belief* in the paranormal and reported paranormal *experiences* may be related. Perception and memory are notoriously inaccurate and unreliable, because they're biased by our expectations and beliefs. So our interpretation of events may be distorted and

According to Groome (2001), given that there's no scientific evidence for astrology, it seems strange that so many people are prepared to believe in it. This apparently irrational belief is of interest to psychologists in its own right, and several studies have been conducted that help to shed some light on the phenomenon.

Snyder and Schenkel (1975, in Groome, 2001) asked a large number of people for their time and date of birth, and then presented each of them with a personality description allegedly based on their horoscope. In reality, all the participants were given exactly the same personality profile; despite this, most participants agreed that the profile described them quite accurately. Similarly, French *et al.* (1991, in Groome, 2001) found that most participants accepted a description of their personality as being 'good' or even 'excellent', despite the fact that it contained both extremes of each personality dimension (for example, 'at times you are extraverted … while at other times you are introverted').

These experiments illustrate the so-called 'Barnum effect', named after the famous showman who claimed that people will believe anything about themselves provided it includes 'a little something for everybody'. The trick is to say things that virtually anyone could identify with (for example, 'you feel at times that some people do not appreciate you enough'), and to keep the content as vague and non-specific as possible. Astrologers also tend to focus on the more flattering aspects of the reader's personality, so that individuals are being told what they want to hear.

imprecise. (As we saw above, this can apply to participants and investigators alike.) If you have a strong belief in the reality of ESP (you're a 'sheep'), you may interpret an ambiguous occurrence (for example, a coincidence between a dream and a subsequent telephone call) as being due to ESP. But if you're a highly sceptical 'goat', you're likely to reject the ESP explanation as improbable or impossible (Watt, 2001).

How Science Works
Practical Learning Activity 10.10

- If you're not convinced that these tactics really work on people, you might like to try reading through the horoscope columns of your daily newspaper.
- If you try hard enough, you'll find some snippets in all 12 zodiac signs that you can recognise in yourself (Groome, 2001).

One possible motive for accepting the tenets of astrology so uncritically is that most individuals are looking for both an understanding of their lives and an insight into the minds of others. The rather limited knowledge offered by psychologists isn't sufficient for many people, who find it frustrating to have no satisfactory framework that enables them to make sense of others: 'Those who simply cannot accept our incomplete knowledge of people and events will readily grasp at a system such as astrology which promises to give them the insights that they require.'

The cultural significance of beliefs in the paranormal

How Science Works
Practical Learning Activity 10.11

- Before reading on, write a story in which you're abducted by aliens. Take as much time as you like, and try to include as much detail as you can. Describe both the sequence of events and your reactions to them (French, 2001).
- Compare your account with those of others in your class – and with French's account below.

You are driving along in a car at night on a lonely isolated road when you notice a strange light in the sky. At first you do not pay it much attention, but gradually you begin to suspect that the light is actually following your car – and it does not look like any conventional aircraft! As the craft gets nearer to your car, you can see that it is definitely circular in shape. You cannot believe your eyes, as your fear turns to terror. You put your foot on the accelerator, in a desperate attempt to outrun the alien craft. A brilliant beam of light engulfs your car and the engine suddenly cuts out completely. You lose consciousness.

The next thing you remember is that you are lying on your back on some kind of examination table inside a circular, dimly lit room. A number of beings … are standing around you. You try to look closely at their faces, but the whole scene has a strange dream-like quality, as if you had been drugged. The beings appear to be humanoid and around 4 feet tall. They have hairless grey skin and very large heads. Their piercing eyes are large and black, but they have very small noses and mouths. One of them looks you directly in the eye and telepathically tells you not to be afraid. You realize that you are naked and that you cannot move. The aliens carry out a detailed examination using strange pieces of equipment which cause you intense, almost unbearable pain. You cannot scream. They seem to be particularly interested in your genitals and use a probe to extract ova or sperm. Finally, they insert some kind of small metallic implant into your brain by forcing a long probe up your nose. Your mind is filled with such intense pain that you again lose consciousness. When you wake up you are back inside your car beside the road. You look at your watch. Over three hours have passed since you first noticed the strange light in the sky.

According to French, your story is unlikely to have been identical to the one above, but the chances are there were some strong similarities. Although there are many variations on this basic theme, alien abduction (AA) experiences typically include capture by aliens and medical examination. These days, the aliens – and the whole abduction scenario – most often correspond to the description given above, and it's not difficult to see why. This standard AA story is now well known in our culture thanks to popular TV series like *The X-Files* and movies such as *Communion* and *Fire in the Sky*.

Many thousands of people worldwide (who are consumers of these US-made programmes/films) are convinced they really have undergone AA, and they have clear and vivid 'memories' to back them up. Newspapers, magazines, TV and radio documentaries and chat shows have all reported many such claims as fact (indeed, the two films referred to above are both based on allegedly true accounts). Coverage is typically uncritical and sensationalised (French, 2001).

Alien abduction and sleep paralysis

According to Hopkins *et al.* (1992, in French, 2001), the most frequently endorsed item given as evidence of AA is 'Waking up paralyzed with a sense of a strange person or presence or something else in the room.' This, in fact, is a concise description of the experience of *sleep paralysis* (a standard symptom of *narcolepsy*, but which can occur quite commonly in the general population). Although it's known that the muscles are paralysed during rapid eye movement (REM) sleep (see Chapter 1), during sleep paralysis (SP) one is aware of not being able to move; there's also a terrifying sense of a malign presence.

SP is likely to be accompanied by *hypnogogic* and *hypnopompic* imagery; this consists of anomalous sensory experiences that occur either prior to sleep or on waking, respectively. These sensations include both auditory and visual hallucinations (often of lights or strange figures in the bedroom), pressure on the chest and floating sensations (including out-of-body experiences / OBEs; see below).

The same core experience has been reported throughout history, in many different cultures, although the interpretation of the experience may vary. Despite having a relatively high incidence in the general population, the existence of SP isn't widely known or understood. Anyone who has experienced this terrifying (although temporary) ordeal is likely to want to explain it; widely shared knowledge of AA provides a very convenient explanation, at least for members of western society. According to French (2001):

Accounts of alien abduction, including the unusual sensations described above, are far more common in modern Western society (e.g. Whitley Strieber's best-selling book, Communion: A True Story*) than scientific accounts of sleep paralysis. In the absence of the latter, many people are likely to believe either that they were going mad or that they genuinely experienced intruders from another world. Not surprisingly, they marginally prefer to believe that they are sane …*

Many researchers believe that SP is at the heart of many, if not most, AA claims (e.g. Blackmore, 1994). Another example of how culture can impact on the content and significance of paranormal beliefs are *near-death experiences* (NDEs); these are discussed in the final section, pages 481–486).

The psychology of deception and self-deception, superstition and coincidence

✔ Specification Hint

Deception was discussed above in relation to 'psychic fraud' by fake psychics (Wiseman, 2001; see pages 465–469). This was described as an unusual form of deception. Self-deception can be understood in various ways, including *defensiveness* (see above, page 471–472) and believers' (that is, sheeps') willingness to be guided by their beliefs in astrology or explain unusual (and frightening) experiences in terms of AA (see above). Superstition can be seen as a belief that arises from people's mistaken understanding of *coincidence*; this is discussed in the following section.

Probability and coincidence

Unexpected events happen from time to time. When they do, we might explain them as coincidences (literally, a coincidence means two/more events occurring together – 'coinciding' – which usually do not); this implies that, although unexpected, the probability of their occurrence is sufficiently high that we don't need a 'special' explanation (such as ESP). These two explanations correspond to 'chance' and 'paranormal', respectively.

For example, we might think of an old friend we've lost touch with and not thought about in years, only to receive an email or telephone call the same day to inform us that they have just died (Milton, 2005). Either we label this as 'mere' coincidence (a 'chance' occurrence) or we decide that the chance of the two events happening together is so slim that it cannot be dismissed as coincidence (rather, some paranormal phenomenon, such as ESP, must be involved).

In all these examples, we're faced with the same basic dilemma: can the events be dismissed as mere chance, or were they just too improbable for such a mundane explanation? This question is really quite fundamental to every claim of a psychic or paranormal experience; in order to answer it we need to be able to judge how probable it was that such an event could have occurred by chance alone. In some cases, this level of probability (p) can be precisely measured, and is usually expressed

How Science Works

Practical Learning Activity 10.12

- Consider the following three examples, and try to decide whether they offer support for the occurrence of paranormal phenomena or whether they can be dismissed as merely chance events (Esgate and Groome, 2001).

1. In an experiment on ESP, the experimenter turns over playing cards one at a time and tries to convey to a partner whether she's looking at a red or a black one. Although the partner cannot see the cards, he begins the experiment by guessing the correct colour three times in a row. Is this just luck or was it due to ESP?
2. A student looking through his list of classmates discovers that one of the other students has the same birthday as him. There are only 23 people in the class, so would you regard this as a fairly amazing coincidence?
3. A man dreams about a plane crash, and then wakes the next day to read in the newspaper that there actually has been a real plane crash. Was the dream a premonition or just a coincidence?

- How did you arrive at your decision?

as either a percentage or a fraction. For example, the p of a coin landing 'heads' is one chance in two (50 per cent, or $p = 0.5$). However, in other cases (such as a plane crash) we're dealing with events that *cannot* be easily measured or quantified. This is one of the problems with everyday life events (as opposed to controlled events in the laboratory).

So what probability estimates can we make for the three examples below?

1. The probability of guessing the colour (red or black) of each card correctly is 0.5 (50 per cent), so the chances of guessing a whole series of cards correctly will be halved with each card selected. This means that there's a 50 per cent chance of guessing the first card correctly, a 25 per cent chance of guessing two in a row correctly, and a 12.5 per cent chance of guessing three in a row correctly. From this we can conclude that there's actually a fairly high probability of making three correct guesses in a row by sheer chance ($p = 0.125$); so there's no need to look for any other explanations.

2. Calculating the probability of two people sharing the same birthday from a group of a given size involves considering every possible comparison between each member of the group (in this case, all 23 students). This produces a surprisingly large number of pair comparisons, and, consequently, the probability of a shared birthday is 50 per cent higher than most people would think. So such a coincidence is far from remarkable and can be expected to occur as often as not. This illustrates how people tend to underestimate the chances of an event happening where there are a large number of possibilities or combinations to take into account (Esgate and Groome, 2001).

3. In order to tell *how surprising* a coincidence is, it's necessary to know how often the observed event would be expected to happen by chance alone. In order to calculate this, we need to know how often the two events that make up the coincidence occur. As we've seen, it's often difficult to calculate the probability of many everyday events. If we cannot calculate an exact probability, we have to accept a fairly rough estimate. We know that plane crashes are reported in the media fairly regularly, and dreams of disasters and accidents are also quite common. Given that both events have a high probability of occurring, the likelihood of their coinciding by sheer chance will also be reasonably high. Esgate and Groome conclude, therefore, that the dream / plane crash coincidence can be adequately explained by chance without any need to assume any psychic or paranormal explanation (such as a premonition).

Probability judgements and belief in the paranormal

The three examples above highlight the basic question we must ask when investigating claims of paranormal experiences: we need to estimate the probability of the particular event occurring by chance alone. As Esgate and Groome say:

> We should only consider the possibility of a non-chance explanation (e.g. the intervention of psychic forces) when the probability of a chance occurrence is extremely low. Even then, of course, we should not automatically accept a paranormal explanation, as there may be other possible causes which need to be ruled out ..., So-called 'paranormal' experiences often turn out to have a normal and straightforward explanation, so it is necessary to look carefully for these before we consider paranormal explanations.

One attempt to calculate precise probabilities of everyday events involved thinking about any of the people we know by chance alone within five minutes of learning of their death. Zusne and Jones (1989, in Milton, 2005) calculate this as being about one in 30,000 per year. Although this would be a rare event for any individual, in a country the size of the USA, about 3000 adults would have such an experience by chance alone in any given year – so it shouldn't be too surprising to hear of such instances. As Milton (2005) says: 'This shows clearly how even what appear to be remarkable coincidences may not be the strong evidence for ESP that they may at first appear.'

How Science Works

Practical Learning Activity 10.13

● If people very often shout at their computers and computers very often break down quite randomly, then by chance alone the two events will occur together relatively often in a large enough sample (Milton, 2005).
● What superstitious belief might someone derive from this coincidence?
● Try to think of any superstitious beliefs you have. Can you account for how you come to have them?
● Try defining the term 'superstition' / 'superstitious belief'.

Individual differences

It seems that people in general, including statisticians, tend to make inaccurate probability judgements in everyday situations, typically underestimating the frequency with which surprising events occur by chance alone (Nisbett and Ross, 1980; Kahneman *et al.*, 1982; see Gross, 2005). In addition, there's some evidence that people who believe in the paranormal may be less accurate in making probability judgements than non-believers (Blackmore and Troscianko, 1985). Specifically, the believers are more likely to *underestimate* the probability of a chance event; this might explain why they're more likely to accept a paranormal explanation of their experiences: they're more likely to consider an unusual event to be so improbable as to be beyond coincidence. In contrast, those with a more accurate grasp of probability would judge the same event to fall within the bounds of chance.

While Blackmore and Troscianko used computer-controlled coin tossing, other researchers have used random number generation and estimations of shared birthdays. While these studies provided some support for the 'probability misjudgement' theory of paranormal belief, not all studies have done so (Blackmore, 1997); believers may be prone to misjudgements in some situations but not in others (Esgate and Groome, 2001).

BELIEF IN EXCEPTIONAL EXPERIENCE

Research into psychic healing

✔ Specification Hint

Psychic healing (abbreviated to just 'healing') was discussed above in the context of psychic fraud. Depending on the particular question, evidence relating to fraud in healing may be just as relevant as the material that follows. Note, too, that Benor's (2005) definition of healing makes reference to any living system as the potential beneficiary of healing (the 'healee'), although most research has focused on human healees.

What is psychic healing?

According to Benor (2005), *healing* is:

> the systematic, intentional intervention by one or more persons to alter the condition of another living being or beings (person, animal, plant or other living system), by means of focused intention, hand contact, or 'passes', without apparently producing the influence through known, conventional physical or energetic means ...

This may involve the invocation of belief systems, including;

- external agents such as God, Christ, other 'higher powers', spirits, universal or cosmic forces or energies

- special healing energies or forces residing in the healer

- PK

- self-healing powers or energies latent in the healee.

Healing may be done by healers touching or passing their hands near the healee's body or may be projected by intention, meditation, or prayer from a distance.

Healing has been described in Ancient Egyptian and Greek texts and is found in every culture studied by modern social sciences. Healers generally claim they can improve the conditions of 80 per cent of people who seek their help, and virtually every known disease has been reported by healers as responsive to their treatments. Unfortunately, most healers keep few, if any, records, and most of those who do have no medical or technical training that would make their observations sufficiently precise to be of any scientific value (Benor, 2005).

Varieties of healing

These range from prayer healing through therapeutic touch to psychic surgery. LeShan (1974, in Benor, 2005) found the most common kinds of healers to be:

- type 1 healers, who see themselves as mentally uniting with the healee, generally in an altered state of consciousness

- type 2 healers, who see themselves as a channel for healing energy

- type 3 healers, who see themselves as working with

spirits; in countries such as the Philippines and Brazil, these healers have been reported to perform surgery with their bare hands or with crude, non-sterile instruments – with outstanding success, involving no pain, bleeding or infection; these haven't been systematically investigated but have been the subject of much controversy (see the discussion of psychic fraud above).

During healing treatments, healers and healees commonly report heat, cold, tingling, vibrations and other sensations at the site of treatment. Though people may subjectively feel heat when focusing on parts of their body, the sensations experienced during healing seem to be quite different from such self-induced sensations. They also vary from person to person, and from one occasion to another for the same person. The sensations experienced during healing indicate that an 'exchange of energy' may be taking place, usually attributed to a healing energy directly *from* or channelled from outside forces *through* the healer. Healees also often report a generalised warmth, relaxation, release of anxieties and tensions, and general well-being during and following healing (Benor, 2005).

Research into healing
Controlled studies
In his review of the research, Benor (2005) states that research since the early 1960s has demonstrated highly significant effects of healing in controlled trials with enzymes, yeasts, bacteria, cell structures *in vitro* (in test tubes), plants, non-human animals and humans. For example, laboratory studies have shown that the growth of bacterial and fungal infections has been slowed down, and haemoglobin levels *in vivo* (in living animals) have been increased.

In a series of experiments, Grad (1977) slowed the growth of goitres (visible swellings of the thyroid gland in the neck) in rats fed an iodine-deprived diet and fed thiouracil to induce goitre. In addition, water held by healers has been shown to change (using infrared spectrophotometry), suggesting an alteration in hydrogen bonding (e.g. Grad, 1965).

A review of over 150 studies, most of them published in parapsychology journals, found that over half were statistically significant, with over 40 per cent being significant at $p <0.01$ (Benor, 1993, in Benor, 2005). Benor refers to two independent reviews of clinical healing studies, which agree that the evidence indicates a real effect. Although some of the studies have been criticised on methodological grounds, a substantial number of sound studies remain to suggest that healing is a potent intervention.

Two further reviews by Benor, conducted in 2001, of almost 200 distant healing and controlled studies of healing with humans, animals and plants, found that 60 per cent produced significant results. About 40 per cent of these were significant at the 0.01 level; a further 20 per cent at the 0.5 level. The studies were included on the basis of their attention to high technical standards of research, including the use of 'double-blind controls' (where human participants are involved), randomisation and the use of statistical analysis of results.

How Science Works
Practical Learning Activity 10.14

- Explain what's meant by (a) 'double-blind' controls and (b) randomisation in the context of human experimentation.
- What does a 'single-blind' control involve?
- Describe how these would work in the context of healing experiments.

Prayer
One well-known study of distant healing produced significant effects in patients with cardiac problems. Byrd (1988, in Benor, 2005) arranged for prayer healing to be sent to 192 patients on a coronary care unit, while another 201 patients served as controls. This was done with a double-blind design, where neither the patients nor the treating or evaluating doctors knew which patients were sent the healing and which weren't. The patients were randomly assigned to the two groups. No significant differences between the two groups were found on several variables, but highly significant effects were found in the treated group, namely, lower incidence of intubation/ventilation, use of antibiotics, cardiopulmonary arrest, congestive heart failure, pneumonia and the use of diuretics. A well-controlled replication by Harris (1999, in Benor, 2005) also showed positive effects for the treatment group.

Sicher *et al.* (1998, in Benor, 2005) matched 20 pairs of AIDS patient volunteers and, using a double-blind control, used experienced healers to give half the group distant healing over a ten-week period. Both groups received standard medical treatment. After six months, the treatment group had significantly fewer AIDS-related symptoms ($p = 0.04$), lower severity of illnesses ($p = 0.02$), made fewer visits to the doctor ($p = 0.01$), and had fewer days in hospital ($p = 0.04$).

Benor (2000, in Benor, 2005) reviewed 61 reports of distant healing studies where healers sent an intent, wish or prayer to the healee; sometimes the healee was present, sometimes they were thousands of miles away. Distance didn't appear to affect the outcome. Benor also observed that there's no research evidence showing that healing through prayer is any more effective than healing attempted outside a religious context.

Meta-analyses

Benor (2005) cites a number of MAs of healing in humans, including prayer healing, distant healing, contact and non-contact therapeutic touch. Braud and Schlitz's (1989) MA focused on *electrodermal activity* (EDA or galvanic skin response/GSR), a measure of the skin's resistance to electricity: resistance decreases with increased sweating, an indicator of tension or anxiety. Healers have been able to selectively raise and lower EDA, aided by feedback from a meter attached to the healee's skin. Braud and Schlitz analysed 15 studies, involving 323 sessions, four experimenters, 62 influencers and 271 participants. A total of 40 per cent of the studies produced significant results; of the 323 sessions, 57 per cent were successful ($p = 0.000023$). In other words, such results could have occurred by chance alone only 23 times in a million. Similar results were found in a later MA of 19 experiments involving EDA (Schlitz and Braud, 1997, in Benor, 2005).

How can these results be explained?

Is healing a 'mere' placebo?

One sceptical claim is that healing represents, at best, a *placebo*. But not only is the placebo effect a very real – and very powerful – biological phenomenon (see Chapter 7), but this explanation cannot account for the significant healing effects found in double-blind trials (i.e. neither the healee nor the experimenter / doctor assessing the healee knows who's receiving the healing and who isn't).

If healing actually works, what biological mechanisms are involved?

Although the ultimate mechanism for the healer–healee intervention, as with other psi phenomena, is unknown, several possible contenders have been suggested, by a variety of researchers (Benor, 2005). These include (a) altered hydrogen bonding in water (the body is 65 per cent water); (b) enhanced action of enzymes and hormones; (c) raised haemoglobin levels; (d) slowing of the growth of infectious organisms; (e) lowered blood pressure; (f) reduced pain and anxiety.

In biological organisms, especially humans, healing might act through two or more of these mechanisms. In turn, these could produce a variety of beneficial effects on hormonal and immune functions, improving attitude, hope and spirituality.

The primary role of psychological harmony

Many healers believe that the physical effects of their treatments are of secondary importance to the changes in awareness they bring about in the healee. If illness is a product of disharmony and/or disease on physical, emotional, mental and/or spiritual levels (as healers claim), then the manifestations of illness are meant to draw people's attention to the disharmonies in their lives, and the crucial aspect of the healing process is to enhance awareness of the causal stresses or attitudes that underlie the symptoms. Healing, then, aims at helping people find better ways of coping with / accepting their problems and help them towards lessons that transcend the physical existence of a single lifetime.

Healers may help people to die more peacefully; this, too, is seen as a healing. According to Benor:

> Increasing and enhancing awareness of transpersonal dimensions becomes a major component of many healers' interventions. This may be subsumed under religious activities or may involve a personal spirituality – an intuitive awareness of one's connectedness with nature, Gaia, Christ consciousness, and the All.

The role of energy in healing

Healing seems to occur through intention and subtle energies. The subjective sensations described above suggest an exchange of energies between healer and healee; 'subtle energies' is the term used by healers to acknowledge the lack of identified healing energies. While conventional (allopathic) medicine continues to regard the body primarily as matter, healers have been saying for a very long time that they address the *energy body* when they do healings. Allopathic and energy medicine approaches may simply correspond to these two different aspects – matter and energy (Benor, 2005).

In the mid-1970s, healers in the UK formed an organisation that lobbied the government to allow them to treat patients in NHS hospitals; 1,500 hospitals were subsequently opened to healers. In the early 1980s, healers agreed a code of conduct that was sent to various medical, nursing and midwifery associations for review; it was given their approval. Since 1988, the Doctor–Healer Network (DHN) has provided a forum for doctors, nurses and other conventional healthcare professionals to meet with healers, and other complementary therapists and clergy to explore how healing may be integrated with conventional medical care. Not only have doctors trained to develop their healing skills, but healers have worked regularly in hospital pain clinics, cancer units, a rheumatology ward and a cardiac rehabilitation centre (Benor, 2005).

Research into out-of-body and near-death experiences

✔ Specification Hint

Because out-of-body experiences (OBEs) form a central feature of near-death experiences (NDEs), we've decided here to focus on NDEs; the latter are also more interesting in terms of the issues they raise and the controversy they've caused. For example, NDEs illustrate very well how it's possible to interpret the 'same' experience in radically different ways.

🔍 How Science Works

Practical Learning Activity 10.15

- Do you believe in life after death? Why / why not?
- What do you understand by the terms 'out-of-body experience' and 'near-death experience'?
- Conduct a survey of adults, asking them these same two questions.

What are near-death experiences?

According to Greyson (2000), near-death experiences (NDEs) are 'profound psychological events with transcendental and mystical elements, typically occurring to individuals close to death or in situations of intense physical or emotional danger'. NDEs were popularised by Moody, an American psychiatrist, in his book *Life After Life* (1975). Based on accounts of numerous survivors of cardiac arrest and other life-threatening situations, Moody presented a description that included:

- experiences of floating along a dark tunnel with a bright light at the end

- leaving the body and being able to watch the proceedings from above (an out-of-body experience/OBE)

- meeting a 'being of light' who helped them review their past life

- feeling as if they are passing into another world (the light) where some final barrier marked the return from joy, love and peace to pain, fear or sickness; in these cases, the person had to choose between carrying on into the light and returning to life's pain or suffering.

Although these experiences were often difficult to talk about, they often left people feeling they'd changed for the better – less materialistic and with reduced fear of death.

Explaining NDEs

These accounts promoted the popular view that NDEs must be evidence for life after death. But many scientists and doctors rejected the experiences as, at best, drug-induced hallucinations or, at worst, pure invention. However, the 'truth' seems to lie somewhere in between these extremes (Blackmore, 2005).

In a review of the evidence, entitled 'Visions from the dying brain: near-death experiences may tell us more about consciousness and the brain than about what lies beyond the grave', Blackmore (1988) considers alternative explanations of NDEs in terms of known or hypothesised *physiological processes*, in particular those relating to brain mechanisms. She argues that before interpreting NDEs as evidence of life after death, we need to rule out explanations – both physiological and

481

psychological; not only can we apply what we already know (about the brain) to these experiences, but they can also teach us much about the brain. Such scientific explanations allow testable predictions to be made, but they must also make sense to the people who have had NDEs.

Blackmore cites research, both that of others and her own conducted in the Brain and Perception Laboratory at the University of Bristol Medical School. Box 10.8 gives a brief example of an NDE sent to Blackmore by a woman in Cyprus.

Figure 10.9 A representation of near-death experience (NDE) (© Liz Pyle, 1988)

Box 10.8: A first-hand account of an NDE

An emergency mastectomy was performed. On the fourth day following the operation I went into shock and became unconscious for several hours ... Although thought to be unconscious I remembered, for years afterwards, the entire, detailed conversation that passed between the surgeon and anaesthetist present ... I was lying above my own body, totally free of pain and looking down at my own self with compassion for the agony I could see on the face; I was floating peacefully. Then ... I was going elsewhere, floating towards a dark, but not frightening, curtain-like area ... then I felt total peace ... Suddenly it all changed – I was slammed back into my body again, very much aware of the agony again.

These experiences seem very real. The tunnel is so convincing that people often assume it's some 'real' passageway to the next life. The OBE is so realistic that people are convinced their spirit has left their body and can see and move without it. The positive emotions are so strong that many don't want to 'come back'. For those who reach the final stage, it often seems as though a conscious decision has been made to return to life and responsibilities rather than remain in bliss and peace.

Explaining the tunnel

Blackmore cites the astronomer Carl Sagan, according to whom the only way of explaining the universal

nature of NDEs is by reference to the one experience all human beings share – namely, birth. The tunnel is 'really' the birth canal, and the tunnel experience and the OBEs are a reliving of one's birth. Similar arguments have given rise to the 'rebirthing' business, regression and all sorts of other 'New Age' techniques.

But the birth canal is nothing like a tunnel, even if the foetus went actually face-first and open-eyed into it. Also, the newborn's cognitive abilities wouldn't allow us to remember our birth in a meaningful way as adults. Studies of so-called 'age regression' under hypnosis show that people generally invent superficially plausible experiences. However, at least the 'birth theory' can be tested. If tunnels and OBEs are a re-experience of birth, then people born by Caesarean section (CS) shouldn't have them. Blackmore gave a questionnaire to 254 people, 36 of whom had been born by CS. Both groups reported the same proportion of OBEs and tunnel experiences. It could be that these experiences are based on the *idea of birth in general* – but this drastically weakens the theory.

The tunnel seems to have a rather interesting origin in the structure of the visual system. It's not confined to NDEs but can occur in epilepsy and migraine, when falling asleep, meditating or just relaxing, when pressure is put on both eyes, or with certain drugs (such as LSD, psilocybin or mescaline). Why do such different conditions produce the same hallucinations?

The visual cortex, which processes both visions and

How Science Works

Practical Learning Activity 10.16

- Are the data consistent with Blackmore's predictions?
- Are there different types of memory that could explain the link between the birth experience and tunnel experiences? (See Gross, 2005, 2008; Gross and Rolls, 2008).
- Does Sagan's theory (and related New Age techniques) necessarily overestimate the capacities of newborns? (See Gross, 2008.)

visual imagination, is usually in a stable state; this is a result of neurons that inhibit the action of others. But many of the conditions listed above reduce or interfere with these inhibitory neurons. LSD, for example, suppresses the action of the raphe cells, which regulate activity in the visual cortex. Any interference with inhibition may produce a highly excitable state: there will be *random* firing of cells. The visual cortex is organised so that many cells are devoted to the centre of the visual field and a few to the periphery. Random firing of cells will produce the effect of a bright light in the centre fading out towards darkness; in other words, a tunnel effect. But no one has yet tested this hypothesis.

However, this doesn't explain why the tunnel experience, if it is a hallucination, seems so real. Blackmore suggests that the answer may lie in asking what makes *anything* so real. The distinction between 'out there' and 'in my mind' isn't an easy one as far as the nervous system is concerned. Almost as soon as visual or auditory processing starts, information from memory is mixed in with the sensory input. It seems unlikely that any simple tag could be attached that says 'this came from outside' or 'this is hallucination'. Blackmore believes the decision is made at a much higher level. The system simply takes the most stable model of the world it has at any one time and calls that 'reality'. Normally, there's one 'model of reality' that's overwhelmingly stable, coherent and complex. It's the one built up from sensory input – 'me, here, now'.

Visions from the dying brain

But what about the dying system, a brain with massive dis-inhibition, beset with noise and danger, or failing altogether to produce a workable model of reality? The system will try to restore stability as soon as possible,

and one way of doing this would be to rely on memory: to ask, as it were, 'Who am I?, Where am I? What am I doing?' The answers will be there in memory, provided enough capacity remains for processing. One interesting feature of memory models is that they're often in bird's eye view.

Suppose that a dying woman's system constructs a model of what she knows should be happening: her body on the operating table, the surgeons around her, the lights above and the apparatus around. This may well be in a bird's eye view – from the ceiling. This model may work rather well. It may also incorporate some input, such as the sounds of the people talking or the clink of instruments on the trolley, as well as the jolts of attempts to resuscitate her. In this way, a mental model could be produced that is not only convincing but actually contains some correct details about the events going on at the time – and is a bird's eye view. If this is the best model the system has at the time, it will seem perfectly real.

This explanation suggests several testable predictions. For example, people who have OBEs ought to be those who can more easily imagine scenes from a bird's eye view, or more easily switch viewpoints mentally. Blackmore found support for this in several experiments (1987). Blackmore and Irwin (in Blackmore, 1988) also found that people with OBEs tend to recall dreams in bird's eye view – though not events from waking life. Although the reasons for this are unclear, this approach seems to be more productive than the belief that something leaves the body.

However, Sabom (1982), an American cardiologist, has claimed that patients have seen things during NDEs that they couldn't possibly have reconstructed from hearing or from what they previously knew about resuscitation techniques. As well as collecting anecdotes, such as that of a shoe seen on an inaccessible window ledge, he asked participants to imagine going through a resuscitation procedure and to tell him what they 'saw'. They represented a control group. What they told him was nothing like the detailed and correct descriptions of apparatus or the movement of needles on dials that people with NDEs saw from out of the body. Blackmore believes that a better control group in Sabom's work would be composed of people who'd actually been through the full procedure and experienced the actions and conversations of staff. The behaviour of the needles should be recorded precisely for comparison with the patient's account.

Conclusions

Blackmore concludes her review by saying that there are good physiological and cognitive reasons why NDEs seem so real and have such a profound and lasting effect on the people who have them. But they're not as mysterious as they might appear. NDEs may tell us more about consciousness and the brain than about what may or may not happen beyond the grave. Its many components can be seen as changes in mental models brought about by dis-inhibition of the cortex and the breakdown of the usual model of normality driven by sensory input. But they shouldn't be dismissed as 'just hallucinations': they're life-transforming and important hallucinations that we should try to understand.

Blackmore (2005) considers a number of alternative explanations in addition to those discussed in the 1988 article.

- *Expectation* certainly affects NDEs, in two ways. First, as we have seen above, they often happen to people who *think* they're dying: you don't have to be physically close to death to have an NDE. Indeed, some aspects of the NDE, such as the OBE, can occur at any time and to perfectly healthy people. The examples given below of cultural and religious differences in the content of NDEs reflect differences in expectations about death. But since the general pattern seems to be similar across cultures, religious expectations cannot be responsible for the entire experience or most of its common features. We might also expect suicide attempters to have more hellish experiences, but their NDEs are much like others' – and they tend to reduce future suicide attempts.

- When under stress, the brain releases chemicals that act to reduce pain or help us cope with the stress. These include *endorphins*, the brain's own morphine-like drugs. It's been suggested that endorphins could account for the NDE. Stressors can include both actual physical trauma and extreme fear – such as the fear of dying. Endorphins can block pain and induce feelings of well-being, acceptance and even intense pleasure. While this might account for the positive experiences that are characteristic of NDEs, some researchers argue that 'hellish' NDEs are far more common than previously thought. Also, it's been argued that serotonin plays a more important

role than endorphins, and that the drug ketamine can induce states similar to NDEs.

- *Anoxia* (lack of oxygen to the brain) has been put forward as causing NDEs. But this is implausible, given that so many NDEs occur in the absence of anoxia (such as when people only *think* they're dying). However, anoxia causes dis-inhibition in the cortex, which Blackmore argues may be responsible for the tunnel and the light. In other words, it's the dis-inhibition (not the anoxia itself) that is responsible for much of the NDE (Blackmore, 1993). Hypercarbia (increased carbon dioxide in the blood) is also thought to play a role in NDEs and has long been known to induce visions, lights, mystical experiences and OBEs.

- The *temporal lobe* is sensitive to anoxia, and stimulating it artificially induces hallucinations, memory flashbacks, body distortions and OBEs. The limbic system is also sensitive to anoxia and is involved in the organisation of emotions and memory. Endorphins increase the chance of seizures in the temporal lobe and limbic system, so they might produce the same effects as anoxia. Also, research looking for an 'NDE-prone personality' has found that those most likely to have NDEs may have more unstable temporal lobes (high lability); but it's unclear whether this is a cause or an effect of NDE.

Methodological issues

NDEs have been reported following resuscitation (after the person had been pronounced clinically dead), by people who actually died but were able to describe their experiences in their final moments, as well as by individuals who, in the course of accidents or illness, simply *feared* they were near to death (Greyson, 2000). According to Roe (2001), in all three types of case it could be claimed that the experience has more to do with the *process* of dying than with the end point of death itself. Roe poses the fundamental question: 'Are people who have NDEs really dead?' The answer he gives is: 'It depends on how you define "dead".'

Initially, doctors determined death by checking for pulse, respiration and pupil reaction to light. With the invention of the stethoscope, the focus shifted to the heart. Later, cardiopulmonary resuscitation showed that people who'd been pronounced dead could be brought back to life. So attention has shifted to brain function. Yet a lack of cortical activity – and even brain stem quiescence – may only be symptomatic of *dying*, rather than an indicator of actual death. In each case, there may be a suspicion that some remnant of life may be going undetected that is capable of maintaining some kind of phenomenological experience.

These shifts in focus show how difficult it is to identify any single event as defining death. As Roe (2001) points out, 'death is a process that takes time, and if the appropriate action is taken then the dying process can be reversed'.

STRETCH AND CHALLENGE: What do we do about spontaneous occurrences?

By their very nature, NDEs and OBEs are *spontaneous* occurrences: people are unlikely to volunteer for experiments in which they're brought to the brink of death and most researchers wouldn't think such experiments ethically acceptable even if such volunteers could be found!

According to Colman (1987), spontaneous cases aren't generally regarded as scientific evidence for the existence of paranormal phenomena or the hypothesised mechanism underlying them (Blackmore, 1995). There are three major reasons for this.

1. They're unrepeatable, making it impossible for independent researchers to check them (unlike general psychology or experimental parapsychology). There's also a lack of theory as to when and where spontaneous psi should occur.
2. It's impossible to *exclude* a normal explanation – that is, some perfectly normal process (such as falling asleep and dreaming) could account for the apparently paranormal experience. In 27 years of psychoanalytic work with patients, Freud never encountered a paranormal dream. Also, the accumulation of similar cases doesn't necessarily strengthen the case for psi. However, in the case of NDEs, reports have been widespread through many ages and cultures (Blackmore, 2005). Long before Moody's *Life After Life* (1975), there'd been similar descriptions of deathbed experiences (when the patient did go on to die) in the psychical research literature. Dying patients often described wonderful visions to those sitting at their bedside; these visions included heavenly scenes, bright light, and deceased friends or relatives coming to help them. As far as culture is concerned, the evidence for consistency is patchy. Blackmore (1993) refers to studies carried out in India, Africa and Mesopotamia, which found some important differences in the content of NDEs compared with those reported by Moody. For example, American NDEs typically involved images of the person's dead mother, while female figures were extremely rare among Indians, especially males. Indians usually saw religious figures, who differed according to their particular faith. Also, while Americans were usually happy to go with their dead relatives or visionary angels (Gabriel or St Peter at his gates), Indians were more likely to refuse to go. Blackmore (1993) concludes that NDEs seem to be *universal* in the sense that something like the modern NDE has been reported in many ages and cultures. They are also reported by children. However, even if the content of NDEs was *consistent* across time, culture and intervals, this wouldn't in itself point to any particular *explanation*.
3. Most importantly, cases of spontaneous psi rely unavoidably on the testimony of those who report them. Colman believes that since paranormal events are literally contrary to the laws of nature, there are never good grounds for believing the testimony. But this argument is based on his definition of paranormal, which isn't accepted by most researchers in the field (see text above).

Roberts and Owen (1988) give an extreme definition of death, involving an irreversible – and permanent – loss of organ functions. Accordingly, all NDE reports refer to the experiences of people who have remained alive. If NDEs really do indicate what happens after we die (as many who report them believe), then we might expect to find differences between those who were actually near death and those who merely *thought* they were. But there's very little evidence to support this claim. The fact that virtually identical NDEs can be induced by perceived threat (i.e. fear of being near death) needs to be taken into account in any potential explanation (Roe, 2001; see below).

Research into psychic mediumship

✔ Specification Hint

As with healing, mediumship was discussed above in relation to psychic fraud (Wiseman, 2001). Also as with healing, depending on the wording of the examination question, that material may be as relevant as the material that follows.

Mediums and psychical research

Gauld (2005) defines mediums as 'individuals through whose agency or through whose organisms there are ostensibly received communications from deceased human beings or other supposed disembodied or remote entities …'.

The phenomenon of mediumship has been reported in one form or another from a large proportion of the past and present societies for which records exist. Often they've become institutionalised, as in Siberian and North American *shamanism* (shamans are defined as socially designated practitioners who claim to deliberately alter their consciousness to obtain information or exert influence in ways useful to their social group, and in ways not ordinarily available to their peers; Krippner, 2005) and western spiritualism (Gauld, 2005).

As we saw at the beginning of the chapter, mediumship played a central role in spiritualism and spiritualistic research. We noted that the frequent exposure of mediums as fraudulent resulted (by 1900) in scientific interest moving away from seances towards, first, 'psychical research', then PP as we know it today.

The eminent psychologists Myers, William James, Jung and Freud were all early members of the Society for Psychical Research (SPR) in London. The SPR investigated both *physical mediums*, who appeared to cause the movement of objects, materialisations, levitation and so on, and *mental mediums*, who, in trance, seemed to have access to information that they wouldn't normally possess. The controls used to stop mediums cheating included physical restraint (such as holding the medium's hands and feet throughout the experiment), and insisting the experiment take place in a room provided by the researchers.

While most turned out to be frauds, a few stand out as genuine. For example, Daniel Dunglas Home apparently produced a range of phenomena, over a 20-year period, including table raps, levitation, elongating his neck and handling burning coals; these sometimes occurred in well-lit conditions. Some of the most impressive mental (or 'trance') mediums were the British Mrs Gladys Leonard (1882–1968) and the American Leonara Piper (1859–1950), both of whom submitted to numerous tests over a 60-year period (Henry, 2005a). As trance mediums, their normal personalities were apparently displaced by those of the communicating entities. Mrs Leonard was particularly noted for her successful 'proxy' sittings – that is, sittings in which the sitter actually present hopes to obtain communications for an absent third party of whose concerns s/he knows little or nothing (Gauld, 2005).

Mediums and 'survival'

Gauld (2005) discusses mediumship in the context of 'survival' – that is, survival of bodily death. While there's an extensive literature on the supposed evidence for survival, an initial – and quite fundamental – difficulty is the lack of any clear agreement as to what would count as evidence. Some credulous people accept almost any odd phenomenon, however trivial, as the work of 'the spirits', while others claim, for various reasons, that no empirical findings whatsoever could constitute evidence for survival.

Under these circumstances, Gauld believes that the simplest course is to identify those categories of phenomena that have most often been supposed to provide evidence for survival. Apart from mediumship, he identifies (a) children who supposedly remember previous lives; (b) possession; (c) apparitions of the dead; and (d) spontaneous OBEs and NDEs (see above).

Cross-correspondences

In a small number of cases of alleged communication through mediums, there's evidence not just of identity but apparent evidence that the communicator is pursuing a characteristic purpose independent of any that might be attributed to the medium or sitters. The best-known cases of this kind are the '*cross-correspondences*'

manifested between 1901 and 1930 in the automatic writings of a number of automatists associated with the SPR (Gauld, 2005). The idea was that different parts of a message should be communicated through *different* mediums in such a way that the contribution of each should remain meaningless and the whole only make sense when the parts were brought together.

SUMMARY

CHAPTER

Theoretical and methodological issues in the study of anomalistic experience

- **Parapsychology** is the study of **psychic phenomena**, which involve interaction between an organism and its environment without the mediation of the **sensory systems** commonly believed to be the only means of acquiring information about the environment.

- **Anomalous** phenomena (commonly referred to as **paranormal** or '**psi**') involve meaningful exchanges of information while appearing to exceed the known capacities of the sensory (and motor) systems.

- The subject matter of parapsychology comprises **extrasensory perception** (ESP) (a general term that covers **telepathy**, **clairvoyance**, **precognition** and **retrocognition**), **psychokinesis (PK)** (**macro**, **micro** and **recurrent spontaneous PKY / RSPK**), **apparitional phenomena**, and **anomalous/exceptional phenomena** (such as **out-of-body experiences / OBEs, near-death experiences / NDEs, coincidence experiences / CEs**).

- The history of parapsychology can be divided into three overlapping phases: **spiritualistic research / spiritualism**, **psychical research** and **modern parapsychology**.

- The founding of modern parapsychology (and the first use of the term) is usually credited to J.B. and Louisa Rhine, although the latter isn't mentioned; this illustrates **sexism** within the psychology profession as a whole.

- Parapsychology is concerned with those phenomena that 'mainstream'/'regular' psychology cannot explain using its currently available models and theories. Phenomena that used to be part of parapsychology (such as hypnosis) have become part of the mainstream, so 'paranormal' implies 'understandable / scientifically explicable **in principle**' (as opposed to 'supernatural').

- The Rhines' early study of telepathy involved the use of **Zener** ('ESP') **cards**, allowing the experimenter to compare the results achieved with what would be expected by chance. The cards were also used to study clairvoyance and precognition.

- The Rhines claimed that they'd established the existence of ESP, but critics raised a number of methodological objections. After tightening up their procedures, above-chance results were still obtained.

- However, a significant factor that emerged was the **experimenter's attitude**: 'goats' (who are sceptical or dismissive of psi) might have a 'negative effect' on the results compared with 'sheep' (who believe in psi).

- Another major controversy that has dogged modern parapsychology (as well as its earlier forms) is the problem of **experimenter fraud**. Despite some notable examples, fraud hasn't been rife within parapsychology, nor is it confined to parapsychology.

- Unlike medicine and other sciences where experimenter fraud occurs, parapsychology may also be open to **participant fraud**: certain psi effects can be replicated by magicians, fakers and stage psychics.

- Although the experimental controls used in modern parapsychological experiments are designed to rule out fraud as an explanation, many of the most significant results have been reported by a relatively small number of experimenters.

- New statistical techniques for analysing and interpreting data in the social sciences and medicine (including parapsychology) have been developed, notably **meta-analysis (MA)**. This involves combining the results of several studies in order to provide an overall picture.

- Compared with traditional 'research reviews', MA offers advantages in relation to **cumulative probability, file-drawer estimate, effect size, study quality** and **replicability**.

- The most successful **free-response ESP** method has been the **Ganzfeld**. This involves a form of sensory deprivation, in which the **receiver** is deprived of patterned light, which encourages internal imagery. A **sender**, in a separate, acoustically isolated room, selects a **target** visual stimulus, which the receiver tries to describe through a continuous verbal commentary. Finally, the receiver has to choose one of four stimuli (one being the target) that most closely matches his/her imagery.

- The 'Ganzfeld debate', involving Honorton ('sheep') and Hyman ('goat'), resulted in a **fully automated** Ganzfeld, leaving little scope for human error or deliberate fraud. Despite this, and its use producing many significant results, the debate goes on.

- Research into **psychokinesis (PK)** involves **macro-PK** and **micro-PK** studies, **bio-PK** or **distant influence upon living systems (DMILS)**, and a **micro-electronic random event generator (REG)** or **random number generator (RNG)**.

- The history of parapsychology highlights a number of methodological issues that are relevant to psychology in general, in particular, (a) the question of the '**conclusive**' experiment, (b) the **replication problem**, (c) **publication bias** (or the '**file-drawer**' problem), (d) the **inadequacy of controls**, and (e) **experimenter effects**.

Factors underlying anomalous experience

- **Cognitive factors** include '**psychic fraud**', an unusual form of deception that refers to people's claims to possess psychic abilities (such as faith healing and psychic surgeons, psychic reading and mediumship).

- Experiments have tested the efficacy of various strategies used by fake psychics, including **misframing**, **attention** and **distraction**, **switching methods**, **controlling performing conditions**, and having ready '**outs**' in the event of things going wrong.

- Many parapsychologists have noted the often striking parallels between ESP and **perception without awareness** (PWA) (preconscious processing or subliminal perception).

- **Defensiveness** is a major **personality factor** associated with both ESP and PWA. **Extraversion** represents a psi-conducive state.

- **Biological factors** that have been investigated include **conscious awareness during anaesthesia** (**CADA**), **electrophysiological markers of non-conscious processing** (Libet), **prepulse inhibition of the startle response**, and **blindsight** (Weiskrantz).

- Numerous polls and surveys have shown that paranormal beliefs are widely held, across a variety of cultures, ages, educational achievements and religious beliefs. People believe in psi (such as **astrology**) for many different reasons, helping them to make important life decisions and make sense of certain events and experiences.

- The **cultural** significance of beliefs in the paranormal are demonstrated by **alien abduction**, which has much in common with **sleep paralysis** (a standard symptom of **narcolepsy** and often involving **hypnogogic/hypnopompic** imagery).

- A ('mere') coincidence is defined as a 'chance event' that, while improbable, doesn't require a 'special' explanation (such as ESP). In order to determine this, we need to estimate the **probability** that the event could have occurred by chance alone.

- While the probability of some events can be precisely assessed (as in cointossing), many everyday occurrences are difficult to assess in this way. Only when the probability of a chance occurrence is **extremely low** should we consider the possibility of the intervention of psi.

- Not only do people in general underestimate the frequency with which surprising events occur by chance alone, but 'sheep' are **more likely** to do so.

Belief in exceptional experience

- Varieties of **psychic healing** range from distant (prayer) healing through therapeutic touch to psychic surgery. Research since the early 1960s has demonstrated highly significant effects of healing in controlled trials with enzymes, yeasts, bacteria, cell structures in test tubes, plants, non-human animals and people.

- Explanations of these effects include (a) healing as a 'mere' **placebo**; (b) the involvement of a variety of **biological mechanisms** (such as enhanced enzyme and hormone activity, and reduced blood pressure); (c) the role of **psychological harmony**; and (d) the role of **energy exchanges** between healer and healee.

- **Out-of-body experiences** (**OBEs**) are a central feature of **near-death experiences** (**NDEs**). Detailed accounts of the latter promoted the popular view that they testify to life after death.

- Blackmore argues that NDEs tell us more about consciousness and the brain than about the afterlife. She explains them by reference to known or hypothesised **physiological** – and **cognitive** – **processes** (such as the tunnel experience in terms of the activity of the **visual cortex**, and drawing on **memory models** of reality).

- Other explanations include **expectation**, the release of **endorphins** under stress, **anoxia**, which stimulates the **temporal lobe** resulting in hallucinations, memory flashbacks, body distortions and OBEs.

- A crucial **methodological issue** concerns the **definition of death**. This has changed over the years and death is best seen as a **process** as opposed to an event.

- The **spontaneous** nature of OBEs and NDEs makes them difficult to accept as scientific evidence for the existence of psi. While they're much more common than originally thought, this might reflect their portrayal in popular culture.

Essay Questions

Theoretical and methodological issues in the study of anomalistic experience

1. Critically consider issues of pseudoscience and scientific fraud in anomalistic psychology.
(25 marks)

2a. Outline findings from studies of ESP and/or psychokinesis using the Ganzfeld technique.
(10 marks)

2b. Critically consider controversies relating to such Ganzfeld studies.   (15 marks)

Factors underlying anomalous experience

3a. Describe some cognitive and/or biological factors underlying anomalous experience.   (9 marks)

3b. Discuss the psychology of coincidence.   (16 marks)

4. 'Even if paranormal phenomena do not exist, paranormal experiences do, as surveys have shown that a considerable number of people report experiences which they interpret as paranormal' (Watt, 2001). Discuss the functions of belief in paranormal and related phenomena.
(25 marks)

Belief in exceptional experience

5. Critically consider explanations of out-of-body and near-death experiences.   (25 marks)
6. Discuss research into psychic healing and/or psychic mediumship.   (25 marks)

It should take you 40 minutes to answer each question.

A2 Unit 4

Psychological research and scientific method

11 Chapter

What's covered in this chapter?

You need to know about:

Psychological research and scientific method
For A2, you will also need to know all the material on research methods covered in AS Unit 1 (see pages 494–521). This is as follows:

Methods and techniques: knowledge and understanding of the following research methods, their advantages and weaknesses
- Experimental method including laboratory, field and natural experiments
- Studies using a correlational analysis
- Observational techniques
- Self-report techniques including questionnaire and interview
- Case studies

Investigation design
- Aims
- Hypotheses, including directional and non-directional
- Experimental design (independent groups, repeated measures and matched participants)
- Design of naturalistic observations including the development and use of behavioural categories
- Design of questionnaires and interviews
- Operationalisation of variables, including independent and dependent variables
- Pilot studies
- Control of extraneous variables
- Reliability and validity
- Awareness of the BPS Code of Ethics
- Ethical issues and ways in which psychologists deal with them
- Selection of participants and sampling techniques, including random, opportunity and volunteer sampling
- Demand characteristics and investigator effects

Data analysis and presentation
- Presentation and interpretation of quantitative data, including graphs, scattergrams and tables
- Analysis and interpretation of quantitative data
- Measures of central tendency, including median, mean and mode
- Measures of dispersion, including ranges and standard deviation

- Analysis and interpretation of correlational data; positive and negative correlations and the interpretation of correlation coefficients
- Analysis and presentation of qualitative data, including the processes involved in content analysis

In addition, at A2, you will need to:
  – understand the application of scientific method in psychology
  – design investigations
  – understand how to analyse and interpret data arising from such investigations
  – report on practical investigations

You also need to know about:

The application of the scientific method in psychology
- The major features of science – for example, replicability, objectivity
- The scientific process, including theory construction, hypothesis testing, use of empirical methods, generation of laws/principles (e.g. Popper, Kuhn)
- Validating new knowledge and the role of peer review

Designing psychological investigations
- Selection and application of appropriate research methods
- Implications of sampling strategies – for example, bias and generalising
- Issues of reliability, including types of reliability, assessment of reliability, improving reliability
- Assessing and improving validity (internal and external)
- Ethical considerations in design and conduct of psychological research

Data analysis and reporting on investigations
- Appropriate selection of graphical representations
- Probability and significance, including the interpretation of significance and Type 1 / Type 2 errors
- Factors affecting choice of statistical test, including levels of measurement
- The use of inferential analysis, including Spearman's rho, Mann-Whitney, Wilcoxon, Chi-squared
- Analysis and interpretation of qualitative data
- Conventions of reporting on psychological investigations

✔ Specification Hint

As noted above, in the 'What's covered in this chapter?' section, at A2 you also need to know all the AS material concerned with research methods. For this reason, we have included in this chapter all the AS research methods material that you should already know (see pages 493–522). The new A2 research methods material starts on page 522. Even if you gained a grade A at AS, it is worth refamiliarising yourself with the AS material before learning the A2 research methods material. Remember, in the A2 examination, the examiners can ask questions drawn from both the AS and A2 Specifications.

RESEARCH METHODS AND TECHNIQUES

There are a number of different research methods in psychology. Like the carpenter who selects the most appropriate tool for the job, psychologists choose the most appropriate method for their research. No single method is perfect or better than another. You need to know what these methods are and what their advantages and weaknesses are.

Quantitative research methods allow the numerical measurement of *how much* there is of something (i.e. the quantity). Qualitative research methods allow for the measurement of *what* something is like (i.e. the quality). An example of quantitative data would be the *number* of stressful incidents per day, whereas qualitative data would involve a *description* of these incidents.

Experimental method

The experimental method refers to a research method using random assignment of participants (see pages 513–514 for information on sampling techniques) and the manipulation of variables in order to determine cause and effect. A variable is any object, characteristic or event that changes or varies in some way. Experiments are the most widely used method in psychology.

The experimenter manipulates an independent variable (IV) to see its effect on the dependent variable (DV). The IV is the variable that's manipulated or altered by the experimenter to see its effect on the DV. The DV is the measured result of the experiment. Any change in the DV should be as a result of the manipulation of the IV. For example, alcohol consumption (IV) could be manipulated to see its effect on reaction time (the DV).

Extraneous variables are any other variables that may have an effect on the DV (see page 510). Controls are employed to prevent extraneous variables spoiling the results. Any extraneous variables that aren't controlled can become confounding variables, so called because they 'confound' (that is, confuse) the results.

There are several types of experiment, as described below.

Laboratory experiments

Here the researcher controls as many variables as possible. There's control over the 'who, what, when, where and how'. This is *usually* done in a laboratory using standardised procedures, but can be conducted anywhere provided it's in a controlled environment.

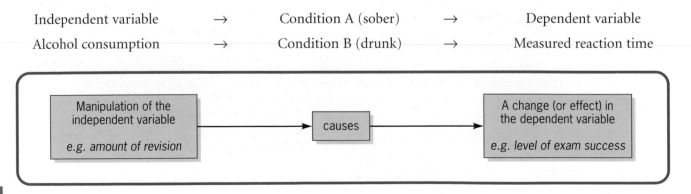

Independent variable → Condition A (sober) → Dependent variable

Alcohol consumption → Condition B (drunk) → Measured reaction time

| Manipulation of the independent variable *e.g. amount of revision* | causes | A change (or effect) in the dependent variable *e.g. level of exam success* |

Figure 11.1 The causal link between an IV and DV in an experiment

Participants should also be randomly allocated to experimental groups.

Research examples

- Bandura's (1965) bobo doll study.

- Milgram's (1963) study of destructive obedience (see Gross and Rolls, 2008).

Advantages

- **High degree of control:** experimenters can control all variables in the situation. For example, the IV and DV can be very precisely defined (or operationalised – see pages 509–510) and measured. This leads to greater accuracy and objectivity.

- **Replication:** other researchers can easily repeat the experiment and check results. This is an important factor of the experimental method.

- **Cause and effect:** it should be possible to determine the cause-and-effect relationship between the IV and DV, provided that the experiment is well designed.

- **Technical equipment:** it's easier to use complicated technical equipment in a laboratory.

- **Stronger effects outside the lab?** Laboratory experiments are often criticised for being artificial, but it may be the case that some laboratory effects are even stronger outside the lab than those recorded within it. For example, Milgram's study of destructive obedience (1963) demonstrated high levels of obedience in the lab situation, but it is likely that the effects are even stronger outside the laboratory, where obedience is associated with social pressure and a likelihood of painful sanctions from authority figures (Coolican, 2004).

Weaknesses

- **Experimenter bias:** sometimes an experimenter's expectations about the study can affect results. Participants may be influenced by these expectations (see pages 514–515).

- **Problems operationalising the IV and DV:** sometimes, in order to gain a precise measure of behaviour, the measure itself becomes too specific and doesn't relate to wider behaviour. For example, Bandura's measures of aggression involved only a very narrow range of the kind of hostile behaviour of which children are capable (Coolican, 2004).

- **Low external (ecological) validity:** the high degree of control can make the experimental situation artificial and unlike real life. As such, it may be difficult to generalise results to other settings. A laboratory setting can be a strange and intimidating place. As such, people may be overly worried by the surroundings and not act in a way that is representative of their normal everyday behaviour (see page 514).

- **Demand characteristics (Orne, 1962):** sometimes participants try to guess the purpose of the experiment and then act according to the 'demands' of the experiment. In contrast, the 'screw you' effect refers to situations where participants guess the purpose of an experiment and act in a deliberately contradictory way (see pages 510–511).

How Science Works

Practical Learning Activity 11.1: A laboratory experiment into the effects of caffeine on reaction times

It's generally believed that caffeine decreases reaction times (i.e. makes people react faster). Some studies indicate that the effect is most marked at lower doses – for example, one or two cups of coffee per day.

- Devise a laboratory experiment to test this.
- Carry out this study and write up the experiment. Include sections such as Introduction, Method (Design, Sample, Procedure, Ethical Issues), Results and Conclusion.

Field experiments

A field experiment is an experiment performed in the 'real world' rather than the laboratory. The IV is still manipulated by the experimenter and as many other variables as possible are controlled.

Research example

● Piliavin *et al.*'s (1969) New York Subway study.

Natural experiments

Here, the IV occurs naturally, it's not manipulated by the experimenter. The experimenter merely records the effect on the DV. An advantage here is that the effect of an IV can be studied where it would be unethical to deliberately manipulate it (e.g. create family stress). Strictly speaking, this is a quasi-experiment since the random allocation of participants is not possible.

Research example

● Hodges and Tizard's (1989) study of teenagers raised in orphanages.

Advantages (can apply to both field and natural experiments)

● **High ecological validity:** due to the 'real world' environment, or naturally occurring environment, results are more likely to relate to everyday behaviour and can be generalised to other settings.

● **No demand characteristics:** often, participants are unaware of the experiment, and so there are no demand characteristics.

Weaknesses

● **Less control:** it's far more difficult to control extraneous variables, either 'in the field' or in naturally occurring situations.

● **Replication:** it's difficult to *precisely* replicate field or natural experiments since the conditions will never be exactly the same again.

● **Ethics:** there are ethical issues (e.g. informed consent, deception) when participants aren't aware that they are taking part in the experiment. This applies more to field experiments, since in natural experiments the independent variable occurs naturally and isn't manipulated by the experimenter.

● **Sample bias:** since participants aren't randomly allocated to groups, there may be some sample bias.

● **Time consuming and expensive:** experiments in the real world can often take more time and involve more costs than those in the laboratory. Researchers often have to consider many other aspects of the design and how it may affect other people in the vicinity of the experiment, which they don't have to do in the comfort of their laboratory.

Studies using correlational analysis

This isn't a research method as such, but a method of data analysis. It involves measuring the strength of the relationship between two or more variables (co-variables) to see if a trend or pattern exists between them.

● A **positive correlation** is where one variable increases

Type of experiment	Variable details	Environment
Laboratory	Manipulation of IV Measure DV	Controlled
Field	Manipulation of IV Measure DV	Real life
Natural	IV occurs naturally Measure DV	Real life

Table 11.1: Summary of experimental research methods

as the other variable increases (e.g. ice cream sales increase as temperature increases).

- A **negative correlation** is where one variable increases while the other variable decreases (e.g. raincoat sales decrease as temperature increases).

- A **correlation coefficient** is a number that expresses the degree to which the two variables are related. The measurement ranges from +1 (perfect positive correlation) to -1 (perfect negative correlation). The closer the correlation to a perfect correlation, the stronger the relationship between the two variables. If there's no correlation, the result will be near to zero (0.0) (see Figure 11.10, page 520).

Research example

- Anderson's (2004) study into violent video game playing found a positive correlation with real-life violence.

Advantages

- **Allows predictions to be made:** once a correlation has been found, we can make predictions about one variable from the other (e.g. we can predict the number of ice creams sold on hot days).

- **Allows quantification of relationships:** correlations can show the strength of the relationship between two co-variables. A correlation of +0.9 means a high positive correlation; a correlation of -0.3 indicates a fairly weak negative correlation.

- **No manipulation:** correlations don't require the manipulation of behaviour, and so can be a quick and ethical method of data collection and analysis.

Weaknesses

- **Quantification problem:** it is worth noting that sometimes correlations that appear to be quite low (e.g. +0.28) can be meaningful or significant if the number of scores recorded is quite high. Conversely, with a large number of recorded scores, correlations that are quite high (e.g. +0.76) are not always stat-

How Science Works

Practical learning Activity 11.2: Positive and negative correlations

Examine the following made-up statements.
1. Older people are more forgetful.
2. Beautiful people are more successful in their careers.
3. Poorer people have a lower level of education.
4. The longer you spend revising, the less worried you become.
5. The better the teaching, the fewer the number of failures.

- Decide which of these statements are positive or negative correlations.
- Think up some other examples of positive and negative correlations.
- Try to think of some examples from research you have studied previously.

Now, imagine that a local head teacher has found research evidence in her school which suggests that larger class sizes are positively correlated to exam success.

- Try to criticise this research and think of all the arguments you might give to argue that smaller class sizes are actually of greater benefit to schoolchildren.
- Consider any extraneous or confounding variables that might have affected the head teacher's research.

istically significant or meaningful. You must be aware of this when interpreting correlation coefficient scores.

- **Cause and effect:** it cannot be assumed that one variable caused the other. Interpretation of results is made difficult since there's no cause and effect in a correlation (see Practical Learning Activity 11.3). It could be that both co-variables are influenced by some other variable(s).

- **Extraneous relationships:** other variables may influence both measured variables (e.g. most holidays are taken in the (hot?) summer and people eat ice creams on holiday). Therefore, the variable 'holiday' is related to both temperature and ice cream sales.

- **Only works for linear relationships:** correlations measure only linear (straight-line) relationships. The relationship between temperature and aggression is a *curvilinear* relationship. This would be a zero correlation, and yet there's an obvious relationship or pattern between these two variables.

How Science Works

Practical Learning Activity 11.3: Causation in a correlation

We have already stated that we cannot assume that one variable caused the second variable in a correlation and that other variables may have played a part. Try to think up some other variables that may have played a causative part in the following correlations:

- lower-income parents have more children
- older people make poorer eyewitnesses
- sales of running shoes have increased at the same rate as sales of personal computers.

Think up some hypothetical correlations and try to think of other variables that might be able to explain the link between them.

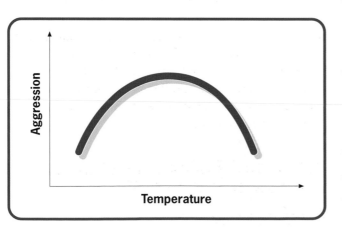

Figure 11.2 Graph showing the curvilinear relationship between temperature and aggression

Observational techniques

To some extent, most psychological studies involve some observation of behaviour, whether it be observing children playing in a school playground or observing the speed of a person's reaction in a laboratory. Observation can occur as part of a laboratory study, as in Milgram's (1963) study of destructive obedience and Bandura's (1965) study of aggression through imitation. However, when one talks of observational techniques this usually refers to a study where observation is the main research method involving the precise (objective) measurement of naturally occurring and relatively unconstrained behaviour. Moreover, the observation usually occurs in the participant's own natural environment.

There are two main types of observation.

1. **Participant observation** involves the observer becoming actively involved in the activities of the people being studied. Instead of merely observing, the psychologist can experience a more 'hands on' perspective on the people and the behaviour being observed. She or he becomes a 'participant' in the research. Participant observation can either be disclosed (people are told they are being observed) or undisclosed (participants remain unaware of being observed).

2. **Non-participant observation** involves the researcher observing the behaviour from a distance; they do not become actively involved in the behaviour to be studied.

Research examples

- Participant observation: Rosenhan's (1973) study entitled 'Being sane in insane places' (see pages 184–186 in Gross and Rolls, 2008).

- Non-participant observation: Griffiths and Parke's (2005) observational study of the effect of music in gambling environments such as casinos and amusement arcades.

The distinction between participant and non-participant observation is not always clear-cut since it may be difficult for an observer to participate fully in some behaviours (e.g. criminal activities); conversely, a non-participant observer is unlikely to have no impact whatsoever on a situation. Think of the example of a football referee. Are they a non-participant or participant observer of the match?

Figure 11.3 A football referee: a participant or non-participant observer?

✔ Specification Hint

Although there are differences between the advantages and weaknesses of participant and non-participant observation, the examiner cannot ask specifically about these types in an exam. This is because they are not specifically named in the specification. The examiner can only ask about observational techniques in general and, for this reason, we have dealt with advantages and weaknesses common to both types.

Advantages

- **High external validity:** since observed behaviour takes place in the natural environment, participants tend to behave naturally and results can usually be generalised to other settings.

- **Practical method:** can be used in situations where deliberate manipulation would be unethical or impractical (e.g. a study of soccer hooliganism). It is useful where cooperation from those being observed is unlikely and where the full social context for behaviour is needed. It's particularly useful for studying animals or children (Coolican, 2004).

- **Few demand characteristics:** participants are often unaware of the observation and so there are few demand characteristics (see page 514).

Weaknesses

- **Cause and effect:** this cannot be inferred, since the variables are only observed, not manipulated. There is also little control of extraneous variables.

- **Observer bias:** if observers know the purpose of the study, they may see what they want to see. Observers need to produce reliable results. Where there is more than one observer, the observational records of one observer can be checked or correlated against another to see if they are observing in the same way. A comparison such as this is called inter-rater reliability (*inter = across*). Sometimes one observer changes their method of observation over time. For example, the behavioural categories that they were using to do the observation at the beginning of the study may alter by the end of the study. A comparison from the start of the observation to the end of the observation would check this; this is called intra-rater reliability (*intra = within*).

- **Replication:** despite the possibility of checking for both inter- and intra-rater reliability, in practice it's often difficult to accurately check the reliability and validity (see pages 510–511) of observations, since a lack of control means conditions can never be repeated accurately.

- **Ethics:** if participants are unaware of being observed, issues of invasion of privacy and informed consent arise. If participants are informed of the study, then there is a possibility of demand characteristics.

- **Practical problems:** sometimes it is difficult to remain unobserved and there are practical problems making recordings (e.g. video/audio) of some behaviours. Furthermore, it is often difficult to categorise the observed behaviours accurately (see Practical Learning Activity 11.4).

Self-report techniques, including questionnaires and interviews

Questionnaires

Questionnaires are a written method of data collection where respondents record their own answers to a pre-

How Science Works

Practical Learning Activity 11.4: Classroom observation

Imagine you are a government inspector of psychology classes. You decide to use a non-participant observation technique.

● Outline exactly how you would observe a psychology lesson.
● Decide on the behavioural categories that you might use to measure a successful lesson. You might consider the number of times students contribute to the lesson, how frequently they take notes, their levels of engagement. How would you record these behaviours?
● Ask to observe a psychology lesson and write up your experiences.
● How successful were you at assessing a lesson?
● What would you do differently next time?

set list of questions. They're usually concerned with people's behaviour, opinions and attitudes. Two main types of question are used.

1. **Closed (fixed) questions:** responses are fixed by the researcher. They usually involve 'tick boxes' (e.g. 'yes' or 'no') or a range of fixed responses (e.g. 'always', 'usually', 'sometimes', 'never'). Such answers are easy to quantify, but restrict participants' answers.

2. **Open questions:** these allow participants to answer in their own words. They're more difficult to analyse, but allow freedom of expression and obtain greater depth.

Examples of closed and open questions:

● **Closed question:** Do you enjoy psychology? YES/NO* (*delete as appropriate).

● **Open question:** Which aspects of psychology do you enjoy and why?

✔ Specification Hint

Although there are differences between the advantages and weaknesses of closed and open-ended questionnaires, the examiner cannot ask specifically about these types in an exam. This is because they are not named in the specification. The examiner can ask only about questionnaires in general and, for this reason, we have dealt with advantages and weaknesses common to both types of question.

Advantages

● **Quick and cheap:** a large amount of information can be gathered in a relatively short period of time. As such, they're quick and cheap in comparison to other methods.

● **Large samples:** questionnaires can be completed without the researcher present. Postal questionnaires can be used to gain very large samples for the cost of a stamp.

● **Quantitative and qualitative analysis:** it's easy to statistically analyse 'closed' questions. Answers can be pre-coded on questionnaires for computer input and instant analysis. Open-ended questions provide richer, fuller detail and the respondent does not feel constrained in his or her answers.

● **Replication:** since questionnaires use standardised questions, it's fairly easy to replicate studies. This is particularly true of questionnaires that use closed questions.

Weaknesses

● **Misunderstanding:** designing a questionnaire is a highly skilled job. Participants may misunderstand or misinterpret questions. For example, what do you mean when you say you 'usually' do your homework? There are problems with the use of complex technical terms, emotive language and leading questions (see the section on Loftus and Palmer, 1974).

Figure 11.4 Social desirability: in the 1980s voters were reluctant to admit that they were Conservatives – but the Tories kept on winning!

- **Biased samples:** questionnaires are suitable only for people who are literate, and willing and able to spend time filling them in. It may be that certain groups of people are more willing to find the time to fill in questionnaires.

- **Low response rates:** some questionnaires have been known to obtain as little as a 5 per cent return rate. Might these 5 per cent of people differ from the other 95 per cent of the population who do not fill in the questionnaire?

- **Superficial issues:** questionnaires, particularly those that predominantly use closed questions, aren't suitable for more sensitive issues that require detailed understanding.

- **Social desirability:** participants may present themselves in a positive light. Indeed, they may lie on particularly sensitive issues (e.g. to do with sexual behaviour).

Interviews

Interviews involve researchers asking questions in a face-to-face situation. They can be very different but there are two broad types.

1. **Structured (or formal) interviews:** a questionnaire is read to participants and the interviewer writes down their responses. These interviews are identical for all participants and tend to involve more simple, quantitative questions. Interviewers don't need a lot of training, since they are fairly easy to conduct.

2. **Unstructured (or informal) interviews:** these are less controlled and involve an informal discussion on a particular topic. However, while the topic is predetermined the direction of the interview isn't. This allows the interviewer to explore the areas of greatest interest. Friendly rapport between the interviewer and respondent is important in order to gain the required level of detail and understanding. Interviewers need considerable training and expertise to conduct such interviews.

Interviews can combine these two types in **semi-structured interviews**.

✔ Specification Hint

Although there are differences between the advantages and weaknesses of structured and unstructured interviews, the examiner cannot ask specifically about these types in an exam. This is because they are not named in the Specification. The examiner can ask only about interviews in general and, for this reason, we have dealt with advantages and weaknesses common to both types of question.

Advantages

- **Complex issues:** complicated or sensitive issues are best dealt with in face-to-face interviews. This is particularly true of unstructured interviews, where a natural flow of conversation is likely to make the respondent feel more relaxed and will thus enhance the quality of the answers.

- **Ease misunderstandings:** any ambiguity or misunderstanding can be clarified within the interview. Interviewers can follow up on any interesting answers and explore them more fully. Questions can be adapted to the individual needs of the respondents, and this should make the interview process more productive for all concerned.

- **Data analysis:** the variety and flexibility of interviews allows for the analysis of both quantitative and qualitative data. Structured interviews in particular produce data that can be analysed in quantitative form fairly easily.

- **Replication:** the more standardised or structured the interview, the easier it is to replicate. Unstructured interviews are less easy to replicate but it should still be possible for other researchers to review the data produced.

Weaknesses

- **Interviewer effects:** interviewers may inadvertently bias the respondent's answers. This could even occur because of the interviewer's appearance. For example, would a white person be less willing to admit to being racist to a black interviewer? Interviews are subject to demand characteristics and social desirability bias.

- **Interview training:** with structured interviews there is less training required. However, a great deal of skill is required to carry out unstructured interviews, par-

ticularly those concerned with sensitive issues. It is not always easy to obtain highly trained interviewers.

- **Ethical issues:** these can arise when participants don't know the true purpose of the interview. There is also a danger that participants may reveal more than they wish to.

- **Respondent answers:** respondents may be unable to put into words their true feelings about a particular topic. For obvious reasons, this applies mainly to structured interviews.

Case studies

A case study is the in-depth, detailed investigation of an individual or group. It would usually include biographical details as well as details of behaviour or experiences of interest. Case studies allow a researcher to examine a particular individual in far greater depth than experimental methods of investigation. So-called qualitative methods tend to be followed that are not easily quantified through the use of statistics. Explanations of behaviour are outlined in written descriptive ways. Subjective reports are often used. These outline what the person feels or believes about a particular issue. Bromley (1986) has argued that case studies are 'the bedrock of scientific investigation' and

Figure 11.5 In this unstructured interview, the interviewer has limited opportunity to ask the right questions

How Science Works

Practical Learning Activity 11.5: Questionnaire or interview?

Choose a topic to research. For example, you might want to investigate people's views on the monarchy or the use of animals in psychological research.

- Half the class could investigate the topic using a questionnaire, with the other half using interviews. Compare the results of the two groups.
- Discuss the advantages and weaknesses of each method for that particular research topic.

that psychologists' preoccupation with experimental procedures has led to a neglect of this area. Coolican (2004) cites a clever example in defence of individual case studies, or the single participant design as he terms it. If only one rock was collected from the moon for study, would scientists discard it claiming that it would be unlikely to be representative of other rocks that exist on the moon?

Advantages

- **Rich detail:** case studies can help to shed light on both specific and general psychological issues. For example, Freud developed his psychoanalytic theory of human development based on his own patients' case histories. Case studies have the advantage of providing greater depth and understanding about an individual, and acknowledge and celebrate human diversity. Because case studies are about 'real, genuine people' they have a special feeling of truth about them.

- **The only possible method to use:** case studies allow psychologists to study behaviours or experiences that are so unique that they could not have been studied in any other way. These case studies allow the researcher to explore possibilities in human behaviour that may not previously have been considered or thought possible.

- **Useful for theory contradiction:** one case study may be enough to contradict a theory. The case study of Genie (Curtiss, 1977) helped to question the evidence regarding critical stages of language development.

Weaknesses

- **Unreliable:** case studies are criticised for being unreliable (no two case studies are alike) and therefore results cannot easily be generalised to other people. The question arises as to whether we do always *have* to find out universal truths of behaviour.

- **Researcher bias:** a further criticism levelled at case studies is that sometimes the researcher conducting the study may be biased in their interpretations or reporting method. This 'subjectivity' means that it could be difficult to determine factual information

✔ Assessment Check 11.1

1. Discuss ONE advantage and one weakness of field experiments. (3 + 3 marks)
2. Outline ONE difference between a laboratory and natural experiment. (3 marks)
3. Give ONE criticism of studies that use correlational analysis. (2 marks)
4. Explain ONE weakness of using a questionnaire to collect data. (2 marks)
5. Explain ONE advantage of using a case study research method. (2 marks)

from researcher inference. An awareness of this does not detract from the stories that emerge. Indeed, much of the rich detail from first-hand accounts would not have been possible had the researcher(s) not formed warm and friendly relationships with the main protagonists.

Research examples

- S.B. (Gregory and Wallace, 1963), who was blind almost from birth but recovered his sight at the age of 52.

- Phineas Gage, who blew a six-foot metal bar through his head and yet lived to tell the tale.

For more details of these and other cases, see Rolls (2005).

INVESTIGATION DESIGN

Aims

An **aim** is a reasonably precise statement of *why* a study is taking place (e.g. to investigate the effect of alcohol on reaction times). It should include what's being studied and what the study is trying to achieve.

Hypotheses, including directional and non-directional

A **hypothesis** is much more precise than an aim and predicts what's expected to happen (e.g. alcohol consumption will significantly affect reaction times). Hypotheses are testable statements. There are two types.

1. **Experimental** (or **alternative**) **hypothesis**: this predicts significant differences in the dependent variable (the variable that is measured) as a result of manipulation of the independent variable (the variable that the experimenter alters). It predicts that any difference or effect found will not be due to chance (e.g. there will be a significant difference in reaction times as a result of alcohol consumption). (Note: the term 'experimental hypothesis' should be used only with the experimental method. For all other research methods, 'alternative hypothesis' should be used.)

2. **Null hypothesis**: this is the 'hypothesis of no differences'. It predicts that the IV will not affect the DV. It predicts that results will simply be due to chance (e.g. there will be no (significant) difference in reaction times as a result of alcohol consumption). (Note: the inclusion of the word 'significant' in the null hypothesis is still being argued about by psychologists.)

One of these hypotheses will be supported by the findings.

Specification Hint

The term 'null hypothesis' is not actually mentioned in the AS specification, so the examiner could not ask a question asking you to identify the null hypothesis. However, it plays an important part in scientific research and therefore we felt it was important to include it here.

There are also two types of experimental (or alternative) hypotheses.

1. **Directional** (also called 'one-tailed'): this states the direction of the results (e.g. there will be a significant *slowing* in the speed of reaction times as a result of alcohol consumption). It is called directional because it states one direction in which the results can go.

2. **Non-directional** (also called 'two-tailed'): this states that there will be a difference, but doesn't state the direction of the results (e.g. there will be a significant *difference* in the speed of reaction times as a result of alcohol consumption); in this example, reaction times could either get quicker or slower, and so they are referred to as 'non-directional' hypotheses.

Directional hypotheses are used when previous research evidence suggests that it's possible to make a clear prediction, or when you're replicating a previous study that has also used a directional hypothesis.

EXPERIMENTAL DESIGN

There are three main types of experimental design, each of which is described below.

Repeated measures design

The same participants are tested in the two (or more) conditions. Each participant *repeats* the study in each condition.

Advantages

- **Group differences:** the same person is measured in both conditions; there are *no* individual differences between the groups. Extraneous variables are kept constant (controlled) between the conditions.

- **Fewer participants:** half as many participants are needed with repeated measures when compared to independent measures design. If you need 10 scores, then 10 participants undertaking both conditions will suffice with repeated measures. With independent groups design, you'd need 20 participants, 10 for each condition. It's not always that easy to get participants for psychology experiments and finding more participants is always time consuming.

Weaknesses

- **Order effects:** when participants repeat a task, results can be affected by **order effects**. On the second task, participants either:
  (a) do worse due to fatigue or boredom, or
  (b) improve through practice in the first condition.

This can be controlled by *counterbalancing,* where half the participants do Condition A followed by Condition B, and the other half do Condition B and then Condition A. This counterbalancing procedure is known as 'ABBA', for obvious reasons.

- **Lost participants:** if a participant drops out of the study, they are 'lost' from both conditions.

- **Guess aim of study:** by participating in all conditions of the experiment, it's far more likely that the participant may guess the purpose of the study. This may make demand characteristics more common.

- **Takes more time:** a gap may need to be given between conditions, perhaps to try to counter the effects of fatigue or boredom. If participants are taking part in both conditions of the experiment, different materials need to be produced for each condition. In a memory test, for example, you could not simply use the same list of words for both conditions. Inevitably these issues involve more time and money.

Independent groups design

Different participants are used in each of the conditions. Each group of participants is *independent* of the other. Participants are usually **randomly allocated** to each condition to try to balance out any differences (see the section on 'Sampling', below).

Advantages

- **Order effects:** there are *no* order effects.

- **Demand characteristics:** participants take part in one condition only. This means there's less chance of participants guessing the purpose of the study.

- **Time saved:** both sets of participants can be tested at the same time. This saves time and money.

Weaknesses

- **More participants:** with participants in only one condition, you need twice as many participants as for repeated measures design.

- **Group differences:** any differences between the groups may be due to individual differences that are distinct from the IV. This can be minimised by the random allocation of participants to each group.

Matched pairs design

Different, but similar, participants are used in each of the conditions. Participants are matched across the groups on any characteristics judged to be important for that particular study. These are typically age, gender and ethnicity. Identical (monozygotic) twins are the perfect matched pair at birth since they share identical genetic characteristics. Later in life, identical twins are still likely to be closely matched on many important characteristics, even in cases where they have been reared apart.

Advantages (see also independent groups design)

- **Group differences:** participant variables are more closely matched between conditions than in independent groups design.

Weaknesses (see also independent groups design)

- **Matching is difficult:** it's impossible to match *all* variables between participants. The one variable missed might be vitally important.

- **Time consuming:** it takes a long time to accurately match participants on *all* variables. This task can become almost a research study in itself!

✔ Specification Hint

You'll notice that many of the weaknesses of one sort of experimental design are advantages of other experimental designs. For example, a weakness of independent groups design is likely to be an advantage of repeated measures design.

How Science Works

Practical Learning Activity 11.6: Summary of the advantages and weaknesses of experimental designs

Devise a table (using the template below for guidance) and complete it as thoroughly as you can. In the final column, consider alternative designs or techniques you might use to overcome some of the weaknesses noted in the previous column.

Design	Advantages	Weaknesses	Possible remedy?
Independent groups			
Repeated measures			
Matched pairs			

Once completed, you *must* learn this table.

Design of naturalistic observations, including the development and use of behavioural categories

We have already noted what we mean by naturalistic observation, and the advantages and weaknesses of this research method (see pages 498–499). One difficulty with naturalistic observations involves the development and use of appropriate behavioural categories. There are several ways that data can be gathered in a naturalistic observation. These include the use of visual recordings (video or still), audio recordings or 'on-the-spot' note taking using previously agreed rating scales or coding categories. The use of video or audio recordings tends to result in later analysis back in the lab, using coding categories.

Behavioural categories

Observers have to agree on a grid or coding sheet on which to record the behaviour they wish to study. The behavioural categories chosen will depend on the subject matter under study. For example, if observers

are interested in the effect of age and sex on the speed of car diving, they might want to develop behavioural categories such as those shown in the table below.

Rather than writing a detailed description of all behaviour observed, it is often easier to code or rate behaviour according to a previously agreed scale. Coding might simply involve numbers (such as age of driver) or letters to describe participant characteristics (such as M = male) or observed behaviours (such as T = talking, M-P = using mobile phone). Observed behaviour can also be rated on a structured scale (such as 1–5 on a scale of 'safe driving').

In practice, it is difficult to achieve standardisation between the different observers, and considerable training is required before the actual observational sessions occur. Checks that all observers are coding behaviour in the same way ensure inter-observer reliability. One way to assess inter-observer reliability is to conduct a correlation of all the observers' scores. If there is a high agreement (or correlation) between observers then it is clear that they are observing and categorising the behaviours in the same way. We

Driver	Sex?	Age? (estimate)	Number of passengers?	Observed behaviour	Type of car?	Speed? (estimate km per hour)	Safe driving rating? 1 = very unsafe 5 = very safe
A	M	55	0	M-P	Saloon	40	2
B	F	21	2	T	Hatch	30	5
C							
D etc.							

Observed behaviour code:
D = Distracted
T = Talking
M-P = Using mobile phone
... and so on

Table 11.2: Example of a Behavioural category table related to driving behaviour

How Science Works

Practical Learning Activity 11.7: Investigating flirting behaviour

Let's assume you wish to investigate whether people flirt with other people of roughly the same level of attractiveness as themselves.

● Devise an observational study using appropriate behavioural categories to examine this. You would need to have some categories to operationalise flirting behaviour and some way of assessing levels of attractiveness.
● Should you consider 'non-verbal' or only 'verbal' flirting?
● You could conduct the observation in any place where you consider flirting occurs – at a café, a party, the canteen, the classroom and so on.
● Always ensure that you do not breach any ethical guidelines associated with psychological research and check that the research method is appropriate with a friend or your teacher. The first rule of observations is to stay safe and follow the ethical guidelines.
● Record your results and feed them back to the rest of the class.

The UK Social Issues Research Centre at Oxford has a fascinating website on the subject of flirting, which is worth a look: http://www.sirc.org/publik/flirt.html.

cannot be sure that they are observing behaviour *correctly*, but we can be sure they are doing it *consistently* as a group (Coolican, 2004).

Design of questionnaires

With some questionnaires suffering from a response rate of as little as 5 per cent, it is essential that a questionnaire is well designed. There are a number of essential factors in questionnaire design.

- **Aims:** knowing exactly what the aim of the research is should help the questionnaire design. Determining the use of any information gained will ensure that only questions that address these aims are asked.

- **Length:** the longer the questionnaire, the more likely people will not complete it. Questionnaires should be short and to the point. Any superfluous questions must be deleted.

- **Advice:** when designing a questionnaire, advice should be sought from experts in the field. Examples of questionnaires that have proved successful in the past should be used as a basis for the questionnaire design.

- **Statistical analysis:** even at the design stage, the statistical analysis of the questionnaire responses should be considered. If a question is not going to be analysed, then it should be omitted.

- **Presentation:** looks matter! Questionnaires should look professional, include clear and concise instructions and, if sent through the post, should be in an envelope that doesn't immediately signify 'junk mail'! Spaces should be left in the design of each page for respondents to include comments to questions as they see fit.

- **Question order:** it is useful to start with some simple factual biographical questions before moving on to more probing questions. However, the first questions also need to be interesting enough to keep the respondents engaged while completing the rest of the questionnaire. It is usually best to put the essential questions in the first half of the questionnaire since respondents often send them back half completed.

- **Question formulation:** questions should be simple,

to the point and easily understood. In order to avoid ambiguity, complicated terms should be avoided. Questions must probe only one dimension. For example, a question that asks 'Do you like the content and design of this book?' is poorly phrased. If a respondent answers 'yes', we cannot be sure if they like the content, the design or both.

- **Incentives:** offering an incentive for questionnaire completion can help to provide additional motivation to respondents. It should also be extremely convenient for respondents to return the questionnaire. A pre-paid envelope is often used to achieve this.

- **Pilot study:** a test of the questionnaire should be done on people who can provide detailed and honest feedback on all aspects of the questionnaire design.

- **Measurement scales:** some questionnaires use measurement scales in order to assess psychological characteristics or attitudes. These often involve statements on which respondents rate their level of agreement (or disagreement). For example:

Rate your level of agreement with the following statement:

'The prime minister is doing a good job'

1	-	2	-	3	-	4	-	5
strongly agree		agree		undecided		disagree		strongly disagree

Usually, there are a number of statements on a particular topic and the answers to all these statements would be combined to determine a single score of attitude strength. There are a few problems with this approach. First, it isn't always easy for respondents to judge their answer and many respondents choose the middle score (in this case 'undecided'). When this happens it is impossible to know whether they have no opinion on the subject or cannot decide between their attitudes in both directions. Perhaps the best known of these attitude scales is the Likert scale.

Design of interviews

The first decision when designing an interview is whether to choose a structured interview (where every participant answers the same questions) or an unstructured interview (where different questions on the general topic are asked) or indeed some combination of both. We have already discussed the relative merits of these approaches (see pages 501–502). There is also the decision regarding the use of 'open' and 'closed' questions.

An important factor in the design of interviews is to consider who will be the interviewer. Decisions as to the most appropriate type of interviewer can depend on what type of person is being interviewed, but there are a number of general interpersonal variables that might be considered. These include the following.

- **Gender and age:** several studies have demonstrated that the sex and age of the interviewer affect the answers of respondents when the topic is of a sensitive sexual nature (Wilson *et al.*, 2002), but these effects are less obvious with less personal topics.

- **Ethnicity:** perhaps due to cultural upbringing, sometimes interviewers have more difficulty interviewing people drawn from a different ethnic group to themselves. Word *et al.* (1974) found white participants spent 25 per cent less time interviewing black job applicants than they did white applicants.

- **Personal characteristics and adopted role:** some people are just easier to get on with than others! Interviewers can also adopt different roles within the interview setting. Use of formal language, accent and appearance (e.g. clothing) can also affect how someone comes across to the interviewee.

How Science Works

Practical Learning Activity 11.8: Questionnaire design

With a partner, decide on a topic that you wish to investigate. Perhaps you might research people's views of the fox-hunting ban, car choice preferences, favourite advertising campaigns or an assessment of government performance.

- Devise two versions of a questionnaire that investigates your chosen topic. One version should include examples of poor questionnaire design and the other should encompass good design.
- Annotate on the questionnaire the reasons why one version is superior to the other.

Interviewer training is an essential factor in successful interviewing. Interviewers need to listen appropriately and learn when and when not to speak. Non-verbal communication is also important in helping to relax the interviewee so that they will give more natural answers. More difficult or probing questions about feelings or emotions are usually best left to the end of the interview, whereas initial questions are better for ascertaining factual information.

How Science Works

Practical Learning Activity 11.9: The preferred interviewer?

- Try to make a list of various factors that you believe might alter an interviewee's response to questions.
- Imagine that you are carrying out research into the following topics and describe the kind of interviewer that you would want to conduct the interviews. State whether you would favour structured or unstructured interviews and explain your choice:
  (a) post-natal depression
  (b) football fan rivalry
  (c) men's role in the upbringing of children
  (d) children's experiences of primary school
  (e) drivers' views of speed cameras
  (f) chocolate bar preferences.

Operationalisation of variables, including independent (IV) and dependent variables (DV)

The term '**operationalisation**' means being able to define variables simply and easily in order to manipulate them (IV) and measure them (DV). Sometimes, this is very easily done. For example, if we were investigating the effect of alcohol consumption on reaction times we could 'operationalise' the IV as the number of alcohol units consumed and the DV could be the speed of response to a flashing light. However, on other occasions this is more difficult. For example, how would you 'operationalise' anger or stress levels? There isn't always a 'best way' of operationalising complex variables. The researcher has to make a judgement as to whether they're actually measuring the variables they hope to be measuring, and present their arguments to support their decision. A major problem with the operationalisation of complex variables is that they often only measure *one* aspect of the variable.

Both IV and DV need to be 'operationalised' accurately and objectively to maintain the integrity of any research study. Without accurate operationalisation, results may not be reliable or valid, and certainly cannot be checked or replicated.

Pilot studies

These are small-scale 'practice' investigations, where researchers can check all aspects of their research. Changes to the design, method, analysis and so on can be made in the light of this. Pilot studies should improve the quality of the research, help avoid unnecessary work, and save time and money. Participants may be able to suggest appropriate changes for the real study. For example, participants may admit that they guessed the purpose of the study and acted accordingly (demand characteristics).

The control of extraneous variables

In any experiment, the IV is manipulated and the DV is measured. It's assumed that the IV causes any change or effect in the DV. However, there can be other variables that may affect the DV. These are called **extraneous variables**.

Extraneous variables must be carefully and systematically controlled so they don't vary across any of the experimental conditions or, indeed, between participants. When designing an experiment, researchers should consider three main areas where extraneous variables may arise.

1. **Participant variables**: participants' age, intelligence, personality and so on should be controlled across the different groups taking part.

2. **Situational variables**: the experimental setting and surrounding environment must be controlled. This may even include the temperature or noise effects.

3. **Experimenter variables**: the personality, appearance and conduct of the researcher. Any change in these across conditions might affect the results. For example, would a female experimenter have recorded lower levels of obedience in Milgram's obedience to authority studies (see pages 157–161 in Gross and Rolls, 2008).

Extraneous variables aren't a problem unless they're not controlled. If they aren't carefully controlled then they may adversely affect or confound the results. They may systematically vary from one condition to another. If this happens we can no longer be sure whether any change in the DV is solely due to the manipulation of the IV or due to the presence of these other 'changing variables'. If this happens, they're called **confounding variables**. The presence of confounding variables minimises the value of any results and are a serious problem.

For example, if researchers wished to investigate the effect of background music (Condition 1) or silence (Condition 2) on homework performance using two classes, they'd have to control a number of possible extraneous variables. These might include age, homework difficulty and so on. If these were all successfully controlled, then the results would probably be worthwhile. However, if the researchers discovered that those in Condition 1 were considerably brighter than those in Condition 2, then intelligence would be acting as a confounding variable. The researchers could no longer be sure whether any differences in homework performance were due to the presence of the music or due to intelligence levels. Results would be confounded and worthless.

Reliability and validity

Researchers try to produce results that are both reliable and valid. If results are reliable, they're said to be *consistent*. If a study was repeated using the same method, design and measurements, you'd expect to get similar results. If this occurs, the results can be described as reliable.

Reliability in science is essential. If results are unreliable, they cannot be trusted and so will be ignored. However, results can be reliable (i.e. consistent) but still not be accurate. Sometimes measuring instruments may be reliably producing inaccurate results. You may feel this is the case when you consistently get poor marks for your psychology homework: the teacher marks reliably but inaccurately.

Research results must also measure what they're supposed to be measuring (i.e. **validity**). If they do this and they're accurate, they're said to be valid. In effect, the measures can be described as 'true'. For example, is your teacher measuring your work according to exam board guidelines? If not, then their marking may be reliable but not valid.

It's possible to test both reliability and validity, as described below.

- **Internal reliability**: whether a test is consistent within itself. For example, a set of scales should measure the same weight between 50 and 100 grams as between 150 and 200 grams.

- **External reliability**: whether a test measures consistently over time. An IQ (intelligence) test should produce roughly the same measure for the same participant at different time intervals. This is called the test–retest method. Obviously, you'd have to ensure that participants don't remember the answers from their previous test.

- **Internal validity**: whether the results are valid (see above) and can be directly attributed to the manipulation of the IV. Results are internally valid if they've not been affected by any confounding variables. Are the results valid *within* the confines of the experimental setting? Various characteristics are required in order for an experiment to be internally valid. These are:
  (a) no investigator effects (see page 514)
  (b) no demand characteristics
  (c) use of standardised instructions
  (d) use of a random sample (see page 513).

- **External (or ecological) validity**: whether the results are valid *beyond* the confines of the experimental setting. Can the results be generalised to the wider population or to different settings or different historical times? It's difficult to test whether a study has high external validity. It often only becomes clear when research findings are found to either apply or not apply to different situations. Field and natural experiments, and naturalistic observations, are usually regarded as being high in external validity. This is because the results can more easily be generalised to other real-life settings. Milgram's obedience experiments have low external validity on all three counts outlined above. The sample was predominantly male (cannot be generalised to females); it involved an artificial setting (Yale University laboratory), and it took place in a different historical time (1960s) to today. Bearing this in mind, we can question whether the results are still valid today.

Awareness of the BPS Code of Ethics and the ways in which psychologists deal with ethics

High-quality research should involve good ethical practice. Ethics should be of paramount importance and before any psychological work is conducted its ethical implications should be considered. In addition to formal professional ethical guidelines, most research institutions, such as universities, have their own ethical committees, which meet to consider all research projects before they commence. The British Psychological Society (BPS) publishes a Code of Ethics that all psychologists should follow (BPS 2007). The informal basis of the code is 'do unto others as you would be done by'. The Code includes the following information.

- **Informed consent**: whenever possible, the investigator should inform all participants of the objectives of the investigation. Parental consent should be obtained in the case of children (under 16 years). In addition, consent should also be obtained from children who are old enough to understand the study.

- **Avoidance of deception**: the withholding of information or the misleading of participants is unacceptable if the participants are likely to object or show unease once debriefed. Intentional deception of the participants over the purpose and general nature of the investigation should be avoided whenever possible. Participants should never be deliberately misled without extremely strong scientific or medical justification. However, there may be occasions where some deception is unavoidable. There are a number of possible ways to try to deal with the problem of deception.
  (a) **Presumptive consent**: this could be gained from people of a similar background to the participants in the study. If they state that they'd have been willing to participate, it's likely that you'll not upset the actual participants (too much).
  (b) **Prior general consent**: this involves participants agreeing to being deceived without knowing how they will be deceived. This can be done some time before the start of the research. Of course participants might suspect deception and this might affect the results, but at least they would have given a form of consent to participate in the study.

(c) **Retrospective consent**: this involves asking participants for consent after they have participated in the study. Of course, a major problem here is that they may not agree to it and yet they have already taken part!

If deception is used, participants should be told immediately afterwards and given the chance to withhold their data from the study. Before conducting such a study, the investigator has a special responsibility to:

(a) determine that alternative procedures avoiding deception are not available

(b) ensure that the participants are provided with sufficient information at the earliest stage

(c) consult appropriately upon the way that the withholding of information or deliberate deception will be received.

● **Adequate briefing/debriefing**: all relevant details of the study should be explained to participants both before and after the study. The debrief is particularly important if deception has been used. Participants should leave the study feeling the same (or better) about themselves as when they started the study. Debriefing does not provide a justification for any unethical aspects of the procedure.

● **Protection of participants**: investigators have a primary responsibility to protect participants from physical and mental harm during the investigation. Normally, the risk of harm must be no greater than in ordinary life (i.e. participants should not be exposed to risks greater than, or in addition to, those encountered in their normal lifestyles).

● **Right to withdraw**: participants should always be aware that they can leave the study at any time, regardless of whether or not any payment or inducement has been offered. This can be particularly difficult to implement during observations. Participants should also be aware that they can withdraw their data at any point in the future.

● **Confidentiality**: participants' data should be treated as confidential and not disclosed to anyone, unless a different arrangement has been agreed in advance. Numbers should be allocated immediately, and used instead of names, and these should be used throughout by the research team and in any subsequent published articles. It's easy to confuse confidentiality with anonymity. Confidentiality means that data can be traced back to names,

Research method	Ethical issues
Laboratory experiments	● Participants *feel pressure* to act in a particular way ● Reluctance of participants to exercise their *right to withdraw* ● Experimental situation can be *stressful*
Field/natural experiments	● *Informed consent* is difficult to obtain ● Participants are unlikely to know of the *right to withdraw* ● *Debriefing* is difficult
Observations	● If participants do not know they are being observed, there are issues of *informed consent, confidentiality* and *invasion of privacy*
Correlational analysis	● Interpretation of results: the public may *interpret correlations incorrectly*
Questionnaires/interviews	● *Confidentiality* must be maintained ● *Right to withhold information* on embarrassing topics
Case studies	● *Issues of confidentiality* and *invasion of privacy*

Table 11.3: Summary of ethical issues with different research methods

whereas anonymous data cannot, since no names are collected by the research team. Confidential data collection is preferable in cases where participants might be followed up later.

- **Observational research:** observations should only be made in public places where people might expect to be seen by strangers.

- **Giving advice:** during research, an investigator may obtain evidence of psychological or physical problems of which a participant is, apparently, unaware. In such a case, the investigator has a responsibility to inform the participant if she or he believes that by not doing so the participant's future well-being may be endangered.

- **Colleagues:** investigators share responsibility for the ethical treatment of research participants with their collaborators, assistants, students and employees. A psychologist who believes that another psychologist or investigator may be conducting research that is not in accordance with the ethical principles should encourage that investigator to re-evaluate the research.

Before any research is conducted, psychologists must seek peer guidance, consult likely participants for their views, follow the BPS Code of Ethics, consider alternative research methodologies, establish a cost/benefit analysis of both short-term and long-term consequences, assume responsibility for the research, and gain approval from any ethical committees that monitor their research. If, during the research process, it becomes clear that there are negative consequences as a result of the research, the research should be stopped and every effort should be made to correct for these adverse consequences. Any researcher that has ethical concerns about a colleague should contact them in the first instance, and if their concerns are not allayed they should then contact the BPS.

The selection of participants, and sampling techniques

Psychological studies usually involve **samples** drawn from larger **populations**. Sampling is essential to avoid the need to study entire populations. The selected sample should be **representative** of this wider population. Representative samples *represent* the target population and should share (some of) the same important characteristics. It's called a **target population** because this is the group of people whom the researcher is hoping to *target* or generalise the results to. In general, the larger the sample, the better it is. However, the larger the sample, the more costly or time consuming it is, too. Psychologists use a number of sampling techniques to try to obtain unbiased samples; some of these are described below.

- **Random sampling:** this is the best-known method. It's where every member of the population has an equal chance of being selected. The easiest way to do this is to place all names from the target population in a hat and draw out the required sample number. Computer programs can also generate random lists. This will result in a sample *selected* in an unbiased way. However, it can still result in a biased sample. For example, if ten boys' and ten girls' names were placed in a hat, there is a (small) chance that the first ten drawn from the hat could be boys' names. Selection would have been unbiased, but the sample would still be biased. A special form of random sampling involves the random allocation of participants to different conditions in independent groups design (see page 505).

How Science Works

Practical Learning Activity 11.10: Milgram and ethical issues

Review Milgram's (1963) Study of Destructive Obedience and consider his procedure in the light of the ethical issues in the BPS Guidelines.

- Which guidelines did Milgram break?
- Could he have conducted the study in a different way? Outline some suggestions.
- Why couldn't he have actually broken the BPS Guidelines at the time of his research?

Take a look at http://www.sbg.ac.at/kriterion/documents/14/14patry.pdf for more details on the ethical issues concerned with Milgram (Patry, 2001).

Evaluation of random sampling

✔ The sample is likely to be representative and therefore results can be generalised to the wider population.

✘ It's sometimes difficult to get details of the wider population in order to select the sample.

Evaluation of opportunity and volunteer sampling

✔ The easiest, most practical and cheapest methods to ensure large samples.

✘ The sample is likely to be biased in some (important) way. Thus the findings may not be generalised to the wider population. Volunteers may be more motivated and thus perform differently from randomly selected participants. Bauman (1973) found different results on reported sexual knowledge, attitudes and behaviour of undergraduate students dependent on whether they were willing or non-willing volunteers.

● **Opportunity sampling:** involves selecting participants who are readily available and willing to take part. This could simply involve asking anybody who's passing. A surprising number of university research studies (75 per cent) use undergraduates as participants simply for the sake of convenience (Sear, 1986).

● **Volunteer sampling:** involves people volunteering to participate. They select themselves as participants, often by replying to adverts. This sampling method was used by Milgram (1963) in his Destructive Obedience Study.

Demand characteristics

Any social interaction affects people's behaviour. Conducting research is no different. It doesn't take place in a 'social vacuum', and involves some interaction between the researcher and the participant. Such interaction can therefore affect the research findings.

Orne (1962) believed that there are many features in research studies that enable the participants to guess what the study is about and what is expected of them. These **demand characteristics** can involve participants:

● guessing the purpose of the research and trying to please the researcher by giving the 'right' results

● guessing the purpose of the research and trying to annoy the researcher by giving them the wrong results; this is called the '**screw you**' **effect** (for obvious reasons!)

● acting unnaturally out of nervousness for fear of being thought 'abnormal'

● acting unnaturally in order to 'look good' (**social desirability bias**).

We've already noted the effect of demand characteristics in different research methods (see pages 494–502).

A technique that reduces demand characteristics is the **single-blind procedure**. This is where participants have no idea which condition of the study they're in. In drug trials, they wouldn't know whether they're being given the real drug or the placebo drug ('sugar pill').

Investigator effects

Investigators may inadvertently influence the results in their research. This can occur in a number of ways, some of which are described below.

● Certain physical characteristics of the investigator may influence results. Such factors might include age, ethnicity, appearance, attractiveness and so on. For example, male participants may be unwilling to admit their sexist views to a female researcher.

● Other less obvious personal characteristics of the investigator, such as accent, tone of voice or non-verbal communication (eye contact, smiling), can influence results. Participants may pick up on this and not act as they normally would.

- The investigator may also be biased in their interpretation of the data. This, of course, should never be deliberate. It is claimed that Burt (1955) made up some of his evidence on the influence of heredity on intelligence.

A technique that reduces investigator effects is the **double-blind procedure**. This is where neither the participant nor the investigator knows which condition the participant is in. They are both 'blind' to this knowledge. This prevents the investigator from inadvertently giving the participant clues as to which condition they are in and therefore reduces demand characteristics. (Obviously, there is an investigator in overall charge who is aware of the allocation to conditions.)

✔ Assessment Check 11.2

1. A researcher wanted to investigate if age affects forgetting. Write a suitable directional hypothesis for such a study. (2 marks)
2. Explain why a directional hypothesis might be chosen. (2 marks)
3. Outline ONE advantage and ONE weakness of using a repeated measures design. (2 + 2 marks)
4. Explain how ONE weakness of independent groups design could be dealt with. (2 marks)
5. Outline any TWO factors that researchers need to consider in the design of a questionnaire. (2 + 2 marks)
6. A researcher wished to investigate the effect of diet on intelligence. Outline ONE possible extraneous variable that she should consider when designing such a study. (2 marks)
7. What is meant by the term reliability? (2 marks)
8. Outline ONE way of assessing reliability. (2 marks)
9. Outline the purpose of a pilot study. (3 marks)
10. Describe ONE ethical issue in psychological research and outline ONE possible way that psychologists have attempted to deal with this issue. (2 + 2 marks)
11. Describe ONE way that psychologists might select a random sample. (2 marks)
12. What is meant by the term 'demand characteristics'? (2 marks)
13. Give an example of investigator effects in an interview situation. (3 marks)

DATA ANALYSIS AND PRESENTATION

Research involves the collection of data. Data can be analysed both quantitatively and qualitatively.

Psychologists are still debating the merits of each approach. Generally, qualitative studies produce subjective, detailed, less reliable data, whereas quantitative studies produce objective, less detailed, more reliable data.

Qualitative data	Quantitative data
Subjective	Objective
Imprecise measures used	Precise measures used
Rich and detailed	Lacks detail
Low in reliability	High in reliability
Used for attitudes, opinions, beliefs	Used for behaviour
Collected in 'real life' setting	Collected in 'artificial' setting

Table 11.4: *General summary of quantitative and qualitative data*

Analysis and interpretation of quantitative data, including graphs, scattergrams and tables

Psychological data can be presented in a number of ways. Although psychology as a science places the emphasis on statistical analysis, data should also be presented in a visually meaningful way. Graphs and charts enable the reader to 'eyeball' the data and help to illustrate any patterns in the data. The use and interpretation of scattergrams is dealt with below (see page 520). Other types of graphs include those described below.

Bar charts

These show data in the form of categories that the researcher wishes to compare (e.g. males, females) (see Figure 11.6). These categories should be placed on the x axis ('x is across'). The columns of bar charts should all be of the same width and separated by a space. The use of a space illustrates that the variable on the x axis is not continuous. It is 'discrete' data such as the mean score of several groups. It can also involve percentages, totals, ratios and so on. A bar chart can display two values together – for example, if the male and female groups shown in Figure 11.6 were divided into a

How Science Works

Practical Learning Activity 11.11: Misleading bar charts

Imagine you are a supporter of either Political Party A or Political Party Z and you are presented with the following data table.

Percentage increase in crime, year on year, during Party A and Party Z governments
Party A: 1983: +10% Party Z: 1997: +3% Party A: 1987: +5% Party Z: 2002: +14% Party A: 1992: +3% Party Z: 2007: +1%

- Choose an appropriate graph to illustrate these figures. Draw up a graph (or two graphs) that you would use if you were a Party A or Party Z supporter.
- How might you explain such figures?
- Consider in your answers issues such as policing funding and the public's willingness to report minor crimes.

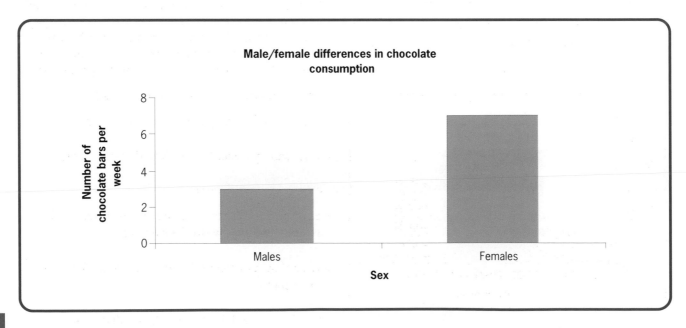

Figure 11.6 Example of a bar chart

further two groups: under and over 20 years of age. Notice that the different y axis gives a different impression of the results. This is something to be aware of when designing a bar **chart.**

Histograms

Students often confuse histograms and bar charts. The main difference is that histograms are used for continuous data (e.g. test scores) like the example in Figure 11.7. These continuous scores or values should ascend along the x axis. The frequency of these values is shown on the y axis. There should be no spaces between the bars since the data are continuous. The column width for each value on the x axis should be the same width per equal category interval. Thus the area of each column is proportional to the number of cases it represents throughout the histogram.

Frequency polygon (or line graph)

This is very similar to a histogram in that the data on the x axes must be continuous. A frequency polygon can be produced by drawing a line from the midpoint top of each bar in a histogram. The one real advantage of a frequency polygon is that two or more frequency distributions can be displayed on the same graph for comparison (see Figure 11.8).

General points to consider with presentation of graphs and charts

- All graphs and charts must be fully labelled with an appropriate title, and the x and y axes should be labelled accurately.

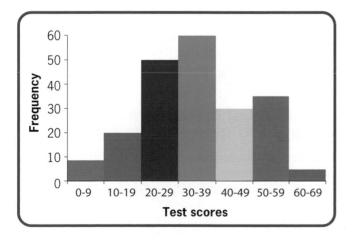

Figure 11.7 Example of a histogram

- Graphs and charts generally look best if the y axis height is three-quarters the x axis width.

- Only one graph or chart should be used to illustrate a set of data. (Many students produce different graphs or charts of the same data.)

- Use an appropriate scale on the axes. Do not mislead people by using an inappropriate scale. Political parties often do this and it's best not to follow their example.

- Do not draw the raw data. A chart or graph should be a summary of the data. Do not be tempted to include each individual score. The raw data table will already have shown this.

Analysis and interpretation of quantitative data

Measures of central tendency are used to summarise large amounts of data into a typical value or average. They are ways of estimating the midpoint of scores. There are three averages: the median, the mean and the mode.

The median

This is the central score in a list of rank-ordered scores. With an odd number of scores, the median is the middle number. With an even number of scores, the median is the midpoint between the two middle scores and therefore may not be one of the original scores.

The advantages of this measure are that:

- it is not affected by extreme 'freak' scores

- it is usually easier to calculate than the mean.

The weaknesses are that:

- it is not as sensitive as the mean, because the raw scores are not used in the calculation

- it can be unrepresentative in a small data set. For example:

 1 1 2 3 4 5 6 7 8 – the median is 4

 2 3 4 6 8 9 19 30 – the median is 7

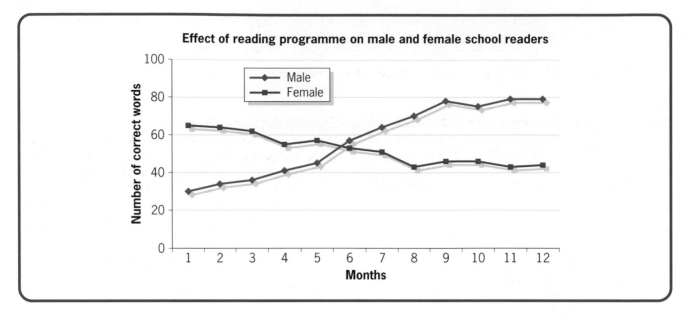

Figure 11.8 Example of a frequency polygon

The mean

This is where all the scores are added up and divided by the total number of scores. It is the exact midpoint of all the combined values.

The advantages of this measure are that:

● it is a very sensitive measure and the most accurate of the measures of central tendency outlined here because it works at the interval level of measurement

● it includes all the information from the raw scores.

The weaknesses are that:

● it is less useful if some of the scores are skewed – that is, if there are very large or small scores in the distribution of scores

● often, the mean score is not one of the original scores.

The mode

This is the most common, or 'popular', number in a set of scores.

The advantages of this measure are that:

● it is not affected by extreme scores in one direction

● it sometimes makes more sense than the other measures of central tendency – for example, the average number of children in a British family is better described as 2 (the mode) rather 2.4 children (mean).

The weaknesses are that:

● there can be more than one mode in a set of data (e.g. 2 3 6 7 7 7 9 15 16 16 16 20 – modes are 7 and 16)

● it doesn't take into account the exact distances between all the values.

Measures of dispersion, including ranges and standard deviation

Measures of dispersion are measures of the variability or spread of scores. They include the range, semi-interquartile range and standard deviation.

The range

This is calculated by taking away the lowest value from the highest value in a set of scores and then adding 1.

| 1 | 2 | 4 | 6 | 7 | 8 | 9 | 12 | 14 | 16 | 19 |

Q1————————this is the inter-quartile range————Q3

Q3 – Q1 = 14 – 4 = 10. 10 divided by 2 = 5 = semi-interquartile range

The advantages of this measure are that:

● it is fairly easy and quick to work out

● it includes extreme values, but does not incorporate individual values.

The weaknesses are that:

● it can be distorted by extreme 'freak' values and does not show whether data are clustered or spread evenly around the mean (e.g. 2 3 4 5 5 6 7 8 9 21 and 2 5 8 9 10 12 13 15 16 18 21 – the range of these two sets of data is the same, despite the data being very different).

Semi-interquartile range

This shows the middle 50 per cent of a set of scores. When the scores are in rank order, the first 'quartile' (Q1) is the first 25 per cent of scores. The third quartile (Q3) includes the first 75 per cent of scores. The inter-quartile range is half the distance between Q1 and Q3. To obtain this, you subtract Q1 from Q3 and divide by two. For example:

The advantages of this measure are that:

● it is fairly easy to calculate

● it is not affected by extreme scores.

The weaknesses are that:

● it doesn't take into account extreme scores

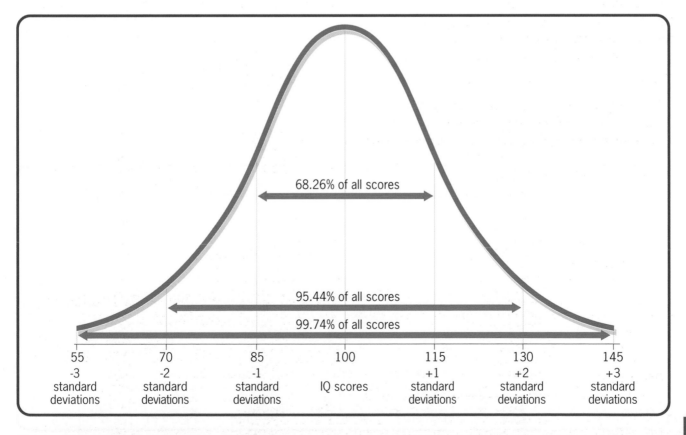

Figure 11.9 Standard deviation: IQ scores

- it is inaccurate if there are large intervals between the scores.

Standard deviation

This is a measure of the spread or variability of a set of scores from the mean. The larger the standard deviation, the larger the spread of scores.

The advantages of this measure are that:

- it is a more sensitive dispersion measure than the range since all scores are used in its calculation

- it allows for the interpretation of an individual's score; thus in Figure 11.9, anybody with an IQ of 121 is in the top 5 per cent of the population (between +2 and +3 standard deviations of the mean).

The weaknesses are that:

- it is more complicated to calculate

- it is less meaningful if data are not normally distributed (Figure 11.9 shows a normal distribution).

Specification Hint

You do not need to know how to calculate any of the measures of central tendency or dispersion for the AS exam.

Analysis and interpretation of correlational data

Positive and negative correlations and the interpretation of correlation coefficients

Correlational methods have been mentioned above (see pages 496–498). Correlations can be either positive or negative, or show no correlation. The stronger the correlation, the nearer it is to +1 or -1. Scattergrams (or scattergraphs) are useful techniques that show at a glance how two variables are correlated. However, a statistical test or correlation coefficient has to be calculated to determine the exact nature of the correlation. Given a scattergram or a correlational coefficient (e.g. +0.7), you should be able to determine the strength and direction of the correlation (see Figure 11.10).

Analysis and presentation of qualitative data, including awareness of the processes involved in content analysis

Qualitative data involves people's meanings, experiences and descriptions. It is particularly good for researching attitudes, opinions and beliefs. Data usually consist of verbal or written descriptions. The qualitative approach suggests that information about human events and experience loses much of its meaning and value when reduced to numerical form (Coolican, 2004).

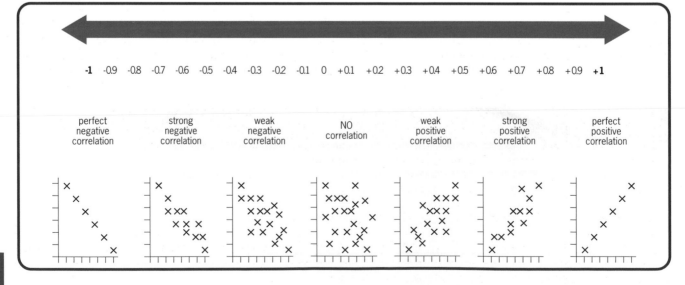

Figure 11.10 Scattergrams and correlational strength

There is no one agreed way to analyse qualitative data. Each researcher has his or her own ideas for the best way to do it. The analysis of qualitative data is a fairly new field and new methods are emerging and developing. Some of the ways to analyse qualitative data include those described below.

Content analysis

This is most commonly done within media research. Strictly speaking, it actually involves the quantification of qualitative material – that is, it analyses in a numerical way written, verbal or visual communication. It can involve the analysis of speeches, graffiti, newspapers, TV adverts and so on. Waynforth and Dunbar (1995) analysed the content of 'lonely hearts' columns to see if men and women were looking for the same things in life.

Content analysis requires coding units to be developed where analysed material can be categorised. For instance, the number of times women appear as housewives in TV adverts. Analysis can involve words, themes, characters or time and space. The number of times these things do not occur can also be important.

Categorising

This involves the grouping of common items together. For example, it might be possible to group students' perceptions of their psychology course into: resources (books, DVDs), peer/teacher relationships, teacher knowledge, delivery and so forth. It's often difficult to decide on the categories to use.

Quotations

Word-for-word quotations are often used to bring the research findings to life. The quotes should 'tell it like it is'. They should typify what others have said during the research.

Qualitative data and naturalistic observations

Observers typically give a running commentary into a tape recorder as they observe behaviour. This produces qualitative data. Such data can be coded or categorised (see above) and can help to add detail to quantitative data. The **diary method** is another technique where observers can take notes on behaviour. This can be self-reported behaviour. The diary method has the advantage of providing genuine information in the participants' own surroundings. However, participants often find it difficult to complete on a long-term basis.

Qualitative data and questionnaire surveys

Qualitative data are mainly collected from open-ended questions where participants are invited to give an answer using their own words. Such data are less likely to be biased by the interviewers' preconceived ideas. Analysis of this data can involve content analysis, categorisation or the use of quotations, as described above.

Qualitative data and interviews

Interviews are likely to be transcribed and can then be analysed using many of the qualitative techniques described above. Unstructured interviews are most suitable for qualitative analysis. The interpretation of interview data is open to subjective interpretation. However, this lack of objectivity may be overcome by the detail that such a method allows.

Evaluation of qualitative data analysis

Qualitative data analysis tends to be subjective, although there are methods for checking both reliability (through replication) and validity (through the use of other methods). In any case, many qualitative

Unit	Examples
Word	Count the number of slang words used
Theme	The amount of violence on TV
Character	The number of female bosses there are in TV programmes
Time and space	The amount of time (on TV) and space (in newspapers) dedicated to famine in Africa

Table 11.5: Possible coding units for content analysis

researchers argue that subjectivity and the personal opinion of a participant are extremely valuable and strengthen any research study. Qualitative data analysis can, however, be extremely time consuming.

Assessment Check 11.3

1. Name ONE measure of central tendency and give ONE reason why it might be used. (2 + 3 marks)
2. Outline ONE weakness of the 'mode'. (2 marks)
3. Explain what standard deviation tells us about a set of data. (3 marks)
4. Describe the type of correlation that you would have if the correlation coefficient was +0.87. (2 marks)

UNIT 4: PSYA4 PSYCHOPATHOLOGY, PSYCHOLOGY IN ACTION AND RESEARCH METHODS

Specification Hint

Questions about the following material can be asked only in Unit 4 (PSYA4).

THE APPLICATION OF THE SCIENTIFIC METHOD IN PSYCHOLOGY

Science is understanding, prediction and control above the levels achieved by unaided common sense – Allport (1947)

Psychology tends to follow the scientific method used in many other sciences, such as chemistry and biology. Briefly this involves observation leading to the formulation of explanatory theories, the development of testable hypotheses, subsequent research testing (using objective measures, and both experimental and non-experimental techniques) and then support or rejection (or modification) of the theory. There are continuing arguments about what kind of science psychology should be, but the key requirements of the science of psychology are that it must be objective, controlled and checkable (Coolican, 2008).

The scientific process

One way to examine behaviour is to gather large amounts of data and then examine these data in order to formulate a theory or reach a conclusion. This approach is called the empirical method. The empirical method is part of the scientific method and is sometimes simply regarded as being the same as the experimental method, which involves the deliberate manipulation of one variable while keeping all others constant, and the random allocation of participants to conditions. In this way, the experimental method can determine cause and effect, and includes laboratory and field experiments.

Psychology tends to rely heavily on a method to test theories called the hypothetico-deductive method. This involves testing theories by generating hypotheses. Hypotheses are predictions generated from theories. For example, if we propose a theory that girls are more intelligent than boys (it's only a theory!), we might test this by generating a more specific testable hypothesis such as 'Girls will achieve significantly higher intelligence test (IQ) scores than boys'.

How Science Works

Practical Learning Activity 11.12: Develop a research proposal to test the so-called Mozart effect

The 'Mozart effect' is a theory which states that listening to Mozart can enhance intellectual function. Devise a study that could test this effect. Formulate a suitable hypothesis and suggest an appropriate method to test this.

Replication

Replication is considered essential in scientific research. There is little point in claiming some scientific effect unless it can be repeated. In order for replication to be possible, all details of the original study must be published, including the data, procedures and results.

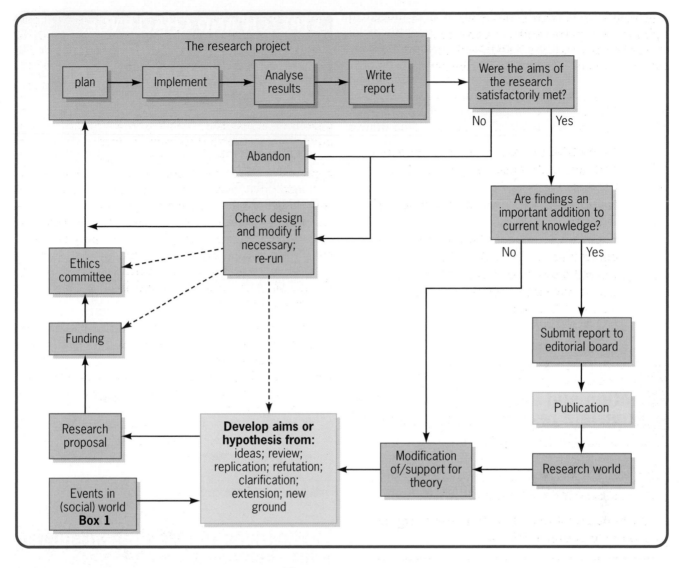

Figure 11.11 The research cycle – start at Box 1

Objectivity

Objectivity is another requisite in scientific research. The term relates to a judgement, theory, explanation, findings and so on, based on observable phenomena and uninfluenced by emotions or personal prejudices.

Validating new knowledge and the role of peer review

One of the final stages in the research cycle involves the publication of the research. However, there are a number of stages that the researcher needs to go through before this occurs. Once the report is written,

researchers may submit their work for publication in an appropriate journal (for example, the *International Journal of Psychology*). Once the research report is received by the journal a process of peer review begins. Peer review (also called 'refereeing') is the process whereby the research is subjected to the scrutiny of other experts in the field. Referees are usually not aware of the identity of the researchers, although it is often possible to guess! Peer review is used by the editors of the journals to select the highest-quality research papers that are most suitable for publication. It is generally agreed that journal articles that are published after a process of peer review are of greater merit than those published in journals not subject to peer review. Research is published only if it is judged to make an important contribution to the scientific field, and the research process has been methodologically and ethically sound. One criticism made of the peer review process is that non-significant findings and replications of earlier studies are judged less likely to be published than more original, significant findings. This is sometimes referred to as the 'file-drawer problem', meaning that many non-significant findings get put away in the filing cabinet and are never submitted to journals for publication. Given Popper's ideas on the importance of falsifying theories, this is unfortunate.

DESIGNING PSYCHOLOGICAL INVESTIGATIONS

The research process in psychology is well illustrated in Figure 11.11 (Coolican, 2004), which shows the complicated nature of any research. It is easy to see that research is one long continuous cycle and doesn't involve separate research projects.

Selection and application of appropriate research methods

There are a number of different research methods available to the research psychologist. Just like the golfer who has a bag full of clubs suitable for different shots, the psychologist has a number of different research methods suitable for different types of research. Psychology places an emphasis on scientific methods, so many psychologists may favour an experimental approach, but in reality all the methods have their strengths and weaknesses and the best method to choose is dependent on the hypothesis being tested. Indeed, good research has often employed more than one method for data collection – for example, a laboratory experiment may be supported by a detailed interview or questionnaire.

✔ Specification Hint

You need to review the advantages and weaknesses of the various research methods detailed on pages 494–503.

STRETCH AND CHALLENGE: Combining the findings from lots of previous research

Sometimes it may appear that half the research findings seem to predict one result and the other half the opposite! This can often be annoying or frustrating, but the study of human behaviour is never going to be straightforward. One way to try to tackle conflicting research findings is to conduct a meta-analysis. This is where the results of numerous studies into the same topic (or more accurately the same research hypothesis) are combined into a single statistical analysis. In a single research study, lots of participants supply the data but in a meta-analysis the data is provided by lots of studies conducted previously. Meta-analyses are a good method of finding out what the majority of research findings show.

- Have a look at the internet and type 'meta-analysis psychology' into a search engine; read about the use of meta-analysis in psychology.

Implications of sampling strategies – for example, bias and generalising

Whenever a psychologist conducts research she or he has to consider what type of people they want to study. The key point here is to decide on the target population that you want to find out about. For instance, you might want to find out about the different reading material of adolescent boys and girls. Your target population is adolescent boy and girl readers but it would be impossible to test all such people in the target population, so a sample group of adolescents would have to be chosen using an appropriate sampling method. This selected group would represent the target population.

There are a number of different methods available to psychologists. Random, opportunity and volunteer sampling have already been dealt with on page 513.

All sampling techniques can result in a biased sample, but certain techniques, such as random sampling, are unbiased in the way that participants are selected for the sample. For example, if I were to select five names out of a hat as a sample to represent my mixed psychology class and all five were males, then the sample would be biased even though I used an unbiased method of selecting the sample. Techniques such as volunteer and opportunity sampling are more likely to result in a biased sample but they are often more convenient than more complicated techniques. Once a suitable sampling method has been selected, then the size of the sample has to be considered. Sample size usually depends on the size of the target population, the resources available and the sampling method chosen. With these considerations in mind, a larger sample is often preferred to a smaller one, but the size of the sample does not necessarily overcome biased sampling techniques. A biased sampling technique allied to a small sample size is likely to invalidate any results obtained, and thus findings cannot be generalised to the target population.

How Science Works

Practical Learning Activity 11.13

● Find out about stratified, systematic and quota sampling. Use the internet or a psychology dictionary. Write a short description of each.
● Devise a table that summarises all these sampling methods (including those you learnt for AS – namely random, opportunity and volunteer), and includes two advantages and weaknesses of each technique. Rank-order the methods in terms of the likelihood of a biased sample occurring and ease of use. What do you find?

Issues of reliability

Reliability is essential in psychological research and has already been dealt with on pages 510–511. If research results are consistent and can be replicated, then the results can be said to be reliable. There are various methods for assessing reliability, as discussed below.

Inter-rater reliability

This refers to the degree to which different raters/observers give consistent estimates of the same object or phenomenon (Figure 11.12). It is particularly useful in observational research. If agreement is high between observers, then inter-rater reliability has been achieved. Depending on the measure of agreement, a correlation coefficient can be used to assess how high the reliability measure is.

Test-retest reliability

This is when the same test is given to the same sample on two different occasions (Figure 11.13). It is assumed that there is no substantial change in the construct being measured between the two time periods. The

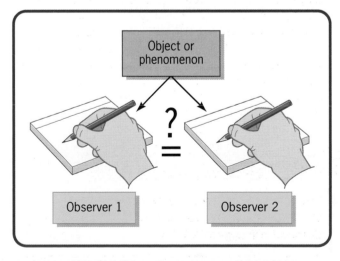

Figure 11.12 Inter-rater reliability is particularly useful in observational research

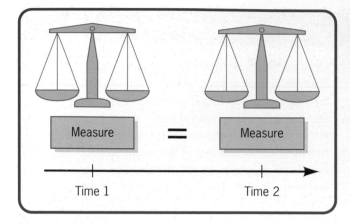

Figure 11.13 Test-retest reliability is when the same test is given to the same sample on two different occasions and the result is similar

degree of correlation between the two measures allows us to estimate the degree of test-retest reliability. The time gap between the two measures is crucial. With a shorter time gap, the degree of correlation should be higher.

Assessing and improving validity

Validity is concerned with whether the research has been successful at measuring accurately what the researchers set out to measure. Different types of validity (internal and external) have been discussed on page 511.

Internal validity is concerned with whether the effect observed in the research is entirely due to the manipulation of the independent variable. This can be improved by an improvement with certain aspects of the research such as the minimisation of investigator

How Science Works
Practical Learning Activity 11.14

Imagine you are taught by two psychology teachers. Teacher X always gives you a grade B for your work. Teacher Z usually gives you a grade E. Devise a procedure where you might check whether the teachers' marking is reliable and/or valid.

effects, reduction of demand characteristics, the use of standardised instructions and the use of a random sample. All these factors will ensure that the study is highly controlled and thus there are fewer areas to doubt that any effect observed is due to poor methodology and is not attributable to the change in the independent variable.

External (or ecological validity) refers to whether the results of a study can be generalised beyond the confines of the experimental setting. It is difficult to assess this until the findings have been shown to be applicable beyond the research setting. One way to improve external validity is to try to set experiments in more naturalistic settings – for example, as is the case with field experiments.

Ethical considerations in the design and conduct of psychological research

The BPS Code of Ethics for those involved in conducting psychological research has been dealt with previously (see pages 511–513). All these ethical

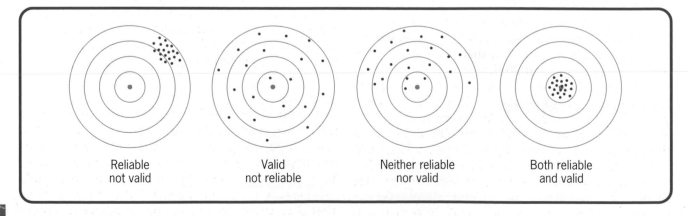

Reliable not valid   Valid not reliable   Neither reliable nor valid   Both reliable and valid

Figure 11.14 The relationship between reliability and validity

STRETCH AND CHALLENGE

Rate how often the following events are likely to occur. Give each a mark out of 100, with 0 being not at all likely and 100 being very likely.

- You will complete your homework.
- The England Football team will win the World Cup.
- A tossed coin will end up heads.
- You will have a salad for lunch today.
- You will win the lottery next week.

We can calculate the probability of these events happening. First take your numbers and divide them by 100 to obtain a decimal. For example, there have been 18 World Cups since 1930 and England have won once. So you could say that England have a 1 in 18 chance of winning, or a 5.5 per cent chance (expressed as a decimal as 0.055). You probably gave a tossed coin a rating of 50 (50 per cent, or 0.5). So for some of these occurrences we can calculate the logical probability of the event happening (e.g. tossed coin), whereas with others (e.g. a future England World Cup win) we have to rely on data in the past to estimate the future empirical probability (Coolican, 2004).

aspects must be considered carefully prior to the design and conduct of any psychological investigation. Much research takes place at universities, all of which would also have ethical committees set up to vet and advise potential research projects.

Probability and significance, and the interpretation of significance

Probability (denoted by the symbol p) refers to how likely something is to happen. This is expressed as a number between 0 and 1. A probability of 1 is that it is certain to happen, whereas a probability of 0 is that it is impossible.

Measuring probability and significance

Generally psychologists use a $p <= 0.05$ (also expressed as 5 per cent) level of significance. Why? Well, statisticians have made the decision that if a result can be repeated 19 times out of 20 then it probably isn't any longer just a coincidence. If I could hit the bull's eye in darts 19 times out of 20 you would probably agree it isn't a fluke and you'd accept my assertion or hypothesis that I'm a good darts player. An observed result of this magnitude is regarded by psychologists as statistically significant – not a mere fluke – since it has only a 5 per cent or smaller likelihood of occurring by mere chance. This 1 in 20 measure can also be expressed as a percentage (5 per cent) or on a scale of 0 to 1, it is expressed as $p \leq 0.05$. Remember, I might do better at

darts and only miss one bull's eye out of 100, which would mean I have achieved an even higher level of probability, which would be 1 per cent, or 0.01. As is obvious, the 1 per cent significance level is much harder to achieve.

There are occasions when we may wish to use a more stringent level of significance (say 0.01, or 1 per cent level) when we want to be more certain of our results. This may occur when we are challenging a well-established theory or well-known piece of research. Adopting a 1 per cent or 0.01 significance level gives us greater confidence in the research findings. Findings at this level of significance are said to be 'highly significant', whereas those that achieve the 5 per cent or $p \leq 0.05$ level are said to 'significant'. When research findings have the potential to have a serious impact on human behaviour – for example, with drug testing or other health issues – then an even higher level of significance is sometimes required.

Note

When the probability level for the alternative hypothesis is achieved (at the required level of $p \leq 0.05$), many students incorrectly state that the alternative hypothesis has been proved true. This is not correct; we have merely found support for the alternative hypothesis because the results suggest that it is very unlikely that they could have been due to chance or coincidence. Significance at the $p \leq 0.05$ level still means that

527

there is a 5 per cent chance that your result was really due to coincidence or chance. Do not use the word 'prove' – after all, even significant results may be just a fluke.

Type 1 and Type 2 errors

There are two kinds of errors that can be made in significance testing. A null hypothesis that is true can be rejected (Type 1 error) and a false null hypothesis can fail to be rejected when it should have been (a false positive). These two types of errors are shown in Table 11.5.

Statistical decision	True state of the null hypothesis	
	H0 True	H0 False
Reject H0	Type 1 error (false positive)	Correct
Do not reject H0	Correct	Type 2 error (false negative)

Table 11.6: Type 1 and Type 2 errors

Obviously, in research we would hope that we are producing accurate results all the time. However, there may be occasions when we reject the null hypothesis when it is in fact true. For example, a pregnancy test that indicates a woman is pregnant when she is not is an indication of a false positive or Type 1 error. A pregnancy test that indicates a woman is not pregnant when in fact she is, is an example of a Type 2 error (false positive).

If we make the significance level very strict (e.g. lower it to $p \leq 0.01$), then we lower the chance of making a Type 1 error, but increase the chance of a Type 2 error. One way to reduce the chance of making errors is to increase the sample size.

Factors affecting choice of statistical test, including levels of measurement

Once psychologists have collected their data, they need to conduct a statistical test to see if the data collected are significant or not. In order to decide which statistical test to use they have to know whether they were looking for a test of difference between samples of scores or a test of correlation between one (or more) pairs of scores. Next they have to decide what level of measurement their data is. There are three basic levels of measurement: nominal, ordinal, and interval or ratio.

1. **Nominal data:** the simplest type, which involves counting of frequency data. For example, how many days of the week were rainy, how many were sunny? How many men and how many women were there? Tally charts are often used to record this type of basic data. With nominal variables, there is a qualitative difference between values, not a quantitative one.

2. **Ordinal data:** this involves the rank-ordering of data and thus one value is greater or larger or better than the other. Rating scales are often used. For example, rate (on a scale of 1 = awful and 10 = brilliant) certain television programmes. With ordinal scales, we only know that a rating of 2 is better than 1, or 10 is better than 9 (in this example); but we do not know by *how much* they are better. The distance between 1 and 2 may be shorter than between 9 and 10, and my subjective rating of 7 may be very different to your rating of 7. Ordinal data is more detailed than nominal data.

3. **Interval or ratio data:** this is the most accurate measurement because it is precise and uses equal measurement intervals. Standardised measurement units such as time, weight, temperature and distance are interval/ratio measures. The same statistic tests are chosen regardless of whether you have interval or ratio data hence, in practice, ratio/interval data are often

Nominal	Ordinal	Interval	Ratio
Gender Ethnicity Marital status	Scale ratings (e.g. 1 = not at all, 5 = very much) The rank order of anything	Temperature Most personality and IQ measures	Annual salary Weight, time, length

Table 11.7: Examples of measurement scales

classified together. The only difference with interval data is that the measurement scale has an arbitrary zero point, whereas ratio data has an absolute zero point. For example, zero degrees temperature does not mean there is no temperature (interval data), whereas having zero pounds in your bank account would mean you have no money (ratio data).

One can think of nominal, ordinal, interval and interval/ratio as being ranked in their relation to one another, getting gradually more sophisticated each time. The mnemonic NOIR (Nominal, Ordinal, Interval/Ratio) is often used to remember this order.

The final factor that determines the choice of statistical test is whether the research design is related (repeated) measures or unrelated (or independent) measures (see pages 504–505).

Once we know the nature of the hypothesis, the level of measurement and the type of research design, we can choose the appropriate statistical test (see Table 11.7).

Specification Hint

You do not need to know how to carry out any of these statistical tests. The tests in red in the table below are specifically mentioned in the Specification and therefore you should learn *when* these statistical tests should be used but not *how* to conduct them.

CONVENTIONS OF REPORTING ON PSYCHOLOGICAL INVESTIGATIONS

Progress in science depends on active communication between research workers in the same and in related fields. It's therefore essential to describe the results of empirical research as accurately and as effectively as possible. All psychologists hope to get their research published in eminent peer-reviewed journals. They have to write up the report according to the conventions of each journal. Although each journal often has its own specific style, the main sections of a psychology report are the same. Some general advice on writing experimental reports is given below, including some of the conventions that apply to scientific reporting.

Introduction

Replicability is essential in scientific inquiry. In principle, it should be possible for someone else to repeat your experiment. Report-writing skills are one of the main skills that psychologists have to learn.

Purpose of a coursework write-up

Put simply, it is the place in which you tell the story of your study:

- what was done

- why it was done

Nature of hypothesis	Level of measurement	Type of research design	
		Independent (unrelated)	**Repeated (related)**
Differences	Nominal data	**Chi-square**	Sign test
	Ordinal data	**Mann-Whitney U test**	**Wilcoxon (matched pairs)**
	Interval data	Independent t test	Related t test
Correlation	Ordinal data		**Spearman's rho**
	Interval data		Pearson product moment

Table 11.8: Choosing the appropriate statistical test (learn the ones in red)

● what was found

● what it means.

This should be done clearly and concisely. The aim is to be explicit and avoid ambiguity. The reader will then be able to repeat the study in all its essential procedural features. Sometimes quite similar studies report different results. In order to work out why this has happened, one needs full information about *what* was done.

Setting out your report

There's no single correct way to set out scientific reports. In many cases it would be foolish to impose a rigid format since, for some areas of psychology, this could be quite impractical. The format suggested below should be taken as a general guide for reporting on psychological investigations. The basic structure is:

● title

● abstract

● introduction

● method

● results

● discussion

● references

● appendices.

How to write up a psychological investigation

It is usual to write up research in continuous prose, in the past tense, and to avoid colloquialisms. Reports usually have the following subheadings.

Title

This should be precise enough to give the reader a good idea of the topic you are investigating.

Table of contents

This is optional, but is best included, along with page numbers.

Abstract

This is a summary (approximately 150 words) of your coursework and informs the reader whether it is worth reading any further. (Obviously, the examiner will read on regardless!) The abstract should include approximately two sentences from each of the other sections in your report: the theoretical background, the aim and hypothesis, the design method and participants, a brief outline of the results, the conclusion, and suggestions for future research. Although the abstract appears first, it's usually best to leave writing it until the end.

Introduction

This answers *why* you carried out the study. It should include general theoretical background, identifying the main theories, controversies and investigations of the chosen topic. It's important to concentrate on relevant material. This section is very much like a 'funnel', whereby it starts off with a broad perspective and should lead on to the more precise aims and hypotheses under study.

Aims

The overall aim(s) of the study should be mentioned.

Hypotheses

The precise experimental/alternative hypotheses should be included, along with the null hypothesis. These should be as precise and unambiguous as possible. A justification of the direction of hypotheses should be included (i.e. one-tailed or two-tailed).

The minimum acceptable level of significance should be stated, this is normally 5 per cent ($p < 0.05$).

Method

This covers what you did. All details of the method should be reported so that other researchers can replicate the study should they so wish. Materials used in the study, such as questionnaires, observation checklists and standardised instructions, should be included in the appendices. The 'Method' section is split into several sub-sections.

Design

There are no hard-and-fast rules about what goes in the design section and what goes in the procedure section. The design section should cover:

- the choice of method, such as laboratory experiment, observation and so on

- the type of design you used (e.g. repeated/independent measures or matched pairs)

- the choice of observational technique (if applicable) (e.g. time or event sampling)

- the identification of variables such as the independent variables, dependent variable and extraneous variables

- ethical considerations.

Participants

This is where you describe your sample. This section should cover:

- the target population described in terms of relevant variables such as age, gender, socio-economic group and so on

- the method you used to obtain your sample (e.g. random, opportunity)

- the actual sample in terms of how many participants there were, how they were selected and recruited, and described in terms of any relevant variables outlined above

- whether participants were naive as to the purpose of the study, and whether any participants refused to take part or subsequently dropped out

- how participants were allocated to conditions.

Apparatus/materials

This section should include a description of any technical equipment involved and how it was used. The main point of this section is relevance. Only include materials that are directly relevant to the investigation, not trivial inclusions such as 'pencil and paper'

(although these may be crucial to some studies!). Include relevant mark schemes for any tests or questionnaires in the 'Appendix'.

Standardised procedure

The aim of this section is to allow precise replication of your study. It's a step-by-step description of exactly how your study was conducted. You need to describe what happened in the order it happened. You ought to include details of where the study took place, any standardised instructions and debriefing procedures. If the instructions are lengthy, then it may be better to place them in an appendix. Try not to repeat information that has appeared elsewhere in your 'Method' section.

Controls

Sometimes this information is included in the 'Design' section. Controls to be mentioned would include counterbalancing, random allocation of participants to groups, single- or double-blind procedures, control of extraneous variables, and what steps were taken to avoid bias in the sampling or experimental procedures.

Results

This covers what you found, and it's where you present the data you've collected. It needs to be presented clearly so that others can evaluate your work. The section should be written in connected prose with the support of tables and/or figures (graphs), which are referred to in your text. The main features of this section are described in more detail below.

There's an art in tabulating your data. If you organise yourself fully before you run your study, there should be no need to write out your raw data more than once. *Don't* insert it in the body of the text, but possibly in an appendix. Tables and figures in the text will typically be very abbreviated or summary versions of the raw data. Each summary table should be clearly headed.

Don't include any names of participants in answer sheets or on questionnaires. Names should be treated as confidential information. One example answer sheet, questionnaire and so on should be included in the appendix.

Descriptive statistics

Descriptive statistics are essential and give the reader a chance to 'eyeball' the data. You should try to summarise your results in the most appropriate graphical form. You could include numerical statistics such as measures of central tendency (mean, mode or median), measures of dispersion (range, standard deviation). Your aim must be to present the key findings in the most straightforward manner. Sometimes the choice of graph is a difficult one. Don't be tempted to include a number of graphs of the same data. Label tables and figures clearly so that the reader understands what the values represent (always specify measurement units), and number these tables and figures so that they can be easily referred to in the text. Tables should be numbered and titled above the table, figures and graphs below. Labels on axes should be unambiguous. Do not insert too much information. Make sure the figure makes optimum use of the space available. Join points on line plots with straight lines, not meandering curves. Try to make figures (graphs, histograms etc.) as visually pleasing as possible (not easy!). Don't label figures or tables 'Figure to show ...'. Use a simple but informative title about the variables displayed. Describe the key features briefly in the text, where appropriate. Don't provide both a table and a figure of the same data; this is wasteful of time and space. Decide which works best and choose that one.

Inferential statistics

When statistical tests or analyses of the data are conducted, you should state clearly why you chose a particular test and what it tests for (see above). Calculations should not appear in the body of the text but should be shown clearly in an appendix so that a reader can follow them easily if necessary. Be clear about the outcome of the statistical analyses. In the main text summarise the key findings and cite test statistics. You should include a statement on the observed and critical table values of the test, the significance level and whether the test was one-tailed or two-tailed. You must show that you understand what the results of your statistical tests mean. Do the results mean that you accept or reject your null hypothesis? Don't attempt to interpret the results at this stage; leave that to the 'Discussion' section.

Discussion
This covers what you think the results mean.

Explanation of findings
This must begin with a clear description of the key findings. The findings should be stated in psychological terms in relation to the aims/hypotheses identified earlier. What bearings do your findings have upon the original hypotheses? State what your

most important finding is and explain what this illustrates. *All* results are results. You must never ignore or dismiss findings that don't fit with previous findings. Science would not progress if scientists dismissed every finding that they weren't looking for. You should show why you obtained the results you did and what they show. A good researcher will themselves act as a participant before conducting a study. Alternatively, you may have conducted a pilot study. Reports by the participants themselves can be most informative. Often they give information about possible sources of error in the design or procedure. Also, participants tend to adopt different strategies, changing course in the middle of a study. They may not do what you want or expect them to do, and such information can be included in the 'Discussion' section, either here in the 'Explanation of findings' section or in the 'Limitations and modifications' section (or both).

Relationship to background research
This is where you account for and discuss your results in terms of previous research findings. You should refer back to the relevant research studies mentioned in your 'Introduction'. Mention any aspects of your design that may account for any differences in your findings and previous ones. If your results support previous reviewed work, then this section may be quite short, although it's still worth emphasising any design or procedural differences that there may be.

Limitations and modifications
Don't sidestep embarrassing findings or paradoxical results. If the study went 'wrong' try to locate possible sources of error. These might include measurement techniques, poor sampling, lack of controls and/or poor procedures. Even the best-designed study is likely to have some flaws or could have been conducted in a better way. Outline what was done, what was intended (these may not be the same), and how things might have been improved or modified.

Implications and suggestions for further research
Questions to consider in this section include: If you were to repeat the study, would you alter the methodology in any way, and why? What further experiments are suggested to you by this experiment and its findings? Can you think of better ways of testing the hypotheses? Do you think that standard studies in the

literature might be improved? Are there any other applications or implications that arise as a result of your findings?

When making suggestions for further research, only do so if they arise directly out of your results. Try to be precise with your suggestions and do not make general statements such as, 'A lot more work needs to be done in this area.' Specific suggestions such as using more participants, eliminating confounding variables such as background environmental noise, and improving standardised instructions are fine provided you have demonstrated that some of these factors have affected your findings in some way.

Conclusion

You might end with a paragraph that recapitulates the key findings and conclusions that can be drawn from the study.

References

In the text itself, you should cite *only* authors' names and dates of publication. In this section you should list full details of *all* references that you have cited in the text. The purpose of a reference list is to enable others to research the references, thus, if in doubt, give as much information as possible.

Use the following standard formats for your list of references

Journal articles

Author's name(s) and initial(s), year of publication, title of article (lower case preferred), title of journal (in full), volume number, page numbers. For example:

Shepard, R.N. and Metzler, J. (1971) Mental rotation of three-dimensional objects. *Science*, *171*, 701–703.

Books

Author's name(s) and initial(s), year of publication, title of book (initial capitals for key words), place of publication, publisher. For example:

Gross, R. and Rolls, G. (2003) *Essential AS Psychology*. London: Hodder & Stoughton.

Chapters in books

Combine aspects of what you would do for journal articles and books (see above), by giving the author of the chapter and his/her chapter title first followed by 'In A. Smith (ed.) …', etc. For example:

Cohen, G. (1982) Theoretical interpretations of visual asymmetries. In J.G. Beaumont (ed.) *Divided Visual Field Studies of Cerebral Organisation*. London: Academic Press.

STRETCH AND CHALLENGE

There is a wonderful web resource called *Classics in the History of Psychology*, which stores original psychology papers. As the website's creator, Dr Christopher Green, states: 'One of the primary goals of the "Classics" web site is to encourage instructors of history of psychology courses to assign primary source reading to their students. Secondary textbooks are useful for giving general overviews and setting contexts, but they cannot replace reading the original words of important thinkers.' Take a look at the site and choose one paper to read and summarise for your studies. The site can be accessed at: http://psychclassics.yorku.ca/index.htm.

The following papers are particularly noteworthy:

Triplett, Norman (1898) The dynamogenic factors in pacemaking and competition. *American Journal of Psychology*, *9*, 507–533. [Often called the first social psychology experiment; social facilitation among bicycle riders.]

Jones, Mary Cover (1924) A laboratory study of fear: the case of Peter. *Pedagogical Seminary*, *31*, 308–315.

Watson, John B. and Rayner, Rosalie (1920) Conditioned emotional reactions. *Journal of Experimental Psychology*, *3*, 1–14. [The famous 'Little Albert' study.]

STRETCH AND CHALLENGE

Conduct your own research study on a topic that you have already investigated or on a topic that you know you will be studying later on in the course.

You could investigate anything you choose. For example:

- the effect of an audience on task performance
- the effect of a placebo (pretend caffeine) on reaction time
- the existence of telepathy or ESP.

The results you obtain are unimportant; it is the process of carrying out the research that is valuable.

Many academics present their work at conferences where they talk about their research to fellow academics. In order to do this, academics put forward a proposal about their talk. Sometimes, for various reasons, researchers do not get invited to give a talk but can arrange to give a poster presentation of their work. This is usually an A2 or A3 size poster, which gives summary details of their research.

An excellent site offering advice on poster presentations and how to present your work is available at: http://www.muhlenberg.edu/depts/psychology/Posters.htm.

It suggests your poster might look like the one shown in Figure 11.15.

Try to design a poster that summarises your research.

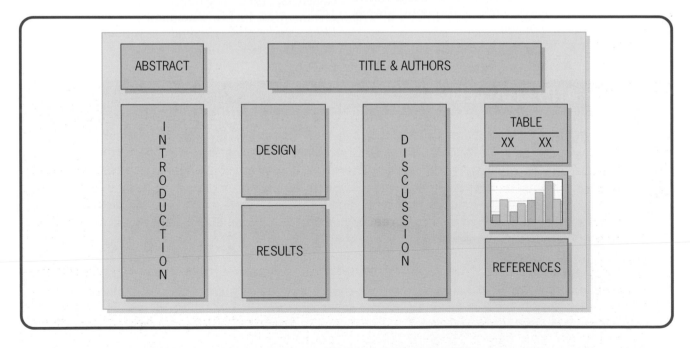

Figure 11.15 Suggested layout of psychology poster presentation

Websites
Author of article or group or organisation. Title of article. Website reference. Date accessed. For example: Psi Chi. *Tips for Psychology Poster Presentations.* www.psichi.org/conventions/presentation_tips.asp Poster. Accessed 9th December 2008.

Appendices
As mentioned earlier, you should provide appendices containing the full instructions given to subjects, the raw data, and calculations for statistical analyses. In addition, if you've generated lists of words or other stimulus materials for use in your study they should be included as an appendix. The different information should be put in numbered appendices so that you can refer to them easily in your text. This isn't a rough work section, and all information should be presented clearly and unambiguously; it's perhaps unfortunate that such sections don't appear in published journal articles.

General considerations and style
This kind of report writing is somewhat specialised. Clear and lucid descriptions are required, and unsupported personal opinions and over-generalisations should be avoided. Only those conclusions warranted by your results should be drawn, and where speculations are made these should be made clear to the reader. You should write in connected prose throughout the report; *never* let it degenerate into a series of notes. It's preferable to write in the third person, past tense. This, along with many of the other points made in these notes, is a convention of scientific writing. Try to avoid slang, stereotyped phrases; these are often vague and ambiguous. However, reports do require imagination and creativity; they needn't be dull and tedious. Remember that it's doubtful that we ever 'prove' anything in psychology. Results may support a hypothesis, but 'prove' is definitely a word to avoid.

SUMMARY

CHAPTER

Methods and techniques

- Psychologists use a range of different **research methods**. Each has its own strengths and weaknesses.

- **A laboratory experiment** takes place in a **controlled environment** where the **IV** is manipulated and the DV is measured.

- **A field experiment** takes place in a **real-life setting** where the IV is manipulated and the DV is measured.

- A **natural experiment** takes place in a real-life setting where the **IV occurs naturally** and the DV is measured.

- **Correlational analysis** allows the **strength of the relationship** between two variables to be measured.

- **Observational techniques** involve the precise (objective) measuring of naturally occurring behaviour. They tend to take place in a natural setting and can involve **participant** or **non-participant observation**.

- **Questionnaires** involve the systematic large-scale collection of data. A questionnaire is a **pre-set list of questions**. They can include **open and closed questions**.

- **Interviews** involve researchers **asking questions in a face-to-face way**. They range from **unstructured to fully structured interviews**.

- **Case studies** involve the in-depth, detailed investigation of an individual or group.

- Each of the research methods has different ethical problems associated with it.

Investigation design

- **Aims** give an indication of why a study is taking place.

- A **hypothesis** is a testable statement and predicts what might happen. **An alternative or experimental hypothesis** predicts significant differences in the DV as a result of manipulation of the IV. These can be **directional or non-directional**. A **null hypothesis** predicts that any results will simply occur as a result of chance.

- There are **three types** of **experimental design**:

  1. **Independent groups design** is where different participants are used in each condition of the study.
  2. **Matched participants design** is where similar, matched pairs of participants are allocated to each of the conditions.
  3. **Repeated measures design** is where the same participants take part in all the conditions.

- There are advantages and disadvantages to each of the designs. **Counterbalancing** can help to overcome the problem of **order effects** with repeated measures design.

- The **operationalisation** of variables refers to the need to define and measure the variables (IV and DV) being studied simply and easily.

- **Pilot studies** are small-scale 'practice' investigations. They are done prior to the actual research and help to identify potential problems.

- **Extraneous variables** are variables that might affect the DV other than the IV. They must be controlled in any study. If they are not controlled, they will adversely affect the results. They are then called **confounding variables** because they 'confound' the results.

- Results should be checked for **reliability (i.e. consistency)** and **validity (i.e. accuracy)**. There are a number of ways to test this, including **internal reliability** and **external reliability** and **internal validity** and **external (ecological) validity**. External (ecological) validity refers to whether or not the results can be generalised beyond the confines of the experimental setting.

- All psychological research must be carried out ethically according **to BPS guidelines**. The main issues involve: informed consent, protection from harm, avoidance of deception and the right to withdraw.

- The selection of participants in psychological research can be done in many ways. These include **random, opportunity and volunteer sampling. Random sampling** is the best known and is where every member of the target population has an equal chance of being selected. It is important to try to obtain a representative sample. **Opportunity sampling** involves asking anybody who is passing to participate. **Volunteer sampling** involves advertising for participants to come forward.

- The relationship between researchers and participants can affect the results obtained. **Demand characteristics** occur when participants try to guess the purpose of the study and then try to give the 'right' results.

- **Investigator effects** occur when some aspects of the investigator (e.g. appearance, gender, ethnicity) influence participants' answers. **Single- and double-blind procedures** can help to overcome these problems.

Data analysis and presentation

- **Quantitative data** involves the numerical analysis of data.

- **Graphs and charts** illustrate patterns in data at a glance. The strength and direction of a correlation can be seen in a **scattergram. A perfect positive correlation is +1** with a **perfect negative correlation being -1. Bar charts, histograms and frequency polygons** are other graphical techniques used for quantitative data.

- **Measures of central tendency** are used to illustrate the average values of data. These include **the mean** (all scores added and divided by the number of scores), **the mode** (the most common score) and **the median** (the middle score).

- **Measures of dispersion** show the variability of a spread of scores. These include **the range, the semi-interquartile range and standard deviation**.

- **Qualitative data** involve people's meanings, experiences and descriptions. They are subjective, but rich and detailed. There is no agreed way to code qualitative data, but it often involves **categorisation of common themes** and the use of direct, illustrative quotations. **Content analysis** involves the quantification of qualitative written material.

The application of the scientific method in psychology

- Psychology follows the **scientific method** just like other sciences such as chemistry and biology. The scientific method involves **hypothesis testing**, and **the experimental method**, where one variable is manipulated while all others are kept constant, is the preferred method and allows for cause and effect determination. **Replication and objectivity** are two other requisites of the scientific method.

- **Peer review** is a vital process that maintains the quality of academic research papers, which are subjected to scrutiny by other experts in the field before being published or rejected.

- **Different sampling strategies** have different strengths and weaknesses. For example, random sampling is an unbiased method of obtaining a sample but it can be time consuming and can still result in a biased sample.

- **Inter-rater reliability** refers to the extent to which two raters or observers agree when rating the same behaviour. **Test-retest reliability** simply determines the degree of similarity between two scores on the same test given at different times. Correlation coefficients can show how reliable the measures are. A correlation measure close to +1.0 suggests a high degree of reliability.

- **Probability** is denoted by the symbol p. Generally, psychologists use a significance level of $p = <0.05$. This means that a result has only a 1 in 20 (or less) possibility of it being the result of chance. Sometimes an even more stringent level of probability is used ($p = <0.01$) when results might have a serious impact on human behaviour, such as is the case with drug trials. **Type 1 errors** occur when a null hypothesis that is really true is rejected (a false positive), and **Type 2 errors** occur when a false null hypothesis is not rejected (a false negative).

- There are three levels of measurement. These are:

  1. **nominal data** – frequency or counting data
  2. **ordinal data** – ordered or ranked data (e.g. first, second, third)
  3. **interval/ratio data** – the most accurate measure, which uses standardised measurement units and equal measurement intervals (e.g. time and weight).

- Each unit of measurement can be remembered using the acronym **NOIR**.

- There are many different statistical tests used to analyse data collected in psychology research. **The Chi-square test** is used for nominal data and independent (unrelated) measures design. **The Mann-Whitney U test** is used for ordinal data and independent (unrelated) measures design. **The Wilcoxon (matched pairs) test** is used for ordinal data and repeated (related) measures design. The Spearman's rho is a test of correlation and used with ordinal data and repeated (related) design.

- Each psychology journal has its own 'in-house' style used to write up psychological research. However, they all have a number of common features. These are:
  - title
  - abstract (or summary)
  - introduction
  - method
  - results
  - discussion
  - references
  - appendices.

FURTHER READING

Coolican, H. (2008) *Research Methods and Statistics in Psychology* (5th edn). London: Hodder Education.

Gross, R. (2007) *Key Studies in Psychology*. London: Hodder Education.

Rolls, G. (2005) *Classic Case Studies in Psychology*. London: Hodder Education.

✔ Specification Hint

You have to answer a research methods question in Unit 4: Section C. This question is compulsory and worth more marks than any other question on the paper (35 marks). Other essays on this paper are worth only 25 marks. Therefore it is obvious that considerable time should be spent revising this topic.

Essay Questions

A sports psychologist wanted to investigate whether the presence of an audience has a beneficial or negative effect on a sports performance. She arranged for 40 cyclists to go to their local cycling track and race against the clock over 20 laps. All the cyclists raced twice, once in the presence of spectators who cheered them on, and once with no spectators present. The times of the cyclists were recorded.

A statistical test was conducted to see if there was a significant difference between the two groups. A significant difference was found at the 1 per cent level of significance ($p = {<}0.01$) for a two-tailed (non-directional) test.

	Audience present	No audience present
Mean time for 20 laps	910 secs	1140 secs
Standard deviation	20	50

1. Identify the type of experimental design used in this study. (1 mark)
2. Identify two extraneous variables in the study that the sports psychologist might have identified and accounted for in the design of the study. (6 marks)
3. Name an appropriate statistical test that could be used for analysing the data. Justify the use of this test. (4 marks)
4. Explain what is meant by $p = {<}0.01$ (2 marks)
5. With reference to the table above, outline and discuss the findings of the study. (8 marks)
6. What would be the most suitable chart or graph to illustrate the data? (2 marks)
7. The sports psychologist noticed that experienced riders performed better in the presence of an audience than less experienced riders. Design a study that would incorporate the relationship between audience effects and rider experience. Include the hypothesis, variables, design, sampling and procedure details in your answer. (12 marks)

Index

Index

Index

Index